THE GREEK ANTHOLOGY

AP xv. 15 by 'the humble Constantine the Rhodian' in the hand of J (Par. gr. suppl. 384, p. 667, lines 14–20): see pp. 301–6. Photo courtesy of Bibliothèque nationale, Paris.

THE GREEK ANTHOLOGY

from Meleager to Planudes

ALAN CAMERON

CLARENDON PRESS · OXFORD

This book has been printed digitally and produced in a standard specification
in order to ensure its continuing availability

OXFORD
UNIVERSITY PRESS

Great Clarendon Street, Oxford OX2 6DP

Oxford University Press is a department of the University of Oxford.
It furthers the University's objective of excellence in research, scholarship,
and education by publishing worldwide in

Oxford New York

Auckland Bangkok Buenos Aires Cape Town Chennai
Dar es Salaam Delhi Hong Kong Istanbul Karachi Kolkata
Kuala Lumpur Madrid Melbourne Mexico City Mumbai Nairobi
São Paulo Shanghai Taipei Tokyo Toronto

Oxford is a registered trade mark of Oxford University Press
in the UK and in certain other countries

Published in the United States
by Oxford University Press Inc., New York

ISBN 0-19-814023-1

For
Dani and Sophie

PREFACE

MY interest in the Greek Anthology was first kindled at St Paul's School in 1951, where at the age of thirteen I first heard epigrams by Callimachus and Lucillius declaimed in a sonorous Irish brogue by Mr M. S. McIntosh. It was thus peculiarly satisfying to discover that the first High Master of St Paul's was one of the first European scholars to lay his hands on the Palatine manuscript during its so far undocumented wanderings between Constantinople and Heidelberg (Ch. VIII).

But it was not till I read Gow's monograph of 1958 and Aubreton's paper of 1968 that I was first impelled to penetrate the deeper mysteries of structure and sources. Some preliminary results were published in my earlier book *Porphyrius the Charioteer* (1973). It will be obvious that I came to reject Aubreton's methods and conclusions in their entirety, so it is proper to acknowledge here that without the stimulation of his work I might never have formulated my own approach or reached my own conclusions. Among earlier works, I owe most to a perceptive 1917 Berlin dissertation by the South African schoolmaster Johannes Basson, apparently his only academic publication.

This is an austere study, but the growth of so fascinating and influential a book was worth working out in detail, and the job had not been done before. For centuries, the Greek Anthology was synonymous with the name of that remarkable polymath Maximus Planudes. Yet he did little but reorganize systematically a preexisting collection. It was high time to tell the story in a longer perspective, assigning the credit variously due to such lesser figures as Meleager, Philip, Cephalas, Constantine the Rhodian, and John Clement.

For assistance of various sorts I am grateful to Robert Aubreton, Hermann Beckby, Darice Birge, Aubrey Diller, Hermann Harrauer, Jean Irigoin, Christopher Jones, Dirk Obbink, Peter Parsons, John Van Sickle, Paul Speck, Alexander Turyn, and especially to Carlotta Dionisotti, Anthony Grafton, Alan Griffiths, Cyril Mango, Leonardo and Sonya Tarán, Martin West, and Nigel

Wilson, who were kind enough to read portions of earlier drafts. Peter Knox read the proofs with his customary vigilance.

The core of the book was written in the late 1970s. Indeed, the manuscript was submitted to the Press as long ago as 1980, and languished in the limbo of copy-editing for a record decade, while I made fitful additions in the intervals of pursuing other projects, hopefully not overlooking any important recent discoveries or discussions. To Debra Nails, whose gentle persistence was instrumental in resurrecting and revising a manuscript which both Press and author had despaired of ever seeing in print, readers of this book should be suitably grateful.

A.C.

Institute for Advanced Study, Princeton
April 1991

CONTENTS

ABBREVIATIONS

For books and articles cited in abbreviated form or by author's name alone, see the bibliography. Most other abbreviations are fairly standard.

AJP	*American Journal of Philology*
L'Ant. class.	*L'Antiquité classique*
AP	*Anthologia Palatina*
APl	*Anthologia Planudea*
Arch. Eph.	*Ἀρχαιολογικὴ 'Εφημερίς*
Berl. Phil. Woch.	*Berliner Philologische Wochenschrift*
BICS	*Bulletin of the Institute of Classical Studies,* London
BKT	*Berliner Klassikertexte, herausgegeben von der Generalverwaltung der Kgl. Museen zu Berlin*
Boll. Class. Lincei	*Bollettino dei Classici a cura del Comitato per la preparazione dell'edizione nazionale dei classici greci e latini,* Accademia Nazionale dei Lincei
BZ	*Byzantinische Zeitschrift*
CP	*Classical Philology*
CQ	*Classical Quarterly*
CR	*Classical Review*
CRAI	*Comptes Rendus de l'Académie des Inscriptions et Belles-Lettres*
DOP	*Dumbarton Oaks Papers*
EEBS	*'Επετηρὶς 'Εταιρείας Βυζαντίνων Σπουδῶν*
FGE	D. L. Page, *Further Greek Epigrams* (Cambridge 1981)
FGrH	F. Jacoby, *Die Fragmente der griechischen Historiker* (Berlin 1926–58)
Frag. Hist. Graec.	C. Müller, *Fragmenta Historicorum Graecorum,* 5 vols. (Paris 1878–85)
GGA	*Göttingische gelehrte Anzeigen*

GP	A. S. F. Gow and D. L. Page, *The Greek Anthology: the Garland of Philip* (Cambridge 1968)
GRBS	*Greek, Roman and Byzantine Studies*
HE	A. S. F. Gow and D. L. Page, *The Greek Anthology: Hellenistic Epigrams* (Cambridge 1965)
HSCP	*Harvard Studies in Classical Philology*
IG	*Inscriptiones Graecae*
JHS	*Journal of Hellenic Studies*
JJP	*Journal of Juristic Papyrology*
JÖB	*Jahrbuch für österreichische Byzantinistik*
JRS	*Journal of Roman Studies*
LSJ	Liddell and Scott, *Greek–English Lexicon*, 9th edn., rev. by H. Stuart Jones
PG	*Patrologia Graeca*
PLG	T. Bergk, *Poetae Lyrici Graeci*⁴ (Leipzig 1882)
PLRE	*Prosopography of the Later Roman Empire*
PW	A. Pauly, G. Wissowa, and W. Kroll, *Real-Encyclopädie d. klassischen Altertumswissenschaft* (Stuttgart 1893–1980)
RAC	*Reallexikon für Antike und Christentum*
RÉA	*Revue des études anciennes*
RÉB	*Revue des études byzantines*
RÉG	*Revue des études grecques*
RÉL	*Revue des études latines*
RhM	*Rheinisches Museum für Philologie*
SIFC	*Studi italiani di filologia classica*
SH	H. Lloyd-Jones and P. Parsons, *Supplementum Hellenisticum* (Berlin and New York 1983)
TAPA	*Transactions of the American Philological Association*
Viz. vrem.	*Vizantijskij vremennik*
Wien. Stud.	*Wiener Studien*
YCS	*Yale Classical Studies*
ZPE	*Zeitschrift für Papyrologie und Epigraphik*

EDITIONS

For the purposes of this book only three editions of the Anthology are of any importance:

    (i) H. Stadtmueller's Teubner edition, of which only three volumes appeared: i (*AP* i–vi), 1894; ii. 1 (*AP* vii), 1899; iii. 1 (*AP* ix. 1–563), 1906.

    (ii) The Budé edition was begun in 1928 by P. Waltz, who with various collaborators published seven volumes (*AP* i–ix. 358) by 1957; viii (*AP* ix. 359–827) was completed by J. Irigoin and P. Laurens (1974); x (*AP* xi) was edited by R. Aubreton (1972); xii (*AP* xiii–xv) by F. Buffière (1970); xii (*APl*) by Aubreton and Buffière (1980). Volumes ix (*AP* x) and xi (*AP* xii) have yet to appear.

    (iii) The only complete modern edition, with invaluable indexes, is that by H. Beckby in four volumes, 2nd edn. 1967–8.

An indispensable complement to these editions is C. Preisendanz, *Anthologia Palatina: codex Palatinus et codex Parisinus phototypice editi* i–ii (Leiden 1911), with very full introduction in volume i; and the successive volumes of selections by A. S. F. Gow and D. L. Page (*HE*, *GP* and *FGE*).

SIGLA

ABV Appendix Barberino-Vaticana (s. xiv)
Q   Brit. Mus. Add. 16409 (*c*.1301)
E   Sylloge Euphemiana (s. x)
J   Redactor Palatini (930/40)
P   Palatinus 23 + Paris. suppl. gr. 384 (930/40)
    A, A2, B, B2, B3 = librarii Palatini
    C = corrector Palatini (*c*.950)
Pl   Anthologia Planudea = Ven. Marc. gr. 481 (1301)
    Pla = Planudis fons primus
    Plb = Planudis fons alter
S   Sylloge Parisina = Paris. suppl. gr. 352 et Paris. gr. 1630
    (s. xiii)
Σ   Sylloge praemissa Euphemianae (s. xiv/xv)
Σᵖ   Sylloge praemissa Palatino (s. xii)

TABLE

Structure of the Cephalan books (v–vii, ix–xiv) of AP *(adapted from F. Lenzinger,*
Zur griechischen Anthologie *[Zurich 1975], Tafel 1)*

	Agathias	Palatine Anthology				
Erotica	vi	v	Rufinus and others (Meleager, Philip and Diogenian) 1–103		Philip 104–33	Melea, 134–2
Anathematica	i	vi	thematic arrangement 1–53	Agathias 54–86	Philip 87–108	Melea, 109–5
Epitymbia	iii	vii	thematic arrangement 1–363		Philip 364–405	Melea, 406–5c
Epideictica and Ecphrastica	ii	ix	thematic arrangement 1–214		Philip 215–312	Melea, 313–3
Protreptica	iv	x	thematic arrangement 1–16 (Philip, 4–13, out of alphabetical sequence)		Philip 17–25	mainly Lucian 26–43
Sympotica and Scoptica	v/vii	xi	Diogenian 1–22		Philip 23–46	
Paederastica		xii	Strato 1–11		miscellaneous 12–35	Meleag 36–174
Polymetra		xiii	stichic metres, 1–10;		strophic/epodic metres, 11–	
Aenigmata		xiv	arithmetical puzzles and riddles 1–64		oracles 65–102	

						Planudean Anthology
	Agathias 216–302	miscellaneous 303–9				vii
miscellaneous 158–78	thematic arrangement 179–226	Philip 227–61	Meleager 262–313	miscellaneous 314–58 (anastrephonta, 314–20; isopsepha, 321–9; Meleager, 351–8)		vi
miscellaneous 507–50	Agathias 551–614	Diogenes Laertius 615–20	Philip 622–45	Meleager 646–65	miscellaneous 666–748 (Meleager, 707–40)	iii
miscellaneous 339–63	Agathias 364–401	miscellaneous 402–583 (Philip, 402–23 and 541–62; Agathias, 442–7; Meleager, 563–8)	Lacuna of c.450 epigrams	thematic arrangement 584–827		i/iv
Palladas 44–63	Agathias 64–76	Palladas 77–99	Philip 100–3	miscellaneous 104–26		i
miscellaneous 47–53	Agathias 57–64	Diogenian 65–255 (Lucillius, 75–81, 83–95, 99–107, 111–16, 131–43, 159–65, 171–9, 205–18)	miscellaneous 256–442 (Palladas, 280–93, 299–307; Lucillius, 308–15; Philip, 318–27; Nicarchus, 328–32; Agathias and Palladas, 349–57 and 365–88; Lucillius, 388–93; Lucian, 396–405 and 427–36)			ii
Strato 175–255			concluding poems (Meleager, 256–7; Strato, 258)			vii
riddles 103–11	oracles 112–15	arithmetical puzzles 116–47		oracles 148–50		

I

Epigram and Anthology

AN epigram was originally nothing more than a legend designed to be written on an object, 'to say whose it is, or who made it, or who has dedicated it to which god, or who is buried underneath it'.[1] The earliest so far found are in verse, and by convention (how early is uncertain) the term came to be limited to inscriptions in verse, by the fifth century BC predominantly in the metre with which it was to be forever associated, the elegiac couplet.

The earliest epigrams are quite impersonal. The first poet who became known for his epigrams was Simonides of Ceos, though only one, the noble epitaph on the seer Megistias, is ascribed to him by a writer of the fifth century, and then only from oral tradition some forty years after the event.[2] The first epigram ascribed to its composer is a dedication at Delphi from the second half of the fourth century by Ion of Samos.[3] It was perhaps another century before there was any general interest in discovering and preserving the authorship of so brief and functional a piece of writing. Collections of epigraphic verses were available as early as Aeschines, late in the fourth century.[4]

By then early epigrams tended as a matter of course to be ascribed to Simonides, the only known specialist. A collection of *Simonidea* which contained much demonstrably later in date than Simonides appeared no earlier than the fourth century and more probably in the hellenistic age. Some are inscriptions dating from the period of Simonides' lifetime, more or less; others are inscrip-

---

[1] M. L. West (1974), 2.

[2] Herodotus, vii. 228. 4; for the details, Page, *FGE* 196.

[3] The monument dates from soon after Aegospotami (405), but the epigram, long thought original, is probably 50–100 years later: P. A. Hansen, *Carm. epigr. graeca*, ii (1989), no. 819, pp. 224–8. We may therefore disregard Wilamowitz' fanciful reconstruction of Ion's life and works: *PW* s.v. Ion 12; Page, *FGE* 157. For another, perhaps earlier signed epigram, Hansen no. 888. ii.

[4] H. T. Wade-Gery, *JHS* liii (1933), 94.

tions of appreciably later date; and many are obviously literary
exercises of hellenistic inspiration. There may even have been
more than one such *Sylloge Simonidea*. Examples of every category
are to be found in Meleager's *Garland*. Meleager seems also to
have used a collection of epigrams ascribed to Anacreon, probably
no earlier (and no more authentic).[5] There is some evidence of an
alphabetical arrangement in the Simonidean and Anacreontic
sequences in the *Anthologia Palatina* (*AP*), presumably a reflection of the source used by Meleager.

By the fourth century inscriptional epigrams became more
elaborate, and there also grew up the practice of writing 'fictitious'
epigrams, poems in the form of dedications and epitaphs (sometimes ironic) but not intended for inscription.[6] The idea was not
new, if the mock epitaph on the early fifth-century poet Timocreon
of Rhodes (*AP* vii. 348) is contemporary, whether or not by
Simonides. A securely dated early example is the abusive mock
funerary poem on Aristotle's friend Hermias, the tyrant of Atar-
neus, *c*.344.[7] But by the third century it had developed into a
regular genre. The pioneer was perhaps Anyte of Tegea. Its most
celebrated and influential exponent was Leonidas of Tarentum, in
whose hands the epigram became a vehicle for describing, in
ornate language, the lives and deaths of simple people.

That the epitaph and dedication should evolve in this way was
understandable. More surprising is the sudden emergence at about
the same time of the sympotic and erotic epigram, already per-
fected by its first identifiable practitioners, Asclepiades and Callimachus. Though naturally much indebted to the traditions of

---

[5] M. Boas (1905), *passim*; the issues are set out with his customary clarity by
Page, *FGE* 119–23 and 124–5; see too P. Friedländer and H. Hoffleit, *Epigrammata*
(1948), 68 f.

[6] This is not the place to give a history of the Greek epigram. The fullest and
most illuminating account of its early stages remains Reitzenstein's *Epigramm und
Skolion* (1893); see also Reitzenstein's entry 'Epigramm' in *PW* and R. Keydell's in
RAC; W. Seelbach in *Kleines Wörterbuch des Hellenismus*, ed. H. H. Schmitt and
E. Vogt (1988), 157–84; Wilamowitz, *Hellenistische Dichtung* ii (1924), 119 f.;
Beckby i. 12–67; Raubitschek, Gentili, and Giangrande in *L'Épigramme grecque*
(1968); J. Ebert, *Griech. Epigramme auf Sieger an gymnischen und hippischen Agonen*
(1972); P. M. Fraser, *Ptolemaic Alexandria*, i (1972), 553–617; West (1974), 18 f.;
G. M. Kirkwood, *Early Greek Monody* (1974), 194 f.; M. Lausberg, *Das Einzeldisti-
chon: Studien zum antiken Epigramm* (1982); P. Bing, *The Well-Read Muse* (1988),
39 f., 58 f. What follows is merely designed to sketch in the background to the
development of anthologies.

[7] Page, *FGE* 93–5; for the date, M. Sordi, *Kokalos* v (1959), 107–18.

sympotic elegy and lyric, the Alexandrians were selective in the motifs they treated, and invested them from the beginning with that combination of allusiveness, conciseness, and wit that were to become the hallmarks of the genre.[8] It is not because of their subject-matter or quality that we must pronounce the love epigrams ascribed to Plato inauthentic (four or five are very fine). It is simply that, writing when he did, Plato would not have expressed such themes in such a way in the form of epigrams. They are, as W. Ludwig put it, 'based substantially on a literary development which was not to take place, so far as we know, before *c*.300 BC.'[9]

The epigram rapidly became one of the most popular hellenistic art forms. Leonidas was known only for epigrams, and Posidippus of Pella was publicly honoured as 'the epigrammatist'.[10] Poets began to publish collections of their own epigrams: to name only those for whom books called 'epigrammata' are expressly attested, Callimachus, Hedylus, Mnasalces, Nicaenetus, Nicander, Philetas, Posidippus.[11]

A recent find has presented us with the opening of just such a collected edition, P. Köln 204, a fragmentary papyrus which cannot be much later in date than the collection itself.[12] Dated on the basis of the script to the middle of the second century BC, the papyrus carries the remains of six epigrams beneath the heading Μ[ν]ασάλκου, 'Of Mnasalces', a Dorian epigrammatist of the late third century BC. Nos. I and II are unknown; III is *AP* vii. 488, transmitted in *AP* under the name of Mnasalces; IV appears to be *AP* vi. 266, transmitted in *AP* under the name of Hegesippus; V and VI are both unknown. Style, theme, and dialect of the unknown epigrams are all consistent with the ascription to Mnasalces.

No. IV is something of a puzzle, since the title implies that the entire collection will be the work of Mnasalces. Very little sur-

---

[8] Giangrande, *L'Épigramme grecque* (1968), 93–177; Cameron, *Reflections of Women in Antiquity*, ed. H. P. Foley (1981), 275–302; G. O. Hutchinson, *Hellenistic Poetry* (1988), 20–5, 73–6, 264–76.

[9] *GRBS* iv (1963), 59–82 (here 62); Page, *FGE* 135–7.

[10] Below, p. 371. Note too the appearance of commentaries on epigrams, proved for the late third/early second century already by the oyster papyrus (Parsons, *ZPE* xxiv (1977), 1–12).

[11] The evidence is collected by P. M. Fraser, *Ptolemaic Alexandria*, ii (1972), 859 n. 405.

[12] Edited with useful commentary by M. Gronewald in *Kölner Papyri* v (1985), 22–32.

vives, little more than the first two words of each of the four lines,
the opening words of the four lines of *AP* vi. 266 by Hegesippus—
but with one major exception. For the proper name Damaretos in
l. 3 of Hegesippus, the papyrus offers Nikaretos or Nikarete. As
Gronewald has already seen, there are two possible explanations.
First, like so many other epigrams in our manuscript tradition, vi.
266 may simply be wrongly ascribed in *AP*. It may really be by
Mnasalces after all. Alternatively, the papyrus version may
actually be a different poem, a variation or adaptation of Hegesippus'. There would in fact be an exact parallel. Another of Mnasalces' poems (XVII GP) is just such a minimal adaptation of a
poem of Asclepiades (*AP* vii. 145), virtually identical except,
significantly, for the substitution of new names.[13] Furthermore,
there are traces of letters written in smaller script above this alone
of the six epigrams. Gronewald doubts whether these traces can be
read as ['Ηγησί]ππου, but acknowledges that the first letter is
probably a π; the third seems to be an ε. A possibility he does not
consider is that the scribe wrote Hegesippus' name in abbreviated
form, as normally in the ascriptions of *AP* and the *Anthologia
Planudea* (*APl*): e.g. ['Ηγησίπ]π. ἐ[πίγρ.] or something similar. In
any case, it is not unreasonable to guess that this exceptional
interlinear lemma explained in some way the presence of a poem
written by or adapted from another poet in an edition of Mnasalces. P. Köln 204 is of great interest as our first fragment of a
collected edition of a poet's epigrams. But it is not an anthology in
the sense here defined.

Fifty or even a hundred epigrams will have made a very slim
book, and too many by the same writer on the same sort of themes,
however excellent in themselves, might become monotonous. The
epigram was in fact destined by its very nature to be *anthologized*.

There is some evidence that there was a joint edition of epigrams
by Asclepiades, Posidippus, and Hedylus, possibly known as
Σωρός, /Heap' (? of grain), perhaps compiled by Hedylus, the latest
of the three.[14] There may have been other such joint editions; it
would explain the survival of small batches of epigrams by minor

---

[13] For some other hellenistic examples of this sort of minimal variation, see
Appendix VII.

[14] For the Soros, see Appendix V.

figures. But a joint edition by contemporaries is hardly an antho-logy.[15]

Polemo of Ilium, the 'Periegete', put together early in the second century a Περὶ τῶν κατὰ πόλεις ἐπιγραμμάτων, 'On epigrams by cities'. To judge from the title and the brief extracts quoted by Athenaeus[16] (all relating to drunkenness), this was less a literary anthology than a selection of (? anonymous) epigrams illustrating, often humorously, the (alleged) characteristics and customs of various cities. We know even less of the Περὶ ἐπιγραμμάτων of the third-century Neoptolemus of Parium.[17] To judge from the title again it was less a collection of epigrams than (more interestingly) a book about them, though our only fragment does in fact quote an epigram, the epitaph said to have been engraved on the tomb of Thrasymachus at Chalcedon. The Ἀττικὰ ἐπιγράμματα of the rather earlier Philochorus of Athens, often quoted as the first anthology of epigrams, may, given the interests of its compiler, have included prose as well as verse inscriptions, perhaps too primarily political rather than literary.[18]

The first comprehensive anthology of epigrams known to us is Meleager's *Garland*, compiled (it seems) on Cos not long after 100 BC. The word 'anthology' itself is not attested before Diogenian in the second century AD (see Ch. IV), and even there it may be a later lexicographer's description rather than Diogenian's own title. But the idea itself, the 'gathering of flowers' (ἄνθη λέγειν), clearly underlies Meleager's enterprise:[19] in his preface he assigns each of his authors a flower (some more appropriate than others). In fact he developed the metaphor one stage further: again and again he says that he has 'entwined' these flowers into a 'garland'— whence (of course) his title. Thus his achievement was twofold. Not only did he assemble perhaps as many as a thousand epigrams;

[15] For example, even if A. D. Knox's thesis were accepted in its entirety (and see E. A. Barber, *CR* xxxix (1925), 28–9; Guéraud and Jouget [n. 22], pp. xxix–xxx), he would only have proved that Cercidas published an edition of ethical (chol)iambics by himself and others, not remotely justifying his title *The First Greek Anthologist* (Cambridge 1923).

[16] For the fragments, C. Müller, *Frag. Hist. Graec.* iii. 138–9; cf. R. Pfeiffer, *History of Classical Scholarship* (Oxford 1968), 247–9, 290; P. Oxy. 2535 is a commentary of some sort that quotes a sixth-century historical epigram, perhaps Simonides, and possibly Polemo too.

[17] C. O. Brink, *Horace on Poetry* (Cambridge 1963), 47, 52 f.

[18] F. Jacoby, *FGrH* 328 T 1, with Commentary (iiiB, suppl. i, 1954), 375 n. 19.

[19] See Gow and Page, *HE* ii. 594 f.

he also arranged them artistically. Like a true garland, Meleager's book was meant to be admired for itself, not just for its individual flowers.

There has of late been a tendency to play down both the originality and the importance of Meleager's *Garland*. As Gow and Page succinctly put it: 'the belief once held that he was the first anthologist is no longer tenable. Papyrus scraps of sufficiently early date make it plain that he had predecessors'.[20] According to A. Barigazzi the papyri provide 'decisive proof' that there were pre-Meleagrian anthologies 'similar to Meleager's only smaller'.[21] D. O. Ross has recently gone much further in an attempt to minimize the impact of the appearance of the *Garland* on Roman poetry of the first century BC (Ch. III. 1).

But it depends what is meant by 'anthology'. It is true that there are a great many papyri so classified in R. A. Pack's *Greek and Latin literary texts from Greco-Roman Egypt*[2] (1965), but very few have any bearing on our inquiry. From this point of view, the only relevant criterion is that of purpose. Some have the modest aim of preserving a few of the writer's favourite texts. But by far the majority have an avowedly didactic purpose, whether to improve the mind, the morals, or literary style.[22] The Greeks often compared this process of collecting improving texts to the activity of the bee, laboriously gathering pollen from every sort of flower to transform into something useful. It is precisely this comparison that underlines the difference between Meleager's *Garland* and almost all other anthologies. Plutarch (for example) contrasts the virtuous bee with 'women who pluck flowers and sweet-scented leaves and intertwine and plait them, producing something which is pleasant enough, but short lived and fruitless'.[23] In the *Garland*, as John Barns has well put it,[24]

however edifying the content of some of the epigrams may be, the general aim of the compiler has plainly been, not to educate, but to give delight to his reader; each poem is a flower to be woven, as Plutarch describes, into a

[20] *HE* i, p. xvi.

[21] *Hermes* lxxx (1952), 494 n. 1.

[22] See O. Guéraud and P. Jouget, *Un livre d'écolier du IIIe siècle avant J.-C.* (Cairo 1938), xxiv–xxxi; H. Chadwick, 'Florilegium' in *RAC* vii. 1131 f.; for a full collection of examples and discussion, J. Barns, *CQ*, xliv (1950), 132–7 and NS i (1951), 1–19; E. G. Turner, *Greek Papyri*[2] (1980), 91–2.

[23] *de recta ratione audiendi* 41 FG; cf. *quomodo adulescens* 31 E and other texts quoted by Barns (1950), 132–5, to whose learned discussion I am much indebted.

[24] Barns (1950), 135.

garland, that symbol of idle pleasure to which Clement of Alexandria devotes chapters of condemnation.

It will take more than the odd epigram to turn a papyrus into a forerunner of Meleager; it must in addition have absolutely no redeeming utilitarian purpose. Of papyri that contain epigrams, significantly enough only the post-Meleagrian bear any similarity to Meleager.

There are a dozen or so pre-Meleagrian epigram papyri of one sort or another. We may begin with P. Firmin Didot and its two long epigrams by Posidippus on the Pharos at Alexandria and the temple of Arsinoe-Aphrodite Zephyritis. But the other texts included are extracts of Aeschylus, Euripides, and Menander. This is neither an anthology of epigrams nor even a true 'book'; rather a few favourite passages, some (as the idiosyncratic variants in the *Medea* prologue suggest) actually copied from memory. As it happens we know the names and a fair amount about the lives of its two scribes, Ptolemaios and his younger brother Apollonios, Macedonians living on the edge of the Egyptian desert. A fascinating paper by Dorothy J. Thompson has shown that each extract reflects some aspect of their lives as exiles in a new land. This was a very personal anthology.[25]

The papyrus most often quoted is P. Petrie 2.49(*a*) of *c*.250 BC,[26] containing on the recto an elegiac epithalamium on Queen Arsinoe (?II) in at least 13 couplets, and on the verso the heading 'Miscellaneous Epigrams: Posidippus . . .'. The implication is that the first poem is by Posidippus and that the copyist could not be bothered (or forgot) to finish his table of contents. It is an attractive and reasonable conjecture that the collection was presented to Arsinoe on the occasion of her marriage to Ptolemy II some time before 274/3. To the question of the description of these long elegiac poems as 'epigrams' at all we shall shortly be returning. For the moment it will suffice to warn that we are not entitled to assume that this collection continued with the wide chronological and thematic range characteristic of the *Garland*, rather than more of

---

[25] Pack (1965), nos. 31, 401, 1319–20, 1435; cf. U. Wilcken, *Urkunden der Ptolemäerzeit*, i (1927), 111 f.; D. J. Thompson, *Proc. Camb. Phil. Soc.* ccxiii (1987), 105–21; *Memphis under the Ptolemies* (Princeton 1988), 212–65, esp. 259 f. Oddly enough, she does not point out that Posidippus may have been selected because he was a fellow Macedonian.

[26] See now *SH* 961. The other names F. Lasserre fancied he could read on the verso have not been confirmed.

these long, relatively homogeneous court poems, quite uncharac-
teristic of the *Garland*. Nor again is it clear that this is a published
anthology rather than a private selection, or that it contained
poems by anyone other than Posidippus.

Then there is P. Petrie 2.49(*b*), again of the third century,
fragments of nine quatrains on tragedies and comedies, each on a
particular play, each with a separate heading. The best preserved
headings are to nos. III, '[On the Achill]es of Aristarchus]', and IV,
'[On the Hector] of Astydamas'.[27] Achilles followed by Hector
suggests art rather than coincidence, and it may also be more than
coincidence that the three identifiable dramatists' names all begin
with alpha. This was surely a published book, set out with some
care. On the other hand, while there are headings to each poem,
there are no authors' names. Apparently all nine are the work of a
single poet, in which case this would not be an anthology at all.
These are the sort of epigrams we might expect to find prefixed to
copies of individual plays. Many such originally written for this
purpose are preserved in the Anthology (though no others on
dramas), usefully collected by M. Gabathuler, *Hellenistische Epigramme auf Dichter* (Basle 1937). This might be a selection culled
from somebody's Greek drama library. Such a series of epigrams
of the same type, whether or not all by the same poet, can hardly be
considered a forerunner of the *Garland*. Even if the complete text
ran to a hundred or more epigrams (and for all we know there may
only have been a couple of dozen), it would still be more like the
series of distichs on Greek and Trojan heroes in the late-second- or
first-century-BC pseudo-Aristotelian *Peplos*, or the series of polymetric epigrams on philosophers written two or three centuries
later by Diogenes Laertius (Appendix VIII). It is rather the sort of
homogeneous collection from which Meleager plucked his flowers
than a 'Garland' itself.

There are two new funerary epigrams on the Petrie papyrus
of *c*.100 BC published by E. G. Turner,[28] but the heading ἄλλο
ἐπίγραμμα (rather than the standard ἄλλο) suggests the possibility
that the preceding columns contained material other than epigrams. P. Harris 56, as reinterpreted and redated (to the mid
second century) by C. H. Roberts,[29] contains one epigram on

---

[27] *SH* 985; R. Reitzenstein, *Berl. Phil. Woch.* xiv (1894), 155–9.

[28] *JJP* iv (1950), 235–8 = *SH* 986.

[29] *JJP* iv (1950), 214–17 = *SH* 981.

Apelles with the heading ἄλλο. The third-century *BKT* v. 1. 77 was formerly thought to contain one long poem, but M. Gronewald has recently recognized it as a sequence of three different epigrams, the first now identified as *AP* vi. 3, a dedication to Heracles, followed by two epigrams on statues, the third being on the Anadyomene of Apelles (like *APl* 178–82).[30] The mixture of dedicatory and ecphrastic epigrams here should be noticed. The absence of poets' names between the successive epigrams does not support the idea that this is an anthology of different poets.

We hardly needed papyri to tell us that Meleager was not the first person to make a collection of his favourite epigrams. Some of these papyri were personal copies, never intended for publication—and probably of very limited scope and compass. For example, a recently published papyrus of the late first century BC or early first AD (P. Köln iii. 128) contains two unknown funerary epigrams with interlinear corrections which can only be the author's own. This must be the poet's autograph, perhaps (as the editors suggest) drafts of the version he eventually had engraved on a tombstone. *SH* 977 carries two funerary epigrams on a dog—presumably the poet's own, since they are written and corrected in the same hand. It must also be remembered that already by the third century many poets were publishing collections of their own epigrams; some of our papyri may be fragments from such editions. Others again are likely to have been genuine miscellanies,[31] like P. Tebt. 1 (Page, *GLP*, no. 92), a 'curiously heterogeneous collection', containing a 'lyric' lament by Helen, a 'dithyrambic' description of dawn, and some erotic couplets of 'an epigrammatic sort' in various metres. It was not obvious or inevitable that epigrams had only to be anthologized with other epigrams. Indeed, so varied was their subject-matter that they could fit into any context. We certainly cannot exclude the possibility of a large and comprehensive pre-Meleagrian anthology. But it cannot be said that the papyri so far found lend any real support to the hypothesis.

What may well turn out to be the most important of all epigram

---

[30] *ZPE* xii (1973), 91–8; Ebert, *APF* xiii (1974), 255 = *SH* 974.
[31] For such miscellaneous collections see G. M. Kirkwood, *TAPA* xcii (1961), 267 f.; for the many 'gnomic' miscellanies, full of Menandrean sententiae, see Barns (1950).

papyri has yet to be published—or even fully deciphered.[32] It is a badly worn mid-third-century roll containing the first line plus line total (but no authors' names) of about 240 epigrams, divided up into several books (i–iv, as far as the roll goes). Only one has so far been identified, *AP* xii. 46 by Asclepiades. This document will no doubt cast many a tantalizing shaft of light on the history of early hellenistic epigram. But it is legitimate to doubt whether it will have much to tell us about epigram anthologies. It appears to be a librarian's (or scholar's) list of desiderata (ἐπιζητούμενα), poems that are 'missing' or 'required', presumably for the purpose of checking a corrupt or defective text. So far as the papyrus has been deciphered, there are no signs of either thematic or verbal links between successive first lines. But the title at the beginning of the roll reads τὰ ἐπιζητούμενα τῶν ἐπιγραμμάτων ἐν τῇ αʹ βύβλῳ, 'Required epigrams in book i', which implies that only the 'required' epigrams are here recorded, not the full contents of the books referred to. It might seem natural to infer the existence of a multi-book anthology behind such a list, but this is by no means the only alternative. The numbered books do not have to be thought of as the successive subdivisions of one comprehensive, artistically arranged, multi-book anthology. They need be no more than a series of rolls containing epigrams as numbered in some library. By the mid-third century, when collections of epigrams, too small for a separate roll of their own, must have become quite common, a librarian might well have had them copied seriatim into a series of consecutively numbered rolls without ever contemplating the drastic step (and extra labour) of amalgamating and rearranging the work of different poets. Nor, so long as the only line identified is by Asclepiades, can we exclude the possibility that *all* the incipits are Asclepiades; that the Vienna papyrus is simply an index of first lines of epigrams by Asclepiades. Unexpected support for this possibility has come from P. Oxy. 3724, fragments of a first century AD roll listing the incipits of some 175 epigrams. Of these, 31 can be identified, of which at least 25 and probably more are by Philodemus. Indeed they may *all* be by Philodemus (App. VII).

It was not just the size of Meleager's *Garland* (800 poems even in

[32] For my knowledge of this document, mostly still undeciphered, I am indebted to Herman Harrauer; see his 'Vorbericht', *Proceedings of the XVI International Congress of Papyrology* (Chico 1981), 49–53. See now addenda.

AP, 4 papyrus rolls); or its artistic arrangement (the collections of individual epigrammatists were presumably arranged on some artistic principle or other); it was in its comprehensive range, chronological, geographic, and thematic alike, that its true novelty and importance lay. Meleager collected material from all areas of the Greek world, from Italy to Syria; from Simonides and Anacreon down to Antipater and Archias; from the sympotic and erotic to the dedicatory, anathematic, and funerary; from the most humdrum inscriptions to the purest poetry.

There remain five papyri that do have affinities with the *Garland*. But not one is earlier than the first century BC; that is to say, all either could be or (in two cases) demonstrably are influenced by Meleager. First and most obviously *BKT* v. 1. 75–6 of the first century AD, with *AP* xii. 76, 77, 78; ix. 15; xii. 106; v. 151; xii. 19. The facts that (*a*) all seven reappear in *AP*; (*b*) three are in the same order as in *AP*; and (*c*) four out of the seven are by Meleager himself (two anon. and the other by Asclepiades or Posidippus) make it all but certain that this is an extract from the erotic section of Meleager's *Garland*. It is a tiny roll, no wider than 4–5 cm, and clearly not a complete Meleager.[33] But the poems are all ascribed to their authors. Another such extract (lacking ascriptions) is P. Oxy. 3324 of about the same date, containing four erotic epigrams, all by Meleager (ix. 16; v. 190; xii. 157; v. 152) and the concluding word (Ζέφυρος) of an unknown poem.

P. Oxy. 662 also contains seven epigrams, all with ascriptions, only two of which reappear in *AP*: first *AP* vii. 162 and 163 by Leonidas and Antipater of Sidon on the death of a Samian lady called Prexo; a new epigram on the same by a certain Amyntas; another by Amyntas on Philopoemen's capture of Sparta in 188 BC (an imitation of *AP* vii. 723); new epitaphs on a hunter called Glenis by (again) Leonidas and Antipater; and the beginning of another poem by Leonidas, of which the scribe wrote only the first word. A. Wifstrand has suggested that Amyntas, evidently an early second-century poet, was himself the compiler of this anthology, which would therefore have been pre-Meleagrian.[34] Amyntas, he argued, was an inferior poet, such as Meleager would have spurned. Yet the incompetence of the scribe makes it difficult to

---

[33] 'Ein Poesiebuch, das eine elegante Dame rasch in dem Busen verbergen konnte', Wilamowitz, p. 75.

[34] Wifstrand (1926), 33–9.

judge the competence of the poet, and Wifstrand overlooked the
fact that Amyntas does in fact appear in a Meleagrian sequence in
AP: the so-called Corrector ascribes to him *AP* vi. 114, a poem on
Philip V of Macedon (221–179 BC).[35] This is obviously preferable
to the original ascription in *AP* (and Planudes) to the third-century
poet Simmias and renders unnecessary the modern conjecture
Samius. If accepted, then Amyntas would be appreciably older
than Antipater (who lived till *c*.100 BC) and so could hardly have
included Antipater in an anthology of his own. Indeed the inclusion of Antipater, an older contemporary of Meleager, scarcely
leaves room for the hypothesis that the anthology is pre-Meleagrian, and the papyrus itself is a good century later than Meleager.
We shall see in the next chapter that the thematic groupings and
author alternation are highly characteristic of Meleager, and the
obvious conclusion is surely that P. Oxy. 662 is in fact an excerpt
from a funerary section in Meleager.[36] The presence of material
not known from *AP* merely confirms (as we shall see later) that the
original text of the *Garland* had suffered substantial abridgement
by the Byzantine age.

There is less to be said about the two other documents; P. Tebt.
I. 3[37] (first century BC), with the Meleagrian *AP* ix. 588 (the early
second-century Alcaeus of Messene) and three new poems, including one each (it seems) by Asclepiades and Posidippus, a pair well
represented in the *Garland*; and P. Freib. 4 of the same date, with
two known Meleagrian poems, *APl* 119 (Posidippus) and ix. 743
(Theodoridas), and an epigram on Homer known from an ostracon
(all three on statues).[38] No poets' names can be read, but space was
left for them between the epigrams. Given the early date of both
papyri, it is certainly possible that one or both reflect a pre-
Meleagrian anthology that influenced Meleager. It would be
implausible and unnecessary to insist in such cases. But given the
undoubted loss of original Meleagrian material and the fact that
their date allows of derivation from the *Garland*, they are a fragile
basis on which to construct a pre-Meleagrian anthology.

Whatever earlier anthologies may have existed, Meleager's
surely eclipsed them by far in scope and design. But this is not the

---

[35] Cf. G. Luck, *GGA* (1967), 39 f.   [36] See Ch. II.
[37] *SH* 988.   [38] *SH* 973; cf. too *BKT* v. 78.

only respect in which he left his personal impress on the tradition
of the ancient epigram. Evidence outside what we might call the
Meleagrian tradition suggests that in the early hellenistic age
epigrams were often of considerable length[39] and written in a
variety of metres. Gow and Page, for example, wrote of the long
elegiac epithalamium that opens the 'Miscellaneous Epigrams' of
P. Petrie 2. 49(*a*) that 'despite the inscription the first poem is in no
sense an epigram'. Similarly, while allowing that it may have been
included among his epigrams 'for want of a better place', they
insist that Callimachus' sixteen-line poem on Pittacus' advice
about marriage (vii. 89) has 'no claim to be called an epigram at
all'. Perhaps they do not look like epigrams to us, but this is
because our definition of the hellenistic epigram is essentially
Meleager's. The line totals of the Vienna list give valuable new
information about the length of poems a third-century scholar
would call epigrams. Out of 173 line totals so far deciphered there
are thirteen with 2 lines; 106 with 4; twenty with 6; nine with 8; one
with 10; two with 12; two with 20; and one each with 21, 40, and 52
lines. Obviously quatrains were most popular, but it is striking to
see poems of 40 and 52 lines described as epigrams. How should
we classify the so-called *Seal* of Posidippus, an elegiac poem of (it
seems) 28 lines? Is it (as generally assumed) the concluding poem
of a book of elegies for which we have no evidence—or of the book
of epigrams we know Posidippus to have published?[40]

As for metre, while the elegiac couplet predominated by far, up
till and including the third century BC a variety of other (often
mixed) metres were occasionally employed both for the literary
and the inscriptional epigram, sometimes to accommodate intrac-
table proper names (as occasionally in the archaic period), more
often simply for the sake of virtuosity.[41] Very few of these unusual
combinations are later than the third century. Two out of the six
epigrams on the new Mnasalces papyrus are not in elegiacs. But by
Meleager's day the elegiac couplet was all but universal, and only a
handful of non-elegiac epigrams are included in the *Garland*. Most

---

[39] e.g., in addition to the examples quoted below, *SH* 977 (12) and 978 (at least 15
lines).

[40] A possibility mentioned by Lloyd-Jones, *JHS* lxxxiii (1963), 96 (whose
identification of the poet with the third-century epigrammatist is now generally
accepted); see now *SH* 705.

[41] Page, *Wien. Stud.* lxxxix (1976), 165 f.; West, *Greek Metre* (1982), 150–1;
Kassel, *ZPE* lxxxiv (1990), 299–300.

hellenistic epigrams in non-elegiac metres that have come down to us are preserved on stone, in the metrical writers, or in *AP* xiii, which was probably compiled from a metrical treatise (Ch. VI). Thus to name only the most prominent, Callimachus and Theocritus wrote epigrams in a dozen metres other than elegiacs.[42] The 21-line epigram of the Vienna list cannot have been in elegiac couplets.

Another omission concerns the erotic and sympotic category. By Meleager's day the line between elegy, skolion, and epigram had long been firmly drawn. Thus while including dedications by (or at any rate ascribed to) Anacreon, he has nothing from his more famous sympotica in the same metre (e.g. the quatrain *eleg.* fr. 2 West). The former were undoubtedly epigrams, the latter elegy and so excluded. It is no doubt also significant that Meleager did not include any of the dozens of early sympotic and erotic poems of epigram length incorporated in the Theognidean *Sylloge*—a strong argument for dating the *Sylloge* in something like its present form before Meleager.[43] Though a much smaller and more homogeneous collection, the Theognidean *Sylloge* is in fact the closest extant parallel to Meleager's *Garland*.

Reitzenstein once made a similar suggestion[44] about the 'omission' from the *Garland* of hellenistic satirical epigrams, whose existence he inferred from Roman epigram and the Greek scoptic epigram of the early empire. But we must not underestimate the originality of either Roman or later Greek epigrammatists, and here too we have a problem of genre demarcation. The vehicle for invective in the hellenistic as in the archaic age was the iambus.[45] And while Meleager includes occasional iambic epigrams, iambus proper was not epigram. A case in point is the second-century poet Alcaeus of Messene, who wrote invective in both epigram and iambus.[46] Meleager has only the former. The truth is that there

---

[42] R. Pfeiffer, *Callimachus*, i (1949), 326–7; Gow and Page, *HE* ii. 217 f., 537 f.

[43] There is of course no agreement about the date and creation of the Theognidean *Sylloge*: J. Carrière, *Théognis de Mégare* (1948), 14–136; A. Lesky, *History of Greek Literature* (ET 1966), 171; West (1974), 43 f. On the similarities (and differences) between Theognis and hellenistic epigram see especially Giangrande (1968), 95 f.; cf. Ludwig, *GRBS* iv (1963), 61; Henrichs, *HSCP* lxxxiii (1979), 209 f.

[44] (1893), 93 n. 1.

[45] West, *Greek Metre*, 160.

[46] Gow and Page, *HE* ii. 8.

was probably very little hellenistic invective that Meleager would have counted as epigram.

Back in the third century, however, 'epigram' seems to have covered occasional poetry of various sorts in various styles, lengths, and metres. It was Meleager's *selection* from this material that has shaped our perception of the character and limitations of the classical epigram. It was Meleager's selection that influenced the practice of later epigrammatists; Meleager's *Garland* that determined the character of later anthologies. The next, a second *Garland*, was published by Philip of Thessalonica in the reign of the Emperor Nero. It included most epigrammatists of any consequence since Meleager, the earliest being his fellow-Gadarene the Epicurean Philodemus. This work of the Roman period reveals a striking change of direction, away from the erotic and sympotic (with the exception of Philodemus) to the ecphrastic and epideictic—in a word to rhetoric.[47] Some of Philip's poets (especially Philip himself) cultivated the iambic trimeter, a few Phalaecians; but elegiacs predominated; the old rules of metre and prosody were somewhat relaxed, but we begin to find indications of accent regulation.[48] Like Meleager, Philip was a major contributor to his *Garland*, and took great pains to arrange it artistically. As yet no papyrus has been found (or recognized), but the second *Garland* was widely read in the following centuries, particularly during the age of Justinian.[49]

The main development in the generation after Philip was the satiric epigram, best represented by the Neronian Lucillius: attacks on the faults, not of individuals, but of whole professions and classes (doctors, athletes, fat men, thin men . . .).[50] There was also a revival of the erotic with Rufinus and the pederastic with

---

[47] P. Laurens, *RÉL* xliii (1965), 315 f. In *Die griech. und latein. Literatur der Kaiserzeit* (1989), 138, A. Dihle inexplicably claims that Philip's *Garland* was merely an expanded version of Meleager's.

[48] Gow and Page, *GP* i, pp. xxxviii–xlv; West, *Greek Metre*, 167 n. 14 and 181–3. By the second century hexameter epigrams became fashionable, on stone as well as in literature.

[49] A. Mattson, *Untersuchungen zur Epigrammsammlung des Agathias* (1942), 21 f., 75 f.

[50] See L. Robert's wonderful chapter in *L'Épigramme grecque* (1968), 181–293; W. Burnikel, *Untersuchungen zur Struktur des Witzepigramms bei Lukillios und Martial* (Palingenesia 15; 1980). There is also much useful information in I. G. Galli Calderini, 'L'epigramma greco tardoantico: tradizione e innovazione', *Vichiana* xvi (1987), 103–34. On Gregory Nazianzen, F. E. Consolino, *Athenaeum* lxv (1987), 407–25.

Strato of Sardis under Hadrian. Strato's 'Boyish Muse' survives almost entire in *AP* xii. But no comprehensive new anthology was compiled till the shadowy *Anthologion* of Diogenian, perhaps under Antoninus Pius.[51] Diogenian was a scholar, not a poet, and there is no indication that he contributed epigrams of his own or left any individual stamp on his collection. While the anthologies of Meleager and Philip survived into the Byzantine age, Diogenian's did not.

The next centuries saw a remarkable revival of genuine inscriptional epigrams, some of very high quality, but little of note at the literary level. Palladas of Alexandria published a collection of mainly satirical epigrams *c.*400, and Gregory of Nazianzus a volume of funerary epigrams a decade or two earlier. The evidence for a new anthology of *c.*400 will be presented in Ch. IV; it seems to have been compiled from existing anthologies, with the addition of one or two epigrams by Palladas. Once again, not a work of any individuality in its own right. The last ancient anthology we can identify and date is the *Cycle* of Agathias, put together in the reign of Justin II *c.*568, closely modelled on Meleager's *Garland*. It contains the epigrams of a number of Byzantine civil servants and professional men in a remarkably homogeneous style, a fascinating illustration of the fusion of all the traditions of the classical epigram with the bombast and verbosity of the Egyptian epic poet Nonnus.[52] This was the end of creative writing in the genre. For more than three centuries there was no more interest in the epigram than in any other classical literary form at Byzantium. Then *c.*900 came the largest and most comprehensive anthology of ancient epigrams ever compiled, the work of the protopapas Constantine Cephalas, the main subject of this book.

Not one of these ancient collections survives to this day in its original form, not even Cephalas'. For our knowledge of them, indeed for our knowledge of virtually the entire history of the classical epigram, we are dependent on two celebrated and remarkable manuscripts: the so-called Palatine Anthology (*AP*), a unique tenth-century codex now divided between Heidelberg and Paris; and the Planudean Anthology (*APl*), of which we possess in Venice the editor's signed and dated (September 1301) autograph copy.

[51] E. L. Bowie, in *Antonine Literature*, ed. D. A. Russell (1990), 55–6.
[52] For the influence of Nonnus, see Mattsson (1942), 112–71, and the commentaries on Agathias (1967) and Paul the Silentiary (1963) by G. Viansino.

Until the extraordinarily belated (and even then indirect) publication of the Palatine codex at the beginning of the nineteenth century,[53] the smaller and vastly inferior compilation of Planudes was *the* Greek Anthology. When F. Jacobs's second edition of 1813–17 appeared, reproducing for the first time the arrangement as well as the contents of *AP*, it became clear that Planudes had substantially rearranged his material. *APl* was in many ways easier to consult than its predecessors (as Planudes justifiably claimed), but as soon as serious work on the sources of the Anthology began it was realized that it was *AP* iv (which Planudes omitted) and the arrangement of *AP* (which Planudes had systematically broken up) that were the two major clues to its sources.

AP iv consists of the prefaces to the two *Garlands* and the *Cycle*. By great good fortune both Meleager and (less fully) Philip list the names of their contributors. Now it so happens that there occur at intervals in the major books of *AP* long sequences consisting entirely or almost entirely of poems ascribed to names in these two lists. There is no such list in Agathias' preface, but there are similar sequences in the same books that by analogy we can recognize as Agathian, thanks to routine addition of early Byzantine titles after the poet's name (scholasticus, antecessor, and the like). The names of Paul and Macedonius are also confirmed by the entry 'Agathias' in the Suda lexicon.

These extracts, sometimes consisting of a hundred or more poems in apparently uninterrupted sequence, will henceforth be called 'Meleagrian', 'Philippan', and 'Agathian' respectively, as (when appropriate) as will poets who regularly appear in such sequences.[54] Outside the main sequences there are also a certain number of shorter, sometimes 'broken' or 'impure' sequences. This is a constant feature of the larger books of *AP*, and as we proceed it will become clear that it is a consequence of the fortunately rather mechanical method of Constantine Cephalas. Our task is twofold: to recover what we can of the contents and arrangement of the *Garlands* and the *Cycle* (and the other ancient

[53] For its strange wanderings behind the scenes throughout the Renaissance, see below, Ch. VIII.

[54] For lists of the contributors to the two *Garlands* see Gow and Page, *HE* i, pp. xxi–xxvii (with Luck, *GGA* 1967, 25 f.) and *GP* i, p. xxi; for the contributors to the *Cycle*, Averil Cameron and myself, *JHS* lxxxvi (1966), 8. The best brief introduction to the subject is by Anna Meschini, in *Antologia Palatina*, ed. F. M. Pontani, i (Turin 1978), pp. xxxi–lvi.

collections); and to reconstruct the activity and influence of Cephalas. For not only does *AP* tell us all we are ever likely to know about Cephalas' predecessors in the ancient world, from Meleager to Agathias (but for *AP* we should never even have heard of either *Garland*): it also enables us to chart the rediscovery of the classical epigram at Byzantium and to write a new chapter in the history of the Macedonian Renaissance. A fresh study of the whereabouts of *AP* during the Italian Renaissance (by way of England) and some newly discovered apographs of the Planudean Anthology will round the story off down to the beginning of the seventeenth century.

II

The *Garlands* and the *Cycle*

MELEAGER: I

ACCORDING to the Palatine lemmatist (hereafter J), Meleager's *Garland* was arranged alphabetically, that is to say according to the initial letter of the first word of each poem. There is no corresponding lemma to Philip's *Garland*, but there are unmistakable alphabetical traces in all the major and most of the minor Philippan sequences in *AP*. The problem is that, despite J's statement about Meleager, there are no comparable alphabetical traces in *any* of the Meleagrian sequences.

Furthermore, in 1895 K. Radinger showed that there were unmistakable traces of two quite different but complementary methods of arrangement in at any rate the longer Meleagrian sequences, especially those of *AP* v, vii, and xii. First, poems by the more prolific poets recur in a sort of rhythmical alternation, with the work of lesser figures distributed evenly between. Second, poems are grouped according to subject-matter (epitaphs on philosophers, soldiers, and so on together: imitations follow the original), and there are sometimes verbal parallels linking poems on different themes. The latter pattern was discovered independently by R. Weisshäupl two years later, who showed that the three successive Meleagrian sequences in *AP* vii (406–506, 646–64, 707–40) had certain obvious similarities both in overall pattern and individual subjects, suggesting the conclusion that all three were different excerpts from the same source—presumably the *Garland* itself. Then A. Wifstrand traced similar parallelisms of arrangement between the Meleagrian sequences of *AP* v and xii, suggesting that heterosexual and homosexual erotica were originally not so divided, and that the Meleagrian sequences in v and xii derived from a common source (presumably again the *Garland* itself) containing both sorts mixed up together.[1]

[1] Wifstrand (1926), 5–29, with a useful summary of the results of Radinger (88–107) and Weisshäupl.

If both *Garlands* had been arranged alphabetically, why is it that only the Philippan sequences preserve the traces? It is a question that has far-reaching implications and must be squarely faced. In the first place, there is considerable current interest in the structure of Graeco-Roman poetry books[2] and it would be important if we could recover the rationale of so influential a specimen as Meleager's *Garland*. Secondly, and more relevant to this study, if Meleager's arrangement *was* alphabetical, then we should be forced to conclude that Cephalas broke it up completely (while leaving Philip's virtually intact) and substituted another of his own. If this is really what he did, then we could have little confidence in any attempt to analyse the sources of *AP*.

According to one recent critic, the 'surmise' (as he calls it) of a thematic arrangement for Meleager's *Garland* 'is contradicted by the evidence of alphabetical order present in the texts as well as by the explicit statement made by the lemmatist, which supports such evidence'.[3]

First the alleged traces of alphabetical order. From *AP* vii (omitting, for the sake of brevity, authors' names): 194 (opening ἀκρίδα), 195 (ἀκρίς), 196 (ἀχήεις τέττιξ); then 200–3, all opening οὐκέτι; then 265–6 (both ναυηγοῦ), 207 (ναυτίλοι), and 208 (ναυηγόν). From *AP* v. 136–7 (both ἔγχει); 172 (ὄρθρε, τί μοι), 173 (ὄρθρε, τί νῦν). G. Luck[4] refers to v. 139 (ἡδὺ μέλος) and 140 (ἡδυμελεῖς), not noticing that *AP* offers ἁδὺ in 139. 1 (ἡδὺ only Planudes); and suggests emending οἰνοπόται at xii. 85 to ᾠνοπόται (ᾧ οἰν.), in order to provide an alphabetical link with xii. 84 (ὤνθρωποι).

Luck goes on to ask whether this is a coincidence. The question needs to be formulated more precisely. The juxtaposition of these poems is not itself (of course) accidental. But the editor responsible did not juxtapose them because they began with the same letter of the alphabet, but because they began with the same word. And that makes all the difference. In every case the primary link is not alphabetical but thematic.

There is nothing remarkable in two out of seven poems (vii. 192–8) on ἀκρίδες (grasshoppers) beginning with the word (and as

---

[2] See especially J. B. Van Sickle (1980).
[3] G. Giangrande, *CR* 1973, 136 n. 1. Cf. A. Lesky, *History of Greek Literature*, tr. J. Willis and C. de Heer (London 1966), 741: 'We may believe the lemmatist' without further comment. More surprisingly, so too A. Dihle, *Die griech. und latein. Literatur der Kaiserzeit* (1989), 138.
[4] 1967, 51–2.

for 196, it is a bold critic who would stake his life that Meleager did not in fact write ἠχήεις). As for vii. 265–8, naturally they are all epitaphs for sailors. The οὐκέτι poems vii. 200–3 are all epitaphs on birds who 'no longer' do what they did in life. *AP* v. 136–7 (ἔγχει) are both toasts; v. 172–3 (ὄρθρε) both apostrophes to Dawn. And even if we allow Luck's ᾠνοπόται at xii. 85, the primary link with xii. 84 is the poet's appeal to his friends. The same applies to the sequence xii. 75–8, all beginning with εἰ; they all describe a lover so beautiful that 'if' he had wings and a bow he would be taken for Cupid. The repetition of εἰ, in a way the key structural element in the poems, instantly prepares the reader for the repetition of the theme. It might be added that all the examples alleged from *AP* vii occur in what are in any case very brief and dubious Meleagrian sequences; for example, the four οὐκέτι epitaphs on birds are followed by a fifth (vii. 204) by Agathias. It is legitimate to wonder whether in this case the grouping may not be the work of Cephalas rather than Meleager.

So the alphabetical traces hitherto adduced are simply irrelevant to the question whether the *Garland* as a whole was arranged alphabetically. What would be needed is not groups of poems beginning with the same word, but (*a*) groups beginning with the same letter when it is *not* the beginning of the same word; and (*b*) a succession of poems or groups of poems beginning with successive letters of the alphabet.[5] Both are conspicuous by their absence.

Finally, there is the decisive but neglected point made by J. Basson (pp. 36–7): the first and last poems of an alphabetically-arranged collection must (inescapably) have begun with an alpha and omega respectively. It happens that we possess the first and last poems of Meleager's *Garland* (*AP* iv. 1 and xii. 257, the latter

---

[5] Beckby i². 70 (after many others) includes without comment as alphabetical Meleagrian sequences the Anacreon sequence vi. 134–42 (α η ο π π π π ρ σ) and the Simonides sequence vii. 507–16 (α ο π σ σ σ τ φ α α ο). Since Meleager's clearly and repeatedly expressed purpose was to 'interweave' the work of different poets (iv. 1, 5, 9, 15, 18, 21, 25, 31, 35, 37, 41, 45), homogeneous sequences by just one poet can hardly be used to illustrate his method when the 'interweaving' so apparent in all the other Meleagrian sequences tells such a different story. As Gow and Page conclude (*HE* i. p. xviii n. 2), 'if they are Meleagrian they probably owe their arrangement to earlier homogeneous sources from which Meleager derived them.' It should be added that if the Simonides sequence *is* accepted as Meleagrian, then we can hardly refuse to consider the immediately following homogeneous Callimachus sequence (vii. 517–25) Meleagrian too; but there is no trace of alphabetical order here (η α δ η κ τ ο η ο). See too Page, *Epigrammata Graeca* (1975), vi–viii.

explicitly described by Meleager as his *coronis*). They begin with a mu and (of all letters) an alpha! By contrast, Philip's preface begins (of course) with an alpha.

It might be argued as a last resort that Cephalas excerpted Philip's *Garland* direct but only knew Meleager's at second or third hand, much as he only knew the Anthology of Diogenian through the fourth-century intermediary postulated in Ch. IV. But even this will not really work. For the result in the case of Diogenian is that the traces of his Anthology in *AP* can only be guessed at. No recognizable sequences, only brief thematic (re)classifications probably to be ascribed to Cephalas (pp. 88–9). Yet the general outline of Meleager's *Garland* is just as clear-cut in *AP* as Philip's; the Meleagrian sequences can be delimited just as sharply as the Philippan; Meleager's preface is quoted together with Philip's in *AP* iv; and we also have (xii. 257) Meleager's conclusion (though not Philip's). The only way out would be to postulate that Cephalas directly excerpted a redaction of Meleager's *Garland* already systematically rearranged on the thematic principles now apparent in the Meleagrian sequences of *AP*.

Why go to such lengths to save the credit of what a moment's reflection will reveal to be no more than a guess on the part of J? The *Garlands* of Meleager and Philip are nowhere mentioned by any writer extant today, and it is not likely that any more information was available to J, writing in only the early stages of the revival of classical scholarship at Byzantium. The absence of entries for Meleager and Philip in the Suda lexicon (perhaps a generation later than J) suggests that there was no biographical tradition stemming from antiquity.[6] The rest of J's statements about both *Garlands* are clearly just inferences from the text of poems quoted in *AP*. For example, at the bottom of p. 82 he wrote to himself the revealing little note 'look up Meleager's home town in the *Garland*'. This he duly did and correctly added 'Gadarene' (from *AP* vii. 417–19) beneath his query. Evidently his exemplar did not supply even the most basic facts. Nor is there any

---

[6] Biographical entries in the Suda derive from a mid-ninth-century revision of Hesychius of Miletus' *Onomatologos* (West, *Studies in Greek Elegy and Iambus* (1974), 44). It might be added that the Suda drew heavily on a redaction of Cephalas very closely akin to *AP*; it is thus the more striking that there is no entry for Meleager and Philip, names evidently no less familiar to the compilers than Agathias (who has quite an adequate entry).

indication (or probability) that J consulted an original text of the *Garland*;[7] we shall soon see that he had no other text against which to check his exemplar.

Where then did he obtain his information about the arrangement of the *Garland*? Like the rest of his comments on the *Garlands*, it is surely just an inference. I used to subscribe to the traditional view that J simply confused the two *Garlands*, but this does not do justice to the facts. It cannot be that he is carelessly identifying the manifestly alphabetical Philippan extracts as Meleagrian, for he goes on to say that it was Cephalas who 'mixed up' (συνέχεεν) Meleager's original arrangement by his own thematic organization 'as in the present book'. That is to say, he was arguing from the *absence* of alphabetization in the Meleagrian sequences rather than its presence in the Philippan sequences. Because he saw (rightly—up to a point) Philip's *Garland* as an 'imitation' of Meleager's, he inferred (wrongly) that *both* had been arranged alphabetically. But since there were no traces of alphabetization in the Meleagrian sequences of *AP* ('in the present book'), he simply assumed that they had been broken up by Cephalas.

It was not a foolish guess, but it was a guess none the less—a mistaken guess. No one who has studied the tables of Radinger, Weisshäupl, and Wifstrand with any care will find it easy to ascribe the simple but skilful and consistent twofold pattern they trace through all the substantial Meleagrian sequences of *AP* either to chance or to the infinitely cruder mind of Cephalas.

The more so since A. Mattsson has demonstrated beyond question that precisely the same twofold system was followed by Agathias for his *Cycle*.[8] And though there must always be reservations about Cephalas' handling of his Meleagrian material, we can at least be sure that he did not significantly rearrange his Agathian material. For we know from Agathias' preface that he employed a third, more basic device as well. He divided his material between seven books according to subject matter: anathematica, epideictica, epitymbia, protreptica, sympotica, erotica, and scoptica. Cephalas took over these convenient basic divisions for his own *Anthology*, and thus we can have every confidence that the Agathian runs in the major Cephalan books directly reflect the order and arrangement of the original Agathian books.

---

[7] I much regret having ever suggested that he did (*GRBS* 1968, 330–1).

[8] Mattsson (1942), 1–16.

It can easily be shown that Agathias and his fellow poets were influenced by the poets of Meleager's *Garland*,[9] and it would not be surprising if Agathias himself had imitated its arrangement. We find precisely the same grouping according to theme and verbal links and the same rhythmic procession of 'Hauptdichter' (Paul, Macedonius, Julian the Egyptian, and Agathias instead of Callimachus, Asclepiades, Leonidas, and Meleager) that Radinger, Weisshäupl, and Wifstrand (curiously but significantly enough without reference to the striking Agathian parallel)[10] detected in Meleager.

MELEAGER: II

There is one further point about Meleager's *Garland* on which a little more light can perhaps be cast before we move on to Philip's. How many and what sort of books went to make up the *Garland*? Gow and Page included 4,749 lines of hellenistic epigram in their collection. Even if we exclude from this total the 23 poems of Theocritus which Meleager apparently omitted[11] and the 35 by Meleagrian authors not included in *AP* or *APl* (some of which may nevertheless have stood in the *Garland* itself), that still leaves *c.* 4,500 lines. Then we must make some sort of allowance for the Meleagrian poems lost in the huge lacuna in *AP* ix (see Ch. X), and there must be many more Meleagrian anonyma in *AP* and *APl* not guaranteed as such by their context. Then there are the substantial losses suffered by the *Garland* between the first century BC and the probably sixth-century copies used by Cephalas, of which more below. Finally, there is the question of titles and ascriptions to individual poems. In *AP* and *APl* they are normally written in the margin, but in all epigram-papyri that carry them at all, on a separate line between poems.[12] On the Gallus papyrus, of *c.*50–25 BC, about three times the normal line space was left between epigrams.[13] In Greek papyri it seems to have been normal

---

[9] Mattsson (1942), 17 f., and see G. Viansino's commentaries on the epigrams of Paul the Silentiary (Turin 1963) and Agathias (Milan 1967).

[10] Except for a brief aside by Radinger (1895), 103 n. 1.

[11] Despite Luck's protest (1967, 31–2) the arguments of Gow and Page seem unanswerable on this point (*HE* ii. 525).

[12] Gow (1958), p. 16, to which add Pack 1602–3.

[13] P. J. Parsons, *JRS* lxix (1979), 129 with pl. IV. There is a gap and a paragraphos separating the two epigrams on the newly published P. Köln iii. 128.

to write ἄλλο between epigrams even if they were anonymous (or a sequence by the same author).[14] If this is how Meleager wrote his ascriptions, that means the best part of another 1,000 lines.

The original total can scarcely have been less than *c.* 6,000 lines, many times longer than any known Greek poetry book (seldom more than *c.* 1,500 lines, often less), and far beyond the capacity of one ordinary papyrus roll.[15] In what must be the last poem in the entire *Garland*, its *sphragis* or seal, the 'coronis', the final flourish that marks the end of the book, is represented as saying (*AP* xii. 257. 3–5):[16]

φαμὶ τὸν ἐκ πάντων ἠθροισμένον εἰς ἕνα μόχθον
　ὑμνοθετᾶν, βύβλῳ τᾷδ' ἐνελιξάμενον,
ἐκτελέσαι Μελέαγρον.

I say that Meleager, who assembled the work of all poets into one work, who rolled them up in this book, has finished his task.

These lines have been interpreted as a statement that the *Garland* consisted of one roll.[17] But that is to combine in one literal interpretation two quite separate metaphors: first, Meleager claims to have 'assembled' his poets (as one might soldiers); next to have 'rolled them up in' his book (conceived, naturally enough, as a papyrus roll). There is an antithesis between the 'one book' and 'all the poets', between the multiplicity of his material and the unification of the poet. Obviously it is the large number of poets he has included rather than the smallness of his book of which Meleager is proud. We might compare the epigram describing how Artemidorus of Tarsus gathered 'all the bucolic muses together in one fold' (*AP* ix. 205). The bucolic corpus might have fitted on one roll, but once again the emphasis clearly lies on the gathering together of previously scattered items. Meleager's βύβλος need not refer to one roll rather than one work divided into several books and written on several rolls. The 5,835 lines of Apollonius'

---

[14] Gow (1958), p. 29; there are many examples on tombstones engraved with more than one epitaph.

[15] On poetry books and papyrus rolls, see Birt, *Das antike Buchwesen* (1882), 289 f.; Irigoin, *Histoire du Texte de Pindare* (1952), 38 f.; more recently, Van Sickle (1980), 7–16; M. S. Santirocco, *Unity and Design in Horace's Odes* (1986), 5–13.

[16] On the personification of the coronis, see P. Bing, *The Well-Read Muse* (1988), 33–5.

[17] E. A. Schmidt, *Philologus* cxxvii (1979), 218–19, using so long a book to support the fashionable but improbable hypothesis that the extant Catullan corpus was so arranged by its author as one 'book'.

Argonautica are divided into four books, one of them the longest extant (1,781 lines). We are surely entitled to assume that Meleager's *Garland* was similarly divided.

Following and developing some hints of Wifstrand we can profitably guess at least at the principle of book-division Meleager used, which will in turn suggest a number. The most obvious and easy principle would have been that followed by Agathias: division by subject matter. There are in *AP* something like 270 Meleagrian erotica, 290 epitymbia, 135 anathematica, and 50 epideictica (to which we can add another 45 from *APl*). These are the only four of the seven Agathian divisions to which Meleagrian poets made any contributions. There are no Meleagrian poems at all in *AP* x and xi. Scoptica, protreptica, and straightforward sympotica seem not to have been to their taste (such as we do find are generally classified under one or other of the other four: for example, most Meleagrian sympotica are also erotic and so in *AP* v). Split up into these four divisions, the 6,000-odd lines of the *Garland* would have comprised four books which would have satisfied both contemporary canons for the length of a poetic book and the size of an average papyrus roll.

We have seen that the twofold system discovered by Radinger—regular alternation of major poets together with verbal and thematic links—is paralleled by the same twofold pattern in sequences from Agathias' *Cycle*. Now the Agathian sequences we know to have been originally divided by Agathias himself into subject categories, the same categories as *AP*, into which they were presumably transferred more or less as they stood, with a minimum of Cephalan reclassification. If the division of Meleagrian poems between these Palatine categories was entirely the work of Cephalas, how is it possible that such clear traces of so subtle a twofold system managed to survive?

Some of the briefer and more obvious thematic groupings would have survived easily enough. When he found suitable thematic groups Cephalas naturally adapted them (as Planudes did later) for his own thematic categories: for example, the seven Meleagrian poems on grasshoppers at vii. 189–98. But the regular alternation of authors could hardly have survived such piecemeal reclassification. It is the *combination* of the two systems which suggests that at least the longer Meleagrian sequences are still relatively undisturbed.

Then there is the parallel arrangement of homo- and heterosexual erotica in *AP* v and xii. The continuous run of mixed
Meleagrian erotica (*AP* xii. 76, 77, 78; ix. 15; xii. 106; v. 152;
xii. 19) in *BKT* v. i. 75–6 was rightly held by Wifstrand to support
his view[18] that the Meleagrian sequences in v and xii are complementary excerpts from an originally combined homo- and heterosexual sequence. Further and stronger support is now supplied by
the similar unbroken erotic sequence in P. Oxy. 3324 (*AP* ix. 16; v.
190; xii. 157; and again v. 152). Wifstrand long ago observed that
in such a combined sequence one would expect to find v. 190 next
to xii. 157 (p. 21), linked by the common motif of the lover
compared to the storm-tossed sailor. In P. Oxy. 3324, v. 190 and
xii. 157 do indeed stand next to each other. It is also noteworthy
that in *BKT* v. i. 75–6, ix. 15 stands one poem away from v. 152,
while in P. Oxy. 3324 ix. 16 stands two away from v. 152. *AP* ix.
15–16 are an erotic pair misclassified (as even J observed in his
lemmata) among the epideictica. There was never any reason to
doubt that they originally belonged with the rest of the Meleagrian
erotica, and we can now add that they probably stood together in
the neighbourhood of v. 152.

Both papyri are undoubtedly excerpts from the *Garland* rather
than unabridged fragments. For example both lack v. 151, the
sister poem to v. 152 (though it might conceivably have followed
152 in P. Oxy.); only one of the pair ix. 15–16 appears in each;
BKT has xii. 76–8 but not 79, the pair to ix. 15 (both on the conceit
of the flame in the lover's heart setting fire to objects); ix. 16, which
has no link with the poems that follow it in P. Oxy., has a clear link
by contrast with xii. 106, the successor to ix. 15 in *BKT* (ix. 16 on
the poet's one heart pierced by three arrows; xii. 106 on the one
object of the poet's affections); more generally, of course, none of
the five poems that precede v. 152 in *BKT* appear in P. Oxy., and
none of the four that precede the same poem in P. Oxy. appears in
BKT. None the less the clear parallels in the sequence of poems
between the two papyri on the one hand and *AP* v and xii on the
other cannot be coincidental. The natural conclusion is that the
papyri and the Palatine books alike are all excerpts from the same

---

[18] Above, p. 11. Luck (1967, 51–2) was rash to claim alphabetical traces in the
seven epigrams of this papyrus, or rather in the first three, the *thematically* linked εἰ
poems xii. 76–9 discussed above.

unbroken, sexually undifferentiated erotic sequence in Meleager's
Garland.

There are also the three successive Meleagrian sequences in *AP*
vii. To what might have seemed the natural implication that these
are three successive excerpts from the same original continuous
sequence of epitymbia, Lenzinger objected (p. 13) that other sorts
of epigrams must have been intermingled among the epitymbia,
for (he argued) if all the Meleagrian epitymbia had been concentrated in one section of the *Garland*, Cephalas would not have had
to conduct more than one search for them. He contrasted the one
Agathian sequence in vii. But we do not know that Cephalas 'had
to' look more than once for Meleagrian epitymbia: we shall soon
see that there is an entirely different explanation for the successive
excerpts. And further support is provided by our third (probably)
Meleagrian papyrus, P. Oxy. 662. Not only is there an unbroken
sequence of seven funerary poems; it is subdivided (like *BKT* v. i.
75–6 and P. Oxy. 3324) into smaller thematic groups (three
epitaphs on Prexo, two on Glenis), and there is also regular author
alternation (Leonidas, Antipater, Amyntas, Leonidas, Antipater,
Leonidas). We have already seen that the inclusion of Antipater
virtually excludes the possibility that this anthology is pre-Meleagrian. It would be an extraordinary coincidence if it had been the
three different excerptors responsible for these three Meleagrian
papyri who introduced these features so characteristic of the
Meleagrian extracts of *AP*. The natural conclusion is surely that
the continuous erotic and funerary sequences are likewise Meleagrian. That P. Oxy. 662 is an excerpt is proved by the omission of
vii. 723 next to its imitation by Amyntas, though the question is
somewhat academic, given that the scribe abandoned his task in
mid poem in the course of the fragment, which is written on the
back of an edition of Pindar.

Wifstrand himself, while canvassing in a tentative parenthesis
the possibility that the erotica comprised a separate book of their
own and admitting too that there appeared to have been another
such section (he avoided the word book) comprised mainly of
epitymbia, was nevertheless loath to suggest a formal division of
the Meleagrian material into books. His reason was the presence
of what he was inclined to regard as alien matter—viz. a lacing
of votive and epideictic poems—matter which in some cases at
least there was reason to believe Meleagrian (rather than Cephalan

insertion). The answer, I think, is that Meleager interpreted these classifications rather more liberally than we might suppose.[19] Indeed, he doubtless interpreted them as broad guidelines rather than hard and fast categories, with non-committal headings such as βίβλος α', β', γ', δ' (like the Vienna list).

Wifstrand lists a number of poems in the Meleagrian sequences of vii which are not sepulchral: for example, 409 on Antimachus, 410 on Thespis, 411 on Aeschylus, 709 on Alcman, 713 on Erinna. Yet are these really intruders? One of the commonest types among the epitymbia included in vii is the poem on a famous writer cast in the form of a fictitious epitaph. Many are really no more sepulchral than those mentioned above. So unless Meleager was going to be pedantic, it might well have seemed more appropriate to include poems on writers which did not even pretend to be sepulchral along with those that did. While they might be more correctly placed among the epideictica, they would then be in a non-literary context, away from their natural fellows. Similarly with vii. 723, a lament for the defeat of Sparta: not an epitaph proper, but not altogether out of place among the epitaphs. Its imitation by Amyntas was already so placed in the funerary sequence of P. Oxy. 662. Strictly speaking, vii. 193 by Simmias should have been classified as epideictic and 195–6 by Meleager as erotic. But they fit harmoniously enough in a sequence of epitaphs for grasshoppers that emphasize their sweet music; in 193 the grasshopper is still performing in a cage, and in Meleager's two poems the music is assuaging the pangs of love. 'Intruders' are alleged in v too. Gow, for example (Gow and Page, *HE* ii. 171), states that v. 146 (Callimachus) on a statue of Berenice is 'evidently misplaced' in v and 'should have been' in ix. But the poem describes her beauty and concludes by saying that without her οὐδ' αὐταὶ ταὶ Χάριτες Χάριτες. This conceit links it closely with 148 (where Heliodora is said to excel αὐτὰς τὰς Χάριτας χάρισιν) and 149. 4 (καὐτὰν τὰν χάριν

---

[19] Giangrande, N.S. xxiii *CR* 1973, 136 n. 1, alleges that my original remarks in *GRBS* 1968, 329 'postulate that Meleager was not precise in evaluating the "formal features" of epigrams'. I did not (of course) mean that Meleager could not tell an erotic from a funerary poem. But as Giangrande's own work in particular has shown, hellenistic epigrams are subtle products of many traditions, often falling between the crude classifications here at issue. For example, vii. 195–6 satisfy every thematic qualification for inclusion in their present context but one—the funerary. It is in such cases (in my view) that Meleager used his judgement, in the last analysis putting literary considerations first, aiming at variety rather than homogeneity. See now addenda.

ἐν χάριτι), both by Meleager himself. In fact, it is clear that Meleager derived this motif directly from Callimachus' poem. This, surely, is why he placed it before his own poems. It was not a true eroticon, but it had some of the characteristics thereof, and as the model for later erotica was more appropriately placed among them than with the anathematica or epideictica, where this connection would be obscured. Epigram 205 might from the formal point of view be classified as an anathematicon, but the object dedicated is a love charm: 206 is a dedication of musical instruments, but by girls bearing names suitable for hetaerae (Gow and Page, *HE* ii. 353), one of them being described as φιλέρως and a willing performer at revels. Here again the erotic and sympotic elements may in Meleager's judgement have outweighed the anathematic form. There are similar apparent 'intruders' in Agathian sections, where we can be certain that the selection was Agathias' own. For example, v. 217 and 218, though concerned with love, are both really epideictic. Epigram 222 on a κιθαριστρίς might have been more appropriately placed together with Leontius' run of poems on dancing girls, presumably included among Agathias' ecphrastica, though now preserved only in *APl* iv. Yet obviously in Agathias' eyes the erotic element predominated in all three.

I would suggest, then, that there is no real alien matter in these four Meleagrian categories as represented in *AP*. It is just that, like Agathias, Meleager was prepared to include 'formal intruders' if for some other reason they seemed to him more suitably placed elsewhere than in their formally correct context. Indeed, I would go further. It seems to me that the absence of glaring misfits in Meleagrian sequences is a strong argument in favour of the thesis of fourfold division by subject. For as we shall see time and again in the pages that follow, there are frequent and startling misclassifications in the Palatine books, errors which cannot have been made by the original editors and must be laid at Cephalas' door.

For example, *AP* vii. 641 (by Antiphilus) Cephalas classified as an epitymbion, evidently supposing that its opening word σῆμα referred to a tomb. Had he taken the trouble to read (rather than merely transcribe) the rest of the poem, he would have seen that it referred in fact to a water clock. It was presumably likewise the mention of a 'mound' (χῶμα) in l. 1 that led him to put vii. 379 by the same Antiphilus among the epitymbia, though this time if he had read on he would have discovered that the reference was to a

mole in the harbour at Puteoli! Then there is ix. 554 by Marcus
Argentarius, a satirical poem on a *fellatrix* called Heracleia,
absurdly out of place in an epideictic sequence on cities. The
explanation is as certain as it is revealing: Heracleia is a commoner
name for cities than girls, and, further misled by πόλις at the end of
l. 2, Cephalas so took it here. *AP* vii. 742 by Apollonides is about a
blind woman who gave birth to twins; it owes its place among the
epitymbia to a misinterpretation of φάος ὤλεσας, 'lost your *sight*', in
l. 1. Then there is the plainly epideictic poem by Antipater on
Amphipolis, which should have been with Heracleia in ix but was
evidently put in vii through a misunderstanding of the description
of the city as the 'tomb of Phyllis', its eponymous hero. *AP* vi. 256
and 257 and vii. 626 are all likewise epideictic; vi. 88 and x. 20 and
21 are no less clearly erotic. Many less conspicuous examples could
be added, such as the two erotic poems ix. 15–16, whose mispla-
cing in the epideictic book 'thanks to the stupidity of the excerptor'
was already noted by J and has been confirmed by their appearance
in their original erotic context in the two papyri discussed above.
Epigram 15 begins (accepting Scaliger's emendation) οὗτος ὁ, one
of the stock openings of ecphrastic epigrams, and 16, opening
τρισσαὶ μὲν χάριτες, referring to the poet's three loves, was no doubt
interpreted as a poem about the Graces.

   There are no such gross misclassifications in the Meleagrian
sequences. Or rather such cases as there are are confined to
Cephalas' own division of the Meleagrian erotica into two categories, heterosexual and homosexual. An easy enough task, one might
have thought. Yet there are numerous homosexual poems in v and
scores of heterosexual poems in xii. This was the result when
Cephalas was faced with thematically undifferentiated material
and had to do his own categorizing. Yet though he made such a
sorry mess of the Meleagrian erotica, he apparently managed to
deal with the Meleagrian anathematica, epideictica, and epitymbia
without making a single mistake of this order or nature, mistakes of
a sort he regularly made when distributing the undifferentiated
Philippan poems under these headings. And the explanation of this
is, surely, not that for once Cephalas was extra-careful and
managed to avoid error, but that he found the Meleagrian anathematica, epideictica, and epitymbia *already* differentiated in his
source—the *Garland* itself.

   So it was not only the alternation of 'Hauptdichter' and thematic linking that Agathias took over from Meleager, but also the preliminary subdivision according to type. Hitherto it has been supposed that this preliminary subdivision was a new departure of Agathias'. I would suggest, rather, that all Agathias did was to add three more headings to cover the wider scope of the work of himself and his friends.

Thanks to P. Köln 204, this conclusion can now be reinforced in part by the evidence of one of Meleager's predecessors, Mnasalces. Before the discovery of this papyrus, Luck pointed out that 10 of the 18 (then) extant epigrams of Mnasalces began with the letter α, too high a number (he argued) to be due to coincidence. More specifically, 6 of these αs occur in what Luck described as a reverse alphabetical sequence in *AP* vii (491, 488, 212, 194, 171, 54). Luck's explanation was that Meleager had excerpted the beginning of an alphabetically arranged collection of Mnasalces' funerary epigrams.[20] What he did not notice is that this 'alphabetical sequence' is twice broken by poems of Mnasalces that do *not* begin with an α (192 and 242, both beginning with an o). What he could not then know is that we would recover the beginning of a pre-Meleagrian collection of Mnasalces' epigrams in which the first four poems began with the letters o, σ, α, and τ. And one of this opening quartet turns out to be none other than the second in Luck's 'alphabetic sequence' (vii. 488), standing between a σ and a τ.

No display of ingenuity is required to discern clear thematic links between the three successive pairs on what remains of the papyrus. No. I is a dedicatory poem about a shield never used in war; II a funerary poem on a warrior; III (*AP* vii. 488) a funerary poem on a girl who died before marriage; IV (? *AP* vi. 266) on an altar dedicated by a girl before marriage; the very fragmentary V and VI are apparently funerary poems on a woman and a (male) poet who were both fond of the bottle in life. But there was no preliminary subdivision between funerary and dedicatory.

The poems in Luck's sequence in *AP* vii are where they are because of similar *thematic* links with adjacent poems by other poets. Thus 488 and 491 are two of 7 Meleagrian poems on girls dying before marriage; 194 is one of 7 Meleagrian poems on crickets and cicadas—192 being another by Mnasalces beginning with o; 54 is one of four poems (not all even Meleagrian) on

[20] *GGA* ccix (1967), 52.

Hesiod. There are no traces of alphabetical sequence in P. Köln 204, and those in *AP* vii must be put down to pure coincidence. But it is obviously more than coincidence that Meleager and Mnasalces share these thematic links between adjacent poems. Alternation between poets and preliminary subdivision by type were additional measures forced on Meleager by the much greater bulk of material he had to deal with.

PHILIP: I

As early as the first serious attempt to analyse the sources of *AP* (Passow's *De vestigiis Coronarum* of 1827) it was realized that all the substantial Philippan sequences in *AP* are arranged alphabetically. A convenient table of all these sequences[21] together with the first word of each poem will be found at pp. 13–20 of Weisshäupl's *Grabgedichte*, and one scarcely needs even to read through to the end to see that there is no possibility of error or denial.[22] This was a discovery of the first importance, since it means that if the first word of any poem inside a Philippan sequence is even one letter out, it can be regarded with confidence as an intruder into that sequence—a confidence unfortunately never attainable in Meleagrian or even Agathian sequences. But it was also a discovery which put an end to further inquiry about the arrangement of the *Garland*, since the last word appeared to have been said.

There seemed only one question left to ask. Was there more than one book, and if so, did the alphabetical order run from the

---

[21] See too the table on p. xvi above.

[22] At both vi. 239 and ix. 410 a sigma (σμήνεος and σμίνθος respectively) occurs between epsilon and eta. The solution is obvious enough: what Philip wrote in both places was an initial zeta (Ζμήνεος and Ζμίνθος), just as Catullus' friend Cinna wrote *Zmyrna* for *Smyrna*. Editors have been curiously reluctant to admit this certain correction (certain in so far as it must be what Philip wrote for the purposes of his alphabetical order: whether the actual authors, Tullius Sabinus and Apollonides, used the *zeta* is another matter) to their texts (not one so far). Though advanced already by F. Passow, 8–9, and repeated by Wiegand in *RhM* iii (1845), 542, it was proposed again by P. Friedlaender (*ap.* Maas) in *Gnomon* vii (1931), 578, then again by A. Wilhelm in *L'Ant. class.* iv (1935), 251 (both for vi. 239 only), and yet again now by R. Merkelbach in *Glotta* xlv (1967), 39–40 (with a *Nachtrag* acknowledging Passow's priority, but no reference to Friedlaender or Wilhelm). A *zeta* now appears in the addenda to Beckby's second edition (though only for vi. 239), the credit being assigned there to Friedlaender (to whom, rather than to Passow, he was referred by Luck in *Gnomon* xxx (1958), 272).

beginning of the first book to the end of the last, or did each individual book run from alpha to omega? Since something like 3,000 Philippan lines survive in *AP* and *APl*, there was probably (though not necessarily) more than one book. As before, we must allow for titles and for omissions by Cephalas. Even so, it looks as though Philip's *Garland* was a little shorter than Meleager's. Indeed, it is commonly believed that Philip himself admitted as much, but this notion is based on a misinterpretation of Philip's preface. 'Familiar as you are with the fame of the older poets [i.e. the Meleagrian poets],' writes Philip to his patron Camillus, γνῶθι καὶ ὁπλοτέρων τὴν ὀλιγοστιχίην (*AP* iv. 2. 6). 'Learn to know the less *abundant* verses of our younger ones', translates Paton; 'lern auch die *knappere Kunst* jüngerer Dichter nunmehr', Beckby (in both cases my italics). 'Doch war der Umfang der Sammlung bedeutend geringer als der des Meleagrischen Stephanos' writes Radinger, quoting this line. In fact there can be no doubt whatever that Philip is alluding to the brevity of the epigram as a literary genre, not to the small number of them included in his *Garland*. In the first place there is no comparative. In the second, compare *AP* ix. 342 by Parmenion, one of the very poets Philip included, and one mentioned in his preface: φημὶ πολυστιχίην ἐπιγράμματος οὐ κατὰ Μούσας / εἶναι . . .

To return to the question of the individual books of the *Garland*. In the course of that tireless search for Graeco-Roman poetry books which eventually filled out a dossier of almost 150, Theodor Birt pounced on the long Philippan sequence at *AP* ix. 215–312, 596 lines (or 694 counting titles), and declared it a book.[23] This view was rejected almost at once by Weisshäupl[24] on two counts, neither of them cogent. His first objection was based on the once fashionable but now generally (and rightly) rejected belief that Cephalas did not himself use the original collections of Meleager or Philip (or even the relatively recent Agathias) at first hand. His second was what he (for no stated reason) apparently regarded as the absurdity of each book having its own complete alphabetical sequence.

If Birt were right, we should be able to conclude that Philip's *Garland* was divided, like the collections of both his predecessor and successor, according to subject matter, each book being

---

[23] Birt (1882), 388–9.   [24] Weisshäupl (1889), 26 n. 1.

arranged alphabetically. But (as we have seen) there are misfits in
almost every Philippan sequence in *AP*, clearly the result of
Cephalas' carelessness. No one will believe that Philip himself took
the *fellatrix* Heracleia for a city or the mole of Puteoli for a
tombstone. Yet every poem is correctly placed in an alphabetical
sequence. So they cannot be intruders inserted by Cephalas. On
the contrary, they are all integral links of the original *Garland*,
which Cephalas mistakenly *retained*. Obviously, then, the original
Garland must have been thematically undifferentiated. It was
Cephalas who did the distributing of individual poems into his
own categories, sometimes getting it wrong and giving the game
away.

So Birt was wrong to suppose that Philippan books were
arranged alphabetically according to subject matter. But the possibility that there were several alphabetical books, *not* arranged
according to subject matter, was left open by Radinger's argument.
True, Radinger seemed to think that the presence of two or three
Philippan sequences per book of *AP* was further evidence against
such a view, but might it not in fact be possible to see here a trace
of two or three such undifferentiated books successively excerpted
by Cephalas? Perhaps. But this possibility too can be put out of
court by a consideration long noted but never apparently exploited
in this connection. *AP* vi. 106, firmly embedded in an alphabetical
sequence, appears again after vi. 255, where it is again firmly
embedded in an alphabetical sequence. There is only one possible
explanation. Originally both these alphabetical sequences formed
one and the same sequence. Cephalas excerpted it *twice*, and
absent-mindedly included the same poem twice in both the result-
ing sequences (which, since the original was alphabetical, would
naturally both be alphabetical themselves).

Thanks to Cephalas' inattentiveness the conclusion seems inescapable that Philip's original *Garland* comprised one long alphabetical series without regard to subject matter; erotica, anathematica, epitymbia, etc. all together. So the Philippan sequences of
erotica, anathematica, epitymbia, etc. which we read in the various
books of *AP* are a series of excerpts of the Philippan poems which
Cephalas thought (sometimes mistakenly) to be concerned with
these subjects. If Philip divided his material into separate bodies,
he perhaps did it on the same principle as the fascicules of an
alphabetical reference work today—three books (say) comprising

$a-\theta$, $\iota-\pi$, $\rho-\omega$. On the other hand, since there were in a sense twenty-four 'books' already (the letters of the alphabet), further formal subdivision may not have been felt necessary. The distribution between papyrus rolls may have varied from copy to copy.

This has a major consequence which does not seem to have been drawn. Even the cautious Gow was for once incautious enough to write of the Meleagrian, Philippan, and Agathian sequences in *AP* in the same terms as 'blocks of epigrams ... transferred more or less unaltered from their respective sources.'[25] We have seen that there are good reasons for supposing this to be the case with the Agathian sequences, and probably too with the Meleagrian sequences (but only if, as argued above, they derive from thematically divided books). But it should be obvious that the Philippan sequences are on a completely different footing. Not one of them can be even relatively 'unaltered'.

The sequence of erotic poems (*AP* v. 104–33), for example, is simply an excerpt of all the erotic poems which Cephalas could find (or deemed good for us) scattered throughout the 3,000-odd lines of the *Garland*. A mere 29 poems, 76 lines, out of 3,000. And since they range from alpha to omega, they must have been culled evenly from all parts of the original. It is theoretically possible that each poem in the present sequence in *AP* v was in the original *Garland* separated by as many as ten or twenty poems from its present neighbours.[26] The fullest of the Philippan sequences in *AP*, the nearly 100 poems and 600 lines of ix. 215–312, again ranging all the way from alpha to omega, is still no more than an excerpt of one poem in six from the original *Garland*. So much for Birt's 'book'.

We could get a better idea of the appearance of the *Garland* proper if we could *amalgamate* all the different sequences in the different books of *AP*. Since the principle of arrangement is alphabetical, it might seem that this could be done easily enough: indeed that one could even intercalate in the appropriate alphabetical position all the 'loose' Philippan poems in both *AP* and *APl*.

---

[25] *HE* i, pp. xvii–xviii.

[26] This consideration also vitiates the discussion in *GP* i, pp. xvi f. on whether or not Philip 'might ... be expected to arrange the authors alphabetically under each epigram initial'. Cephalas' division of the original Philippan sequence between his own categories will inevitably have broken up the traces of such an author distribution.

Unfortunately this would be impossible, because of a point which has no doubt occurred to others before me, but which I have not seen set down in print.

Philip did *not* in fact arrange his material on a thorough-going alphabetical principle. He merely divided it into twenty-four groups according to the initial letter of the first word of each poem. All the poems whose first word begins with alpha come before all those whose first word begins with beta (and so on), but *inside* each letter group no consistent attempt was made to arrange individual poems in alphabetical order. Compare the sequence *AP* vi. 227–61. While no initial letter occurs before a preceding letter of the alphabet, inside letter groups no fewer than 13 out of a total of 34 are out of place. In the sequence vii. 364–405 no fewer than 17 out of 41 are out of place inside letter groups. The proportion is approximately 1:3 in both cases. Take the fullest sequence for one letter which we have: ix. 215–36, 22 consecutive poems opening with an alpha. Here are the first words: αἰεί, ἁρμονίης, αἱ, ἀβάλε, αἰγιβότου, ἁ, αὐγάζω, ἀνέρα, ἀγγελίην, αἶγα, Ἀσωπίς, αἱ, ἀκταίην, ἀγγελίης, ἀρχαίη, ἀμβαίνων, αὔην, Ἀδριακοῖο, αὖα, ἄχρι, ἄγχουροι, ἄρρηκτοι. It would be difficult to say how many were out of place here, for there is not even an approximate tendency towards alphabetical order. After the initial alpha we have a rho in second position and a delta and gamma (in that order) towards the end.

This cannot be merely one of the results of Cephalas' carelessness. His carelessness (which should not be exaggerated) takes other forms—misunderstanding, inaccurate classification, false ascriptions. He usually copies his sources accurately enough except for errors of this sort. If we credit him with the disorder inside these Philippan letter groups, we should also have to expect up to one in three poems to be misplaced by several positions in Meleagrian and Agathian sequences too. Yet this is plainly not so. The subtle twofold pattern still discernible in those sequences could never have survived such treatment. There is, fortunately, one opportunity to check Cephalas' accuracy in this respect when copying from his sources. For vii. 83–133, no fewer than fifty consecutive poems, are copied directly from a work which happily survives—Diogenes Laertius' *Lives of the Philosophers*. All but one appear in *AP* in the same order as in Diogenes.[27] Obviously it

---

[27] Weisshäupl (1889), 34–8.

would be very singular if Cephalas had juggled around in this way
with his Philippan material alone.

Let us suppose for a moment that Philip *did* arrange his material
in perfect alphabetical order, taking first and second letters into
account where necessary. Either Cephalas would have noticed, in
which case his juggling about would be inexplicable. Or he would
not have noticed, and his juggling about would not have been
confined to letter groups. We should expect to find the odd beta
among the alphas and gammas. Why should the juggling, whether
deliberate or accidental, be confined to the letter groups?

Proof positive is provided by the poem which occurs in two
Philippan sequences, vi. 106, opening τοῦτό τοι. As vi. 106 it comes
in a sequence of alphabetically arranged letter groups after a poem
opening Τρίγλαν and before an upsilon. By Philippan standards it is
in position inside a group of taus (whose order inside the group is
in fact in reverse alphabetical order). At its second occurrence after
vi. 255, it comes after poems opening τήν (254) and τοῦτο Σάων
(255), and before Ταύρου (256) and then τίς (257), τάς (258), and τίς
again (259)—again, inside a group of taus which are not themselves
in alphabetical order. If the poem stands out of absolute alphabetical place in both these excerpts from the *Garland*, clearly it must
have stood out of place in the *Garland* itself. If these two sequences
were united, the disorder would become even more marked. The
case of the alphas in ix. 205 f. shows that the more poems inside a
letter group, the greater the disorder. So when we find letter
groups of only (say) two or three poems in the shorter sequences in
other books of *AP* which happen to be in absolute alphabetical
order, this may be just coincidence. If we could collect all the
groups of this letter from all the sequences, we should probably
find the same pattern of disorder.

One final point. We happen to have Philip's preface (*AP* iv. 2),
which for obvious reasons will have headed the whole collection.
So the initial letter of its first word will have been the very first
letter of the *Garland*. It is an alpha,[28] but after that only a nu
(ἄνθεα). There are fourteen alphas from the ix. 205 f. sequence
alone which on alphabetical considerations should have preceded
the preface.

---

[28] For this reason alone (though there are others) we may safely ignore L.
Herrmann's proposal (*L'Ant. class.* xxvii (1958), 98–9) to transfer the first two lines
of Meleager's preface to stand in front of Philip's. Meleager's preface begins Μοῦσα.

It seems clear then that Philip made no attempt to arrange poems alphabetically inside letter groups.[29] This need cause no surprise. Rather it would be surprising if he had. For obvious though the principle of alphabetization might seem, it was not employed either early or consistently in ancient times. And alphabetization after the first letter was particularly late in arriving. The earliest attested examples of second-letter order are the glossary P. Oxy. 1801 and a Bodleian papyrus of Apollonius' *Homeric Lexicon*,[30] both mid first century. By the second century there are several more: P. Oxy. 1802, Galen's work on Hippocratic glosses, and the *Lexicon* of Harpocration, which appears to be the earliest example of absolute alphabetization.[31] So the principle was certainly known by Philip's day. Yet it was obviously a principle devised in the first instance by lexicographers, dealing with so much material that the inadequacies of alphabetization by first letter alone were revealed at a practical level.

It may be instructive to compare the other examples of alphabetical ordering in the editing of poetical texts. There is some evidence that Alexandrian editors alphabetized Sappho and Bacchylides by the first word of each poem; and the plays of Aeschylus, Euripides, Aristophanes, and Menander may early have been listed in alphabetical sequence of title.[32] But this was a purely external classification, adding nothing to the appreciation of the texts. Rather different are the so-called Menandrean *Monosticha*, sometimes found on papyri in runs of 24, one line for each letter in sequence (II, IV, VIII Jäkel).[33] This was no doubt intended as a mnemonic, to help the student remember his lines (II begins significantly ἀρχὴ μεγίστη τοῦ φρονεῖν τὰ γράμματα), but again adds nothing to the appreciation of the text.

---

[29] This point at least is surely self-evident, whatever further conclusions may be drawn. I cannot understand Giangrande's objection that Philip was 'going against contemporary practice' (*CR* 1973, 136).

[30] For the few irregularities, see J. J. Keaney, *GRBS* xiv (1973), 415–23.

[31] Cf. E. W. B. Nicholson, *CR* xi (1897), 390–3. I gratefully borrow my information on this subject from Lloyd W. Daly, *Contributions to a History of Alphabetization in Antiquity and the Middle Ages* (Collection Latomus 90), 1967, and K. Alpers, *Gnomon*, xlvii (1975), 113–17.

[32] See Daly (1967), 23–4.

[33] In later papyri and the medieval MSS we find more and more in each letter category, eventually 95 lines beginning with alpha before 40 beginning with beta, and so on (in first-letter order): for all the details, see S. Jäkel, *Menandri Sententiae* (1964).

Philip's purpose was neither to instruct nor merely to classify, but (of course) to entertain. Can we really believe that he was content to put 120 poems beginning with alpha together in no order whatever before passing on to treat poems beginning with beta the same way, and so on?[34]

The grouping of poems by initial letter was merely a preliminary, the external framework of his system. It was Philip's variation on Meleager's preliminary division of material into four basic categories before addressing himself to the more subtle task of arranging the individual poems inside those categories. Philip too had an internal *and* an external system. He may well have rejected Meleager's external division as being too crude. By contrast he hit on the ingenious idea of dividing his material alphabetically in the first instance. The arbitrariness of the procedure would ensure that each letter group contained a good cross-section of poems of every genre, thus avoiding the monotony of long stretches of unrelieved erotica (or whatever). Inside these groups he could employ an internal system (no doubt very similar to Meleager's) of linking by community (or contrast) of theme or verbal parallel. The rejection of second and third letter alphabetization, so far from being a shortcoming, actually gave him more room to manœuvre within letter groups.

PHILIP: II

One of the most characteristic features of Philip's own contribution to his *Garland* is his variations on the poems of his fellow contributors.[35] Now a quite disproportionately high number of these variations begin with the same letter of the alphabet as their model.[36]

In a few cases variation and model begin with the same word, e.g. vii. 233 (Apollonides) and 234 (Philip) on the general who

---

[34] Reitzenstein, *RE* vi (1909), col. 105, had harsh words for the crudity of Philip's system.

[35] See now for all the details (though not the general point) Gow and Page, *GP* ii. 327–71.

[36] For a more adventurous formulation see E. Hirsch (1966), not known to me when I first published an earlier version of this section in *GRBS* 1968, 339 f. He goes so far as to classify *all* Philippan poems in 24 groups by initial letter and announces that half to two-thirds 'liess sich mit einiger Wahrscheinlichkeit inhaltlich zusammenstellen' (p. 415).

committed suicide (both beginning Αἴλιος); or ix. 321 (Philip) and
322 (Antiphilus) on pedantic grammarians (γραμματικοί/ῶν). But
(unlike the examples discussed above from Meleager's *Garland*)
most do not. In such cases the reader is constantly made aware of
the ingenuity of the combined alphabetical and thematic link. This
is one case where alphabetization does add something to the
appreciation of the texts alphabetized. Here is a by no means
exhaustive list of the more obvious examples:

1. ix. 415 (ἤμην) and 416 (ἡ ναῦς) by Antiphilus and Philip on the
Good Ship Venus
2. vii. 236 (οὐχί) and 237 (οὔρεα) by Antipater and Philip (or
Alpheius) on the grave of Themistocles
3. *APl* 176 (καί) and 177 (Κύπρις), by Antipater and Philip again,
on Aphrodite in Sparta
4. ix. 293 (πουλύ) and 294 (πορφυρέαν) by Philip and Antiphilus on
Xerxes and Leonidas
5. *APl* 215 (συλήσαντες) and 216 (σκυλοφαρεῖς) by Secundus and
Philip on Erotes in the armour of the Olympians
6. *APl* 136 (τάν) and 137 (τίς) by Antiphilus and Philip on the
Medea of Timomachus
7. ix. 250 (ἔστην) and 253 (ἐν) by Honestus and Philip on Tragedy
at Thebes
8. *APl* 103 ("Ηρακλες) and 104 ("Ηρη) by Tullius Geminus and
Philip on Heracles disarmed by Eros
9. *APl* 240 (ὡραίας), 241 (ὥριμος) and 242 (ὡς βαρύ) on Priapus by
Philip, Argentarius, and Erycius
10. vii. 382 (ἠπείρῳ) and 383 (ἠιόνιον), two variations by Philip
himself on a shipwreck
11. Finally, Philip's pair (ix. 708, ἔζευξ') to Antiphilus' poem (vii.
379, εἶπέ) on the Puteoli mole so egregiously misplaced by Cephalas.

We may add ix. 257 (ἡ καθαρή) and 258 (ἡ πάρος), variations by two
other Philippan authors, Apollonides and Antiphanes, on the pure
fountain defiled by blood washed from a murderer's hands; and
APl 198 (κλαῖε) and 199 (καί), variations by Maecius and Crinagoras on Eros in chains.[37] Nor is it easy to believe that it is by

---

[37] This pair is immediately preceded (in the same Planudean chapter) by three
more poems on the same theme, 195 (τέχνη), 196 (τὰν), and 197 (τίς). The poems are
ascribed by Planudes to Satyrus, Alcaeus, and Antipater. Little is known of

coincidence that vii. 385 (ἥρως) and vii. 141 (Θεσσαλέ), variations by Philip and Antiphilus on the allegedly angry trees around Protesilaus' grave, begin with *consecutive* letters of the alphabet.

I will add two illustrations of the more complex interweaving of different motifs we might expect to find more often if we had the *Garland* intact. First, vi. 240–4: 240 (Ζηνός) is a dedication by Philip to Artemis, daughter of Zeus; 242 (ἡ), by Crinagoras, is another dedication to Artemis, coupled with Zeus Teleius, on the occasion of the birth of a child; 243 (ἡ), by Diodorus, and 244 (Ἥρη), by Crinagoras, are again both addresses to Hera, the second to Hera Teleia as goddess of childbirth—coupled with Zeus. Thus 244 has one sort of link with 243 and another with 242; 242 in turn, in addition to its link with 244, has another sort of link with 240.

Then a perhaps more fragile chain, forged by the more hazardous procedure of hopping between sequences. *AP* vi. 89 (ἀκταίης) and 90 (ἄγχυραν), by Maecius and Philip, are both dedications by fishermen: the first of a shell to Priapus, 'who delights in the rocks', the second of an anchor to Poseidon. In the second Philippan sequence in the same book we find at vi. 230 (ἀκρείτᾳ) another poem by Maecius: another dedication of a shell by a fisherman, this time to Apollo. Epigram 230, in turn, is linked to 231 (Philip) by the fact that both are dedications by a fisherman called Damis. Nor is this the last link in the chain. Earlier in the book there is another poem by the same Maecius (this time outside a sequence), vi. 33 (αἰγιαλῖτα): another dedication by a fisherman to Priapus of the shore, only this time of a bowl, stool, and wine-cup. It is very tempting to conclude that all three of Maecius' poems stood together in the *Garland*. All three are dedications by fishermen. But over and above this common feature vi. 89 is linked to 230 by

Satyrus. But at x. 6 he appears as one half of an alphabetical pair (both opening ἤδη) with the probably Philippan Thyillus, both variations on Leonidas' famous spring poem (x. 1). And surely he is to be identified with the author of vi. 11, ascribed to 'Satrius' in *AP* but to 'Satyrius' by Planudes, another variation on Leonidas' hardly less popular poem vi. 13. Antipater could be the Meleagrian from Sidon or the Philippan from Thessalonica equally. Luck (1967, 46–7) opts for the former because it suits a theory of his about the Sidonian. Gow, more cautiously (*HE* ii. 23), leaves the choice entirely open. There is no reason to rule out the Thessalonican. This leaves Alcaeus. 196 bears little resemblance to the work of Alcaeus of Messene, but it does bear a strong resemblance to the closely parallel poem sixteen later in this same chapter of Planudes (212), this time on a sleeping Eros, by the Philippan poet Alpheius of Mytilene. The alphabetical sequence (neglected by Luck and Gow) extending to three, and the close parallelism between 195–7 all on the same subject, seem to me to point clearly to a Philippan group.

the dedicated object (a shell), while at the same time having a different link, the dedicatee (Priapus), with 33.

The chances against such a variety of thematic links coinciding with the alphabetical links should be high. If there were many more examples of this sort of nexus, then it was not merely in imitation of Meleager and not entirely without justification that Philip too called his collection a *Garland*.

CEPHALAS' TEXTS OF THE *GARLANDS* AND *CYCLE*

If we are on the right lines so far, we can perhaps gain a rather clearer picture of the *Garlands* of Meleager and Philip than has hitherto been supposed. But we must not flatter ourselves that we can come anywhere near *reconstructing* them.

It has long been realized that much of the contents of the *Garlands* may have been lost long before Cephalas made the excerpts we read in *AP*.[38] Three of the poets named in Meleager's preface are not represented in *AP*—unless some of the adespota are theirs. Then there is P. Oxy. 662, a fragment of an anthology which (as we saw in the last chapter) is more likely than not to be an excerpt from Meleager's *Garland*. Of its seven funerary epigrams only two survive in *AP*. But *BKT* v. 1. 75–6, with its seven erotic Meleagrian epigrams, *all* in *AP*, warns against taking too pessimistic a view of Meleagrian losses. Three smaller fragments of less certain Meleagrian credentials confirm the general picture: P. Freib. 4 with three epigrams, two in *AP*; P. Tebt. I. 3 with three, only one in *AP*; and *Gr. Ostr.* ii. 1488 with the opening words of six, two in *AP*. There is also the observation by Gow and Page that some initial letters in Philippan sequences seem to be disproportionately under-represented, though in such a consideration we must make due allowance for chance.

But the most important piece of evidence has been staring us in the face all along, in *AP* itself. Reference has already been made to a Philippan epigram repeated in two different Philippan sequences. There are in fact quite a number of epigrams duplicated in *AP*. That these duplications were already a feature of Cephalas is proved by the fact that many of them appear twice in *APl* too.

---

[38] We might compare the similar losses suffered down the centuries by the Theognidean *sylloge*: cf. West (1974), 45.

Now there are five Meleagrian duplications, two of which appear both times in Meleagrian sequences. Gow found it 'hard to resist the conclusion that some at any rate of these epigrams appeared twice in Meleager's *Garland*.'[39] This is surely most improbable. Meleager was not only a far more sophisticated and careful anthologist than Cephalas; he was operating with a far smaller number of poems, poems which he knew well and constantly imitated in his own compositions. How could he have failed to spot and eliminate such frequent repetitions? There is also the one Philippan duplication, in perfect alphabetical position in two Philippan sequences. In Philip the alphabetical arrangement must have made it impossible for duplications to pass unnoticed.

It should have been observed that the duplication of individual Meleagrian and Philippan poems is not a problem that can be solved on its own. It is obviously related to the more general question of the duplication of Meleagrian and Philippan *sequences* in *AP*.

We have already noticed Weisshäupl's discovery that the three Meleagrian sequences in *AP* vii—406–506, 646–65, and 707–40— are organized on the same pattern and may be taken to be three successive excerpts from the same original, fuller Meleagrian sequence. But *why* three successive excerpts? And why the two Philippan sequences (vii. 364–405, 622–45)? Why the double Meleagrian (109–57, 262–313) and Philippan (87–108, 227–61) sequences in *AP* vi?

One might guess that this was Cephalas' way of breaking the monotony of what would otherwise have been rather long sequences. But the simplest way of achieving this would have been just to divide the material into two parts, whereas the two Philippan sequences in *AP* vi run from α–ω and α–χ, clearly independent excerpts from the entire original Philippan sequence—the same pattern as the successive Meleagrian sequences in *AP* vii.

It needs only to be pointed out that on every occasion when the repeated poem appears both times embedded in a *Garland* sequence there are textual variants and the answer is obvious. Cephalas had *two different copies* of both *Garlands*. Both had been somewhat abridged with the passage of time and so he had to excerpt both from start to finish to be sure of not missing anything.

[39] Gow (1958), 61.

It would have meant a lot more work (harmonizing their thematic and alphabetical arrangements) to integrate his two sets of excerpts into one sequence, so he left them separate. The repeated poems he absent-mindedly copied twice, once from each exemplar.

Here is the evidence for the textual variations (omitting a few minor details), P¹ denoting the first occurrence of each poem and P² the second:

vi. 146 (Callimachus), again after 274 (both times appropriately in a context of healing and childbirth):

	P¹	P²
1	καλεύσῃς	καλούσῃς
2	εὐτοκίῃ	εὐτυχίῃ
3	τοι	τόδε

vii. 462 (Dionysius), again after 728 (on death in childbirth, both times followed by another poem on the same theme):

	P¹	P²
1	κρύφε (ἔκρυφε, C)	κρύψε (and *APl*)
2	ἐστενάχησε	ἐστονάχησε

vi. 106 (Zonas), again after 255:

	P¹	P²
1	σοι (and *APl*)	τοι
	ἀγρειάδος	ἀγριάδος (*APl*)
4	χειρός	χερὸς (*APl*)
6	εὐαγρεῖ (*APl*)	εὐάγρῃ

There are five more Meleagrian repetitions (all with textual differences and one a different ascription), but they do not have probative value since they appear only once in a sequence.[40] But there is one further candidate for inclusion in the list: vii. 502 by Nicaenetus appears only once in *AP* in a Meleagrian sequence, but twice (with substantial variations)[41] in *APl*. First (fo. 37ᵛ) after 499–501 and before 503–4, all (like 502) on cenotaphs of sailors who died at sea; and again on fo. 101ʳ after vii. 653–4. Now 651–4

---

[40] vi. 144 (repeated after 481); vii. 170 (after 481); vii. 229 (after 721); vii. 231 (after 438); vii. 270 (after 650). The Philippan vii. 161 reappears after 344, in neither place in a sequence but unquestionably from two different sources (see Gow and Page, *GP* ii. 220).

[41] Given in full below, p. 346; remarkably enough, the repetition of the poem in *APl* has never been noticed and the variants never published.

(the second substantial Meleagrian sequence in *AP* vii) provide an equally appropriate context, again, like 502, on cenotaphs of sailors who died at sea, with similar evocation of destructive winds and distressed parents. The probability is that the poem originally stood twice in Cephalas, in both these two Meleagrian sequences, each of which reproduced a part (different except for 502) of the original, fuller Meleagrian sequence on sailors' cenotaphs. Planudes did not notice the duplication but the Palatine scribe (or his source) for once did and eliminated the second occurrence.

However this may be, the first three examples are decisive enough, and a number of important conclusions follow.

In the first place, as late as 900 Cephalas could apparently lay his hand on two copies of both *Garlands*. This is not altogether surprising, since they were evidently known intimately to Agathias and his friends, all men of position who could doubtless afford to have their own copies made. Together with Homer and Nonnus, the *Garlands* may well have been the most popular classical poetry books in mid-sixth-century Constantinople.

Next, Cephalas' activity is not to be dissociated from the 'Macedonian Renaissance' and the transliteration of the old uncial manuscripts into the handier minuscule script. It is often assumed that only one uncial manuscript survived the 'dark ages' and that the process of transliteration was performed only once. In many cases both propositions were probably true,[42] but they should not perhaps be thought of as necessarily synonymous. Cephalas' Anthology doubtless embodied the first and only transliteration of both *Garlands*. But that transliteration was surely based on a collation of *two* uncial copies. The not infrequent variants, in most cases clearly transmitted readings rather than conjectures, that we find in the margins of *AP*, especially in the hand of the so-called Corrector, are no doubt the fruits of this collation.

The curious fact that throughout the major Cephalan books of *AP* Philippan sequences *precede* Meleagrian sequences suggests that this was the order in which they were bound in both Cephalas' copies (though the prefaces in *AP* iv are quoted in correct chronological order).

Most important and relevant to the present investigation, however, is the obvious implication that both Cephalas' copies were much reduced versions of the original *Garlands*. For example (not

[42] See Reynolds and Wilson (1974), 53 f.

counting short 'broken' runs and numerous 'loose' Meleagrian poems scattered throughout both books), the first Meleagrian sequence in *AP* vi contains 48 poems, the second 51; in *AP* vii the first sequence 100, the second and third 19 and 33. By themselves these figures prove little, since we do not know how exhaustively Cephalas excerpted his first copy or how many (beyond the duplications) of his first sequences were repeated in his second copy.

The inevitable, indeed startlingly close parallel is the two sets of excerpts, taken (as he states) from different sources, that go to make up Planudes' Anthology. The parallel structure of the two sets of excerpts, the numerous duplications, and the comparison with *AP* make it clear that both Planudes' sources were reduced redactions of Cephalas, partly but not entirely overlapping in their contents. The second excerpts add more than 500 epigrams to the *c.*1,900 in the first excerpts, and though again we do not know how many of these 1,900 also appeared in the second source, it does at least seem clear that the 500 did not appear in the first source. The implication is that the second source was at any rate not much smaller than the first and that each contained much not in the other.

The same is surely true of Cephalas' two copies of the *Garlands*. Later chapters will trace the successive abridgements of Cephalas, and it is not surprising to discover that the *Garlands* suffered the same fate. Successive copyists are bound to have dropped first one and then another of the interminable variations on the same themes, and the joint Meleagrian/Philippan practice of juxtaposing poems with similar openings virtually ensured a large number of accidental omissions.

To judge from papyrus fragments, abridged Meleagers were circulating as early as the first century of our era. Anthologies were not unified texts protected by the ordinary principles of literary ownership and propriety, and it is likely that no two abridgements were the same. The process itself is illustrated in the pages of *AP*. The Corrector C added poems here and there and marked others for deletion: if a copy was ever made it was not identical to *AP*. It would not be surprising if the differing abridgements used by Cephalas went right back to the circle of Agathias.

By contrast, Agathias' own *Cycle* enjoyed only the briefest of vogues. The revival of the elegiac epigram was shortlived (see

Ch. XVI). The classicizing Indian summer was rapidly followed by a Christian winter, and it is not likely that there was any call for fresh copies or even abridgements after *c*.600.[43] So Cephalas' copy of the *Cycle* may well have been not much later than Agathias' own lifetime. This is no doubt why the text of *Cycle* authors is relatively free from serious corruption. Apart from perhaps a few dozen ecphrastic poems lost in the lacuna in *AP* ix, *AP* may well preserve the *Cycle* (evidently much smaller than either *Garland*) almost complete. As Mattsson has already remarked, *AP* v. 216–302 may be Agathias' erotic book virtually intact.

---

[43] On this sudden (and complex) cultural shift at Byzantium see Averil Cameron, 'Images of Authority: elites and icons in late sixth-century Byzantium', *Past and Present* lxxxiv (August 1979), esp. pp. 24 f.

III

Some Dates

I. MELEAGER

It is unfortunate that the only ancient writer to offer a date for Meleager should be two centuries in error. According to Diogenes Laertius (*Vit. Phil.* vi. 99), the books of the Cynic philosopher Menippus (who lived in the early third century) 'overflow with laughter, much the same as those of his contemporary Meleager.' But although a recent work on the hellenistic love epigram leaves the possibility open,[1] Meleager simply cannot have lived that early. At least seven *Garland*-poets—Alcaeus, Amyntas, Antipater of Sidon, Moschus, Nicander, Polystratus, and Samius—wrote in the second century.[2] The obvious connection between Meleager and Menippus is not their date but their native city: both were Gadarenes. The most natural solution is that Diogenes misunderstood some such reference to their connection in his source.[3]

The only other explicit text we have is J's statement that Meleager 'flourished under the last Seleucus'. The last ruler of the Seleucid house to bear that name was Seleucus VI Epiphanes Nicator, a short-lived and unsuccessful claimant to the Seleucid throne in the period 96/5 to 95/4 BC. As Gow and Page remark, 'a *floruit* pinned to a single year is not very helpful.' Meleager might have mentioned a Seleucus in an epigram now lost or in his lost (prose) *Charites*, and the date itself is perfectly acceptable. But it is not easy to see how such a reference could have been so precisely identified. Indeed, it is not easy to single out one among a succession of pretenders as 'the last Seleucus' while the dynasty was crumbling to its inglorious end. Nor could such a retrospective

---

[1] Daniel H. Garrison, *Mild Frenzy* (Hermes Einzelschr. 14, 1978), 9 n. 9.
[2] For a list of *Garland* authors in chronological order, see Luck (1967), 25–40.
[3] For other possible explanations of Diogenes' error see J. Mejer, *Diogenes Laertius and his Hellenistic Background* (Hermes Einzelschr. 40, 1978), 43.

judgement well have been made before the eventual establishment of Syria as a Roman province in 64—surely too late for Meleager. And it might further be asked, when everything else J has to offer on Meleager (and Philip) is such patent guesswork, how did he come by so exact a piece of information as this?

Surely it is just another guess, as its context would in any case imply (the words *immediately* follow J's statement, confessedly an inference from Meleager's poems, that he 'was a Gadarene'). J lived in an age when all the classical historians were being rediscovered and excerpted at the bidding of the imperial historian Constantine VII.[4] He knew his Josephus on the fall of the Seleucids. Now among the many pretty boys Meleager names in his pederastic poems was one Antiochus, a name borne by thirteen Seleucid rulers. Of the twelfth, (86–85, again only one year) Josephus wrote (not quite accurately) that he was 'last of those descended from Seleucus' (*BJ* i. 99). J was perhaps historian enough to see that this was approximately the right period. It will hardly be necessary to add that, however suitable the date, the basis of the guess is unsound. Antiochus XII is not likely to have been Meleager's lover. J's note is probably best forgotten.

It has hitherto been generally assumed that the latest datable poet included in the *Garland* is Antipater of Sidon, who is held by Gow and Page to have died *c.*125.[5] But an honorific inscription at Delos signed 'Antipater of Sidon', on the base of a statue of Philostratus, a well-known banker from Ascalon, points somewhat later than this.[6] Philostratus' activity at Delos can be fixed fairly precisely: dated inscriptions attest his presence between 108 and 92 BC. Mancinetti Santamaria was prepared to allow that he might have come to Delos as early as 130/120, which is an obvious possibility, but the documents lend no direct support and his son Theophilus was no older than an ephebe in 93/2, and so born on Delos *c.*113/12. Antipater's poem might easily be as late as 105/100.[7]

---

[4] Ch. XIV.

[5] *HE* i. xvi, cf. ii. 32; exploited by D. O. Ross (n. 12) for his early dating of Aedituus and Catulus.

[6] *I. Délos* 2549; W. Peek, *Philologus* ci (1957), 101–12; J. and L. Robert, *RÉG* lxxi (1958), 287–9; G. Mancinetti Santamaria, *Delo e l'Italia*, ed. F. Coarelli, D. Musti, H. Solin (Opusc. Inst. Rom. Finl. 2; 1982), 79–89, with a full account of Philostratus' career and connections.

[7] It should be noted that Mancinetti Santamaria's *terminus post quem* of 102 is based on a misunderstanding: her remark 'sappiamo che Archia ancora *adulescens* ebbe modo di conoscere Antipatro *senem* e questo non può essere avvenuto se non

The poet lived to a great age, we are told,[8] suffering only one day's illness a year—regularly on his birthday. Inevitably, it was on his birthday that he finally died. Since Meleager includes his own epitaph on Antipater, a date before *c*.100 seems unlikely. Furthermore, Gow and Page have now (rightly, it seems) decided that it is to the first rather than second *Garland* that one (at least) of the epigrammatists called Archias should be assigned.[9] Now this Archias is plainly much indebted to the epigrams of Antipater of Sidon.[10] So if Meleagrian, he must be the *latest* Meleagrian poet. If so, then who can he be but the poet Archias of Antioch immortalized by Cicero? Cicero's Archias was born *c*.120 BC and arrived at Rome in 102. Even if he was the child prodigy Cicero represents him, a *Garland* that included his work can scarcely have appeared before 100 BC.

Now it has long been recognized that there are a number of striking affinities between the erotic epigrams of the *Garland* and the small corpus of early Latin erotic epigrams by Valerius Aedituus, Porcius Licinus, and Q. Lutatius Catulus (cos. 102) quoted by A. Gellius (*NA* xix. 9. 10–14) and supplemented by Cicero (*De Nat. Deor.* i. 79). Hence the neat and attractive suggestion of A. A. Day that 'when Archias came to Rome in 102 he brought with him a copy of the *Garland*'.[11]

D. O. Ross has vigorously objected:[12] 'It is not necessary to argue that Meleager's *Garland* was important for the beginnings of hellenistic epigram at Rome: Antipater had preceded it by at least a quarter of a century, and other anthologies had no doubt been circulating.' Then to clinch his case he coolly pushed Aedituus and Licinus back to *c*.150 BC, concluding that 'it seems safe to say . . . that by 150 BC hellenistic epigram was being imitated by Roman poets' (p. 141).

---

dopo il 102' (p. 81, n. 9, cf. p. 88), seems to misread as Ciceronian rhetoric T. Reinach's suggestion, 'hunc adolescens senem potuit etiam videre' (*De Archia poeta* [Paris 1890], 3). The claim at *de orat*. iii. 194 that Catulus 'well *remembers* Antipater' (*quem tu probe, Catule, meministi*), implies (*a*) that Antipater was known to Catulus personally and (*b*) that he was dead by the dialogue's dramatic date of 91. But nothing is known of the date or duration of his Roman stay; he may have made the trip to Delos from Rome.

[8] Valerius Max. i. 8. 16; cf. Pliny, *NH* vii. 172.
[9] *GP* ii. 432–5.
[10] *GP* ii. 434 f., and H. H. Law, *CP* xxxi (1936), 233–7.
[11] *The Origins of Latin Love-Elegy* (1938), 104.
[12] *Style and Tradition in Catullus* (1969), 143; cf. *YCS* xxi (1969), 141.

But the fact that Gellius applied the term *vetus poeta* to Aedituus, the first of the three he happens to mention, need not (as Ross
assumes) imply that he was appreciably earlier than the other two;
indeed in the context the opposition is clearly between this whole
group of 'old' poets and the generation of Catullus and Calvus. A
poet of *c.*90 BC would certainly be 'old' compared with Catullus
and Calvus. The existence of pre-Meleagrian anthologies such as
Ross postulated has already been shown to be more than doubtful.
And whether or not Antipater was in residence at Rome by *c.*125
(which is quite uncertain), it is clear from his substantial contribution to the *Garland* that he had no interest in the *erotic* epigram, the
sole interest of our three Roman poets. Nor Archias either, if Gow
and Page were right to withold from him *AP* v. 57–8. Above all,
however, Ross's case founders on the fact that it is not 'hellenistic
epigram' in general that inspired the Roman poets, but precisely
Meleager's epigrams.

For example, with Catulus II (on the actor Roscius outshining
the rising sun) compare Meleager, *AP* xii. 59:

ἁβρούς, ναὶ τὸν Ἔρωτα, τρέφει Τύρος· ἀλλὰ Μυΐσκος
ἔσβεσεν ἐκλάμψας ἀστέρας ἠέλιος.

Or with Catulus' last line, 'mortalis visus pulchrior esse deo', cf.
Meleager, *AP* xii. 54. 4, εὕρηται κρείσσων οὗτος Ἔρωτος Ἔρως
(where the second 'Eros' is the poet's beloved). With Aedituus II
(no need for a torch when there is so bright a flame in my heart) cf.
AP ix. 15, οὗτος ὁ πῦρ καύσειν διζήμενος . . . δεῦρ' ἀπ' ἐμῆς ψυχῆς ἄψον
σέλας. Day remarks that ix. 15 is 'unfortunately anonymous'; but
he might have added that it appears in *BKT* v. 1. 75 f. in a
sequence of undoubted Meleagrian erotica and, whoever the
author, certainly stood in the *Garland*.

The most valuable part of Ross's discussion is his emphasis on the
original and Roman elements in the five poems, though it is going
too far to assert that 'no single hellenistic epigram . . . can be said to
be the original from which any of these Latin epigrams were
translated' (p. 150). We cannot assume that there were no closer
parallels in the original *Garland*. And if Catulus I, 'Aufugit mi
animus', is not a word-for-word translation of Callimachus xii. 73,
that is only because Catulus was unable to reproduce all the
subtleties of his original. He was certainly trying.

Far-reaching chronological deductions have been drawn from Catulus' epigram on the famous actor Roscius. Writer after writer has asserted with the utmost confidence that Roscius was born *c.*135,[13] and that, since the poem 'betrays a youthful admiration',[14] it should be dated *c.*120/115, when Roscius was still in his teens and Catulus a long way from his consulship (102). There are at least three questionable assumptions here. First, there is no real evidence that Roscius was born this early. All we know is that three passages of the *De Oratore* represent him as an established star at the dramatic date of the dialogue in 91; and that when he died shortly before 62, Cicero referred to him as old.[15] Moderns tend to apply anachronistic standards to such terms, but the fact is that, in antiquity as at the Renaissance, men and women began to be considered old from the age of fifty.[16] These various passages in Cicero need not imply that Roscius was more than (say) sixty in 61, and so born no earlier than 120. Second, Roscius' connection with a Roman noble surely followed rather than preceded his fame as an actor. We cannot assume either that he took to the stage in his teens or that he was an overnight success.

Third, the assumption that he must have been a pretty young boy to inspire such passion presupposes that the poem is an autobiographical document. Now Catulus may or may not have been attracted by handsome young actors. It is not his sexual preference that is at issue, but the likelihood that he would have written such a poem if contemporaries were likely to read it as autobiography.[17] In fact the epigram clearly owes more to art than

---

[13] From C. Cichorius, *Untersuchungen zu Lucilius* (Berlin 1908), 291 ('zwischen 134 und 130') to H. Bardon, *Les Études classiques*, xviii (1950), 147 ('vers 134'); H. Dahlmann, *Gymnasium* lxxxviii (1981), 24–5 ('um 135'); C. Garton, *Personal Aspects of the Roman Theatre* (Toronto 1972), 48 ('about 132/1'). Catulus' birth can be fixed fairly precisely in 150/49 (Cichorius 151).

[14] A. L. Wheeler, *Catulus and the Traditions of Ancient Poetry* (1934), 69; 257 n. 17.

[15] *cum esset senex mortuus, pro Archia* 17; *De Orat.* 1. 130, 221, 254; there is also a reference to his acting style changing with *senectus* in *De Leg.* 1. 11: G. K. G. Henry, *Studies in Philology* xvi (1919), 343–4.

[16] C. Gilbert, 'When did a Man in the Renaissance Grow Old?', *Studies in the Renaissance* xiv (1967), 7–32; Cameron, *Callimachus and his Critics*, forthcoming, Ch. IV.

[17] Despite the claims of John Boswell to the contrary (*Christianity, Social Tolerance and Homosexuality* [Chicago 1980], passim), there can be little doubt that open homosexual liaisons were disapproved of in late Republican Rome: R. MacMullen, 'Greek Love at Rome', *Historia* xxxi (1982), 484–502.

heart—more precisely to the art of Meleager. It may be relevant to
quote Denys Page on Meleager himself:[18]

Myiscus and Heliodora, Zenophila and Heraclitus, and the rest, were
presumably real persons, not fictitious; and Meleager's passions and
jealousies were presumably as strong as those of other men. But whatever
he may have felt, he has seldom expressed it in these epigrams.

So too Catulus. A similar problem arises in the case of an epigram
that has unfortunately not survived: one Cicero wrote on his slave
(later freedman) Tiro, to which Pliny alludes in a well-known
poem of his own.[19] Cicero (he claims)

> queritur quod fraude mala frustratus amantem
> paucula cenato sibi debita savia Tiro
> tempore nocturno subtraxerit.

> For Tully, grave Tully, in amorous strains
> of the frauds of his paramour Tiro complains,
> that faithless to love and to pleasure untrue,
> from his promis'd embrace the arch wanton withdrew.

Pliny goes on to proclaim the favours 'of his own Tiro', with
similar talk of wiles and flames in the best hellenistic style.
Shackleton Bailey has amusingly catalogued the desperate attempts of moderns to save Cicero's reputation by exposing this
epigram as a forgery.[20] Yet it is clear that Pliny did not see it as a
blemish on the great man's name. On the contrary, he 'began to
reflect upon the fact all the greatest orators had amused themselves
with this kind of writing, and had seen merit in doing so'.
Elsewhere Pliny includes Catulus too in his list of Roman erotic
poets (*Ep.* 5. 3. 5).

Whether or not Catulus and his peers amused themselves with
slave boys and actors, slave boys and actors were hardly in a
position to play the haughty games described in these verses. The
love epigrams of Catulus and Cicero transpose ordinary friend-
ships into the extravagant conceits of Meleager.[21] As Pliny saw, it

---

[18] *HE* ii. 592; even the more sympathetic D. Garrison concludes that 'the
autobiographical content of those epigrams is incidental to their poetical content'
(*Mild Frenzy: A Reading of the Hellenistic Love Epigram*, Hermes Einzelschr. 41,
Wiesbaden 1978, 91).

[19] *Ep.* vii. 4, with the charming translation of W. Melmoth, reprinted in the
original (1915) Loeb.

[20] *Profile of Horace* (London 1982), 71-4.

[21] Compare too the erotic overtones in Catullus 50 on Calvus: *atque illinc abii tuo
lepore / incensus, Licini, facetiisque, / ut nec me miserum cibus iuvaret . . .*

was 'playful sport' (*lascivum lusum*), and contemporaries were not likely to misunderstand the conventions. There is no serious reason to refer the Roscius poem to the youth of either Catulus or Roscius. And if Roscius was indeed born a decade or so later than hitherto supposed, their relationship cannot have begun before Catulus' series of bids for the consulship, when he was already in his mid forties. Catulus was not the last of Roscius' prominent Roman admirers. Some twenty years later he was a favourite of Sulla,[22] and later still he is described as Cicero's *amores ac deliciae*.[23] The sculptor Pasiteles made a silver image of a famous incident from his childhood, and Archias wrote a poem on it. Archias' poem cannot have been earlier than *c.*100, and Pasiteles' *floruit* fell 'in the age of Pompey', that is to say, between about 80 and 48.[24] More than two centuries later, the future Emperor Marcus adapted Catulus' translation of the (again, ostensibly pederastic) Callimachus epigram to express his affection for his teacher Fronto.[25] I submit that there is nothing in the Roscius epigram that warrants dating Meleager's arrival in Rome before the 90s.

Ross also argued that 'the period of activity spanned by our three poets must have been a long one' (p. 142). Given both the obvious stylistic similarities between the Latin epigrams and their common inspiration by the same range of hellenistic erotica, it is surely more natural to conclude that they were written at more or less the same time, in a moment of common discovery.[26] To suggest that Aedituus, Licinus, and Catulus were contemporaries and friends does not in itself imply recognition of the literary circle that used to be associated with Catulus' name.[27] But Apuleius cites the three

[22] Plutarch, *Sulla* 36; Macrob. 3. 14. 13; Cic. *De Leg.* 1. 11; the theme is imaginatively developed in Garton, *Personal Aspects*, 141–67.

[23] By Q. Cicero in *De Div.* 1. 79; as Pease's commentary shows, Cicero used such extravagant language fairly freely, without the slightest hint of pederasty.

[24] Pliny, *NH* 33. 130 and 156; according to 36. 40, he won Roman citizenship in 90.

[25] *at ego ubi animus meus sit nescio: nisi hoc scio, ilico nescio quo < modo > ad te profectum eum esse* (*Ep.* 1. 2, p. 2. 6 van den Hout[2]; but, unlike him, I accept Jacobs's supplement and correction of the MS *illo*); this is much closer to Catulus' version (*aufugit mi animus; credo, ut solet, ad Theotimum | devenit*) than to the original.

[26] Compare the nine fragmentary epigrams inscribed on a wall of the Sullan theatre at Pompeii, republished by Ross, *Yale Class. Stud.* xxi (1969), 127 f. As Ross himself emphasizes, they are 'remarkably similar' to the poems by Aedituus, Licinus, and Catulus—and share their interest in Meleagrian pederastic epigram. Yet they cannot be earlier than the age of Sulla.

[27] On which see Bardon, *Les Ét. Class.* xviii (1950), 145–64.

poets in the same order as Gellius, who quotes four epigrams by them in a way that suggests that he found them together in a single volume.[28] It is an old and natural conjecture that they published an anthology of their work—naturally enough on the model of Meleager's *Garland*.

We do not have to believe that it was Archias in person who brought the *Garland* to Rome, whether in 102 or on a subsequent visit. But it is chronologically possible and would nicely explain why it was in the circle of Catulus that hellenistic epigram was discovered at Rome. Catulus died in 87 and Archias was born *c*.118. The *Garland* cannot have been published more than a year or so before 100 or after 90 BC.

II. PHILIP

Philip's *Garland* has long been assigned to the brief reign of the emperor Gaius, more precisely to AD 40. The standard discussions are those of Hillscher,[29] Cichorius,[30] and Gow and Page.[31] The key poem is Antiphilus VI Gow–Page (*AP* ix. 178):

'Ὡς πάρος Ἀελίου, νῦν Καίσαρος ἁ Ῥόδος εἰμὶ
νᾶσος, ἴσον δ' αὐχῶ φέγγος ἀπ' ἀμφοτέρων·
ἤδη σβεννυμέναν με νέα κατεφώτισεν ἀκτίς,
Ἅλιε, καὶ παρὰ σὸν φέγγος ἔλαμψε Νέρων.
πῶς εἴπω, τίνι μᾶλλον ὀφείλομαι; ὃς μὲν ἔδειξεν
ἐξ ἁλός, ὃς δ' ἤδη ῥύσατο δυομέναν.

I, Rhodes, once the Sun's island, am now Caesar's, and I boast of equal light from both. Just as my fire was dying a new radiance illumined me: O Sun, surpassing your light, Nero shone forth. How shall I say to whom I owe more? The one revealed me from the sea, the other rescued me just as I was sinking.

Hillscher argued that the Nero Caesar here so effusively thanked by the Rhodians was not the (future) Emperor Nero but Tiberius

[28] H. Usener, *Rhein. Mus.* viii (1865), 150. Bardon's counter-argument from 'la nonchalance' of Gellius' method of citation (p. 149) ignores his artistic purpose.

[29] A. Hillscher, 'Hominum literatorum Gaecorum ante Tiberii mortem in urbe Roma commoratorum historia critica', *Jahrb. f. klass. Philologie*, Supp. xviii (1892), 416–17.

[30] *Römische Studien: Historisches, Epigrapisches, Literaturgeschichtliches aus vier Jahrhunderten Roms* (1922), 341–65.

[31] *GP* i, pp. xlvi–xlix.

Claudius Nero, the (future) Emperor Tiberius. It is true that Tiberius lived at Rhodes from 6 BC to AD 2. But he did not become Caesar till after his adoption by Augustus in AD 4, after which he dropped the names Claudius and Nero.[32] The inexact nomenclature one might forgive a poet, but more important is the fact that there is no known way in which Tiberius could be said to have 'saved' Rhodes. Beyond question Antiphilus is alluding to the speech the young Nero made in 53 successfully urging the restoration to the Rhodians of the liberty Claudius had taken away from them in 44 (Tacitus, *Ann.* xii. 53. 2). A commemorative Rhodian coin 'portrays Nero crowned with laurel and with the sun's rayed halo, inscribed Καῖσαρ αὐτοκράτωρ Νέρων' (Gow and Page, *GP* ii. 120, with a good summary of the debate).

This explanation Gow and Page quite rightly accepted without demur—while continuing to uphold the traditional Gaian date for the *Garland*. They observed that the poem does not occur in a Philippan alphabetical sequence and might therefore 'have been taken into the Anthology from some other source' (i, pp. xlvii–xlviii). It 'must not be used as evidence that Philip's *Garland* was first published later than the principate of Gaius' (cf. ii. 334 for another reference to the 'first' publication of the *Garland*). That is to say they offer two quite different lines of defence: either Antiphilus VI was never in the *Garland* at all or it was first added in a hypothetical 'second' edition later than AD 40. They did not develop either of these suggestions, and it must at once be said that both run into virtually insurmountable difficulties.

There is almost always a simpler explanation than the second edition editors are so fond of postulating to account for textual variants and chronological problems.[33] In this case the only reason is the apparent conflict between a poem that cannot have been written earlier than 53 and this alleged publication date of 40. The hypothesis of publication in 40 rests heavily on the identification of Philip's dedicatee Camillus with L. Arruntius Camillus Scribonianus cos. 32, the unsuccessful rebel against Claudius who died in 42. Yet if this is the Camillus of Philip's dedication (i. 5), then the edition drawn on by the Anthology must be the *first* edition. We

---

[32] *Die Epigramme des Antiphilos von Byzanz* (Berlin 1935), 14–21: on Rhodes at this time, see C. P. Jones, *The Roman World of Dio Chrysostom* (1978), 26 f.

[33] See the usually sensible discussion of the many suggested cases in H. Emonds, *Zweite Auflage im Altertum* (Bonn 1937).

may be sure that Philip would have eliminated an unsuccessful usurper from the preface to a second edition published in the 50s. So we should have to assume that the alphabetical sequences in *AP* derived from the first edition while Antiphilus VI was a lone relic of the second.

The alphabetical sequences yield 334 Philippan poems; nearly 100 occur in short or broken sequences; and between 100 and 150 more by Philippan authors in no very close connection with other *Garland* epigrams, some completely isolated (Gow and Page, *GP* i, pp. xii f.). Obviously it is possible that some of these isolated poems came from a source other than the *Garland* itself. But the implications of this possibility need to be further explored.

Meleager's *Garland* contains work by some celebrated and influential poets, Asclepiades, Posidippus, Callimachus, Leonidas, and Meleager himself. The earlier poets at least certainly published their own collections, and some of their epigrams would doubtless have survived even if they had not been anthologized by Meleager. Philip's labours, by contrast, bestowed an unexpected and in many cases quite undeserved immortality on his poets. And while he no doubt used separate editions of such substantial earlier figures as Philodemus and Crinagoras, many of his smaller contributions by lesser, especially contemporary, figures he must have collected himself from private sources. It is significant that so many of his poets are fellow-countrymen (Antipater and Epigonus from Thessalonica; Adaeus, Antiphanes, and Parmenio all described as Macedonians). Antiphilus came from Byzantium; he was clearly a contemporary of Philip's, and his epigrams show an unusually high number of links with Philip's. We cannot safely assume that Antiphilus ever published a separate edition of his own poems. If he did, it is scarcely likely that so slim a volume would have long continued to circulate alongside the ample selection included in the *Garland*. It is conceivable that a poem like VI might have been quoted by a biographer of Nero (such as Plutarch whose *Nero* is unfortunately lost) but on balance it seems most unlikely that Cephalas in the tenth century was able to find a poem by Antiphilus not included by Philip.

About fifty epigrams are attributed to Antiphilus. Of these, thirty occur in the main alphabetical sequences; five in shorter sequences; two more with a related poem by Philodemus at the end of *AP* v; three in a disordered block of mostly Philippan poems;

another in a small group of mixed Philippan and Meleagrian poems (Gow and Page ii. 115–16 for the details). 'The remainder' (they conclude) 'are placed according to theme (vii. 41) or are quite isolated (ix. 71, 73, 156, 178, 192).' In fact, of the 5 last quoted ix. 156 on Troy was clearly so placed to follow 4 poems by Agathias on Troy, while 192, on the Iliad and Odyssey, fits well enough in a long series on famous books (184–214). *AP* ix. 71 and 73 do not occur in either an alphabetical or a clear-cut thematic sequence, but in a sequence which none the less contains a preponderance of Philippan poems (14 between ix. 69 and 89). *AP* ix. 178—none other than the poem on Nero and Rhodes—seems to be the only Antiphilan poem that is 'completely isolated'.

Yet 'isolation' from a Philippan context does not in itself constitute proof or even probability of non-Philippan origin. My own researches have led me to a conclusion close to the suggestion made by Gow and Page (i, p. xviii), that 'the combination of order and disorder in the Palatine (manuscript) may suggest that Cephalas inherited a conglomerate anthology in which Philip's authors were represented by the more or less isolated epigrams and that he added the main alphabetical sequences from an independently surviving copy of the *Garland*.' The next chapter will postulate just such an anthology compiled in the late fourth century, an anthology which incorporated material from both the *Garlands* together with selections from the later collections of Diogenianus and Palladas. I have no doubt that many of the 'isolated' epigrams by Meleagrian and Philippan poets that we find in *AP* derive from some such secondary source. But this does not mean that they did not *originally* come from one or another of the *Garlands*. In the case (say) of so widely read and quoted a poet as Callimachus there is a definite possibility of non-Meleagrian origin for isolated epigrams. But for the obscure Antiphilus the chances are negligible.

Gow and Page were right to be cautious. But caution is not to be placed above probability, and it is surely more probable than not that Antiphilus VI was originally included in Philip's *Garland*. The only positive objection that can be brought is the hypothesis under discussion that the *Garland* was published thirteen years before Antiphilus VI was written. But a chronological hypothesis that has to eliminate on chronological grounds the only piece of evidence that can decisively refute it cannot be said to stand on a strong foundation. If another, unquestionably Philippan, poem can be shown to postdate 40, there will be no case left to answer.

There is in fact an uncomfortably large number of poems which could as easily be Claudian or Neronian as Gaian or Tiberian, where the decision has often been made on the basis of the assumption that the *Garland* was published under Gaius. I have discussed a number of cases in a paper published in 1980.[34] Here it will be enough to reconsider one of the poems discussed there, and to add one new example. Both are test cases, since both are embedded in solid alphabetical sequences, of 35 and 42 poems respectively. There can be no doubt that both poems stood in Philip's *Garland*. First the new poem, Antiphilus III (*AP* vii. 379):

—εἰπέ, Δικαιάρχεια, τί σοι τόσον εἰς ἄλα χῶμα
βέβληται μέσσου γευόμενον πελάγους;
Κυκλώπων τάδε χεῖρες ἐνιδρύσαντο θαλάσσῃ
τείχεα· μέχρι πόσου, Γαῖα, βιαζόμεθα;
—κόσμου νηίτην δέχομαι στόλον· εἴσιδε Ῥώμην
ἔγγυθεν, εἰ ταύτης μέτρον ἔχω λιμένα.

—Tell me, Dicarcheia, why have you cast so great a mole into the waters, touching mid-ocean? Cyclopean were the hands that planted these walls on the sea. How far, Earth, must we suffer your violence?
—I am harbour to the world's fleet of ships. Look at Rome nearby, and judge if I have not a haven the measure of hers.

The first speaker is evidently the sea (l. 4), the second the city of Dicarcheia (Puteoli). According to Gow and Page, 'It is improbable that a court poet would speak of Puteoli in these terms later than AD 42', the year in which Claudius began to build the new harbour for Rome at Ostia. But this is to misunderstand both the historical situation and Antiphilus' poem. As R. Meiggs has put it, if it was Claudius' intention that Ostia would 'make Rome independent of Puteoli . . . it was not realized'. If not the 'harbour of the world', Puteoli long remained the main destination of eastern traffic in Italy.[35] Furthermore, the nature of her boast surely

---

[34] 'The Garland of Philip', *GRBS* xxxi (1980), 43–62; K. Hartigan, *The Poets and the Cities* (Beiträge zur Klass. Philologie 87, 1979), 108–9, also opted for publication under Nero, but without going into the question of *Garland* sequences; see too L. Robert, *Journal des savants* 1982, 139–62, arguing that vi. 240 and ix. 543 by Philip concern King Rhoetomalcas III of Thrace (who died in AD 44), but not disputing my conclusion that the *Garland* itself was published later than this (cf. pp. 140–1).

[35] *Roman Ostia*² (Oxford 1972), 56 f.

implies that the poem was written *after* 42. It would be pointless for Puteoli to have claimed equality with the harbour of Rome at a time when Rome had no harbour to speak of at all. The boast only makes sense once Ostia was finished and functioning, but *still* no match for Puteoli. M. Griffin has recently suggested that the poem is 'a tribute to the favour Puteoli had found with Nero, from whom it received in 60 colonial status and a new name'.[36] But there is no hint of enhanced status or new name in either Antiphilus' poem or the companion piece by Philip (LVII = *AP* ix. 708), also in a (shorter but undisturbed) alphabetical sequence (ix. 706–9). Here Page's translation will suffice):

The barbarian, with a fool's audacity, yoked the Hellespont, but Time has undone all those great labours. Now Dicarcheia has made the sea a mainland and has reshaped the deeps to the land's form. She has rooted monstrous stones, a deep foundation, and with Giant's hands has put the waters in their place below. One could always sail the sea; inconstant when traversed by sailors, it has agreed to stay firm for those on foot.

Both poets are commemorating the completion of a mole in the harbour of Puteoli. It has hitherto been assumed that this mole was Augustan,[37] but it is at least as likely that it was undertaken in imitation of the two huge moles built to create the new harbour at Ostia, no doubt utilizing the techniques developed there. The harbour at Ostia may have been in use before Claudius' death, but there was no commemorative coinage before 64, implying that much work remained to be done in the early years of Nero.[38] The probability is that both poems are Neronian.

Next, Thallus II (*AP* vi. 235):

Ἑσπερίοις μέγα χάρμα καὶ ἠῴοις περάτεσσιν,
　Καῖσαρ, ἀνικάτων ἔκγονε Ῥωμυλιδῶν,
αἰθερίην γένεσιν σέο μέλπομεν, ἀμφὶ δὲ βωμοῖς
　γηθοσύνους λοιβὰς σπένδομεν ἀθανάτοις.
ἀλλὰ σὺ παππῴοις ἐπὶ βήμασιν ἴχνος ἐρείδων
　εὐχομένοις ἡμῖν πουλὺ μέλοις ἐπ' ἔτος.

---

[36] *Nero, The End of a Dynasty* (London 1984), 149, cf. 274–5. The new name was Colonia Claudia Neronis, but we now know that Puteoli was already an Augustan colony (M. Frederiksen, *Roman Campania*, ed. N. Purcell [1984], 331–2); Nero must have renewed its colonial status.

[37] M. W. Frederiksen, *PW* s.v. Puteoli 2055–6.

[38] Meiggs, *Roman Ostia*², 55; Hartigan (*The Poets and the Cities*, 108) also uses the evidence of the coinage, but on the assumption that, though writing under Nero, Antiphilus wrote *AP* vii. 385 *before* Ostia was finished.

Great joy to the farthest West and East, Caesar, descendant of Romulus'
unconquerable sons, your heavenly birth we sing, and around the altars we
pour glad libations to the immortals. Do you tread firm in your grandfather's steps, and be the subject of our prayers for many a year.

Who is Caesar? The man who writes a poem for so specific an
occasion as the emperor's birthday[39] does not need to say which
birthday, much less which emperor. He will flatter and exaggerate.
But there are some things he must get right if he mentions them at
all. And we are surely entitled to assume that he is at least equipped
with the *tact* that his delicate task requires.

Gow and Page eliminated one candidate on the grounds that he
is not known to have been accorded divine honours in his lifetime.
But there is nothing in the second couplet to suggest that the gods
to whom the poet poured out his libations included Caesar. Nor
(with Cichorius, p. 357) can we safely infer any real or recent
conquests from the first couplet. It seems to me that there is only
one firm indication in the poem. You do not tell a man to follow in
his grandfather's footsteps if his father's would have done as well.
There must have been some important and obvious respect in
which Caesar's father could not provide the necessary example.
And if l. 5 is read in conjunction with l. 6 it will be clear that it is
not grandfather's kingly qualities and achievements that Caesar is
being exhorted to emulate, but his *longevity*. From this point of
view it makes no difference whether we accept C's μένοις ('abide
with us') or (with Gow and Page) keep the 'more exquisite' μέλοις
('be in our thoughts'). There is no implication that father had
failed to live up to grandfather's standards; merely that he had not
lived so long. Thallus' birthday wish is simply: 'may you have as
many happy returns as your grandfather'. Now the only Julio-
Claudian grandfathers who lived to any age at all were Augustus
(77) and Tiberius (78). Given the semi-official nature of Thallus'
poem we must certainly consider their legal as well as their
biological grandchildren.

For example, Gaius and Lucius, the sons of the elder Julia and
Agrippa, were certainly Augustus' grandchildren, but it was not
till he adopted them (in 17 BC) that they took the name Caesar.
After then they were officially his *sons*, as illustrated by Antipater
of Thessalonica's propempticon for Gaius' Parthian expedition of

[39] On the celebration of the emperor's birthday see W. Schmidt in *RE* s.v.
γενέθλιος ἡμέρα, 1138 f.; S. Weinstock, *Divus Julius* (Oxford 1971), 209–12.

1 BC, πατρῴων ἄρξαι ἀπ' ἐντολέων, 'rule in accord with your *father's* precepts' (ix. 297. 4)—and indeed by Ovid, writing of the same expedition (*AA* i. 191), 'auspiciis animisque *patris* puer arma movebis'. As for Germanicus, it is true that he was a (step)grandson of Augustus through his short-lived father Drusus, but he too only became a Caesar on his adoption (in AD 4) by Tiberius. Tiberius not only did not die young: he outlived Germanicus. In any age it would be tactless to exhort a man with a still living father in his 50s or early 60s to live as long as his grandfather: whatever the poet's intention, whichever genealogy he had in mind, the implication is there that the father's life may be shorter than the grandfather's. Who would have risked so ill-omened an interpretation when there was a living 'father' who was a notoriously suspicious and superstitious emperor much given to anxious study of his horoscope?[40]

It might be further objected against Gaius and Lucius (who both died before Augustus) that it would have been hardly less ill-omened to hold up the longevity of the equally superstitious Augustus as exemplary during his lifetime, since it might be thought to suggest that he had lived long enough already.

Nero, grandson of the short-lived Germanicus, can be eliminated without discussion. Caligula too, grandson of the equally short-lived Drusus, fails on his biological genealogy. But as Germanicus' son he was by adoption *Tiberius'* grandson. His correct and invariable official style was 'C. Caesar, Germanici filius, Tiberii Augusti nepos, divi Augusti pronepos'. But even with a short-lived father and a long-lived grandfather there are problems with the identification of Thallus' Caesar with Gaius.

Cichorius weakly argued that it was Tiberius rather than Germanicus that the poet quoted as model because Germanicus, not having actually been emperor, was 'not suitable'. But Tiberius died hated by his people—above all by his grandson and successor. He was not deified by the new regime, and it was naturally and appropriately Germanicus whose memory was refurbished and whose example was held up before the new emperor and his people. To quote a minor but significant example, one of Gaius' earliest acts was to rename September Germanicus—evidently rejecting the proposal turned down by Tiberius himself that it

---

[40] R. Syme, *Tacitus*, ii (Oxford 1958), 525.

should be called Tiberius.[41] Who would have been so tactless as to refer Gaius to Tiberius rather than Germanicus as a model for anything? And why of all things should courtiers with a receptive young ruler to flatter have chosen to evoke the seemingly never-ending old age of his abominated predecessor, reviving all too fresh memories of the debaucheries and cruelties of Capri? Moreover, it was Tiberius who was popularly believed to have been responsible for the fact that Germanicus did not live to a ripe old age. All in all, in this context Thallus' poem could only seem ill-omened—if not deliberately and dangerously ironic.

That leaves only Claudius. With a short-lived father (Drusus) and a long-lived *step*-grandfather in Augustus (his natural grand-mother was Augustus's second wife Livia), he fits the formal requirements to perfection. And Augustus's footsteps would certainly have been more auspicious than Tiberius'. Furthermore, all the other Caesars we have been considering were men in their twenties or thirties, an age when one does not usually worry about living to be seventy or eighty. But in the case of an older man like Claudius, who had always enjoyed poor health and was already fifty at his accession, Thallus' birthday wish would have been both more understandable and more appropriate. Of course, strictly speaking Claudius was *not* Augustus's grandson. Indeed, he was evidently only too conscious that he did not stand in the direct line of descent from Augustus by either birth or adoption.[42] That could not be changed, but he could at least change his nomenclature to suggest that he did: Ti. Claudius Nero Germanicus became Ti. Claudius *Caesar Augustus* Germanicus. Thallus might well have been alluding to the assumption of Augustus's names by the new emperor.[43] Add to this the fact that Claudius' birthday fell on the first of the month renamed after the first princeps, and it could be suggested that the poem was written precisely for 1 August 41. In any case, Thallus does not identify his subject straightforwardly as the grandson of his long-lived predecessor. He wishes only that he might step in 'grandfatherly footsteps' ($\pi\alpha\pi\pi\dot\omega\omega\iota\varsigma\ \dot\epsilon\pi\dot\iota\ \beta\dot\eta\mu\alpha\sigma\iota$). This could easily include Livia as well—and no less appropriately, given her 87 years.

---

[41] Weinstock, *Divus Julius*, 154–5.

[42] Nor did Augustus so regard him: surviving letters to Livia refer to Claudius as 'nepos *tuus*' (*Claud.* 4–5).

[43] So Griffin, *Nero* (1984), 192, 288 n. 13.

That makes one Claudian poem in a solid *Garland* sequence, and the two on Puteoli that are more likely to be Neronian than Claudian. Since Antiphilus VI on Rhodes was written barely a year before Claudius' death, it seems reasonable to conclude that the *Garland* itself was assembled and published under Nero.

It is no objection to this inference that there is no *Garland* poem unmistakably referable to Nero as emperor. Epigrams that name or address reigning emperors normally and naturally refer only to 'Caesar'. It was only by a process of elimination that we identified Claudius in Thallus II, and four out of five of the references to Nero in Lucillius are just to 'Caesar'. It is perfectly possible that the 'Caesar' of Philip III, IV, or V or the anonymous *Garland* poem *AP* vii. 626 is Nero—just as the 'queen' of Antiphilus II could be Octavia. The 'Caesar' of Philip VI (*AP* ix. 778), recipient of a present from the wife of Herod Agrippa, is (despite the commentators) much more likely to be Herod's lifelong friend Claudius than Gaius. If Philip does not thank Nero for his favour, as Lucillius does (ix. 572), he does not thank or reveal personal familiarity with any other emperor either. It is none the less probable that, like many other Greek men of letters, Philip should have sought (and perhaps won) the philhellene Nero's patronage with his *Garland*.

III. STRATO AND RUFINUS

Strato's date has been recently discussed in relation to Rufinus' by Denys Page,[44] who put Rufinus in the fourth century AD but left the question of his relationship with Strato open. Since Rufinus and Strato were the only two erotic epigrammatists between the age of Augustus and Justinian, we might expect the later to be familiar with the work of the earlier. There are numerous parallels between them, and I have elsewhere shown that it is Strato who is the borrower[45]—and so the later of the two. Rufinus is Neronian.

Strato has usually been put under Hadrian, though there has of late been a movement to take him back to the reign of Nero.[46] It

[44] Page (1978), 23–7.

[45] *CQ*, NS xxxii (1982), 162–73. Much the same conclusions about the date of Rufinus were also reached by L. Robert, *CRAI* 1982, 50–63.

[46] e.g. R. Keydell, *Hermes* lxxx (1952), 499: *CQ* loc. cit.

seems to me that the Hadrianic date can be more persuasively formulated than it has been hitherto. Here is the key poem, a lampoon on an incompetent eye-doctor called Capito (*AP* xi. 317):

Ἰητρὸς Καπίτων Χρύσην ἐνέχρισεν ὁρῶντα
ὀκτὼ μὲν μακρὸν πύργον ἀπὸ σταδίων,
ἄνδρα δ' ἀπὸ σταδίου, διὰ δώδεκα δ' ὄρτυγα πηχῶν,
φθεῖρα δ' ἀπὸ σπιθαμῶν καὶ δύο δερκόμενον.
νῦν δ' ἀπὸ μὲν σταδίου πόλιν οὐ βλέπει, ἐκ δὲ διπλέθρου
καιόμενον κατιδεῖν τὸν φάρον οὐ δύναται·
ἵππον ἀπὸ σπιθαμῆς δὲ μόλις βλέπει, ἀντὶ δὲ τοῦ πρὶν
ὄρτυγος οὐδὲ μέγαν στρουθὸν ἰδεῖν δύναται.
ἂν δὲ προσεγχρίσας αὐτὸν φθάσῃ, οὐδ' ἐλέφαντα
οὐκέτι μήποτ' ἴδῃ πλησίον ἑσταότα.

When Capito the doctor put his ointment on Chryses' eyes he could see [before the treatment] a high tower from 8 stades [1416 m.], a man from 1 stade [177 m.], a quail from 12 cubits [5.28 m.] and a louse from 2 spans [0.44 m.]. Now he cannot see the city from 1 stade [177 m.] or the lighthouse fire from 2 plethra [59.2 m.]. He can scarcely see a horse at 1 span [0.22 m.] nor a large ostrich where he could previously see a quail [at 12 cubits, 5.28 m.]. If Capito continues with his ointment, Chryses won't be able to see an elephant standing right in front of him.

It was J. G. Schneider who first suggested that Artemidorus Capito, a medical scholar whose edition of Hippocrates won the favour of Hadrian (Galen, xv. 21 Kühn), was the Capito of this poem. Both the identification and Strato's authorship of the poem have been denied.

Keydell and Page both object that this is the only non-pederastic poem transmitted under Strato's name, both strongly suspecting that the ascription is erroneous. R. Aubreton, editor of the Budé *AP* xi, athetizes without argument ('titulum Stratoni perperam tributum'). Yet it is clearly ascribed to Strato in both *AP* and *APl*, and it seems unreasonable to exclude on principle the possibility that an erotic poet might also on occasion write a satirical poem. That it is an unexpected ascription is in its favour rather than the reverse; it would not have been an obvious guess—or even error. The poem would not of course have been included in the μοῦσα παιδική. Most probably, like other scoptica of the late first and early second century in *AP* xi, it was taken by Cephalas from the 'Anthology of epigrams' of Diogenianus of Heraclea. Diogenianus' Anthology may have appeared under Marcus, though his earliest works go back to Hadrian. Obviously such a person would have been in a particularly good position to lay his hands on an occasional poem by a contemporary poet about a contemporary figure—an argument in favour of the authenticity of poem and subject alike.

Page also argues (*a*) that the 40-odd names in Strato's pederastic poems are likely to be fictitious, and (*b*) that most of the names in the scoptica of *AP* xi are also fictitious, concluding that the Capito of xi. 117 (whoever wrote it) is 'at least as likely to be fictitious as real' (p. 27). But the fact that Strato no doubt used a series of fictitious names for his ἐρώμενοι hardly proves that he would not have used a real name when writing satire. It is true that xi. 117 is embedded in a series of scoptica on doctors (xi. 112–26), most of which are certainly directed against types rather than individuals. But it is fair to point out that 117 stands out from the rest in the mildness and nature of its satire. Most of the others are variations on the monotonous theme of the doctor having only to touch the patient to kill or blind him. In 126, for example, the doctor uses a fork instead of a spatula to anoint his patient's eye and yanks it out. We hardly need to study the stock names to see that these are not poems about real doctors and real patients. 117 is a refreshing change. The sharpness of Chryses' sight before treatment is not exaggerated; after all he must have gone to the doctor for help, and if he could only just make out a man at 177 m. and a louse at 44 cm., then he needed help. Nor is the deterioration noted after treatment even grotesque, much less (as usual) fatal. The highest extent of the hyperbole is the prospect of not being able to identify an elephant *if* he continues with the treatment. The humour of the poem turns less on the doctor's incompetence, in fact, than on the incongruous series of objects by which the patient's vision is measured. Now while the fact that Capito is not demonstrably a 'type' like the doctors of Lucillius and Nicarchus does not in itself guarantee that he was a real person, it does eliminate the only serious argument against. There are other real doctors among the 'types' of *AP* xi. For example, *AP* xi. 281 by Palladas on Magnus: a stock name, it might have been assumed, if we did not know Palladas' dates exactly enough to be able to identify with his celebrated contemporary Magnus of Nisibis, like Palladas a holder of a public chair at Alexandria.[47]

[47] *PLRE* i, s.v. Magnus 7, p. 534.

Keydell raised another, quite different sort of objection: the reference to the lighthouse (φάρον) in l. 6, he argued, points to Alexandria, whereas on the evidence of the epigrams Strato's world was bounded by Sardis, Smyrna,[48] and Ephesus (xii. 193, 202, 226). But the anonymous inscriptional epigram *AP* ix. 671 commemorates the building of a lighthouse precisely at Smyrna. The man who built it is generally identified, on grounds that are less than compelling, with a proconsul of the same name (Ambrosius) who rebuilt the theatre at Ephesus in the fourth century.[49] Even so, at that date his achievement would surely have been the rebuilding rather than the building of a lighthouse at so important a port; any first- or second-century erection would have fallen in the earthquake that destroyed Smyrna in 178. *AP* ix. 675 also commemorates the erection of a pharos at Smyrna, this time by the 'Asclepiadai'—perhaps the one destroyed in 178. So inasmuch as the poet presupposes a lighthouse as a conspicuous local landmark (τὸν φάρον, 'the lighthouse'), and there was one at Smyrna, Keydell's observation tells in favour rather than against the ascription to Strato and the circumstantial nature of the epigram.

Page argues that 'the medical scholar who enjoyed the patronage of the emperor was not a likely target for satire of this kind', but we do not know how seriously the satire was intended, how long Capito enjoyed the emperor's favour, or what Strato's social position was. V. Buchheit objected that the name Capito was 'im römischen Reich nicht gerade selten'.[50] Over the length and breadth of the Roman world, no doubt, but the question is, how many Greek doctors in the early Empire were called Capito?

To be sure, the editor of Hippocrates does not look much like the bad eye-doctor of *AP* xi. 117. But no one who has ever discussed the identification has ever referred to Book iv. 7 of Galen's *De Compositione Medicamentorum secundum Locos* (xii. 731–2 Kühn), where a Capito is twice quoted for medicinal compounds designed to cure sore eyes. There is no direct proof that this is the editor of Hippocrates, but it should be noted that after introducing Artemidorus Capito in full as Ἀρτεμίδωρος ὁ ἐπικληθεὶς Καπίτων (xv. 21; cf. xvii. B. 631, xix. 83), Galen regularly elsewhere refers to him as

---

[48] The reference to the twin Nemeses of Smyrna in xii. 193 suggests local knowledge: cf. C. J. Cadoux, *Ancient Smyrna* (1938), 220–3.

[49] L. Robert, *Hellenica*, iv (1948), 62; *PLRE* i, p. 52.

[50] *Studien zum Corpus Priapeorum* (Zetemata 28, Munich 1962), 111, alleging also that it is a 'sprechender Name'.

simply Καπίτων (xv. 24, 358; xvi. 485, 837; xvii. A. 154, 730, 795; xvii. B. 97–8, 104, 310), just like the eye-doctor of xii. 731–2. There is no good reason to doubt that they are one and the same man. There would be nothing surprising in the same man being both scholar and practitioner. Galen himself was at once an enormously productive scholar (*inter alia* he criticized Capito's edition of Hippocrates)[51] and a highly successful practitioner. Medical books did not pay the rent, nor was imperial patronage a dependable source of income.

Greek eye-doctors called Capito are surely not to be multiplied beyond necessity—and it would not be surprising if the unpromising-looking remedies reported by Galen had worked as badly as Strato describes. For what solid grounds are there for doubting Strato's authorship of *AP* xi. 117? If so, then Strato wrote in the age of Hadrian, who reigned from 117 to 138. And Rufinus cannot have written much after AD 100, quite possibly a few decades earlier. I have argued elsewhere that two epigrams of Rufinus (v. 47; v. 35) were known to and imitated by Martial (i. 57; xi. 100), in which case he might be Neronian rather than Flavian (no earlier, or he could hardly have failed to make Philip's *Garland*).

IV. DIOGENIAN AND PALLADAS

Concerning the date of Diogenian's Anthology, there is no need to anticipate the conclusions of the following chapter. Concerning Palladas I need only reaffirm my acceptance of Bowra's date of 391 (or soon after) for *AP* x. 97, written when he was 72. If so, then he was born *c*.319 (see p. 90). In Chapter XV I shall be adducing further support for Luck's discovery that *AP* ix. 400, the main foundation of the later chronology, is a Christian poem many centuries later than Palladas.

V. AGATHIAS

We have seen that in the case of Meleager and Philip, J had no information beyond the bare texts supplied by Cephalas. With

---

[51] Whence all our knowledge of the man: see the passages from Galen collected by J. Ilberg, 'Die Hippokratesausgaben des Artemidorus Kapiton und Dioskurides', *Rheinisches Museum* xlv (1890), 111–37; cf. too F. Pfaff, 'Die Überlieferung des Corpus Hippocraticum in der nachalexandrinischen Zeit', *Wien. Studien* l (1932), 67–82.

Agathias he was in a slightly better position. In the first place, the text Cephalas used was probably not more than a generation or so later than Agathias (Ch. II), as the authoritative heading to *AP* iv. 3 suggests: 'Agathias Scholasticus of Myrina in Asia: collection of new epigrams presented in Constantinople to Theodore, son of Cosmas, the decurion. The proems were spoken after the frequent recitations given at that time.'

The double ethnic Ἀσιανοῦ Μυριναίου is sufficiently explained by Agathias' own remark in the preface to his history: 'By Myrina I do not mean the town in Thrace nor any other in Europe or Africa that happens to be called by this name, but the one in Asia colonized long ago by the Aeolians'. Surely the double ethnic in *AP* derives direct from Agathias, here too anxious that no one should be in any doubt about the location of his home town. The last sentence looks as if it were written by someone who knew something about the original circumstances of recitation. And the identification, complete with office and patronymic, of Agathias' dedicatee bears every mark of authenticity.

It is a pity that this well-informed person did not go on to identify the emperor addressed in the second half of Agathias' preface. It was only J, in a marginal note, who added the name Justinian. Not a stupid guess; the first text in *AP* is the well-known ecphrasis of Hagia Sophia by Agathias' most prolific contributor, Paul the Silentiary, and its preface is addressed to Justinian. J also mentions Agathias' history, a continuation of Procopius' history of the wars of Justinian. None the less, as Averil Cameron and I first pointed out in 1966, the Cycle was unquestionably published early in the reign of Justin II, *c*.567/8.[52]

The proof is very simple. At least three *Cycle*-poems clearly name or allude to Justin II and/or his Empress Sophia: *AP* ix. 657 is by Marianus scholasticus; 658 by Paul; and 659 by Theaetetus scholasticus. Since doubts have been expressed about this conclusion (most recently by Barry Baldwin),[53] it will not be irrelevant to restate the case.

Marianus' poem describes the Sophianae palace that Justin built for his empress on the far side of the Bosporus. The reference in lines 3–4 to the 'far-famed Queen Sophia' proves that the unnamed

---

[52] *JHS* lxxxvi (1966), 6 f.

[53] *BZ* lxx (1977), 298–301; lxxiii (1980), 334–40.

emperor is Justin II. The date of the completion of the palace can be fixed on other evidence to 566/7.[54]

AP ix. 658–9 by Paul and Theaetetus both commemorate the renovation of the Great Praetorium by a certain Domninus under an emperor called Justin. That he is Justin II (and not Justin I as previously supposed) is proved by a second pair of epigrams commemorating statues of Justin and Sophia erected by Domninus in front of the same building later in the book (ix. 812–13). In 1966 we were inclined to assign ix. 812–13 too to the *Cycle*, but R. C. McCail rightly objected that the context is almost entirely epigraphic; in fact that 'the whole series from 799 to 822 has the appearance of an inscriptional sylloge put together by Cephalas from non-literary sources'.[55] Quoting McCail, Baldwin argues that all four Praetorium poems (and the Sophianae poem) 'could have been brought together directly from inscriptions by Cephalas'.[56] Yet McCail's observation actually supports our main contention that 658–9 derive from the *Cycle*. For if all four Praetorium poems had reached Cephalas from the same source (whether literary or epigraphic), we should have expected to find them all together. As it is, the two ascribed to *Cycle* poets (658–9) appear with other *Cycle* poets whereas the two anonyma (812–13) appear with other epigraphic anonyma. The obvious inference is that Cephalas found the first pair in the *Cycle* and the second pair on the original monuments.

It must be conceded that our three poems do not occur in any unbroken Agathian sequence. ix. 606–69 is a long thematically arranged sequence, including a few anonymous inscriptional poems as well as poems by *Cycle* authors, all on early Byzantine buildings. But it is from these two sources alone (it seems) that the sequence derives. Poems with ascriptions are ascribed only to known or likely *Cycle* authors (Baldwin ignores the fact that inscriptional poems are normally anonymous). The presumption is that the thematic classification is Agathias' own, and that Cephalas simply added a few inscriptional poems on similar themes that fitted these categories.

Now all we know about Marianus (apart from the datable ix. 656) is that he is always given the title *scholasticus* borne by at least

[54] Averil Cameron, *Byzantion* xxxvii (1967), 11 f.
[55] *JHS* lxxxix (1969), 94.
[56] *BZ* lxxiii (1980), 335.

six other *Cycle* poets and that four of his five other extant poems occur (like ix. 656) in solid *Cycle* groupings. As with the Philippan Antiphilus, the chances of any poem by him that was not included in the only known anthology of the age surviving to the tenth century are remote. A new argument can be added here. *AP* ix. 657 is quoted in full in the early twelfth-century *Epitome Historiarum* of John Zonaras (xiv. 10)—though ascribed to Agathias. There seems no call to doubt the combined ascription to Marianus in *AP* and *APl*, and the obvious explanation is that Zonaras took his quotation from the *Cycle* itself and carelessly assumed that Agathias himself was the author. A few pages earlier in the same book (xiv. 7) Zonaras quotes another *Cycle* poem in full (ix. 641), Agathias' piece on the bridge over the river Sangarius. There is certainly no reason to doubt that this poem (written in 559–60) was included in the *Cycle*. It seems improbable in the extreme that Zonaras (who wrote his history in a remote island monastery) should have copied either poem from the original monument. If he had, it would be an extraordinary coincidence if he had come up in both cases with an ascription to *Cycle* poets—in one case to the wrong one. There is in fact a clear proof that his source was literary: in each poem Zonaras' text offers a corruption also present in *AP* (in 641. 4 οὕτως where metre requires οὕτω; and in 657. 6 the third person δέρκεται where the second person δέρκεαι is obviously required). Each is the merest of slips, easy enough to correct, and the corrections are in fact already to be found in Planudes. We can hardly doubt that both errors stood in Cephalas' text—and perhaps also Zonaras' text of the *Cycle*.

There is one further proof, a poem by Agathias (*AP* i. 36) describing a painting that showed the presentation of the insignia of master of offices to a certain Theodorus. It appears in a brief sequence (i. 33–6) on archangels whose Cyclic provenance can be better discussed in a later chapter. The relevant lines are 3–4:

ἐκ σέο γὰρ Θεόδωρος ἔχει ζωστῆρα μαγίστρου
καὶ δὶς ἀεθλεύει πρὸς θρόνον ἀνθυπάτων.

Despite Baldwin's assertion to the contrary (contradicted by the very sources he quotes), at this period the word μάγιστρος without further qualification always denotes the *magister officiorum*. Now between 539 (when Agathias was about seven years old) and 565 the mastership of the offices was held continuously by the celebrated scholar and diplomat Peter the Patrician. On his death it passed briefly to a man called Anastasius, and then in 566 to Peter's son Theodorus,[57] both date and relationship being securely attested in Corippus' panegyric on the new Emperor Justin II (*Laud. Just.* i. 26–7):

> successorque boni recidivaque gloria Petri
> hinc Theodorus adest, patria gravitate magister.

The son of Peter is the only Theodorus *magister* Agathias can ever have known.

McCail and Baldwin would prefer the Theodorus of this poem to be the Theodorus *decurio* (head of the palace silentiaries) to whom Agathias dedicated the *Cycle*. McCail ingeniously points out that decurions 'were allowed on retirement to assume the title of ex-Master of the Offices' but 'could be recalled to active service, which in the case of Theodorus would have taken the form of two proconsular governorships'.[58] Such a titular master of offices might seem to fit the bill, but there is a fatal objection none the less. The painting Agathias' epigram describes showed Theodorus receiving the insignia of office: evidently then it commemorated his *appointment* as master of offices. Yet it is clear from l. 4 (despite the 'poetic' present tense) that he has *already* held his two proconsulates. McCail's hypothesis requires the reverse, namely that he won his proconsulates *after* receipt of his insignia as titular master of offices. It would also be surprising for the epigram (and painting) to make no reference to Theodorus' period as *decurio*, the office (on McCail's hypothesis) he was holding when he received the dedication of the *Cycle*. McCail also has to dismiss as 'someone else altogether' the probably Agathian 'Theodorus the proconsul' of *AP* vii. 556, in whom it is more tempting to recognize the future master of offices while still holding one of his proconsulships. As for Theodorus the *decurio*, is he not the former *decurio* Theodorus who is attested by an inscription on the island of Philae (G. Lefebvre, *Inscriptions grecques-chrétiennes d'Égypte* (1907), no. 584) as *dux Augustalis* of the Thebaid in 577? There were only three decurions of the silentiaries at a time, and it was not a post with a rapid turnover. Thus a former decurion of 577 was almost

---

[57] On whom see Averil Cameron, *F. Cresconius Corippus, In laudem Iustini Augusti Minoris libri IV* (1976), p. 128.

[58] *JHS* lxxxix (1969), 93–4.

certainly active as a decurion in the 560s. So unless we are prepared to accept two contemporary or consecutive decurions of the same name, this man is surely Agathias' dedicatee. Naturally, the fact that he was still active as late as 577 favours a date under Justin II for the *Cycle*.

It follows that the Theodorus of i. 36 can only be the son of Peter the Patrician, and that in all probability Agathias' poem dates from the year of Theodorus' appointment, namely 566. In the case of Philip's *Garland*, there was only one epigram by a Philippan poet that unmistakably referred to Nero. Here we have no fewer than four poems by four different Agathian poets that unmistakably date from 566/7.[59] Is it really possible to believe that not one of them was included in the *Cycle*?

There remains Agathias' preface, the second part of which (*AP* iv. 3. 43–98) is in effect a panegyric of the (unfortunately unnamed) emperor. Since the main theme of this panegyric is the extent of the emperor's conquests in Persia, Africa, and the West, it is not surprising that, before closer study of the *Cycle* as a whole, commentators from J on took it for granted that Justinian was meant. But what was the panegyrist of Justin II to say? Was he to admit that Justinian's successor was a lesser man with no achievements of his own? In fact Agathias did exactly what Corippus did in his panegyric on the same emperor published within a year of Agathias' own. Both solved their problem by concentrating on the glory of Byzantine power at Justin's accession, as though it was Justin's name that struck terror into every barbarian heart.[60] Both in fact offer a highly generalized development on the power of Roman arms and the extent of Roman peace. Baldwin argues that the same applies to the panegyrical portions of Paul the Silentiary's *Ecphrasis* of Hagia Sophia recited before Justinian in 563. But this is not altogether true; Paul three times directly praises his emperor's triumphs. Agathias is never so explicit. Baldwin objects that Agathias does not name Justin—but then he does not name Justinian either! As for the argument that this or that detail suits Justinian better, this may well be true enough—but irrelevant. For

---

[59] There are also several anonyma dating from 566/7 with a claim for inclusion: see *BICS* xiii (1966), 103 (with *CR* xviii (1968), 21–2); *Byz.* xlvii (1977), 63–4. And in *Mnemosyne* xxi (1968), 76–8 McCail advanced an ingenious and convincing argument for assigning a post-Justinianic date to another epigram of Agathias (vii. 596).

[60] Averil Cameron, op. cit. n. 37, 118–19.

Agathias' audience was not (like us) reduced to guessing at the identity of the emperor. They knew—and understood Agathias' predicament. Moreover, there is one passage that is better suited to Justin, lines 98–100:

> τοὔνεκεν, ὅππότε πάντα φίλης πέπληθε γαλήνης,
> ὅππότε καὶ ξείνοιο καὶ ἐνδαπίοιο κυδοιμοῦ
> ἐλπίδες ἐθραύσθησαν ὑφ᾽ ἡμετέρῳ βασιλῆι . . .

So now that the whole earth is full of kindly peace, now that hopes of war at home and abroad have been shattered by our emperor . . .

The 'hopes for war at home' can be identified either (for Justinian) as the so-called bankers' conspiracy of 562 (see the allusion in Paul, *Ecphr.* 137) or (for Justin II) as the conspiracy of Aetherius and Addaeus (Corippus, i. 60–1). But what of the 'hopes for war abroad'? Justinian's long and (more or less) successful campaigns on many frontiers did far more than dash *hopes*. But this was the limit of Justin's contribution thus far. Hoping to take advantage of Justinian's death, the Avars and Persians at once sent envoys demanding better terms. Justin dismissed such demands with disdain—and much publicity.[61] So the one act Agathias specifically attributes to the emperor he is addressing is pitched rather low—and corresponds exactly with the extent of Justin's diplomatic achievement.

So the *Cycle* was not published before c.567—and probably not much later. The description of the West as a 'handmaiden' is not likely to have been written after the fall of Italy to the Lombards, which began in 568. By 570 Agathias must have been immersed in the research for the history which was to occupy such free time as his busy legal business left him until his early death.

VI. CEPHALAS AND PLANUDES

On the date of Cephalas, c.900, there is no need to anticipate the argument of Chapter XI.

Planudes' is the one anthology for which we have a precise date accurate to a month, added in duplicate in the compiler's own signed subscription. Yet even here there is a problem. And since I

---

[61] A. H. M. Jones, *Later Roman Empire*, i (1964), 304.

have changed my own mind on this much debated issue, it may be useful to set out the details.

Like most dated manuscripts, Marc. 481 is dated by both world and indiction years: to September in year 13 of the indiction (1299), 6810 (1301) of the world. As so often, the two dates conflict. There are three possible solutions:

(a) September 1299 was meant;

(b) September 1301 was meant;

(c) Planudes originally dated the manuscript to 1299 and then, after revising it two years later, deliberately changed the date to 1301. So Gallavotti 1959, 30; Turyn, *Dated Greek MSS* (1972), 91–2; and E. Mioni (1975), 266 and *Codices Graeci manuscripti Bibl. Divi Marci Venetiarum* II (1985), 276.

According to Gallavotti and Turyn the last element in the *anno mundi* date (ϛώ δεκ(ά)τ(ου)) is written over an erasure (which is why, they suggest, it was written out in full). They assume that Planudes had originally written ϛώή, 6808 (= 1299, in harmony with the indiction date), and then erased the last figure so that he could alter the date. It seems to me that there are two strong objections to this hypothesis.

Byzantine manuscripts were not normally redated after revision, and while this does not mean that it never happened, the only other example Turyn was able to quote is not at all parallel to what is supposed to have happened here; in Vat. gr. 256 an extra figure has been added by a different hand in a different ink, adding nine years to the original date. A meticulous scribe (or later owner) might reasonably wish to indicate the fact if he had done substantial fresh work on a manuscript at a later date, but it is difficult to see why Planudes should have wanted to *erase* the original date. Furthermore, what Planudes actually did would have been a most unsatisfactory way of redating the manuscript. A confusion when writing the original date would be understandable, but it is less easy to believe that when deliberately altering the *anno mundi* figure two years later Planudes failed to realize that the indiction year would need to be altered as well. As it is he left a direct conflict, with no way for anyone to know which he intended (there is no such unclarity in Vatic. gr. 256). The present form of the subscription is the standard way of indicating a single date.

Lastly, the subscription was written at the end of Nonnus' *Paraphrase of St John*, which in turn was written *after* Planudes had compiled the addenda to his anthology. There are signs that he did make one or two subsequent corrections (see App. II), but little to warrant redating the manuscript as a whole.[62]

Of the two other alternatives, in 1973 (*Porphyrius the Charioteer*, p. 96 n. 1) I opted for 1299 on general grounds: a man writing in September, when the new year began, might be expected to get the new indiction number (the simpler and more widely used system) correct while absent-mindedly repeating an old *anno mundi* figure. I now believe that there are two pointers to 1301.

In the first place, the correction of the last figure in the *anno mundi* date. If we may exclude the deliberate redating hypothesis, the natural implication (as with J's correction to his note on *AP* i. 10, Ch. V. 3) is that Planudes simply made a slip in the original figure which he recognized and corrected at once. If so, then this fact alone suggests that it was the second of the two dates to which he was giving his attention and which might therefore be presumed to be correct.

Secondly, there is the happy discovery of B. Hemmerdinger,[63] confirmed by Preisendanz, that MS S of Thucydides (Cassell. Ms. hist. fol. 3) is annotated in Planudes' own hand, the first of his comments being dated precisely on fo. 183ᵛ to 3 July ἰνδ. ί ἔτους ͵ςωί, the same world year (6810) as Marc. 481, though because of the month here denoting 1302. But the indiction year, it will be observed, is 10, properly denoting 1297—double the discrepancy of Marc. 481. Now Planudes also owned another manuscript of Thucydides, F (Monac. gr. 430), which contains on one of the flyleaves a note in Planudes' hand recording (in a for once perfectly harmonized date) the death of the princess Theodora Raoulena on 6 Dec. ἔτει ͵ςωθ (6809 = 1300) ἰνδ. ιδ (14 = 1300). While there is of course no proof here, there is a certain presumption that this note was made when Planudes was annotating not only this but also his other Thucydides manuscript.[64] If so, then we should probably follow the *anno mundi* 1302 for S and, by analogy and in the light of the correction, 1301 for Marc. 481.

---

[62] I cannot see that there is any justification for Mioni's suggestion that *API* had been complete for 'perhaps a decade' when Planudes added the Nonnus. There is a good chance that he found the Nonnus in his second epigram source: it once stood in *AP* (see p. 139).

[63] *Essai sur le texte de Thucydide* (Paris 1955) 45.

[64] All his work on Plutarch seems to belong to the same period 1294–6: Turyn, *Dated Greek MSS* (1972), 81–3; Wilson, *GRBS* xvi (1975), 95.

IV

Rufinus, Diogenian, Ausonius
A Fourth-Century Greek
Anthology

THE uncertain evidence about the so-called *Sylloge Rufiniana* was submitted to a characteristically sensible and efficient but basically inconclusive re-examination by Denys Page.[1] More progress can be made once it is realized that the problems of the *Sylloge Rufiniana* are linked to that other mysterious anthology of the early empire, the *Anthologion* of Diogenian of Heraclea. But first Rufinus.

I. RUFINUS

Not counting the introductory poem of Cephalas and 303–9, a miscellaneous conclusion, *AP* v divides naturally into four parts,[2] the last three of which can be traced to their sources without difficulty: 104–33 is an extract from the *Garland* of Philip, 134–215 from the *Garland* of Meleager, and 216–302 from the *Cycle* of Agathias; 2–103 is not nearly so well-defined a sequence, but it does have one unifying feature: 36 of its 101 poems are by Rufinus, who is nowhere else represented in the Anthology. Despite the fact that the remaining poems are by a most heterogeneous variety of authors, some anonymous (see the list below), it has generally been felt that *AP* v. 2–103 constitute a sequence that must be analysed as a whole. The following seem to me the most important considerations:

1. A poem by Rufinus (103) closes the sequence, and M. Boas[3]

---

[1] *The Epigrams of Rufinus* (1978), 3–18.
[2] See the useful analysis in Lenzinger, 4–5.
[3] *Philologus* lxxiii (1914), 1–18.

argued on stylistic grounds that the first, v. 2, though anonymous in *AP* and ascribed to Meleager in *APl*, is also by Rufinus. He compared the pederastic book *AP* xii, which, while containing many poems by a variety of authors, begins and ends with Strato, who is also far and away the biggest single contributor to the book. While conceding (as I would) that the stylistic argument is strong of its kind, Page was content to conclude that it cannot be considered more than 'a likely guess' which 'ought not to be used as a basis for the reconstruction of a *Sylloge Rufiniana*' (p. 7). That is sound scholarly caution, but suppose the 'likely guess' received the support of (say) a new papyrus find; how valid would the comparison with *AP* xii be then? It would in fact still be a very inexact and misleading comparison. For xii. 1–2 (a complementary pair) and 258 are quite clearly the original introduction and conclusion to Strato's μοῦσα παιδική. *AP* v. 2, on the advantages of dreaming about an inaccessible girlfriend, and 103, a warning to a girl who says no, would not make a suitable introduction or conclusion to any book of poems and were certainly not designed for either purpose. On the contrary, one could make out a better case for supposing that v. 9 was meant (though not necessarily by Rufinus himself) to mark the beginning of the Rufinian series; it is the most autobiographical of Rufinus' poems and the only one in which he refers to himself by name (῾Ρουφῖνος τῇ 'μῇ γλυκερωτάτῃ Ἐλπίδι πολλά / χαίρειν). Furthermore, the most natural explanation of the present character of *AP* xii is that Cephalas amplified an original collection of poems by Strato with the pederastic poems he had subtracted from the *Garlands* of Meleager and Philip.[4] The relationship between Rufinian and non-Rufinian poems in *AP* v. 2–103 is not to be explained by so straightforward an operation. Whether or not we ascribe v. 2 to Rufinus and even if we agree with Boas that the sequence 2–103 as a whole is the 'Überrest einer *Sylloge Rufiniana*', there is little in the present arrangement of the sequence to suggest any significant traces of the original *Sylloge*.

2. While Boas was able to point to several groups of two and sometimes more poems on similar themes, Page rightly objected that 'more striking are the numerous missed opportunities', quoting many examples where epigrams on the same theme are 'more or less widely separated', while Rufinus' own poems on linked themes are 'not as a rule put together' (p. 12). But he did not draw

---

[4] See below, p. 240.

the further inference that this lack of a thoroughgoing thematic arrangement suggests.

AP v has much the same structure as the other major 'Cephalan' books of *AP* (e.g. vi, vii, and ix): that is to say its central core consists of extracts from the *Garlands* of Meleager and Philip and Agathias' *Cycle*, in each case preceded by a thematically arranged miscellany,[5] which we may surely ascribe to one and the same Byzantine editor, namely Constantine Cephalas. These thematic categories are fairly methodically worked out. The introductory miscellany of *AP* vii, for example (1–363), begins with epitaphs on poets (1–55), prose-writers (56–78), and philosophers (79–135), with further subdivisions inside each major division (e.g. 1–7 on Homer, 8–10 on Orpheus, 11–13 on Erinna, 14–17 on Sappho). The much less systematic arrangement of v. 2–103 does not look like the work of the same anthologist. That is to say, it might be that instead of making his own thematic miscellany of erotica, Cephalas on this occasion made use of a pre-existing miscellany which seemed adequate for his purpose—the *Sylloge Rufiniana*.

3. This leads us to R. Weisshäupl's observation,[6] repeated by Page (p. 13), that there is no Agathian poem in the sequence. If the selection had been made *after* the sixth century, that is to say by Cephalas or some other Byzantine editor, it is hard to see why the selector should have included Meleagrian, Philippan, and a variety of other poems but nothing (in so long a sequence) from the *Cycle*. This is a further pointer to a pre-Cephalan origin for the sequence.

4. The latest datable poet included in the sequence (71–2) is the late fourth-century *grammaticus* Palladas (for precise details see below)—unless the Claudian who wrote 86 is to be identified with the court poet of Honorius (died *c*.404), which is possible but quite uncertain. For Page Rufinus himself wrote in the fourth century, but all the evidence points to the first.

At all events, a terminus of *c*.400. Now it so happens that there was a sudden flowering of interest in Greek epigrams at precisely this period in Gaul and Italy. Ausonius translated or paraphrased almost fifty, and the various contributors to the recently discovered *Epigrammata Bobiensia*, among whom we can identify Naucellius and Anicius Probinus, cos. 395, almost forty (for brevity's sake I shall style them collectively *EB*). Both Ausonius

---

[5] See below, pp. 122–3.   [6] *Grabgedichte d. griech. Anthologie* (1889), 38 f.

and the *EB* seem to have been active between about 390 and 400 (for details, see below, pp. 90–1).

A certain amount of attention has been paid to these translations as translations, but almost none to the source of their Greek originals. Writing long before the publication of the *EB*, P. Sakolowski assumed that Ausonius directly consulted the *Garlands* of Meleager and Philip and the Anthology of Diogenian.[7] No one seems to have questioned this assumption; indeed, since his further argument that it was in Diogenian that Ausonius read Rufinus has been generally rejected, the implication would seem to be that Ausonius had a text of Rufinus as well. And he certainly knew Palladas.

We are now in a position to add that the *EB* show familiarity with material from *exactly* the same range of epigrammatic collections: Meleager, Philip, Diogenian (on whom see further below), Rufinus, and Palladas. In view of the general decline of Greek studies in the late fourth-century west, it does not seem very likely that all five of these books were available in both Gaul and Italy at this time. Naucellius and his friends might conceivably have used the same copies, but it would hardly be safe to assume that they borrowed or inherited them from Ausonius. And while the more literate and scholarly Ausonius might at least have been capable of mastering such a quantity of this sophisticated and allusive poetry, the same could hardly be said of Naucellius and his friends. Furthermore, if both Ausonius and the *EB* had enjoyed independent access to the rich variety of the original collections, it would be surprising indeed if they had independently arrived at so similar and narrow a selection of poets (only Antipater of Sidon, Lucillius, and 'Plato' appear more than three times) and themes (mainly epideictic and satirical).

It is more natural and economical to suppose that both parties were using one later anthology, a common source that presented them with a ready-made selection from the five earlier anthologies.

For our present purpose it will be enough to list the most obvious pointers to this common source:

(*a*) Out of nearly fifty epigrams translated by Ausonius and forty by the *EB*, ten are translated by *both*—though in each case differently. Even if we allow (what, if likely enough on general grounds, is certainly not demonstrable) that the *EB* were familiar

---

[7] *De anthologia Palatina quaestiones* (Diss. Lips. 1893), 67.

with the work of Ausonius, so large an area of coincidence in so small a sample would be remarkable if both parties had had full access to the several thousand epigrams in the original collections.

(*b*) *AP* ix. 713–42 is a sequence of twenty-nine epigrams on the theme of Myron's lifelike cow, with ascriptions ranging from Anacreon to Julian the Egyptian. Since Meleager claims to have included poems by Anacreon (*AP* iv. 1. 35–6), 715–16 may have been Meleagrian even though, since Anacreon died before Myron was born, they cannot be authentic (for this reason, together with the 'Plato' epigrams, they should have been included in the *Hellenistic Epigrams* of Gow and Page). Apart from the demonstrably Meleagrian and Philippan poems in the sequence, there are twelve with no ascription, and while some may be Meleagrian or Philippan, it is hardly reasonable to insist that all are; in addition there is one by the undatable Demetrius of Bithynia, often (not by Gow and Page) though without sufficient reason claimed as Meleagrian.

Ausonius produced eight versions (*Epigr.* 56–63 Schenkl), most of them not directly referable to any extant original in the Palatine sequence, though his first is clearly based on no fewer than three, ix. 713, 726 (both anon.), and 730 (Demetrius), and the third seems to be a free variation on 721 (by the Meleagrian Antipater). The others may be based on lost models but are at least as likely to be Ausonius' original variations. The *EB* offer four translations, all from different originals: one from 'Anacreon', two from Antipater, and one from the Philippan Euenus. It would hardly be plausible to suppose that both Ausonius and the *EB* independently combed several different anthologies for variations on this theme. Indeed, the very fact that each wrote a regular cycle of variations suggests of itself that they were confronted by a cycle of variations in their sources. Surely there was just the one source, containing a comprehensive sequence (like *AP* ix. 713 f.) compiled from a number of different anthologies. It is also perhaps more than a coincidence that Ausonius' first poem opens exactly like the first in the Palatine sequence (bucula sum . . . Myronis / βοίδιόν εἰμι Μύρωνος) and the first in the *EB* sequence is a translation of only the third in the Palatine sequence. Students of the Anthology have tended to assume that Cephalas made up his own thematic sequences, but in this case it looks as if he found ready-made a sequence very like the one used five hundred years earlier by Ausonius and the *EB*. All

Cephalas did, as he so often did with ready-made sequences, was to incorporate it whole into a suitable part of his own epideictic book, merely adding a few later examples of the theme—most obviously the two poems by Julian, significantly almost at the end of the sequence (ix. 738–9).

(*c*) In addition to the epigrams they share, it is noteworthy that both Ausonius and the *EB* also translate, quite differently and apparently independently, the same five-line fragment of Hesiod (fr. 171 Rz = 304 M–W). It is tempting to conjecture that this too was a component in their common source; there are many such gnomic hexameter fragments in *AP*.

(*d*) We return at last to Rufinus. It has not so far been observed that all the erotic epigrams Ausonius and the *EB* translate occur in our 'Rufinian' sequence *AP* v. 2–103. Ausonius tried his hand at 21 and 42 (both Rufinus), 68 (Lucillius or Polemo) and 88 (Rufinus); the *EB* 80 ('Plato'), 95 (anon. in *AP*, Rufinus—probably mistakenly—in *APl*) and 96 (Meleager). Munari thought that *EB* 33

> Tres fuerant Charites, sed, dum mea Lesbia vixit,
> quattuor. at periit: tres numerantur item

might be an imitation of *AP* v. 146 (Callimachus) or ix. 515 (Crinagoras), both on the theme of the girl (in Callimachus' case, queen) fit to be numbered as the fourth Grace. But the point of *EB* 33, underlined by its title *de amissa puella*, is that the girl has *died*. The poem is in fact a disguised epitaph, and if it is a translation, the original has not survived.

A more talented contemporary, Claudian, also dabbled in epigrams. Only one (*carm. min.* 16, cf. 17) is a translation of a particular Greek model, again, suggestively enough, from the Rufinian sequence: v. 50 by Rufinus (on the ascription, see Page, pp. 21–3). And at *In Eutrop.* i. 90–4 he clearly alludes to the famous poem (vi. 1) on Lais and her mirror ascribed to Plato. Epigrams ascribed to Plato were especial favourites with Ausonius and the *EB* (seven between them), and this very poem is translated in full by Ausonius. May we not conjecture that the anthology used by Ausonius, the *EB*, and perhaps Claudian too contained as its erotic section something very like the Rufinian sequence of *AP* v? For what it is worth note too that Ausonius' translations (*Epigr.* 12, 36, 82, 83) appear in the same order as their models in *AP* (v. 21, 42, 68, 88). And while this is not also true of the *EB* sequence, the erotica in *EB* are all clustered together (30, 32, 34–5), as are their models (80, 95–6, translated in the order 96, 80, 95).

The fact that no erotic epigram known to Ausonius or the *EB* appears in the main core of *AP* v, the Philippan and Meleagrian sequences 104–33 and 134–215, is exactly paralleled in the category best represented in Ausonius and the *EB*, epideictica. They translate or otherwise show knowledge of the following poems from the epideictic part of *AP* ix (1–583): Ausonius 17, 18, 44, 45, 145, 159, 357, 359, 366, 489, 504, 506; *EB* 3, 12, 17, 18, 44, 108, 359, 360, 515. There is nothing from either the Meleagrian sequence 313–41 or the particularly long Philippan sequence 215–312. This can hardly be coincidence.

I suggest that, alongside his other sources, Cephalas used an anthology that was close kin to the common source of Ausonius and the *EB*. This anthology was the only source he could lay his hands on in the tenth century that contained epigrams by Rufinus. It was probably divided up into basic general categories such as erotic, epideictic, and scoptic, but not systematically subclassified within these categories.

Cephalas made use of it for his thematic sequences, amplifying it from a variety of other sources, most notably from the original *Garlands* of Meleager and Philip and Agathias' *Cycle*. His usual method was to begin a book with a thematic sequence and to follow it up with successive *Garland* and *Cycle* extracts, naturally omitting from the *Garland* extracts Meleagrian or Philippan poems that had already appeared in the thematic sequence—when he remembered. There are in fact one or two tell-tale repetitions: 121–2 reappear after 339 at the end of the Meleagrian sequence, and 123, by Leonidas of Alexandria, reappears embedded in a sequence of poems by Leonidas after 344.

II. DIOGENIAN

The other category of epigrams translated in any number (twelve) by both Ausonius and the *EB* is scoptic, from originals in the sceptic portion of *AP* (xi. 65–441). Here analysis of sequences cannot provide such clear-cut results, since there are no unbroken *Garland* extracts of any length in *AP* xi. Worse, we plunge straight into the cloudy waters of the Anthology of Diogenian.

There has been no full discussion of Diogenian's Anthology since that of P. Sakolowski, which, while far from satisfactory in many ways, makes two important points that have been unjustly neglected. The remarks in the preface to R. Aubreton's Budé edition of *AP* xi (1972) represent no advance.

If we are honest we must admit that we have no direct information beyond the statement in Diogenian's Suda-entry that he 'flourished' under Hadrian and produced, among other works, an ἐπιγραμμάτων Ἀνθολόγιον.

The assumptions that are commonly made are less secure than tends to be supposed. For example, it is not self-evident that Diogenian would have restricted his scope to epigrams written after the publication of Philip's *Garland* (under Nero). Working as he was in the archaizing atmosphere of the Second Sophistic and an antiquarian himself, might he not have been more interested in the classical age? Secondly, the fact that he (naturally and appropriately) used alphabetical order for such philological works as a *Varieties of Diction* and a collection of proverbs (Suda, s.v.) does not prove that he would have used the same method for an anthology of epigrams.

None the less, prima-facie confirmation of both these assumptions is probably to be found in three brief alphabetical sequences in *AP* xi (388–98, α–τ; 399–413, γ–ω; and 417–36, α–θ) containing poems by a variety of late first- and early second-century epigrammatists, Lucillius, Nicarchus, Ammianus, and even one by the Emperor Trajan. There are also a few even briefer and less clearcut alphabetical runs (three to five poems) inside the long thematic sequence xi. 65–255, mainly by Lucillius: for example, in the section 127–37 on poets, the opening (ε ε π τ) and closing (α μ ο ω) four poems; the brief section 138–40 on grammarians (α γ τ); 174–84 on thieves, after four poems beginning with τ, has the run β ε ε η χ; 185–7 on singers (ε ν σ); and 226–9 (ε θ μ ο) inside the sequence 226–38 on bad men. And then a few more in the heterogeneous section between 256 and 387, again mostly Lucillius (with Nicarchus): 309–12 (θ η ο ο), 313–16 (α ε ε ε), 329–33 (δ ε ε ο φ). Obviously some of these briefer alphabetical runs may be due to mere chance, but it seems unlikely that all are.

So we have to postulate an alphabetically arranged source for this period anyway. But there are problems in identifying it with Diogenian. In each of the three longer alphabetical sequences appear poems ascribed to Lucian, and if even some of these are really by Lucian of Samosata, then not even the most juvenile products of one who outlived the Emperor Marcus (161–80) are likely to have been anthologized under Hadrian (117–38). The favourite solution is either to postulate another Lucian or to emend *ΛΟΥΚΙΑΝΟΥ* to *ΛΟΥΚΙΛΛΙΟΥ* throughout (see Sakolowski). The least popular is to deny that the anthology in question is Diogenian's. The simplest and most satisfactory has yet to be proposed: Diogenian published his anthology much later than hitherto supposed.

The Hadrianic *floruit* rests on no firmer foundation than a γέγονε date in the Suda. Now everyone knows that γέγονε in Suda-biographies sometimes means 'was born', sometimes 'flourished', often no more than that one book or event in the man's life fell in the period specified. To go no further afield, the Lucian entry says that he γέγονε in the reign of Trajan (98–117), presumably here meaning 'born'—and at the end of the reign (some scholars place even his birth under Hadrian).[8]

Earlier scepticism about the authenticity of the Lucian epigrams seems to be on the wane among those who know their Lucian best,[9] and for my part I can see no valid reason to doubt that *AP* xi. 274, a satirical epitaph on the sophist Lollianus of Ephesus, was written by Lucian of Samosata. Lollianus taught for many years at Athens and Lucian too spent much time in Athens. Furthermore, C. P. Jones has recently made it probable that the sophist Lucian satirized under the name Lexiphanes in the dialogue of that name is Philagrus of Cilicia, one of Lollianus' star pupils.[10] Lucian might well have been in Athens when Lollianus died, perhaps in the late 150s.[11] If Lucian's epigrams were written in the first half of his career (by *c*.160), there is no reason why they should not have appeared in an anthology published early in the reign of Marcus.

But there is another objection. If Cephalas consulted this alphabetically arranged anthology direct, why is it that even the longer alphabetical extracts are so meagre and incomplete? Let us

---

[8] J. Hall, *Lucian's Satire* (New York 1981), 6–16; C. P. Jones, *Culture and Society in Lucian* (Cambridge, Mass. 1986), 8.
[9] B. Baldwin, 'The Epigrams of Lucian', *Phoenix* xxix (1972), 311–35; E. L. Bowie, *ANRW* II. 31. 1 (1989), 251–3; see too M. D. MacLeod, *Luciani opera* (Oxford 1987), iv, p. xviii.
[10] 'Two enemies of Lucian', *GRBS* xiii (1972), 476–8.
[11] O. Schissel, 'Lollianus auf Ephesos', *Philologus* lxxxii (1926), 181.

examine the structure of the book as a whole (for which purpose we may disregard xi. 1–64, which in *AP* itself are clearly marked out with a separate heading of their own as sympotic, distinct from the scoptic book constituted by 65–441).

The book opens like all the major Cephalan books of *AP* (v, vi, vii, ix), with a long thematically arranged sequence. Then comes a long miscellaneous section, 256–387 (including material from both *Garlands*, the *Cycle*, and Palladas as well as Diogenian) before the three successive alphabetical sequences (388–98, 399–413, and 417–36) that we have tentatively claimed for Diogenian.

Community of themes and style and the same selection of authors makes it probable that most of the poems in the thematic categories derive from the same source as the alphabetical sequences between 388 and 436—presumably Diogenian. Numerous poems from 388–436 might more suitably have been united with their natural fellows in the thematic categories: for example, 405–6 on long noses with 198–200 on the same theme; 391 and 397 on misers with 165–73; 392 on a rhetor with 141–52; 394 on a poet with 127–37; 402 on a glutton with 205–9; and so forth.

Here as (for example) in the case of Philip's *Garland* it is clearly the thematic categories, not the alphabetical sequences, that are the work of the Byzantine editor. It will be sufficient to quote the misclassification of xi. 97, by the early first-century (and surely Diogenianian) Ammianus in the category of oddly proportioned people:

> τῷ Στρατονικείῳ πόλιν ἄλλην οἰκοδομεῖτε,
> ἢ τούτοις ἄλλην οἰκοδομεῖτε πόλιν.

AP xi. 91 is on a man called Stratonikos so light that when he hanged himself with a hair from a corn stalk, his body floated upwards! It is plain that the editor who put 97 in this company (87–111) took l. 1 to refer to a *man* called Stratonikeios so huge that he needed a whole city to himself—a hyperbole in itself no more grotesque than that of 91 and several similar. In fact, as Louis Robert pointed out,[12] the reference is to a temple of Queen Stratonice (wife successively of Seleucus I and Antiochus I) at Smyrna (Ammianus' native city):

---

[12] 'Les épigrammes satiriques de Lucillius sur les athlètes: parodie et réalités', *L'Épigramme grecque* (Fondation Hardt Entretiens xiv, 1968), 283.

Au IIe siècle p.C., on a voulu transformer le sanctuaire en un bâtiment colossal à la mode du temps, comme on voit les énormes édifices d'alors à Ephèse, à Pergame et ailleurs. Le poète juge cela disproportionné dans le cadre de sa ville et il adjure ironiquement: 'Bâtissez pour le Stratoniceum une autre ville, ou à ceux-ci (les habitants de Smyrne) construisez une autre ville.'

If the poem is reread in the light of some of Ammianus' other poems, there can be no doubt that this is the correct interpretation. The gross misinterpretation implicit in its position in *AP* (made explicit by its inclusion in Planudes' section εἰς μακρούς, 'on tall people') is scarcely to be laid at the door of Diogenian—or even of the fourth-century anthologist we shall be postulating (though his own rearrangement of Diogenian's material may have involved some thematic classification). We have already attributed numerous such misclassifications to Cephalas.

We may assume that, here as elsewhere, the thematic categories were compiled by Cephalas with material he had excerpted for the purpose from his main alphabetical source. This would explain why there are still some traces of alphabetical order in the thematic categories. If Cephalas excerpted poems on (say) misers in the order he found them, where he did not rearrange them for his own thematic categories some alphabetical traces might be expected to survive.

This brings us back to the problem from which we digressed. In the other major Cephalan books of *AP*, the opening thematic sequence is succeeded by substantial extracts from the *Garlands* and *Cycle*, fifty to a hundred or more poems in uninterrupted original sequence.

As we shall see in detail later (pp. 126–7), Cephalas had two basic, alternating methods of arrangements: the first to rearrange his material in thematic categories, the second to take over the arrangement of his source more or less unaltered. In addition to the recurring extracts from the *Garlands* and *Cycle*, there is (for instance) the sequence of 49 epigrams on philosophers taken from Diogenes Laertius at *AP* vii. 83–133, 46 of which are still in their original sequence. And the same applies to the sequence of 54 charioteer epigrams preserved in *APl*.

So why is there no substantial, uninterrupted sequence from Diogenian? Why is it that, when the two *Garlands* and *Cycle* have left such clear traces in *AP*, the *Anthologion* of Diogenian has not?

The answer, I would suggest, is that Cephalas was able to apply his two methods *direct* to the original texts of the two *Garlands* and the *Cycle*: but (as Sakolowski rightly suspected) he did *not* have the original text of Diogenian. He had only an interpolated and rather haphazardly rearranged later redaction; in fact (I further suggest) the *same* fourth-century anthology we have already conjectured to have been his source for Rufinus.

This leads us to another suggestion of Sakolowski's (p. 68) that has been equally ignored: that it was in Diogenian that Cephalas found the epigrams of Rufinus. As he rightly observed, the Rufinian sequence in *AP* v contains, in addition to a number of poems from the *Garlands*, several by 'Diogenianian' authors, most of whom do not appear elsewhere in *AP*: namely Callicter (assuming that the Cillactor of v. 29 and 45 is to be identified with the Callicter of xi. 2, 5–6, 118–22, 333); Dionysius (v. 81, ?82, 83: cf. xi. 182); Gaetulicus (v. 68: cf. xi *passim*); Nicarchus (v. 38–40: cf. xi *passim*); and Lucillius (v. 68: cf. xi *passim*). Callicter, Dionysius, and Gaetulicus are insignificant figures, and it would be surprising if their few lines (or even the more numerous poems of Lucillius and Nicarchus) had reached Cephalas by two separate routes.

If Rufinus wrote (as seems most likely) in the late first century,[13] then he would have been an obvious candidate for inclusion in a second-century anthology. To Boas's objection to Sakolowski, 'that in the undoubtedly Diogenianian parts of the Anthology there is no trace of Rufinus', there is a simple and satisfactory answer. All Rufinus' poems are erotic and erotic poems belong in *AP* v. Boas's claim that some would have fitted in xi equally well is quite unjustified. When the Palatine corrector wrote χλευαστικόν, 'mocking', in the margin by v. 41, he was not amending its classification from erotic to scoptic but merely commenting on the fact that it mocks a wife punished for her infidelity (like 218 and 220, similarly and properly put in v).

Of course, both Rufinus and Lucillius will have published their own editions of their poems (Martial, for example, seems to have read them both well before Diogenian), but it is clear that Cephalas did not have access to these books at least. The first stage of their journey into the Byzantine world might well have been via Diogenian. But both passed through at least one other stage before they reached Cephalas. And the anthology we are in any case

[13] See 'Strato and Rufinus', *CQ*, NS xxxii (1982), 162–73.

obliged to postulate as the common source of Ausonius and the *EB*
is surely the first and most important of these other stages: a
selection from Meleager, Philip, Diogenian (if it was indeed
Diogenian who anthologized the first-century satirists and Rufinus), and various other minor and later sources. Anthologies not
being by their very nature 'protected' texts, it is more than likely
that this fourth-century compilation suffered both gains and losses
in the course of the five centuries before it reached Cephalas. None
the less, an anthology of approximately this scope and date would
seem to provide the simplest and most economical solution to a
number of related problems in the long story of the growth of the
Greek Anthology.

THE FOURTH-CENTURY ANTHOLOGY

The date of this compilation can be fixed within fairly narrow
limits. The latest Greek epigrammatist known to both the *EB*
(47 ~ Dübner–Cougny III. iii. 145; 50 ~ *AP* xi. 292) and Ausonius
(*epigr.* 46 ~ *AP* ix. 489; 48 ~ *APl* 317) is Palladas. And while it is
theoretically possible that separate copies of so recent a poet might
have made their way to the West, the facts (*a*) that both parties
knew him, (*b*) that 2 poems by him appear in the 'Rufinian'
sequence (v. 71–2), and (*c*) that his name several times alternates
with that of Lucillius in *AP* xi (255, 263, 280–1; cf. 299–317)
would seem to put it beyond reasonable doubt that some of his
poems were included in our anthology.

Now Palladas lived to be at least 70 (x. 97), and there are
grounds for dating the poem in which he makes this claim to 391
and so to place his birth in 319.[14] The poem (xi. 292) of which *EB*
must be acknowledged a translation (a translation accurate enough
to enable us to correct the Palatine and Planudean text of the
original)[15] can be dated with virtual certainty to 384 or early 385
(the original was inspired by Themistius' *Orat.* xxxiv defending
his tenure of the prefecture of Constantinople in 384).[16] It has been
argued that one at least of the *EB* was writing as late as 417
(Speyer's edition, p. viii), but Naucellius was already 90 by 400

---

[14] C. M. Bowra, *Proc. Brit. Acad.* xlv (1959), 266–7.
[15] Cf. *CQ*, NS xv (1965), 225–6.
[16] *PLRE* i. 892, with *CQ*, NS xv (1963), 221–3.

(Munari's edition, p. 23), and Ausonius is not likely to have long survived his last datable work, written in 393 when he was over 80. This anthology must have been put together in the late 380s, and evidently had an immediate impact in the West. Ausonius' *Epitaphia*, which contain two close translations (of *AP* vii. 64 and 228), were certainly written after 385. The preface informs us that the *Epitaphia* were added as a sort of appendix to the *Professores*, which in turn are plainly linked to the *Parentalia*. They are a series of verse commemorations of, respectively, professors at Ausonius' native Bordeaux and all the relatives he could muster, many in the form of epigrams, though some rather longer and in metres other than the elegiac couplet. The *Professores* at least were written after 385, since v. 38 alludes to the death in that year of Delphidius' wife Euchrotia, executed with the heretic Priscillian. The *Caesares* too, a series of tetrastichs on the Roman emperors from Caesar to at any rate Elagabalus,[17] belong late in Ausonius' career and fit in the same context.

It looks as if Ausonius did not become seriously interested in the epigram till his old age. Some of the individual items in his *epigrammaton liber* are earlier *pièces d'occasion*, such as 4–5 on Valentinian's Alamannic victory of 368 and 7 on Gratian (at any rate earlier than his death in 383), but the majority, those of Greek inspiration, could be among the last of his works. It is significant that there is no trace of Greek influence in the *Professores*, *Parentalia*, or *Caesares*. Indeed, they were almost certainly written under the influence of a specific Latin model, the *Imagines* or *Hebdomades* of Varro, a collection of pictures of famous Romans, each equipped with a metrical *elogium*.[18] That Ausonius was familiar with the *Hebdomades* is proved by an explicit reference to it in his *Mosella* (l. 305), composed between 371 and 375. And in 375 the orator Symmachus (cos. 391), a friend of Ausonius, received a letter from his father (*Epp.* i. 2) announcing that he, Symmachus *père*, had just undertaken a modern version of Varro's work, enclosing epigrams on five great Romans of the early fourth century as a specimen.

For his *Epitaphia*, epitaphs on Trojan heroes, Ausonius turned to a Greek source we can identify. He explains in his preface that they are translated from 'ancient' poems he found 'in some

[17] See R. P. H. Green, *CQ*, NS xxxi (1981), 226–36.
[18] For all the details, see App. VIII.

scholar'. They derive ultimately from the pseudo-Aristotelian *Peplos*, but Ausonius seems to have found them quoted in the *Homeric Researches* of Porphyry, the scholar he mentions.[19] Towards the end we find translations of two epitaphs that were later to turn up as *AP* vii. 64 and 228. These did not come from Porphyry. We may assume that he found them in the postulated fourth-century anthology.

The sheer crudity of the reaction of Ausonius and his contemporaries to their Greek models lends support to the hypothesis that they had suddenly been introduced to something quite new. The high-water mark of the epigram in Latin, as represented by Martial, has a character all its own, one element of which is a thorough mastery of the themes and techniques of hellenistic and early imperial Greek epigram. It is striking how utterly unlike Martial Ausonius and the *EB* are. One thinks rather of the unoriginal adaptations from Callimachus and Meleager by Q. Lutatius Catulus, Valerius Aedituus, and Porcius Licinus in the 90s BC (p. 51)—the reaction of men with a limited Greek culture suddenly confronted with the whole panorama of hellenistic epigram in the newly published *Garland* of Meleager. Ausonius and his fellows had precisely the same experience. It is not enough to say, with Munari, that Ausonius, 'unlike Martial, was no born epigrammatist'.[20] This is no doubt true enough, but no less obvious and important is the fact that, unlike Martial, Ausonius had simply not yet digested and absorbed the themes and techniques of seven centuries of Greek epigram. Where he does not translate fairly literally he produces a synthesis of two or three Greek poems, or writes free but thoroughly derivative variations of his own. Naucellius and his friends do exactly the same. The epigram had been little cultivated in the West since Martial, and there is certainly nothing to suggest any interest in Greek epigrams in the third- and early fourth-century West. I suggest that Ausonius and his contemporaries had little knowledge of hellenistic and early imperial Greek epigram until the sudden appearance of our postulated anthology *c.*390.

But if Greek epigrams were a new phenomenon in the late fourth-century West, the revival had begun much earlier in the East. The epigram as a literary genre evolved from the verse

[19] A. Momigliano, *Quinto contributo alla storia degli studi classici* (1975), 54.
[20] 'Ausonio e gli epigrammi greci', *SIFC* xxvii/xxviii (1956), 308 f.

inscription, and by the Byzantine age it had largely resumed this original function. Between the fourth and sixth centuries AD there is an enormous upsurge in inscriptional poetry.

Pendant cette époque [writes Louis Robert] les gouverneurs sont ordinairement honorés par des inscriptions d'un type tout différent de celles que l'on gravait à la gloire de leurs prédécesseurs du Haut-Empire. Les unes et les autres accompagnaient des statues, sur la base desquelles elles étaient gravées. Mais sous le Haut-Empire ces inscriptions publiques sont presque toujours en prose. Sous le Bas-Empire elles sont normalement des épigrammes.[21]

At a more literary level, the culmination of this development, given fresh impetus by the stylistic and metrical innovations of Nonnus, was the work collected in Agathias' *Cycle*, much of it authentic inscriptional poetry of the age.

But even at the lowest level, a surprisingly large number of these epigrams are competently done. Particular attention must have been paid to the art at school. And it was only natural that sooner or later some enterprising person would collect together into one anthology a comprehensive and representative selection of hellenistic and imperial epigrams, as much to teach as to entertain.

The inclusion of the perhaps still living Alexandrian epigrammatist Palladas need not mean that our anthologist lived or worked in Alexandria, though obviously this is a serious possibility. Consider, however, *EB* 51:

> frendentem Scyllam metus est prope litoris oram
>   sic sisti, Caesar: vincula necte prius.
> nam potis est virtus spirantis fallere aeni,
>   ut prius astringat, navita quam caveat.

The poet warns the emperor that the 'breathing bronze' Scylla placed by the sea-shore may lure unwary sailors to their doom; perhaps he should chain it down. At first sight the unusually precise lemma 'In Scyllam Constantinopolitanam in circo' might seem to contradict the natural inference that a statue of Scylla had been erected by the sea. But the hippodrome of Constantinople was built on high ground close to and overlooking the sea. And from *AP* ix. 271–2 we learn of a statue of Anastasius (491–518) erected next to a bronze Scylla 'on the Euripus', that is to say what

---

[21] 'Épigrammes du Bas-Empire', *Hellenica* iv (1948), 109.

is more generally called the *spina* in the hippodrome,[22] a statue that was still there for the Crusaders to destroy in 1204.[23] Then there is *AP* ix. 755, celebrating a bronze Scylla:

Εἰ μὴ χαλκὸς ἔλαμπεν, ἐμάνυε δ᾽ ἔργον ἄνακτος
ἔμμεναι Ἡφαίστου δαιδαλέοιο τέχνας,
αὐτὴν ἄν τις Σκύλλαν ὀΐσσατο τηλόθι λεύσσων
ἑστάμεν, ἐκ πόντου γαῖαν ἀμειψαμέναν·
τόσσον ἐπισσείει, τόσσον κότον ἀντία φαίνει,
οἷον ἀπὸ πελάγευς συγκλονέουσα νέας.

Unless the bronze glistened and betrayed the work to be a product of Hephaestus' cunning art, one looking from afar would think that Scylla herself stood here, transferred from sea to land, so threatening is her gesture, such wrath does she exhibit, as if dashing ships to pieces in the sea!

No helpful lemma this time, but the implication of l. 3 is perhaps that this is a very large, elevated statue, such as might be 'seen from afar'. Many of the larger statues that decorated the *spina* were placed on tall columns, as can be seen from a number of early travellers' sketches of the hippodrome.[24]

A large statue of a raging Scylla as described in *EB* 51 (cf. *frendentem*, l. 1) and *AP* ix. 755 (cf. τόσσον κότον ἀντία φαίνει, l. 5) elevated on a tall column in the hippodrome of Constantinople overlooking the sea might easily have suggested to a poet the fancy that it was still a menace to shipping. Given the parallel of ix. 755 and the fact that even the lemma corresponds exactly to the form found constantly for early Byzantine monuments in the Anthology,[25] no one is likely to question Munari's verdict that *EB* 51 is a translation of a Greek original. I will only add that it must have been a fourth-century original. The hippodrome of Constantinople is supposed to have been begun by Severus, but it was not till Constantine that it was completed on a scale and style befitting an

---

[22] C. Mango, *RÉB* vi (1949), 180 f.

[23] Nicetas Choniates, *de signis*, 7; cf. Cameron (1973), 184–5. This Scylla and its various copies and presumed original have been much discussed in recent years, since the discovery of fragments signed by the Rhodian trio Agesander, Polydorus, and Athenodorus in the Sperlonga Caves: e.g. B. Andreae and B. Conticello, *Skylla und Charybdis: zur Skylla-Gruppe von Sperlonga* (Abh. Mainz 1987); B. Andreae, *Laokoon und die Gründung Roms* (Mainz 1988); B. S. Ridgway, *Journal of Roman Archaeology* ii (1989), 172–81.

[24] References in Cameron (1973), 6–7.

[25] W. Speyer, *Naucellius und sein Kreis* (Zetemata 21, 1959), 84.

imperial capital,[26] and it was Constantine and his immediate successors who adorned it with the stolen statuary of the entire Graeco-Roman world.[27] The apostrophe of the emperor in l. 2 is the clinching touch. The fact that it is the emperor the poet warns about the *location* of the statue clearly implies that the emperor in question (regrettably unnamed—at least in the translation) had just had it put on that very spot. The original of *EB* 51 might even have been inscribed on the base of the column, in which case our anthologist presumably copied it *in situ*. The lemma shows that he knew exactly where the statue stood. Of course, the fact that he copied one epigram in Constantinople does not prove that he compiled the whole anthology there, but he must at any rate have lived there for a while.

One last speculation. If I am right, this postulated anthology contained a number of poems by both Palladas and Lucian. Now by the anonymous epitaph *AP* vii. 339 the lemmatist J wrote the following note: ἄδηλον ἐπὶ τίνι τοῦτο γέγραπται, πλὴν ὅτι ἐν τοῖς τοῦ Παλλαδᾶ ἐπιγράμμασιν εὑρέθη κείμενον· μήποτε δὲ Λουκιανοῦ ἐστιν. 'Unclear who this was written about, except that it was found [? just 'appears'] among the epigrams of Palladas; perhaps it is by Lucian.'

If this poem had been transmitted under the name of Palladas no one would have been likely to dispute the ascription. But it is not so ascribed here, and there is nothing by either Palladas or Lucian anywhere in the vicinity in *AP*. It seems clear that J is referring to *another* manuscript to which he had access, in which this poem, evidently still anonymous, appeared among the poems of Palladas. It has often been assumed that this was a text of Palladas. Yet J evidently doubted that vii. 339 was by Palladas, or he would not have added his guess that it might be by Lucian. And why did he guess Lucian? Hardly on the basis of style or subject-matter; there are some similarities, but vii. 339 does not look at all like Lucian. Was it then a combined edition of Lucian and Palladas, so that if a poem was not by the one it was bound to be by the other?

We can hardly do more than guess, and a better-grounded guess than most must now be the fourth-century anthology that we have conjectured on other grounds to contain (among other poets) a selection of poems by both Lucian and Palladas. If this anthology

[26] R. Guilland, *Byzantinoslavica* xxxi (1970), 182 f.
[27] Mango, *DOP* xvii (1963), 57–8.

was still extant *c.*900 for Cephalas to use, there is no reason why it should not still have been available a generation later for J.

There is also another text where these two poets are linked—and confused: the *Gnomologium* of Johannes Georgides the monk, a collection of moral utterances from classical and patristic authors (the latest John Damascene) that can hardly be earlier than the tenth century. Georgides quotes two epigrams[28] (= *AP* x. 28 and 58) which reappear in the long sequence of epigrams by Lucian and Palladas in *AP* x, ascribing both to Lucian. The second is in fact by Palladas. The slip would be easily explained if he had been using the source here postulated.

---

[28] J. F. Boissonade, *Anecdota Nova* i (1829), 22 and 91 (= *PG* cxvii. 1079 and 1147).

V

The Palatine Manuscript
and its Scribes

I. THE PROBLEM

WE have so far been working on the assumption that behind *AP*,
APl, and five minor collections not so far mentioned lies the lost
anthology of Constantine Cephalas. It is now time to justify this
assumption, often made, never fully worked out, and recently
challenged.

The basis of the assumption may be summarized as follows. The
mid-tenth-century *AP* refers several times to the anthology of
Cephalas. *APl* was compiled from two manuscripts which were
very close kin of *AP* in content and arrangement, both apparently
somewhat smaller than *AP* yet containing a number of epigrams
absent from *AP*. The minor collections are: The *Sylloge Euphemiana* (E) of the early tenth century; *Sylloge Σ^π* of the twelfth or
thirteenth century; *Sylloge Laurentiana* (L), also compiled by
Planudes, of *c*.1280; *Appendix Barberino-Vaticana* (*ABV*) of the
early fourteenth century; and the *Sylloge Parisina* (S), of unknown
date but certainly earlier than the thirteenth century manuscript
that contains it. All these collections contain a majority of epigrams
duplicated in *AP* and/or *APl* together with a small but significant
minority absent therefrom.

The substantial core common to all and the fact that each
contains at least one epigram absent from the rest are the classic
pointers to an earlier and fuller common source. Hence the
traditional (and reasonable) scholarly assumption that Cephalas,
known to have been at any rate a major source of *AP*, was the
common source of all the rest. If so, it follows that Cephalas'
anthology must have been, in point both of size and date, the
definitive Byzantine anthology of classical epigrams.

R. Aubreton issued a forthright challenge.[1] The cornerstone of his challenge is his redating of the Palatine manuscript, long assigned to the second half of the tenth century, to the second half of the eleventh century. During the period of more than 150 years that (on this hypothesis) separates *AP* from Cephalas, Aubreton reckons that substantial additions to and modifications of the original Cephalan nucleus occurred. As for our other supposed witnesses to Cephalas, the *syllogae minores*, these Aubreton asserts to be either independent of or actually earlier than Cephalas. For Aubreton, then, Cephalas' book was not at all the definitive Byzantine anthology. It is *AP* rather that he sees as the great original collection of ancient epigrams, a massive amplification of Cephalas' fairly modest effort. Those who produced the manuscript—B, B2, B3, A, and J as they have been known since Preisendanz[2]—are held to be more its compilers than its copyists.

The palaeographical grounds on which Aubreton reached his eleventh-century date have not so far been clearly formulated or supported by dated parallels. Meanwhile, the reaction of other palaeographers has been uniformly negative.[3] Unaware of Aubreton's redating, A. Diller found even the *c*.980 canonized in the standard editions of P. Waltz and H. Beckby almost half a century too late. Diller's verdict was based on a systematic study both of dated manuscripts of the period and of a number of other undated manuscripts, like *AP* assigned to the late tenth or eleventh century by earlier scholars unfamiliar with 'the broader array of dated and datable manuscripts made available for study by photography'.[4] Nigel Wilson states firmly that 'present knowledge can hardly justify a date later than 930–60',[5] J. Irigoin took a very similar position,[6] and a detailed recent study by Maria Luisa Agati places the compilation of *AP* between 955 and 970.[7]

Fortunately, however, we are not reduced to weighing one

[1] Aubreton (1968), 32–82.

[2] Preisendanz (1911) did not distinguish B3, recognized independently and almost simultaneously by A. Diller (private communication) and J. Irigoin (1975), though doubts had already been expressed about the identification of the hand of pp. 705–6 and 693–5 with B2.

[3] e.g. H. Hunger, *BZ* lxiii (1970), 370.

[4] Diller (1974), 520–1.

[5] Personal communication; cf. also N. G. Wilson, *Scholars of Byzantium* (1983), 138 ('probably *c*.930–950').

[6] (1977), 284.

[7] *Boll. Class. Lincei*, 3rd ser., v (1984), 43–59, with pls. 1–10.

palaeographer against another. All that we know of Cephalas derives from the scholia of *AP*, texts long known but never adequately exploited for their chronological implications.[8] When taken together they point to an interval between Cephalas and *AP* of not 150 but at most 30 or 40 years. That is to say, given a date *c*.900 for Cephalas (Ch. XI), *AP* will have been put together by *c*.940, a date in perfect harmony with current palaeographical opinion.

II. THE PALATINE MANUSCRIPT

The Palatine manuscript has a complicated structure—though not perhaps quite so complicated as editors have supposed. It consists of two main blocks: Pa (pp. 1–452), written in the main by the scribe known as A; and Pb (pp. 453–706), written in the main by the scribes B, B2, and B3. Almost all the rest, the beginning, middle, and end of the manuscript, was written by J, who also wrote lemmata and annotated the manuscript throughout.[9] Later (though, as we shall see not much later) another person, C, took the book in hand and made a considerable number of important corrections, limited to Pa, from another manuscript. I set out below the distribution of hands, restoring the true order of pages in the last quaternion (the outside leaves of which, that is to say pp. 691–2 and 705–6, were accidentally folded wrong during binding):[10]

1–50	J
51–61	A
62–3	J
64–423, l. 25	A
423, ll. 26–452	J
453–517	B
518–24, l. 21	B2

---

[8] They are quoted in full by Preisendanz (1911), cols. lxxv–cxl, and (as far as it goes) in Stadtmueller's edition. Other editions quote only an arbitrary selection.

[9] Like most writers since Preisendanz, I accept his identification (cols. lxxviii f.) of the hand of the text scribe J with that of the lemmatist, called L by Stadtmueller (ii. 1, viii f.).

[10] The binding error is treated in detail by Preisendanz (pp. xxvii–xxix), Buffière (Budé xii. 106–7), and Irigoin (1977, 285–6).

524, ll. 21–621	B
622–42	B3
643–8, l. 9	J
648, ll. 10–664, l. 20	A2
664, ll. 22–690	J
705–6, 693–5, l. 13	B3
695, ll. 14–704, 691–2	J

Preisendanz recognized three distinct stages in the composition of the manuscript. The oldest, he claims, is the contribution of B, B2, and B3 (pp. 453–642 plus the short section 705–6 and 693–5), older indeed by some fifty years than A. A originally wrote the whole of pp. 49–452, but the first and last pages of the fourth quaternion (49–50, 62–3), which had presumably got damaged, were removed and replaced by J. From this Preisendanz inferred that J's contribution was later than A's.

The blocks written by A and B, B2 and B3 respectively were originally (he argues) independent fragments from two separate copies of Cephalas. It was J who united them in one volume, after using another, complete Cephalas to cobble the gaps between them and at both ends. On this hypothesis at least four different (though not necessarily all overlapping) copies of Cephalas lie behind *AP*: the respective exemplars of A, B, J, and finally C.

Remarkably enough, this museum piece of reasoning seems never to have been seriously questioned. Even the sagacious and independent Gow took it for granted that A, B, and J were not contemporary.[11]

But this half-century that is supposed to have elapsed between A and B rests solely on a now almost universally rejected palaeographical judgement by a scholar who professed no palaeographical expertise—and dropped a whole century while reading his proofs.[12] And a palaeographical judgement that gives rise to so many improbabilities deserves at least to be questioned.

---

[11] *The Greek Anthology* (1958), 10–11.

[12] It is Preisendanz that Aubreton holds responsible for the prevalence of the tenth-century date among editors (p. 49), and it is indeed to his authority that they all appeal. Neither editors nor Aubreton seem to have noticed that in the addendum on cols. cxlviii–cxlix (cf. his *Carmina Anacreontea* (1912), p. xvii) Preisendanz abandoned the tenth century for the eleventh without comment on *non*-palaeographical grounds—the misinterpretation of J's note on *AP* i. 10. 28–9 discussed below, pp. 114–15.

If Preisendanz is correct, then at the beginning of his task J had on his desk (*a*) one complete text of what (without prejudging its relationship to the original) we will call Cephalas, and (*b*) fragmentary portions of two other such texts, A and B. Not only did A not overlap with either B fragment; the two B fragments themselves were not continuous. More remarkable still, the A fragment and the second B fragment were both apparently left unfinished by their original scribes. For J takes over from B3 halfway down p. 695 (l. 14), and from A in mid-epigram (ix. 384.8) at p. 423, l. 26. We are dealing then, not just with two fragments, but with two separate unfinished fragments.

For the supposed gap between A and J we do not even have a palaeographical *fiat*. J's repairs to the fourth quaternion prove nothing, of course. How did a quaternion *inside* a book come to get damaged at both ends? Preisendanz improbably suggests that it once circulated separately, but whatever the relationship of A to J, we are surely bound to assume (what the quaternion numbers in any case prove) that A's contribution was written consecutively and bound together. If so, then the probability is that the fourth quaternion was damaged accidentally *before* binding. We know from his attempt to remedy the binding error in the last quaternion that J himself supervised the binding;[13] so the presumption is surely that J and A were contemporaries.

Preisendanz further pointed to a series of numbers in the top corners of most quaternions in A which are seven in advance of the present quaternion numbers in *AP*. These he assumed to be the quaternion numbers of the manuscript to which A had originally belonged. But (as Aubreton has seen) we know from J's index to *AP* that it originally began with Nonnus' *Paraphrase of St John*. Now 7 quaternions making 112 pages with (as in *AP*) between 32 and 34 lines to the page would have taken 3,696 lines (112 × 33), that is to say, if we add in book headings and the like, almost exactly the 3,665 lines of Nonnus' *Paraphrase*. We can hardly doubt that A's numbers are the *original* quaternion numbers of *AP* *before* the first 7 quaternions were detached by some aficionado of Nonnus. In other words, here is proof that A was one of the original contributors to *AP*.

[13] V. Gardthausen (*Griechische Palaeographie*, i² (1911), 181) points out that such evidence as we have on bookbinding suggests that Byzantine books were bound by the monks who wrote them. But J was a man of standing who used others to do the bulk of his copying; perhaps his binding too.

We need not be surprised then to find that pp. 648–64, following and followed by blocks written by J, are written in a hand (A2) that is very similar to (though probably not identical with) A.[14] A2 was no doubt an apprentice of A, both evidently collaborators of J.

What then of B, B2, and B3? If we may for the moment disregard the supposed palaeographical objection, the natural implication of the fact that J finishes a quaternion begun by B3, as he did earlier for A, is that B3, like A, was a contemporary and collaborator of J. And if J was contemporary with B3, then since B3 was evidently contemporary with B (he finishes a block begun by B), it would follow that J and B were likewise contemporaries.

Soon after the beginning of his contribution (on p. 453 with *AP* ix. 563), B wrote the lemma to *AP* ix. 583 and then left a blank space, in which J wrote the poem itself. Now all modern students of the Anthology, from Preisendanz to Aubreton, have taken it for granted that J had an exemplar of his own *different* from the exemplar used by A and B.[15] It was from this exemplar (they assume) that J copied on the one hand his own contributions to the text of *AP* and on the other the lemmata and sundry other annotations with which he filled the margins of A and B. This is of course a natural consequence of the original assumption that A and B are fragments of separate anthologies put together by J. I propose that we abandon both assumptions; I suggest instead that J, A, B, B2, and B3 were a team who all used the same exemplar in turn.[16] Unlike C (whose activity is discussed below), J never introduces into the contributions of A and B the sort of corrections and supplements that need to be referred to another source.

J's editorial activity is almost entirely limited to providing lemmata (titles or explanatory headings) and, much less often, ascriptions (authors' names). The lemmata occasionally preserve information of independent value but most are only too obviously made up by J himself, their modest purpose being to give the casual reader an idea what the poems are about. The ascriptions are quite a different matter. Here, unlike his modern successors, J was mercifully reluctant to guess; if he had no information he conscientiously left a blank.

[14] Stadtmueller and others identified A2 with A (cf. Waltz, Budé i, p. xli, n. 3), but Preisendanz did not nor does Irigoin.

[15] e.g. even Gow (1958): 'J supplements and corrects both A and BB2 and evidently derives from a third source' (p. 11).

[16] Or rather different parts of the same exemplar simultaneously: see p. 108.

The distribution of J's additions to the work of A is instructive.[17] Take *AP* vii. For poems 1–155 both ascriptions and lemmata are in A's hand; thereafter the lemmata are written by J and the ascriptions by C. It looks as if the energy of the scribe responsible for A's exemplar flagged early, and he left 156–738 without either lemmata or ascriptions. J (who on my hypothesis was using the same exemplar as A) could do nothing about the ascriptions (which C was later able to supply from a fuller exemplar) but could provide lemmata easily enough. In ix. 1–383 there are hardly any ascriptions by A; once more it is C, not J, who supplies them. In vi likewise it is C, not J, who supplements A's ascriptions. Elsewhere J does provide a fair number of ascriptions, but distributed in such a way that the most natural explanation is that he is simply repairing omissions and errors made by the unquestionably careless and inaccurate A, drawing on a more thorough reading of their joint exemplar.

As for J's improvements to the text, while they are by no means negligible, few if any suggest, again, anything more than the correction of A's carelessness on the basis of a more accurate and intelligent reading of their shared exemplar. C's corrections make a striking contrast. Not only are they more numerous and substantial; many clearly reflect a quite different text. More suggestive still, C's corrections frequently agree with the text of Planudes (less often with other witnesses like the Suda). For example, to take a sequence more or less at random, in the second half of *AP* v (150–303) there are at least fifty major corrections by C, nearly half of which coincide with Planudes (sometimes in error: for example, v. 28. 8; 302. 14).

Furthermore, while C's usual practice was simply to correct A's text, often erasing it for the purpose, occasionally he writes an alternative in the margin as well (or instead), prefaced by the abbreviation γρ. In C's case γρ. fairly clearly signifies, not γράφε, the sign of a personal conjecture, but γράφεται, indicating an alternative transmitted reading. I suggest, in fact, that Cephalas equipped his text with marginal variants (in some cases at least perhaps from his two copies of the two *Garlands*). This would explain why Planudes sometimes has the original reading of P, sometimes C's correction; the Suda too sometimes agrees with P, sometimes with C.

---

[17] See the prefaces to individual books in Stadtmueller, Waltz, and Beckby.

I give just one illustration of C's variants. At vii. 164. 3, for the words ἔχων σε, which make no sense in the context, C made in the text the slight but certain correction ἔχωσε, 'piled'. He then added γρ. ἔδειμε in the margin. Now if C had been intelligent enough to have conjectured ἔχωσε himself, he would have realized that ἔδειμε was merely an inferior attempt to solve the same corruption. Evidently both are *transmitted* readings.[18]

One of the clearest proofs that J did not have another exemplar is the fact that he was unable to fill the not infrequent lacunae left by A. Consider the following list (which lays no claim to completeness), where in every case it was C, not J, who repaired the gap. Lacuna of one word in *AP* ii. 137 (Pl); v. 50. 1; 150. 2; 210. 1 (Pl); 274. 1 (Pl); 279. 5; vi. 99. 6; vii. 408. 3; ix. 264. 5. Lacuna of two words in vii. 275. 5 (Pl) and ix. 236. 2; of a whole line in vi. 186. 3 and vii. 363. 4; and of two lines at vi. 309. 1–2. A particularly interesting case is vii. 305. 3, where instead of writing his supplement (not a conjecture, since it is shared by Planudes) in the vacant space left by A (and J), C added it in the margin with a γρ. Presumably this is how it appeared in his exemplar, which doubtless offered the same gap in the text as A and J. Contrast from the second half of *AP* ix the gap of two lines left by B after writing the lemma εἰς ἑτέραν καμάραν after ix. 785. As usual, there was nothing J could do, and since by now C had abandoned his task, the gap remains unexplained and unfilled.

Naturally, the supplements prove that C had an independent exemplar. No less obviously, the gaps prove that J did not. It would be absurd to suppose that he had an exemplar that shared every one of these lacunae, especially since C's supplements, which often coincide with Planudes', prove that they are not common to the whole Cephalan tradition—unique, rather, to the Palatine branch.

---

[18] A thorough and detailed comparison of the corrections and annotations of J and C would be well worth undertaking. My own impression is that the more substantial corrections C offers are more likely to be transmitted readings than personal conjectures. Both J and C perpetrate or perpetuate far too many metrical and other blunders to suggest any deep understanding of the style and metre of ancient epigram. There is also a quite different point about C's exemplar that would bear careful investigation. When he is at his most attentive and active, we find traces of C's pen on virtually every line: clearly at times he collated every word in *AP* with his exemplar: see p. 116. So when he leaves alone some obvious corruption in the hand of A, or some correction of J, with all due caution we may perhaps presume that this was what he read in his exemplar.

Gow has already remarked that since J contributed so little to the blocks written by B, B2, and B3, 'it could perhaps be maintained that he no longer had another copy before him'.[19] On this hypothesis J's exemplar, like A and B, must be supposed defective (C's contribution also stops with the A block, whence the standard inference that his exemplar too was defective; indeed, C has been credited with no fewer than four defective exemplars, making a grand total of eight variously mutilated manuscripts conjured up by modern students of the Anthology—within only two or three decades of their common source in Cephalas). But we have seen that J's activity is not to be interpreted in isolation; it is necessarily a function of the activity of the original text scribes. Now it has long been recognized that B, B2, and B3 are much more conscientious and accurate scribes than A. With the exception under discussion, they provide both ascriptions and lemmata, the latter often worthless, of course, but not infrequently deriving at any rate from their common exemplar of Cephalas (to judge from the fact that many reappear verbatim in Planudes). Is it so very surprising that J should find less to correct and supplement in their work? He added no ascriptions because B, B2, and B3 were faithfully copying what ascriptions their exemplar offered; and he simply could not be bothered to go on inventing lemmata where the exemplar lacked them.

Contrary to what has so far been supposed, it is the way J handles the gap left by B after the lemma to ix. 583 that provides the most decisive proof that he did *not* have a separate exemplar of his own. As we shall see in more detail later on (Ch. X), it is between ix. 583 and 584 that we are obliged to postulate the lacuna (a loss of three or more probably four whole quaternions) in which the 450-odd Cephalan ecphrastica preserved in *APl* fell out of the source of *AP*. Now is it really just a coincidence that it is at precisely this point that there should be a lacuna in *AP* itself, if only of four lines? It may well be, as Wifstrand thought,[20] that the text of *AP*'s exemplar broke off with the lemma to ix. 583, 'on the book of Thucydides', and began again with 584. Now on my assumption that B and J shared the same exemplar, J should not have been in a position to supply the missing poem—his one and only substantial textual supplement to the work of his primary

---

[19] Op. cit., p. 55 n. 2; cf. Preisendanz (1911), col. cv.   [20] (1926), 81.

copyists. Where then did he find 583? How was it that on this one occasion he *was* able to fill a gap in *AP*?

The great majority of epigrams in *AP* would not be traceable from their lemmata alone, but B's εἰς Θουκυδίδου βιβλίον clearly points to a poem written for a manuscript of Thucydides' *History*. All J had to do was look up a manuscript of Thucydides. As it happens the earliest extant manuscript of Thucydides, the early tenth-century C (Laur. 69. 2) 'which stands nearer to the minuscule archetype than any other MS'[21] does carry the poem, as do a number of manuscripts of the eleventh century and later.[22] It was no doubt from a manuscript of Thucydides that Cephalas himself took the same poem in the first place. That J did indeed find the right poem on Thucydides is confirmed by its appearance in *APl*, there at least almost certainly taken from Cephalas.

It seems to me that there is one decisive argument—over and above the more general objections already presented—against the conventional assumption that J took the poem from another, more complete text of Cephalas. If he had possessed such a text, then it would surely have contained not only ix. 583 but some or all of the 450 other missing poems. Is it really credible that he had another text that contained only *one* of the missing poems—and apparently shared all the lacunae of his main source?

The only reasonable conclusion, as Irigoin conceded, is that J was unable to repair and perhaps even unaware of the major lacuna here because he was using the same defective exemplar as B. All he was able to do was supply ix. 583 by his own researches from the clue given in the lemma—and add lemmata of his own invention for 581–2 and 584 while he was about it.

Now on my assumption that B, like A, was J's contemporary and colleague, it is perfectly reasonable and natural to suppose that all three used the same exemplar. But on the conventional assumption (to which Irigoin still adheres) that the B blocks are independent of and earlier than A and J, this supposition must surely be held less natural and less reasonable. We are asked to believe that J found the two B blocks *together with their exemplar*, the exemplar being

---

[21] J. E. Powell, *CQ* xxxii (1938), 79.

[22] For a full list of the Thucydides MSS that carry it, C. Gallavotti, *Rivista di studi bizantini e neoellenici* xxii/3 (1985/6), 196–201. Note C's well-informed comment on vii. 430 (Dioscorides on the battle of Thyrea): 'I think this story is in Thucydides Bk. iv'.

complete but the apograph not only defective but actually unfinished.

There is no need to deny that the B blocks were written independently of the A and J blocks. As Preisendanz has observed, there are signs that J was cramming more into his pages as he neared the end of quaternion 28, evidently so that he could end it at a predetermined point—where B takes over at ix. 564. In the event he did not calculate quite right, and repeated the last line of ix. 563 to square the final page off to his satisfaction. But neither this nor the slightly thicker parchment on which they are written necessarily implies that the B blocks were actually written *earlier* than—or indeed separately from—the A and J blocks. There is a perfectly acceptable alternative consonant with normal scribal practice:[23] in the interests of speed J divided his exemplar into two at ix. 563 and gave one half to A and the other to B and his assistants B2 and B3 (who happened at that moment to be using a different quality of parchment) so that both could work simultaneously. This would explain why it is that we find J finishing off both portions; the A block so that he could use his greater experience to adjust the remaining material to fill the quaternion exactly, and the B block (as we shall see in Ch. XV) so as to add some new material of his own.[24]

Indeed, there is a hitherto unexplained fact that lends considerable support to this hypothesis. *AP* viii, written by A on pp. 326–58, contains 260[25] sepulchral epigrams by Gregory of

[23] For two later cases where the details of the distribution of labour have been meticulously worked out, see A. Turyn, *Dated Greek MSS* (1972), 23–4 (Ambr. I. 4 sup.) and *Codices Vaticani Graeci* (1964), 104–5 (Vat. gr. 2220). With the change of just one letter Turyn's account of the scribes of the latter manuscript could be applied to *AP*: 'necesse est concedamus librarios illos aequales fuisse, qui sive codicis partes scribendo se exciperent sive etiam intra quaterniones interdum alius alii succederent. Tum universos fasciculos librarius J coagmentavit et indice praefixo instruxit' (p. 105).

[24] Note too that the epigrammatic portion of *AP* begins with a new quaternion on p. 49; most of the three preceding quaternions are occupied with Paul the Silentiary's two ecphraseis, though pp. 41–8 contain a selection of Gregory Nazianzen's *dogmatica* (shared with L, see Ch. IX). Are not the latter perhaps makeweights to fill out the quaternion, just as J fills out the last quaternion with more Gregory? If so, then perhaps J did it because A had already begun the epigrams on a different quaternion. That is to say, maybe all three sets of scribes, J, A, and BB2B3, were working simultaneously, J copying Nonnus and Paul while the others copied the epigrams.

[25] Approximately; owing to insoluble problems of poem division 'il n'est pas possible d'en determiner le nombre avec une précision rigoureuse' (Waltz, Budé vi, pp. 3–4).

Nazianzus. At the very end of the manuscript (pp. 695–704 and 691–2) no fewer than 68, more than a quarter of them, are repeated in the hand of J. In the margin of p. 691 he ruefully remarked προεγράφησαν ἅπαντα εἰς τὰ λοιπὰ ἐπιγράμματα εἰς τὸ τέλος τῶν ἐπιτυμβίων—evidently a later addition, since it was not till after the binding error in the last quaternion already mentioned (pp. 4 and 188 f.) that 691 became the first instead of the last-but-one page of the second Gregorian sequence. So it was apparently not till *after* the manuscript (or at least this part of it) had already been bound up that he even noticed the duplication. But how could he possibly have missed the first Gregorian batch if he had ever even glanced at pp. 326 ff. before writing pp. 695 ff.? It follows, paradoxically enough, that he must have *written* pp. 695 ff. before he had *read* pp. 326 ff. Now if J had divided his exemplar of Cephalas between his two sets of scribes, then since A wrote nearly twice as much as B and his colleagues (almost 400 as against less than 200 pages), J will have been able to revise and make his own additions to the already finished B blocks while A was still working on his portion. Since he was intending to collate the work of his scribes against the exemplar when they had finished, it would not be surprising if he had not taken the trouble to read it carefully before they started. Thus it is perfectly possible that he did not discover the existence of *AP* viii until he began to revise A's contribution, *after* he had already written pp. 695 ff.

If this simple, economical, and reasonable explanation is accepted, then we no longer have separate, successive texts of Cephalas copied by A and B to fit in between J and Cephalas himself. And it is to the question of the relationship between J and Cephalas that we now turn.

III. J AND C

After remarking that the latest poets to contribute to *AP* were 'Arethas and his contemporaries', Diller adds that 'the scribes A and J may well have remembered these men personally, and the scribe B would be even closer.'[26] This was, of course, an inference from the date he had assigned the scribes on palaeographical grounds. But the proximity of J and even the later C to not only

---

[26] (1974), 521.

Arethas but Cephalas himself as well is strikingly borne out by a series of informative marginalia.

We may begin with the successive annotations of A, J, and C on p. 207. First, by way of title to *AP* vii, A wrote the words ἀρχὴ τῶν ἐπιτυμβίων ἐπιγραμμάτων. J then added in the margin ὧν ἐσχεδίασεν ὁ [Κεφαλᾶς]. C then erased the last word (which must have been Κεφαλᾶς) and added Κύρις Κωνσταντῖνος ὁ Κεφαλᾶς ὁ μακάριος καὶ ἀείμνηστος καὶ τριπόθητος ἄνθρωπος. What inspired C to add this extravagant tribute to Cephalas at this point? μακάριος in such contexts normally bears the same meaning as μακαρίτης, 'of blessed memory', 'the late', referring to someone recently dead.[27] That it does so here is confirmed by the two other epithets, 'ever to be remembered' and 'thrice missed'. One does not write so of a man (on Aubreton's hypothesis) dead for a century and a half. It seems to me that the natural interpretation of C's emotional outburst is that Cephalas was a man known personally to him who had only recently died. His literary achievement scarcely merited such eulogies; it is his personal qualities that C is commemorating.

AP vii. 429 is a fictitious epitaph by Alcaeus of Messene apparently inspired by a tomb inscribed simply with the letter Φ written twice, a riddling representation of the name Pheidis (φεῖ δίς). According to C, τοῦτο τὸ ἐπίγραμμα ὁ Κεφαλᾶς προεβάλετο ἐν τῇ σχολῇ τῆς νέας ἐκκλησίας ἐπὶ τοῦ μακαρίου Γρηγορίου μαγίστορος. This passage is of some importance for the student of Byzantine education during the 'first Byzantine Renaissance'. The 'New Church' was built by Basil I in the Palace complex and dedicated

---

[27] C. H. Turner, *Journal of Theological Studies* xxiii (1922), 31–5 and G. W. H. Lampe, *Patristic Lexicon*, s.v. μακάριος E and especially s.v. μακαρίτης ('usu. of one lately dead'). For inscriptional examples, see G. Lefebvre, *Recueil des inscriptions grecques-chrétiennes d'Égypte* (1907), p. xxxi. There is an ample collection of examples in L. Dinneen, *Titles of Address in Christian Greek Epistolography* (Diss. Washington 1929), 81–4, concluding that μακαρίτης (applied twice to Gregory of Campsa, see above) is 'used always of deceased persons, apparently of those who were living within the lifetime of the writer' (p. 83). To this material add one particularly clear example combining μακαρίτης with the κυρός which we shall find in several other such scholia: one manuscript of Nicetas Eugenianos' romance *Drusilla and Charicles* preserves the evidently contemporary subtitle, ποίησις κυροῦ Νικήτου τοῦ Εὐγενειανοῦ κατὰ μίμησιν τοῦ μακαρίτου φιλοσόφου τοῦ Προδρόμου. Niketas was evidently a younger contemporary of Theodore Prodromos, whose *Rhodanthe and Dosikles* he so admiringly imitated; for he also wrote a lament for his death, entitled τοῦ Εὐγ. κυροῦ Νικήτα μονῳδία εἰς τὸν μακαριώτατον φιλ. κυρὸν Θεοδ. τὸν Προδρ. (Krumbacher, *Gesch. d. byz. Literatur*² (Munich 1897), 764). See too J. Darrouzès, *Epistoliers byzantins du Xᵉ siècle* (1960), 412.

in 880;[28] the school attached to it (there are other examples at this period)[29] was presumably also built by Basil, at latest by his son Leo VI (886–912). Now προβάλλομαι is the *vox propria* of setting or propounding a riddle, and we can hardly doubt that Cephalas was teacher, not pupil in this school.[30] What then was his relationship there to Gregory 'the master'? P. Speck is probably right to conclude that Cephalas was an assistant teacher, Gregory the headmaster. That Cephalas was Gregory's junior, in years if not in office, is also suggested by the two notes of J to be discussed next, whence we learn that Cephalas drew on a collection of inscriptional epigrams by Gregory. It looks as if it was from Gregory's pioneering work that Cephalas derived his interest in the epigram, later to bear fruit in his own more ambitious anthology.

Now if Cephalas was a teacher, then he will have inflicted hundreds of his favourite epigrams on generations of pupils. But C happened to remember Cephalas expounding this particular poem in this particular classroom, in the days of Gregory. Against vii. 327 it is J again who supplies the information that Casandros, the subject of the poem, was buried in Larissa, adding that it μετεγράφη παρὰ Γρηγορίου τοῦ μακαρίτου διδασκάλου ἐξ αὐτῆς τῆς λάρνακος. Once more, note 'Gregory of blessed memory' identified as a teacher, J's teacher perhaps. According to the same J on vii. 334, ἐγράφη δὲ καὶ τοῦτο παρὰ τοῦ μακαρίτου Γρηγορίου τοῦ Καμφικοῦ· ὅθεν αὐτὸ καὶ ὁ Κεφαλᾶς ἐν τοῖς ἐπιγράμμασιν ἔταξεν. The two pointers to derivation from Gregory are, (*a*) that the poem should appear to be a genuine inscription (and so will normally be anonymous), and (*b*) be equipped with a lemma noting its provenance (in the case of vii. 334 Cyzicus) which could not have been deduced from the poem.[31] Now it is hardly likely that J got his information direct from a text of Gregory. We do not even know whether Gregory published his collection himself, and if J had had a copy to hand we should have expected more full and consistent use of it. In fact, it is C who more often supplies the sort of information that must derive from Gregory's epigraphic forays. For example, εὑρέθη ἐν Θεσσαλονίκῃ on vii. 340 and similar notes on 330 and 331. Note especially vii. 667,

---

[28] R. Janin, *Les Églises et les monastères*[2] (Paris 1969), 361–4 (not mentioning the school).

[29] P. Speck, pp. 12 n. 55, and 67 n. 3.

[30] A possibility canvassed by Speck, p. 61 n. 28, a. See *LSJ* s.v. προβάλλω, II. *b*. 5.

[31] For lists of the places visited by Gregory see R. Weisshäupl, *Die Grabgedichte d. griech. Anthologie* (1889), 29–32; Stadtmueller, ii. 1, pp. ix–x.

where J wrote only the vacuous εἰς . . . θαυμασίην γυναῖκα, while C was able to add the obviously authentic information that her epitaph was now to be found ἐν τῷ ναῷ τῆς ἁγίας Ἀναστασίας ἐν Θεσσαλονίκῃ. There are other inscriptional epigrams from Thessalonica. Compare ix. 686, where B's lemma εἰς τὴν πύλην τὴν ἀνατολικὴν τῆς Θεσσαλονίκης reappears with only a trifling difference of word-order in Planudes, clear proof that it stood in their common source Cephalas. Evidently Cephalas embodied Gregory's notes on the provenance of his epigrams in his own anthology; C's copy preserved them more fully than J's. It was surely while he was copying out from his Cephalas the lemma referring Casandros' moving epitaph (vii. 327) to Larissa that J suddenly recalled his old teacher describing how he had 'copied it from the very coffin'.

A number of notes in *AP* vi and vii show that C also collated P against a copy written by one Michael Chartophylax.[32] For example, on vii. 432: ἕως ὧδε τὰ τοῦ κυροῦ Μιχαὴλ τοῦ μακαρίου περιεῖχον ἐπιγράμματα ἅτινα ἰδιοχείρως αὐτὸς ἔγραψεν ἐκ τῆς βίβλου τοῦ Κεφαλᾶ. The 'Lord Michael of blessed memory' is spoken of with obvious respect as, once more, a man not long dead. He is almost invariably 'the Lord Michael': for example, ἕως ὧδε ἀντεβλήθη ['collated'] πρὸς τὸ ἀντιβόλιν ['copy'] τοῦ κυροῦ Μιχαὴλ at vii. 428 (cf. τοῦ κυροῦ Μιχαηλοῦ at vi. 269 and τοῦ κυροῦ Μιχαὴλ at vii. 450), just as Cephalas is 'the lord Constantine Cephalas' in the heading to *AP* vii. It is not likely that this title either was applied to unknown persons long dead.[33]

This copy of Michael's was written in his own hand (ἰδιοχείρως) and taken direct 'from Cephalas' book'. This undoubtedly means Cephalas' autograph, not just an exemplar of Cephalas. For Cephalas' anthology was not a book to which he could lay claim as author in the ordinary way. He was not even, like Meleager or Philip, a contributor to his anthology; he was just its compiler. All later anthologists pillage the riches he assembled, but none later

---

[32] There is really nothing to be said in favour of G. Luck's suggestion (*HSCP* lxiii (1958), 471) that Michael is to be identified with the Michael credited with a few dodecasyllables in a British Library manuscript of Kasia (cf. Krumbacher's edition, *Sitzungsber. München* 1897, 328–9).

[33] I have been unable to find any study on the use of this title. Krumbacher remarked on the need for one in 1902 ('Die Akrostichis in der griech. Kirchenpoesie', *Sitzungsber. München* 1902, pp. 639–40), when suggesting that hymns introduced by the formula τοῦ κύρου (for the accent, ibid., p. 640 n. 1) Ῥωμανοῦ were written by pupils or disciples of Romanos. For an analysis of its use in tenth-century epistolography see Darrouzès, *Épistoliers byzantins*, p. 412.

than *AP* (not even Planudes) so much as names Cephalas himself. Elsewhere (on vii. 428), remarking that he has made some corrections from Michael's copy, C adds that even this contained errors (πλὴν ὅτι κἀκεῖνο σφάλματα εἶχεν). That is to say, he is surprised to observe that even a direct copy of Cephalas' autograph was not free of error. He should not have been surprised, of course. Cephalas' text could only be as good as the no doubt rather battered texts of Meleager, Philip, and the rest he was able to unearth, and we shall in fact see good reason to suppose that it was often very corrupt indeed. For all their enthusiasm, Cephalas' generation did not (unlike Planudes, for example) have either the stylistic or the metrical equipment to restore classical elegiacs.

Now the clear prima facie implication of these texts is that both J and C were not more than a generation younger than Gregory Magister, Cephalas, and Michael Chartophylax. The only way out is to argue that they are not in fact the personal reminiscences of J and C but notes by earlier scholiasts which they copied mechanically from their exemplars into *AP*. This has long been a favourite approach, less from a deliberate desire to eliminate the scholia as evidence than as a natural consequence of the assumption of late nineteenth-century German scholarship that no one ever wrote even the most mundane marginalia for the first time.

One example has already been quoted: Preisendanz's far-fetched assumption that the quaternion numbers in A refer to a different manuscript—as though J would have allowed the pagination of another manuscript to stand uncorrected in his own! Another and even more outrageous offence against logic and common sense is Stadtmueller's assumption that the numbers added by C to every tenth poem in *AP* vii are the numbers of the poems, not in *AP*, but in Michael's text.[34] Quite apart from the improbability and pointlessness of such an undertaking, Stadtmueller has overlooked the fact that (as we shall see, p. 117) Michael made some changes in the order of the poems. So *his* numeration would have been *different* from that of *AP*; C's numbers, however, as Stadtmueller himself skilfully demonstrated, fit *AP*. C also numbered *AP* v and vi in tens, adding at the end of each book the totals 306 (later corrected to 310) and 360 respectively (true totals 308 and 358). Now we know that Michael omitted at least one poem in vi (269, see below); yet once again it is clear that these totals are based on *AP* (their

---

[34] ii. 1, p. xiii.

very inaccuracy arises out of mistakes in C's numeration of individual poems in *AP*).[35]

It must be firmly stated that neither J nor C were simple scribes who just copied mechanically whatever lay in front of them. Both were scholars, with the scholar's penchant for personal as well as critical annotation. The margins of *AP* are peppered with exclamations of ὡραῖον, θαυμαστόν, ἀναίσχυντον, πορνικώτατον, and the like.[36] C could be very sharp when he chose. For example, when A, perhaps misreading a correction in his exemplar (note that J was unable to correct his error), wrote v. 262. 3 after v. 261. 2 and then left a gap for what he presumed to be the missing pentameter, C deleted the adventitious line and observed 'no lacuna, only a foolish scribe' (οὐδὲν λείπει, πλὴν ὅτι ὁ γράφων ἦν ἀνόητος). Then there is J's note against vii. 472. 7, ζήτει τὸν νοῦν τοῦ ἐπιγράμματος ὅτι ἐσφαλμένος ἐστίν, to which C acidly replied, ἐὰν ἔχῃς νοῦν οὐκ ἔσφαλται.

One of J's more tantalizing asides was inspired by the famous epigram on Timocreon of Rhodes ascribed to Simonides:

πολλὰ πιὼν καὶ πολλὰ φαγὼν καὶ πολλὰ κάκ' εἰπών
ἀνθρώπους κεῖμαι Τιμοκρέων Ῥόδιος. (vii. 348)

'Just the mentality and style of my uncle' (οὗτινος τὴν γνώμην πᾶσαν καὶ τὴν συνήθειαν εἶχεν ὁ θεῖός μου). If only he had named his uncle! It is good to see that in 1962 the veteran Preisendanz was prepared to allow that this was J's uncle rather than Cephalas',[37] but in the same paragraph he still took it for granted that the information about Cephalas teaching in the school of the New Church came from his exemplar. It is a peculiarity of J that he occasionally addresses facetious remarks to the authors of poems. For example, against vii. 23, a poem on Anacreon by Antipater of Sidon, he penned the following dodecasyllable, presumably of his own composition: τὸν σαπρὸν ἄνδρα σαπροῖς ἐπαίνοις στέφεις. Compare his similar metrical sallies against the author of *AP* xv. 37 and 40 (Ch. XV).

It is against this background that we must approach the well-known scholion on *AP* i. 10. 29, claiming that the beauties of the

[35] See Stadtmueller's computations, i. 223, 419; with Preisendanz (1911), col. xxxvii n. 1.
[36] Preisendanz (1911), cols. lxxxvii f.
[37] *Gnomon* xxxiv (1962), 654–5; in 1911, of course, it had been Cephalas' uncle (col. ci n. 2).

(recently excavated) church of St Polyeuctus will last for ever: μένουσιν, ἄριστε, πάντα μέχρι τῆς σήμερον ἔτεσι πεντακοσίοις. After the last word there are some traces *in rasura*, read by Stadtmueller as (καὶ) ***κοντα and supplemented by Preisendanz (καὶ) ⟨ἐξή⟩κοντα, that is to say 560. According to Preisendanz, the 'original' version of the scholion gave just πεντακοσίοις. Sixty years later the scribe of J's exemplar brought the figure up to date. J first copied this figure but then noticed that his 'other exemplar' gave only 500 and erased the 60 to restore the 'original' reading.[38] It need hardly be said that this is neither the only possible nor the most straightforward explanation. To start with, it depends on the more than doubtful assumption that J had two exemplars. Why reject the obvious, that J wrote the only version that ever existed himself? The facetious address to the poet, 'my dear fellow', is entirely in his style.

We now know that the church of St Polyeuctus was built between 524 and 527.[39] On Preisendanz's hypothesis this would place J's exemplar (with its addition of 60 to the 'original' 500) *c.*1085, and J himself scarcely earlier than 1100—a little later even than Aubreton's date for *AP* (though Aubreton himself curiously failed to use this argument). But what did J know of the date of St Polyeuctus? If he got his information, as is most likely, from the standard guide of his day, the *Patria* of Constantinople,[40] then he will have thought that the Juliana who built it was a daughter of Valentinian I (d. 375) instead of granddaughter of Valentinian III. That is to say, he will have assumed a late fourth-century date, in which case even 560 years on takes us no later than *c.*950—almost exactly my date for *AP*. Furthermore, once we abandon the idea of successive redactions of the scholion, then the natural explanation of the erased additional figure is that J made a mistake in his own original calculation, which he immediately recognized and rectified. Since we do not know what number he was starting from and cannot even be sure that the erased figure was ἐξήκοντα rather than

---

[38] Preisendanz (1911), cols. cxlviii–cxlix, and cf. his *Carmina Anacreontea* (1912), p. xvii.

[39] Mango and Ševčenko, *DOP* xv (1961), 245.

[40] *Scriptor. Orig. Cpol.* ii (1907), p. 237; this particular redaction dates from *c.*995, so J must have consulted its source, which probably dates from the eighth or ninth century. Both Maas (*Hermes* xlviii (1913), 295 n. 2 = *Kl. Schr.* (1973), 135 n. 2) and Diller (*Serta Turyniana*, p. 521) saw that it was the patriographical tradition rather than the true date that mattered here, though neither offered an explanation of the erasure.

(say) τριάκοντα, it would be idle to guess what mistake he might have made. Nor, if it *was* just a mistake, does it matter in any case.

There is one other relevant passage, never so far quoted in any discussion of the date of *AP*. ix. 81 by Crinagoras is a poem on the theme that death itself is not always the end of man's sufferings, instancing the example of Nikias, tyrant of Cos under Augustus, whose remains were disinterred and insulted.[41] In the form of a lemma to the poem J penned the following highly rhetorical reflection:

ὅτι καὶ νεκροὶ πολλάκις πάσχουσιν ἀναίσθητα μέν, ἀλλ' ὅμως πάσχουσιν· καὶ βλέπε τὸν Μαυρικίου τάφον καὶ τὸν Ἀμαντίου, ὧν δ μὲν ἐξεβλήθη καὶ κατεσκάφη, ὁ δ' ἐξερρίφη καὶ κατεσπάρη, ὁ μὲν ἐπὶ Λέοντος, ὁ δ' ἐπὶ Ῥωμανοῦ, καὶ ταῦτα βασιλέων· τί δ' ἂν εἴποις περὶ τῶν λοιπῶν ἀνθρώπων;

Corpses often endure sufferings they cannot feel, but they endure them none the less. Take the case of the tombs of Maurice and Amantius; the former was thrown out and dug down, the latter cast out and scattered about, the one under Leo, the other under Romanus—and this although they were emperors. What would you say about the rest of mankind?

Garbled stuff (there was, of course, no emperor 'Amantius', and Leo and Romanus have been confused), but the basic facts alluded to can be made out.[42] In 922 or 923 the Emperor Romanus I Lecapenus had three sarcophagi transferred from the church of St Mamas to his own monastery of Myrelaion, to serve in due course for himself and his family; it was said that they had once contained the bodies of Maurice and his sons (Theophanes continuatus, pp. 403–4). It may be doubted whether Maurice's remains were treated as despitefully as J's rhetoric implies, but we can hardly doubt that this is one of the incidents he had in mind.

As for the other, despite the absurd 'Amantius', the reference is presumably to Leo VI's reuse of the tomb of Justin I for the remains of (? his natural father) Michael III, apparently on the death of his (officially recognized) father Basil I in 886.[43]

The story about Leo (886–912) *could* have been in Cephalas, but not the story about Romanus (920–44), and in any case, the lemma has an obvious stylistic unity. Now there were six emperors called

[41] Gow and Page, *GP* ii. 230–1.
[42] P. Grierson, 'The tombs and obits of the Byzantine emperors', *DOP* xvi (1962), 28 n. 94.
[43] On the family details see now Mango, *Zbornik radova Vizant. Instituta* xiv/xv (1973), 17 f.

Leo and four called Romanus, yet J writes as though there could be no doubt which ones he had in mind. The only period when such confidence would have been justified is the sole reign of Constantine VII Porphyrogenitus, 944–59. At any time under the Macedonian dynasty 'Leo' would inevitably have meant Leo VI. But the reference to Romanus was surely written before the reign of Romanus II (959–63), not to mention those of Romanus III (1028–34) and IV (1068–71). (Aubreton was prepared to bring *AP* down to 1070.) So if it be felt that J's implied criticism of Romanus I is likely to have been written after his fall (944), then *AP* will have been written between 944 and 959.

We may now draw two conclusions about these scholia. First, there is no reason to doubt that they are anything but what they appear to be, the personal observations and reminiscences of J and C themselves. Second, while both refer to Gregory as 'the late', it is only C who so styles Cephalas. Indeed, since C erased part of a note by J to add his tribute to Cephalas' memory, we might infer that Cephalas was still alive when J wrote, which cannot therefore have been much later than *c*.940. Both must have been quite old by the time they worked on *AP*. It may have been after J's death that the manuscript passed into the hands of his slightly younger contemporary.[44]

IV. MICHAEL CHARTOPHYLAX

To judge from the number and distribution of his corrections and supplements to the work of A and J, C collated *AP* very carefully against his copy of Michael Chartophylax. At regular intervals he jotted down a ὧδε or ἕως ὧδε in the margin to remind himself where he had got to each time he stopped.[45] These marks are very frequent; for example, eighteen of them in Book vii, on pp. 219, 228, 235, 238, 240, 243, 244, 254, 264, 266, 268, 271, 273, 274, 281, 284, 286, 288, and 322. Thus it took him no fewer than eighteen sessions to complete his work on this book. Many of the sessions were short, though even the shortest will scarcely have been less

---

[44] Though it might be that C simply borrowed the first volume, which would explain why his annotations stop at the point I suggest for the division; see below, p. 133.

[45] They are listed in Preisendanz (1911), cols. cxvi–cxvii.

than an hour, so it must have taken C this long to collate even a couple of pages. Add to this the fact that he had at his disposal an exemplar copied direct from Cephalas' autograph, and it will be understood that C is a most valuable witness to the relationship of *AP* to Michael and Cephalas.

Against vi. 269 C remarks εἰς τὸ ἀντιβόλιν οὐ κεῖται τοῦ κυροῦ Μιχαηλοῦ· πόθεν οὖν ἐγράφη οὐκ οἶδα. That is to say, presuming that Michael was a better witness to Cephalas than *AP*, C took it for granted that vi. 269 was an interpolation of *AP*, an insertion from some other source. A much simpler and more likely explanation is that Michael omitted the poem. It fits perfectly in its present context in *AP*, the first of six dedications to Artemis by women (269–74) in a long and unbroken extract from Meleager's *Garland* (262–313). With the ascription ὡς Σαπφοῦς, 'in the style of Sappho', we may compare 273 ὡς Νοσσίδος. We can hardly doubt that all six stood together in both Meleager and Cephalas.[46] As it is transmitted in *AP*, however, 269 is barely intelligible; indeed, C wrote ὁλόσφαλτον, 'utterly corrupt', at the end of the poem. There are two other obscure and corrupt poems in the vicinity which, evidently finding little help in Michael, C similarly stigmatized, vi. 297 and 305.[47] If 269 had been corrupt already in Cephalas, then Michael might have omitted it deliberately. We have already noted C's surprise at the bad state of Michael's text, and there are two or three other suggestive points. After both vi. 125 and 143 A left a gap of six lines; C remarks οὐ λείπει, ὡς οἶμαι and οὐ λείπει, ὡς οἶμαι, οὐδὲ ἐνταῦθα ('no lacuna here either') respectively, as though puzzled (note the repeated 'I think'). I suggest that in both places the text was already corrupt in Cephalas; A conscientiously left gaps, in case J might be able to repair them, while Michael just left the poems out (whence C's surprise at the gaps in *AP*). C's comments about the gap after vi. 158 (see below) also look as if they are based on guesswork.

Paradoxically, then, it looks as if Michael is actually a less faithful witness to Cephalas here than *AP*. He omitted at least one poem preserved in *AP* and two or three others where *AP* has at least preserved the traces.

[46] Oddly enough Gow and Page omit 269, while mentioning it in their discussion of the group (*HE* ii. 443).

[47] Not only is 297 very obscure and corrupt; it is further disfigured by the erroneous insertion of a pentameter from 298 after l. 3 (omitted from Beckby's app. crit.; see Gow and Page ad loc.).

This conclusion is reinforced by the note on vii. 450, a poem by Dioscorides on the hetaera Philainis. First C simply remarked νομίζω ὅτι δισσῶς κεῖται τὸ ἐπίγραμμα. He then evidently checked. The epigram is not in fact duplicated in the *text*, but C himself had added it twenty pages earlier in the bottom margin of p. 256 against another poem on Philainis in scazons by Aeschrion, vii. 345. Having discovered this and checked with Michael, C then added: πλὴν ἐν τῇ τάξει τῶν ἐπιγραμμάτων τοῦ κυροῦ Μιχαὴλ οὕτως κεῖται συνηημμένον μετὰ τοῦ ἰαμβικοῦ [Aeschrion's scazons]. Preisendanz interpreted these words to imply that vii. 450 also appeared twice in Michael, and probably Cephalas too.[48] I should have thought the implication was rather that it appeared only once in Michael, next to Aeschrion. It should be added that C added two other poems on Philainis, vii. 477 (Tymnes) and 486 (Anyte), in the margins of the next page. Indeed there are a number of such duplications by C in the margins of this book. By vii. 230 he wrote ix. 61, 397, and 447, all on the theme of cowardly Spartans; vii. 364 is added by 190, both on Myro; 455 by 353, both on the tipsy Maronis; 577 by 315, both on the misanthrope Timon; and 516 by 77, both by Simonides. The object of all this, as Gow has rightly observed, was clearly 'to bring like to like'.[49] But whose object?

While allowing that in writing 450 by 345 C is following Michael's order, Gow assumes that 'in default of other evidence the rest of his repetitions may be attributed to his own observations'. Why assume that the only case where we have evidence is a special case? The purpose of these marginal additions was surely not exegetical but editorial. C did not write 450 on p. 256 to illustrate 345 but because, following Michael, he thought that it belonged there. This is proved by his reaction on encountering it again on p. 278: the note δισσῶς κεῖται (evidently considered undesirable) and the fresh collation with Michael. Contrast too his treatment of the obviously anathematic poem vii. 53. Realizing that it was out of place in vii among the epitumbia he wrote it again more appropriately at the end of vi and marked vii. 53 very clearly for deletion.[50] None of the poems written in the margins of vii are marked for deletion in their original places. What happened, I

---

[48] (1911), col. cxiv n. 2.

[49] Gow (1958), 59.

[50] It is one of the many proofs of the common source behind *AP* and *APl* that this obviously misclassified epigram appears in the same sepulchral context in *APl*; we shall see that this sort of misclassification is typical of Cephalas.

suggest, is that as he collated *AP* with Michael, C noticed the occasional poem in Michael apparently missing from *AP*. These he added in his margin where he thought they had been omitted, not realizing that those listed above were to be found elsewhere in *AP*. But two of these additions, vii. 2*b* and 254*b*, are genuinely absent from *AP*; these he must have found in the corresponding place in Michael. Suggestively enough, after 254*b* he added the note τοῦτο δισσῶς κεῖται. Now this is not true of *AP*, nor is it easy to believe that C would have written the poem where he did if he even suspected it to be true of *AP*. Surely what he means is that (as Basson saw) it appeared twice *in Michael*; that is to say it was one of the epigrams Michael transferred from one place to another, on this occasion forgetting to delete it in its original place. Compare too an even clearer example which Basson missed, C's note on vi. 179: ἀντεβλήθη ἐπιγράμματα θ᾽ ὡς κείμενα ἔμπροσθεν· ζητεῖται κἀκεῖ. The nine epigrams in question are vi. 179–87, and C suspected duplication because all nine are variations on the same famous dedication of Leonidas as vi. 11–16 (obviously C's ἔμπροσθεν). The fifteen poems are barely distinguishable one from another, and it was reasonable for C to check for duplication. In fact none are repeated in *AP*. Yet the finding of C's collation as he himself reports it—ζητεῖται κἀκεῖ—is that all nine *were*. ζητεῖν, as well as being the scholiast's general-purpose word for any sort of error or gap that needs checking, is also used more specifically in cases of transposition, to guide the reader to the place where the desired passage is to be found.[51] The κἀκεῖ, 'there too', makes it clear that the word is so used here. Since this cannot apply to *AP*, we are surely bound to conclude that it is Michael's copy he is referring to. In the light of what we have so far discovered about Michael's method, it is perfectly credible that he transposed the whole sequence 179–87 to follow after their natural fellows 11–16.

Which was Cephalas' order? Once more, surely, the order in *AP*. For although Planudes also united the two sequences (in his vi. 92–106), at first sight strong support for Michael's order, in fact he took not only the nine poems 179–87 C mentions but also the unconnected 188. This suggests that he found the nine, not ready-united with 11–16 at the beginning of Cephalas' dedicatory book, but in their present context in *AP*, where, of course, they are followed by 188. It is difficult to see why, if the sequence had been

---

[51] R. Devreesse, *Introduction à l'étude des manuscrits grecs* (Paris 1954), 86.

united in Cephalas, J's exemplar should have divided it. On the other hand, it is easy to believe that Cephalas himself deliberately divided for the sake of variety what would certainly have made a monotonously long sequence on the one limited theme.

As for the ten poems duplicated by C in the margins of *AP* vii, here again seven are firmly anchored in their original contexts in *AP*: the three on Philainis (vii. 450, 477, and 486) are all embedded in a long Meleagrian sequence, as is 455 by Leonidas on Maronis; 364 by Marcus Argentarius on Myro appears (decisively) at the head of an impeccable alphabetical sequence from Philip's *Garland*; vii. 577 and ix. 447, both by Julian the Egyptian, in Agathian sequences, and ix. 397 by Palladas does at least appear together with other poems by Palladas. Once more, there can be little doubt that all these poems were taken over by Cephalas, in their present contexts, direct into his own anthology from the books of Meleager, Philip, Agathias, and Palladas respectively. It is Michael who transferred them to the positions indicated by C, in a (sometimes misjudged) attempt to tidy up Cephalas' admittedly rather unsatisfactory thematic classification (for example, of the four poems on Philainis, Aeschrion, and Dioscorides—as J's lemmata correctly point out—wrote about quite a different woman from Anyte and Tymnes).

We are now in a position to draw some further conclusions.

1. Michael's book, indisputably, was a copy of Cephalas.

2. If so, then *AP* was another. C collated the two books very carefully, and it is clear from the way he records their few divergences that (in content and arrangement at least) he *expected* them to coincide here as they evidently did elsewhere.

3. Contrary to the conclusion C himself apparently drew, we have seen that in most of these divergences it is *AP* that is closer to Cephalas. On the basis of the information supplied by C, Michael had two poems not in *AP* and *AP* one not in Michael, unmistakable pointers to a common source—in this case (of course) Cephalas.

VI

Cephalas

THE next point to be established is the scope of Michael's book. Stadtmueller thought that it broke off at vii. 432, and few have allowed it to proceed beyond ix. 563, where C's annotations stop. On more general and intangible grounds, Aubreton insists that it did not contain more than a selection of the poems in *AP*. If (as we have been assuming) it can be made probable that Michael's copy was coextensive with the 'Cephalan' parts of *AP* at any rate up to ix. 563, then this would imply that Cephalas too was coextensive with *AP* to this point.

First, however, it will be necessary to offer some general prefatory remarks about the structure of the 'Cephalan' books of *AP*.[1] Scholars have long been perturbed by the sudden switches from order to apparent disorder and from one method of arrangement to another. Some (most notably Aubreton) have supposed that only the more systematically arranged parts derive from Cephalas, the rest being later additions from other hands. Others have taken refuge in Cephalas' undeniable carelessness and concluded, either that he tired of his task and gave up bothering about structure and arrangement long before the end of each book (Waltz), or that, prevented by some external cause, he simply did not finish the job (Preisendanz). The form of the successive books of *AP* is certainly messy and often puzzling, but they do (I think) possess a structural unity of a kind, particularly in respect of the supposed 'additions', that has not been sufficiently taken into account.

We may begin by emphasizing the magnitude and difficulty of the task Cephalas set himself. He did his research thoroughly. There is nothing to be said in favour of the old assumption that he derived his knowledge of Meleager and Philip from some late intermediary. There is no reason to doubt that he excerpted at first

---

[1] See already Ch. IV above.

hand all the main earlier anthologies and collections he could
lay his hands on: Meleager, Philip, Strato, Agathias, (probably)
Palladas, and if not an original text of Diogenian, at any rate the
fourth-century abridgement postulated in Ch. IV. He also
excerpted much of value from a wide variety of prose sources,
notably Diogenes Laertius. His colleague Gregory of Campsa was
able to supply epigraphic material. The completeness of his search
is illustrated by the relatively small number of epigrams from
literary sources other than the Anthology left for T. Preger to
gather in his valuable supplement *Inscriptiones Graecae metricae ex
scriptoribus praeter Anthologiam collectae* (1891). It is from inscriptions that the great modern harvest of ancient epigrams has come.

So much could diligence alone achieve. But on what principle
was he to arrange all this material: thematic, stylistic, chronological, topographical? The varying reviews of a recent modern
attempt, W. Peek's *Griechische Versinschriften* i, well illustrate the
different possibilities.[2] Meleager and (following him) Agathias
grouped by association or contrast of theme and alternation of
authors; Philip by alphabetical order of the initial letter of each
poem and then thematically inside letter groups.[3] All, that is, used
more than one method in conjunction.

Cephalas' first step (as J remarked in his note on *AP* iv. 1) was
broad subject categories: erotic, anathematic, funerary, and so on.
Inside these broad categories he used several further methods of
organization, with the deliberate intention (I would suggest) of
achieving a balance between order and variety. By way of example
let us consider the arrangement of a particular book together
with the arguments that have been addressed against the assumption that the whole book is the work of Cephalas. First vi, anathematica:[4]

1. 1–53:   thematically ordered, that is to say a succession of dedica-
              tions to certain gods or by certain classes of people,
              irrespective of the date or authorship of the individual
              poems
2. 54–86:   unbroken sequence from the *Cycle* of Agathias
3. 87–108:   unbroken sequence from the *Garland* of Philip

---

[2] Notably that by L. Robert, *Gnomon* xxxi (1959), 1–30.
[3] See Ch. II *passim*.
[4] The tables that follow are adapted from those in Lenzinger, which are not
always accurate; see p. xvi.

4. 109–57:   unbroken sequence from the *Garland* of Meleager
5. 158–78:   mixed (but not thematically ordered) group from Meleager, Philip, and Agathias combined
6. 179–226:   thematically ordered section, much like 1–53
7. 227–61:   unbroken sequence from Philip
8. 262–313:   unbroken sequence from Meleager
9. 314–58:   miscellaneous conclusion: anacyclica by Nicodemus of Heraclea (314–20, 323), isopsepha by Leonidas of Alexandria (321–9, though not 323), Theocritus (336–40).

According to Aubreton (p. 66), only the 'parties réellement ordonnées' go back to Cephalas, in the case of vi (he claims) 1–218. Elsewhere (p. 43) he claims that C's corrections from Michael Chartophylax also stop at 218. This might indeed have been reckoned a significant coincidence—if true.

C's corrections continue uninterrupted up to 356, that is to say to within two poems of the end of the book. There is a ὧδε mark after 251 and a direct reference to Michael (who had omitted the poem) against 269. Few of the corrections are especially notable, though few appear to be guesses; those at 228. 2, 302. 7, 303. 2, and 328. 4 agree with the text of Planudes, those at 234. 1, 248. 3, 296. 4, and 298. 3 agree with quotations in the Suda. Since neither Suda nor Planudes drew on *AP*,[5] we can hardly doubt that these at least are authentic readings that C found in his exemplar. Of particular interest is his correction of 317, by Nicodemus of Heraclea:

Πραξιτέλης ἔπλασεν Δανάην καὶ φάρεα Νυμφῶν
λύγδινα καὶ Πέτρης Πάνά με Πεντελικῆς.

C put a deletion sign against the final nu of ἔπλασεν in l. 1, foolishly *contra metrum* at first sight. In fact, the poem is anacyclic and ἔπλασε is required in the reversal:

Πεντελικῆς ἐμὲ Πᾶνα πέτρης καὶ λύγδινα Νυμφῶν
φάρεα καὶ Δανάην ἔπλασε Πραξιτέλης.

Not a guess, since (*a*) Planudes too originally wrote ἔπλασε, before adding a nu *metri causa* during revision; and (*b*) it was left to Brunck to make the other correction required for the reversal, Παν' ἐμέ for Πᾶνά με in l. 2. ἔπλασε at least evidently stood in C's exemplar, as it did in Planudes'.

---

[5] For the Suda, see below, Ch. XII.

Finally and decisively, C was able to add two whole couplets omitted by A and not supplied by J: 288. 9–10 and (confirmed by Planudes) 309. 1–2. Since we know that Michael's exemplar was Cephalas' autograph, there can be no reasonable doubt that *AP* vi stood in Cephalas almost exactly as we have it in *AP*.

As for Aubreton's other argument, it depends on the arbitrary assumption that a mechanical thematic grouping is the only method Cephalas was likely to have used. But Cephalas had studied his Meleager, Philip, and Agathias closely, and must have become aware of their more elaborate principles of organization. It was obviously a pity and a waste to destroy these for the sake of a crude thematic grouping, and Cephalas devised a sensible compromise. A certain number of his Meleagrian, Philippan, and Agathian poems he used together with the rest of the material at his disposal for the book to make his thematic groupings. He then transcribed fairly long extracts from each of the three original collections, *not* because he was too lazy to break them up and continue his thematic groupings, but precisely in order to make their more sophisticated arrangement his own, and, in addition, provide what amounts to a chronological section to balance the thematic grouping of the first part of the book. Inevitably much material he had not been able to fit in his thematic groupings was still left over, and this he put together as best he could in a miscellaneous concluding section.

I am certainly not suggesting that Cephalas' books are masterpieces of organization. Their execution is undeniably careless. One common avoidable consequence of his double treatment of the *Garlands* and the *Cycle* is that a certain number of poems that might best have been put with others on the same theme in the thematic groupings are left in their original contexts in the extracts. It was precisely this shortcoming that we have seen Michael Chartophylax trying to remedy in vii, by transferring poems from Meleagrian, Philippan, and Agathian contexts to the thematic groupings earlier in the book—clear proof that he was confronted with a text arranged, with all its faults, exactly like *AP*. My point is that, if it be accepted that Cephalas was deliberately employing both methods, then neither the variation between them nor even the structureless miscellaneous conclusions provide any argument for post-Cephalan addition.

It will by now be obvious that Aubreton's claim that the 'partie réellement ordonnée' of vi reaches only to 218 does not correspond with the facts. There *is* a break, but it comes at 178, where the book falls into two halves, the second repeating the structure of the first exactly save for the omission of a second extract from Agathias. Lenzinger suggested that it was at 178 that the 'original' vi ended, but if the duplication of the pattern is puzzling, it is no less a puzzle if we ascribe it to a later redactor rather than to Cephalas himself.

There is one final proof. Aubreton claims that a comparison with Planudes and the *syllogae minores* confirms his conclusion about the relationship of *AP* to Cephalas. Had he actually carried out such a comparison he would have discovered that it provides a decisive refutation of his claim.

AP contains *c*.3,700 poems, *c*.1,700 of them absent from *APl*; *APl c*.2,400, 400 of which are absent from *AP*. Aubreton, who does not believe that both derive from a common source in Cephalas, would like to think that the 1,700-odd poems in *AP* missing from *APl* were personally added by the scribes of *AP*. In support of this contention he observes (p. 74) that the minor *syllogae* contain very few epigrams absent from *APl*, proof that 'les additions furent le fait des auteurs du *Palatinus*'. But when the total number of poems offered by the minor *syllogae* is so small (barely 450 all together) and the overlap between *AP* and *APl* so large (more than 2,000), such a statistic proves little; much of the material peculiar to *AP* is trivial and repetitious, and it is hardly surprising that Planudes and the minor collections should often have coincided in their omissions. That the poems in *AP* absent from Planudes were *not* the additions of the Palatine scribes can easily be proved by a glance at their distribution.

AP vi contains 358 anathematic poems, of which 174 are absent from *APl*, a surprisingly high number, proportionately much higher than the 181 missing out of 755 in *AP* vii, 52 out of 441 in xi, or 18 out of 126 in x. But these 174 missing poems are not grouped together in detachable blocks nor are they concentrated towards the end of the book. They occur in groups of two or three, seldom as many as six or seven, scattered evenly throughout the book. Much the longest stretches are 135–51 and 264–83, both in the middle of unbroken extracts from Meleager, 109–57 and 262–313 respectively. That these stretches stood in Cephalas is proved not just by general considerations of probability, but by the fact that both contain poems corrected by C from Michael

Chartophylax *and* poems quoted in the Suda. Now the Suda (which, unlike Basson, I do not believe to have derived its epigram citations from *AP* itself) quotes from 225 poems in *AP* vi, more than Planudes, the first from vi. 3 and the last from 348. The poems taken by Planudes run from vi. 1 to 352. Of the minor *syllogae*, E has 1, 2, 4, 5, 9, and 331 and 332, poems (that is) taken from the beginning and end of the book respectively (note that Planudes has 331 but not 330).

Only one conclusion seems possible. Michael Chartophylax and Planudes, the compilers of *AP*, E, and the Suda, all derive, directly or indirectly, from an identical common source, namely Cephalas.

Save for perhaps just the one poem omitted by Michael (269) and three or four that the scribe A could not decipher (Ch. XI), *AP* vi may be taken to be a more or less exact copy of both the contents and the arrangement of Cephalas' book of anathematica. And if vi is as faithful a witness to Cephalas as this, why not the other Cephalan books of *AP*? Take the much longer vii, for example:

1. 1–363: thematically arranged, incorporating a series on philosophers (83–133) from Diogenes Laertius
2. 364–405: extract from Philip
3. 406–506: extract from Meleager
4. 507–50: mixture from Philip and Meleager
5. 551–614: extract from Agathias
6. 615–20: more on philosophers from Diogenes Laertius
7. 622–45: extract from Philip
8. 646–65: extract from Meleager
9. 666–748: miscellaneous conclusion (707–40 from Meleager)

It will at once be apparent that vii closely parallels vi in both structure and sources. After the same thematic opening there is the same run of extracts from Philip, Meleager, and Agathias and a miscellaneous section before the same pattern, based on the same sources, starts all over again. The only difference is that in vii section 5 follows 4 rather than vice versa as in vi, and section 6 is unexpectedly short. With this arrangement of sections 1–4 compare the structure of *AP* ix. 1–583, which we may presume to represent Cephalas' epideictic book:

1. 1–214: thematically arranged
2. 215–312: extract from Philip

3. 313–38:   extract from Meleager
4. 339–583:   mixture from various sources

No separate Agathian section because there happened to be relatively few Agathian epideictica.[6] It will be noticed that, unlike vi and vii, the pattern appears only once here, for which we may compare the structure of *AP* v:

1. 1–103:   'Sylloge Rufiniana'
2. 104–33:   extract from Philip
3. 134–215:   extract from Meleager
4. 216–302:   extract from Agathias
5. 303–9:   miscellaneous conclusion

It has already been suggested in Ch. IV that 1–103 are an excerpt from a fourth-century anthology embodying excerpts from the second-century anthology of Diogenian, and the rest of the book is very straightforward. It might be conjectured that there is only one set of *Garland* sequences because there were so few Philippan erotica, though it must be borne in mind that there are 162 more Philippan and (mostly) Meleagrian erotica in *AP* xii. It was by sex that Cephalas divided up his erotic material.

According to Aubreton, the 'partie réellement ordonnée' of v is 104–302; of vii, 1–363; and of ix, 1–583 entire. That is to say, he accepts the thematic introduction of vii; the Meleagrian, Philippan, and Agathian extracts of v; and from ix, introduction, extracts, *and* a massive miscellaneous conclusion too! On what principle of logic or consistency can we refuse Cephalas the extracts and conclusion of vii or the introduction and conclusion to v?

The distribution of Planudean omissions in v, vii, and ix follows the same pattern as in vi. No long blocks that could be later insertions, but short stretches of two or three at a time. Throughout the 1,331 poems of vii and ix. 1–583 there are never more than six consecutive poems absent from Planudes, and only one case of as many as eight in vi (198–206, in a Meleagrian extract). We have his own admission that Planudes deliberately passed over a number of erotica on moral grounds, illuminatingly confirmed by the *Appendix Barberino-Vaticana* (*ABV*). This collection (which derives from a redaction of Cephalas in some respects fuller than

---

[6] A. Mattsson (1942), 73.

AP) contains 33 poems from v, 28 of them absent from Planudes (it was in fact designed to make up for his prudery):[7] the list runs from 18 to 305. Planudes' takings from v begin with 2 and end with 308. There can be no doubt that both Planudes and the compiler of *ABV* drew on a sequence of erotica closely similar if not identical to *AP* v—a sequence that included both the introduction and conclusion of *AP* v. It can be added that in his earlier anthology L (based on a different source from *APl*—see Ch. IX) Planudes took v. 229, 236, 291, 297, and 302, only five poems but from the last third of the book. For vii too we have the takings in L, only eleven poems, but significantly distributed among all sections but the last: 126, 309, 327, 336, 339, 400, 476, 576, 586, 630, 650.

For *AP* v we have in addition a hitherto neglected witness of a rather unusual sort in Nicetas Eugenianos' verse romance *Drosilla and Charicles*, which contains a large number of imitations of erotic epigrams. There are no doubt many more than the list given below,[8] but it is full enough to make the point:

AP v.	3 (Antip. Thess.)	= *Dros.*	6. 660–1
	59 (Archias)		8. 103
	67 (Capito)		8. 105–6
	69 (Rufinus)		8. 107–9
	83 (?Dion. Soph.)		8. 110–12
	123 (Philodemus)		8. 113–15
	224 (Macedonius)		3. 253–4
	225 (Macedonius)		3. 251–2
	229 (Macedonius)		6. 614–17
	237 (Agathias)		6. 649–59
	246 (Paul)		6. 624–8
	252 (Paul)		6. 638–41
	253 (Irenaeus)		3. 163–72
	257 (Palladas)		6. 629–32
	258 (Paul)		6. 633–7
	259 (Paul)		3. 243–50
	268 (Paul)		2. 125–8
	273 (Agathias)		3. 176–8
ix.	748 (Plato jun.)		6. 395–6

It must be emphasized that these are not just glancing echoes but

---

[7] See Ch. VIII.
[8] A corrected and expanded version of the list in J. Hutton (1935), 7.

deliberate and often protracted paraphrases.[9] For example, with
Agathias, *AP* v. 237:

πᾶσαν ἐγὼ τὴν νύκτα κινύρομαι· εὖτε δ᾽ ἐπέλῃ
ὄρθρος ἐλινῦσαι μικρὰ χαριζόμενος,
ἀμφιπεριτρύζουσι χελιδόνες . . .

compare *Dros.* 6. 649 f.:

πᾶσαν μὲν ἤδη νύκτα γρηγορῶν μένω·
εἰ δ᾽ ὄρθρος ἤξει μικρὸν ὕπνον ἐγχέων
χελιδόνες τρύζουσιν . . .

Or with Macedonius, v. 224:

λῆξον, Ἔρως, κραδίης τε καὶ ἥπατος· εἰ δ᾽ ἐπιθυμεῖς
βάλλειν, ἄλλο τί μου τῶν μελέων μετάβα,

compare *Dros.* 3. 251–3:

ναὶ παῦσον . . . ἄλλο βάλλε μοι μέρος,
τὸ δ᾽ ἧπαρ ἄφες ἀλλὰ καὶ τὴν καρδίαν.

In the light of his model, it is clear that Nicetas wrote μέλος, not
μέρος, at the end of l. 252.

It will be obvious that there are three passages in particular
(3. 163 f., 6. 614 f., 8. 103 f.) where we can only assume that
Nicetas had a copy of Cephalas open in front of him as he wrote. In
twelve lines of Bk. viii he paraphrases five different poems by five
different poets in the same order in which they appear in *AP*. The
poems he imitates run from 3 to 275 in *AP* v. Nicetas himself
wrote at the end of the twelfth century, but his copy of Cephalas
need not have been so late. It might be added that Nicetas also
imitates the *Anacreontea*, a collection only known to us from *AP*
(Ch. XV).

The evidence of C's corrections is no less clear—as far as they
go. There are four ὧδε marks in v, eight in vi, eighteen (as we saw
earlier) in vii, and three in ix. C's notes, ascriptions, lemmata, and
corrections naturally vary in character and extent according to the
accuracy and fullness both of *AP* and his exemplar at any given
point, not to mention his own no doubt fluctuating vigilance and
diligence. But they appear regularly up to ix. 563. Prima facie,
then, Michael Chartophylax's copy continued to at least this point.

---

[9] For some brief remarks on Nicetas' classical imitations see H. Hunger, *DOP*
xxiii/xxiv (1969/70), 37 f.

There is a complication, however. Against vii. 432 (on p. 273) C first notes in the margin ὧδε Μιχ. τοῦ χαρτοφύλακος, and then again beneath the poem, as though the point needed to be made more fully, a scholion already quoted in another connection: ἕως ὧδε τὰ τοῦ κυροῦ Μιχαὴλ τοῦ μακαρίου περιεῖχον ἐπιγράμματα ἅτινα ἰδιοχείρως αὐτὸς ἔγραψεν ἐκ τῆς βίβλου τοῦ Κεφαλᾶ. Scholars from Stadtmueller (ii. 1, xii) to Aubreton (p. 44) have taken it for granted that this means that Michael's codex broke off at this point; that is to say, either it was defective or this is all that Michael wrote. C's corrections and ὧδε marks, however, continue as before. Against 497 C writes ἕως ὧδε ἀντεβλήθη, whence Stadtmueller inferred that (what he took to be) the new exemplar C had been collating with from 433 had also now given out, after which (since C's corrections still continue, with another two ὧδεs before the end of the book) he used yet another exemplar.

These two further exemplars we may surely reject out of hand. It seems clear from the nature both of his corrections and his queries that C had only been using one exemplar up to 432, and it is scarcely credible that he managed so opportunely to lay his hands on another defective copy that took over, by coincidence, exactly where Michael had broken off—only to break off itself 65 poems later. The use of ἕως ὧδε ἀντεβλήθη at 497 instead of just ὧδε or ἕως ὧδε is surely of no significance; it is also found for example, at vi. 187 and ix. 460, in neither of which places is there any indication or probability of C changing exemplars.

But the problem of the notes on 432 remains. The answer (as so often) was seen by Basson (p. 24). What C means is that this is where Michael *himself* (αὐτός) stopped copying *in his own hand* (ἰδιοχείρως). This, surely, is why C added the second note. He realized that the first might indeed seem to suggest that Michael's copy gave out altogether, so he added what he hoped was a more explicit statement. I suggest, in fact, that C gives as much information as he does here because he is paraphrasing Michael's own colophon, something on the lines of ἕως ὧδε ἰδιοχείρως ἔγραψα ἐκ τῆς βίβλου τοῦ Κεφαλᾶ Μιχαὴλ ὁ χαρτοφύλαξ. We may compare the note on fo. 292 of MS A (Par. suppl. gr. 255) of Thucydides: ἐμετρήθησαν τὰ φύλλα τοῦ παρόντος βιβλίου παρ' ἐμοῦ . . . [several letters illegible] Θεοδώρου καὶ εὑρέθησαν ὄντα διακόσια καὶ ἐνενήκοντα καὶ ἕν· εἰσὶ δὲ ἐξ αὐτῶν κεκομμένα ἐξ ἄκρας δέκα τρία καὶ ἐγράφησαν παρ' ἐμοῦ οἰκειοχείρως διαστι . . . [no more legible]. Whether or not this is the great Theodore Metochites and whatever exactly the note may mean (A contains 292, not 291 folia, and all are written in the hand of the original scribe), it is clear, as B. Hemmerdinger remarks, that 'l'adverbe οἰκειοχείρως, aux antipodes de l'humilité des moines copistes, implique qu'il s'agit d'un grand personnage qui a daigné faire office de copiste'.[10] Theodore had been numbering the pages of a Thucydides manuscript when he discovered that it was defective,[11] and since it was only a matter of eleven pages, he copied them out himself (apparently adding his explanatory note in the exemplar he had used instead of the manuscript he had repaired).

Michael, like Theodore, and indeed like J, was not a professional scribe but a man of letters, who employed others to take over when he had had enough himself. Michael was a man of some consequence, a far more important figure, it might be added, than Cephalas. The chartophylax was not, as generations of editors and commentators have translated the word, an 'archivist', suggesting a bookish figure who earned his living by his pen. He was at this period the head of the patriarchal chancellery.[12] His standing is illustrated by the deferential letter from an anonymous professor of the age to the chartophylax Orestes, thanking him for glancing at a manuscript but quite appreciating that he is far too busy to give it any more attention at present.[13] Even if Cephalas is to be identified with the protopapas of the palace of 917 (see p. 254), this

[10] *Essai sur le texte de Thucydide* (Paris 1955), 43. Arethas (*Scripta minora* i. 228. 15W) uses ἰδιοχείρως (of an alleged forgery by his enemy Anastasius the stammerer, of whom more below). And Alexander of Nicaea (another contemporary we shall meet again) complains of having to write a document αὐτοχειρί (Darrouzès, *Épistoliers byzantins*, p. 69, l. 31) because there was no secretary available. For several other examples of αὐτοχειρίᾳ in tenth-century epistolographers (never in the classical sense 'murder') see Darrouzès' index, p. 400.

[11] Against the identification as Metochites, Ševčenko, *Études sur la polémique entre Théod. Mét. et Nic. Choumnos* (1962), 58 n. 5; Wilson 1983, 258.

[12] J. Darrouzès, *Recherches sur les officia de l'Église byzantine* (Paris 1970), 334f., 508f.

[13] *Epp.* 21 in the corpus discussed by R. Browing in *Byz.* xxiv (1954), 397–452 and published in full by Browning and Laourdas, *Ep. Et. Buz. Spoud.* xxvii (1957), 152–212. In the present context it is worth quoting in full Browning's excellent account of this professor's activity as copyist: 'He appears from his correspondence to have supplied manuscripts to the Patriarch Nicolaus Mysticus (?) (ep. 53, 88), Nicephorus Metropolitan of Philippopolis or Philippi (ep. 63), and probably Leo Metropolitan of Sardis (ep. 85). No doubt it is primarily as a copyist that he is brought into relation with some of his other correspondents. At first sight he seems to be one of the humble instruments without whom the great rebirth of literature and learning in the late ninth and early tenth centuries could not have taken place, a

was not a senior rank in the ecclesiastical hierarchy but an unofficial clerical title of no great distinction conferred personally by the emperor.[14] So just as Theodore copied a mere eleven pages οἰκειοχείρως and J less than 150 of the 700 pages of *AP*, so too Michael wrote only a portion of his manuscript. The rest of the text of what we may still call Michael's copy will have been written, naturally from the same exemplar, by one or more professional scribes, whose work Michael himself no doubt then corrected. This would explain why it is that the character and quality of C's corrections remain unchanged after 432.

We need not doubt, then, that C used the same exemplar right up to ix. 563. But what happened then? According to Aubreton (p. 66) this was as far as Cephalas had got at the time; but why should Michael have wanted to copy Cephalas' book before it was finished, before indeed he had added the last twenty poems to his epideictica? The standard view is that Michael's copy simply broke off at this point—yet another mutilated manuscript to add to the seven already scattered in the dust behind us.

This is not impossible, of course, but it is an odd coincidence that C's exemplar should break off exactly where there is also a major break in *AP*. For it is with ix. 563 that the block written on thicker parchment by BB2B3 begins. Any attempt to link C's defection with the supposed tripartite structure of *AP* is bound to fail. For whenever A and B were written, they must already have been united by J *before* the manuscript came into C's hands (C is unquestionably later than J).

It should perhaps be mentioned that though C wrote lemmata

man such as Baanes and John the Calligrapher, who copied manuscripts for Arethas of Caesarea. Yet closer examination of the letters shows that such an impression would be mistaken. The writer makes no claim to calligraphy, and distinguishes himself sharply from professional scribes (ep. 53). And the task which he reluctantly undertakes for the Patriarch in ep. 88 seems to be more akin to editing than copying, involving as it does choice between variant readings and compilation of some kind of marginal apparatus' (*Byz.* 1954, 438).

[14] I am grateful to Père Darrouzès for confirming this point to me in a letter (10 Nov. 1976), from which I quote: 'En tant que protopapas (=archiprêtre) il a simplement un role liturgique et principalement d'apparat dans le groupe des prêtres qui officient au Palais, ou dans une église desservie par plusieurs prêtres; en plus du protopapas du Palais, il y en avait un à Sainte Sophie, et toute église ou paroisse avec un clergé nombreuse pouvait en avoir un. Dans le clergé impérial, il est probable que la promotion était arbitraire. . . . Les deux mentions de Kephalas peuvent signifier toutefois que la dignité palatine de protopapas, en 917, est comme une récompense, ou une reconnaissance d'une mérite même littéraire (de la part de Léon le Sage?) et d'un personnage probablement âgé.'

regularly up to ix. 562, he had not been making actual corrections for some time by then. And the ὧδε marks become fewer and further between: on pp. 322 (the end of vii), 366, 432, and finally (by ix. 460) 437. C was tiring of his task, covering more ground with less attention per session. Particularly once he had got on to the portion written by the more accurate J, there was less need for close scrutiny of the text. However, the suggestion that he simply abandoned his collation is open to the same two objections as the hypothesis of the defective exemplar. Why at precisely this point? And why did he not write a single word on the remaining 250 pages of the manuscript? It is likely (as we shall see) that C's exemplar did not contain various minor parts of *AP* (i, iii, and viii, for example), but this did not stop him reading through the text and jotting down the odd conjecture in the margin. Even if his exemplar did give out at ix. 562, it would be surprising if he had not read on in *AP* at least to 583, the end of the epideictica. And especially if his own exemplar was defective one might have expected him to read through to the end of Cephalas' Anthology out of interest alone. If he had done this, he would certainly have left his mark in the margin.

I propose a different explanation of C's sudden silence. When complete with the now missing 112 pages of Nonnus, *AP* would have been a fairly bulky volume of 818 pages. It is bound in two volumes today[15] and might well have been so bound by J. If he had thought to do so, the point at which the thicker parchment used by the B scribes began would have been a very suitable point to make the division. We have already seen that the A and B blocks were probably written simultaneously, and if (as J's note about the duplication of the Gregorian epigraphia on p. 691 suggests) the B block was already bound up while the A block was still being written (Ch. X), then naturally it would follow that the manuscript was divided into two volumes at this point. And there is another consideration. At the bottom of p. 452, underneath ix. 562, J wrote ζήτει Νικίου εἰς τὸ ἔαρ. 'Nikias' poem on spring' is in fact the very next poem (ix. 563), the first poem written on p. 453 by B. I have seen no really satisfactory explanation of this note.[16] Nowhere else

---

[15] The present division is very unequal, pp. 1–614 and 615–709, and probably dates from the seventeenth century: see Preisendanz, col. viii, and Waltz, Budé i, p. xxxix. There is no reason to suppose that it is original.

[16] According to Irigoin (p. 287), J's purpose was simply to ensure that the binder assembled the quaternions in the correct order.

does any scribe of *AP* use such a device to link quaternions. Indeed, the catchword (for this is what it is) is a device alien to the practice of Byzantine scribes as a whole. But it would be a very natural and sensible way for J to have indicated to future readers (and indeed reminded himself) how a separately bound volume began. If *AP* was divided into two volumes at this point, then it is perfectly possible that, for whatever reason, C had only volume i at his disposal when he had the chance of collating it against Michael Chartophylax. If so, then we have no means of knowing how much further Michael went.

It remains to consider on our other evidence how far beyond ix. 563 Cephalas went. Between 583 and 584, as Basson and Wifstrand have satisfactorily demonstrated, fell a massive lacuna in the source of *AP*.[17] In this lacuna there disappeared perhaps some 450 ecphrastic poems, of which 381 are preserved in *APl*. For reasons to be presented in Ch. X there can be little doubt that these poems stood in Cephalas.

On the basis of J's remark that Cephalas distributed Meleager's *Garland* into separate categories of erotica, anathematica, epitumbia, and epideictica, it has sometimes been claimed that these were the *only* Cephalan books, and that *AP* i–iv, viii, and x–xv are all post-Cephalan. But (*a*) J did not need to enumerate all the Cephalan categories to make his point; (*b*) he was writing of Meleager, and Meleagrian poems are in fact largely confined to these four categories; and (*c*) all the Cephalan derivatees we shall be discussing in the pages that follow—*ABV*, L, S, E, Σ'', and both sources of *APl*—contain poems that feature in some or all of x, xi, xii, and xiv.

No one in recent years has seriously doubted that x and xi are Cephalan. Aubreton's claim (p. 66) that xi consisted originally of only 1–22 and 65–242 is wholly arbitrary, and contradicted by the typically Cephalan structure of the book as a whole and (as usual) by the distribution of Planudean omissions (only 55 out of 441).[18] It only remains to add that S has seventeen poems from the book,

---

[17] See pp. 219–20 below.

[18] Aubreton has developed his views on the 'growth' of *AP* xi more fully in his edition (Budé x. 28–39). His analysis of the structure of the book has a certain interest and validity, but there is not the slightest justification for his assumption that the different parts were added by different redactors at different times.

running from 47 to 390,[19] and L also seventeen running from 50 to 432.[20]

Book xii has been more often doubted, unjustifiably, but it will be more convenient to demonstrate its Cephalan origin in connection with the *Sylloge Parisina* (S) in Ch. X below.

Book xiv, a collection of riddles, oracles, and arithmetical problems in rather haphazard combination, seems not to have been considered Cephalan by anyone since Krumbacher—mainly on the curious ground that Planudes took only five. If he had taken *none*, that might indeed have seemed a serious (though not fatal) objection (it should be appreciated that Planudes' categories do not cater for puzzles, riddles, and oracles formally so classified). But if he took any at all, then it makes little difference whether he took only five (as in *API*) or the seventeen (plus two more absent from *AP*) that we now know him to have included in L, his earlier essay of 1280. Since, moreover, there are three of xiv's oracles in E and one oracle and six problems (two of them shared with *API*) in B, both anthologies (as we shall see good reason to believe in the pages that follow) Cephalan derivatees no less than L, *API*, and *AP*, then the onus would seem to rest with those who wish to deny that all five here as elsewhere derive from a common source in Cephalas.

Scholars from Wolters to Lenzinger have attached much importance to the fact that *AP* v–xii are relatively homogeneous in both content and structure. But if Cephalas did take it into his head to have a book of riddles, problems, and oracles, then he was bound to have turned to different sources and, given the nature of the material, arrange it differently. In any case, the compiler of xiv did draw on a number of sources that were in fact used extensively by Cephalas: Diodorus, Diogenes Laertius, Pausanias, Plutarch, and above all Herodotus.[21] As for structure, it is clear that the compiler took some pains, as we have seen Cephalas do in the other books, to avoid too mechanical an arrangement of his various component parts.

There is also another line of approach, curiously neglected in recent research. No one has ever doubted that *AP* v is the first Cephalan book. Between v and vi there is written in the text (that is

---

[19] See p. 218.   [20] See p. 203.
[21] For the sources of xiv see Buffière, Budé xii. 34 f.

to say, *not* a scholion) by the main text scribe A the following introduction to vi:

ἀρχὴ μὲν ἡμῖν (ὥς φησιν) ἡ τῶν ἐρωτικῶν ἐπιγραμμάτων ἔκθεσις γεγένηται, σκοπὸν ἔχουσα τὴν σὴν ἐξάψαι διάνοιαν.

My starting point (as he [Cephalas] says) is the series of erotic epigrams, its purpose to arouse your mind.

The notice goes on to say that, if this purpose has been achieved, the reader is to progress to the anathematica. There is no reason to doubt the common assumption that these notices go back to Cephalas himself.[22] There is an exactly similar first-person introduction to vii (καὶ ὁ τῶν ἀναθεματικῶν ἡμῖν ἐπιγραμμάτων χαρακτὴρ πεπλήρωται ἱκανῶς ἔχων ὡς ἐμαυτὸν πείθω. μετιτέον οὖν . . . ἐπιτυμβίων . . .), against which A, J, and C between them have added in the margin, 'beginning of the epitymbia as set out (ἐσχεδίασεν) by Cephalas'. The implication is clearly that the 'I' of the introductory notice is Cephalas. The interesting idea that erotic poetry will make a good beginning by arousing the reader's enthusiasm for the rest of the book is spelled out more fully in the iambic introductory poem to v:

νέοις ἀνάπτων καρδίας σοφὴν ζέσιν
ἀρχὴν Ἔρωτα τῶν λόγων ποιήσομαι·
πυρσὸν γὰρ οὗτος ἐξανάπτει τοῖς λόγοις.

Once more, the usual assumption (supported by its feeble iambics) that this poem is Cephalas' own introduction to his anthology is surely correct.

There are prose introductions to vi, vii, ix, x, xi (two, one to the sympotic and another to the sceptic portions of the book), and xii. All were transcribed in full and translated into French by Aubreton, who freely acknowledged that they were the original Cephalan prefaces.[23] It is thus the more remarkable that he betrayed no

---

[22] Some doubt would seem to be expressed by Gow, p. 54.

[23] pp. 64–5, insisting that they prove that the author's intention was 'nullement de composer une edition complète des épigrammes', but merely to provide a selection for didactic purposes (that is to say, that Cephalas' anthology was much smaller than *AP*). I cannot see that they prove any such thing. The preface to the sympotic part of xi says that the compiler took τὰ ἐμπεσόντα; Aubreton tendentiously translates 'il ne prend que celles "qui lui tombent sous la main"', commenting 'il ne s'agit donc nullement d'une recherche systématique'. But this is surely to read too much into one phrase, and in any case it should be noted that sympotica *are* by far the smallest category in *AP*, a mere 64 compared with the

knowledge of the exactly similar preface to xiv: γυμνασίας χάριν καὶ ταῦτα τοῖς φιλοπόνοις προτίθημι, ἵνα γνῶς τί μὲν παλαιῶν παῖδες, τί δὲ νέων. The first person προτίθημι (cf. ποιήσομαι, pr. v; ἡμῖν, pr. vi, vii; ὑπέταξα, pr. xi. 1; ἐπιδείξομεν, pr. xi. 2; ἐπεκρυψάμην, pr. xii), the second person address to the reader ἵνα γνῶς (cf. ἐπὶ τὴν τῶν ἀναθεματικῶν ἀναγνώρισιν μετάβηθι, pr. vi; ἵν᾽ οὖν μηδὲ τούτων ἀμοιρῇς, pr. xi. 1; ἔχου τοίνυν τῶν ἑξῆς, pr. xii), the reference to the tastes of the παλαιοί (pr. ix; x; xi. 1; xi. 2), all point to pr. xiv likewise being the product of Cephalas' pen. In addition, we have seen that 'propounding' epigrams γυμνασίας χάριν to the young was how Cephalas used to earn his daily bread (it is the νέοι to whom pr. v is addressed). To judge from his silence, J at least saw no reason to suppose that the subject of pr. xiv was different from the subject of pr. v–xii, and the *onus probandi* must surely rest with those who would identify him otherwise.

AP XIII

AP xiii consists of 31 poems in a variety of metres. The earliest are attributed to Anacreon and Simonides, the latest to Philip, and most belong in the third century BC. Each poem is equipped with a lemma identifying the metre, two of them are examples quoted in the extant epitome of Hephaestion's metrical enchiridion, and some are incomplete, as though quoted merely to illustrate the metre. The collection as a whole is systematically arranged: 1–10, stichic metres; 11–31, strophic or epodic metres; and 11–31 may be further divided into five subcategories.[24]

A century ago P. Wolters suggested that the book was simply a

---

600-odd epideictica and ecphrastica and 748 epitumbia. It would not be surprising if in this preface alone Cephalas had used a phrase which implied a small total. Contrast the preface to vii, remarking that the preceding book has given an 'ample fullness' (πεπλήρωται ἱκανῶς) of anathematica.

[24] G. Morelli, 'Origini e formazione del tredicesimo libro dell'*Antologia Palatina*', *RFIC* 113 (1985), 257–96, at p. 266. This is a full and useful study of *AP* xiii to which I am much indebted. But it is prevented by unquestioning acceptance of Preisendanz's theories on the chronology and sources of *AP* from reaching a true appreciation of the relationship of xiii to the rest of *AP*. If I am not mistaken, Morelli refers to Cephalas only once (p. 293 n. 2), alleging that the poverty of the indirect transmission of *AP* xiii makes it likely that it was 'ignota a Costantino Cefala, e prima ancora alle fonti di Cefala'. But why should it have been unknown to Cephalas yet (apparently) known to his disciples J and C?

series of excerpts from a full text of Hephaestion (or some other such manual), and he has been followed in the recent edition of F. Buffière.[25] Against so crude a formulation is the fact that, if a few poems are incomplete, the majority are clearly not. Indeed, some are surely too long for metrical exempla. What metrician would have quoted in full 7- and 8-line poems in such simple stichic metres as xiii. 7 and 8 when one line of each would have sufficed? Or all eight lines of xiii. 12 or (above all) the twelve lines each of xiii. 19 and 28, when two would have sufficed? Of the two poems (xiii. 9 and 25) quoted in the Hephaestion epitome,[26] the first has only two lines (and is obviously incomplete, as the lemmatist remarks) and the second gives only the first three of the six lines offered by *AP*.[27] We need only conclude that the collection was assembled by a metrician, or with the aid of a metrical treatise.

It has long been taken for granted that Bk xiii is not Cephalan, on the weakest of grounds. Lenzinger was disturbed by the presence of polymetric poems in other books of *AP* (p. 27). If the compiler had been Cephalas (he argued), he would either have put all these other polymetric poems in xiii, or else distributed all the poems from xiii among his other books. Why so? The polymetric poems in the other books he no doubt found in the sources he used for those books. Transferring them to xiii would have required the ability to recognize and identify each metre, an ability (as we shall see) that Cephalas may well not have possessed. If he found the contents of xiii ready assembled in a metrical source, why not leave them together as a metrical book?

Planudes 'übergeht diese Gedichte fast ganz', remarks Beckby (iv². 148), adding that (like Planudes' takings from xiv) they only appear in his addenda. Lenzinger too seems to share this feeling that Planudes' addenda are somehow less significant than the material he took from his first source. Yet no one who has seriously studied Basson's analysis could doubt that Planudes' second source was simply a fuller version of his first, and that both were close kin of, though neither derived from, *AP*. In short, two abbreviated copies of Cephalas. Immediately after the addenda follows Nonnus' Paraphrase of St John, which (as we have seen)

---

[25] *Rhein. Museum* xxxviii (1883), 110; Buffière, Budé xii. 5–6.

[26] Not three, as Buffière claims (p. 4).

[27] In addition, the Palatine lemma to the second describes the metre somewhat differently from Hephaestion (p. 55. 13 f. Consbruch).

originally stood at the beginning of *AP*. It was presumably in this second source that Planudes found his Nonnus, in which case it may have resembled *AP* very closely in content. As with the similar argument raised against xiv, if *none* of the poems in xiii had appeared in *APl*, that might have been a real objection. But Planudes does have two (3 and 29). The absence of the rest from the later Cephalan tradition[28] may adequately be accounted for by the difficulty of the metres and the incomplete and corrupt state of some of the poems.

On the positive side, we may begin by noting two unusual features of the book. First, the metrical lemmata are all copied into the main body of the text, not (as elsewhere) in the margin—all in the hand of the text scribe, here B. This suggests that these explanations were not subsequent additions by a well-informed reader, but part and parcel of the original conception of the book. Lemmatist and anthologist were one.

Secondly, the numeration. There are in *AP* xiii 31 epigrams, numbered systematically by B himself from 1 to 26, while 27 is numbered 29, and 28–31 are not numbered at all. Assuming that B did not just miscount, it looks as if two poems (complete with lemmata) were missing (or deleted) in his exemplar. Furthermore, after 27 there is a lemma ('by Callimachus, the same tetrameter followed by a hendecasyllable'), but no corresponding epigram. If B had till 26 been reproducing the numeration of his exemplar, it is not surprising that he should have discontinued it at the point where it obviously broke down.

There are a good many non-elegiac epigrams scattered through the Cephalan books of *AP*. In particular, no fewer than 51 out of the 748 in *AP* vii. But if they are provided with a metrical lemma at all, whether by C or J, it is usually no more informative than a vague ἰαμβικόν for iambic trimeters. By contrast, the lemmata of xiii invariably use the more precise term τρίμετρον (e.g. xiii. 2, 3, 5, 6, 12, 13, 14, 17, 20, 21, 22, 23, 26, 27, 29). With only three exceptions, poems in epodic or strophic metres are never explained at all, much less equipped with precise, technically worded lemmata like those of *AP* xiii. The three exceptions, all in the hand of C, are the lemmata to *AP* vii. 663, 664, and 728. All three are

---

[28] The quotation of xiii. 29. 2 in Suda s.v. ὕδωρ derives from Photius, Lex. s.v. ὕδωρ, not Cephalas. Photius/Suda offer a quite different text and ascription: see Gow and Page, *HE* ii. 419–20.

written in exactly the same style and terminology as the lemmata of xiii. For example, in both sets of lemmata the standard formula for describing 'X followed by Y' is throughout ἐπὶ X Y. For the formula μιᾷ συλλαβῇ πλεονάζων ('with an extra syllable') in vii. 663, cf. xiii. 25 and 28. Instead of the usual ἰαμβικόν, the lemma to vii. 664 uses the technical term τρίμετρον ἄρτιον,[29] 'regular trimeter' (not catalectic or scazon), as xiii. 21, 22, 23 and 27. More striking still is the description of a *catalectic* trimeter (short by one syllable) as a σκάζον (properly a trimeter with a long in place of the last short) shared by the lemmata to vii. 664 and xiii. 20. Both lemmata also call this same line 'Archilochian'. But it is vii. 728 that provides the decisive link between vii and xiii.

We have seen that there were apparently three polymetric epigrams missing from B's exemplar of *AP* xiii, one of them by Callimachus in tetrameters plus hendecasyllables. Now vii. 728 is, precisely, an epigram by Callimachus in tetrameters plus hendecasyllables; its lemma is *identical* with the one B wrote between xiii. 27 and 28: ἐπὶ τῷ αὐτῷ τετραμέτρῳ ἐνδεκασύλλαβον. It is natural and reasonable to infer that vii. 728 is none other than the missing poem between xiii. 28 and 29—and that it is missing there because it was transferred to vii. 728. For the lemma 'the *same* tetrameter followed by a hendecasyllable' only makes sense after xiii. 28, since xiii. 23–7 are all in metres incorporating tetrameters, while the twenty poems that precede vii. 728 are all in elegiacs. It follows that C's lemma to vii. 728 (and presumably the poem too) was taken from xiii (or rather, as we shall see, the source from which *AP* xiii was compiled).

If vii. 728 is one of the three poems missing from xiii, it seems natural to infer that the two others are vii. 663–4. Both are tetrameter combinations, and their original location in xiii would have been between 26 and 27, both again tetrameter combinations. All three would be welcome additions to xiii, since they are in metres not otherwise represented there.

But if all three were once part of a collection of metrical exempla, vii. 663 and 664 are also both preserved in the corpus of Theocritus' epigrams. It will therefore be necessary to outline here the facts about the treatment of the Theocritean corpus in *AP*. Twenty-two epigrams are transmitted in a fixed sequence in the manuscripts that carry the rest of the Bucolic poems. All of these

---

[29] Cf. Hephaestion 5. 1 (p. 15. 20 Cons.); for συλλαβῇ πλεονάζειν, ibid., p. 289. 16.

epigrams plus five more appear in *AP*, but (as Gow put it): 'though it can hardly be doubted that a text of the Theocritean collection not widely different from that of [the Bucolic] MSS contributed to the formation of *AP*, the use there made of it presents problems which appear to be insoluble'.[30] A list of the Theocritean epigrams in *AP* together with their position in the Bucolic sequence is given in Table A. It will be seen that there are some small groups that

TABLE A

Buc	*AP*	Buc	*AP*	Buc	*AP*
2	vi. 177	7	vii. 569	5	ix. 433
1	vi. 336	9	vii. 660		+ 13.3–6
8	vi. 337	11	vii. 661	(27)	ix. 434
10	vi. 338	16	vii. 662	14	ix. 435
12	vi. 339	20	vii. 663	(24)	ix. 436
13	vi. 340.1–2	21	vii. 664	4.1–6	ix. 437
(23)	vii. 262	(26)	ix. 205	22	ix. 598
(25)	vii. 534.1–6	3	ix. 338	17	ix. 599
15	vii. 658	6	ix. 432	18	ix. 600
		4.7–12	[ix. 437][a]	19	xiii. 3
		4.13–18	[ix. 437]		

[a] The 18 lines of Ep. 4 are divided into three parts in *AP*: lines 1–6 stand after ix. 436; 7–12 and 13–18 between 432 and 433, with separate ascriptions and lemmata as if two separate poems. Modern editions print all 18 lines in sequence as vii. 437. Ep. 13 was also split into two, with lines 3–6 mistakenly attached to ix. 433. Theocritean epigrams added to the bucolic sequence by *AP* are shown in brackets. For the purposes of this table I have not indicated *AP*'s ascription of vii. 658–63 to Leonidas, which is surely no more than a mechanical corruption that arose during or after the compilation of Cephalas' funerary book (Gow and Page, *HE* ii. 525).

preserve the bucolic sequence with little or no dislocation (vi. 336–40; vii. 658–64; ix. 598–600), while one group is more seriously disturbed, with one long poem divided into three, all out of sequence, not to mention an intruder from another source (ix. 432–7). There are also several poems scattered singly throughout Bks vi, vii, ix, and xiii.[31]

[30] *Theocritus*, ii (1950), 525.
[31] R. J. Smutny, *The Text History of the Epigrams of Theocritus* (Univ. Cal. Publ. in Class. Phil. 15. 2; 1955), 63 f.; see too C. Gallavotti, *Boll. Class. Lincei*, 3rd ser., vii (1986), 101–23.

Against the widespread modern view (most recently stated by
Beckby) that *AP* xiii is an original compilation of the 'redactor of
AP', Morelli has already pointed to the numerous errors in the
metrical lemmata, banal copying errors imposing the conclusion
that, in its present form, the book is a *copy*, not an original
composition. The confusion in the numeration points in the same
direction. And who is meant by the 'redactor of *AP*'? B is merely a
text scribe. It is undoubtedly J who is the redactor of the collection
as a whole, and yet there is no trace of his hand in *AP* xiii, not even
to correct the most obvious errors. Clearly J had nothing of his
own to contribute to B's far from competent transcription of *AP*
xiii. It follows that the book goes back at any rate to the common
exemplar of B and J.

That it was Cephalas himself rather than a later redactor of his
anthology who inserted the Theocritean epigrams into their present places in *AP* is proved (*a*) by the fact that five appear in
Planudes[32] and one in the Suda; and (*b*) by the corrections and
marginalia appended by C (not least the metrical lemmata to vii.
663–4), taken (as we have seen) from the copy of Michael Chartophylax, a direct copy of Cephalas' autograph. Why Cephalas
should have treated the bucolic sequence in this rather inconsequential way is certainly a puzzle, but the facts speak for themselves.

Yet there is one fact that has not so far been adequately
exploited. All but one of the epigrams from the bucolic sequence
appear in one or another of the main Cephalan books of *AP*,
including vii. 663–4. The one exception is *Ep.* 19, which appears as
xiii. 3. Moreover, this is one of the two poems in xiii that reappear
in Planudes, with readings that agree with *AP* as against the
bucolic manuscripts. On the criteria established in the preceding
chapters, there is a strong presumption that xiii. 3 stood in
Cephalas.

So there is after all a clear link between *AP* xiii and one of the
indisputably Cephalan books of *AP*. That Cephalas himself
actually compiled *AP* xiii seems unlikely, if only because of the
absence of competent metrical lemmata anywhere else in *AP*,
whether in the hands of the text scribes or C or J. It does not look
as if Cephalas had the metrical expertise to write the lemmata of

---

[32] And in vii. 662, Planudes preserves the erroneous ascription to Leonidas that is
best explained as a mechanical error in Cephalas (see p. 141 n. a).

AP xiii himself. And if it was not Cephalas, *a fortiori* it is not likely to have been an earlier Byzantine scholar. It was not for another four centuries, with Planudes and Triclinius, that the Byzantines began to make a serious study of classical Greek metrics. The latest datable writer (conspicuously in first place) is the mid-first-century Philip, and the second century (or not long after) seems the most likely date for the original compilation of the collection.[33]

This original collection included all three Theocritean epigrams.[34] All three were naturally also included in Cephalas' manuscript of the bucolic sequence. We have seen in earlier chapters that Cephalas was careless about duplication; it is C or J who draw attention to the not infrequent duplications in *AP*. But when Cephalas did notice he usually did something about it. This was evidently one such occasion, since these particular epigrams appear only once in *AP*. Since two of them were funerary, Cephalas left them with their Theocritean funerary fellows in a brief sequence in vii (658–64), while the third (also funerary, as it happens) he left in xiii—but deleted from vii.

No other solution can account for all the relevant facts. According to Morelli, it was the scribe B who noticed that vii. 663–4 and 728 had already appeared in vii and so deleted them from xiii.[35] But the text scribes never elsewhere take that sort of editorial initiative,[36] and in any case there is neither evidence nor probability that B was familiar with Book vii, the work of A. It is remotely possible that it was C who transferred the metrical lemma of vii. 728 (though not of course vii. 663–4) from xiii to vii. Against even this minimalist hypothesis is the fact that C seems never to have laid a hand on the part of *AP* that contains xiii, the work of B. And even if C had chanced to look at the end of xiii, the *text* of the three poems and the lemmata to vii. 663–4 are simply not there. Nor can it be C who transferred the poems to vii from the counterpart (if

---

[33] It seems to me a waste of time to speculate (with Morelli, pp. 294–6) about different redactions of this original collection. There is simply no way of telling whether it grew gradually from the hellenistic age or was put together in essentially its present form under the empire.

[34] And no doubt other material now lost or transferred elsewhere in *AP*.

[35] *RFIC* 113 (1985), 279.

[36] Certainly B never elsewhere either deletes or even comments on any of the numerous duplications in *AP*. It is only C and J who pay attention to such matters, and even they normally confine themselves to a δισσῶς in the margin.

there was one) to xiii in his copy of Michael, because the *text* of all three as written in *AP* is due to A; C wrote only the lemmata. And while it is conceivable that C got at any rate his lemmata from Michael's Book xiii (assuming that it still contained all three poems),[37] that would still not explain why B (who wrote before C) came to omit the same three poems from *AP* xiii.

The only satisfactory explanation is that it was Cephalas himself, working with a bucolic manuscript and his metrical source, who noticed when putting together his own metrical book that he now had four duplications: three Theocritean epigrams and one by Callimachus that he had already included in his funerary book. With that editorial whimsy that characterizes his entire anthology, Cephalas left three of the four where he had first put them, adding the detailed metrical descriptions offered by his metrical source—and no doubt one or two variant readings too. But the fourth, xiii. 3, he deleted from his funerary book, letting it stand in his metrical book. Since the Palatine text of xiii. 3 differs in several details from the bucolic text, it may be that here too he incorporated textual variants.[38] If he had a reason at all, it may be that, poor metrician though he was, Cephalas could at least recognize that xiii. 3 was the only choliambic poem in the book, while vii. 663–4 and 728 were but three among many (to Cephalas) baffling tetrameter combinations, more dispensable (in his eyes) than so common a metre as choliambics from a metrical book.

There is no moralizing prose preface to xiii, but this might be explained by the technical rather than moral purpose a metrical book was intended to serve. In any case, if xii and xiv are Cephalan, its position alone strongly suggests that xiii is too. The considerations advanced here surely turn that presumption into something approaching certainty.

The decisive break comes after xiv. There can be no question of xv being Cephalan, as we shall see in Ch. XV. Arguments of

[37] If (as I believe) the transference of the poems to vii had already been made by Cephalas, they will *not* in fact still have been in Michael's counterpart to *AP* xiii.

[38] I have had to leave on one side the large question whether Cephalas himself included textual variants. It is naturally difficult to determine whether any given correction or marginal variant by C reflects (*a*) a transmitted variant; (*b*) C's own conjecture; (*c*) Michael Chartophylax's conjecture; or (*d*) C's correction against the Cephalan text of an error by A, B or J. But a careful and exhaustive study might well repay the effort. Linked to this is the question whether (or how often) Cephalas used more than one text of his (presumably majuscule) sources; see Ch. II, end, for the hypothesis that he used two different exemplars of both *Garlands*.

content and chronology aside, xv does not (as printed editions imply) immediately follow xiv in *AP*. It is separated by the two books and 732 lines of John of Gaza's ecphrasis on the world map in the winter bath of Gaza.

If we put traditional preconceptions to one side and attend instead to the internal arguments here assembled, Cephalas' Anthology would appear to have consisted of *AP* v–xiv. But that is not quite the end of the matter.

AP VIII

First there is *AP* viii, the 260-odd epitaphs by Gregory Nazianzen that follow on after *AP* vii (not counted as a separate book until Jacobs). I would suggest the following five arguments in favour of the long felt suspicion that these poems are not Cephalan:

1. Though classicizing in both style and metre, they constitute a massive and homogeneous block of Christian intruders in the middle of an otherwise secular anthology.

2. Such a long, unbroken sequence of poems on so few themes by one author nowhere else represented would be without parallel in the Cephalan books of *AP*.

3. In view of their number, their complete absence from both *APl* and the minor *syllogae* must be held significant.

4. As we have seen (Ch. V), it is clear from the fact that J unwittingly repeated a selection from these same Gregorian epitaphs himself in the course of his supplement to Cephalas on pp. 695 f., that he had not expected to find any in Cephalas.

5. Though C apparently read these pages and added the odd inconsequential touch here and there, there are no ὧδε marks and no corrections of the substance, calibre, and frequency we encounter on most pages of the preceding and following books. In particular the text-scribe A left 4 lacunae: the whole of viii. 57. 4, all but the first word each of 160. 2 and 3, and the end of 190. 4. The text is not in doubt, since the poems appear in several manuscripts containing the works of Gregory. It is not surprising that J could not repair the gaps; but it would be surprising if C's exemplar had not only offered no better readings in more than 1,000 lines of poetry, but also contained the same lacunae or illegible lines as the common source of A and J.

The conclusion seems almost inescapable that C's exemplar, Michael Chartophylax's copy of Cephalas, went straight from epitymbia (*AP* vii) to epideictica (*AP* ix), with no counterpart to *AP* viii.

But if the Gregorian epitaphs were absent from Cephalas, *AP* was not the first Cephalan redaction in which they appeared. This much is clear from J's evident surprise that his own plan of adding a Gregorian appendix had been anticipated by *AP* viii. Then there is A's note μέρος τι τῶν ἐπιτυμβίων ἐπιγραμμάτων, 'part of the funerary epigrams', added after the title in the upper margin of the page on which *AP* viii begins. The title itself, ἐκ τῶν ἐπῶν τοῦ ἁγίου Γρηγορίου τοῦ Θεολόγου, 'Selections from the poems of the holy Gregory the Theologian', repeated by J above the first poem, presents no problems. But the note 'part of the funerary epigrams' is in no sense a part of this title, but a warning that, despite the comprehensive new title, the poems that follow are not to be considered a new book. It is an editorial note such as we might have expected from J or C, but not from a mere copyist like A— unless he did merely copy it from or at any rate follow some indication in his exemplar. I suggest that it was the compiler of this exemplar who first inserted the Gregorian epitaphs into the Cephalan tradition. And in support I draw attention to the fact that the Gregoriana in *AP* run from p. 326. 11 to p. 358. 2, thirty-two pages all but nine lines; that is to say the equivalent of two quaternions all but nine lines. It is hardly audacious to conjecture that in this exemplar they filled *exactly* two quaternions. I suggest, in fact, that its compiler, having decided to add some Gregory, copied or had copied a *selection* (the title makes clear that only a selection was intended) that filled two quaternions, which he then inserted into his copy of Cephalas with a note to inform the next copyist (or perhaps his own binder) that this extra material was to form 'part of the funerary epigrams'. These instructions were faithfully followed (and reproduced) by A. By way of parallel we might compare another part of J's appendix to *AP*, the *Anacreontea* (pp. 679–90), presumably another selection, unless it was by coincidence that they fill exactly one quaternion. Less prudent, however, than the compiler of the original of *AP* viii, J gave no instructions whereabouts in his appendix the *Anacreontea* were to be placed, and as we shall see (p. 299 below), they were apparently bound up in the completed codex one quaternion too early.

There remain *AP* i–iv. The fact that they precede Cephalas' introduction and the first book would seem to be strongly against them, not to mention the absence of i, iii, and iv from *APl*. But ii, Christodorus of Coptus' ecphrasis of the statues in the Zeuxippus at Constantinople, is an altogether different matter. Planudes incorporated it whole as his Book v. Nor could he have derived it from *AP*, since the *AP* version lacks eight obviously authentic lines (61–4, 222–4, 380) present in *APl*. Now in addition to Christodorus' poem *AP* contains three more early Byzantine ecphraseis, Paul the Silentiary on Hagia Sophia and its ambo and the poem of John of Gaza just mentioned. The two poems by Paul fall in the part of the manuscript corrected by C, and since he left them unattended we may fairly presume that they were not in Michael Chartophylax. Christodorus, however, manifestly has been corrected against a more accurate exemplar.[39]

First, six relatively minor (though certain) corrections at 14, 70, 91, 106, 190, and 239 which need not be quoted. Then there is the alteration of the standard form Φθιώτης at 202 into the (according to *LSJ*) unparalleled Φθιώτιος and the addition of a necessary δὲ in 13 and 244. And finally the addition of the certain supplement χρύσεια in the defective line 137:

μῆλα λεοντοφόνῳ παλάμῃ <   > κομίζων.

That none of these corrections are C's own conjectures is proved by the decisive fact that in every single case the same reading is to be found in Planudes.

It follows that Christodorus' ecphrasis stood in C's exemplar. Now it is always possible either that C did not get it from Michael or that Michael did not get it from Cephalas, but the natural presumption is that both C and Michael were using the only sources we know them to have used and so that Christodorus was already in Cephalas. Such a conclusion is strongly supported by the appearance of the poem in *APl*.

Was it then (as Planudes seems to have thought) actually a part of Cephalas' anthology? It is true that it is more a series of ecphrastic epigrams on the individual statues of the Zeuxippus than a continuous ecphrasis, but it would still be surprising if Cephalas had formally so treated the poem, quite apart from its

[39] Not even Lenzinger (p. 2) seems to have perceived this decisive fact.

location *before* Cephalas' Book i in *AP*. The answer may lie in the difference between the Byzantine and modern book. Cephalas' anthology need not have been the *only* work in its codex—as indeed it is not in *AP*. It is possible, likely even, that other associated texts both preceded and followed it in his manuscript. Nonnus' paraphrase of St John, found in both *AP* and (probably) Planudes' second source, may have been one such text. Paul the Silentiary and John of Gaza are certainly post-Cephalan additions (perhaps by J himself) to the corpus, no doubt on the analogy of Christodorus' ecphrasis, but Christodorus himself may well have stood already in Cephalas' manuscript.

What then of i, iii, and iv? They are clearly not parts of Cephalas' anthology proper. Their absence from *APl*, the all but complete absence of corrections from C, and their position in *AP* are decisive here. It remains possible none the less that they formed part of his manuscript.

AP iii is a collection of 19 epigrams from a temple in Cyzicus, of very low quality and very corrupt. There is a marked (and understandable) tendency in the Cephalan tradition for corrupt poems to be omitted. *AP* i consists of Christian epigrams, a valuable collection but not necessarily of interest to an enthusiast for *classical* epigrams. *AP* iv contains only the prefaces of Meleager, Philip, and Agathias, the first two being little but lists of the names of the contributors to the two *Garlands*. Once more, of no great interest as specimens of the classical epigram.

Concerning iii, we do not know when either the epigrams or the unusually informative lemmata were written or when the collection was put together. The temple was erected in honour of Queen Apollonis of Pergamum between 175 and 159 BC, but the epigrams, which describe the bas-reliefs on the columns in the temple, were apparently added much later, perhaps five or six hundred years later.[40] Only two relevant points can be made: (*a*) the corrupt state of the epigrams and above all the fact that no. 17 is almost entirely missing proves that they were at any rate not put together by the Palatine scribes; and (*b*) the only person we know to have copied epigrams from monuments in Cyzicus (cf. *AP* vii. 334) is Gregory Magister. If it was Gregory who copied *AP* iii and perhaps also

---

[40] H. Van Looy and K. Demoen, *Epigraphica Anatolica* viii (1986), 133–42; K. Demoen, *L'Ant. class.* lviii (1988), 231–48.

wrote the lemmata, then obviously the book might well have been included in Cephalas' manuscript.

As for iv, the only person of the age we know to have studied the two *Garlands* and the *Cycle* at first hand is Cephalas; he must have embodied all three in his own collection virtually complete. The prefaces are not really epigrams and certainly did not fit any of his categories, but it must have seemed a pity just to omit three documents of such interest and importance for anyone (like Cephalas) concerned with the work of the writers there listed. It is easy to believe that he solved his problem by placing them together before, and therefore strictly outside, his anthology to serve as a sort of informal extra introduction. But precisely because it was not a formal part of the anthology, it is no less easy to see why others may have left it out. I personally find it rather harder to imagine some later figure conducting a fresh first-hand study of the *Garlands* and *Cycle* to excerpt the prefaces when the massive recent efforts of Cephalas would seem to have made such a task so unnecessary. It was not in the style of Byzantine scholarship to duplicate such projects.

Then there is the consideration that an anonymous epigram written in the reign of Leo VI (886–912) contains a clear echo of Agathias' preface. The epigram is one of three that introduce a redaction or epitome of the late fifth-century *Tacticon* of Urbicius. The first (which also appears as *AP* ix. 210) was evidently written for the original edition of the work in the mid 490s. Since these little-known poems[41] are interesting specimens of the revival of hexametric epigram in the age of Cephalas, it will do no harm to set them out here:

A βίβλου τῆσδ᾽ ἐπέεσσι τέον νόον ἔνθεο χαίρων
Αὐσονίων σκηπτοῦχε Λέων, καὶ μίμνεο φρεσσὶ
τάξιν ὅπως πτολέμοιο θέης γλαφυρῆς ἀπὸ τέχνης
καὶ τάχυ βάρβαρα φῦλα τεῆς διὰ χειρὸς ὀλέσσῃς
ὅσσα βόρεια νότου τε ἀλαζονῆας [?-έας] Σαρακηνούς.

Attend gladly to the words of this book, Leo emperor of the Romans, and learn how to arrange a battle line with subtle skill, and how to destroy barbarian tribes swiftly, those from the North and the South and the braggart Saracens.

---

[41] R. Förster, *Hermes* xii (1877), 467 f.; Dain, *RÉB* xxvi (1968), 125.

B Οὐρβίκιος σὺν ταῖσδε βίου δρόμον αἰὲν ὁδεύων
   σημαίνων θ' ἅμα πᾶσιν ὑπερμένεας μετ' ἄνακτας,
   εἰκόνας ἀρχαίων πολέμων ἐκέλευσε γενέσθαι,
   χαλκοτόροις στρατιῇσι σοφὸν μίμημα κυδοιμῶν.

Urbicus travelled through his life always with this < book >, expounding
to all in the company of mighty princes; he bade the images of ancient wars
be revived, a skilful imitation of battles for the bronze-covered hosts.

It is well known that a veritable corpus of military writings[42]
appeared under Leo VI (some of it ascribed to the emperor
himself), and there can be little doubt that he is the Leo addressed.
Nor that (1) and (2) were written at the same time for the same
edition—if indeed they are not to be taken as one long epigram, a
dedication to the reigning emperor followed by an account of the
book dedicated, just like the twelve lines of *AP* ix. 210.

With σοφὸν μίμημα in (2.4) compare now Agathias, *AP* iv. 3.
115–16 (quoted in a fuller context below, p. 157):

καὶ γὰρ ἐῴκει
γράμματος ἀρχαίοιο σοφὸν μίμημα φυλάξαι.

More than just the verbal coincidence is involved. Both writers are
claiming that their own efforts are a 'skilful imitation' of the work
of the masters of old.[43] It is not impossible that our anonymous
armchair tactitian took his reminiscence direct from a copy of the
Cycle, but far more likely that he got it from a more recent and
accessible collection such as the anthology of Cephalas, published,
as we shall see (pp. 245–5), about half-way through the reign of
Leo VI, shortly before 900. It was no doubt from a study of the
material collected by Cephalas that he developed his own (passing
over 1.5) relative fluency in the metre.

AP i (assuming that it is a unity) can be dated within fairly
narrow limits. *AP* i. 1 was inscribed all the way round the face of
the apse semidome in St Sophia; indeed, unknown to editors, the
first three and last nine letters are still to be read there, in dark blue
glass letters 0.40 m. high set in a gold background:

ἃς οἱ πλάνοι καθεῖλον ἐνθάδ' εἰκόνας,
ἄνακτες ἐστήλωσαν εὐσεβεῖς πάλιν.

---

[42] A. Dain, 'Les stratégistes byzantins', *Travaux et mémoires*, ii (1967), 317–92.

[43] The writer evidently took σοφὸν in Agathias with μίμημα and not ἐῴκει, as
suggested by G. Luck, *Gnomon* xxx (1950), 273; cf. Averil Cameron, *Agathias*
(Oxford 1970), 16 n. 4. See too addenda.

It celebrates the restoration of the icons. The unveiling of the mosaic of the Virgin and child to which it specifically refers, the mosaic that still stands in the apse semidome, can be dated precisely by a homily of Photius to 29 March 867. The 'pious emperors' are therefore Basil I and Michael III.[44]

AP i. 109 by Ignatius Magister was clearly written during the joint reign of Basil I and his sons Constantine and Leo, that is to say between 870 and 879.

AP i. 122 is by none other than Michael Chartophylax. All we know of Michael's dates is that he outlived the completion of Cephalas' anthology, though of course this poem might have been written well before then. It evidently commemorates a picture of the Virgin carrying the infant Jesus:

αὕτη τεκοῦσα παρθένος πάλιν μένει·
καὶ μὴ θροηθῇς· ἔστι γὰρ τὸ παιδίον
Θεὸς θελήσας προσλαβέσθαι σαρκίον.

Naturally there must have been countless pictures of the Virgin and child in late ninth- and early tenth-century Constantinople,[45] but after *AP* i. 1 it is tempting to guess that perhaps it was the St Sophia apse mosaic that Michael had in mind.

AP i. 4, 34 (three times) and 99 are quoted in the Suda, which took its epigrams from a near twin of *AP*, a twin that evidently carried a selection of the same Christian epigrams as *AP* (Ch. XII).

That the book is not as late as the Palatine scribes is proved by the defective state of i. 18, 48, and 99. Of 48 A wrote only a lemma and the traces Ἀδὰμ ἦν ζο before leaving the next line blank; of 18 he wrote a manifestly corrupt lemma and then two disconnected lines with a blank space for four lines between. Evidently his exemplar was defective or illegible, and J could not make good the gaps.[46] Since only about thirty years separate J and Cephalas, the

---

[44] C. Mango and E. J. W. Hawkins, 'The Apse Mosaic of St Sophia in Istanbul: Report on work carried out in 1964', *DOP* xix (1965), 125, 144.

[45] Compare the similar poem by Leo Choirosphactes published by G. Kolias, *Léon Choirosphaktès* (Athens 1939), 131 and the anonymous piece dated to c.900 published by R. Browning, *Byz.* xxxiii (1963), 297.

[46] Most of the headings and lemmata were written by A (except for the pages repaired by J), and where J adds them there is little to suggest that he had another exemplar to hand. For example, the ascription of 90 and 123 to Sophronius is probably (as I shall be arguing elsewhere) no more than a guess (the first wrong), and J may well have known Michael Chartophylax, the author of i. 122. On the interpretation of these epigrams, J. Bauer, JÖB ix (1960), 31–40; x (1961), 31–7.

compiler cannot have been more than a few years either older or younger than Cephalas.

The answer perhaps lies in i. 32–6, a succession of poems on the Archangel Michael, 32 anonymous, 34–6 by Agathias, and 33 by one Neilus Scholasticus (to judge from his title, style, subject matter, and conjunction with Agathias in the sequence *APl* 244–7 a contributor to the *Cycle*). How do these poems come to be in *AP* i?

In a note to 36 J wrote ταῦτα ἐν 'Εφέσῳ γέγραπται ἐν τῷ νάρθηκι τοῦ Θεολόγου, 'This was written in Ephesus, in the narthex of the Theologian', that is to say in the narthex of the church of St John the Theologian, the Evangelist. R. C. McCail has inferred that 'since J knew the inscription's exact location inside the Church of St John, it is overwhelmingly likely that it had been copied *in situ* by Gregory of Campsa or some other collector, and had come thence into the Palatine MS'.[47] 'The locations of the other two Agathian poems', he continues, 'are also preserved by the lemmata, though in less detail, and these poems doubtless entered P in the same way.' This is not a hypothesis to be dismissed out of hand. It is not in itself improbable that the epigraphical material in *AP* i derives from the researches of Gregory. Of the four or five other poems in the book which do not come either from manuscript sources or buildings in Constantinople, three are inscriptions from Ephesus (50, 91, and 95),[48] and a fourth is an inscription from the lintel of a house in that known haunt of Gregory, Cyzicus (103). There is a considerable number of inscriptional poems from Smyrna in *AP* ix and *APl* iv[49] for many of which we are no doubt in Gregory's debt, and when so close he is bound to have visited the church of St John of Ephesus, the goal of countless medieval pilgrims.[50] None the less, there are serious objections to the supposition that i. 32–6 were all chance epigraphic finds made *in situ*.

---

[47] *JHS* lxxxviii (1968), 92–3.

[48] N. Bees, *Arch. Eph.* liv (1953), 266, argues that the entire series *AP* i. 37–89 are inscriptions to mosaics and frescoes in the church of St John at Ephesus—and further ascribes them all to Agathias. There is not the slightest justification for either claim. Some of the epigrams are far below Agathias' stylistic and metrical standards, and the sequence i. 78 f. (and perhaps others) were surely written for illuminated manuscripts.

[49] See Beckby's index nominum (iv². 687–8) s.v. Smyrna.

[50] C. Foss, *Ephesus after Antiquity* (Cambridge 1979), 126; St John himself was believed to have been buried beneath the high altar.

In the first place, the locations given in the lemmata to i. 34 and 35 are not nearly so specific (merely ἐν Πλάτῃ, ἐν τῷ Σωσθενίῳ, districts of Constantinople), and 32 (anon.) and 33 by Neilus are assigned no location at all, though both clearly refer to specific icons of the Archangel. As for 36, the actual title to the poem, as written by the text scribe A, runs as follows: εἰς εἰκόνα Θεοδώρου ἰλλουστρίου καὶ δὶς ἀνθυπάτου, ἐν ᾗ γέγραπται παρὰ τοῦ ἀρχαγγέλου δεχόμενος τὰς ἀξίας ἐν Ἐφέσῳ 'On an icon of Theodore *illustris* and twice proconsul, in which he is painted receiving the insignia of office from the Archangel, in Ephesus'. On McCail's hypothesis, this would reflect Gregory's description of the icon itself, seen *in situ*. But an important recent paper by P. Speck has shown that the icon itself cannot have represented the Archangel actually handing over the insignia of office.[51] In the light of Speck's work, it will be worth reconsidering the poem as a whole. Here is the text, followed by a version that attempts to interpret rather than just to translate Agathias' epigrammatic rhetoric:

Ἴλαθι μορφωθείς, ἀρχάγγελε· σὴ γὰρ ὀπωπή
ἄσκοπος, ἀλλὰ βροτῶν δῶρα πέλουσι τάδε.
ἐκ σέο γὰρ Θεόδωρος ἔχει ζωστῆρα μαγίστρου
καὶ δὶς ἀεθλεύει πρὸς θρόνον ἀνθυπάτων.
τῆς δ' εὐγνωμοσύνης μάρτυς γραφίς· ὑμετέρην γὰρ
χρώμασι μιμηλὴν ἀντετύπωσε χάριν.

Archangel, be gracious, shown as you are here in mortal form. Your appearance cannot be seen by us, but these are gifts from mortals. It is because of you that Theodorus has won the insignia of the master of offices and twice held the judicial seat of proconsul. The painting bears witness to his gratitude. He has depicted your grace in colours that reflect its nature.[52]

There would be no parallel in the art of the age for a painting that showed an angel investing a human being with the insignia of office. The second couplet implies nothing more than that Theodorus owes his office to the Archangel. To Speck's arguments we can add that line 4 attributes the two proconsulates to the Archangel no less than the mastership of the offices. Obviously the

---

[51] 'Ein Bild des Erzengels Michael in Ephesos', *Poikilia Byzantina* vi (Freie Universität Berlin: Byz.-neugriech. Seminar; Bonn 1987), 357–62.

[52] Mango translates: 'By means of colours he has faithfully reproduced thy favour' (*Art of the Byzantine Empire: 312–1453* [1972], 118, but this gives a very flat conclusion to the poem. The point is surely that the brilliance of the colours gives mortal men some sense of the essence of the Archangel; so Speck, p. 359.

painting would not have shown the Archangel giving Theodorus the insignia of two earlier offices as well as his current rank. It represented the Archangel alone: no Theodorus, no investiture. But by the tenth century there were parallels for such investitures, and Cephalas seems so to have misunderstood Agathias' original lemma, which must have run somewhat as follows: 'on a picture dedicated by Theodorus, when he received the insignia . . .' That is to say, the lemma in *AP* did not derive from autopsy in Ephesus. Indeed, it matches exactly the style of the lemmata to 34 and 35 — as indeed the lemmata to scores of indisputable *Cycle* epigrams, which give similar details about subject and provenance in similar fashion. For example, ix. 642 Agathias, εἰς . . . ἐν Σμύρνῃ; ix. 648 by Macedonius, εἰς . . . ἐν Κιβύρᾳ; ix. 668 by Marianus, εἰς . . . ἐν Ἀμασείᾳ. Compare too the lemma to the only other poem we have by Neilus, in a section of *Cycle* poems about statues or pictures of Satyrs: εἰς εἰκόνα Σατύρου ἀπὸ ψηφῖδος [in mosaic] ἐν Ἀντιοχείᾳ. We may surely presume that these lemmata, with their uniformly unspecific references to provenances, are Agathias' own. These lemmata of Agathias are preserved only fitfully in *AP* and *APl* — exactly as in *AP* i. Those to 33–5 are intact, but Neilus' poem has only its ascription, and 32 neither ascription nor lemma. Poems in *AP* i taken directly from monuments are invariably anonymous and usually equipped with more circumstantial details of subject and provenance. Now the information about the narthex of the church of St John has nothing to do with the main lemma to 36. It comes in a quite separate note by J written in the top margin of the following page. I suggest that it derives from another source altogether and has no bearing on the source of the block of archangel epigrams i. 32–6.

We have already seen that the name of the author of an inscriptional epigram is not normally given on the inscription itself. It is true, as McCail observes, that examples do exist, but it is simply incredible that four supposedly chance epigraphic finds from at least three different places devoted to the same subject should all turn out to carry an ascription—three to the same poet and the fourth to one of the contributors to an anthology compiled by that poet. It remains only to add that Agathias' poem i. 34 is surely an expansion of the brief but striking 33 by Neilus:[53]

[53] For some interesting remarks on these poems see E. Kitzinger, *DOP* viii (1954), 139, and R. C. McCail, *Byz.* xli (1971), 241 f., with a different argument for the priority of Neilus.

Ὡς θρασὺ μορφῶσαι τὸν ἀσώματον· ἀλλὰ καὶ εἰκὼν
ἐς νοερὴν ἀνάγει μνῆστιν ἐπουρανίων. (Neilos)

How daring it is to picture the incorporeal! But yet the image leads us up
to spiritual recollection of celestial beings.

Ἄσκοπον ἀγγελίαρχον, ἀσώματον εἴδεϊ μορφῆς,
   ἃ μέγα τολμήεις κηρὸς ἀπεπλάσατο·
ἔμπης οὐκ ἀχάριστον, ἐπεὶ βροτὸς εἰκόνα λεύσσων
   θυμὸν ἀπιθύνει κρέσσονι φαντασίῃ·
οὐκέτι δ᾽ ἀλλοπρόσσαλλον ἔχει σέβας, ἀλλ᾽ ἐν ἑαυτῷ
   τὸν τύπον ἐγγράψας ὡς παρεόντα τρέμει·
ὄμματα δ᾽ ὀτρύνουσι βαθὺν νόον· οἶδε δὲ τέχνη
   χρώμασι πορθμεῦσαι τὴν φρενὸς ἱκεσίην. (Agathias)

Greatly daring was the wax that formed the image of the invisible Prince
of the Angels, incorporeal in the essence of his form. But yet it is welcome;
for a man looking at the image directs his mind to a higher contemplation.
No longer has he a confused veneration, but imprinting the image in
himself, he fears him as if he were present. The eyes stir up the depths of
the spirit, and Art can convey by colours the prayers of the soul.

It is surely far more probable that all four—and no doubt the
stylistically similar anonymous 32 as well—were taken from the
Cycle itself, where Agathias (as so often Meleager and Philip
before him) had placed his model in sequence before his own
variation. It remains to account for J's additional information
about the church of St John. Perhaps he got it from Gregory of
Campsa. Or he may have been to Ephesus himself, as is strongly
suggested by his lemma to ix. 58, a poem by Antipater of
Thessalonica on the Artemision at Ephesus: 'On the temple of
Artemis in Ephesus, < saying > that it excelled all sights', after
which he added the more personal reflection, 'But now it is the
most deserted and ill-starred of all, thanks to the grace of Christ
and John the Theologian.' To have made this connection J must
surely himself have gazed upon the ruins of the pagan temple and
noted the reassuring proximity of the church of St John.[54] Note too
J's remark on Leonidas' epitaph vii. 657, νομίζω δ᾽ ὅτι ἐν Ἐφέσῳ
κεῖται ταῦτα, 'I think this is to be found in Ephesus'. Whether or
not this poem of Leonidas was really engraved in Ephesus, the
remark does suggest that J recalled having seen something similar
there himself. When inside the church he naturally examined the

---

[54] The church was in fact built right next to the ruins of the Artemision. See Foss
(op. cit. 9–36) for Justinian's rebuilding of the church, 'the last great public
monument of Ephesus to be built for 800 years'. See too below, p. 327.

mosaics and read the inscriptions. It hardly strains credulity that when reading *AP* years later he should have recalled seeing Agathias' poem and the mosaic it celebrated *in situ* and added what detail he could from memory.

McCail objects that the explicitly Christian character of i. 34–6 'renders them totally different from any other epigram known for certain to be Cyclic'. This is a misleading argument. There is no such explicitly Christian epigram anywhere in the Cephalan books *AP* v–xiv.[55] But this is surely because Cephalas wanted his anthology to be an anthology of *classical* epigrams (in his prefaces he regularly speaks of οἱ παλαιοί, 'the ancients'). If (as I believe) he put such Christian poems as he found in *AP* i, then it is not surprising that there are no *Cycle* poems on archangels in v–xiv.

Agathias lived in an age when savage persecutions of pagans were still a regular occurrence: for example, in 529, 546, 562, and 580. It is expressly recorded that among those denounced, tortured, and imprisoned in 546 was 'a crowd of grammarians, sophists, lawyers, and physicians'—precisely the professional circles in which Agathias moved.[56] In 562 pagan books were burned; in 580 it was the accused pagans themselves who were consigned to the flames or to wild beasts. These were not risks to be run lightly. And what better handle to offer the accusation of paganism than to publish a book of purely pagan poetry?[57] Surely it would have been prudent for Agathias to go out of his way to include a certain number of Christian poems (especially from the editor's own pen), suitably insulated from any blasphemous proximity to pagan dedications or erotic material. Note the cautious and apologetic tone of Agathias' own account of his first book, the anathematica (*AP* iv. 3. 113–16):

πρῶτα δέ σοι λέξαιμι, παλαιγενέεσσιν ἐρίζων
ὅσσαπερ ἐγράψαντο νέης γενετῆρες ἀοιδῆς

---

[55] Though there are of course many classicizing epigrams by Christian authors which incidentally betray their author's religion (e.g. ix. 615). The only poems in v–xiv that would have been more at home in i are ix. 817–19, three sets of Byzantine dodecasyllables on Christian religious objects (studied by P. Waltz in *RÉG* lviii (1945), 105–17, perhaps (since they occur at the very end of the book and are absent from *APl*) post-Cephalan accretions.

[56] P. Chuvin, *Chronicle of the Last Pagans* (Cambridge, Mass., 1990), 143–7; G. W. Bowersock, *Hellenism in Late Antiquity* (Ann Arbor, Mich., 1990), 1 f.

[57] For the long-standing connection between classicizing poetry and paganism see *Historia* xiv (1965), 471 f.

ὡς προτέροις μακάρεσσιν ἀνειμένα· καὶ γὰρ ἐῴκει
γράμματος ἀρχαίοιο σοφὸν μίμημα φυλάξαι.

I will first select for you, competing with the men of olden times all that
the fathers of the new song wrote *as though offered to the old gods.* For it
seemed suitable to preserve a skilful imitation of the classical style.

It was naturally the dedications 'to the old gods' that were most
likely to lend colour to any suspicions about Agathias' religious
views; there is no implication that this apology is meant to apply to
the other books. Strictly speaking, i. 35 is a dedication to the
Archangel, though we may doubt whether Agathias put it in his
Book i. In all probability he put all five poems on the Archangel
together in some suitable part of his ecphrastic book, whence they
were extracted (? by Cephalas) and inserted into *AP* i.

We may compare the rather cruder precautions taken by J
(surely his own rather than copied from his exemplar); living in an
age when paganism proper had been dead for centuries he still felt
it prudent to place his Christian epigrams in front of the other
books, all inevitably more or less pagan in character, prefaced by
the following heading: τὰ τῶν Χριστιανῶν προτετάχθω εὐσεβῆ τε καὶ
θεῖα ἐπιγράμματα, κἂν οἱ Ἕλληνες ἀπαρέσκωνται, 'Let the pious and
godly Christian epigrams come first—even if the pagans are upset!'
Nor were such precautions superfluous even at this date. J's
slightly older contemporary Arethas was twice formally indicted
for impiety on the strength of his interest in classical writers
(*Scripta minora* ii, pp. 49 f. and 108 f. Westerink). Arethas in turn
attacked the poet, philosopher, and diplomat Leo Choirosphactes
inter alia for his devotion to pagan philosophy (ibid. i, p. 212). A
generation or so earlier Leo the mathematician was accused of
'hellenism', and in a later chapter we shall be examining the
attempts of one of his former pupils to defend himself against the
same accusation (Ch. X). Like Arethas in his Lucian, J periodically
fills the margins of *AP* with anti-pagan invectives (Ch. XV). Such
abuse, as Westerink has recently remarked, 'besides relieving the
critic's ambivalent emotions, had the twofold practical advantage
of protecting both the owner and the book. The owner, if accused
of too much interest in pernicious literature, would find it useful to
have a written record of his better judgement.'[58] Books, being rare
and expensive items, were frequently lent, and in so small a society

[58] L. G. Westerink, *Byzantion* xlii (1972), 201.

so ridden with feuds and intrigues, it was wise for a man to protect himself.

Agathias no more wanted to be taken for a 'hellene' than J or Arethas. Even at a purely literary level, such fine poems as i. 33–4 (quoted above) provide an excellent illustration of the transformation of the ancient genre of epigram to the needs of the new religion—and so, incidentally, a justification of the practice.

There was another pressing reason for the inclusion of at any rate i. 34 in the *Cycle*. Its subject can be certainly identified: Theodore, son of Peter the patrician, promoted to the mastership of the offices held by his father before him in 566[59] only a year before the publication of the *Cycle*. Agathias' poem describes a mosaic representation of this promotion. Naturally mention is made of the role there attributed to the Archangel, but in other respects the poem is simply a glorification of Theodore, very similar to *APl* 37 on Peter Barsymes. I can see no possible literary or religious objection strong enough to outweigh the offence likely to be given to probably the most important man Agathias knew by its omission.

If 32–6 come from the *Cycle*, then naturally the probability is high that they were excerpted thence by Cephalas. Not only because of his known familiarity with the *Cycle*, but also because, if *AP* i is a separate later effort by another, it is difficult to see why Cephalas did not put them together with their fellows among his ecphrastica. Doubtless aided by his colleague Gregory he is bound to have turned up a fair number of Christian epigrams in the course of his research. For example, epigrams from the monuments of Constantinople and on ancient books are both well represented in *AP* ix, epigrams from the *churches* of Constantinople and on *Christian* books are to be found in *AP* i: the material was presumably all collected together. Cephalas judged that Christian poems did not fit either the categories or the ethos he had planned for his anthology proper, so he put them together in a separate book.

I suggest, then, that we need not think of Cephalas' epigrammatic activity in terms of one clearly defined anthology of which some Palatine books form part while others do not. It was a corpus rather,

[59] *JHS* lxxxvi (1966), 22–3; Averil Cameron, *Corippus, In laudem Iustini minoris* (London 1976), 128.

a corpus which (for all we know) may originally have been larger still. *AP* iii perhaps, and viii probably may be post-Cephalan additions, but I can see no arguments against supposing i, ii and iv Cephalan (in this wide sense) as good as those for.

H. Hunger, assuming the old date of *c*.980 for *AP*, has recently argued that J added the Christian epigrams and early Byzantine ecphraseis 'in order to provide a contrast' to Cephalas and 'shift the weight within the structure of the collection by relying more on Byzantine antiquity, i.e. the 5th and 6th centuries, instead of the purely pagan past of the "wreaths" from Antiquity'.[60] With Hunger's general point that the Byzantines felt closer to late Antiquity than to pagan Antiquity I have no quarrel, but there is no real basis for supposing that *AP* is significantly more Christian or Byzantine than Cephalas.

Hunger refers to the 'hundreds of Christian epigrams ... in books i, ii, and viii'. There are (of course) no Christian epigrams in book ii, a late antique ecphrasis of statues from classical myth and history already present in Michael's exemplar and, like i, perhaps also in Cephalas. Book viii was also in at any rate *AP*'s source. As for the late antique material J added, Agathias' *Cycle* and a substantial selection of early Byzantine inscriptional epigrams were already an integral part of Cephalas. And while Paul's two ecphraseis treat Christian themes, John of Gaza's does not; indeed it opens by invoking the Sirens and Apollo. Hunger has also forgotten that the other text we can be reasonably sure J himself added to the tradition was the purely pagan *Anacreontea*. Finally, the collective ministrations of J and C reveal a desire to make as full and accurate a copy as possible of Cephalas. We have seen how deeply both admired him as a man and teacher, and there is certainly no sign that they did not share his enthusiasm for classical epigram.

---

[60] *17th International Byzantine Congress Major Papers* (New York 1986), 518–19.

VII

The *Syllogae Minores*

THERE is a sense in which Aubreton's attempt to dethrone Cephalas from his central position in the Byzantine epigram tradition is neither radical nor even original. For he is quite happy to allow that all the anthologies under discussion derive from an anonymous earlier collection which he calls simply 'Anthologie perdue Xs'. That is to say, for a lost source we know to have existed he has substituted another, hypothetical source. This was in fact the common assumption before Basson's epoch-making Berlin dissertation of 1917. Schneidewin, for example, discussing S in 1855 and Dilthey E in 1887, struck by the close parallelism of arrangement between their respective collections and *AP*/*APl*, both postulated a lost common source. 'Habemus', wrote Wolters of the *syllogae minores* in 1882, 'vestigia luculenta vastae cuiusdam epigrammatum conlectionis, unde et Cephalas et alii sua epigrammata deprompserunt.'

The difference is that Aubreton is less concerned than his German predecessors (to whose authority he makes no appeal) to stress the dominance of this 'vasta collectio' in the whole subsequent Byzantine epigram tradition. This is in part because he believes *AP* to be the product of fresh research continuing into the eleventh century, but also because he seems to attribute less importance than his predecessors to coincidence of content and parallelism of arrangement between the various collections. This point is never explicitly made, but in practice (for example in his discussions of S and E) Aubreton pays little attention to such considerations. He emphasizes instead the 'leçons personnelles' peculiar to individual *syllogae*, proof (he imagines) of their relative independence.

It must be said at once that this is a criterion which Aubreton systematically misuses. Idiosyncratic readings do *not* in themselves prove independence; what matters is whether they are true or false.

Shared false readings are prima-facie proof of dependence, idio-syncratic true readings of independence. Shared true readings and idiosyncratic false readings are proof of nothing but a good or bad scribe.

Take Σ, which Stadtmueller argued (and Basson confirmed) to have been derived from *APl* and therefore of no independent value. Aubreton treats it with great respect, on the ground that it has many 'leçons particulières'. But anyone who takes the trouble to follow up the list will discover that without exception they are either careless errors or futile conjectures. Not a shadow of an idiosyncratic true reading. On the other hand, it shares a great many Planudean readings, true and false alike, that can only be regarded as Planudes' own conjectures, often demonstrably guesses (sometimes intelligent, sometimes misguided) to heal faulty metre (e.g. vii. 44. 4, 489. 3; ix. 26. 10, 116. 2, 504. 10, 576. 2). This is the more striking in that many of the idiosyncratic readings of Σ betray no understanding of metre at all (e.g. vii. 148. 2; ix. 18. 1; *APl* 276. 2, 303. 2–3). With just four exceptions the contents of Σ all appear (as we should expect) in *APl*. Of these four, it has long been recognized that two (ix. 205 and 434) were taken from the Scholia to Theocritus. It can now be added that the other two (ix. 388–9) appear in the margin of the copy of *APl* made by Demetrius Chalcondyles in 1460, Laur. 31. 28, and in several later Planudean apographs. So Σ is not only post-Planudean; it is as much as two centuries later. Indeed, since it only exists in two manuscripts written by the same man at the same place at the same time, Bartolomeo Comparini at Florence in 1493—a scholar who had earlier made another excerpt from *APl* which shows the influence of Laur. 31. 28—there is much to be said for E. Mioni's attractive suggestion that the compiler of Σ was none other than Bartolomeo himself.[1]

By contrast, there is *ABV*, a collection late in itself (post-Planudean) and transmitted in even later manuscripts in a very corrupt state. It has often been dismissed as worthless. In fact, it offers half a dozen readings of such manifest superiority to the text of *AP* (no editor has hesitated to print them) that they must be presumed to derive from a manuscript independent of *AP*—a conclusion that is amply borne out by considerations of content (see Ch. VIII).

[1] Mioni (1975), 278.

Just the opposite is true of L, the earlier anthology made by Planudes and much the largest of the minor *syllogae*. Arguments from content and arrangement prove that its source was not *AP* or (more surprisingly) either of the two manuscripts used by Planudes for *APl*. And contrary to the tendency to agreement with *APl* (Ch. IX) that Aubreton claims to detect in the minor *syllogae*, L's affiliations are all with *AP* rather than *APl*. Like *ABV*, it contains several items absent from both *AP* and *APl* and must be held (like *ABV*) to derive, if only indirectly, from a fuller redaction of Cephalas than *AP*. Textually speaking, however, the manuscript is all but worthless. It is full of new errors, but in 167 epigrams has only one good reading to offer not otherwise known. Since Planudes himself was normally a careful copyist, the only conclusion these errors warrant is that L's source must already have been very carelessly written.

S, E, and Σ'' are all in a similar position. Each has idiosyncratic errors, to be sure, but (*pace* Aubreton) they are no proof of independence. More important, all share a number of errors with *AP/APl* while also offering two or three true readings of their own. S, for example, has superior readings at ix. 363. 4 and xii. 118. 2–3; add xii. 209. 3 and *APl* 197. 1 where Σ'' is at any rate less corrupt than *AP* and allowed Brunck and Meineke respectively to restore the truth. E is better at xiv. 71. 1, 10 and 74. 4; Σ'' at xv. 46. 1, 47. 5, 49. 6, and probably 4. 13 and *APl* 278. 5. Coincidence in error and occasional idiosyncratic true readings are prima-facie pointers to a lost common source. Such a conclusion naturally lends strong support to the hypothesis that all derive from Cephalas. It falls short of proof, however, since it is theoretically possible that the source was earlier than Cephalas and consulted independently by S, E, Σ'', *AP*, *APl*, *and* Cephalas.

Only in the case of the relationship between E and Σ'' are more positive results to be won by this method. Their coincidence throughout, in truth and falsehood alike (note especially ix. 127. 3 and 748. 2), goes a long way to confirm Basson's suggestion on grounds of content and arrangement that Σ'' is in fact an excerpt from a fuller version of E.

In general, however, it is not by study of textual variants that we are going to be able to determine the relationship between the minor *syllogae* and Cephalas. There are three more promising approaches, in combination decisive.

First, sequence of poems. None of the minor *syllogae* follows Palatine order exactly, but Aubreton exaggerates the differences. There are enough coincidences (even in E and Σ^{π}) with the often arbitrary order of *AP* to establish dependence.

Second, the minor *syllogae* all draw on the same range of sources as *AP*—the two *Garlands*, the *Cycle*, Diogenian, Strato, Palladas, a variety of lesser individuals and prose works, and (most telling of all) occasional traces of the epigraphic material privately communicated to Cephalas by Gregory Magister.

Third, it was Cephalas who originated the thematic categories into which *AP* is divided. The equation is explicitly made by his pupil J: Cephalas 'divided between different chapters (κεφάλαια) . . . as in the present book'. Many poems naturally fall into one or another of these categories, but as we saw in Ch. II, there is a persistent pattern of *mis*classification running through the major books of *AP*, ranging from the grotesque (the water clock taken for a tombstone, the *fellatrix* taken for a city) down to the merely eccentric. All the minor *syllogae* (and *APl*) have a certain number of these misclassified poems identically misclassified.

Now if (as Aubreton maintains) the *syllogae minores* are all pre-Cephalan, we should have to conclude that they drew on an earlier source or sources that had anticipated Cephalas in sequence, classification, and first-hand study of exactly the same range of minor authors in an age when they were not in fashion and cannot have been easy of access. Logic and common sense cry out for the application of Occam's razor. The common source we are obliged to postulate can only have been Cephalas.

VIII

The *Appendix Barberino-Vaticana*

THE cumbersomely entitled *Appendix Barberino-Vaticana* (hereafter *ABV*)[1] consists of fifty-four epigrams transmitted in three manuscripts: Vat. gr. 240 (hereafter V) written *c*.1560; Vat. Barb. gr. 123 (hereafter M), copied for Janus Lascaris, the first editor of the Planudean Anthology (1494), between 1504 and 1509, though the pages that carry *ABV* were not (as formerly believed) written in his own hand;[2] and Par. Suppl. gr. 1199 (hereafter K), written on paper datable between 1480 and 1500, an important new witness first published in 1978 by E. Mioni and—independently— R. Aubreton.[3]

All fifty-four epigrams are erotic; almost all are absent from *APl*, and all but two appear in *AP*. There can be little doubt that *ABV* was designed as an erotic appendix to *APl*, an attempt to supply some of the 'many' erotic poems in his source that Planudes, in the preface to Book vii, explicitly states that he omitted *pudoris causa*.

Here is a list of its contents:

1	xi. 108	19	v. 37	37	v. 252
2	xii. 69	20	259	38	246
3	65	21	243	39	289
4	1	22	232	40	272
5	2	23	77	41	242

[1] Elaborately published, with invaluable introduction and commentary, by L. Sternbach (1890).

[2] Anna Meschini (1975), 56–70. Equally mistaken is Sternbach's view (cf. Hutton (1935), 32, 245) that the manuscript was written by Fulvio Orsini, whence (adding in Orsini's reference to A. Colocci discussed later in this chapter) P. Waltz compounded the error by claiming (i. lvi, n. 4): 'Le *Barb.* est de F. Orsini, qui déclare l'avoir copié sur un manuscrit de la bibliothèque d'A. Colocci.'

[3] Mioni, *Miscellanea*, i (1978), 69–79 and Aubreton, *RÉA* lxxx (1978), 228–38. Mioni dubbed the new manuscript S, but since this letter has long been appropriated for the *Sylloge Parisina* (Ch. X), I have used K instead. I have also followed traditional practice in calling Barb. gr. 123 M rather than (as Mioni, giving no reason for the unnecessary change) B. See too the discussion by Gallavotti, *Boll. Class. Lincei*, 3rd ser., iv (1983), 117–23 (who also introduces new sigla).

6	4	24	255	42	294
7	Cento	25	258	43	305
8	xii. 237	26	285	44	xii. 17
9	v. 172	27	275	45	Numenius
10	31	28	xii. 20	46	ix. 361
11	xii. 173	28	77	47	381
12	v. 82	30	75	48	v. 18
13	35	31	76	49	50
14 (= 49a)	60	32	86	49a (= 14)	60 *bis*
15	41	33	196	50	96
16	135	34	59	51	158
17	128	35	79	52	186
18	99	36	v. 244	53	187
				54	71

Fifty-two of these fifty-four epigrams appear in *AP*. Sternbach and Basson[4] argued that V and M were independent copies of a source similar to but not identical with *AP*. But Stadtmueller,[5] followed by Beckby,[6] claimed that M derived from *AP* itself and that V was merely an apograph of M. Aubreton took it as proven that M was the original *ABV*.[7] Even before the discovery of K, this is a hypothesis that could not for one moment have survived a study of the actual text presented by M and V.

To start with, V cannot possibly be a copy of M. To quote only the most conspicuous proofs, M omits twelve words in four lines of *AP* v. 289, all of which are present in V; M omits a whole line of v. 242 present in V; M omits two lines of v. 41 present in V. Secondly, the combination of these omissions and scores of gross miscopyings[8] has reduced entire poems in M to pure gibberish. As Anna Meschini has remarked, one must doubt whether its scribe was even Greek[9] (or knew Greek). It follows that both manuscripts must derive from a common source which the later V reproduced more fully and accurately.

Mioni argues that K is the original, the common (and direct) source of both V and M. K is certainly the most complete and probably the earliest of our three extant manuscripts of *ABV*.

[4] See particularly Basson, 64–70.
[5] *Berl. Phil. Woch.* x (1890), 1391 f.
[6] Beckby i². 83; against, briefly, Gallavotti (1983), 119–20.
[7] *Byz.* xxxix (1969), 50 (a very confused page).
[8] Conveniently listed by Mioni (1978), 72–4.
[9] Meschini (1975), 61.

None the less, it cannot be the sole or direct source of either M or K.

The case for M turns on one word, but when so much of its text is unmetrical, ungrammatical nonsense, the preservation of even one word omitted by K and V is significant. The text of P is as follows (*AP* v. 272. 1–2):

μαζοὺς χερσὶν ἔχω, στόματι στόμα, καὶ περὶ δειρὴν
ἄσχετα λυσσώων βόσκομαι ἀργυφέην . . .

I press her breasts with my hands, her mouth with my mouth, and feed in unrestrained frenzy on her silvery neck . . .

In l. 1 KV offer just στόμα, M just στόματι. That is to say, KV has one half, M the other half of what is obviously the full text. Both omissions destroy the metre, though M's text ('I press your breasts with my hands, with my mouth') makes a sense of sorts, while KV's ('I press your breasts, your mouth, with my hands') does not. Yet who can believe the incompetent scribe of M capable of so improving the text of K, if that had been his source? On the other hand, who can believe that it was nothing more than his usual carelessness that resulted in a miscopying coincidentally identical with one half of the full text of *AP*? The most probable explanation is that M and KV drew on a common source offering the same text as *AP*, of which each omitted half.

There are rather more cases, equally telling, where V offers a better text than K. Mioni remarks, without argument, that the scribe of V 'sembra talora un dotto che interviene a modificare K' (p. 75). Consider first two omissions in K (and M) where V offers the same complete text as *AP*:

> *AP* v. 77. 1   εἶχε PV   om. KM
> *AP* v. 272. 5   ἄρ' PV   om. KM.

Both are easy supplements and the agreement with P *could* be coincidence. But omissions of this sort are very characteristic of *ABV*: for example, xii. 4. 3 (om. τά), 5 (δέ); v. 289. 9 (τόν); v. 272. 6 (μέσσος); 294. 14 (τῆς); xii. 17. 12 (καί); 158. 3 (διόλου). The scribe of V repairs none of these gaps; indeed he adds more of his own: v. 259. 5 (om. μέν); v. 252. 2 (γυίοις), 3 (τό). This is not a man who was in the habit of making supplements *metri gratia*.

Then there is v. 18. 3 (Rufinus), τῇ μὲν γὰρ λείπει σαρκῶν χύσις (of a thin girl), where PV have σαρκῶν, KM σαρκός. The plural has a more literary flavour (*LSJ* s.v.), and given the superior authority of P, editors have never hesitated to print it here. But the singular is common enough too (Rufinus himself uses it at v. 35. 5), and there is no reason why, if presented with σαρκός in K, the scribe of V should have changed it to the plural.

The fact that in almost every other detail V agrees with K, in both truth and error, only proves that both are very careful copies of the common source we are now obliged to postulate, a source which in these three cases V reproduces more accurately than K.

We come now to the reason why Z, our postulated source of *ABV*, cannot have been *AP*. Many of the corruptions and omissions in K, M, and V are doubtless due to the carelessness of successive scribes, but it is fairly clear that even the original was a pretty feeble piece of work. It is therefore the more surprising to discover, sparkling amid the dung, an imposing series of true readings not in *AP*. A certain number *could* be intelligent corrections: for example, δὲ for P's γε at v. 96. 2; ἱμείρω for ἱμειρών at v. 258. 2; κάμνω for κάμνων at v. 272. 3; πάλι for πάλιν at xii. 20. 1; κελεύθου for κέλευθον at v. 275. 3. The all but certain metrical supplements of ἐνὶ in xii. 65. 3 and τὸ in xii. 69. 4 could theoretically be intelligent guesses, and the insertion of οὕτως in v. 82. 1 is perhaps less certain. But we have already noted that unmetrical omissions are more characteristic of *ABV* than metrical supplements; the compiler may well have been quite ignorant of metre.

AP's εἰ δ' ἐπὶ πρεσβυτέρους τις ἔχει πόθον at xii. 4. 7 (Strato) makes tolerable sense, though there appears to be no exact parallel for πόθον ἔχειν ἐπί τινα, and in the preceding list of the pederast's differing reactions to boys of six different age groups from 12 to 17 the reference has always been in the singular, as in the resumptive τὸν δέ in l. 8. It was on grounds of sense and style alone that K. Schwenck made his elegant and generally accepted conjecture ἔτι πρεσβυτέρου, love 'of one even older' (*Rhein. Mus.* NF ii (1843), 464–5). This was before the revelation of *ABV*'s εἰ δ' ἔτι πρεσβυτέρους ζητεῖ πόθον. ζητεῖ (an anticipation of ζητεῖ in l. 8) is *ABV*'s eighth major blunder in the eight lines of this poem, and no sense can be made of the two accusatives. But there is Schwenk's ἔτι, conceivably just a miscopying of ἐπί but certainly not a conjecture. Compare v. 255. 3 (Paul), where for *AP*'s οὐ κόρον εἶχον ἔρωτος ἀφηδέος, *ABV* offers the (in the context) obviously correct ἀφειδέος, 'relentless'. *AP*'s reading is no more than an etacism, to be sure, but even so it is unlikely that *ABV*'s ἀφειδέος is a conjecture. For the text scribe's original *vox nihili* ἀφηδέος had already been neatly emended by the corrector C to ἀφ᾽ ἡδέος, 'sweet' love. Though inferior to ἀφειδέος, this makes quite good enough sense to obviate the need for further conjecture. In both these cases *ABV* surely offers transmitted truth, not conjecture.

And it is surely impossible to believe that it was by conjecture that our anthologist anticipated Salmasius' λευκῇ . . . εὐαφίη for the λευκή . . . εὐαφίην of P and the Suda, still less the same scholar's brilliant πύργος for the πυρί of *AP* and the Suda[10] (contrast the other conjectures—made before the publication of *ABV*—discussed by F. Jacobs, *Animadv. in Anth. Gr.* iii. 1 [vol. xi] (1802), p. 52, rightly following Salmasius). The probability is that most if not all these readings go back to Z.

Now Z, though independent of *AP*, was clearly very close kin. All but two of the poems contained in *ABV* reappear in *AP*, and they are drawn from the same wide and varied range of authors: from Meleager's *Garland*, Asclepiades, Posidippus, Meleager; from Philip's, Antipater of Thessalonica, Marcus Argentarius, and Philodemus; from the *Cycle*, Agathias, Eratosthenes, Macedonius, and Paul; from their own collections, Leonidas, Palladas, Rufinus, and Strato; and such obscure 'loners' as Cillactor, Dionysius the Sophist, Leo the Philosopher, and Numenius of Tarsus. All these poets contributed other epigrams to *AP*, and we can hardly resist the conclusion that all were featured in Cephalas. There is also the evidence of shared false readings, such as the mysterious nonsense word χρονέεσκεν at v. 77. 2 in both *AP* and *ABV*, where Meineke's κόρον ἔσκεν is generally accepted. In *AP* the last line of v. 186 by Posidippus runs as follows: φιλεῖν ἂν ἔφης μεῖζον κεῖνον ἐμοῦ. C made the obvious correction to restore the metre, ἐκεῖνον. *ABV*'s κεῖνον μεῖζον ἐμοῦ points to the same corrupt text, with the words merely shuffled into their more natural order.

Since *ABV* is restricted in scope to erotic poetry, with one or

---

[10] *AP* and the Suda are closely linked (Ch. XII), and presumably both derive from an exemplar where the end of πύργος was illegible. Alan Griffiths remarks that a damaged gamma would be more easily read as iota in an uncial than a minuscule manuscript, that is to say (since Cephalas was surely written in minuscule) implying a pre-Cephalan uncial archetype. Yet it is equally possible that the scribe of the source of *AP* and Suda was confronted with only the traces πυρ and supplied the iota by conjecture.

two minor exceptions, we can only compare it to *AP* v and xii. But this very restriction can have its advantages. As we shall see in Ch. X, it was Cephalas, not some earlier anthologist, who divided this varied erotic material into separate hetero- and homosexual categories. Here we do find an obvious attempt to produce variety by alternating hetero- and homosexual sequences, but there can be little doubt that the excerptor was faced with sequences already divided as in *AP*. And though he did not transcribe his sequences in perfect Palatine order, there are clear traces of that order, modified according to the excerptor's own taste and purpose. For example, nos. 13, 14, and 15, *AP* v. 82, 35, and 60, are thus juxtaposed because all are by Rufinus. And when 14 is repeated as 49*a*, it again appears in a sequence corresponding to the early part of *AP* v (v. 18, 50, 60, 96), again following another poem by Rufinus. Evidently our excerptor excerpted the same sequence in Z twice. Note too that the three 'intruders' from Palatine books other than v and xii (on which see further below) stand separately from the material from v and xii, xi. 108 at the very beginning and ix. 361 and 381 together between sequences from v and xii.

It is the ascriptions in *ABV* that are most helpful for our purpose. First and most obviously, it is clear that, unlike S (for example), and most later anthologies, Z was equipped with ascriptions throughout. Out of 54 epigrams only two lack ascriptions, and one of those (53) because the beginning of the poem is defective. In no fewer than thirty cases the ascription is identical to that of *AP* (in some cases as supplemented or corrected by J), including such freak double ascriptions as Ἀσκληπιάδου ἢ Ποσειδίππου, for 29 and also 44, which is ἄδηλον in *AP* (xii. 17). Gow and Page (*HE* ii. 142) decide that 'despite the idiomatic heading it seems doubtful whether [xii. 17] is by either Asclepiades or Poseidippus'. This may be so—though one wonders whether such doubts would have been expressed if this had been the ascription to *AP*—but it may none the less have been so ascribed in Cephalas. And if it is an error in *ABV*, then it is presumably a mechanical error (though there is no obvious explanation in the context of *AP*).

There are at least two cases of disagreement between *AP* and *ABV* where it is probably *ABV* that is to be preferred. First v. 50, where *ABV*'s ascription to Rufinus (ἀδέσποτον in *AP*), though not free of doubt, seems acceptable. On the other hand the three hexameter lines ascribed to Rufinus in *AP* (ἄδηλον in *ABV*) can hardly be by him, and on this occasion it was probably *AP* where a series of τοῦ αὐτοῦ headings (v. 73–6 are all ascribed to Rufinus) was continued one too far.

Elsewhere, as Page rightly remarks,[11] *ABV* 'comes off badly' in cases of disagreement. It was only to be expected that its compiler would demonstrate his incompetence in the ascriptions no less than in the text of the poems he selected. But two reservations are in order. In the first place, if Z is *not* identified with *AP*, then the thirty-two agreements become more significant. In the second, the erroneous ascriptions are actually a more revealing clue to the nature of Z than the true ones. For example, 10 (*AP* v. 31) is attributed in *ABV* to Cillactor, in *AP* to Antipater of Thessalonica, which (in the light of its pair v. 30) is certainly correct. But v. 29 is ascribed to Cillactor in *AP*. Basson assumes that the compiler of *ABV* carelessly took this ascription for v. 31 instead of that to v. 30. But we shall soon see that Z was less full than *AP*. If 30 had been omitted from Z, and the ascription τοῦ αὐτοῦ of 31 left unaltered, it would have seemed to refer to Cillactor, the ascription of 29. *AP* v. 244, 243, and 246 are ascribed in *AP* to Paul, Macedonius, and Paul respectively; in *ABV* all three are ascribed to Eratosthenes. Once more the same explanation offers; the preceding poem in *AP*, v. 242 (not in *ABV*), *is* ascribed to Eratosthenes. Presumably 243, 244, and 246 had lost their ascriptions in Z and picked up the heading to 242 instead. *ABV* 35 (*AP* xii. 79), ἄδηλον in *AP*, is ascribed to Meleager in *ABV*, perhaps taken from the ascription of *AP* xii. 78 to Meleager (not in *ABV*)— though perhaps it is simply true. *ABV* 43 (*AP* v. 305), ἄδηλον in *AP* and *APl*, is ascribed to Agathias in *ABV*. Once more perhaps from v. 302 (Agathias)—though again (as Sternbach argued) perhaps true. *ABV* 49 (*AP* v. 50) is ἄδηλον in *AP*, Rufinus in *ABV*; once more, *AP* v. 47–8 are by Rufinus. Then there is the ascription of *ABV* 12 (*AP* v. 82) to Dionysius, ἀδέσποτον in *AP*. Not only is *AP* v. 81 (not in *ABV*) given to Dionysius in *AP*; v. 83 (ἀδέσποτον in *AP*, not in *ABV*) is given to Dionysius in *APl*. In all these cases, the false ascriptions in *ABV* (if indeed they are false) may be explained by assuming that *ABV* was excerpted from a fuller sequence of erotic poems arranged in the same order as and (if

---

[11] Page (1978), 22–3, with a useful tabulation of differing ascriptions in *AP* and *ABV*.

perhaps with some omissions) equipped with the same ascriptions as *AP*.

Particularly revealing from two points of view is the case of *ABV* 54 (*AP* v. 71), correctly ascribed in *ABV* to Palladas (cf. *AP* xi. 378. 5). In *AP* the original text-scribe A marked it down with a τοῦ αὐτοῦ to Rufinus, the author of 69 and 70. J erased this and substituted Παλλαδᾶ Ἀλεξ. Then came C, who reinstated A's τοῦ αὐτοῦ and added a οἱ δὲ before J's ascription, thereby nicely demonstrating how a double ascription can arise. This complicated state of affairs is to be explained as follows. We have already seen that J used the same exemplar as A; this (and v. 72, which he also ascribed to Palladas) is the only poem in the whole of *AP* v (or vi, for that matter) for which J was able to correct an attribution provided by A. It was not from their usual joint exemplar that J took his information, but from the separate exemplar of Palladas we know him to have used (Ch. IV, end). C's exemplar, like A and J's, apparently gave only Rufinus' name, but realizing that J must have had some reason for not merely adding but substituting Palladas' name, he left it as an alternative (his οἱ δὲ, in fact, means J). It follows that the exemplars of both J and C illustrate the very error we have been postulating in *ABV*: in both, *AP* v. 71 had already acquired the ascription of its immediate predecessor, while *ABV* for once preserves what must have stood in Cephalas. To judge from C, the first person to make the mistake was Michael Chartophylax, copying direct from Cephalas' autograph, but the copyist responsible for Z did not make it.

So Z preserves at least two or three true ascriptions (and perhaps a few more that might now be taken more seriously) and a series of true readings unknown to either J or C, both younger contemporaries of Cephalas.

We come now to the two poems (not one, as most editors suppose) in *ABV* that are missing from *AP*. First *ABV* 45, ascribed to Numenius:

ἢν ἐσίδω ταύτην, τά γε πάνθ' ὁρῶ· ἂν δὲ τὰ πάντα
βλέψω, τήνδε δὲ μή, τοὔμπαλιν οὐδὲν ὁρῶ.

If I see her, I see all things; but if I see all things and not her, contrariwise I see nothing.

Beckby, the only modern editor of *AP* xii, assumes that this is merely a corrupt version, or rather bowdlerization, of *AP* xii. 60, ascribed (as also by Planudes) to Meleager:

ἢν ἐσίδω θήρωνα, τὰ πάνθ᾽ ὁρῶ· ἢν δὲ τὰ πάντα
βλέψω, τόνδε δὲ μή, τἄμπαλιν οὐδὲν ὁρῶ.

Such editorial bowdlerization would not in itself be incredible, but whence the ascription to Numenius? In *AP*—and, it may be added, elsewhere in Greek literature at large—Numenius is known as the author of only one pederastic poem of two lines, *AP* xii. 28 (left anonymous in *APl*). In *ABV*, however, he is credited with xii. 237 (Strato in *AP*) as well as the poem quoted above. Whether or not either of these ascriptions is correct, the implication is at least that *ABV* derived from a source that did feature erotic poems by Numenius. I suggest that Cephalas included both xii. 60 by Meleager *and* Numenius' feeble heterosexualization of it, and that *AP* and Z took the first and second respectively.

The other new poem in *ABV* consists of seven lines of epic cento, taken mainly from Quintus of Smyrna (i. 235–43) with the odd Homeric tag thrown in:[12]

αἶψα δ᾽ ὅγ᾽ ἀντιθέην κούρην βάλε· τῆς δὲ διαπρὸ
ἦλθε δόρυ στιβαρὸν κατὰ νηδύος, ἐκ δέ οἱ ὦκα
κήκιεν αἷμα μέλαν, φορύνοντό τε δέμνια φίλα·
ἔγχει δ᾽ ὀξυόεντι μεσηγὺ κόρην βάλε μηρῶν
εὔσφυρον, ἀδμῆτιν, διὰ δὲ φλέβας αἱματοέσσας
κέρσε· μέλαν δέ οἱ αἷμα δι᾽ ἕλκεος οὐταμένοιο
ἔβλυσεν ἐσσυμένως, δάμνα δέ ἑ νεύρινον ἔγχος·

Swiftly he pierced the godlike maiden. His stout spear went right through her belly and dark blood gurgled out and her dear bed was stained. With sharp spear he pierced the maid betwixt her thighs, her with the fair ankles, unwed, and cut through her blood-filled veins, and the dark blood bubbled swiftly through the wound that had been dealt, and the sinewy spear brought her low.

Poor stuff—and scarcely a run-of-the-mill erotic poem. But there are two other very similar erotic epic centos in *AP*, ix. 361 and 381—both of which were included in *ABV*. Epigram ix. 361, indeed, appears in *AP*, *ABV*, and E too with the same ascription, to the ninth-century polymath Leo the Philosopher, and the identical lemma, εἰς παρθένον φθαρεῖσαν. In Latin literature Ausonius' *Nuptial Cento* from Vergil (imitated by Luxorius) is notorious, but these three fragments appear to be the only extant

---

[12] See Sternbach's full commentary, pp. 7–11.

examples of erotic cento in Greek.[13] It would thus be a very surprising coincidence if the compiler of *ABV* had happened to find them in two different sources. It seems more reasonable to assume that all three appeared in Cephalas (presumably together among the epideictica) and that one was omitted from *AP*.[14]

So Z contained readings, ascriptions, and poems absent from both *AP* and (so far as C allows us to judge) Michael Chartophylax. These features must derive from a very early and accurate apograph of Cephalas. But it need not follow that Z itself was actually a complete Cephalas. If the scribe of *ABV* had been compiling his supplement from a redaction as full as *AP* he could have produced a far larger crop of addenda than he did (*AP* contains 150 hetero- and 242 homosexual erotica in *AP* v and xii alone that are not in *APl* vii). In his search for erotica in Z he did more than just excerpt its counterparts to *AP* v and xii. He looked among the sceptica for a poem on cunnilingus (*AP* xi. 108) in addition to the three erotic centos he dug out from the epideictica. Of course he may have done this for the sake of variety rather than out of a desire to be exhaustive, but there is a presumption, I would suggest, that Z did actually contain fewer erotica than *AP*.

This would be likely enough. *AP* is by far the fullest redaction of Cephalas of which we have any knowledge. But there are (as we shall see) a number of much smaller editions, most of which contain the odd poem not in *AP*. To have contained as many as 54 erotica not in *APl*, Z must have been on a much larger scale than these. We do in fact know of two such collections that answer exactly to the specifications here drawn up for Z, the only two

---

[13] Hunger (ii. 98 f.) quotes no example of any sort of Homeric cento between the fifth and twelfth century, strangely taking the 'Leo philosophus' of ix. 361 and 382 as an otherwise unknown poet of the fifth century. On Leo, see further below.

[14] The use of the same Homeric tag in both 361. 3 and 381. 7 suggests that 381 too is by Leo. *ABV* 7 is surely of the same period. It is for this reason that I have rejected most of Sternbach's tamperings with the text: that is to say his φύροντο δὲ and καλά for φίλα in l. 3. φορύνω is used at least twice by Quintus (ii. 356, iii. 604) and, quantity aside, would be ideal. There is even less call to take exception to the quantity φῖλα in view of the Homeric vocative φῖλε and *Od*. viii. 277 φίλα δέμνια. Nor is there any reason to write ἀδμήτην in l. 5, in view of the v.l. ἀδμῆτιν at *Il*. xxiii. 655 and the entry ἀδμῆτις in Zonaras, the Suda, and *Etym. Magn.*, all quoted by Sternbach. I have printed his δάμνα for the ἐδάμνα of M and V in l. 7, but would not rule out the possibility that the writer (who seems metrically less competent than Leo) thought that the first could be scanned short. It would not be surprising if later anthologists had deliberately omitted such a piece. Lines 1–3 and 4–6 look like alternative versions of the same idea rather than one continuous programme.

redactions of Cephalas (other than *AP*) known to have survived till
at any rate 1300: the two sources used by Planudes for his own
Anthology. Both had close affinities with *AP* and contained
material absent from it, but in general were obviously much
smaller. One of his two redactions of Cephalas Planudes presumably returned to his friend Theodore Xanthopoulos from whom he
had borrowed it,[15] but the other may have remained (for a while at
least) in the library of the Akataleptos monastery where he signed
Marc. 481.

It has so far been universally assumed that *ABV* is no earlier
than the beginning of the sixteenth century. Its two manuscripts
datable to *c.*1500—K and M—have successively been claimed as
the original compilation. We have now seen that neither can be the
source of the other two manuscripts and that there must have been
at least one further manuscript earlier than both K and M. It is not
obvious why this missing manuscript must be dated to *c.*1490
rather than 1390—or indeed earlier still. The most likely moment
for the confection of such an appendix was surely during the
period of the first diffusion of the Planudean anthology it was
designed to supplement, when Planudes had on the one hand
whetted people's appetites for classical epigrams—and yet frus-
trated them by deliberately withholding the spiciest items: and
when there was still a chance of getting hold of the book he had
bowdlerized. Whether or not Z was actually one of Planudes'
sources, it was clearly a substantial redaction of Cephalas. On our
present evidence it is difficult to believe that any such anthology
was still available as late as 1500.

There is indeed one pointer to the immediate post-Planudean
age. On fo. 28ᵛ of Paris. gr. 2744, an early fourteenth-century copy
of *APl*, a scribe whom A. Turyn has recently identified as Nicolaus
Triclines, added *AP* v. 18 at the end of the erotic book.[16] Where
did he find this poem? It is tempting to guess that he found it in
ABV, where it appears as no. 48.[17] If so, then *ABV* existed by
*c.*1320.

---

[15] *Ep.* 28, p. 45 Treu; cf. Turyn, *Dated Greek MSS* (1972), 75. There are two
poems (v. 35 and 258) in *ABV* which also appear (though less fully) in *APl*, thus
giving us the chance to compare the text of *ABV* with one of Planudes' manuscripts. There are a couple of variants, but they are hardly significant and in any
case *ABV* might equally have been drawn from the other manuscript.

[16] Turyn (1973), 412.

[17] Turyn (and, for a similar view, Mioni (1975), 288) supposes that Nicolaus
Triclines drew v. 18 from one of the sources used by Planudes, though against this

Gallavotti has recently made the surprising suggestion that *ABV* might be earlier than Planudes, on the basis of its links with *AP*: 'not an appendix or supplement to *APl*, but a random selection of erotic epigrams made for personal use according to the taste of the times.'[18] But *APl* derives from Cephalas no less than *ABV* does—and *AP* too. All derive from different redactions of Cephalas, made, and used, at different times. The fact that *ABV* derives from a redaction of Cephalas independent of *AP* does not in itself imply either that this redaction was of the tenth rather than (say) the twelfth century, or that the copy Z was made in (say) the twelfth rather than the fourteenth century. And if *ABV* was a copy made without reference to or (especially) before *APl*, it would be a curious double coincidence that it consisted (*a*) exclusively of erotica, and (*b*) exclusively of erotica omitted by Planudes. As we shall see in what follows, Planudes' bowdlerization was to become notorious in the fifteenth and sixteenth centuries.

It is mainly because they have derived *ABV* from *AP* that scholars have tended to date it so late. For these same scholars (notably Gallavotti and Mioni) have also argued that it was *c*.1500 that *AP* arrived in Rome. If *AP* had been so centrally available at this time, one might indeed have expected its riches to be tapped in an age so fascinated (as Hutton's *Greek Anthology in Italy* illustrates) by the classical epigram.

Gallavotti[19] went so far as to argue that J. Lascaris already knew of *AP* when he published his *editio princeps* of the Anthology, taken (as Turyn has shown) from a late and poor Planudean apograph. Since his reasoning has been widely approved, a few reservations will not be irrelevant.

In the preface to his edition Lascaris writes:

Illud unum non praetermittam, hoc epigrammatum Ἀνθολόγιον ab Agathia concinnatum esse, praestantissimo historico et poeta sui temporis, non a Planude, ut nonnullis est temere persuasum. Planudes enim monachus, ut eum appellant, non magis disposuit quam mutilavit et, ut ita dicam, castravit hunc librum detractis lascivioribus epigrammatis, ut ipse gloriatur.

---

see below. Mioni (1978), 75 argues that, on the contrary, the compiler of *ABV* got it from the appendix to the Aldine *Planudea* of 1503. It will not be necessary to repeat that *ABV* can scarcely be as late as this.

[18] *Boll. Class. Lincei*, 3rd ser., iv (1983), 121.

[19] *Boll. Class. Lincei*, 1960, 18–19; 1982, 69.

This criticism is largely justified. Planudes did just rearrange[20] and edit the results of another's research. But it was not Agathias' Anthology he so treated, but Cephalas'. How did Lascaris come to make this mistake?

While admitting the possibility that he simply guessed on the basis of the Suda entry for Agathias, Gallavotti felt that the assurance and precision with which Lascaris attributed Planudes' editorial activity to Agathias suggested that he had confronted *APl* with a pre-Planudean redaction of Cephalas. In fact with *AP* itself, whose iv incorporates Agathias' own preface to his *Cycle*, revealing that it was arranged in seven categories, the same number as Planudes'.

But Planudes' seven categories are not the same as Agathias'— and the number seven is obvious enough in any case. More important, if Lascaris ever had *AP* in his hands, why did he not use it to improve the Planudean Anthology he so despised? He refers only to the omission of erotica, which Planudes had admitted. Comparison with *AP* would have revealed other substantial omissions; for example, *APl* lacks nearly 200 of the sepulchral poems in *AP* vii. He could also have added many hundreds of ascriptions for poems left anonymous by Planudes, not to mention countless superior readings. But there is a more decisive objection still.

If Lascaris had done no more than glance at *AP* iv, he would have realized that Agathias' was not the only anthology to be taken into account. He would have discovered that, while *APl* was indeed merely a reworking of something like *AP*, *AP* itself was based on the *Garlands* of Meleager and Philip, not to mention numerous lesser but still substantial collections such as Strato, in addition to Agathias. Since the prefaces of Meleager and Philip list the poets they included, he would easily have been able to estimate the extent of their contribution to *AP*. Above all, he would have discovered from *AP* the existence of the anthology of Cephalas— most obviously from the conspicuous scholion to *AP* iv, a clear statement that the categories of 'the present book' were the work of 'Constantine called Cephalas'. Nor could he have missed the introductory lemma to *AP* vii making the same point.[21]

---

[20] His criticisms of the haphazard arrangement of his exemplar—an abbreviated Cephalas—are quoted by Gallavotti (1959), 31.

[21] Gallavotti incredibly writes that the first part of *AP*, bks. i–xiii, 'non differisce molto dalla Planudea per la sostanza' (1960, 21).

It is quite clear that Lascaris knew nothing of Cephalas. And he knew nothing of Cephalas precisely because he had *not* seen a pre-Planudean redaction of Cephalas such as *AP*, the source of all our own knowledge of Cephalas.

It was from the Suda (which he certainly knew)[22] that Lascaris discovered about the Anthology of Agathias (there are of course no Suda entries for Meleager or Cephalas). He saw there that it had contained poems by Agathias himself, Paul the Silentiary, and Macedonius the consul. These names recur throughout the Planudean Anthology, in six of Planudes' seven categories, and he simply guessed that it was Agathias' Anthology that Planudes had made his own. He obviously had no idea that Planudes' Agathian poems were taken at second hand from Cephalas.

The second pillar of Gallavotti's argument is a marginal note[23] written by Fulvio Orsini in a copy of the first Aldine Anthology of 1503, against the reference to Planudes' omissions in the printed heading to *API* vii: ἀλλὰ καὶ ταῦτα ἐν παλαιῷ εἰσιν παρ' ἐμοὶ γεγραμμένα ἀντιγράφῳ συλλεχθέντα παρὰ Ἀγγέλου τοῦ Κολλωτίου, οὗ καὶ τὸ βιβλίον ἐτύγχανεν ὄν. This 'old copy' (παλαιὸν ἀντίγραφον), suggests Gallavotti, was none other than *AP*, and Mioni has recently sought to strengthen the case.[24] Here too there are serious objections.

First and perhaps most subjective, as Sternbach saw, Orsini's words imply a brief erotic appendix such as *ABV* rather than anything so substantial and general as *AP*.

Second, we are lucky enough to possess a copy of Orsini's own inventory of his extensive library, and there is nothing that could possibly be taken as a description of *AP*. Furthermore, while Orsini was no more expert a palaeographer than most of his contemporaries, P. de Nolhac rightly observed a clear and consistent distinction in his terminology: 'Le mot *antico* indique des manuscrits antérieurs au xve siècle, le mot *antichissimo* des manuscrits antérieurs au xive siècle.'[25] Orsini owned only two Greek manuscripts older than *AP*, the Vatican Ptolemy and the Vatican

[22] Gallavotti (1960), 19 n. 5.

[23] This note has long been known in an abbreviated form; it was Gallavotti who rediscovered the original in a Vatican Aldine (1960, 20).

[24] Mioni (1975), 296–307.

[25] de Nolhac, *La bibliothèque de Fulvio Orsini* (Paris 1887), 275. See S. Rizzo, *Il lessico filologico degli umanisti* (1973), 147–68: only Politian made careful distinctions (147–64); other humanists were generally much vaguer.

Dio fragments, which he placed at the head of his collection, well aware of their exceptional antiquity. Of the rest, all of the four-teenth century or older are duly described as *antichissimi*.[26] We cannot exclude the possibility that he sold or gave away or was robbed of *AP* before compiling his inventory, but even so it seems unlikely that he would have described so venerable and unique a manuscript as merely παλαιόν (*antico*) rather than παλαιότατον (*antichissimo*).

Third, the hypothesis that *AP* was in Rome *c.* 1500 ignores solid evidence which places it on the other side of Europe during the early sixteenth century.

AP IN THE SIXTEENTH CENTURY

There should no longer be any serious doubt that *AP* was in Louvain *c.* 1550, where the young Henri Estienne, or Stephanus (as he preferred to be known), copied from it the *Anacreontea*. The *Anacreontea* are preserved in no manuscript other than *AP*, and the text of Stephanus' edition (1554), and still more the text of his own manuscript copy now in Leiden, agree in all significant respects with *AP*.[27] This conclusion editors have been curiously reluctant to concede, preferring either to suppose that Clement had only vol. ii of *AP* (how then did it first lose and then rejoin vol. i?), or else to postulate a twin of *AP* now lost without trace. But it would have to have been an identical twin. For after copying out the *Anacreontea* on fos. 29ʳ–35ʳ of his apograph, Stephanus left the next six pages blank, repeated a couple of lines from the *Anacreontea* on fo. 38ᵛ, and then on fo. 39ʳ wrote the words Δοσιάδα βωμός, 'Dosiadas' altar'. It is as though he had been intending to copy this poem but then changed his mind, perhaps remembering that it had already been published. Now on p. 673 of *AP*, two pages before the *Anacreontea* (pp. 675–90), stands 'Dosiadas' altar' (*AP* xv. 26). It is easy to see why Stephanus should have formed the idea of copying it: unlike the other figure-poems on adjacent pages in *AP* (xv. 21–5, 27), its unusual shape is not obscured by closely written

---

[26] See the invaluable annotated edition of the inventory by P. de Nolhac 1887.

[27] For Stephanus and the *Anacreontea* see the successive Teubner editions of V. Rose (¹1868; ³1890), K. Preisendanz (1912), and M. L. West (1984), with Rose and West accepting and Preisendanz denying that he used *AP*.

surrounding scholia. Though published in Calliergis' 1516 edition of Theocritus, the poem was not there ascribed to Dosiadas. Furthermore, even in these two words Stephanus shares with *AP* not only the rare spelling with omicron (*Δο*- rather than *Δω*-) but also the genitive in -*α* rather than (as in all Bucolic manuscripts and all other sources) -*ου*.

For whatever reason, in his edition of 1554 Stephanus did not say where he found the *Anacreontea*.[28] Soon after making his copy, Stephanus chanced to meet P. Vettori, the greatest scholar of the age, and showed him his find. Vettori quotes *Anacr.* 7 in his *Variarum lectionum libri XXV* (xx. 17, p. 313) of 1553, adding that the precocious youth 'said he had found it by chance hidden in an old book' (*inventum a se forte (ut aiebat) in antiqui libri tegmine*).[29] Twelve years later in his edition of the Planudean Anthology (1566), Stephanus added near the end (pp. 532–3) six riddle poems, again material not to be found anywhere but in *AP* (xiv. 52, 56, 57, 58, 60, 62). This time he states that he found them in a 'vetus codex epigrammatum' in the possession of 'Iohannes Clemens Anglus' at Louvain. John Clement was a doctor who numbered Cardinal Wolsey and King Henry VIII among his patients, and also played a distinguished part in the first Aldine edition of the Greek text of Galen.[30] Stephanus passed through Louvain on his return from a trip to England in 1551, and Clement is known to have been at Louvain between 1549 and 1553, a Catholic exile from the repressive religious policy of Edward VI. Although absent from *APl* (and so unknown when he published them), the last five of Stephanus' six do appear in the riddle section of L, written in Planudes' hand, but in a different sequence, with a number of variants—and without xiv. 52. Except for a few obvious errors that Stephanus corrected in his regular way, his text agrees with *AP* in every detail, usually against L, even in error: e.g. ἐείδομαι against L's ἐρείδομαι at 58. 3; the unmetrical μοῦνα at 57. 4

---

[28] No reason is needed: sixteenth-century French editors did not 'cite, evaluate, and report on their manuscripts in the manner that the Italians thought proper' (A. Grafton, *Joseph Scaliger* [Oxford 1983], 85).

[29] Hutton (1935), 211; Grafton, *Joseph Scaliger*, i. 265, n. 81.

[30] V. Rose (1890), pp. i–xxiv; E. Wenkebach, *John Clement: ein englischer Humanist und Arzt des sechzehnten Jahrhunderts* (Studien zur Geschichte der Medizin 14; Leipzig 1925); V. Nutton, *John Caius and the Manuscripts of Galen* (*Cambridge Philological Society Supplement* 13; 1987), 58–9, 84–5; R. W. Hunt, *Studia Patristica*, xviii (1982), 367–71.

against L's obviously correct μοῦνον; ἐκαινούργει at 60. 1 against L's certain καινούργησεν; down to such trifles as *AP*'s ἄν and καὶ ἐγώ in 56. 1 against L's ἤν and κἀγώ. At 52. 5, where we do not have L, Stephanus simply repeats *AP*'s unmetrical nonsense.

That Clement's manuscript was indeed *AP* is confirmed by the inventory of Clement's books prepared by his son Thomas in 1572, the year of John's death, still in exile, at Malines (Mechlen). Among his manuscripts is listed an *epigrammatum liber magnus et perantiquus* that contained 'twice as many epigrams as the Aldine Anthology and many more even than Stephanus' Anthology'.[31] Now Stephanus' edition of the Planudean Anthology (1566) was enriched by much additional material, and was by far the largest Greek Anthology then available.

Third, there is a note written by Gerard Falkenburg of Nijmegen, editor of Nonnus' *Dionysiaca* (1569), on the title page of his copy of the Juntine Planudean Anthology (1519) *c.*1566 (the date he wrote his name on the flyleaf).[32] 'Huius florilegii collector fuit Planudes, qui, e vetere circulo, epigrammata obscoeniora sustulit, quae etiamnum hodie apud Io. Clementem Britannum exstant.' The book is full of marginalia in Falkenburg's hand, but no new poems or readings from *AP*. Indeed his claim that Clement's manuscript contained merely the 'naughtier' poems that Planudes had omitted proves that he had no idea of the true extent of its superiority. But the little he did know of Clement's Anthology is accurate as far as it goes, and certainly confirms that it was *AP*. A 'very old' anthology of epigrams that was larger than Stephanus' and contained in addition riddle poems, the *Anacreontea* and numerous erotic poems omitted by Planudes simply has to have been *AP*.

So by at any rate 1551 John Clement owned *AP* and let Stephanus consult it at Louvain. At the time Stephanus' interest was caught by the *Anacreontea*, which he at once recognized to be unpublished. Given the immense overlap between *AP* and *APl*, it

---

[31] *duplo plura quam Aldi liber, et multo plura quam Henr. Stephani liber continens*: for the inventory, with a full account of the latter stages of Clement's life and library, see G. Mercati, 'Sopra Giovanni Clement e i suoi manoscritti', *La Bibliofilia* xxviii (1926), 81–9 = *Opere Minori*, iv (Vatican 1937), 292–315. An inventory of the books he left behind in London (naturally the less valuable part of his collection) was published by A. W. Reed, 'John Clement and his Books', *The Library*, 4th ser., vi (1926), 329–39.

[32] Now in the Bodleian Library, Auct. S. 5. 33.

would have taken a very detailed comparison by an experienced scholar to discover the full extent of *AP*'s superiority. Stephanus was only twenty at the time, and it is possible that he only examined vol. ii. The other material he copied from *AP*, the six riddle poems from book xiv and the title of Dosiadas' Altar, all came from vol. ii. He evidently did not have a chance to re-examine the manuscript for his edition of the Anthology fifteen years later, or it would have worn a very different look. There is only one detail that suggests any knowledge of vol. i:[33] to *AP* vii. 339 (on p. 178) Stephanus added the heading, ἄδηλον, οἱ δὲ Παλλαδᾶ, where Planudes had offered only ἄδηλον. Palladas does not seem at all an obvious guess, and in any case the form of the heading suggests an alternative tradition. Perhaps Stephanus had jotted down among his notes the unusual heading in *AP*, ἄδηλον, πλὴν ὅτι ἐν τοῖς τοῦ Παλλαδᾶ ἐπιγράμμασιν εὑρέθη.[34] Rather than infer that the two volumes had become separated, it may be that Stephanus did not pay much attention to vol. i, mistakenly (but not unnaturally) supposing that it was simply a copy of *APl*, which he was not directly concerned with at the time.

That *AP* was in Clement's possession between *c.*1550 and 1572 we may surely regard as certain. But how, when and where did he get hold of it? During a visit to Rome between 1522 and 1525, on the conventional view, first set out by V. Rose.[35] Yet, not to mention the fact that there is no real evidence that *AP* was ever in Rome, there are serious grounds for questioning this hypothesis.

Clement is the first identifiable pupil at St Paul's School in London, founded by John Colet with the backing of Erasmus and

---

[33] I have not collated Stephanus' edition against *AP*; a detailed examination might well disclose further traces. He clearly took notes for further use in 1551, as shown by the six riddle poems he was able to produce in 1566.

[34] On the next page, Stephanus suggests 'idem titulus' for *AP* x. 118 on the grounds that it repeats two lines of vii. 339—presumably this time just a guess. For Preisendanz this was proof that Stephanus was guessing in *both* places, but why assign both poems to Palladas out of the blue? Surely the guess about x. 118 was inspired by his knowledge of the ascription to vii. 339.

[35] *Anacreontea*³ (1890), pp. vi–vii, xx–xxiv; see too Preisendanz' edition (1912), pp. v–vi, and now M. L. West, *Carmina Anacreontea* (Leipzig 1984), pp. v–ix (referring to an earlier version of this chapter). I am puzzled by R. Pfeiffer's reference to Stephanus discovering 'the *codex unicus* . . . in Italy some time before 1549' (*History of Classical Scholarship from 1300 to 1850*, 1976, 107) since on p. 109 n. 3 he claims to be following Preisendanz and concludes that the 'original cod. Palatinus plays no part in the story'.

More in 1509.[36] In 1516 he lived as a page in the house of his patron, Thomas More. He is mentioned that year in the dedicatory letter prefixed to More's *Utopia* as 'my boy' (*puer meus*), and in similar terms in a letter to Erasmus of the same year, describing him as a youth 'making such progress in both Latin and Greek that I hope for great things from him'.[37] In due course he married More's foster-daughter Margaret Giggs and rose to be president of the Royal College of Physicians. But his first and perhaps only visit to Italy (1522–5) was undertaken to study medicine and medical manuscripts in Padua and Siena (where he received his degree in 1525). Although still a student it was during this period that he laid the foundations of what was eventually to become an impressive collection of Greek and Latin manuscripts, but his earliest acquisitions seem to have been texts of Galen, which were used for the *editio princeps* of 1525.[38] It seems unlikely that a medical student had the interest, the connections, or the resources to acquire so valuable a text as *AP*, though the primary objection is actually chronological.

Clement did not reach Italy till March 1522.[39] But there is evidence, hitherto overlooked, that places *AP* in England at least five and more likely ten or twelve years earlier than this. More himself was keenly interested in ancient Greek epigrams, and in 1518 published some Latin translations from the Anthology jointly with William Lily, the first high master of St Paul's School, under the title *Progymnasmata Thomae Mori et Gulielmi Lilii Sodalium*. All but one of the Greek epigrams translated were taken, predictably enough, from the Planudean Anthology.[40] The exception is *Progymnasmata*, no. 18. Since More and Lily quote the Greek original, there can be no doubt about the identification of the poem they translated: Simonides, *Ep.* 186 Bergk = 55 Page:

---

[36] J. H. Lupton, *A Life of John Colet, D.D.* (London 1887), 154–77, with Appendices A–C; M. F. J. McDonnell, *A History of St. Paul's School* (London 1909), 1–68.

[37] *Utopia*, in *Complete Works of St Thomas More*, iv, ed. E. Surtz and J. H. Hexter (New Haven 1965), p. 40; P. S. Allen (ed.), *Opus Epistolarum Des. Erasmi*, ii (1910), no. 468.

[38] Nutton (1987), 58–9, 84–5.

[39] Rose (1890), pp. vii, xvii–xxiv; Wenkebach (1925), 10.

[40] C. H. Miller, L. Bradner, C. A. Lynch, and R. P. Oliver, *Latin Poems, Complete Works of St. Thomas More*, iii. 2 (New Haven 1984), arguing (pp. 14–17) that More and Lily worked from a selection made from *APl* rather than directly from a text of *APl*.

ΣΙΜΩΝΙΔΟΥ

δῆμος Ἀθηναίων σε, Νεοπτόλεμ', εἰκόνι τῇδε
τίμησ' εὐνοίης εὐσεβίης θ' ἕνεκα.

T. MORI

Cecropis urbs te tota, Neoptoleme, hac statua ornat.
ut faciat, faciunt hinc amor hinc pietas.

G. LILII

hoc te donarat propter pietatem et amorem
signo Cecropidum turba, Neoptoleme.

This poem is absent from both *AP* and *APl*. It appears only in the
minor *syllogae* E and *Σ*ᵖ.

Of the four manuscripts that contain E, Laur. 57. 29 was not
written till after 1580;[41] Par. gr. 1773 was copied by Bartolomeo
Comparini in 1493; Par. gr. 2720 by Scipione Carteromaco
(† 1515); and Vat. gr. 1949 is of more or less the same period. The
last three must all have been in private hands in Italy during the
first two decades of the sixteenth century. Since More himself
never visited Italy, he cannot have inspected any of them in
person. His collaborator Lily did spend two years in Italy, but not
only was he barely twenty when he arrived in 1489; he was back in
London by 1492,[42] a year before at least two and perhaps all four
extant copies of E were made. *Σ*ᵖ, on the other hand, is the small
collection written in blank spaces of *AP*. The page that carries the
poem in question was pasted on to the first quaternion of *AP*.
More need only have opened the manuscript at its very first page of
text to be confronted with it. And if we grant that More's protégé
Clement had *AP* by 1550, why should not More himself have had
it a few decades earlier?

We know from Erasmus that most of More's translations were
made many years before they were finally published in 1518; the
Yale editors argue that they were written between *c*.1501 and
1510.[43] If so, More must have had access to *AP* long before
Clement reached Italy in 1522.

Before proceeding with More, it is time to mention the important discovery published by E. Mioni in 1975: a selection from a
corpus of notes on the Anthology contained in two Vatican

---

[41] Aubreton (1968), 70, n. 3; Gallavotti, *Boll. Class. Lincei*, 3rd ser., iii (1982), 79.

[42] G. B. Parks, *The English Traveler to Italy*, i (Stanford 1954), 463–6.

[43] Miller *et al.*, pp. 10–14.

manuscripts (Vatic. gr. 1169, fos. 66–91 and 1416, fos. 236–9). These manuscripts, written in different hands, are headed respectively 'Iohannis Lascaris et Musuri notae et animadversiones in epigrammata graeca variorum auctorum' and ἐκ τοῦ Μουσούρου καὶ ἄλλων εἰς τὴν τῶν ἐπιγραμμάτων ἀνθολογίαν.[44] There can be no doubt that these notes include readings, ascriptions, and even whole poems from *AP*, and it is to be hoped that they will soon be published in full. It is difficult to doubt that one or both of these scholars had made a close study of *AP*, and since we have already seen reason to doubt that Lascaris knew anything of *AP*, that leaves Musurus.

Mioni himself assumed, on inadequate grounds and in ignorance of the evidence about Clement and More, that it was in Rome that Musurus consulted *AP*. But it was not till 1516 that Musurus visited Rome, and he was dead by 1517. If More did indeed consult *AP*, he did so before then. There is another possibility. In 1507 Musurus gave widely reported lectures on the Anthology at Padua.[45] He also lectured there on Theocritus and Anacreon.[46] Since there was precious little Anacreon in print by then, it is tempting to wonder (with M. Sicherl) whether this in fact means the *Anacreontea*, which Musurus (like Stephanus a generation later) had read in *AP*. It has long been suspected that he drew on *AP* during his work on the epigrams of Theocritus.[47] If so, then as Sicherl has already argued against Mioni, it must have been at Padua that Musurus studied *AP*, *c.*1507.

Now this happens to have been the very date and place where More's great friend Erasmus got to know Musurus. One of his letters records a visit to Musurus' house for dinner one day in November 1508.[48] In December of that year Erasmus left Padua for a brief stay in Rome, and then, early in 1509, to England—and More.[49] It is obviously possible that Musurus showed *AP* to

---

[44] E. Mioni, 'L'Antologia greca da Massimo Planude a Marco Musuro', *Scritti in onore di Carlo Diano* (Bologna 1975), at pp. 296–307. See addenda.

[45] Hutton (1935), 155; M. Sicherl, *Joannes Cuno* (Heidelberg 1978), 97–100. For Musurus' period in Padua, see D. J. Geanakoplos, *Greek Scholars in Venice* (Harvard 1962), 133–9.

[46] Sicherl, 88, 100.

[47] J. Irigoin, *Rev. de Phil.* xxxiii (1959), 60–1, arguing against R. J. Smutny, *Text History of the Epigrams of Theocritus* (Berkeley 1955), 59.

[48] *Opus epistolarum Erasmi*, v 244 Allen.

[49] Erasmus was not the only friend of More in Italy at the turn of the century. Two who can be identified are Thomas Linacre (between 1487 and 1499) and

Erasmus during his stay in Padua. That he *gave* it to him might seem less likely. But in a famous passage of his *Adagia* (*festina lente*), Erasmus describes the generosity with which the member's of Aldus' circle lent him valuable manuscripts during his stay in Venice, even of unpublished works. Musurus is mentioned by name.[50] But Musurus may not have been the owner; it might have been in the possession of some private collector, perhaps unaware of its value,[51] who took a fancy to Erasmus and gave—or perhaps simply lent—it to him.[52] We learn from the reports of scholars like Manutius, Musurus, and Politian of many a valuable Greek codex then in private hands that has now disappeared. We also hear of manuscripts borrowed from the poorly policed recent bequest of Cardinal Bessarion that were never returned—some of them seen for sale in the local bookstalls.[53] We shall see that some of Clement's other manuscripts (a valuable Tertullian, for instance) suffered a similar fate. *AP* has at least survived. If he saw a chance of acquiring such a treasure, Erasmus would surely have seized it. The surprise is more that, having acquired it, he gave it to More. But then we know that he had a deep admiration and affection for More, whom he knew to be interested in Greek epigrams. On this hypothesis, Clement simply inherited *AP* from his father-in-law, as we know he did a valuable Greek Octateuch.[54]

The hypothesis that *AP* was in London and the Low Countries between 1509 and 1572 would kill two birds with one stone. It would explain how early Renaissance scholars in Italy knew *something* of *AP* (Musurus' notes); but also why they knew no

William Latimer (between 1498 and 1505): Parks, *The English Traveler to Italy*, i (1954), 457–8 and 467–9. Both got to know Aldus Manutius (M. Lowry, *The World of Aldus Manutius: Business and Scholarship in Renaissance Venice* (Cornell 1979), 259–63), but Linacre was mainly interested in medicine, and both left Italy at a time when (on the evidence of Musurus) *AP* was still there. It may (of course) have been some other friend of More, now unidentifiable, who picked up *AP* and brought it to London, but Erasmus' movements best fit the available evidence.

[50] For the details, D. J. Geanokoplos, 'Erasmus and the Aldine Academy', *GRBS* iii (1960), 121–3.

[51] Given the entirely different arrangement of *AP* and the Planudean Anthology, it would (as already remarked) have taken an expert a good deal of time to establish the extent of *AP*'s superiority. Musurus seems to have made this discovery, but he may not have been consulted and *AP*'s owner may not have been so perceptive.

[52] His ever straitened financial circumstances make it unlikely that Erasmus could have bought it at anything approaching a fair market value.

[53] See M. Lowry, *The World of Aldus Manutius*, 230–3.

[54] For the Octateuch, see below, p. 195. More was executed on 6 July 1535.

more. It is not merely that no one published any of the otherwise unknown texts in this unique manuscript. Two remarkable books by James Hutton have traced in immense detail the quite extraordinary vogue of the Greek Anthology throughout Europe during the Renaissance.[55] Everyone with any pretensions to letters took care to signal his familiarity with the Anthology by producing translations or variations in Latin. A student of Scaliger described his daily regimen as follows:[56] 'Every evening, as he went to bed, he translated one or two of the epigrams from Book VII of the Anthology for me word for word [in Planudes the erotic book]. I was to return them to him the next day in Latin verse.' This means that knowledge of individual epigrams can be documented in an unusually precise way, which can be followed the more easily through the very full indexes to Hutton's two books. It may thus be asserted with considerable confidence that, throughout the Renaissance, the Greek Anthology was the Planudean Anthology. The many hundreds of poems in *AP* unknown to Planudes remained unknown down to the seventeenth century. If *AP* had remained in Italy, even unpublished, some of its new epigrams would have begun to circulate in manuscript and be translated into Latin. The fact that Hutton's collections show not a single case is the argument from silence at its strongest. And we now know why. *AP* was far away, inaccessible in England.

Thus far I have deliberately left on one side the well-known letter of Scaliger hitherto held to be the key document on the whereabouts of *AP* at this period, a reply to a letter from J. Gruter about Salmasius' rediscovery of *AP* at Heidelberg, dated 20 February 1607. Gruter had sent him a transcription of a few unknown (presumably pederastic) epigrams by Callimachus to 'whet his appetite' (*quantam salivam mihi movisti!*). On the basis of this sample Scaliger conjectured that *AP* must be a manuscript he had heard of long ago:[57]

[55] *The Greek Anthology in Italy* (1936) and *The Greek Anthology in France and the Latin Writers of the Netherlands* (1946); he never published the projected third volume on England.

[56] I use the translation by A. Grafton, *Joseph Scaliger*, i. 180.

[57] 'audivi non semel ex Francisco Porto Cretensi, optimo et eruditissimo sene, se in manibus Nicolai Sophiani hominis Graeci integrum ἀνθολογίας codicem summae vetustatis vidisse: in quo omnia illa Epigrammata, quae narras, exstabant, quae non dubium est, propter praetextata verba et obscenitatem a Planude monacho damnata fuisse': *Iosephi Scaligeri Epistulae* (Leiden 1627), *Ep.* 430, p. 789; cf. Hutton (1946), 156–7.

Francesco Porto the Cretan, an excellent and learned old gentleman, told
me often that he had seen a complete codex of the Anthology of great
antiquity in the hands of Nicholaus Sophianus the Greek. In it stood all
the epigrams you tell me about, undoubtedly those condemned by
Planudes the monk for their explicit language and obscenity.

Hitherto this letter has been accorded something like the status of
an eyewitness report.[58] But it is Porto,[59] not Scaliger, who is
supposed to have seen this manuscript. And while Porto might
have copied some poems and later shown them to Scaliger, it
should be emphasized that this is not what Scaliger says. He does
not say that Porto showed him a transcript: his words are 'heard'
and 'seen'. He represents himself recollecting what was already a
recollection by Porto. We must bear in mind that each of these
recollections was twenty or thirty years old. Clearly Scaliger
cannot (as he implies) have *recognized* the epigrams Gruter sent
him.

More disquieting still is Scaliger's next letter to Gruter (21
June), evidently in response to a request for further information
about Porto's story:[60]

I now see that this is the same codex as the one Nicolaus Sophianus had.
In addition to others he had a complete codex of the *Ethnica* of Stephanus
of Byzantium, with the whole of K and L, which (as you know) are
incomplete in the standard editions. Sophianus also had a manuscript of
Isocrates which offered the *Panathenaïcus* with three folia more than
current editions. Henricus Stephanus was there, and Sophianus showed
him a printed text lacking those folia, and told him to say what it meant.

---

[58] 'témoignage contemporain', Aubreton (1980), 4.
[59] For the career and works of F. Porto, see E. Legrand, *Bibliographie hellén-
ique . . . aux XVᵉ et XVIᵉ siècles*, i (Paris 1885), pp. vii–xx.
[60] 'Iam video illum codicem eundem esse, quem Nic. Sophianus habebat. Nam
praeter alios codices inerat et integer Stephanus ἐθνικογράφος, cum toto K. et L.
quae hodie imperfecta circumferri non ignoras. Sed codicem Isocratis idem
Sophianus habebat, qui Panathenaicum tribus foliis auctiorem continebat quam qui
hodie in manibus nostris versatur. Praesens aderat Henricus Stephanus. Impressum illi Panegyricum Sophianus ostendit locum, a quo absunt illa folia, interpretari
iubet, quem quum diligenter is perpendisset, palam, se non intelligere professus
est, quum tamen antea suspectus ipsi non fuisset. Postea, explicato codice Graeco,
indicavit quantum in vulgatis editionibus deesset. An ille codex nunc in Bibliotheca
extet, magni fecerim scire: et, si ita est, cum vulgatis conferre Salmasius poterit; ne
tibi homini in melioribus occupato tantum taedium deuorandum sit. Aliquando ex
ipso Stephano audiui, propter hanc lacunam se editione Isocratis deterritum fuisse:
quam tamen postea cum interpretatione Latina excudit. Isti Sophiano idem et
nomen et cognomen commune cum eo fuit, qui Graeciae tabulam confecit, ne forte
quis eundem putarit': *Ep.* 431, p. 725.

Stephanus thought hard about it for a while and then frankly admitted that he could not understand the passage, despite having had no previous doubts about it. Sophianus then opened the Greek manuscript, demonstrating how much it differed from the standard editions. I would love to know if this manuscript is in the [Palatine] Library. . . . I once (*aliquando*) heard from Stephanus himself that he had been deterred from editing Isocrates by this lacuna, though he later published a text and Latin translation. This Sophianus had the same name and surname (*nomen et cognomen*) as the man who published the map of Greece, in case anyone confuses them.

Once again, this is all presented as personal recollections, whereas at best it is (as before) recollections of recollections. The different nature of the second reference to Stephanus (*aliquando ex ipso Stephano audivi*) makes it clear that Stephanus was not his source for what precedes, not even for the story about Stephanus and Sophianus. The natural assumption is that Scaliger is again drawing on those distant conversations with Porto. Fortunately, the three main claims he makes in the second letter can all be checked, and it has to be said at once that all three are in varying degrees and ways mistaken.

First of all, who is this Sophianus? Nicolaus Sophianus of Corfu, who lived from *c.*1500 to *c.*1552;[61] or Michael Sophianus of Chios, who lived from *c.*1515 to 1565?[62] Both collected Greek manuscripts and spent much time in or near Venice. If we had only Scaliger's letter to go on, there might have seemed little doubt that Nicolaus was meant. But he was not alone even among contemporaries in his inability to distinguish the two Sophiani. The polymath K. Gesner claimed in his *Bibliotheca Universalis* of 1545 to have met 'Nicolaus Sophianus of Corcyra a year and a half ago in Venice' (p. 520*a*), and mentions him more than once as an owner

---

[61] A. Moustoxidis, Ἑλληνομνήμων, i (1843), 236–64; Legrand i. pp. clxxvii–cxciv; M. Vogel and V. Gardthausen, *Die griechischen Schreiber des Mittelalters und der Renaissance* (Leipzig 1909), 356–7 (14 manuscripts, the two with dates being 1533 and 1534); Geanakoplos, *Greek Scholars in Venice* 295. Nicolaus was a printer as well as copyist: W. A. Pettas, *The Library*, xxix (1974), 206–13. And in 1533 he collaborated with a medical student to write a comedy containing the earliest extant conversational modern Greek: Mario Vitti, *Nicolao Sofiano e la commedia dei 'Tre tiranni' di A. Ricchi* (Naples 1966).

[62] Legrand ii. 168–76; Vogel and Gardthausen 320–1 (10 manuscripts, with dates ranging from 1546 to 1560); Moustoxidis, l.c.; and see further below. According to G. Uhlig (p. 189 n. 65 below), P. Mazzuccelli, Librarian of the Ambrosiana from 1823 to 1829, wrote detailed 'Memorie intorno ai Sofiani', distinguishing 16, of whom Michael is no. 11 (Ambr. 179. sup. f. 53ᵛ ff.).

and connoisseur of rare manuscripts. Scaliger's man, it might seem. But take the most circumstantial example Gesner quotes, in his entry for Apollonius Dyscolus: 'Nicolaus Sophianus, vir Graecus . . . ostendit mihi Venetiis exemplar suum impressum, cui multa folia, quae deficiebant, manu ascripta erant.' No fewer than three such printed copies of Apollonius (Aldines), supplemented exactly as Gesner describes, are extant. But all of them bear the name *Michael* Sophianus. R. 44 sup (713) in the Ambrosian Library at Milan has a subscription describing how Michael and the Belgian scholar Nicaise van Ellebode († 1577) devoted a whole year to this difficult text at Padua in 1562/3. Michael and Ellebode worked together on another grammatical treatise (by Michael Syncellus), and both also did valuable work on Aristotle. Ellebode's paraphrase of the *Poetics* was rescued from oblivion by B. Weinberg in 1961,[63] and the following year R. Kassel resuscitated a series of penetrating conjectures on the text made jointly by Ellebode and Michael.[64] Michael died soon after his labours on Apollonius, but one of those who saw to it that they were not wasted was none other than Francesco Porto.[65] Between 1546 and 1554 Porto worked at Ferrara, where Michael died in 1565. Porto left Ferrara (and Italy) in 1554 on turning Calvinist, and since the preface to his work on Apollonius (dated 1580) states that he found his *multo plenius exemplar* in Italy, it was presumably before 1554 that he and Michael talked about the Greek Anthology.[66] It was therefore at least twenty years later that he told Scaliger about it, while they were at Geneva together between 1572 and 1574.[67] By the time Scaliger wrote to Gruter in 1607, more than half a century

---

[63] *A History of Literary Criticism in the Renaissance*, i (Chicago 1961), 519–23. On Ellebode, see too D. Wagner, *Zur Biographie des Nicasius Ellebodius* (Sitz. Heidelberg 1973, 5), *passim* (pp. 11–13 on his relations with Sophianus). Also D. Donnet, *Byzantion* xlii (1972), 490–6; *L'Antiquité classique* liv (1975), 654–63; *Bulletin de l'Histoire belge de Rome* xliii (1973), 404–5.

[64] 'Unbeachtete Renaissance-Emendationen zur Aristotelischen Poetik', *Rhein. Museum* cv (1962), 111–21.

[65] For the whole story see G. Uhlig's edition of Apollonius Dyscolus (*Grammatici Graeci* II. 2, 1910), pp. xvi–xix; xlv–li; lxix–lxxiii. The relevance of this connection between F. Porto and Michael Sophianus to the story of *AP* seems not to have been perceived.

[66] These collective labours on Apollonius did not in fact see the light of day till after Porto's death as well, in the edition of F. Sylburg (1590): Uhlig, p. lxxiii.

[67] The two men remained close; Porto sent Scaliger a valuable computus manuscript shortly before his death, in Geneva, on 7 June 1581 (A. Grafton, *Journ. Warb. Inst.* 48 [1985], 136).

had passed since the original conversation between Michael and Porto.

What about the Isocrates manuscript? On the testimony of his close friend P. Vettori (who cites two witnesses by name), it was *Michael* Sophianus who owned a manuscript of Isocrates that contained material missing in the current editions;[68] and the Map of Greece was certainly published by the only *Nicolaus* Sophianus we know of, the Corfiote.[69] Even Scaliger's further remark that H. Stephanus had seen this Isocrates manuscript points to Michael, whom Stephanus knew well,[70] rather than the older Nicolaus, whom he may never have met.

Indeed the Isocrates question can be settled in a way that nicely illustrates the shortcomings in detail of Scaliger's marvellous memory. For it was the text, not of the *Panathenaïcus*, but of the *Antidosis* that was defective. It was not until 1812 that A. Moustoxidis (after a search inspired by Scaliger's letter to Gruter) published the complete text, from two manuscripts, Laurentianus LXXXVII. 14 and Ambrosianus O. 144.[71] The latter, a codex of the fifteenth century, carries on the title page the legend: *ex insula Chio advectus. fuit ex libris Michaelis Sophiani*; and on the top margin of fo. 207^r: Μιχαήλου σοφιανοῦ καὶ τῶν ὄντως φίλων. On fo. 206^v stands a scholion in a sixteenth-century hand as follows: 'in every other manuscript I have come across the speech on the exchange is defective'.[72] According to the Budé editor G. Mathieu, till that moment 'seul J. Scaliger . . . avait cru à une lacune'.[73] We can now add that this was not an inspired conjecture on Scaliger's part. He knew, whether from Vettori or Porto, that there was a fuller manuscript in existence. But he got the details all wrong, confusing the two Sophiani and two different works of Isocrates. Under the circumstances, we may perhaps be sceptical about some

[68] P. Victorius, *Commentarii in III libros Aristotelis de arte dicendi* (Florence 1579), 718.

[69] A. Diller, *The Tradition of the Minor Greek Geographers* (1952), 16–17.

[70] Legrand ii. 169.

[71] As his dedicatory letter to Koraes describes, he had been searching in Italian libraries εἴ που τῶν ἰσοκράτους ἀπογράφων, οὕτω μακρὸν, ἡλίκον ἰωσὴφ ὁ σκαλιγέρος δεῖξαι νικόλαον τὸν σοφιανὸν μαρτυρεῖ ἐῤῥίκῳ τῷ στεφάνῳ . . . (Milan 1812), p. v.

[72] ὅτι ἐν ἅπασιν οἷς ἐνέτυχον ἀντιγράφοις ἐλλείπως ἔχει ὁ περὶ τῆς ἀντιδόσεως λόγος; A. Martini and D. Bassi, *Catalogus codicum Graecorum Bibliothecae Ambrosianae*, ii (Milan 1906), pp. 697–8, no. 602; E. Drerup, *Leipziger Studien* xvii (1895), 26–39. Neither indicates whether the hand of this scholion is Michael's.

[73] G. Mathieu, *Isocrate: Discours*, iii^2 (Paris 1950), 101–2.

of the other circumstantial details in Scaliger's report—like
Sophianus making Stephanus construe the printed text in front of
the assembled company.

That leaves the manuscript of Stephanus of Byzantium. That
Michael owned a manuscript of Stephanus is likely enough. It may
be the fifteenth century Ambrosianus 449 (H 117 sup.), for it was
in the Ambrosian Library in Milan that Michael's collection found
its permanent home.[74] But it did not contain the missing parts of K
and L. There is as yet no critical edition of Stephanus, but Aubrey
Diller examined all the extant manuscripts (including Ambr. 449),
and they all have the same gaps.[75] It may have been Michael who
exaggerated the value of his own manuscript, but more probably
Scaliger got confused over the years about which of Sophianus'
manuscripts supplemented texts known to be defective.

For there were many stories about Michael's manuscript discoveries. But they did not always concern manuscripts that he owned
himself. A story told by H. Stephanus provides a good illustration:[76]

I have put Musaeus after Tryphiodorus because, like Tryphiodorus, he
too was a grammarian. For Michael Sophianus once told me in the
presence of several others that at Genoa he had seen an old text that
contained that poem along with some others, with the title 'The Hero and
Leander of Musaeus the grammarian'. And he named the owner.

Michael was more than a collector and a copyist. He was a serious
scholar who won the respect of Robortello, Vettori, and Stephanus; at least ten of his conjectures are to be found in any modern
text of Aeschylus.[77] He examined old manuscripts wherever he

[74] Martini and Bassi, i. 540. On Michael's collection, see Martini and Bassi, i, pp.
xv–xvi: 22 manuscripts owned by Michael, 15 by Manuel Sophianus (presumably
the kinsman who inherited) and 2 by Theodorus Sophianus (see ii. 1276 for the
list). They are all said to have come *ex ins(ula) Chio*. There is no indication in the
brief entry for Ambr. 449 that it either belonged to Michael or came from Chios,
but we must presumably allow for the possibility that not all his manuscripts bore
explicit notes of provenance.

[75] 'The Tradition of Stephanus Byzantius', *TAPA* lxix (1938), 333–48, reprinted
with one or two additions in his *Studies in Greek Manuscript Tradition* (Amsterdam
1983), 183–98. At p. 344 n. 22 he cites Scaliger's letter as the source of 'a rumor of a
codex of Stephanus that did not have these lacunae'.

[76] *Poetae Graeci principes heroici carminis* (Geneva 1566) ii. 487; I have adapted
the translation from A. Grafton, *Defenders of the Text* (Cambridge, Mass., 1991),
155.

[77] See R. Kassel, *Rhein. Museum* cv (1962), 113 for the list—all in M. L. West's
text of 1990.

found them and knew what to look for: the title 'grammarian' has now long since been confirmed for Musaeus from a number of manuscripts.[78]

Scaliger was much given to reminiscences about eyewitnesses who could corroborate otherwise undocumented claims. H. J. de Jonge quotes a whole series from the *Scaligerana*: 'Monsieur Cujas me dit l'avoir veu'; 'hoc mihi narravit qui vidit'; 'ce m'a dit Felix de Nismes'; 'Poloni qui ibi fuerant mihi retulerunt'; 'Lingelshemius dixit mihi'.[79] De Jonge has discussed one of these cases in detail. According to the *Secunda Scaligerana*, Scaliger once claimed that 'there was once (*il y avoit*) a Gothic New Testament in the Palatine Library. Gruter says it is no longer there, and I know a man who has seen it. Vulcanius has given us a specimen. . . .' The manuscript to which he refers must be the so-called *Codex Argenteus*, which was never in the Palatine Library. De Jonge has ingeniously and convincingly explained Scaliger's error.[80] In 1597 Bonaventura Vulcanius mistakenly applied the name *Codex Argenteus* to a manuscript containing *notae Lombardicae*, and then went on to say that he had heard there was also (*etiam*) a work *de notis veterum Romanorum* in the Palatine Library. A careless reading of this might have been thought to imply that the *Codex Argenteus* was there as well. De Jonge also points out that Scaliger did in fact know a man, Marnix of St Aldegonde, who had seen the real *Codex Argenteus* with his own eyes—but in a different library. Scaliger presumably fused all these details together in his 'recollection'.

It should by now be clear that Scaliger's recollections about the whereabouts and contents of unpublished manuscripts are far from trustworthy. I submit that all we can be reasonably sure of is that Porto told Scaliger *something* about Sophianus seeing an old Anthology manuscript containing erotic poems not in Planudes. But we can have no confidence that Porto himself ever saw it, or that Sophianus ever had it in his possession.

---

[78] See the new edition by E. Livrea and P. Eleuteri (1982), p. 1. It was this discovery that confirmed Stephanus in his feeling that Musaeus wrote under the Roman Empire, not in the days of Orpheus.

[79] *Secunda Scaligerana*, pp. 328–9, 362, 364, 389, 396, 434, 461, 483, 553, all cited by de Jonge, p. 291.

[80] 'J. J. Scaligers Nachrichten über den Codex Argenteus in Heidelberg', *Bibliothèque d'Humanisme et Renaissance* xxxix (1977), 285–94.

We may now turn to the identity of this manuscript. Scarcely *ABV*. For although *ABV* contains erotic material absent from *APl*, it has no epigrams by Callimachus, nor could it have been called either 'extremely old' (the three extant copies are all of the sixteenth century) or a 'complete text of the Anthology'. One possibility is the *Sylloge Parisina* (S), whose final, erotic section includes 25 pederastic poems absent from *APl* (Ch. X). The very fact that most of its 90 other epigrams are Planudean might have seemed to reinforce the guess that these were the very poems that Planudes had so notoriously boasted of suppressing ('mutilavit et . . . castravit hunc librum', in the words of Lascaris). By *integrum codicem* Porto might have meant no more than a manuscript containing those obscene poems. Its only manuscript (Par. suppl. gr. 352) is of the thirteenth century, hardly *summae vetustatis* but certainly old. That leaves the standard (if most problematic) assumption: that what Sophianus saw was *AP*.

AP cannot have been in Ferrara between 1546 and 1554 when Michael and Porto were together there. Throughout this period it was in Belgium with the Clements, at any rate up to John's death in 1572. And in case it be suggested that Thomas' list includes items lost or disposed of before then, the comparison with Stephanus' edition of 1566 proves that it was still in Clement's possession until then, a year after Michael's death.

But Sophianus might have heard of Clement's manuscript. The two men had a mutual friend in Stephanus, who knew that Clement owned *AP* and might easily have passed the information on to Michael. Michael's closest friend was Pier Vettori,[81] whom Stephanus had told about *AP* and presumably Clement as well. And we have already seen that Michael was on close terms with the Belgian scholar Ellebode, who might also have known Clement during his Belgian exile. More than one channel existed through which contact could have been made.

But would Clement have lent one of his treasures? He had built up his library with great care and at no small expense, and maintained it 'like a rich treasure' (*divitis . . . thesauri instar*), as Simon Grynaeus put it as early as 1531.[82] Grynaeus, a professor at

[81] Legrand i. 173–5.

[82] Despite its obvious flattery, it seems worth quoting the relevant part of Grynaeus' dedication in full, the only account we have of the growth of Clement's library, evidently already an impressive collection: 'non monumenta solum, quae

Basle, had copied Clement's manuscript of Proclus *de motu* and published the *editio princeps* of the work later that year in Basle. Unfortunately his preface does not make clear whether he came to London for the purpose or discovered the existence of Clement's manuscript by chance when there. If we can put any weight on Vettori's *forte*, it was by chance that Stephanus heard of Clement's *Anacreontea*. In his edition of Cyprian (1568), Jacobus Pamelius reports that Clement 'sent him some *castigationes*'. Since in the lexicon of the humanists *castigatio* implies corrections rather than merely manuscript readings,[83] it might be inferred that it was Clement rather than Pamelius who actually did the collating. In his Tertullian (1584), published after Clement's death, Pamelius refers, echoing Grynaeus' phrase, to the manuscript 'which John Clement used to keep in his house like a treasure' (*quem thesauri loco penes se adservabat quondam Joan. Clemens Anglus*, p. 8). That too suggests that he was not allowed to take the precious text away. And the Tertullian may indeed have been very old and valuable, if (as seems likely) it is the manuscript recorded in an old library catalogue at Corbie.[84] But in 1568 it was Clement who took the initiative in offering to lend some manuscripts to the Antwerp printer C. Plantin for his Polyglot Bible. Plantin records a letter from Clement listing among other manuscripts *une partie de la*

plurima veterum apud te habes, mira diligentia pervestigata, mox ingenti cum labore et sumptu conquisita, ac divitis demum thesauri instar conservata destinasti, sed studium praeterea omne tuum eodem conferre libenter soles: quippe cui non satis fuit ad certum patriae et amicorum solatium, ex utriusque linguae fontibus et diuturna inter exteros peregrinatione, per incredibiles labores absolutam artis medicae notitiam comparasse, nisi eosdem autores unde praeclare tu profecisti, optimos illos, velut viam rectam, mortalibus etiam caeteris comunicasses: de Galeno loquor, cui tu, cum per tot saecula sepultus iacuisset, ut typis aliquando descriptus reviviscere, et princeps in omni philosophia vir, in manus mortalium restitueretur, non obstetricatus es solum, sed passim per Italiam velut ossa et membra eius disiecta colligens, per ALDI officinam, autorem nobilem ab internicie vindicatum, aeternitati consecrasti: principes ipsos hac in re, privatus homo, memorabili conatu supergressus: nam horum munus erat puto, sapientiam in coetus hominum revocare praeclarum magis quam regna de manibus hostium eruere' (*Procli insignis philosophi . . . de motu* [Basle 1531], 3–5).

[83] 'Il sostantivo *castigatio*, usato dagli umanisti come sinonimo di *correctio*, indica sia l'azione del correggere che il resultato dell'azione, la correzione', Silvia Rizzo, *Il lessico filologico degli umanisti* (Rome 1973), 276, citing examples.

[84] Ae. Kroymann, *Tertulliani opera*, ii. 2 (1952), pp. xxvi–xxvii; cf. Mai, *Spic. Rom.* v. 203. The name of 'Clemens Anglus' and his siglum C appear often in the app. crit. of the relevant treatises of Tertullian, where 'nonnumquam in vera scriptura indaganda haud contemnendam adferant opem' (G. Wissowa, *Tertull. opera*, i [1890], p. xi).

Bible grecque jusques au livres des Roix, qui est très ancienne et beaucoup différente de celles qui sont imprimées.[85] Plantin's editor, Arias Montanus, wrote as follows in his preface: 'est etiam nobis a Clemente Anglo, philosophiae et medicinae doctore, qui in hisce regionibus propter Christianam religionem exulat, exhibitum Pentateuchi Graeci, *ex Thomae Mori bibliotheca,* elegantissimum exemplar.' Even so, we cannot assume that Clement let this precious book[86] out of his sight. Vulcanius was delighted when, after the second sack of Malines in April 1580, he managed to acquire from Thomas two manuscripts, Leidensis 54 (the *Histories* of Agathias) and 56 (the *De Thematibus* of Constantine Porphyrogenitus), from which he published the *editiones principes* of both texts (1588 and 1594). Neither manuscript is earlier than the fourteenth century, and other manuscripts of both works soon turned up,[87] but at the time they were unique. In his dedicatory letter of 1588 Vulcanius describes himself as freeing the books from 'many years of lurking in the dust and squalor' of Clement's library.[88] This was hardly fair. Clement was an informed collector, well aware of the value of his acquisitions, and in his day made good use of his Galen manuscripts in editing Galen. But the fact remains that if *AP* had been allowed to remain in Venice or Padua, its new texts would surely have been published within a few years, and the subsequent history of the Greek Anthology would have been very different.

Clement may have allowed and occasionally invited scholars and publishers to examine his treasures, but not on a regular basis. He seems to have taken no steps to have any more of the new texts in *AP* published. If Sophianus' manuscript was indeed *AP*, it must

[85] Wenkebach p. 67 n. 88.

[86] This is presumably the Greek Octateuch bearing a dedication from John Clement now in the Glasgow University Library: Wenkebach 67; Mercati 306–7 and J. Baldwin, *The Bibliotheck* viii (1977), 130 and 147, with pl. 5. But there are problems. The date of the dedication is 7 Oct. 1563, five years before the letter to Plantin. But, like Par. gr. 2168, the dedication is to Clement's old college, Corpus Christi, Oxford, just as Leiden 16 is dedicated to New College, Oxford; and since none of these manuscripts is now or perhaps ever has been in any of those colleges, it seems that, for whatever reason, he changed his mind. This is the only direct evidence that Clement inherited manuscripts from his father-in-law.

[87] R. Keydell, *Agathiae Historiae* (Berlin 1967), pp. xiii f. (mistakenly criticizing Vulcanius for referring to Thomas rather than John Clement); A. Pertusi, *Constantino Porfirogenito De Thematibus* (Vatican 1952), 9 f.

[88] 'apud medicum quendam Anglum, Thomam Clementem, parum clementer habitus multos annos in bibliothecae vel βιβλιοπέδης potius squalore et pulvere latuit' [sc. Constantinus].

have been in Belgium that he saw it, perhaps on a visit to his friend Ellebode, perhaps on a special trip to see Clement's collection.

There is one final, curious detail. Leidensis BPG 34b is a codex in which Scaliger himself copied in his own hand[89] a good selection of the non-Planudean material from *AP* (presumably from information supplied by Gruter, since he never saw *AP* himself). At the end of his selection stand the following words: *haec tria ultima Epigrammata attulit e Graecia Michael Sophianos, qui obiit Ferrariae anno DCLXV xv Augusti.* There follow three epigrams, all of epigraphic origin, all of the late Hellenistic or Roman period. One is stated to have been copied from a marble plaque on show in Venice, where it was later copied by Scipione Maffei;[90] another is said to have come from Chios;[91] and the last was copied from a cave in Crete by Cyriacus Ancona before Sophianus.[92] Interestingly enough, this is the only surviving evidence for the exact date of Michael's death. The other evidence is two letters to the Duke of Ferrara, Michael's patron, by his secretary, Lucio Paganucci:[93] the first, dated 5 August 1565, informs the Duke that Michael has suffered an aneurism and is not expected to live; the second, dated 22 August, announces his death. Scaliger's 15 August is clearly based on good information, and we may presume that the epigrams do indeed derive from copies made by Sophianus on his travels. So do we have a link between Michael Sophianus and Scaliger himself? Surely not. Since Scaliger was so emphatic that the Sophianus who knew Porto was called Nicholas, he may well have thought that Michael was a different man. The natural assumption is that he derived these epigrams from the same source as all the

---

[89] As kindly confirmed for me by H. J. de Jonge (letter to A. Grafton, 4 Apr. 1991).

[90] I have brought up to date the antiquated references given by Aubreton (1980), 22 n. 4: see *CIG* ii. 2415 = Kaibel 218 = *IG* xii. 5. 310 = Peek *GV* 1871; see too M. Guarducci, *RIA* ix (1942), 39 f.; E. L. Bowie, in D. A. Russell (ed.), *Antonine Literature* (1990), 58.

[91] *CIG* ii. 2240 = Kaibel 233 = *GV* 1420. According to Boeckh, written with the lemma εὑρέθη ἐν Χίῳ in a copy of Lascaris' 1544 Anthology (misunderstood by Aubreton [1980], 22 n. 4). Whether this copy was independent of Michael Sophianus is unclear. Chian provenance is supported by the fact that Protarchos is a name found on Chios: P. M. Fraser and E. Matthews, *Lexicon of Greek Proper Names*, i (Oxford 1987), 389, citing *SEG* xxxv (1988), 930 and one or two other texts.

[92] Gruter, *Thesaurus*, p. mlxviii = *CIG* ii. 2569 = Kaibel 815 = *Inscr. Cret.* ii. 302–4 (with bibliography of the early copies, but not mentioning Michael).

[93] Published by G. Bertoni, *La Rinascità* iv (1941), 890–1.

others copied into the manuscript: from Gruter. Indeed, Gruter had only recently published the last of the three in his *Thesaurus* (1602–3). Eager to satisfy Scaliger's enthusiasm for new epigrams, Gruter sent him all he could find. So no link between Scaliger and Sophianus. And if this is a fair sample of Sophianus' Greek epigram collection, it looks as if his primary interest lay in epigraphic poetry.

At all events, whether or not Michael Sophianus ever had *AP* in his hands, there seems no reason to doubt that it was still in Belgium in 1572—and in all probability till the second sack of Malines in 1580, after which Clement's collection was dispersed.[94] The exact date of its acquisition by the Palatine library in Heidelberg is unknown. Though absent from F. Sylburg's inventories of 1584 and 1591, it seems to have been in Sylburg's private library till his death in 1596.[95] His personal copy of the second Aldine contains a partial collation of *AP* in his own hand.[96] It is also said that he made the influential complete apograph known as the 'codex Vossianus'.[97] Salmasius always gets the credit for 'discovering' *AP*, but Sylburg (like Thomas Clement) was evidently aware of its superiority to existing editions. He may have got hold of it in or soon after 1580.

It was not till the nineteenth century that *AP* found a permanent home. If books could write, it would tell of wanderings worthy of Sinbad. Scarcely installed in Heidelberg, it was carried to Rome as the spoils of war in 1623; then to Paris as spoils of another war in 1797; finally, in 1815, back again to Heidelberg—at least for vol. i. By some oversight, vol. ii remained in the Bibliothèque Nationale, and by the time the oversight was noticed in Heidelberg, the French refused to surrender it. That is how vol. ii became Parisinus graecus 384. How vol. i became Palatinus graecus 23 is a bizarre if minor puzzle recently solved by P. Canart. The original

---

[94] Mercati 302–3.

[95] Preisendanz (1911), col. v; Aubreton (1980), 5; P. Canart, *Scriptorium* xxxv (1981), 227–8; H. Görgemanns, in *Bibliotheca Palatina*, ed. E. Mittler (Heidelberg 1986), 486. For another manuscript known to have been in Sylburg's private possession before being acquired by the Library, Pal. gr. 417, see Görgemanns, ibid. 78 and 438.

[96] Said by Preisendanz in 1911 to have disappeared, but on show in the exhibition of 1986: Görgemanns, *Bibliotheca Palatina*, 487–8. On the careers and activity of Sylburg and Gruter at Heidelberg, see the various articles by various scholars in this useful catalogue, pp. 435–57.

[97] Hutton (1946), 8–9; Aubreton (1980), 6–9.

number assigned by Gruter was 443, for which L. Allaci in Rome substituted 33. But during rebinding in the late eighteenth century, a gilder in error stamped 213 on the spine of vol. ii. This was 'corrected' by pasting a bit of parchment over the 1, thus leaving 23. The correct 33 on vol. ii was then altered to 23 to harmonize![98]

The final puzzle is the further delay of two centuries before publication—indeed of three and a half centuries (almost to the year) before the first complete edition of the Anthology directly based on *AP*. Given the long search for all those sexy poems Planudes had cut out, and given the earlier huge success of Stephanus' *Anacreontea*, we might have expected the remaining new poems to be published without delay. Many plans were formed, many manuscript copies (mostly excerpts) were made, now for the first time studied in detail by R. Aubreton.[99] But for one reason or another they all came to nought. It was not till the beginning of the nineteenth century that the epigrammatic parts of *AP* were finally published in full (by F. Jacobs, 1813–17), though even then not from *AP* itself. It was not till 1957–8 that Hermann Beckby published an edition that could really be said to report the contents and text of *AP* with any degree of accuracy and completeness.

But however remarkable, the vicissitudes of *AP* since 1607 are at least well documented. What remain to be determined are its whereabouts during the sixteenth century. The traditional view, first propounded (it seems) by P. Herbert and maintained in our own times by Gallavotti, Aubreton, Mioni, and Görgemanns, is that it passed from Colocci either to Orsini or to N. Sophianus (or to both in succession) and then to his kinsman M. Sophianus; then to Francesco Porto and finally to Francesco's son Emilio, who lived in Heidelberg at the beginning of the seventeenth century and might therefore be claimed as the channel whereby *AP* eventually reached the Palatine Library. Mioni calls this a 'viaggio . . . assai fantasioso'. It is not in fact more fantastic than the wanderings described in this chapter: from Padua to London and then, driven by religious persecution to Louvain and Malines before finally surfacing in Heidelberg. The objection to the traditional view is rather its fragility. To say no more at this point of the

[98] P. Canart, 'Les cotes du manuscrit palatin de l'*Anthologie*', *Scriptorium* xxxv (1981), 227–40; I am simplifying an even more complex series of renumberings and misnumberings.

[99] Aubreton (1980), 1–53; (1981), 1–46.

problem of identifying Orsini's 'old book' with *AP*, Nicolaus
Sophianus, cataloguer (with Matthew Devaris) of the Greek
manuscripts of Cardinal Ridolfi and the only link with Orsini's
circle at Rome, is best eliminated from the picture altogether. The
idea that Michael was Nicolaus' son goes back to Humphrey
Hody's *De Graecis Illustribus* of 1742 (p. 311). In fact Michael's
father was called George.[100] Others have claimed Nicolaus as
Michael's uncle (Waltz as his grandfather!). But the fact that
Michael is regularly styled Chian and Nicolaus Corfiote would
seem to rule out the possibility of any blood relationship (which is
never even hinted at by contemporaries). Nicholas must surely be
excluded from future discussion: although Scaliger wrote Nicolaus, he clearly meant Michael. And if Porto had himself inherited
from Michael the treasure about which he (allegedly) so often told
Scaliger, why tell him only that he saw it 'in manibus Sophiani'? If
Porto ever owned *AP*, he would already have had it by the time he
met Scaliger. And if it had been Emilio Porto who presented *AP* to
the Palatine Library, then surely Gruter or Salmasius would have
known and Scaliger would not have been reduced to guesswork; he
would have told Gruter to check with Emilio, who was actually
living in Heidelberg at the time.[101] There is no reason to suppose
that Porto père acquired any of Michael's manuscripts, which
(according to Vettori) passed into the hands of a kinsman who lived
abroad, a merchant. In 1606, as we have already seen, they were
acquired by the Ambrosian Library in Milan. No Anthology
manuscript was among them.

Furthermore, on the evidence of another unpublished
commentary it can now be added with confidence that Emilio
Porto had no knowledge of *AP*. There are in the Bodleian Library
extensive notes on the Anthology in Emilio's own hand (MS
D'Orville 277), written at Heidelberg between November 1604
and January 1605, on the very eve of the rediscovery of *AP* in the
Palatine Library.[102] There is not one Palatine poem or reading or

---

[100] Moustoxidis, Ἑλληνομνήμων (1843), 264.

[101] On Emilio Porto, see Hutton (1935), 253–4; H. D. Saffrey and L. G.
Westerink, *Proclus: Théologie platonicienne*, i (Paris 1968), pp. xciii–xciv.

[102] F. Madan, *A Summary Catalogue of Western Manuscripts in the Bodleian
Library* IV (1897), 101, no. 17155. I examined the manuscript in Jan. 1980. There
are various indications (notably the casual and often trifling author-corrections on
every page) that the book is an autograph. Emilio's hand is in any case known from
other manuscripts in the Bodleian and elsewhere.

ascription to be found throughout the hundred pages of Emilio's notes. Time and again where comparison with *AP* would have brought instant illumination, it is clear that Emilio knew nothing that was not in Stephanus' Anthology, his base text.

If Orsini's παλαιὸν ἀντίγραφον was, as the context implies, an erotic appendix to *APl*, then it was most likely *ABV*. If we may infer from the 'old' that the manuscript was no later than the fourteenth century, then it was a much earlier witness than our three extant manuscripts. An ἀντίγραφον need not have been a separate volume. Orsini's inventory lists separately numerous items bound up together with other texts. Can we in fact identify this ἀντίγραφον with an item in the inventory? Hutton drew attention to no. 65 (not identified by de Nolhac) in the list of Greek printed books: 'Epigrammatorio d'Aldo, con un quinterno d'epigrammi non impressi.' But a gathering bound up with a printed book is likely to have been written later than the book (1503)—unless its pages just happened to match the small format of the Aldine. Furthermore, no one seems to have compared the suspiciously similar entry no. 118 on the list of Greek manuscripts: 'quinterno di epigrammi Graeci antichi oltre li stampati dal Planude, inserto in un' epigrammatario in -4° stampato et tocco dal Lascari [i.e. Lascaris' edition of 1494].' It would be an odd coincidence for Orsini to have possessed two printed editions bound up with a 'quinterno' of unpublished epigrams not in Planudes. De Nolhac has pointed out that Orsini was more careless than one might have expected in drawing up the inventory of so valuable and familiar a collection, and it is surely more likely that, while (quite reasonably) entering this hybrid item under both manuscripts and printed books, he mistakenly wrote Aldo for Lascari the second time—the more understandably in that the four preceding items in the printed book list, 61–4, are all Aldine Anthologies. If so, then the book in question can be identified with certainty as *Vatic. incun.* III. 81, and the 'quinterno' (a term Orsini used loosely for gatherings of varying size) of unpublished epigrams has nothing to do with *ABV*. It is no more than a miscellany of epigrams from other classical sources, especially Pausanias.[103]

But this cannot have been the παλαιὸν ἀντίγραφον. It is not old enough, nor does it contain the non-Planudean erotica Orsini cites it for. The only extant collection other than *AP* of any antiquity

[103] de Nolhac (1887), 159; Mioni (1975), 294–5.

(thirteenth century) with a substantial number of non-Planudean erotica is the *sylloge Parisina* (Ch. X), the final section of which contains 31 pederastic poems, all absent from Planudes. It is not absolutely impossible that this was Orsini's manuscript, but there is nothing positive to link it with Colocci (or Orsini), and there is also another objection.

As Michael Reeve pointed out,[104] there seems to be a distinction in Orsini's note (quoted p. 177) between the erotic epigrams 'collected by Colocci' and the 'old manuscript' in which they were written. Since Colocci knew little Greek,[105] it is unlikely that he made any such collection himself. But Orsini may have meant a collection added to an old manuscript of Colocci's in a sixteenth-century hand that he mistakenly identified as Colocci's. That would rule out both *AP* and the *sylloge Parisina*, but it would fit a copy of *ABV* well enough—though hardly the fourteenth-century original postulated in this chapter.

---

[104] 'I don't see how things συλλεχθέντα παρὰ Ἀγγέλου τοῦ Κολλωτίου can have been in the παλαιὸν ἀντίγραφον by the original hand', letter dated 28-2-80.

[105] *Dizionario biografico degli Italiani* xxvii (1982), 108.

IX

Laurentianus XXXII. 16

THIS celebrated codex (hereafter L), compiled by Planudes between 1280 and 1283 (and subsequently bought by Filelfo in 1423 from the widow of J. Chrysoloras in Constantinople), is well known to all serious students of Greek epic.[1] As a light relief an anthology of minor poetry was added, comprising some Phocylides, selected dogmatic poems by Gregory Nazianzen, and two short collections of epigrams. Despite attracting the attention of such cognoscenti as C. Wendel[2] and C. Gallavotti,[3] the epigrams have been curiously neglected by students of the Anthology. Only one editor has read the manuscript at all, H. Beckby for his second edition of 1967–8.

As remarked already, the text presented by L is almost entirely valueless. Its importance lies in (*a*) the recent identification of the hand in which the epigram sections are written as Planudes' own, and (*b*) the question of the relationship of the two collections both to *AP* and to the sources later used by Planudes for his major anthology of 1301 (*APl*).

Here is a full list of the various parts of the epigrammatic corpus in L:[4]

---

[1] See the full description and bibliography given by A. Turyn, *Dated Greek MSS* (1972), 228–39.

[2] 'Planudea', *BZ* xl (1940), at pp. 423–5.

[3] *Boll. Class. Lincei*, NS vii (1959), 37–50.

[4] I have corrected the few inaccuracies in Gallavotti's list (*Boll. Class. Lincei*, NS vii [1959], 45–6); those published by A. Chiari (*Raccolta . . . F. Ramorino* (1927), 572) and Wendel (1940) are quite unusable. From the top of fo. 5ᵛ Gallavotti gives x. 37–9 and 41 for x. 37, 38, 40, and 41; and claims that on fo. 384ʳ Cougny VII. 29 is written between *AP* xiv. 56. 1–2 and lines 3–4 of the same poem—a curious slip (inexcusably perpetuated by Buffière ad loc.), since Cougny VII. 29 *is AP* xiv. 56. 3–4.

Part I (fos. 3ʳ–6ᵛ)

AP			AP			AP		
	v.	297		x.	27		v.	229
		302			28			236
	vii.	56			29			291. 5–6
		89			30	fo. 5ᵛ	x.	37
	xi.	395			31			38
	vii.	126			32			40
	ix.	61	[Paroem. II. 167. 11]					41
	vii.	309			34			42
		327			35. 3–4			45
fo. 3ᵛ		336	fo. 4ᵛ	ix.	43			46
	ix.	394			74			47
		499			80			51
		527			120			52
		573			133			54
		642			138			57
		768			165			58
		769			166			59
	x.	98			167			60
		104			172			61
	xi.	50			359			62
		61			360	fo. 6ʳ		63
		156		vii.	586. 3–4			64
		193			620			65
fo. 4ʳ		238		ix.	23. 7–8			66
		251	fo. 5ʳ	vii.	339			69
		292. 3–4			400. 3–4			72
		293			476. 7–10			73
		294			476. 3–4			76
		303			567			77
		349			630			78
		381			650			79
		391		xv.	9 (εἰς			80
		401	τὸν βασιλέα Θεοδόσιον)			fo. 6ᵛ		84
		428	Cougny II. 732					85
		432	AP	xv.	29			36

[APl 27
(ἐπιγραφὴ εἰς τὸν
τάφον
Σαρδαναπάλου)]

Part II *(fos. 381ᵛ–384ʳ)*

(a) ἐκ τῆς Θεοσοφίας (with detailed individual lemmata for each oracle)

Cougny VI. 140	Cougny VI. 153
148	154
149	184
150	185
144	261
151	*AP* x. 108
152	Cougny VI. 155

(b) αἰνίγματα (with occasional lemmata)

Cougny VII. 31	Cougny VII. 23
AP xiv. 19	*AP* xiv. 9
26	12
30	20
32	22
35	56
41	61
42	
57⁵	
58	
60	
62	

(c) Ἐπιγράμματα δι᾽ ἡρωελεγείων εἰς τὰς ἐν τῷ Ἱπποδρόμῳ Κωνσταντινου-
πόλεως ἱσταμένας στήλας τῶν ἐν αὐτῷ νικησάντων τεθρίππῳ ὧν καὶ τὰ
ὀνόματα δηλοῦνται ἐν τοῖς αὐτοῖς ἐπιγράμμασιν

APl	335	*APl*	347
	338		363
	337	*AP* xv.	43 (365a)
	336	*APl*	366
	339	*AP* xv.	41 (364a)
	353	*APl*	371
	355		374
AP xv.	44 (346a)		373
APl	348	*AP* xv.	45 (378a)
	361		49 (375a)
	358		48 (377a)
	359	*APl*	377
	360		376
	361 *bis*		

⁵ In fact only the first couplets of 57 and 58 are written here: the second couplets
follow after Cougny VII. 23, but since it is clear from the symbols in the margin
that the omissions were accidental, for the sake of simplicity I have restored
Planudes' intended order.

Both Wendel and Gallavotti remarked in very general terms on the obvious affinity between L and *AP* (to which we shall return), but neither went into the question of the sources of *APl*. One might have expected to find that L and *APl* were based on the same source; that L contained a briefer selection from one (presumably the first) of the two sources of *APl*. Surprisingly enough such is not the case.

Of the 105 epigrams in Part I of L, almost all reappear in *APl*. But (not to mention the run of riddle epigrams and oracles in Part II) five do not: namely *AP* v. 291, vii. 620, xv. 9, xv. 29, and Cougny II. 732. And while most of the epigrams that do reappear in *APl* occur in the main body of the Anthology, taken from the first of Planudes' sources, four he was only able to add from the second: namely *AP* vii. 339, ix. 527, x. 78, and xi. 401. From this it follows that the source of L must have contained poems absent from *both* the sources of *APl*.

It could be objected that either of the sources of *APl* (let us distinguish them hereafter as Pl*a* and Pl*b*) might have contained all nine of these poems, and that when compiling *APl* Planudes either overlooked or deliberately omitted them. Such a hypothesis would be based on the assumption more often implied than stated that Planudes merely selected from these two sources. It is certainly true (as we have noted on several occasions) that much Palatine material is missing from *APl*. But the fact that Planudes was able to add so much from Pl*b* shows that Pl*a* must already have been a substantially reduced redaction of Cephalas. Whether Pl*b* was itself correspondingly fuller than Pl*a* overall we cannot judge, since obviously it may have lacked much that was included in Pl*a*. There is another point. A not inconsiderable number of the addenda from Pl*b* are in fact duplications of poems already taken from Pl*a*. It is indeed these duplications that form one of the neatest proofs of Basson's demonstration that Pl*a* and Pl*b* were different redactions of the same anthology, namely Cephalas; for comparison of the two contexts together (where possible) with the normally fuller sequences in *AP* shows that Planudes must have found them in the same context in both his sources. For our present purpose, however, what they illustrate best is Planudes' anxiety not to miss a single epigram. This anxiety is further illustrated by the fact that he left blank spaces of up to half a page after each section of his addenda, evidently in the hope that he   .

might come across yet another manuscript and be able to add a few more epigrams. If he had been using one of the same sources as in 1280, it would be surprising if he had overlooked in 1301 as many as five or nine poems (depending whether it was Pl*b* or Pl*a*) that he had thought worth including in his much briefer anthology of 1280. The very fact that he draws attention to his deliberate omission of some of the erotica in Pl*a* suggests that he had *not* been selecting from the other categories.

The presumption is, then, that *APl* reflects the contents of Pl*a* and Pl*b* very closely, and that consequently L is not based on either, a conclusion that is borne out by two quite different considerations. In the first place, the text presented by L is (as we have seen) very corrupt, much poorer than the text of *APl*;[6] in the second, almost none of the poems in Part I of L are provided with ascriptions or lemmata, whereas the majority of poems in Pl*a* and Pl*b* evidently were so provided. Now Planudes was no hack copyist, and it would be quite implausible to ascribe both these features of L to haste and inaccuracy on his part. And even if some of the errors had been due to his inaccuracy, it would be astonishing, if he had been using the same source, that he should have repeated *none* of them when copying *APl* twenty years later. The conclusion seems inescapable that the source of L was *not* either Pl*a* or Pl*b*, but some other less full, less accurately copied anthology which offered fewer ascriptions and lemmata.

That this anthology—like Pl*a* and Pl*b*—was yet another redaction of Cephalas is indicated by the very close parallelism between L and *AP*. The table of contents reveals two interesting things about Part I: first, that it consists of a series of often short sequences in Palatine order from six of the Palatine categories; and second, on closer inspection, that these short sequences are for the most part arbitrarily rearranged fragments from originally longer sequences. This is particularly clear in the case of the protreptica (*AP* x). Col. i of the table contains x. 98 and 104, col. ii (with one omission) 27–35 and iii (with several omissions) 37–85, with 36 (presumably omitted in error from the beginning of the sequence). Finally there is x. 108, a prayer to Zeus, which was held over for the section on oracles on fo. 382[r]. From the sympotica and scoptica (*AP* xi) there is (apart from the isolated xi. 395 on fo. 3[r]) one unbroken sequence, 16 poems running from xi. 50 to xi. 432. But

---

[6] See Cameron (1973), 259–64.

there are similar broken erotic, sepulchral, and epideictic/ecphras-
tic sequences. From *AP* v, for example, there are two brief runs:
297 and 302 in col. i followed by 229, 236, and 291 in col. iii. From
AP vii there are 309–650 in col. ii. From ix, 394–769 in col. i and
43–360 in col. ii. That the breaking up and rearranging of these
sequences is the work of Planudes may be inferred with certainty
from the adjustment of successive instalments of protreptica to the
pages of L: for example, it was precisely at the bottom of fo. 4^r that
he broke off the first long sequence with x. 35 to begin the new
page with epideictica, taking it up again with x. 37 at the top of fo.
5^v. Evidently Planudes was already dissatisfied with the Cephalan
thematic categories, though as yet his only way of coping with their
monotony was to cut the sequences into shorter blocks and mix
them up.

Whether these are all the epigrams that L's source contained or
just a selection there is no means of judging.[7] The fact that
Planudes did not use it for *APl* may mean no more than that it was
no longer available to him in 1301. On the other hand it may be
that he deliberately ignored it precisely because in both scope and
execution it was so obviously inferior to Pl*a*. After all, whether or
not he still had access to L's source, he could at least have checked
his own apograph in L, where he would have found the nine
epigrams listed above to add to the tally of Pl*a*.

On balance then I would suggest that the source of Part I of L
was a very much abbreviated redaction of Cephalas, hardly much
larger than L itself. It contained excerpts from the Cephalan
equivalents to *AP* v, vii, ix, x, xi, and apparently xv as well.
Anathematica (*AP* vi) and paederastica (*AP* xii) seem not to have
been represented.

We pass now to the links between Part II of L and *AP* xiv,
already briefly touched upon above (p. 135). *AP* xiv is a tripartite
anthology of riddles, oracles, and arithmetical problems. Part II of
L is another tripartite anthology, of riddles, oracles, and epigrams
on charioteers. Now by a lucky chance the whole series of
charioteer epigrams, just as they were transcribed direct from the

---

[7] *AP* ix. 440 (Moschus' 'Runaway Love') appears on fo. 297^v in Planudes' hand,
on which see below. In addition, ix. 495. 3 (see P. Maas, *Kl. Schr.* (Munich 1973),
168) is quoted in the margin by Nonnus, *Dion.* xxxiii. 316 on fo. 114^v, once more
perhaps (like several other scholia on Nonnus: Turyn, *Dated Greek MSS* (1972),
32) in Planudes' hand.

original monuments, is preserved in Planudes' later definitive anthology of 1301 (Marc. 481, fos. 43ᵛ–45ᵛ, split up in modern editions between *AP* xv. 41–50 and *APl* 335–78). Thus it is possible to see that the series in L is just a selection from this fuller series, with no additions from elsewhere.[8] What now of the two other sections?

A glance at the list of riddles (fo. 382ᵛ) as set out on p. 204 above will show that those in the first column follow the order of *AP* exactly, and though the seven in the second break the original sequence, they are still in the order of *AP*. It looks as if Planudes excerpted the same original sequence twice. Having copied out his first choice of a dozen riddles (the riddle sequence ends at xiv. 64 and the last poem in L is xiv. 62), Planudes decided to fill up his page with a few more (all but two of the second batch are distichs, and they do reach exactly to the bottom of the page). So he skimmed through his exemplar again from the beginning, adding a few he had missed the first time round (for example, having originally passed from 60 to 62, he now took 61).

The implication is that Planudes had before him a sequence of riddles arranged in exactly the same order as the sequence in *AP* xiv. What now of Cougny VII. 31 and 23, known to us (in the Anthology tradition) only from L? Both *could*, of course, be additions from another source, but the single sources employed for both the charioteer epigrams and (as we shall see) the oracles render this most unlikely.

And a closer look at the riddle sequence will reveal that Cougny VII. 23 is not in fact a riddle. Now it would be odd for Planudes to have gone to the trouble of consulting another source for his riddle sequence and then add a poem which was not a riddle at all. On the other hand, it would *not* be odd for the compiler of the original riddle series to have included Cougny VII. 23, since the sequence in *AP* xiv includes no fewer than three poems which, though mildly puzzling, are no more riddles than Cougny VII. 23: nos. 8, 10, and 15.

In this connection, it is particularly instructive to see that L includes xiv. 9, which is not a riddle but an arithmetical puzzle. Now *AP* xiv contains an approximately equal number each of riddles, oracles, and arithmetical problems. Basically, the oracles occupy the middle of the book (65–100), and the problems the end

---

[8] I have demonstrated this in detail in Cameron (1973), Chs. III–IV.

(116–46), though between 101 and 115 there is a mixture of riddles and oracles. Basically, the rest of the book consists of riddles, though most of 1–13 are problems (1–4, 6–7, 11–13), as also are 48–51—not to mention the three that are neither riddles nor problems (8, 10, 15). That is to say, the book is not divided cleanly and straightforwardly (like the tripartite anthology in L) into its three component parts. Some attempt has been made to provide short mixed sections, without however breaking up all the material in this way. Now Aubreton, for whom the Palatine scribes are the compilers rather than just the copyists of *AP* xiv, would ascribe this idiosyncratic and haphazard method of arrangement to those scribes rather than to their sources, since in his view they made additions to whatever sources they may have used at irregular intervals throughout.[9] Yet here we have L evidently drawing on a source which is not *AP* but which nevertheless already contained the idiosyncratic *mélange* of riddles and problems *AP* xiv. 1–13. If it can be shown that L's source was *fuller* than *AP* xiv, then it would have to be a source which was *earlier* than *AP* xiv. And if L's source contained Cougny VII. 31 and 23, then it *was* fuller than *AP* xiv.

For the moment let us call this postulated common source *X*. Now the riddle sequence proper in *AP* xiv runs from xiv. 14 to 64. With the exception of xiv. 9 from the mixed sequence 1–13, all the riddles in L are from this main sequence, running from 19 to 62. Now since Cougny VII. 31 stands before xiv. 19 in L, presumably it also stood before 19 in *X*—probably before 14 and 19.

Here is the poem:

Πέντ' ἄνδρες δέκα νηυσὶ κατήλυθον εἰς ἕνα χῶρον,
ἐν δὲ λίθοις ἐμάχοντο, λίθον δ' οὐκ ἦν ἀνελέσθαι·
δίψῃ δ' ἐξώλλυντο, ὕδωρ δ' ὑπερεῖχε γένεια.

Not of course a real shipwreck, which would not explain why there are twice as many ships as sailors in l. 1. The answer, as my former student Mark Caponigro ingeniously pointed out, is bitter almonds.[10] A man takes a handful—to be precise five—splits them into five kernels and ten half-shells, the five 'sailors' and ten 'ships' (cf. the 'nut-sailors' in their half-shells of Lucian's *True History* ii. 38), and puts them on 'one place', namely his tongue. The dry taste

---

[9] *L'Ant. class.* xxxviii (1969), 461.
[10] 'Five Men and Ten Ships' in *GRBS* xxv (1984), 285–96.

prompts him to take a sip of water (for the practice of swallowing 'five or six' almonds to induce thirst cf. Athenaeus, ii. 52D), and the sailors 'drown' (go down his throat), after a vain battle with 'unmovable rocks' (his teeth). So the thirst they die of is not theirs but his, and the chin that is covered by water is likewise his.

Is there a suitable context for a riddle like this between xiv. 14 and 19? There is indeed. Compare xiv. 14 itself:

Εἷς ἄνεμος· δύο νῆες· ἐρέττουσιν δέκα ναῦται·
εἰς δὲ κυβερνήτης ἀμφοτέρας ἐλάει.

Answer:[11] the double flute (αὐλός), the ten sailors being the ten fingers and the wind the breath of the player, while the two ships are of course the two pipes. Just like Cougny VII. 31, the point turns on a specified number of 'ships' and 'sailors', who turn out to be something quite different, in contact with the elements. Naturally enough there are many other examples of riddles on the same or linked themes being juxtaposed (for example, xiv. 17–19 on hunting; 23–4 on birth; 32–3 on Nessus the centaur; 40–1 on day and night). Cougny VII. 31 and *AP* xiv. 14 would make highly appropriate neighbours. L omitted one of the pair, *AP* xiv the other. It was only in *X* that both stood together.

Now for Cougny VII. 23:

Κούρη Ἰκαρίοιο περίφρων Πηνελόπεια,
ἐξ ποσὶν ἐμβεβαυῖα, τριδάκτυλος ἐξεφαάνθη.

The point, of course, is not that Penelope herself has six feet and three fingers, but that line 1 (which often occurs in the *Odyssey*) has six metrical feet of which three are dactyls. Its immediate predecessor in L is xiv. 62, one of the last of the riddle sequence in *AP*; its successor xiv. 9, one of the first. In *X*, then, it must have stood either at the very end, or at the very beginning, where Planudes found it his second time round. The beginning is much more likely, since Cougny VII. 23 has nothing in common with the riddles at the end and everything in common with the material at the beginning. It has been remarked already that there are three poems in *AP* xiv that are neither riddles nor puzzles. All occur together at the beginning: 8, 10, and 15. If Cougny VII. 23 came at the beginning in *X*, it would have stood before 9, sandwiched

---

[11] Solved long ago.

between two of these intruders. Here is 8, a similar bit of counting in verse, on the numbers on opposite sides of a die:

ἕξ, ἕν, πέντε, δύο, τρία, τέσσαρα κῦβος ἐλαύνει.

But the one of the trio that best parallels Cougny VII. 23 is *AP* xiv. 15, a strikingly similar schoolmasterly trifle on the same subject, metre (this time the iambic):[12]

ἐξ πόδες ἐν χώραισι τόσαις μετροῦσιν ἴαμβον,
σπονδεῖος, χόριος καὶ δάκτυλος ἠδ' ἀνάπαιστος,
πυρρίχιος καὶ ἴαμβος . . .

It looks as though the compiler of *X* decided to introduce readers gently by diluting his riddles and puzzles with a few less demanding bits of verbal juggling in the early stages of the book.

There is one last argument in favour of placing at any rate Cougny VII. 31 in *X*. It also appears in Athenaeus, 457D. Now *AP* xiv. 64 occurs in this same chapter of Athenaeus (456B). Rather than postulate two separate consultations of this same chapter of Athenaeus, first by the Palatine scribes and then, independently, by Planudes, would it not be both more natural and more economical to suppose that the compiler of *X* found them both there at the same time and transferred them both together into *X*?

Now if *X* is earlier than *AP* it must have been very close in time to Cephalas. The already slim chance that it was an early addition to the Cephalan corpus is further reduced by the appearance of problems, riddles, and even oracles in most of the other Cephalan derivatees. *APl* has four problems (2, 4, 7, 13) and one oracle (74); B[13] one oracle (71), six problems, 1, 2 (shared with *APl*), 7, 12, 13 (shared with *APl*), and 51, and one that is none of the three, 17 (shared with S); E[14] has 71 (shared with B), 72, and 74 (shared with *APl*), that is to say three oracles (note also that E alone preserves the true reading at xiv. 74. 4 and 72. 1 and 10). It is hard to resist the natural presumption that *APl*, L, B, and E all derive from a slightly fuller Cephalan equivalent to *AP* xiv.

The oracles in L are described as being taken ἐκ τῆς Θεοσοφίας. The Theosophia is a late fifth- or early sixth-century Christian work which quotes a number of pagan oracles carefully chosen for

---

[12] Also transmitted in Par. gr. 1409 (s. xiv), attributed to the Emperor Julian: see Bidez and Cumont, *Iuliani Epp. Poem. Leges* (Oxford and Paris 1922), 219–20.

[13] See below, p. 223.

[14] See below, p. 259.

their possible appropriateness to things Christian. It does not survive entire, but we do have manuscripts containing fuller excerpts than those in L (published in H. Erbse's very full and elaborate edition, *Fragmente griechischer Theosophien*, Hamburg 1941). Once more, L's series is simply an excerpt from this one source.

As it happens not one of the thirteen oracles on fo. 381ᵛ of L reappears among the oracles of *AP* xiv. Nevertheless, I venture to suggest that a common source does lie behind the two collections.

In a fascinating study, 'Trois oracles de la Théosophie et un prophète d'Apollon' (*CRAI* 1968, 568–99), Louis Robert has shown that three of the oracles in L (Cougny VI. 152–4 = Erbse 22–4) are authentic oracles from the oracle of Apollo at Didyma concerning leading citizens of Miletus in the second or third centuries. These oracles, complete with the name of the petitioner and his petition written out in full, must originally have been inscribed on stones at Didyma itself or Miletus, where they were copied by Porphyry for his influential interpretative collection *Philosophy from Oracles* (Περὶ τῆς ἐκ λογίων φιλοσοφίας), the main source of the *Theosophia*.

Now in addition to these three, this Tübingen manuscript that forms the basis of Erbse's edition contains one other oracle which, on the evidence of Lactantius, must be assigned to Didyma. Robert has shown that there is no serious reason to question its authenticity.

Almost in passing, Robert drew attention to an oracle *not* included in our *Theosophia* excerpts which (he argued) ought also to be assigned to Apollo of Didyma: *AP* xiv. 72. It is a thirteen-line reply to a certain Rufinus, who had asked the god how to exact an oath from his ship's captain (χρησμὸς ἐρωτήσαντι Ῥουφίνῳ πῶς ἂν λάβοι ὅρκον παρὰ τοῦ ἰδίου ναυκλήρου).

There are three formal points of contact. In the first place the lemma is very similar to Erbse 22, 23, 24, and 37. In all these cases the lemma gives detailed information (the name of the petitioner and the nature of his petition) which could not have been inferred from the oracles and yet has every appearance of authenticity. Erbse 22–3, for example, reflect different stages in the career of the petitioner: Ποπλᾷ τινι τοὔνομα ἐρωτήσαντι εἰ συμφέρει περὶ χρημάτων εἰς φιλοτιμίαν πέμψαι πρὸς βασιλέα, ἀπεκρίνατο οὕτως (22); ἄλλοτε [on another occasion] λυπουμένῳ τῷ Ποπλᾷ ὡς καὶ τῶν πραγμάτων ἐναντιουμένων αὐτῷ καὶ τῆς οὐσίας μειουμένης καὶ τοῦ σώματος οὐκ εὖ ἔχοντος καὶ μαθεῖν ζητοῦντι παρ' οὗ δυνηθείη βοηθείας τυχεῖν, ἔχρησεν οὕτως (23). It seems clear that these lemmata preserve the actual questions posed to the oracle. At Apollo's oracle at Didyma, as we know from a number of extant specimens, the petitioner's name and question were inscribed together with the god's reply; this was not the practice, for example, of Apollo's oracle at Claros.

Second, in Rufinus' case as in three out of the four others (23, 24, 37), the oracle deals with personal problems of the inquirer, not big issues of state.

Third, Rufinus is told to make his captain touch the sea with one hand and land with the other and swear by heaven, earth, the harbours of the sea,

αἰθερίου τε πυρὸς βιοδώτορα ἡγεμονῆα (11).

The second of Poplas' oracles (23) consists of just the one line:

ἱλάσκου Ζηνὸς βιοδώτορος ἀγλαὸν ὄμμα.

The epithet is extremely rare,[15] and the language of oracles is naturally formulaic. For example, with Erbse 23 quoted above compare from the earlier reply to Poplas (22. 2) λισσομένῳ Ζηνὸς πανδερκέος ἄφθιτον ὄμμα, from the reply to Stratonicus (24. 1–2) σεβάζου / ζωοδότου Διὸς ὄμμα, and from an inscriptional example found in the Southern Agora of Miletus (A. Rehm, *Milet* i. 7, *Südmarkt* (1924), no. 205), θοὸν ὄμμα Σαράπιδος ἀρρήτοιο . . . λισσόμενος. βιοδώτωρ was surely a favourite epithet of Didymean Apollo.

But the cornerstone of Robert's attribution is his identification of the Rufinus. An inscription from the Asclepieum of Pergamum mentions an oracle from Didymean Apollo concerning the burial of a 'hero' of Pergamum called Rufinus. The identity of this man can hardly be in doubt, L. Cuspius Pactumeius Rufinus the great second-century benefactor of Pergamum, builder there of a temple of Zeus Asclepius and an Asclepieum that was to be reckoned one of the seven wonders of the Roman world.[16] If Rufinus' fellow citizens consulted Didymean Apollo about his burial, is this not

---

[15] Kaibel, *Epigr. gr.* 820. 2; *Orph. Hy.* 73. 2; Julian. Aeg., *AP* vii. 585. 3.

[16] See H. Hepding, *Philologus* lxxxviii (1933), 90–103; C. Habicht, *Altertümer von Pergamon*, viii. 3 (Berlin 1969), no. 2, pp. 23–6; cf. L. Robert, *CRAI* 1968, 589–90, and *CRAI* 1971, 604 n. 2. The Pergamene inscription reports only the question; the oracle itself is lost.

(suggests Robert) because Rufinus had been in his lifetime one of the oracle's more distinguished patrons (note the length of the oracle designed to ensure the honesty of his ship's captain)?

If *AP* xiv. 72 is indeed an oracle of Didymean Apollo, then the chances are high that it owes its preservation in the Byzantine anthology tradition to being copied, together with Erbse 22–4, by Porphyry and transferred two and a half centuries later to the *Theosophia*.

It would be rather surprising if the combination of oracles and riddles that we find in both L and *AP* xiv had been arrived at independently. That the riddles derive from a common source can hardly be doubted, and we would surely now be justified in assuming that a common source lies behind their oracle sections too, a common source which contained a selection of excerpts from the *Theosophia*. L took Erbse 22–4, *AP* only *AP* xiv. 72, doubtless finding the rest too long or insufficiently puzzling.

There is also one rather different sort of witness, the exiled Peloponnesian nobleman Nicetas magister. In a letter written in 944 he alludes unmistakably to *AP* ix. 137; and in another, written in the winter of 945/6, he quotes directly from the oracle to the Megarians, *AP* xiv. 73.[17] Naturally we cannot be sure that Nicetas got both quotations from the same source nor that this source was Cephalas. But he was writing at a time when Cephalas' anthology was stimulating wide interest in the ancient epigram—and perhaps before the appearance of *AP*. Cephalas or some derivatee thereof is both a possible and a likely source; and if so the second quotation may perhaps be held to suggest that the oracles were already part of the Cephalan tradition by the 940s.

Whether the oracles, riddles, and charioteer epigrams were separately classified in L's source as they are in L is open to doubt. In *AP* xiv the oracles and riddles were mixed together in one book, and though there are no charioteer epigrams in *AP* itself, we can be fairly certain that they originally stood among the large block of ecphrastic epigrams that fell out of *AP*'s source. So it looks as if Planudes extracted them from the ecphrastic section of his source—just as he took *AP* x. 108 from among its protreptica because he thought that it would go better with his oracle section.

We cannot be sure, but it seems a reasonable assumption that

---

[17] L. G. Westerink, *Nicétas Magistros: Lettres d'un exilé* (Paris 1973), pp. 103. 32–3; 113. 10–13.

both parts of the epigrammatic corpus in L derive from the same source, a source that was not just a redaction of Cephalas but a redaction of Cephalas that looked very like *AP*. For the resemblance between L and *AP* is not restricted to their 'Cephalan' epigrammatic material. Pp. 40–8 of *AP* contain an idiosyncratic selection of the dogmatic poems of Gregory Nazianzen, in the following order: 12, 14, 15, 13, 19, 20, 24, 23, 22, 26, 21, 25, 27. On fos. 362–4 of L stand, in this order: 12, *18*, 20, 24, 22, 26, 21, 25, *23*, 27, and then on fo. 385ʳ: 14, 15, 13, and 19. *AP* has put together what appear as two separate extracts in L, in both cases with the same variations from the regular order in complete editions of Gregory's *dogmatica* (the only discrepancies being that *AP* omitted 18 and put 23 after 25 instead of 24). More striking still, both *AP* and L omit the last line of 25. There can be little doubt, as I concluded elsewhere (Cameron (1973), 103, whence I repeat this argument), that here too a common source lies behind L and *AP*, a source that L once again reproduced more fully than *AP*.

L has one other epigram new to the Cephalan tradition, the moving epitaph of the ill-fated Empress Constantina, who ended her days, like her husband, five sons, and three daughters on the executioner's block:

ἅδ' ἐγὼ ἡ τριτάλαινα, καὶ ἀμφοτέρων βασιλήων
　Τιβερίου θυγάτηρ, Μαυρικίου δὲ δάμαρ,
ἡ πολύπαις βασίλεια καλῇ δείξασα λοχείῃ
　ὡς ἀγαθὸν τελέθει καὶ πολυκοιρανίη,
κεῖμαι σὺν τεκέεσσι καὶ ἡμετέρῳ παρακοίτῃ
　δήμου ἀτασθαλίῃ καὶ μανίῃ στρατιῆς.
ἔτλην τῆς Ἑκάβης πολὺ χείρονα τῆς τ' Ἰοκάστης·
　ναὶ ναὶ τῆς Νιόβης ἔμπνοός εἰμι λίθος.
αἰαῖ τὸν γενέτην· τί δὲ καὶ τὰ νεόγν' ἀπέκτειναν
　ἀμπλακίης μερόπων μηδὲν ἐπιστάμενα;
ἡμετέροισι κλάδοισι κατάσκιος οὐκέτι Ῥώμη·
　ῥίζα γὰρ ἐκλάσθη Θρηϊκίοις ἀνέμοις.

This poem too is regularly quoted by the chroniclers, and it may be that Gallavotti was right to suppose that it was from one of them (Zonaras or Cedrenus) that Planudes took it. But it is also quoted separately in a variety of manuscripts, in two of them ascribed to Agathias ('Αγαθίου εἰς Μαυρίκιον βασιλέα, see Preger, *Inscr. gr. metr.*, p. 22). The ascription is certainly false (Agathias had been dead for some twenty-five years at Constantina's execution), and the only plausible explanation is that the excerptors took the poem from an anthology which, like Lascaris (see pp. 175–7), they mistakenly took to be Agathias' rather than Cephalas' (no extant redaction or excerpt of Cephalas save *AP* so much as mentions his name). If it be asked how so long and impressive an epitaph was lost from the whole Cephalan tradition save for L, once again simple parablepsy may be the answer: in *AP* vii there are two other poems that open with the same words ἅδ' ἐγώ ἁ (145, 324), not to mention many similar.

The epitaph does not appear in a regular Palatine sepulchral context, but between two poems known only from the certainly post-Cephalan *AP* xv (Ch. XV), nos. 9 and 29. So even if it is not actually Cephalan, it might still have appeared in the MS *X* we have been postulating, in its original state a somewhat amplified early redaction of Cephalas.[18]

This original *X*, as can be inferred even from its much abbreviated and corrupt descendant L, had so many points of contact with *AP*, though apparently somewhat fuller, that it may actually have been the source of *AP*, or at any rate close kin thereof. At all events, it was a manuscript with enough of the features which Aubreton considered unique to *AP* to show that he was wrong.

---

[18] For the post-Cephalan origin of *API*, see below p. 275.

X

The *Sylloge Parisina*

S is contained in one manuscript of the thirteenth century (Paris. suppl. gr. 352).[1] But there is also one fourteenth-century manuscript (Paris. gr. 1630) that contains what appears in the main to be a rearranged excerpt from S, generally known as B. S has 114 epigrams, B 53 of which 9 are absent from S. Coincidence in error where they overlap removes any possibility of doubt: B is an excerpt from a fuller version of S. Its additional poems, consisting mainly of oracles and problems, have been discussed above. In general, however, the order of the poems in B is too much disturbed to render it of any independent value for study of the poems preserved in S. But it does prove what should already have been inferred from the structure of S itself: that S is incomplete.

S comprises (*a*) 41 epideictic or ecphrastic poems that reappear in *AP* ix or *APl* iv; (*b*) 15 protreptic poems from *AP* x; (*c*) 14 sympotic poems from *AP* xi; (*d*) 3 oracles (*AP* ix. 527; xiv. 17, 71); (*e*) 9 more ecphrastica from *APl*; (*f*) 32 erotic or rather pederastic poems, mainly (though not exclusively) from *AP* xii. That is to say, material from *AP* ix, x, xi, xii, and xiv. Why nothing from v, vi, and vii? Of course mere caprice on the part of the compiler or (that favourite lifebelt) a defective Cephalas are always possibilities, but the natural implication is that what we have is only the second half of an abridged Cephalas. Note too that the epideictic sequence does not begin till as late in *AP* ix as 360, suggesting that the beginning of this section is also missing.

That S's source was indeed Cephalas was long ago made probable by Basson and Waltz. Aubreton, however, who seems not to have read Basson, refers without argument to Waltz's view as a

---

[1] A full description of the manuscript will be published in due course by M. Charles Astruc of the Bibliothèque Nationale, who kindly showed me the relevant part of his forthcoming catalogue. The basic works on S are Basson (37–45), Dilthey, Waltz (i, pp. liii–liv), Wifstrand (76–86), and Gallavotti, *Boll. Class. Lincei*, 3rd ser., iv (1983), 48–56.

'mistake' and, with no more argument than the fallacy of the 'leçons personnelles', takes it for granted that S is pre-Cephalan. The more recent brief discussion of Gallavotti reaches the same conclusion, on the basis of the many epigrams in S unknown to *AP*.

Since the only other lists available, those compiled by Aubreton and Gallavotti, contain a number of errors, I give here a complete inventory of the poems preserved in S in the order in which they appear there:

(1)	*AP* ix. 616	*AP* xi. 48	*AP* xii. 19
AP ix. 360	635	50	21
468	623	227	C. IV. 72
C. III. 174	626	157	*AP* xii. 118
IV. 65	666	255	C. V. 53
V. 52	667	273	*AP* xii. 29
AP ix. 573	669[4]	299	53
564	363	301	58
APl 159	*APl* 13	338	C. IV. 70
161	*AP* ix. 721	349	*AP* xii. 235
182	721*	390	237
C. III. 173	(2)	(4)	241
APl 168	*AP* x. 1	*AP* ix. 527	C. IV. 71
201[2]	26	xiv. 17	III. 171
207	27	71	IV. 69
132	40	(5)	IV. 67
89	42	*APl* 292	III. 170
57	52	96	III. 169
223	64. 1–4	99	*AP* xii. 181
109	58	197	185
74	68	200	209
AP ix. 751	72	203	214
752	73	209	223[5]
680	74	213	224
768	76. 1–2	62	196
333	84	(6)	50. 1–6
637	117	ᾠδάριον ἐρωτικόν	νῦν ὁ καλός
639	(3)	(*PLG* iii.[4] 351–4)	(Cramer iv. 388)
608	*AP* xi. 54. 5–6	C. IV. 73	
610[3]	55	*AP* xi. 51	
607	47	v. 78	
		xii. 18	

It will be simplest to begin with sections (2) and (3). (2) contains a selection of sixteen poems from *AP* x in almost perfect Palatine order, poems by Leonidas of Tarentum, Lucian, Theognis, Palladas, Agathias, Paul the Silentiary, and Phocyllides. That is to say, the same mixture from at least five different original sources in virtually the same order as *AP*. It is even possible to see why 64 (Agathias on Τύχη) was moved back a place—so as to compliment 52 (Palladas on Καιρός). Planudes took 110 poems, from 1–125, for *APl*, and 43, from 27–108, for L. There can be little doubt that *AP* x, *APl* i, L, and S all derive from the same source, and we know that *AP*'s source was Cephalas.

The minor variations from the Palatine order in the sequence from *AP* xi (54–389, B having 390 as well as 389) do nothing to detract from the same conclusion (*APl* has items from 1–437 this time, L from 50–432). (1) is much more interesting, providing as it does confirmation of Wifstrand's hypothesis about the lacuna in the exemplar of *AP*.

The Planudea missing from *AP* are almost all ecphrastic, and derive from exactly the same ancient sources as the Palatine ecphrastica. There is no need to recapitulate Basson's subtle analysis, successively refined by Preisendanz,[6] Wifstrand,[7] and Gow:[8] everything points to the Planudean ecphrastica having fallen out of *AP*'s exemplar in a lacuna early in the second half of ix. The first half of ix consists of epideictica, the second half of ecphrastica. The distinction is not easy to draw but (as Wifstrand saw) Planudes drew it between 583 and 584. Poems up to 583 he put in his Book i, those from 584 to 822 (with one exception) in Book iv together with the ecphrastica peculiar to *APl*.

Gow took a different line. Rather than postulate a lacuna in which all the Planudea once stood, he preferred 'to regard *AP* ix. 584–822 as a selection comparable with that made by Planudes in his Book iv'. To this suggestion it must be objected that since *AP* is in all other respects much the fullest version of Cephalas we

[2] 'Cougny III. 332' (in fact 322), which Aubreton lists between *APl* 201 and 207, is in fact simply the continuation of Marianus' long poem *APl* 201.

[3] In fact l. 1 of 610 and l. 2 of 612.

[4] Once more, 'Cougny III. 172', listed by Aubreton and Gallavotti after ix. 669, is simply the last couplet of another long poem by Marianus, ix. 669.

[5] 'Cougny IV. 66' in Aubreton and Gallavotti is in fact *AP* xii. 223.

[6] *Woch. f. kl. Phil.* 1918, 169 f.

[7] (1926), 66–86.

[8] (1958), 45 f.

have, it would be very surprising if one of its books had been merely a selection.

If Gow were right, we should expect an abridgement which followed the original order in Cephalas fairly faithfully (that is, S) to show a *mixture* of *AP* ix. 584–822 and *APl* iv in its ecphrastic section. If Wifstrand were right, we should expect to find Palatine poems up to the neighbourhood of 583, then a purely Planudean sequence, and then another Palatine sequence from *c.*600 to 822. In either case we should expect the odd poem absent from both *AP* and *APl*: *APl* iv lacks 1 in 5 (48 out of 238) of the ecphrastica preserved in *AP*, which suggests (assuming a uniform rate of reduction) that the 381 Planudean ecphrastica represent a total Palatine loss of at least 450.[9]

A glance at the list will show that Wifstrand was right. Excluding newcomers and the odd misfit (*AP* ix. 363 and *APl* 13 just before the end of the second Palatine sequence) we have: first a Palatine sequence up to 573, then a Planudean sequence, and then another Palatine sequence from 607 to 768. And whatever the reason for the second Planudean sequence in section (5), the absence of Palatine material suggests that it is a second excerpt from the Planudean part of Cephalas' ecphrastica.

The minor variations in Palatine order in the second Palatine sequence prove no more than that our excerptor did not excerpt here quite so mechanically as in sections (2) and (3). For example, he clearly put 607 after 610 because it is on the same theme as 616 (the Graces bathing); 637 and 639 were linked with 608 because all celebrate baths of Aphrodite, and 333 was perhaps moved there from its original context because it described a seaside temple of Aphrodite. The two Planudean sequences are in what appears to be a somewhat broken order, but it must be remembered that, while individual Planudean chapters may preserve some traces of the Cephalan arrangement, the order of the chapters has nothing to do with Cephalas: for example, *APl* 132 is on Tantalus' daughter Niobe, 89, which follows it in S, on Tantalus himself. It is likely that in general S's order reflects Cephalas' order more closely than *APl*.

It should be added that some of these poems could equally have

---

[9] Cf. Gow, 51–2, through his own formulation, 'omitted 48 . . .', 'reduction of the total at his disposal', implies—wrongly I think—that it was Planudes rather than the intermediaries on whom he drew who did the omitting and reducing.

been classified as erotica (for example, *APl* 213) by Strato or Meleager; that S, like *AP*, *APl*, and E, put it with the ecphrastica, is a strong pointer to their common derivation from Cephalas. Furthermore, to judge from its lemma in *AP*, recording an unguessable Antiochene provenance, the anonymous ix. 680 is one of the inscriptions that Cephalas obtained from Gregory of Campsa. So too probably *APl* 62, one of a pair of inscriptions from a monument (62–3) which the Palatine lemma to 62 correctly places in the hippodrome of Constantinople. If so, then this alone would undermine Aubreton's thesis of a *pre*-Cephalan origin for S.

That S was produced by a process of excerpting a larger anthology can actually be proved by an example from this section. *AP* ix. 610 and 612 celebrate a small but beautiful and sweet-smelling bath:

μικρὰ μὲν ἔργα τάδ᾽ ἐστίν, ἔχει δ᾽ ἡδεῖαν ὀπωπήν,
  ὡς ῥόδον ἐν κήποις, ὡς ἴον ἐν ταλάροις   (608)

ὡς κέδρου βραχὺ φύλλον, ἔχει δ᾽ ἡδεῖαν ὀδωδήν,
  οὕτως λουτρὰ τάδε σμικρὰ μέν, ἀλλὰ φίλα   (610)

S presents the first line of 608 (but with ὀδωδήν) and then the second line of 610: evidently the excerptor's eye jumped from the first ἔχει δ᾽ ἡδεῖαν to the second. A similar example is provided by two lemmata in B. In S there are almost no lemmata, in B a fair number; most bear no resemblance to the more authoritative lemmata in *AP* and *APl* which we have assumed to derive from Cephalas (p. 103) and (like many of J's) are obviously later editorial confections. *APl* 74 has the same heading εἰς ἄρχοντα in *APl* and B, despite its vagueness not in fact a particularly obvious inference from the poem. But the two significant examples are *APl* 203 and 209. In B the lemma to 203 is εἰς Πραξιτέλην (εἰς Πραξιτέλους Ἔρωτα, *APl*), to 209 εἰς τὸν αὐτόν (εἰς τὸ αὐτό, *APl*). The first is reasonably accurate, the second quite incorrect: 209 is about neither Praxiteles nor his Eros. Interestingly enough *APl*'s εἰς τὸ αὐτό is equally incorrect, referring as it does back to the lemma of *APl* 208, 'on an Eros sleeping on a pepper-pot' (the point of the poem being that 'though asleep, lifeless, and at a banquet' Eros is still not 'without a fire-scattering nip'). *APl* 209 is not about this either. To judge from its contents it is about a statue or picture of Eros blowing on a torch to light a lamp (the poet suggests that the lamp be lit from the flames in his own soul!). It is obviously most improbable that the compiler of S and Planudes consciously decided that 209 was about the same subject as 203 and 208 respectively. A glance at the Planudean context is enough to show what happened. *APl* 194–215 is a series of poems describing various representations of Eros; S has 197, 200, 203, 209, and 213; B 197, 203, 209, 213. *APl* and S (whence B) drew on a slightly fuller series (namely Cephalas) which contained a pair to 209 with the correct lemma. This poem was dropped, as so often leaving its pair 209 with an uncorrected lemma 'on the same', in *APl* now referring to 208, in B (which omitted more of the series) to 203 (for similar errors in ascription arising from the heading τοῦ αὐτοῦ, see above, p. 171).

The excerpts from *AP* x and xi in sections (2) and (3) were evidently made direct from just one source and there seems no good reason to suppose that the compiler of such a modest collection took the trouble to look elsewhere for the few new-comers in this section (or section (6), to which we shall come next). In the epideictic part of section (1) the newcomers are three poems arbitrarily and unhelpfully distributed in Cougny's edition between three different books as III. 174, IV. 65, and V. 52. Since there is every reason to suppose that they derive from Cephalas it is to be hoped that in future editions of the Anthology they will be appended to *AP* ix. Since they are so little known I transcribe them here with one or two comments:

A. τοσοῦτον ὁ πλοῦς, καὶ μάτην· καὶ ποῦ πλέω·
　ἐρυθριῶ γὰρ ὀλέσας τὴν φιλτάτην
　αἰσχρῶς φανῆναι τοῖς φίλοις ἐν πατρίδι.
　ἆρ' οὖν τις αὐτὴν ἐξέκλεψε τῶν θεῶν
　τεθαυμακὼς τὸ κάλλος· ὤμοι τῶν κακῶν·
　πάλιν τέτρωμαι τῷ πόθῳ διπλασίως,
　τὸ κάλλος εἰπών· τοιγαροῦν σιγητέον.　(III. 174)

Thus far my voyage—and in vain. Where now am I to sail? Having lost my dearest I blush to appear disgraced in the sight of my friends back home. Is it not some god who has stolen her away, struck with wonderment at her beauty? Alas for my woes! The mention of her beauty pierces me again twofold with longing. I must keep silent.

B. Ἥρη παμβασίλεια νεοζυγέων ὑμεναίων,
　δέρκεο λυγρὸν ἔρωτα μαραινομένης Γαλατείης·
　δέρκεο πικρὰ βέλεμνα κορυσσομένης Ἀφροδίτης·
　ὁ πρὶν ἐρωμανέων στυγέει Γαλάτειαν ἰδέσθαι.　(IV. 65)

Hera, queen of the newly-wed, look upon the sad love of Galatea as she wastes away. Look upon the bitter darts of Aphrodite as she arms herself for battle. He who once loved her to distraction now hates even to see Galatea.

C. Τυνδαρέη κρητῆρα κερασσομένη παρὰ δεῖπνον
δάκρυα Τηλεμάχοιο κατέσβεσεν ἐς μίαν ὥρην.
εἰ δὲ ῥόδα προσέμιξε παρηγορέοντι κυπέλλῳ,
εἶχε μένειν ἄκλαυστος, ἕως νόστησεν Ὀδυσσεύς.   (V. 52)

Tyndarus' daughter [Helen] mixed the cup at the feast and extinguished Telemachus' tears for one hour. If she had mixed in roses with her cup of comfort, he could have remained free of tears until Odysseus returned.

A and B are exercises of the τίνας ἂν εἴποι λόγους type of which (as Gow remarks, p. 56) '*AP* ix. 449–80 is a more than sufficient series'. B occurs in S two poems after one of that number, ix. 468, which (like ix. 469) is a speech *by* Hera. This would certainly be an appropriate context for B, which, like many in the series, is clearly post-Nonnian, in fact little more than a Nonnian cento.[10] To judge from its metre (dodecasyllables rather than iambic trimeters) and the quantities ὀλέσας and διπλāσίως, A looks Byzantine.rather than just (like B and C) late Roman, but there are other such iambic fragments in the series in *AP* (ix. 476, 478, 480). In neither B nor A is it clear who the speaker is. C is a suggested improvement on the beverage with which Helen assuaged Telemachus' grief at Sparta in *Od.* iv. 220 f. (the mixing of roses with wine was a well known ancient practice: for example, *Anacreontea* v. 2 f., and for a recipe, Apicius i. 3. 1). Not a speech, but there are many such short mythological hexameter fragments in this part of *AP* (ix. 495, 504, 505, 523, 581). All three would fit perfectly in this epideictic context. As for the newcomer in the Planudean sequence Περσεὺς κῆτος ὄλεσσε καὶ Ἀνδρομέδην ἐσάωσεν (C. III. 173), it is not easy to see what *raison d'être* so short a piece could have except as the caption to a painting, in which case it would be appropriately placed among the ecphrastica rather than epideictica. It is not surprising that Planudes (or his source already) left out such a trifle.

There is not much to be said about section (4), except that its brevity and the six extra oracles provided by B suggest that it is

[10] e.g. νεοζ. ὕμεν. (Dion. 48. 237; 553); initial δέρκεο, *passim*; ἐρωμανέων; it is superfluous to give references since the completion of W. Peek's *Lexicon zu den Dion. des Nonnos* (Berlin 1968–75).

incomplete. The presence of such a section is of course strong
support for the view expressed above that *AP* xiv is Cephalan. Its
(compared with the Palatine order) anomalous position between
excerpts from *AP* x and xi may be not unconnected with the
circumstances that left it incomplete.

We pass to the concluding, pederastic section. Among its thirty-
two poems there are no fewer than twelve absent from *AP/APl*.
Constantine the Sicilian's hundred-line ᾠδάριον ἐρωτικόν may well
have been inserted from elsewhere, but to my mind there can be
little doubt that most if not all of the rest came from the same
source.

Now there are only four newcomers in the rest of S, and as far as
AP is concerned one at least of them will have fallen out in the
lacuna of ix. Why then are there so many new poems in this
section? Assuming that they all originally stood in Cephalas, there
are various ways of explaining how they might have come to be
omitted from *AP*. First, mere oversight; one epigram often looks
much like another and it is likely that as many were accidentally
omitted as are accidentally repeated in the pages of *AP*. Second,
bowdlerization. No fewer than 242 of the 258 pederastica preserved in *AP* xii are absent from *APl*, most (as Planudes himself
admitted) deliberately omitted. The new poems in S are certainly
not more obscene than most of those in *AP* xii, but bowdlerization
is of its very nature subjective and inconsistent (Planudes included
many poems more obscene than many he omitted). Third, something that must often have happened though we can never prove it:
the deliberate omission of poems that were felt to be too trivial or
too similar to what had already been included. Fourth, the tendency we have already noticed for corrupt poems to be omitted;
when scribe A of *AP* omitted poems he was scrupulous enough
(unlike Michael Chartophylax) to leave gaps; perhaps B, who
copied xii, did not. Many of the new paederastica in S are very
corrupt indeed.

But these factors alone are not likely to have been responsible for
quite so many losses. No fewer than six of the twelve occur
together in the middle. Perhaps the truth is that a few more pages
fell out of the source of *AP*. Since the rest of the poems in the
section are not in one continuous Palatine sequence, some of the
other new poems may have come from the same area and disappeared in the same lacuna.

The new poems were first published together with the rest of S by J. A. Cramer in his *Anecdota Parisina* iv (1841), at pp. 380–8, in largely unintelligible form. Some corrections and supplements were made by A. Meineke (*Analecta Alexandrina* (1843), 395 f.) and N. Piccolos (*Supplément à l'anthologie grecque* (1852), 155 f.), and a more accurate collation and some further conjectures were included in K. Dilthey's *De epigrammatum Graecorum syllogis quibusdam minoribus* (Programm Göttingen 1887), unfortunately not known to E. Cougny, who published an improved but still very imperfect (and incomplete) text in 1890, so arbitrarily distributed through his supplement to the Didot Anthology as to render study of the series as a whole impossible. I have therefore printed a completely new text (based on a fresh study of the manuscript) together with some comments and an English translation. These poems are no less worthy of attention that those that have had the better fortune to be included in *AP* xii, and yet they remain almost completely unknown. If I am not mistaken they are nowhere quoted or mentioned in the various works of Gow and Page, although several are Meleagrian in date and at least two almost certainly in authorship too. There is still time for them to be included as an appendix to one of the outstanding volumes of the Budé Anthology.

The series opens with the long 'ode' of Constantine the Sicilian,[11] which on grounds of length, date, and metre alike is unlikely to have featured in Cephalas. Next comes the first newcomer (C. IV. 73):

εἰ μὲν ἀεὶ θάλλεις, τήρει, φίλος· εἰ δὲ μαραίνῃ,
τί φθονέεις τούτου τῷ σε θέλοντι γίσαι;

If you are going to be in bloom for ever, friend, hang on to it; But if you are fading, why do you begrudge this of the man who would enjoy you?

The εἰ clause is ironic, of course; *if* your bloom is imperishable, you can afford to keep it intact; but otherwise . . . For this use of τηρῶ cf. C. III. 171. 1 and 3 (below, p. 232). The theme of the fading (μαραίνειν) of the beloved boy's shortlived charms is a favourite with Strato: cf. xii. 232, 234, and above all 235 (which appears later on in S):

εἰ μὲν γηράσκει τὸ καλόν, μετάδος, πρὶν ἀπέλθῃ·
εἰ δὲ μένει, τί φοβῇ τοῦθ' ὃ μένει, διδόναι;

11 Discussed further below.

The parallel εἰ clauses, picked up respectively by an imperative and a question in both poems, their common use of τοῦτο to refer to the residual charms of the near adult, all support the ascription of IV. 73 to Strato. And while φοβῇ in xii. 235. 2 is perfect in itself, φθονεῖς would have been no less so (as we shall see, Strato would not have minded the shortened τι). Compare xii. 211. 4, τί φθονέεις δοῦναι, again Strato to a reluctant boy. If γίσαι is really what the poet wrote, then its meaning must presumably be inferred from Hesychius s.v. γίσας· φθείρας, possibly an obscene word, which might be thought more typical of Strato (cf. xii. 3 and 7) than the Meleagrian and Philippan poets whose paederastica fill most of the rest of *AP* xii. But a word to continue in some way the metaphors of l. 1 would be preferable, and Martin West suggests βλίσαι (from βλίττω), to take honey from a hive, appositely referring to the comparison of a kiss to a 'honeycomb from a hive' in C. III. 171.

The poem was probably omitted from *AP* through simple parablepsy: note that xii. 235 also opens εἰ μέν—not to mention xii. 108, 118, and 211.

Then comes a poem which appears to be an intruder from another Palatine book:

τῆς ὥρας ἀπόλαυε· παρακμάζει ταχὺ πάντα·
ἓν θέρος ἐξ ἐρίφου τρηχὺν ἔθηκε τράγον. (xi. 51)

Enjoy your season. All things swiftly pass their prime. One summer makes a shaggy goat of a kid.

The homosexual reference here has not, I think, been noticed. The 'kid' is the beloved boy, the 'shaggy goat' the near adult whose cheeks are becoming bristly (on this lamentable phenomenon cf. xii. 27, 31, 33, 35, 36, 39, etc.). The commoner antithesis is between the 'kid' and the 'wolf', the predatory pederast.[12] But is the poem complete? By an intriguing coincidence eight poems later in S comes a distich which comes two poems later than xi. 51 in *AP*:

τὸ [καὶ S] ῥόδον ἀκμάζει βαιὸν χρόνον· ἢν δὲ παρέλθῃ,
ζητῶν εὑρήσεις οὐ ῥόδον, ἀλλὰ βάτον. (xi. 53)

The rose blooms for a short season, and when that passes, you will find not a rose but a thorn.

Taken by themselves these lines have no overt sexual reference,

---

[12] Studied in detail by G. Luck, 'Kids and Wolves', *CQ* NS ix (1959), 34–7.

though a comparison with the last line of the misclassified pederastic poem v. 28 by Rufinus, ἀντὶ ῥόδου γὰρ ἐγὼ τὴν βάτον οὐ δέχομαι (of another bristly boy), certainly makes them seem suggestive. It is not altogether surprising, then, to discover that in S they are joined to an explicitly pederastic poem, xii. 29 by Alcaeus of Messene:

Πρώταρχος καλός ἐστι, καὶ οὐ θέλει· ἀλλὰ θελήσει
ὕστερον· ἡ δ' ὥρη λαμπάδ' ἔχουσα τρέχει.

Protarchus is a pretty boy, and does not want it. But he will later. His youth races on holding a torch.

The reference is to the Lampadedromia, a relay race, held all over the Greek world, in which a burning torch was passed from hand to hand—at Athens thirty-nine times (Gow and Page, *HE* ii. 13–14; Fraenkel, *Aeschylus: Agamemnon*, ii [1950], 166–9). It was not the first runner to reach the altar who was declared the winner, but his whole team. Since it was normally run by ephebes (Jüthner, *PW* xii. 572), depicted naked in art, its power as an image of one male lover succeeding another in rapid succession is obvious. Meineke, Dilthey, and Dübner accepted this combination, and as Gow and Page observe, 'the majority of the epigrams (by very various authors) from 24 to 41 are about the growth of hair, and the couplet would fit the quatrain to its context'. The bristles implied in the first couplet would be picked up by the thorn in the second.

At some stage, then (certainly no later than Cephalas, see below), the second couplet was detached, perhaps deliberately so as to free a nice moralizing distich from a homosexual context.

AP xi. 51 *could* perfectly well be a complete poem in its own right—but it would equally well make a good generalizing final couplet. It would be rash to pick a particular poem in xii which might be incomplete, since if poem and conclusion became separated in the first place, even if deliberately, the link between them cannot have been very strong. But if this is what happened, then neither xi. 51 nor xi. 53 need be seen as an intruder even from another Cephalan book. Interestingly enough, the poem they sandwich between them, xi. 52, is yet another misclassified pederastic piece, addressed to a boy called Thrasybulus. It turns on an elaborately developed fishing metaphor: the poet has been caught in Thrasybulus' net and is gasping like a dolphin on the beach.

This would neatly pick up Strato xii. 241, where the boy, unnamed, is said to have caught the poet on his hook. There are two more pederastica a little earlier in the book, xi. 21 and 22, 21 being a minimal rewriting of xii. 242, likewise ascribed to Strato. It was presumably Cephalas himself who put all five poems in xi, perhaps considering them as much convivial as pederastic, for 51–3 and 22 all reappear in *APl, not* however among the erotica in *APl* vii but in *APl* ia (51–3) and ib (22); the implication is that they were similarly misclassified in *both* Planudes' sources. It is possible that they all originally stood in Cephalas' pederastic book too. Such repetitions arising out of classification problems are common in *AP* and were no doubt commoner still in Cephalas. Since xii follows directly after xi (and was copied by the same scribe in *AP*) they might have been spotted and eliminated in the later book.

Next come three poems in Palatine order—*AP* xii. 18 (Alpheius), 19 (anon.), and 21 (Strato)—before C. IV. 72:

κοῦρε, τί μοι λεπτός, θαλεραὶ δ' οὐχ ὥς ποτε σά⟨ρκες⟩,
οὐδὲ τὸ πρὶν ἐραταῖς [ἐρασταῖς S] ἐν λαγόνεσσι γάνος;
ποῖαί σευ καλὸν [κάλαμον S] ἄνθος ἀποσμύχου⟨σι⟩ μέριμν⟨αι⟩;
μή τι τὸ Ναρκίσσου νᾶμα κατωπτρίσαο;

Boy, why are you growing thin; why is your flesh not sturdy the way it used to be? Nor is there the old delight in your sweet loins. What cares are causing your fair bloom to waste away? Have you perhaps used a Narcissus' pool for a mirror?

No modern scholar would take long to make the necessary corrections and supplements, but if this is how the poem was presented in Cephalas it is not surprising that it was soon omitted from the tradition.

Meineke long ago suggested the name of Strato, and Beckby quoted it in illustration of xii. 176 by Strato:

στυγνὸς δὴ τί, Μένιππε, κατεσκέπασαι μέχρι πέζης
ὁ πρὶν ἐπ' ἰγνύης λῶπος ἀνελκόμενος . . . ;

Why are you draped down to your ankles in that melancholy fashion, Menippus, you who used to tuck your tunic up to your thighs . . .?

But here the situation is different. Menippus is not growing thin but downcast, and we are told why; it is those beastly bristles again. Strato is certainly a possibility, but no more than one of many.

After xii. 118, a pederastic paraclausithuron by Callimachus, comes C. V. 53:

ἠράσθη Κίτυός τις, ὃς οὐκ ἴδεν, οὔατα πεισθείς·
φεῦ κάλλους· ἡμεῖς δ᾿ ὄμμασι μεμφόμεθα.

Someone fell in love with Citys who had not even seen him, convinced by hearsay. Alas for such beauty! I find fault with my eyes [i.e. I wish I had *not* seen him].

Once more, rather a corrupt piece (κίτυος, τίς ὄν . . . φεῦ καλῶς S). Since τις should be the antecedent of the relative, with ὄν it is Citys who has not seen the lover, whereas the sense requires that it should be the lover who has not seen Citys. I have therefore written ὅς.

Next in the sequence, after Alcaeus xii. 29 plus xi. 53 already discussed and Rhianus xii. 58, comes C. IV. 70:

εἶπεν Ἔρως τὸν καλὸν ἰδὼν ⟨παριόντα⟩ Μυΐσκον·
δωροῦμαι τάδε σοι τόξ᾿ ἐμὰ καὶ φαρέτρην·
δωροῦμαι καὶ πτηνὸν ἰδ⟨οῦ βέλος· εἰ δ᾿⟩ ἐπὶ χείλεα
χείλεσί μοι θείης, λάμβανε καὶ πτέρυγας.

Love saw the fair Myiscus approaching and said: 'I give you this my bow and quiver; look, I also give you my winged arrow. If you will put your lips on mine, take my wings too.'

In addition to the lacunae as marked, the MS unmetrically reverses the order of σοι and ἐμά in l. 2, presents only τα γε χείλεα at the end of 3, and χεῖλος ἐμὸν at the beginning of 4. l. 1: παριόντα Dilthey, cf. Meleager, *AP* xii. 121. 1, κιόντι; 127. 1, στείχοντα; Strato, xii. 223. 1–2, προσιόντος . . . παριόντα; ⟨ποτε παῖδα⟩ Fix. l. 3 = ⟨ἐμὸν βέλος . . .⟩ suppl. Fix; ἰδ⟨οῦ καλόν . . .⟩ Dilthey. The restoration of the end of 3 remains most uncertain; I have followed Dilthey, who compares Meleager, *AP* v. 171. 3 εἴθ᾿ ὑπ᾿ [ἐπ᾿ Herwerden] ἐμοῖς νῦν χείλεσι χείλεα θεῖσα. Though not even quoted among the *dubia* by Gow and Page, there can be little doubt that the poem is by none other than Meleager. There are no fewer than twelve poems addressed to a boy called Myiscus in *AP* xii—and every one is by Meleager. Compare particularly 144, in which Eros himself is said, as here, to have fallen captive to the boy's charms. But we can go further. In S the poem's immediate predecessor is by the Meleagrian poet Rhianus. In *AP* Rhianus' poem occurs in a Meleagrian sequence, followed by a poem by Meleager himself on Myiscus

(xii. 59). It is tempting to guess that C. IV. 70 originally stood between xii. 59 and 60.

There follow xii. 235 and 237 (joined together, with the omission of 237. 1 and some rearrangement) and 241, all by Strato, and then another new poem, C. IV. 71:

αὐτοῦ μοι, Κλεόβουλε, παρὰ στροφάλιγγα θυρα⟨ίαν⟩,
κλεπτομένην χάρισαι Κύπριδος εὐφροσύνην.
ὕ⟨βρ⟩ιν ἔρως οὐκ οἶδε πόθου μένος· ἡ γὰρ ἀνάγκης
μῖξις προσπαίοις ἐνδέδεται πάθεσι.
καὶ γὰρ Ζεὺς θεὸς ἦν· ἀλλ' ἡνίκα καιρὸν ἔκλεπ⟨τεν⟩
αἰετὸς ἢ δαμάλης ἢ κύκνος ἐβλέπετο.

Grant me the furtive pleasure of the Cyprian here by the door hinge, Cleobulus. Love does not recognize the force of passion as outrage. Sex born of compulsion is a slave to sudden passions. For Zeus too was a god(?); but when he stole a moment, he appeared as an eagle or a steer or a swan.

A particularly difficult and corrupt poem; it would be idle to pretend that the text and notes here offered provide any final solutions. First details. My own examination of the manuscript confirms that l. 3 did not, as Cramer thought, begin with a beta (whence Cougny's β[ρί]ξαι), but, as Dilthey claimed, with a upsilon. There are traces consistent with a nu to end the first word. On the other hand I cannot confirm Dilthey's θυράων at the end of l. 1, which I find less plausible than Meineke's θυρα⟨ίαν⟩. στροφάλιγξ normally denotes a whirl or curve of some sort, but here apparently means pivot or hinge, which accords ill with the plural θυράων, properly double doors, especially since the poet's purpose is presumably that the pair should make love at the side of the door or perhaps even behind an open door, in a dark corner. The opening of the poem is inspired by Asclepiades, v. 145. 1, αὐτοῦ μοι στέφανοι παρὰ δικλίσι ταῖσδε κρεμαστοί / μίμνετε, where αὐτοῦ similarly refers to a doorway. l. 5: last three letters can no longer be read. l. 6: δάμαλις cod.; obviously δαμάλης (Meineke), as much from considerations of sex as metre.

Now more general interpretation. Given the traces, Dilthey's ὕβριν in l. 3 seems the obvious supplement, the point presumably being that love does not see as outrage what others well might, viz. Cleobulus obliging the poet in a doorway. ἔρως ποθούμενος seems an improbable phrase; the difference in otherwise parallel phrases such as *amatis amantibus* (Catullus 61. 47, cf. 45. 20) and ἀντεφίλησ'

ὁ φιληθείς (Theocritus 12. 16) is the repetition of the *same* word.
The general structure of the clause seems to be supported by what
looks like the imitation by Paul the Silentiary: θεσμὸν Ἔρως οὐκ οἶδε
βιήμαχος (*AP* v. 293. 1). ἀνάγκης μῖξις seems tolerable Greek but
disturbingly prosaic. In l. 4 the manuscript presents προστίμοις
ἐνδέχεται. There is a noun πρόστιμον, 'fine', but πρόστιμος does not
seem a very likely formation for an adjective meaning (as Dilthey
and Cougny wanted) 'subject to punishment or fine'—nor does it
seem likely that the poet would have jeopardized his prospects at
such a moment by reminding Cleobulus that sex in doorways was
against the law. As T. W. Lumb saw, 'the sense of l. 4 is fixed by
αὐτοῦ, l. 1, and by καιρόν, l. 5; *sudden* opportunities create sudden
necessities.'[13] He therefore makes the attractive suggestion
προσπαίοις. It is not difficult to imagine ΠΑΙ in an uncial hand being
misread as ΤΙΜ. However, he kept ἐνδέχεται, translating: 'The
union which necessity offers is possible in sudden fits of passion.'
But what we want is 'is permissible' rather than 'is possible', and
even if ἐνδέχεται could mean this, can the datives be so construed?
The minimal change required by Piccolos' ἐνδέδεται is surely to be
preferred (cf. anon. *AP* xii. 88. 2, δισσαῖς ἐνδέδεμαι μανίαις).

Dilthey thought the last couplet an interpolation, but from ἀλλ'
to ἐβλέπετο it follows on well enough, with ἔκλεπτεν (l. 5) picking up
κλεπτομένην (l. 2). Ordinary mortals wanting an unobserved
'quickie' out of doors have to make do with dark corners whereas
Zeus can simply change his appearance—a characteristic enough
movement from realistic beginning to mythological *exemplum* for a
hellenistic epigram. Dilthey rightly took exception to the γάρ in the
first clause, though the θεός and indeed the καί are no less
problematic. Who needs to be told that Zeus is a god, much less
that Zeus *too* is a god (the ποθούμενος prevents us capitalizing ἔρως
to obtain another god). What we do need to be told is that Zeus too
is a philanderer. I suggest that the poet wrote καὶ Ζεὺς ἦν φιλόπαις
or (better, since the examples in l. 6 are not pederastic) φιλέρως,
used twice by Meleager, *AP* v. 171. 1 and 197. 1. The word may
have been accidentally omitted, and metre repaired with the feeble
stopgaps γάρ and θεός. As for authorship, all that can be said is that
the only other paederastica addressed to a Cleobulus are by
Meleager (xii. 164, 165, and cf. 74), and writers of erotica do not
normally borrow the names of their predecessors (it was different

[13] *Notes on the Greek Anthology* (London 1920), 132.

with anathematica, as the series vi. 11–16 and 179–87 sufficiently illustrates). And Meleager was much given to drawing morals or comparisons from the amorous (and especially pederastic) activities of Zeus (e.g. xii. 53, 65, 67, 68, 101, 117, 122). The poem is neither attractive nor subtle, but Meleager, though usually both, is not always either.

Its successor is a much more graceful piece, C. III. 171:

τηρῶ σου τὸ φίλημα τὸ χρύσεον, ὡς ἀπὸ σίμβλου
κηρίον, ὡς μήλου πνεῦμα πεπαινομένου.
τηρῶ καὶ συνέχω τοῖς χείλεσι, κἤν προσίῃ τις
"χαῖρε" λέγων, εὐθὺς τοῦτον ἀποστρέφομαι.
τοῦτο γὰρ αὐτὸ καθ᾽ αὐτὸ κακὸν μέγα συμβάλλεσθαι
ἐστὶ τὸ σὺν τούτῳ τῷ πυρὶ πῦρ ἕτερον.

I am keeping your golden kiss, like a honeycomb from a hive or the scent of a ripe apple. I am keeping it and holding it between my lips, and if anyone comes up to say 'hello', straightaway I push him on one side. For it is a great crime in itself to join one fire with another.

Fortunately, our enjoyment of this excellent poem is not spoiled by textual corruption (though the emphasis of αὐτὸ καθ ᾽ αὐτὸ in l. 5 is unclear). The honey, the kiss, the fires, and the elegant conciseness all suggest the possibility of Meleager himself. Compare xii. 109 by Meleager, on a pretty boy who is unexpectedly captivated by a girl; 'a new miracle,' exclaims the poet, φλέγεται πῦρ πυρὶ καιόμενον. The last line implies that the passer-by whose kiss the poet will try to duck is another lover, but xii. 109 shows we cannot take it for granted that the kiss being treasured also came from a boy. There are two poems by Strato on greeting pretty boys in the street, xii. 223 (in S) and 227. As Gow and Page observe, 'Strato can write very like Meleager'.

Next C. IV. 69:

ὄρνι, τί μ᾽ ἐξ ὕπνου φρενοθελγέος ἐξεβόησας;
τίπτε δ᾽ ὀνειροπόλου νόσφισας ἀμβροσίης;
αὐτόθι γὰρ γλυκεροῖς περιπλέγμασι παιδὸς ἐχρώμην,
ἐγγὺς ἔχων τὸν ἐμὸν καὶ φιλέων ἕταρον.
ἐξ οἴης μ᾽ ἀπάτης ἀπενόσφισας· ὄρνι, σὺ πᾶσιν
ὤν βαρύς, εἰς ἐμὲ νῦν ὠκυπέτης ἐγένου.

Cock, why did you arouse me from mind-soothing sleep? Why did you tear me away from the ambrosia of dreams? For there I was enjoying the sweet embraces of my boy, holding close and kissing my companion. From what a pleasure you have snatched me! Cock, irksome for all as you are, you have now become a fast-flyer for me.

Not a particularly distinguished variation on the theme of the night
being too short for lovers (Gow and Page, *HE* ii. 622, not quoting
this example) but it can at least be presented (as above) in a
readable text. In lines 1 and 5 both the manuscript and (without a
qualm) all editors present ὕπνε where I have printed ὄρνι. But how
can sleep stir lovers from sleep—or shout, for that matter (l. 1)?
Nor can it be sleep that snatches the poet from the ambrosia of
dreams (2) or beguilement (5), that is to say once more from sleep.
Nor can it be sleep, the great refresher, that is irksome to all (6);
nor, finally, can the poet's complaint be that he fell asleep too
quickly. Clearly the original vocative in both places must have
been a word meaning or standing for *dawn*, the first displaced by
accident (the poem is full of references to sleep), the second
'corrected' to harmonize. There can be little doubt what that word
was. Hardly ὄρθρε, as in the two best known examples of the theme,
by Meleager (v. 172. 1: ὄρθρε, τί μοι, δυσέραστε, ταχὺς περὶ κοῖτον
ἐπέστης; and v. 173. 1: ὄρθρε, τὶ νῦν, δυσέραστε, βραδὺς περὶ κόσμον
ἐλίσσῃ;). For dawn itself does not shout any more than sleep.
Meleager wrote another variation in which it is the noise of the
cockerel that wakes the lovers (xii. 137, cf. anon. xii. 136 and
Antip. Thess. v. 3), but it is Marcus Argentarius (ix. 286. 1) who
supplied what is either the model for or an imitation of our poem:
ὄρνι, τί μοι φίλον ὕπνον ἀφήρπασας;

For the benefit of future critics I warn against the temptation (to
which I briefly succumbed myself) of changing βαρύς in l. 6 to
βραδύς. The superficially neat antithesis between slow and fast
simply does not work here: dawn is coming fast for the poet but not
for that reason slowly for anyone much less everyone (πᾶσιν) else.
Dawn is βραδύς in Meleager v. 172. 1 (cf. Macedonius, v. 223. 4)
because the girl is with another, a quite different theme. As Ovid's
Aurora poem (*Am.* i. 13) illustrates at length, though the arrival of
dawn may be particularly cruel for lovers, it is hard on everybody
else too, from soldiers and farmers to lawyers and schoolboys; in
two words, βαρύς πᾶσιν. l. 3: γ' ἄν MS and edd., but why the γε or
the conditional ἄν? The poet is merely stating what he was doing
until interrupted. There is no need for Meineke's ἔχαιρον at the end
of 3 or ἀγκὰς at the beginning of 4. Line 5: as L. Robert showed,
ἀπάτη in koine Greek means simply 'pleasure', with no connotation
of deception (*Hellenica* xi/xii [1960], 6–15). It was a point that had
to be underlined in the Atticist Lexica: ἀπάτη ἡ πλάνη παρ' Ἀττικοῖς,
ἀπάτη ἡ τέρψις παρ' Ἕλλησι (Moeris).

σκέψαι νάρκισσον, καὶ μηκέτι γαῦρα φρονήσῃς·
τοῦθ' ὑπερηφανίης ἄνθος ἔφυσεν ἔρως.
τίμα τὸν στέργοντα, παλίστροφα ⟨δ'⟩ ἔργα δεδορκώς
πειράθητι φρονεῖν μηδὲν ὑπὲρ τὸ μέτρον.
τοῦθ' ὁ βλέπεις στεφ⟨άν⟩ωμα παρὰ κρήνην ἐπερεισθέν
ἔκλαυσεν μορφῆς εἰκόνας ἀντιτύπους. (C. IV. 67)

Look at the narcissus, and give up these arrogant thoughts. This is the flower of haughtiness that love gave birth to. Be respectful to your lover, and, seeing that things are subject to reversal, try not to entertain ideas beyond the mean. This ring you see jostling round the edge of the spring once wept for the mirror image of its beauty.

I have printed these lines in the order in which they are transmitted, but I am strongly inclined to adopt Martin West's suggestion that the first and second couplets be transposed. First the general principle, and then a story to illustrate it.

Line 1: if Νάρκισσον (Cramer, Cougny) then presumably τόνδ' rather than τοῦθ' in l. 2. But surely the flower is meant.

Line 3: Meineke's τίμα for the MS τινα is certain and his supplement the only plausible way of restoring the metre.

Line 4: the unmetrical φρονέειν of the MS somehow survived till Dilthey.

Line 5: στέφωμα (στεφάνωμα Meineke) παρὰ κρήνην ἐστὶν ἐρησθέν MS (ἐρασθέν incorrectly Cramer). κρήνῃσι θερισθέν Dilthey, i.e. 'plucked'; μαρανθέν Meineke, more plausibly but further from the *ductus litterarum*; I had thought of ἀπŏριφθέν (keeping κρήνην), 'cast down by the spring' (for the prosody and motif alike cf. Strato xii. 234. 2, where the rose, like a boy's charms, is said to fade and be cast away, μαρανθέν ἄφνω σὺν κοπρίοις ἐρίφη). Yet to all these it must be objected that there is nothing in the first two couplets to suggest that the poet is thinking of a garland of *cut* flowers rather than a ring or circle of flowers still growing around the spring—as the Narcissus story itself might lead us to suppose. Indeed, τοῦθ' ὃ βλέπεις στεφάνωμα suggests something the boy has just had pointed out to him rather than something he has just cast down haughtily to wither and is *not* therefore likely to be looking at. Thus I prefer what is in any case the most 'palaeographically' attractive conjecture, West's ἐπερεισθέν (pressed close up against, or leaning over, the spring). The first stage in the corruption could well be the misreading of π as τι in uncials we have already hypothesized for an earlier poem. The point of the last couplet will not then lie in the withering of the narcissi foreshadowing the withering of the boy's beauty, but simply in the allusion to the narcissi having once been beautiful boys punished for their haughtiness. There is more than a chance that this is another poem by Strato. Cf. xii. 193, Strato on another haughty youth:

οὐδὲ Σμυρναῖαι Νεμέσεις ὅτι σοι 'πιλέγουσιν,
Ἀρτεμίδωρε, νοεῖς· ''μηδὲν ὑπὲρ τὸ μέτρον''.

Nor do you heed what the Nemesises of Smyrna tell you, Artemidorus: 'Nothing beyond the mean'.

The same advice, but here it is ascribed to the two Nemesises worshipped at Smyrna. The unattributed advice of IV. 67 may be presumed to be derived from xii. 193, and since no poems in the book are later than Strato it is likely to be another, later variation on the theme by Strato himself. The Meleagrian poets who occupy most of the rest of *AP* xii would never have shortened a vowel before βλέπεις in l. 5 (the only example I have found is Dioscorides, v. 55. 5), whereas there are no fewer than eight examples in Strato (175. 4, 186. 4, 199. 6, 213. 1, 219. 2, 223. 2, 236. 2, 254. 2; otherwise in xii only in the undatable Numenius, 28. 2; in v in Rufinus, 43. 6 and 94. 3). It might be added that this poem has an obvious connection with *AP* v. 74 by Rufinus (XXVIII Page):

πέμπω σοί, Ῥοδόκλεια, τόδε στέφος, ἄνθεσι καλοῖς
αὐτὸς ὑφ' ἡμετέραις πλεξάμενος παλάμαις.
ἔστι κρίνον, ῥοδέη τε κάλυξ, νοτερή τ' ἀνεμώνη,
καὶ νάρκισσος ὑγρός, καὶ κυαναυγὲς ἴον.
ταῦτα στεψαμένη, λῆξον μεγάλαυχος ἐοῦσα·
ἀνθεῖς καὶ λήγεις καὶ σὺ καὶ ὁ στέφανος.

The parallelism between anon. l. 1 and Rufinus l. 5 is so close that it is difficult to believe that if the one wrote σκέψαι, the other wrote στεψαμένη rather than σκεψαμένη. στεψαμένη in Rufinus, though never suspected, makes no better sense than στέψαι would in anon.: just as the boy is being asked to reflect on the lesson of the narcissus, so too is Rhodocleia being asked, not to 'put on' the garland Rufinus 'has sent her (which would imply that he was inviting her to a party), but again to reflect on its lesson. And this lesson, clear enough in the warning λῆξον μεγάλαυχος ἐοῦσα and the final pentameter, is literally spelled out in lines 3–4, as acutely noticed by A. M. Harmon in *Class. Phil.* xxii (1927), 219–20: the initial letters of the first four flowers in the list, κ(ρίνον), ῥ(οδέη κάλυξ), ἀ(νεμώνη) and ν(άρκισσος), together with the whole of the last flower, ἴον, spell κρανίον, 'skull', a *memento mori* symbolizing the theme of the poem, that life is short. Page dismissed this as 'an ingenious but improbable notion', and while it seems hard to believe the appearance of κράνιον in ll. 3–4 a coincidence, none the less it is true that in all the other examples of acrostichs in epigrams discussed by V. Buchheit (*Studien zum corpus Priapeorum* (Zetemata 28; Munich 1962), 84–6—not known to Page) there is some sort of pointer, missing in the transmitted text of Rufinus XXVIII, to ensure that the reader looks for the hidden word. The restoration of σκειψαμένη supplies just the pointer we need, an instruction to 'reflect' on what has just been said.

The fact that the injunction to 'reflect' on the lesson of the narcissus comes near the end of this poem might be thought to lend some support to West's transposition of the first and second couplets of C. IV. 67. The combination of the close verbal and general thematic parallel (the haughty lover who does not realize that his/her beauty will fade like a garland of flowers) strongly suggests that one poet was inspired by the other. But which? There are two hints, no more. First, Rufinus clearly had in mind a regular garland, woven out of a number of different flowers. Yet, as the commentary above indicates, there is some uncertainty about the precise reference of the στεφάνωμα of anon. l. 4, since up to that point the poet has apparently been talking about just one flower.

Second, while it is easy to see how anon., having decided to write on the general theme of Rufinus' poem, might have varied it by focusing on the most promising individual flower in his garland, the narcissus, there is no way of deriving Rufinus' development of the theme from that of anon. Though far from decisive by themselves, these hints would receive strong support if anon., as suggested above, is indeed Strato. For (as I have argued elsewhere, against Page) Rufinus is a late first-century AD poet frequently imitated by the early second-century Strato.[14] But for the more limited purposes of this chapter, it is enough to have underlined once more the close affinities between the 'new' poems offered by S and the demonstrably Cephalan erotica of *AP* v and xii.

The point of the reference to Narcissus in Cougny IV. 72 and Rufinus does not immediately leap to the eye. In the familiar

[14] *CQ* NS xxxii (1982), 162–73.

version, Narcissus simply falls in love with himself. The reference must be to the version in which Narcissus brings down his own doom by first haughtily rejecting love (ὑπερόπτης Ἔρωτός τε καὶ ἐραστῶν, Conon in *FGrH* 26 F 1 § 24; Greve, in Roscher's *Myth. Lexikon* iii. 1. 12). A boy called Ameinias was driven to suicide by unrequited love for Narcissus, calling on Eros to avenge him before he died. In this version, it was Eros who caused Narcissus to waste away, after which 'the Thespians learned to pay more honour to Eros' (Conon, l.c.). There was a cult of Eros by 'the pool of Narcissus' in Thespiae, on Mt Helicon (Pausanias ix. 31. 7). The Emperor Hadrian made a dedication to this Eros, 'dwelling in Heliconian Thespiae, by the burgeoning garden of Narcissus':

ὦ παῖ τοξότα Κύπριδος λιγείης,
Θεσπιαῖς Ἑλικωνίαισι ναίων
Ναρκίσσου παρὰ κῆπον ἀνθέοντα,
ἱλήκοις· τὸ δέ τοι δίδωσι δέξο . . . (Kaibel, *Epigr. gr.* 811).

On the circumstances of this dedication see L. Robert, *Documents d'Asie Mineure* (Paris 1987), 136–7. This version of the story was naturally an appropriate exemplum to hold up to the haughty beloved, whether boy (anon.) or girl (Rufinus).

After this two more new poems (C. III. 170 and 169) before a run of eight, all of which reappear in *AP* xii, and a new concluding couplet (overlooked by Cougny, though printed by Cramer and so not, as Aubreton oddly claimed, 'inédit'), which it will be convenient to take here:

νῦν ὁ καλὸς θάλλει Νικόστρατος, ἀλλ' ἀρύσασθε,
ὡς ἀπὸ κρηνῖδος ψυχρὸν ὕδωρ θέρεος.

The fair Nicostratus is in bloom now, but fill your cup, as though with cool water from a spring in summer.

That is to say, make use of Nicostratus' bloom while it lasts, the point being less that cool water is refreshing (cf. Asclepiades, *AP* v. 169. 1, ἡδὺ θέρους διψῶντι χιὼν πότον) than that in summer it does not stay cool very long. Once more Strato seems the most likely author. Compare xii. 195: Milesius θάλλει like the flowers in spring, spring, not knowing that beauty is killed by hair as a fair flower is by heat. Or xii. 215:

νῦν ἔαρ εἶ, μετέπειτα θέρος· κἄπειτα τί μέλλεις
Κῦρις; βούλευσαι· καὶ καλάμη [stubble] γὰρ ἔσῃ.

Nicostratus does not occur elsewhere as a lover's name, but forty of
Strato's lover-names are used only once (cf. Page, *The Epigrams of
Rufinus*, p. 27).

It should be added that these two lines are written at the bottom
of the last page of a defective manuscript, and lack the colophon
with which the scribe invariably elsewhere indicates the end of a
poem. So although the thought is complete inside the couplet,
some further illustration of the point may have followed.

Now for III. 170 and 169:

ὑπνώσσοις ἐπὶ πουλύν, Ἔρως, χρόνον· ἄχρι γὰρ ἂν ⟨σὺ⟩
εὕδῃς, εἰρήνην σῶν ἔχομεν βελέων·
ἢν δέ σ᾽ ὁ λυσιμελὴς προφύγῃ κόπος, οἰκτρὸς ἐκεῖνος
ὃς πρῶτος σὸν ἴδοι κανθὸν ἀνοιγόμενον. (C. III. 170)

Sleep long, Eros, for while you sleep we have a rest from your arrows. But
if limb-relaxing sleep should leave you, pitiable is he who first sees your
eye open.

οἶος ἀποστάξει μηρῶν πόθος· οἶον ἀκραίων
ὥριον ἐκ λαγόνων ἄνθος ἀποκρέμαται·
οἶον δ᾽ οἱ δροσόεντες ὑποιδαίνουσιν ἀκμαίως
†αὐτοερυθρα† φαιδρὰ σαλευομένης.
τίς πλάστης τοιοῦτο τεχνήσατο; τρισμακάριστος
κεῖνος ὃς ἐργοπόνους τῷδ᾽ ἐπέθηκε χέρας [χεῖρας MS]. (C. III. 169)

What desire drips from the thighs! What fresh bloom hangs from the tips
of the loins. How fully the dewy ⟨?breasts⟩ swell, . . . as she sways(?).
What sculptor fashioned such an object? Thrice blessed he who laid his
craftsman's hands on it!

Line 1: ἀκμαῖον MS (? from l. 3), corr. Piccolos.

Line 4 seems desperate. μαστοὶ ἐρυθραῖοι, Piccolos; breasts are
certainly what is wanted, but the adjective seems only to refer to
the city of Erythrae. ἐρυθρὰ is found meaning 'pimples' in medical
writers (*LSJ* s.v.), and could perhaps be used of nipples or breasts
(less appropriately of statue, though of course they were painted):
cf. Dioscorides, v. 54. 4, σοῦ δε σαλευομένου, of sexual threshing;
with Rufinus, v. 60. 4 σαλευόμεναι referring to erotically wobbling
buttocks; Strato, xi. 225. 4, σαλευόμενον of the man in the middle of
a threesome; and especially Dioscorides again, v. 55. 5, ἀμφισαλευο-
μένης ἔτρεμε πορφύρεα, of a girl's breasts (πορφύρεα presumably
referring to the nipples) swaying during intercourse in the superior

position—whence my (tentative) correction of the MS σαλευό-μενον.[15]

The most interesting thing about the last two poems is that they are *not* pederastic. Nor were they put among the paederastica just for the sake of variety. They have been misunderstood and misclassified. 169 is meant to have a surprise conclusion: the voluptuous description of the first two couplets suggest that the subject is a real person; l. 5 reveals that it is only a statue, though the final two words continue the sexual *double entendre*. The breasts that are dimly discernible through the corruptions in ll. 3–4 suggest a female statue, but the ripe flower hanging from the thighs in l. 2 might have been taken as a fanciful description of a penis, and the same inattentive reader might almost be forgiven for jumping to the conclusion that in τρισμακάριστος / κεῖνος ὅς . . . τῷδ᾽ ἐπέθηκε χέρας, τῷδε referred to a boy and κεῖνος his lucky lover. The more so if he had recently read xii. 217. 5, where ὦ μακάριστος ἐκεῖνος ὅτις ποτέ does indeed refer to the lucky lover of Strato's boy. With rather less justification he might similarly have misunderstood οἰκτρὸς ἐκεῖνος / ὅς . . . in 170, given that he was copying the two poems in sequence.

Now this occasional misclassification of paederastica is also a feature of *AP* xii, and it is at this point that we may appropriately take up again a question shelved on an earlier page: the source or sources of *AP* xii. In keeping with his general thesis, Aubreton[16] disputes the usual assumption that it is basically Cephalan. For him, Cephalas' pederastic book consisted only of poems by Strato, a thesis recently elaborated by W. M. Clarke.[17] It was, they claim, some later redactor, most probably the scribe B who wrote *AP* xii, who added the material from other collections that occupies most of the centre of the book.

There is only one prima facie serious argument in favour of this view. The prose preface, which we have assumed to be Cephalas' own, announces only Strato. Here is the whole of this preface (Paton adapted):

And what kind of man should I be if, after setting forth all that precedes for you to study, I were to conceal the 'Boyish Muse' of Strato of Sardis,

---

[15] Cf. too Archilochus, *fr.* 41W with West (1974), 124.

[16] *Byz.* xxxix (1969), 35–52.

[17] *GRBS* xvii (1976), 371–84; I can only say that I am quite unconvinced by Clarke's ingenious calculations, which only work at all by ignoring the poems in S.

which he used to recite to those about him in sport, taking personal delight in the diction of the epigrams, not in their meaning. So apply yourself to what follows, for 'in dances', as the tragic poet says, 'a chaste woman will not be corrupted' (Eur. *Bacch.* 318).

Admittedly this is not how one might expect an editor to introduce a book that consists of one and a half times as many epigrams by other writers as well. But the compiler of *AP* xii (in my judgement Cephalas) made his own both the concept and the contents of Strato's collection. And though he added a great many new poems, his book begins with Strato's introduction and closes with Strato's conclusion, and Strato remains far and away the biggest single contributor. The book is in effect an expanded edition of Strato's μοῦσα παιδική. Is it really so unreasonable or inappropriate for him to have continued to refer to it as 'Strato's Boyish Muse'? If it *was* some later redactor who added the non-Stratonian material to Cephalas' original pederastic book of 'pure' Strato, it is even more difficult to answer the question (not asked by Aubreton and Clarke) why *he* was content to leave his expanded pederastic book with the same Stratonian title as Cephalas. For the same B who wrote the text of *AP* xii also copied out in full the Cephalan preface quoted above.

As before, the evidence of S is virtually decisive. In the first place, it has, like *AP*, a pederastic section following in order its equivalents to *AP* ix, x, and xi. This section contains paederastica by Alcaeus, Asclepiades, Callimachus, Meleager, Rhianus, and the probably Philippan Alpheius as well as Strato. Here we may compare the contents of *APl* and *ABV*. Although Planudes took only a fraction of the paederastica at his disposal (16 compared with the 258 in *AP* xii), even so he has poems by Asclepiades, Callimachus, and Meleager as well as Strato, the Philippan Euenus, and even the obscure Numenius of Tarsus. *ABV* has seventeen paederastica, Asclepiades and Meleager from the first *Garland*, Philodemus from Philip's, Leonidas of Alexandria from neither, and, suggestively enough, two poems (60 and 237) ascribed to Numenius. There seems no good reason to reject the Palatine ascription of these poems to Meleager and Strato respectively, but whether guess or error, the mention of Numenius points to a source that featured poems by him; *AP* xii has only one, 28, the sole source of our knowledge of the poet. So all three, S, *APl*, and *ABV*, drew on a collection that, like *AP* xii, already contained paederastica from both *Garlands* as well as Strato—and *APl* and *ABV* have the odd piece by other writers too. Prima facie, then, all four collections derive their common features from a common source. And while the possibility of a *post*-Cephalan common source cannot be absolutely excluded, it is obviously most unlikely that all four should have hit on the same post-Cephalan redaction. Aubreton's 'original' Cephalan book containing only Strato is a hypothesis for which there is neither evidence nor room.

The weakness of Aubreton's case throughout is that these supposed later addenda to the original Cephalan core are always drawn from the same sources that Cephalas himself used. In this case he is reduced to the paradoxical conclusion that when Cephalas was putting together his pederastic book he did not know of the existence of the 130-odd Meleagrian paederastica that now fill the centre of the book. But how can we possibly suppose Cephalas ignorant of Meleager's *Garland*?

Aubreton thinks that Meleager published a separate collection of paederastica. But as Wifstrand saw, the poem on which he based his case, xii. 256, proves no such thing (see Gow and Page, *HE* ii. 650); it is no more than a self-contained epigram about the boys of Tyre. It was Wifstrand again who showed that the Meleagrian section of *AP* xii was compiled at the same time and from the same material as *AP* v; and v at least we can be sure was the work of Cephalas.

We have already seen that Philip did not divide his material into thematic categories; and that Meleager at any rate did not divide his erotica according to the sex of the loved one. It must be Cephalas who was responsible for the division between paederastica and ordinary erotica we encounter in *AP*, and on almost every page we catch him *in flagrante delicto*. There are several Meleagrian paederastica in v and rather more Meleagrian erotica in xii. West has recently pointed out that it must have been at about the same time, *c*.900, that the pederastic poems in the Theognidean sylloge were rather inefficiently segregated into a separate section, what we now call 'Book ii'; inefficiently, because 'one or two remain in the body of the sylloge, and not all that were removed need be pederastic'.[18]

[18] West (1974), 44–5.

Some of the misfits in *AP* xii were caused by a failure to realize that neuter-looking forms like Timarion and Phanion were girls' names,[19] though many others can only be ascribed to sheer carelessness. For most of the paederastica in v there is likewise no excuse, though 142 was perhaps put there deliberately because of the heterosexual imitation by Meleager which precedes it—proof in itself that Meleager did not distinguish erotica and paederastica. One interesting example is Meleager's poem v. 215, which reappears in xii after xii. 19—with Ἡλιοδώρου for -δώρας. It is tempting to suppose that the name was adapted *after* the misclassification.

Cephalas' stupidest error was to put Asclepiades' celebration of the healing qualities of drink (xii. 50) in xii. He was evidently misled by the opening masculine vocative, πῖν᾽, Ἀσκληπιάδη—in fact, of course, a *self*-address by the poet! Now this poem is similarly misclassified in both S and *APl*, decisive proof that *AP*, S, and *APl* derive their paederastica no less than their other material from a common source—a common source that can only be Cephalas.

And we have now seen that C. III. 170 and 169 were likewise misclassified among the paederastica. Now Aubreton took it for granted that what we have for convenience's sake been calling the 'new' poems in S were all interpolations, and insists that the order of the section as a whole is 'totalement contraire à la tradition'. The foregoing discussion has attempted to show that they are all written on the same themes, even the same boys, in the same style, and in some if not all cases by the same poets as the rest of the material in xii. The other sections in S appear to derive from just one source. Why should our compiler have turned to another source for his paederastica—and to what source? As for the matter of the arrangement, there are clear enough traces of the Palatine order (18, 19, 21 . . . 235, 237, 241 . . . 181, 185, 209, 214, 223, 224) to make it explanation enough that the variations are deliberate changes made for personal reasons of taste (as with the variations from the Palatine order among the ecphrastica in section 1).

S also offers a handful of true readings where *AP* is corrupt, and given that the text of S is in general more corrupt than that of *AP*, these readings must be presumed transmitted truth rather than conjecture. For example, S offers xii. 223. 1 (τερπνὸν ὅλως τὸ

---

[19] Though it was not a form which fell out of use in the later Greek period. Compare the subscription to Paris. gr. 1750 by our friend Michael Sophianus: he finished copying on 7 Oct. 1561 at Padua, παρῆν δὲ καὶ Λουκρήτιον ἡ ἑταίρα.

πρόσωπον ἐμοὶ προσίοντος ἀπαρκεῖ) with Περπούρου in place of the first two words. τερπνὸν seems very feeble for a face so dazzling the poet cannot take his eyes off it, and a proper name (as often in Strato) would be preferable.

At ix. 363. 4, S alone preserves the certainly correct κόμησε (from κομάω) where both *AP* and *APl* have the corrupt κόμισσε. A more complicated case that deserves fresh discussion is the last couplet of xii. 209. Strato is telling his boyfriend not to lie so sullenly beside him:

> ἔστω που πορνικὰ φιλήματα καὶ τὰ πρὸ ἔργων
> παίγνια, πληκτισμοί, κνίσμα, φίλημα, λόγος.

Early imperial epigrammatists do commit sometimes surprising errors of prosody (listed in Page, *The Epigrams of Rufinus*, 40–3), but there is no parallel in Strato for the apparent lengthening of the iota in πορνῐκά. Editors all print προύν(ε)ῐκα (= 'lewd', virtually indistinguishable in meaning as in appearance) from S's ἔστω προύνεικα πρῶτα φιλήματα, which may well be right. But it has not been noticed that we could restore prosody equally and produce a rather better line by transferring *AP*'s πορνικά to S's version: ἔστω πορνικὰ πρῶτα φιλήματα. *AP*'s που is weak and pointless, and so far from πρῶτα being an anticipation of τὰ πρὸ ἔργων, one might argue that Strato is hammering home the point that he wants *foreplay*, not for the boy to lie there sullen (στυγνὸς . . . κατηφής) and passive until it is all over. If we ask *utrum in alterum*, it is surely more likely that πρῶτα was accidentally omitted by homoioarchon after προύνικα/πορνικά (either of which could have been misread as the other), and που inserted as a stopgap.

However this may be, we are still left with the repetition of φίλημα in 4 after φιλήματα in 3, one of which has surely expelled a different word. Most editors print Jacobs's θιγήματα, 'touchings', in 3; Salmasius had conjectured λαλήματα, but although λαλέω is a favourite word of Strato's for homosexual foreplay (xii. 21. 3; 208. 7; 211. 7; 218. 1; cf. P. G. Maxwell Stuart, *Hermes* 100 (1972), 223–4), it would be an unfortunate anticipation of the final λόγος here. Paton suggested κνίσματα, βλέμμα in 4, which could be right (cf. xii. 7. 4), though a 'look', however potentially arousing, is not really a παίγνιον. I would prefer to write θίγημα in 4, partly because the second φίλημα is more likely to be corrupt than the first, but mainly because this seems to yield a more logical erotic progression: first kisses, the most basic of preliminaries; and then playful blows ('toying', *LSJ*), scratching, touching, and finally (lewd) talk. The last need not be the anticlimax it might seem; at xii. 7. 3 Strato claims that girls cannot compete with boys because they cannot provide λόγος ἡδὺς ἐκεῖνος ὁ πορνικός.[20] θίγημα will here presumably be the explicit genital or anal caress implied by κεῖνα θιγεῖν in the preceding poem, xii. 208. 6.

For our present purpose the main point is simply that S and *AP* share a common error, just as at xii. 224. 4, where both offer the pointless κύρια δ᾽ ἀμφότερα, of love and beauty. No one has ever hesitated to print Brunck's καίρια, meaning 'lasting only for a season'.

Lastly, xii. 118:

εἰ μὲν ἑκών, Ἀρχῖν᾽, ἐπεκώμασα, μύρια μέμφου·
εἰ δ᾽ ἄκων ἥκω, τὴν προπέτειαν ἔα.
ἄκρητος καὶ Ἔρως μ᾽ ἠνάγκασαν· ὧν ὁ μὲν αὐτῶν
εἷλκεν, ὁ δ᾽ οὐκ εἴα τὴν προπέτειαν ἐᾶν.
ἐλθὼν δ᾽ οὐκ ἐβόησα, τίς ἢ τίνος, ἀλλ᾽ ἐφίλησα
τὴν φλιήν· εἰ τοῦτ᾽ ἔστ᾽ ἀδίκημ᾽, ἀδικέω.

The poet apologizes for revelry outside his lover's door, blaming his 'recklessness' on love and wine. The last couplet reveals that in fact he did not so much as raise his voice, but merely planted a kiss on the doorpost. The point of the poem turns on the anticlimax.

The text given above is a conflation of the manuscript tradition with a damaged first-century copy on a wall of a private house in Rome, the so-called Auditorium of Maecenas.[21] The inscription confirms S's ἔα against *AP*'s ὅρα at the end of l. 2, and its fragmentary ετηανεαν at the end of l. 4 was the basis for Dressel's generally accepted conjecture τὴν προπέτειαν ἐᾶν for the quite different versions of both *AP* (σώφρονα θυμὸν ἔχειν) and S (τὴν βίαν ὅσσην ἔχει).[22] The end of l. 2 would mean 'disregard my reckless-ness'; the end of l. 4 something like 'did not allow me to put aside my recklessness'. This strained repetition may well have been what

---

[20] Cf. Juvenal, vi. 196–7: 'quod enim non excitet inguen / vox blanda et nequam?'
[21] Kaibel 1111; cf. *HE* ii. 162–3; Sonya Lida Tarán, *The Art of Variation in the Hellenistic Epigram* (Leiden 1979), 65–8. For the building, O. Murray, *JRS* lxxv (1985), 43, with recent bibliography.
[22] For a detailed discussion coming to a different conclusion, see Tarán, *The Art of Variation in the Hellenistic Epigram*, 65 f.: it seems to me an advantage rather than a fault of Dressel's text that 'it forces us to assign a different meaning to each of the three occurrences of the verb ἐάω: "forgive" in line 2, and "permit" and "leave aside" in line 4' (p. 67).

Callimachus wrote, but it is easy to believe that a scribe might have jumped to the conclusion that l. 4 had been corrupted from l. 2 and supplied a version of his own, or perhaps rather two. *AP*'s version is virtually identical with the first half of Theognis 754, an author being read in the age of Cephalas; and its prosody betrays S's version as a piece of Byzantine composition. Now since *AP*'s ὅρα at the end of l. 1 reflects S's ὅρα at the end of l. 4, it looks as if *AP* derives here from a manuscript which also offered S's version; and since it seems likely that Cephalas was the first Byzantine editor to concern himself with classical epigrams, this manuscript might well have been Cephalas' own. C's supplements from Michael Chartophylax show that Cephalas' manuscript offered a great many variants not reproduced in *AP*, including other such metrical stopgaps (for example, at v. 62. 6).

There is in S only one clearly non-Cephalan poem, the long 'erotic ode', anonymous in S (whence Cramer, IV. 380–2), but (unknown, apparently, to Aubreton) also preserved with other Byzantine anacreontics in another manuscript, whence we learn the author's name, Constantine the philosopher, the Sicilian (Bergk, *PLG* iii⁴, 351–4, the second of two such poems ascribed to Constantine).

There seems no reason to doubt that this is the Constantine the Sicilian who wrote *AP* xv. 13, a footling trifle addressed to his professorial chair, which boasts that it only supports men of learning. A certain Theophanes (on whom see further p. 307) wrote an even feebler 'reply' (ἀντίγραφον), denouncing the chair as an 'empty braggart', in fact a very ordinary, unadorned seat of wood (xv. 14).

Now in Ch. XV we shall see that *AP* xv is a post-Cephalan collection, in all probability put together by J himself in the 940s. Both Theophanes and the Constantine of *AP* xv are described by J (here writing both text and ascriptions) as 'the late' (τοῦ μακαρίου). On this basis Constantine the Sicilian ought to be younger than Cephalas but older than J.

Yet he has hitherto been identified with the Constantine of another group of poems published by P. Matranga in 1850 (*Anecd. graeca*, ii. 555–6), which have still to be properly understood and ascribed. First come three elegiac poems ascribed to a Constantine which attack his recently deceased teacher 'Leo the philosopher' for his 'hellenizing' ways. About the identity of Leo at least there can be no doubt. Certainly not the Emperor Leo the Wise (as Matranga thought) nor the diplomat Leo Choirosphactes, but the influential polymath (and briefly Archbishop of Thessalonica) more generally now known as Leo the philosopher or Leo the mathematician,[23] a man of wide intellectual sympathies who not surprisingly won the suspicious sobriquet 'Hellene' in ninth-century Byzantium (cf. the heading τοῦ ἐπονομαζομένου Ἕλληνος to his poem *AP* xv. 12). It is Zeus, defiler of maidens' beds, that Leo has made his god; let him go down now to his Hades, Constantine cries, and meet his dear Euclids, his Platos, Procluses, Ptolemies, Epicuruses, and so forth (II. 13 f.). Euclid, Plato, Proclus, and Ptolemy are known to have been preoccupations of Leo, and in *AP* xv. 12. 1 he refers gratefully to Fortune's gift to him of the ἀπραγμοσύνη of Epicurus. It was from Leo, Constantine adds (III. 5–6), that he 'drank the milk of Calliope', that is, learned to write poetry:

> ταῦτα δὲ Κωνσταντῖνος, ὁ σῆς γάλα Καλλιοπίης
> καλὸν ἀμελξάμενος, ᾖσεν ἐπισταμένως.

There follows in the manuscript (Vat. gr. 915) another poem (in iambics) headed 'Apology of Leo the philosopher, in which he reveres Christ and belittles the Hellenes'. It is obviously no such thing. The author defends himself against the accusation of attacking Leo, who had been a second father to him, as a blasphemer and apostate—and then renews the attack, defiantly proclaiming himself the 'parricide of an impious teacher, even if the Hellenes burst in twain':

> κἂν εἰ διαρραγεῖεν Ἕλληνες μέσον (34).

Obviously the poet cannot be Leo himself, nor is the poem a defence against Constantine's attack. It was Bury who saw the answer.[24] It is another sally by Constantine, who had been criticized for the vehemence and disloyalty of his attacks on his old teacher. The original title must have been something like ἀπολογία ⟨Κωνσταντίνου κατὰ⟩ Λέοντος, but a copyist was understandably misled by ἀπολογία . . . Λέοντος into expecting *Leo*'s defence.

---

[23] See the account in Lemerle, 148 f.
[24] *Eastern Roman Empire* (London 1912), 441 n. 4; cf. (independently) S. G. Mercati, *Riv. degli Studi Orientali*, x (1923–5), 235 n. 1 (= *Collect. Byz.* i (1970), 296): Lemerle, 172–5; M. D. Spadaro, *Siculorum Gymnasium* xxiv (1971), 175–205.

The 'Hellenes' Constantine had in mind in l. 34 are evidently these critics, men like Leo Choirosphactes, who had penned a very different tribute to the great man's memory:

θεωρίας ὕψωμα, γνώσεως βάθος,
πλάτος λόγων, φρόνησις, ἁπλότης, πόνος,
θρηνοῦσιν, οἰμώζουσιν· οὐ γὰρ ἐν βίῳ
Λέοντα νῦν βλέπουσιν. ὦ τῆς ζημίας.

Choirosphactes himself was ultimately to fall victim to the charge of Hellenism. Was it l. 34 of Constantine's poem that J had in mind when he put Christian epigrams first in *AP*, adding to his heading the words κἂν οἱ Ἕλληνες ἀπαρέσκωνται? Or had it become no more than a standard, if still necessary, saving formula by then?

There follow in the manuscript two distichs under the heading οἷον δὴ καὶ τοῦτο τὸ ἡρωικοελεγεῖον αὐτοῦ:

ἔρρε μοι, ὦ τριτάλαινα Πολύμνια, ἔρρετε μοῦσαι,
    αὐτὰρ ἐγὼν ἀπὸ νῦν ῥητορικῆς ἔραμαι·
Φώτιον ἀρχιερῆα γεροντοδιδάσκαλον εὑρών,
    ὅς με γάλακτι ἔθρεψε θείων ναμάτων.

Scholars have been puzzled by these lines—as they might well be if they supposed them by Leo. Lemerle proposed to transfer them to Constantine. There was little need for the caution with which he advanced this suggestion, self-evident and virtually inescapable as it is. In the first place, if the ἀπολογία is indeed by Constantine (which no one now doubts), then there is a prima-facie presumption that any poem that follows it described as 'another poem of his' is being ascribed to Constantine. Secondly, the heading specifies that it is 'another elegiac poem of his'. Now the ἀπολογία is in iambics. The αὐτοῦ must refer to a poet whose elegiacs have previously been quoted, and that can only be Constantine. This point is confirmed by the next item in the manuscript, a set of iambics duly and explicitly headed ἕτεροι ἰαμβεῖοι τούτου στίχοι. The 'other set of iambics' implied by the ἕτεροι is the ἀπολογία. Thirdly, with the (miserably unmetrical) reference in the last line to the 'milk of Calliope' in III. 5, Constantine is deliberately using the same image to underline the change in his life; for the milk of Calliope he used to drink with Leo he has turned to the milk of the holy streams (that is to say, the Scriptures) with which Photius has now nourished him. He is bidding a final farewell to the paganizing poetry (Polymnia and the Muses) that he now so regrets having wasted his time on. Fourthly, γεροντοδιδάσκαλον. Usage and common sense alike require that the old man should be Constantine, not Photius (it is the pupil, not the teacher, who is normally expected to be young). Why then does the poet draw attention to his ὀψιμαθία? If he is Constantine, surely because he is countering the charge of disloyalty to the master of his youth by pointing out that in his old age he has acquired a new one, none other than the patriarch himself. It is to Photius that his loyalty now belongs.

Everything now falls into place. All six poems published by Matranga (ii. 555–60) are by Constantine. Lemerle assumes that the poet's hostility to Leo was inspired by the 'ardour of the neophyte' who had fallen under the influence of Photius (evidently during his first patriarchate, 858–67, since Leo died some time in the 870s, probably before the second, 877–86). But there may have been another factor too. The greater part of the poem (which runs to seventy-six lines) is devoted, not so much to a defence of his earlier attack on Leo's 'Hellenism' as to a defence of his own Christianity. For example, everything from 36 f.,

καὶ πρῶτα μὲν ζήλῳ γε ῥωσθεὶς ἐνθέῳ
Χριστὸν κριτὴν τίθημι . . .

to the very defensive 66 f.,

ταῦτα φρονῶ ζῶν, καὶ θανὼν ἐκεῖ πάλιν
καυχώμενος λέξαιμι πρόσθεν Ἀγγέλων . . .

It is hard to resist the suspicion that Constantine himself had been accused of pagan ways because of his association with Leo.

Matranga took it for granted that Constantine the pupil of Leo was Constantine the Sicilian, and he has generally been followed. But with the quatrain ἔρρε μοι correctly ascribed, the pupil of Leo is revealed to have been an old man in the 860s. How can he be the man whom J wrote of as recently dead in the 940s? Furthermore, Matranga's original assumption rested on an indefensible misreading of the lemma to *AP* xv. 13, 'on his chair' (εἰς τὸν θρόνον αὐτοῦ). Matranga took the 'his' to refer to Leo, who by what can only be a coincidence happens to be the author of the immediately preceding poem xv. 12. It must in fact refer to the author of 13, namely Constantine.

The fuller title given in both Matranga's manuscript and the index of now lost Byzantine anacreontics in Barb. gr. 310 (246) not only supplies the poet's name but adds that he took his subject from 'some poem or other' (λαβόντος τὴν ὑπόθεσιν ἐκ μελῳδίας τινός). This looks like the residue of a once more informative lemma, and as it happens the poem in question can still be identified: Moschus' 'Runaway Love', no. 1 in the usual numeration of the poems ascribed to Moschus (= *AP*. ix. 440).

This famous little poem presents Aphrodite exhorting someone to catch her runaway son Eros (πλανώμενον . . . ἔρωτα, 2), concluding with a warning of the danger of the enterprise. Constantine's poem describes how the poet heedlessly set out to catch runaway Eros (ἔρωτα τὸν πλανήτην, 59) and suffered the consequences. Over and above the obvious similarity of theme there are a number of certain echoes of Mo(schus)'s poem in Co(nstantine)'s:

Co. 25–8, γυμνός . . . / πυρὶ δ᾽ εἴκελος τὰ πάντα· / ἀπὸ δ᾽ ὀμμάτων βολάων / φλογερὴν ἔπεμπεν αἴγλην ~ Mo. 7–8 πυρὶ δ᾽ εἴκελος· ὄμματα δ᾽ αὐτοῦ / δριμύλα καὶ φλογόεντα, and γυμνὸς in 15.

Co. 33, μικρὸν ἔχει τὸ βέλος, μακρὰ δὲ βάλλει ~ Mo. 13 μικκύλα μὲν τήνῳ τὰ χερύδρια, μακρὰ δὲ βάλλει.

Co. 29, 31, ἐρατὴν φέρεν φαρέτρην . . . ἐπίχρυσον εἶχε τόξον ~ Mo. 20 καὶ χρύσεον περὶ νῶτα φαρέτριον.

Co. 49, 51, καθάπερ ταώς τις ὄρνις . . . ὑπερίπτατο ~ Mo. 16 καὶ πτερόεις ὅσον ὄρνις ἐφίπταται.

Finally, just as Moschus ends with a warning not to touch the boy because everything about him is bathed in fire (29, and cf. 22–3 on his λαμπάς), so Constantine closes by warning that λαμπάδα καιομένην χερσὶ κομίζει.

There can be little doubt that Constantine was influenced in both conception and detail by Moschus. Where did he read the poem? That it was included in Cephalas is proved by its appearance in *AP*, *APl*, and E. That it also appears later in several Bucolic manuscripts might seem to suggest another, independent line of transmission. In fact it was probably via Cephalas that Moschus I entered the Bucolic tradition. The earliest Bucolic manuscript to carry it is Laur. 32. 16, known to editors of Theocritus as S but better known to us as L. The page that carries Moschus I, like those that carry the collection of epigrams discussed in Ch. VII above, was written by Planudes himself. Even before Planudes' hand was recognized, Wilamowitz[25] and Maas[26] had assumed that it was from an anthology source that Moschus I was added here, largely because L's text is so close to that of *AP*. We can now add that Planudes had a (somewhat abridged) copy of Cephalas to hand while he worked on the manuscript and wrote both the relevant parts himself. It would not be surprising if he had transferred Moschus I from the epigram section to a more appropriate home with the other poems attributed to Moschus.

Several fragments 'from the *Bucolica*' of both Moschus and Bion are quoted by Stobaeus (Gow, *Bucolici Graeci* (1952), pp. 151–2, 159–65), but only one complete, authentic poem by either found a place in the Byzantine corpus of the Bucolici. Cephalas had one other poem by Moschus (*APl* 200, also in S), an epigram on 'Love the ploughman' whose authenticity there is no call to doubt and which in all probability he found in Meleager's *Garland*. That 'Runaway Love', 29 lines and hardly an epigram, was also included by Meleager cannot be taken for granted, but in view of the fact that it was the inspiration of one of Meleager's own most characteristic and brilliant epigrams (v. 177), this is at least a serious possibility. At all events, it seems unnecessary to look beyond Cephalas for Constantine the Sicilian's knowledge of 'Runaway Love'.

Consider too lines 77 f. of Constantine's poem (Eros has finally turned and shot the poet):

> συνομηλίκων χορεία,
> συναρήξατε προθύμως . . .
> τί δὲ φάρμακόν ποθ᾽ εὕρω,
> κραδίην ἐμὴν δροσίζον.
> φάρμακον ἐξ Ἑλένης εἴ τις ἐφεύροι
> ἡμετέραις φιάλαις ἐγκαταμῖξαι.

Francis Cairns[27] has recently compared this poem with Propertius i. 1, suggesting that both derive from the same lost hellenistic source. 'Here', writes Cairns (p. 109), 'we have first an appeal to the speaker's contemporaries for help and advice. Then the speaker wishes for a φάρμακον. This word in itself can refer equally to magic or to orthodox medicine. But the phrase ἐξ Ἑλένης which qualifies φάρμακον favours a religious/magical interpretation.' Cairns acknowledges a suggestion of A. J. Beattie 'that Constantine's poem seems to refer to worship of Helen as a love-goddess',

[27] 'Some Observations on Propertius i. i', *CQ* NS xxiv (1974), 108–10; for a preliminary formulation of my interpretation, see *CP* lxxiv (1979), 58–60.

which he takes as a 'further hint of the learned Hellenistic source from which this lyric may ultimately derive'. On this assumption he infers that 'in these lines we have appeals resembling those of Propertius to the witches and to his friends (i. 1. 19–30)', concluding (p. 110) that 'it is impossible to dismiss the thematic correspondences between them as coincidence'. Alas, Constantine's ultimate source can be identified with certainty: none other than Homer. He is alluding to the opiate that Helen, no love-goddess but the reinstated wife of Menelaus, mixed with Telemachus' wine to dissipate his grief at Sparta (*Od.* iv. 220–1). But his immediate source was surely the anonymous but probably Cephalan hexameter epigram suggesting an improvement on Helen's potion (quoted above, p. 223) that appears a few pages earlier in S.

Cairns was right to draw attention to the general hellenistic inspiration of Constantine's poem, though there is no need to postulate any one lost poem. Over and above the echoes of Moschus' 'Runaway Love', there are several other parallels in the extant epigrams collected by Cephalas: for example, with the 'appeal to the speaker's contemporaries', rather than Propertius cf. Meleager, *AP* xii. 84. 1, ὤνθρωποι, βωθεῖτε; with the reference to the 'binding' of Eros (Co. 13), cf. the series *APl* 195–9. We can hardly doubt that one of Constantine's main 'sources' was Cephalas' anthology.

No less obviously, another was surely a corpus of classicizing anacreontic poetry such as we now read as an appendix to Cephalas' anthology in *AP*. The late ninth/early tenth century saw a notable revival of anacreontic poetry (Arethas, Arsenios, Metrophanes, Leo Choirosphactes, even the Emperor Leo VI), but it was almost entirely either religious or ceremonial, following two traditions established in late antiquity, on the one hand the hymns of Synesius and Sophronius, on the other the poems for weddings and other festivals by John of Gaza and George grammaticus.[28] Constantine's poem stands apart from the work of his contemporaries in its frankly pagan and literary inspiration: Eros playing with water-nymphs, his bow and arrow, his torch of love. The Gaza poets had written mythological ethopoiae, 'What Aphrodite would

---

[28] T. Nissen's *Die byzantinischen Anakreonteen* (1940) contains some excellent spadework, but it is high time that a comprehensive edition was undertaken. For the Palatine *Anacreontea* see Máximo Brioso Sánchez, *Anacreontea: un ensayo para su datación* (Salamanca 1970); G. Giangrande, *Quaderni Urbinati*, xix (1975),

say while searching for Adonis', 'What Ares would say if Aphrodite were wounded by a rose-thorn', and the like, which Constantine certainly knew, but he surely also knew the Palatine corpus. There are one or two thematic and verbal parallels: for example with the 'appeal to contemporaries' cf. also *Anacr.* 21. 6, τί μοι μάχεσθ', ἕταιροι; with Co. 40, ὑπεμειδία κραδαίνων, cf. *Anacr.* 29. 9 and 14, κραδαίνων . . . ὑπεμειδίασε (different subjects, but the same positions in the line). Sometimes John or George might equally be his 'source': for example, Constantine 1. 54, λιγυρὸν μέλος λιγαίνω, might seem to recall *Anacr.* 60. 6, λιγυρὸν μέλος κροαίνων, but cf. too John 1. 24, λιγυρὸν μέλος τι μέλπειν, with λιγαίνειν *(-οι)* closing lines 30 and 34. With δότε μοι λόγον, τί ῥέξω, / τί πάθω; (Co. 83–4) cf. John 1. 16 τί πάθω, φίλοι, τί ῥέξω; and for δότε μοι, John 3. 11, 4. 2, George 1. 35. But the emphasis on the mischievous boy Eros recalls the Palatine anacreontics rather than the Gaza school. And to the best of my knowledge it is only in the Palatine anacreontics that we find, virtually as a technical term of the genre, the precise title attested for Constantine's poem by both extant manuscripts and the index in Barb. gr. 310 (246), ᾠδάριον ἐρωτικόν (*Anacr.* 18*a*; 26, 42; 43; cf. 34; 44; 45).

Whether or not it was Cephalas himself who revived erotic anacreontics, we shall not be far from the truth in associating their rediscovery with the revival in interest in the classicizing erotic epigram with which Cephalas is certainly to be credited and which is especially conspicuous in the predominantly erotic selection of S.

Indeed, perhaps we can go one step further. Is it just by coincidence that S contains an epigram on the same theme of Helen's opiate as Constantine's Ode? It might be added that we cannot exclude the possibility that Moschus' 'Runaway Love' originally stood in the now lost first part of S, which is bound to have contained a further (heterosexual) erotic section, correspond-

---

177–210; M. L. West, *Carmina Anacreontea* (Leipzig 1984); id. *CQ* xxxiv (1984), 206–21; for Sophronius', M. Gigante, *Sophronii Anacreontica* (1957), with a valuable metrical appendix and index verborum; see too R. Anastasi, 'Giorgio Grammatico', *Siculorum Gymnasium* 20 (1967), 209–53. References to John of Gaza and George grammaticus, as to Constantine, are to Bergk, *Poetae Lyrici Graeci* iii[4] (1884). For a brief summary, Hunger, ii. 93–5. For Leo Choirosphactes' anacreontic ecphrasis, see P. Magdalino, *Maistor: Classical, Byzantine and Renaissance Studies for Robert Browning* (Canberra 1984), 225–40 and *DOP* xlii (1988), 97–118. For a new edition of Leo VI's anacreontics, F. Ciccolella, *Boll. Class. Lincei*, 3rd ser., x (1989), 17–37.

ing to what we know as *AP* v. Irritatingly enough S as we have it begins at precisely the point where Moschus' poem (*AP* ix. 440) would have come in the Palatine sequence generally observed in S.

The only clearly non-Cephalan poem in S (Constantine's) is the work of a younger contemporary of Cephalas. The same appears to have been true of both the sources later used by Planudes, like S abridged versions of Cephalas: both contain a handful of non-Cephalan poems by or concerning younger contemporaries of Cephalas (Alexander of Nicaea, Thomas the Patrician, Nicholas Mysticus)—but nothing later. The implication (as we shall see) is that all three (like E) are *early* abridgements of Cephalas. The presence in S of at least one poem directly related to Constantine's Ode suggests the possibility that its compiler might have been Constantine himself. Its contents would then naturally reflect Constantine's own interest in hellenistic erotic poetry. If S is indeed the work of Constantine, then since he was dead by the date of *AP*, the compilation of S would fall between Cephalas (*c*.900) and *AP* (*c*.940).

XI

The *Sylloge Euphemiana* and Σ^π

In all probability, then, the full text of the anthology of which S is a fragment was early, perhaps earlier than *AP*. With E we are in a better position; it can be dated to within a decade—though not the decade favoured by modern scholars.

According to Waltz, Cephalas' anthology appeared 'sans doute un peu avant l'an 900', and E about 890, 'légèrement antérieur à celui de Cephalas'. It was E, he suggested, that gave Cephalas the idea of 'une refonte générale' of the earlier collection.[1]

One might be forgiven for supposing that there was some direct evidence for the priority of E. There is none. There are in fact strong external as well as internal grounds for dating Cephalas *before* E.

It has usually been assumed that Cephalas is to be identified with the Κωνσταντίνου πρωτοπαπᾶ τοῦ παλατίου, τοῦ Κεφαλᾶ λεγομένου mentioned in Theophanes Continuatus (p. 388. 24–389. 1 Bonn) under the year 917. This may well be so. Κεφαλᾶς is not a regular proper name but a nickname, 'Bighead'.[2] It does seem reasonable to suppose that there was only one public figure of the age known as Constantine Bighead, though it is strange that those who accept the identification should arbitrarily propose a date for his anthology some 20 years earlier than their only other chronological evidence. Whether or not the anthologist was the protopapas, we shall see that there are in fact one or two pointers to a date *c*.900 none the less. It was apparently in his youth that the anthologist Cephalas taught in the school of the New Church, as an assistant to Gregory Magister (p. 110). Since he was already then occupied with the interpretation of classical epigrams, it is natural to place

---

[1] Budé I, pp. xxvii, lii; cf. Beckby i², 82 ('um 890'), 74 ('die älteste der Spätanthologien').

[2] To quote an almost contemporary example, a physician called Theophilitzes, noticing that the future Basil I had a large head, ἐπέθηκεν αὐτὸν Κεφαλᾶν (Theoph. Cont. 820).

the production of his anthology at this stage of his career. So if he *is* the protopapas of 917, then his anthology might well have appeared as early as *c*.900. It might be added that promotion inside the palace service rather than the regular ecclesiastical hierarchy would be natural and appropriate for a man who had spent many years teaching in a school attached to a palace church.

The evidence for the date of E is provided by the two following epigrams (Cougny III. 256–7):

A   ταῦτά σοι ἐσθλὰ νοῶν, Εὐφήμιε, ἐσθλὰ χαράττει
     μουσοπόλος ξεῖνός σ᾿ ἀμφαγαπαζόμενος,
     ὃς προλέλοιπε πάτρην ἠδ᾿ Ἑλλάδα καλλιγύναικα
     καὶ γλυκερὴν καλύβην Θετταλικῆς Ὑπάτης.
     καὶ νῦν ἄστυ κλυτὸν Βυζάντιον ἀμφιπολεύει
     πιστὸς ἐὼν θεράπων κοιρανίης μεγάλης,
     ἥν ῥα Λέων μεθέπει ὁ σοφώτατος ἐν βασιλεῦσιν,
     ἐν δίκῃ, ἐν σοφίῃ, ἐν πινυταῖς πραπίσιν.

These good ⟨poems⟩, with good intentions, Euphemius, a foreign poet writes in greeting to you. He has left his land and Hellas with its beautiful women and his dear home in Thessalian Hypata and now lives in the famed city of Byzantium, a loyal servant of the mighty rule of Leo, wisest among emperors, in justice, wisdom and prudent counsel.

B   βαιὰ μὲν ἐξ Ἑλικῶνος ἀπηνθισάμην, πανὺ βαιά
     λείρια Μουσάων, Εὐφήμιε, πάγκλυτα δῶρα.

I have plucked these few lilies from Helicon, few indeed, Euphemius, but glorious gifts of the Muses.

The author, addressing presumably a Constantinopolitan born and bred, calls himself a 'foreigner', born in Hypata in Thessaly but now long since domiciled in the capital and a loyal servant of the Emperor Leo VI the Wise. His poems were written during the long reign of Leo VI, that is to say, at any time between 886 and 912. If during the second half of this period, then he might well be later than Cephalas. We have already seen that a military writer of the reign of Leo knew *AP* iv. 3 by Agathias, and we shall see later that Arethas seems to have had a Cephalas by at any rate 907 and perhaps by 900 (Ch. XIII).

Euphemius was presumably a literary man. Perhaps the 'famous grammaticus Euphemius' (Εὐφήμιον ἐκεῖνον τὸν περιβόητον γραμμα-τικόν) who wrote a satirical iambic poem on the arrogant Peloponnesian nobleman, Nicetas Magister, who had married his daughter

Sophia to Christopher, son of the future Emperor Romanus Lecapenus. The marriage took place in 912 and the story is told in the *De Thematibus* of Constantine VII, written probably soon after 934.[3] A literary man who wrote epigrams himself would be a very suitable dedicatee for E. Then there is the Euphemius *mystographus* who built a fortification wall at Attalia in Pamphylia between June 911 and May 912, commemorated in a long and surprisingly competent iambic poem.[4]

It has generally been supposed that the author of these two epigrams was the original compiler of this collection—or at any rate of the original collection from which our fifteenth/sixteenth century excerpts derive. While conceding that they suit an anthology of epigrams very well (note particularly ἀπηνθισάμην), Gallavotti oddly found them ill suited to this particular anthology, claiming that its contents, though short (βαιά), are not 'lilies from Helicon'.[5] But this is an inappropriately subjective criterion to apply to a Byzantine poem. These are simply clichés: for a Byzantine, all epigrams in any anthology would be 'lilies from Helicon'. It seems to me that there are quite insufficient grounds for regarding the Euphemius poems as later insertions in a pre-existing anthology.

There is a strong element of paradox in Gallavotti's position. He argues (or rather asserts) that E is basically of much later date than the reign of Leo VI ('una compilazione del Due o Trecento, se non più tarda'), though he allows that it contains early material. It is not clear just what sort of distinction is being drawn here. That the early material passed through various processes of excerpting and

---

[3] 6. 37 f., p. 91 Pertusi. The verse in question, γαρασδοειδὴς ὄψις ἐσθλαβωμένη, is a notorious puzzle: for a summary of views, see Pertusi's commentary, pp. 173–4. Pertusi argued that *De Them.* ii was not published till *c.*999, partly on the basis of a mistaken argument concerning the marriage in question. But G. Ostrogorsky has shown that there is no good reason to doubt that it was published soon after i—see *Byzantion* 1953, 36 f. On the date of the marriage see now L. G. Westerink, *Nicétas Magistros: lettres d'un exilé (928–946)* (Paris 1973), 23–6.

[4] H. Grégoire, *Recueil des inscriptions grecques chrétiennes d'Asie Mineure* (1922), no. 302, p. 103 (contrast the following metrical inscription from the same place, Grégoire no. 303). The function of the μυστογράφος is unknown, but evidently connected with that of the μυστικός, who was often a man of letters—most relevantly Constantine the philosopher (Speck, 64–5) and Leo Choirosphactes. For a list, see R. Guilland, *RÉB* xxvi (1968), 278–89 (missing Euphemius, the first known); see too N. Oikonomidès, *Les Listes de préséance byzantines des IXe et Xe siècles* (Paris 1972), 324.

[5] *Boll. Class. Lincei*, 3rd ser., iii (1982), 79–86.

redaction at various dates goes without saying. Our earliest datable manuscript can be assigned to 1493. The final redaction may well have been made not long before that, in the light of Gallavotti's discovery that E 82 (the last poem in the collection) is the work of the fifteenth-century Cretan book collector Marcos Mamunas.[6] But no one would wish to place the original redaction of the ancient material that late. For if (as we shall see, following Basson) Σ″ is in fact an excerpt of the same original collection from which the ancient material in E derives, E cannot be later than the date of the hand that wrote Σ″, now generally assigned to the twelfth century.[7] At all events, certainly pre-Planudean. Whether or not the excerpts we have were made in or before the twelfth century, there is nothing that could not have been included in an anthology of the tenth century. The two Euphemius poems clearly derive from a tenth-century anthology. And yet we are asked to believe that this anthology has nothing to do with E; that they are later insertions from some other source.

The relationship of the ancient epigrammatical material in E to Cephalas can only be determined on internal considerations. For Aubreton, E 'présente un ensemble totalement différent de ce que nous connaissons habituellement: les livres sont complètement mélangés, ce qui prouve un travail antérieur à toute classification' (p. 72). It is true that there are no unbroken Palatine sequences as in S, nor even the series of broken Palatine sequences we find in L. There is no such regularity in the arrangement of E, but it is simply not true that there is no arrangement at all. There are in fact a number of short stretches that show unmistakable traces of the (often arbitrary) order of the various Palatine books. There are also similar coincidences with the order of the Planudean ecphrastica

---

[6] P. Canart, 'Les épigrammes de Thomas Trivizanos', *Thesaurismata* viii (1971), 226–7 and 245; for a list of 17 of Mamunas' manuscripts, P. Henry, *Les Manuscrits des Ennéades*[2] (Brussels 1948), 265–9; for a list of 35, Gallavotti, *Rivista di studi bizantini e neollenici* xvii/xix (1982), 237–45; the latest manuscript he owned seems to date to *c.*1415. His fellow Cretan Thomas included the poem in a collection of his epigrams published in 1553/4, with the heading Μάρκου Μαμουνᾶ εἰς τὸν ἀνθρώπινον βίον, followed by a reply of his own, headed ἀπόκρισις Θωμᾶ τοῦ Τριβηζάνου. P. Canart inferred that Mamunas was a contemporary of Thomas (p. 245), mistakenly, since the poem was included in a manuscript of E dated to 1493 (Par. gr. 1773).

[7] Preisendanz (1911), col. xxii; Aubreton (1968), 62 (1070/1080); Gallavotti, *Boll. Class. Lincei*, 1982, 72–5 and 1989, 52 ('dodicesimo secolo'); M. L. Agati, ibid., 1984, 44 ('XII secolo in pieno'), reporting (ibid. n. 10) the agreement of Paul Canart.

absent from *AP* (comparison of *APl* iv with the ecphrastica in *AP*
ix. 584–822 shows that Planudes follows the original, mainly
thematic arrangement of Cephalas more closely here than usual).
Moreover, a number of individual poems in E are equipped with
lemmata explicitly classifying them as (e.g.) ἀναθεματικός (50, 51)
or ἐπιτύμβιον[8] (14, 53, 56, 58), thereby betraying direct knowledge
of the categories we know to have been originated by Cephalas.
Add to this the wide range of authors represented in E, material
from all the major collections, Meleager, Philip, Agathias, Palladas, Lucillius, not to mention epigrams by individual poets from
Simonides and Mimnermus to Nestor of Laranda and Proclus—
exactly the same range that we find in *AP*, taken over from
Cephalas—and there can be little doubt that E too is later than and
dependent on Cephalas.

E is transmitted in four manuscripts of the late fifteenth or
sixteenth century: Par. gr. 2720; Laur. 57. 29; Par. gr. 1773 of
1493; Vat. gr. 1943. The fullest version is contained in 2720,
written by Scipione Carteromaco (Forteguerri, 1466–1515), the
friend of Aldus Manutius and Erasmus. But the relationship
between the four manuscripts cannot be established in any
straightforward way: 57. 29 lacks six poems in 2720 (2, 3, 5, 7, 8,
47); 1773 lacks these six plus three more (22, 60, 73);[9] 1943 lacks all
of these plus three more as far as 35 (where it breaks off), *except* for
3 and 22, and so cannot derive from either 1773 or 57. 29. We have
to postulate at least two other humanist copies, not to mention the
much earlier common source of E and Σ^π.

I give below a complete list of the poems preserved by the four
manuscripts of E,[10] followed by a list of the poems in Σ^π. Poems
in E marked with an asterisk are missing in Paris. gr. 1773 and Laur.

---

[8] Note too the headings ἐρωτικά and ἐπιδεικτικά in Σ^π (below, p. 260).

[9] All save three were included in the post-Planudean anthology Σ, which in
57. 29 and 1773 (and 1943) immediately precedes E; they were therefore deliberately omitted to avoid duplication.

[10] Paris. gr. 1773, Laur. gr. 57. 29 and Par. gr. 2720, all of the sixteenth century;
see (with caution) Aubreton, pp. 70–3. The basic works on E remain Schneidewin's
Progymnasmata in Anthologiam Graecam (1850) and Basson, pp. 51–61. For another
detailed list, Gallavotti (1982), 80–2. Aubreton ends his list with *AP* xi. 61 as no. 82,
but Gallavotti rightly points out (p. 80 n. 2) that this poem should not be regarded
as part of E, but as no. 1 in the brief appendix of epigrams (which Gallavotti calls
MF) added after E in 2720 by Carteromaco. The fourth, Vat. gr. 1949, fos.
174ᵛ–177ᵛ, was first mentioned in a postscript by Gallavotti (p. 86): it is fully
described by P. Canart, *Codices Vaticani Graeci: Codices 1745–1962*, i (Vatican
1970), 742–3.'

57. 29—omitted because they also appear in Σ, which precedes E in both manuscripts, and the copyist eliminated the duplications. Not realizing this, Aubreton (p. 71) states that Par. gr. 2720 'connaît cinq pièces supplémentaires'. Σ^π is written by a perhaps twelfth-century hand in the margins and blank spaces of *AP* (see Cameron (1973), 98); references to *AP* in square brackets are to poems which appear only once in *AP*, in the hand of Σ^π, but have been wrongly classified (since Jacobs) as part of *AP* proper. Other references to *AP* are to poems which appear in both *AP* and Σ^π.

E 49, 50, and 51 are *AP* vi. 2, 4, and 5, by Simonides, Leonidas of Tarentum, and Philip of Thessalonica respectively. What are

E

1	*AP* ix.	52	29	*APl*	230	57	*AP* vii.	311
* 2	ix.	53	30	*AP* ix.	824	58	ix.	49
3	x.	104	31		823	59		44
4	vi.	330	32		825	*60	vi.	331
* 5	ix.	115b/116	33		826	61	C. III.	166
6		125	34		827	62	*AP* ix.	128
* 7		68	35	xv.	51	63		129
* 8		69	36	ix.	632	64	*APl*	318
9	xi.	277	37		683	65		135
10	ix.	126	38	xi.	220	66	*AP* ix.	364
11		515	39		108	67	*APl*	129
12	Simon.	186B	40		106	68	*AP* ix.	489
13	*AP* ix.	54	41		107	69	vi.	9
14	vii.	309	42	ix.	127	70	xiv.	74
15	ix.	62	43	xi.	255	71		71
16	vi.	1	44		293	72		72
17	*APl*	319	45	ix.	361	73	ix.	451
18	*AP* ix.	24	46		50	74	C. III.	145
19	v.	68	*47		51	75	*AP* xi.	378
20	ix.	449	48		748	76	C. IV.	77
21		440	49	vi.	2	77	C. III.	256
22	*APl*	210	50		4	78	C. III.	257
23		213	51		5	79	*AP* x.	28
24	*AP* ix.	456	52	vii.	268	80	Eurip. *fr.*	1042
25	*APl*	11	53		269	81	Eurip. *fr.*	449
26		12	54		310	82	C. IV.	92
27		13	55		155			
28		227	56	*APl*	31			

Σ"

p. α'	APl	246	AP vii.	307			826
	AP x.	104	APl	326			827]
Simon. 186B				275	p. 568 AP ix.		127
	APl	210	p. δ'	46		xi.	255
		213		387c.5		x.	30
		11		192		xi.	294
		12		60		ix.	51
p. β' ἐκ τῶν ἐρωτικῶν			p. ε'	120			748
	APl	152	Simon. 158B			[xi.	442]
		278	APl	182	p. 707	[xv.	41
		277		307			42
		283	C. III.	179			43
		288					44
p. γ ' ἐκ τῶν ἐπιδεικτικῶν			p. ς' APl	52			45
	APl	159	AP vi.	256	p. 708		46
		160	APl	25			47
		161	p. 476 [AP ix.	711]			48
		163	p. 488 [AP ix.	823			49
		164		824	p. 709		50
		115		825			51]

the chances of Cephalas and the compiler of E[11] juxtaposing these three same dedications to three different gods from three different original collections independently? Note too that *AP* vi. 1 and 9 appear as E 16 and 69. It is hard to resist the conclusion that when his thoughts turned to anathematica, our compiler opened Cephalas at the very beginning of the relevant book. His only two other anathematica (E 4 and 60) are likewise neighbours in *AP* vi, 330 and 331, likewise poems by different authors on different subjects from different original sources.

There are several other such short runs. E 38, 39, and 40 are *AP* xi. 108 (anon.) and 106–7, both by Lucillius. *AP* xi. 108, like ix. 361, which appears here as E 45, both reappear in *ABV*, another collection that derives from Cephalas.

E 7 and 8 are *AP* ix. 68 (anon.) and 69 (Parmenio). Both are on the same theme and are clearly linked. Both also begin with the same letter of the alphabet. Parmenio is a Philippan poet and the

---

[11] For the sake of brevity I shall, where no confusion is likely to arise, use the symbol E to denote both the anthology and the compiler.

chances are surely high that both poems originally stood together in Philip's *Garland*,[12] whence they were excerpted, as a pair, successively by Cephalas, E, the Palatine scribes, and finally Planudes (*APl* i*a*. 48. 2–3).

E 52 and 53 are *AP* vii. 268 and 269, both ascribed to Plato. E 54 and 57, on the other hand, are *AP* vii. 310 and 311, both anonymous, and quite unconnected with each other. It is thus the more striking that they too should be adjacent in both E and *AP* and reappear in *APl*.

However we are to solve the problem presented by *AP* ix. 115, 115*b*, and 116 (see the various editors ad loc.), it is clear that the source from which E 5 was copied had the same defective or disordered text as *AP*. Note too that E 6 is *AP* ix. 125, quite a different sort of poem (in fact a fragment from a late epic) but standing on the same page of *AP*. More significant still, *AP* ix. 126 appears as E 10, ix. 127 as E 42, and 128–9 as E 62–3. *AP* ix. 126 is a frivolous bit of declamation; 127 a comparison of wine and life; and 128–9 are not epigrams proper but (again) fragments from late epic, this time Nestor of Laranda. Once more, a farrago of poems randomly associated on the same page or two of *AP* appear scattered evenly through E. Two further examples follow.

E opens with *AP* ix. 52–3, poems by unconnected authors (Carpyllides and Nicodemus or Bassus) on unconnected themes. E 13 is *AP* ix. 55, by Lucillius or Menecrates, on a different theme again. At E 46 and 47 we find *AP* ix. 50 and 51, by Minnermus and Plato, again on quite unconnected themes. Then, at E 58 and 59, we have *AP* ix. 49 (anon.) and 44 (puzzlingly ascribed to either Plato or Statyllius Flaccus). The lack of connection between these poems is underlined by the fact that Planudes put all seven of them in different chapters. It is thus the more striking that they appear in such close proximity in both E and *AP*.

Something too can be won from a comparison of the lemmata in E and *AP*. For example, the first poem in E, ix. 52 by Carpyllides, is equipped in *AP* with the rambling but accurate lemma: 'on a fisherman who caught a human head instead of a fish, and when digging to bury it found buried treasure'. E has the briefer but quite misleading: 'on a fisherman'. There is no direct mention of a

---

[12] Gow and Page, while admitting that 'the pair are obviously rival compositions on the same theme' (*GP* ii. 324) do not even consider this possibility (nor do they note the alphabetical link).

fisherman in the poem and a more suitable short title would be: 'piety rewarded'. E's title is surely a careless abbreviation of a paraphrase such as we now read in *AP*, the work of Cephalas.

E 74 (Cougny III. 145) is a poem on a quarrelsome wife by a grammarian:

"Μῆνιν ἄειδε" μαθὼν καὶ "μῆνιν ἄειδε" διδάξας
"οὐλομένην" γαμετὴν ἠγαγόμην ὁ τάλας·
πᾶν δ' ἦμαρ μάχεται, καὶ παννυχίη πολεμίζει,
ὡς παρὰ τῆς μητρὸς προῖκα λαβοῦσα μάχην.
ἢν δὲ θέλω σιγᾶν καὶ μαρναμένῃ ὑποείκειν,
ὅττι περ οὐ μάχομαι, τοῦδ' ἕνεκεν μάχεται.

It is ascribed to an otherwise unknown Palladius, a name we may confidently correct to Palladas. The next poem (E 75) is a piece by Palladas on the very same subject (*AP* xi. 378, οὐ δύναμαι γαμετῆς καὶ γραμματικῆς ἀνέχεσθαι), and compare too the even closer Palladan parallel, *AP* ix. 168 (Μῆνιν οὐλομένην γαμετὴν ὁ τάλας γεγάμηκα), with 169 (Μῆνις Ἀχιλλῆος καὶ ἐμοὶ πρόφασις γεγένηται). E 74, though absent from *AP*, is transmitted separately in various other manuscripts; in one (which I have been unable to identify) ascribed to Palladas, and in four others (Vindob. 311, Matrit. 4562 [olim xxiv], Paris. 3019, and Venet. 183) ascribed to Agathias.[13] The double ascription (as we shall see) is significant, though our decision cannot be in doubt, for two reasons. First, no. 46 of the recently discovered *Epigrammata Bobiensia* is a loose but unmistakable translation:

'arma virumque' docens atque 'arma virumque' peritus,
    non duxi uxorem sed magis arma domum.
namque dies totos totasque ex ordine noctes
    litibus oppugnat meque meumque larem.
atque ut perpetuis dotata a matre duellis,
    arma in me tollit, nec datur ulla quies.
iamque repugnanti dedam me, ut denique victus
    iurger ob hoc solum, iurgia quod fugiam.[14]

The collection was assembled round about AD 400, a full century and a half before Agathias first put pen to paper. It also contains other versions of Palladas, evidently a popular poet in late fourth-century Italy and Gaul.[15]

---

[13] They are listed by A. Franke, *De Pallada epigrammatographo* (Diss. Leipzig 1899), 19–20.

[14] I have accepted Mariotti's correction *iurger*.   [15] See above, p. 90.

Why then the ascription to Agathias? Perhaps a purely mechanical error. *AP* xi. 378 (οὐ δύναμαι γαμετῆς) appears in *AP* between two poems by Agathias on quite unconnected subjects, xi. 376 and 379, 377 being another poem by Palladas. Let us suppose that E 74 originally preceded xi. 378 in Cephalas as it does now in E. In *AP* 378 bears the heading τοῦ αὐτοῦ, correctly referring to the ascription of 377 to Palladas. E 74 is likely to have borne the same heading. Now if 377 had been omitted (as it was, for example, from the first of Planudes' two exemplars), then τοῦ αὐτοῦ would naturally have been taken to refer to the ascription of 376, namely Agathias. This must be one of the commonest sources of false ascription in the Anthology.[16]

The presumption is, then, not only that E and *AP* derive from a common source here, but that the manuscripts which ascribe the poem to Agathias derive from an abbreviated redaction of the same source. Nor can the identity of this source be in serious doubt. Since poems by Agathias and Palladas sometimes appear in close proximity in *AP*, it has often been hastily assumed that Palladas was one of the contributors to Agathias' *Cycle*. In the first place, however, A. Franke's careful analysis has shown that Palladas' name never appears in undisturbed Agathian sequences; in all the apparent cases the original sequence has clearly been interfered with.[17] Second, Agathias explicitly says that he included *recent* work (τὰ ἀρτιγενῆ καὶ νεώτερα, *Hist. pr.* 6. 11), and by recent (as the

---

[16] Gow, p. 35, discusses a number of examples.

[17] *De Pallada*, 48–60. Thus in the *Cycle* sequence vi. 54–86 it is true that 60 and 61 are by Palladas, but 62 is by Philip of Thessalonica, who was certainly no Agathian poet; presumably all three were inserted by Cephalas. *AP* x. 64–76 is certainly a mixed sequence of Agathian poets and Palladas, but 44–63 and 77–99 are by Palladas alone; here it looks as if Cephalas distributed his few Agathian protreptica among the many by Palladas for the sake of variety. *AP* ix. 481 f. is not a pure *Cycle* sequence. As for v. 257, the lone Palladan presence in an otherwise pure *Cycle* sequence extending from 216 to 302, I cannot believe that it was put there by Agathias; it is a satirical piece, quite unlike the Agathian erotica that surround it, which (as Waltz rightly remarks ad loc.) would have been more at home in xi. It was surely Cephalas who put it here. Aubreton (Budé x, p. 32) claims xi. 54–64 as a *Cycle* sequence. In fact 54 is by Palladas; 55–6 are anonymous but hardly Agathian; 57–61 and 63–4 are Agathian and 62 by Palladas, no doubt inserted here because it is on the same theme as 61 and 63 by Macedonius (incidentally, my remarks in *JHS* lxxvi (1966), 7 which Aubreton quotes in support state the exact opposite of what he implies). It would be unwise to allege a cumulative effect from this multiplication of apparent examples; if Agathias had really counted Palladas among his regular contributors, there should have been numerous quite clearcut examples, admitting of no such explaining away.

other names included make clear) he meant contemporary. He can hardly have counted Palladas, whose *floruit* fell nearly two centuries before the compilation of the *Cycle*, as a contemporary. Third, Agathias states that his material had till then been unpublished or difficult of access (διαλανθάνοντα ἔτι[18] καὶ χύδην οὑτωσὶ παρ᾽ ἐνίοις ὑποψιθυριζόμενα, *Hist.* loc. cit.), whereas the long Palladas sequences in *AP* and the diffusion of his poems in the West make it clear that a separate edition had been in existence since *c*.400.[19]

Cephalas certainly had direct access to a text of Agathias and probably Palladas[20] too. It seems inevitable to conclude that Cephalas was the editor who occasionally juxtaposed the two poets in his own anthology. If so, then the double ascription to Cougny III. 145 is a pointer to Cephalas.

At the end of *AP* ix. 49. 1, Ἐλπὶς καὶ σὺ Τύχη, μεγὰ χαίρετε· τὸν λιμέν᾽ εὗρον (so *AP* and *APl*), E offers τὴν ὁδὸν εὗρον. It looks as if its compiler excerpted the poem from a source which (like *AP*) contained ix. 134, which opens with the same line save for precisely this variation in the closing phrase.

From our point of view the most important sequence in E is 20–34: *AP* ix. 449, 440; *Pl* 210, 213; ix. 456; *Pl* 11, 12, and 13; *Pl* 227, 230; *AP* ix. 824, 823, 825, 826, 827. It must be premised straightaway (*a*) that, despite their conventional numeration in printed editions, *Pl* 11, 12, and 13 originally occur in Planudes' autograph (fo. 49ʳ) between *Pl* 226 and 227; and (*b*) that the poems conventionally numbered *AP* ix. 823–7 do *not* in fact appear in *AP* proper; they are part of the collection Σ″, which was written in blank spaces left in *AP*, in this case on p. 488, after the end of ix. (To Σ″ we shall return; for the moment it will suffice to observe that its ultimate source cannot be in doubt: Cephalas.) Compare now the following sequence from *APl* iva (εἰς Θεούς) 8. 59 f.: *Pl* 210–15 (on Eros); *Pl* 216 (on Hermes); *AP* ix. 589 (Hera suckling Heracles); *Pl* 217 (the Muse Calliope); *Pl* 218 (a singer Calliope); *Pl* 219 (a singer Polyhymnia); *Pl* 220 (the three Muses); *Pl* 221–4 (on Nemesis); *AP* ix. 823, *Pl* 225–6, *AP* ix. 825, *Pl* 12–13 (on Pan); *Pl* 227–8 (on a cool rustic spot); *Pl* 229 (Pan); *Pl* 230 (a cool stream); *Pl* 231, *AP* ix. 824, *Pl* 232–5 (on Pan); *Pl* 236–43 (on Priapus); *AP* ix. 826–7, *Pl* 244–8 (on Satyrs).

---

[18] Not 'oubliés' (Aubreton, Budé x, p. 32 n. 2), as the ἔτι shows.
[19] For the date, see above, p. 90.   [20] See p. 96.

It will be clear that these two sequences are closely related, and since Planudes is unquestionably later than E and each sequence contains material absent from the other, a common source is the only possible explanation. With the sole exception of *AP* ix. 589, all the epigrams in the Planudean sequence are ecphrastic poems absent from *AP*; they may be presumed to have stood originally in the ecphrastic section of Cephalas now missing from *AP*. Now Planudes' Anthology is based on two sources which he excerpted successively (the addenda are expressly stated to have been taken ἐξ ἑτέρου βιβλίου). This sequence comes from his first source, which apparently lacked *Pl* 11. Later, evidently forgetting that he already had *Pl* 12–13, Planudes found both together with 11 in his second source and copied all three out among his addenda as *ib.* 14. 1–3, a chapter on trees. This little group at least, then, stood together in *both* Planudes' sources, both (as we have seen) abbreviated copies of Cephalas.

A comparison of the two sequences will show that E made a balanced *selection* from the material in his source: 210 and 213 on Eros; *Pl* 11–13 on rustic statues of Pan and Hermes; *Pl* 227 and 230 on rustic scenes; *AP* ix. 823–5 on Pan and 826–7 on Satyrs. It was erotic and rustic poems he wanted, not Muses, singers, Nemesis, or Priapus. There is further interesting confirmation here of a common origin for the two sequences. The sixteen poems from *AP* ix. 823 to *Pl* 235 are all classified by Planudes—as presumably by Cephalas before him—under the heading of poems about Pan. *Pl* 227–8 and 230, however, though rustic, do not mention Pan. Inside this group *Pl* 226–31 are probably a block lifted direct from Meleager's *Garland.* Now on the more sophisticated principle of Meleager this makes an excellent rustic sequence precisely because of its variety: poems on cool glades and brooks as well as Pan. But Cephalas was no Meleager; as countless examples show (see above), he worked carelessly and mechanically. Observing the obvious rustic colouring of the block and the mention of Pan at its beginning, middle, and end, he inserted it whole into his section on Pan. Epigrams 227 and 230 appear in both E and Planudes between poems on Pan; both, that is to say, reflect Cephalas' misclassification.

The only poems in the E sequence that appear to be alien from the Planudean sequence are *AP* ix. 449, 440, and 456. These are not ecphrastic but epideictic, and are thus appropriately classified

in the extant epideictic part of *AP* and in the epideictic book of
Planudes (*ia*. 26), where, interestingly enough, they appear in the
same order as E, 449, 440, and 456. Thus they will not have stood
in the same part of Cephalas as the ecphrastic series just considered. It must be the compiler of E who linked the two
sequences, and it is easy to see why. *AP* ix. 449, 440, and 456 are all
speeches to, by, or about Eros, and *Pl* 210 and 213 are also about
Eros. It is even possible (as Basson observed) to see why he
ordered the five poems as he did: ix. 440, offering a reward for the
return of a runaway Eros, has a neater link with 210, on Eros found
asleep, than 449, a simple declamation on the power of Eros. This
is why he transposed the Palatine order. And 456 has a formal link
with 213 in that both are cast in the form of conditionals. But there
seems no reason to doubt that he found them in the same place and
the same way as Planudes, excerpting Cephalas' epideictica for
poems about Eros.

A pattern is beginning to emerge. While there can be little doubt
that E derives from a source common to *AP* and *APl*, its compiler
did not skim through this source evenly taking (say) a poem a page.
He seems rather to have studied two or three pages at a time with
some care and selected a number of associated or at least adjacent
poems from those pages, which he then sometimes rearranged on
his own principles. That is to say, his method was not nearly so
mechanical as that of the compilers of S or L, and it is not
surprising that the traces of Palatine order are less conspicuous.

But before we can reach any final verdict on the matter it will be
necessary to take a closer look at Σ^{π}. For Aubreton, both E and Σ^{π}
were complete and independent anthologies. The evidence
suggests that neither is either.

There are a number of striking coincidences in the sequence of
poems in E and Σ^{π}. Let us begin with the rustic/erotic sequence E
20–34 just discussed. With the run *AP* ix. 824, 823, 825, 826, 827
(E 30–4) compare from Σ^{π}n (p. 488) *AP* ix. 823, 824, 825, 826, 827.
Now these five poems appear evenly distributed through a sequence of twenty-six poems in *APl* iv. 8 (see above, p. 264). Was it
by chance that E and Σ^{π} happened to excerpt the same five? E 22,
23, 25, and 26 are *APl* 210, 213, 11, and 12. Σ^{π} has the same four
epigrams in the same order (p. a'), preceded by *APl* 246, *AP* x.
104, and Simon. 186B (294P). *AP* x. 104 and Simon. 186B appear
in E in the same order as E 3 and 12, and *APl* 246, on a satyr,
would fit the rustic/erotic context to perfection.

We have already examined the contexts in which AP ix. 44, 49, 50, 51, 52, 53, and 59 reappear in E. Look now at the sequence E 42–8, comprising the following arbitrary and heterogeneous selection: AP ix. *127*, xi. *255*, 293, ix. 361, 50, *51*, *748*. Compare Σ^{π} (p. 568): *ix. 127, xi. 255*, x. 30, xi. 294, *ix. 51, 748*, and xi. 442. Σ^{π} lacks ix. 50, 293, and 361, but adds 294, x. 30, and xi. 442. The correspondences point to a common source which neither has fully reproduced, particularly the appearance of ix. 293 in one and 294 in the other—poems which have nothing in common beyond their adjacence in AP.

Now these correspondences occur precisely where E is *not* following the Palatine order. The fuller common source they point to cannot then be Cephalas himself. Ruling out (as we surely must) the possibility of pure coincidence in such arbitrary rearrangement of the Palatine order, there is only one alternative: as Basson suggested (and indeed A. Franke before him),[21] E as we have it and Σ^{π} are both excerpts from one fuller anthology which itself derived from Cephalas: in short both are excerpts from the *original* text of the *sylloge Euphemiana*.

If this is so, then important consequences follow. First, E as we have it must (like S) be incomplete. That this is so can be confirmed on internal grounds. If E were in its original undisturbed state we should hardly expect to find the two dedicatory poems to Euphemius together *inside* the collection (E 77 and 78). If the practice of Meleager and Strato is anything to go by, what we should expect is one at the beginning and the other at the end. The presumption is that a certain amount of at any rate rearranging has taken place. That there have been losses too is shown by the fact that none of the three manuscripts contains the full total of eighty-three poems listed above.[22]

Second, we may presume that most at least of the extra poems in Σ^{π} appeared in the original E, the more confidently in that almost all of them do reappear elsewhere in the Cephalan tradition, in AP or APl. Three sequences in particular call for comment: APl 159, 160, 161, 163, and 164 (p. γ'), all on Praxiteles' Aphrodite; APl 278, 277, 283, and 288 (p. β'), two poems each by Paul the Silentiary and Leontius on lyre-girls and pantomimes; and AP xv. 41–50 (pp. 707–9), on sixth-century charioteer monuments. All are homogeneous sequences which Planudes may confidently be pre-

---

[21] *De Pallada*, p. 59 n. 1; cf. Basson, pp. 56 f.

[22] See p. 258.

sumed to have taken over from Cephalas. It may be added that the last poem in the collection is xv. 51, which reappears in both *APl* and E. These additional examples lend strong support to our original conclusion that E derives from Cephalas.

Then there is a poem that Aubreton missed. In the upper margin of p. 476 by *AP* ix. 710, the scribe of Σ" wrote what since Jacobs has been counted as *AP* ix. 711:

αὐτὴν Γραμματικὴν ὁ ζωγράφος ἤθελε γράψαι·
Βίκτορα δὲ γράψας "τὸν σκοπόν", εἶπεν, "ἔχω."

This poem, by an otherwise unknown Zenobius grammaticus, has obvious similarities to *AP* ix. 712, by Metrodorus grammaticus:

αὐτὸν Ἰωάννην ὁ γέρων ὅτ᾽ ἐδέξατο θεσμός,
εἶπεν ἀνηβήσας "αὖθις ἔχω σε, Σόλων."

On top of the parallelism in structure and use of dialogue, there is the fact that Victor is the archetypal grammarian just as John is the archetypal jurist. It is tempting to conjecture that the poems stood together in Cephalas, whence they were excerpted together by the compiler of the *sylloge Euphemiana*. The scribe of *AP* (or its exemplar), however, accidentally omitted 711, his eye slipping from αὐτὴν to αὐτὸν. The scribe of Σ", collating *AP* against his copy of the *sylloge Euphemiana*, noticed the omission and repaired it. If this is what happened, then it looks as if the original E may have been considerably larger than what we now possess. After all, we must bear in mind that the sole purpose of the scribe of Σ" was to add material missing from *AP*. Naturally therefore the Palatine material in E will be underrepresented in Σ".

Further confirmation of the relationship of Σ" to E and of both to Cephalas is provided by some textual points. For example, x. 104 is preserved in *AP*, *APl*, E, Σ", and (another Cephalan derivatee) L. *AP*, E, Σ", and L all offer the unmetrical uncontracted form τιμόωσιν in l. 3; *APl*'s τιμῶσιν is presumably Planudes' own correction of what he found in his source. More striking still, all five break off at line 3. E, Σ", and *APl* likewise all break off at l. 3 of *AP* ix. 827, here too evidently deriving from the same defective exemplar.

AP xiv. 74 is an oracle about ritual purification which concludes by bidding the wicked to be on their way:

οὔποτε γὰρ σὴν
ψυχὴν ἐκνίψει σῶμα διαινόμενον.

So E. *AP* offers the *vox nihili* διμαινόμενον, for which Planudes made the neat but disastrous conjecture μιαινόμενον. It is not (of course) a *polluted* body that 'will never wash your soul', but a '*washed* body' (from διαίνω, 'moisten').

In *AP* ix. 127. 3, *AP* offers the unmetrical οὕτως ἀπαντλήσας, which Planudes corrected to οὕτως ἀντλήσας. Much neater and better, and surely what stood in Cephalas, is the reading of E and Σ″: οὕτω ἀπαντλησας.[23]

Then there is ix. 748, by 'Plato the younger':

ἁ λίθος ἔστ' ἀμέθυστος,[24] ἐγὼ δ' ὁ πότας Διόνυσος·
ἢ νήφειν πείσει μ' ἢ μαθέτω μεθύειν.

The poem is about the paradox of 'a Dionysus engraved in amethyst' (so the lemma), paradox because the amethyst was supposed to protect against drunkenness (see the Budé note ad loc.). With the text of l. 2 as it is printed above by all recent editors (so P, save for the etacism νείφειν), Dionysus is saying: 'either it [the amethyst] will persuade me to be sober or let it learn to get drunk.' E and Σ″ offer ἢ πεισάτω νήφειν μ' [om. Σ″ μ']; *APl* ἢ πιθέτω νήφειν. The imperative not only gives a far better balance: 'either let it teach me to be sober or learn to get drunk'. It is also more or less guaranteed by the rambling translation preserved as *Epigr. Bob.* 20:[25]

'quis lapis hic?' 'Amethystus.' 'At hic?' 'Ego potor Iacchus . . .
quin igitur *discat* de me lapis ebrius esse,
    aut *doceat* quare sobrius esse queam.'

ἢ πεισάτω stood in Cephalas and was faithfully copied into E and Σ″. Realizing the metrical error, the Palatine scribe (or the scribe of his exemplar) feebly substituted the future πείσει. Planudes made the neater but palaeographically less plausible correction πιθέτω. All we need to do (I was anticipated by Schneidewin) is transpose, πεισάτω ἢ. The original word order was 'corrected' by a scribe

---

[23] Note that what Beckby here classifies as P^b is in fact Σ″. Gallavotti, *Boll. Class. Lincei*, 3rd ser., iii (1982), 73, implausibly sees the text of E and Σ″ as an emendation.

[24] All witnesses, *AP*, *APl*, Σ″, E and even (contrary to what editors report, as P. Speck has kindly confirmed for me) Monac. gr. 157 of Heliodorus (fo. 167^v), offer the unmetrical ἀμέθυσος. Whether or not this is felt to support Meineke's ἀμέθυσσος (in a 'Doric' poem), the common error might well be counted an additional pointer to a common source in Cephalas.

[25] Missed in Gallavotti's discussion of the poem in *Boll. Class. Lincei*, 3rd ser., iii (1982), 72; and by Page, *FGE* 83.

ignorant of metre but sensitive to anaphora, perhaps the school-master Cephalas himself.

Both $\varSigma^\pi$ and E have a certain number of poems absent from the rest of the Cephalan tradition. Some at least of these probably derive from Cephalas none the less. Let us consider just two, Simon. 186B (= 294 Page) (the only one included in both):

δῆμος Ἀθηναίων σε, Νεοπτόλεμ᾽, εἰκόνι τῇδε
τίμησ᾽ εὐνοίης εὐσεβίης θ᾽ ἕνεκα,

and Simonides 158B (= 417 Page), only in $\varSigma^\pi$:

Κρὴς Ἄλκων Διδ⟨ύμου⟩ Φοίβῳ στέφος Ἰσθμι᾽ ἑλὼν πύξ.

Both are ascribed to Simonides, the first certainly in error, the second probably so. But there is no reason to doubt that both featured in the hellenistic collection of Simonidea which was drawn upon by Meleager and, through him, is still well represented in the Cephalan tradition.[26] E 49 is an example where Cephalan provenance is proved by its appearance in the anathematic books of both *AP* (vi. 2) and *APl* (vi. 144). Then there is another case in $\varSigma^\pi$ (p. δ′), reappearing as *APl* 60. In all these attestations the poems are expressly ascribed to Simonides. It would be surprising if the compiler of E had used two different sources for his Simonidea. There is a strong prima-facie presumption that both the poems quoted above stood in Cephalas' anathematic book.

Now for a variety of reasons (pp. 117–9) we are in a position to form a better than average idea of the scope of Cephalas' anathematic book. There is reason to believe that *AP* vi is at least as full a copy of it as that of Michael Chartophylax, made from Cephalas' own autograph.

One further proof of this is the almost complete absence of non-Palatine anathematica elsewhere in the Cephalan tradition. Not one in S, L, or *ABV*. Apart from our two Simonidea in E and $\varSigma^\pi$, there is only one other anathematicon proper, *APl* 291 (Anyte) — though Planudes did include in his Bk. vi eleven palindromes to which we shall be returning.[27]

[26] See M. Boas, *De Epigrammatis Simonideis* (Groningen 1905), 136–94; more briefly D. L. Page, *FGE* 119 f.

[27] Of the non-Palatine Simonidea in *APl*, four (like 158B = 417 Page) celebrate athletic victors (*APl* 2–3, 23–4) but none is dedicatory. *APl* 232, on a statue of Pan erected by Miltiades (presumably after Marathon, cf. Herod. vi. 105–6) might have

It has already been noted (p. 117) that the scribe A left three gaps in his transcription of *AP* vi, with a note to himself to 'check' (ζήτει): 6 lines between vi. 125 and 126; 6 more between 143 and 144; and 7 between 158 and 159. Presumably his exemplar was illegible, corrupt, or defective at these points. The corrector C was apparently puzzled by the first two gaps (p. 117), and against the 7-line gap after 158 made the rather surprising note 'look out for *eleven* lines' (ζήτει στίχους ἕνδεκα). Here then we have 19 lines (at least) which we may presume to have been occupied in Cephalas by anathematica, more than enough room for our three pieces of 1, 2, and 4 lines respectively. Indeed, we can perhaps go further.

AP vi. 144, the poem that follows the second gap, is headed τοῦ αὐτοῦ. By a lucky chance it is repeated after 213, again headed τοῦ αὐτοῦ but this time in a Simonidean context. On the face of it, then, both 144 and the poem or poems that preceded it were ascribed to Simonides. If so, then there is a fair case for inserting one or both of the Simonidea in Σ^{π} and E here.

There is a complication, however, M. Boas, author of the standard work on the epigrams of Simonides, argued that 144 was to be ascribed to Anacreon rather than Simonides, and unfortunately his reasoning has imposed on the latest editor of both poets, D. L. Page.[28] The case runs as follows. *AP* vi. 134 is ascribed to Anacreon and by implication the whole series 135–43 as well, all headed τοῦ αὐτοῦ. Then comes the six-line gap followed by 144, likewise headed τοῦ αὐτοῦ. Boas argues that here too τοῦ αὐτοῦ refers to Anacreon. That is to say he took it for granted that the (probably) two missing dedications were also by Anacreon. It is true (as Boas emphasizes) that the first letters of the first words of the Anacreon series are in alphabetical order, presumably the deliberate intention of its editor. However, the order breaks down with the poem *before* the gap: η, ο, π, π, π, π, π, ρ, σ, ε (εὔχεο, 143), gap, σ (Στροίβου, 144). Boas is reduced to arguing that 143 is an intruder interpolated by Meleager (note too that to maintain the integrity of his alphabetical series down to 144 he is obliged to suppose that the missing poems both began with a sigma). But if we are going to allow Meleager to interpolate at this point, how can

been so counted but was put among the ecphrastica by Planudes (as indeed was the undoubtedly dedicatory poem *APl* 291 by Anyte quoted above, which may therefore have been so classified by Cephalas too).

[28] *Epigr. Graeca*, p. 7, Anacreon XV; for some qualifications Page, *FGE* 142–3.

we insist that the gap did not also contain 'interpolations', a poem or poems by Simonides, for example?

Lastly, argues Boas, if C was of the opinion that there was no lacuna between 143 and 144, then presumably he at least was of the opinion that 144 was by Anacreon. But the reason for C's scepticism about the lacuna is surely that the corrupt poem A found in his exemplar had been simply omitted without comment in C's text (we have seen other examples of this above). If so, then the argument falls to the ground; C had no means of forming a judgement.

What now of the second occurrence of 144 after 213, firmly embedded in an unbroken Simonidean sequence running from 212 to 217? According to Boas, if Meleager had ascribed it to Anacreon once (*if* . . .), then he could not have ascribed it to another poet another time. So he assumes that Meleager deliberately repeated 144 after 213 because of an alleged parallel with 212, but forgot to alter the heading τοῦ αὐτοῦ, with the result that in its new position it now appeared to designate Simonides rather than Anacreon. This is surely very far-fetched, quite apart from the general implausibility of this sort of exegetical explanation of the not infrequent repetitions in *AP*.[29]

Why so much special pleading to escape the natural and harmless enough inference that vi. 144 was ascribed to Simonides? The first distich at least is certainly a genuine archaic dedication (the original stone has been found) by a man called Leocrates, strategos at Athens in 479 and 459 BC, that is to say in the lifetime of both poets.[30] There is, of course, no way of proving that it was actually *written* by either. But the appearance of a Leocrates among Simonides' patrons in a well-informed passage of Quintilian (xi. 2. 14) would seem to tilt the balance in his favour. Wilamowitz was right to object that we cannot be *sure* this was the same Leocrates.[31] But the coincidence of name is bound to have ensured that an archaic dedication by a Leocrates was at least *ascribed* to Simonides rather than to *any* other poet.

I suggest then that 144 should be so ascribed and that one or both of our two Simonidea from E and Σ'' be assumed to have once

---

[29] Cf. p. 373.

[30] See P. Friedländer and H. B. Hoffleit, *Epigrammata* (1948), no. 119, pp. 113–14; cf. Page, *FGE* 144–6.

[31] *Sappho und Simonides* (1913), 146.

stood in the gap before it. *APl* 291, a rustic dedication by the Meleagrian Anyte, would fit tolerably if not admirably in the gap between 125 and 126, in a Meleagrian sequence (123 is another piece by Anyte), though better contexts could be imagined, from which it might have fallen out for a variety of accidental reasons.

It is the seven-line gap between 158 and 159, or rather C's treatment of it, that presents something of a puzzle. One might have expected C either to indicate that his exemplar had no lacuna there (as he did with A's other two gaps) or to fill it in from his own text, if that had been complete. He did neither. He made a note to himself to look out for eleven lines, four more than A had left room for. Assuming that he did not simply make a slip or miscount, the implication is that on the one hand his exemplar did contain *something* between 158 and 159, though eleven rather than seven lines; but that here too they appeared corrupt or incomplete, not fit to be copied into *AP* as they stood. It is this conclusion that prompts me to give more serious consideration than Preisendanz or Gow to Basson's suggestion that what C had in mind was the ten palindromes Planudes put in his anathematic book (vi. 87), which amount to exactly eleven lines.[32] They are not anathematic, to be sure, but neither are the ἀναστρέφοντα of Nicodemus of Heraclea, which Planudes likewise included in his anathematic book (vi. 22–8). He did so in this case because they were already so classified in Cephalas, as we can see from their appearance as *AP* vi. 314–20. That the palindromes did appear in Cephalas is supported by the presence of the eighth of them[33] in Σ^π (*APl* 387 *c*.5), and by analogy with the ἀναστρέφοντα we may reasonably assume that they too stood in his anathematic book. Now if C was the sort of man who liked what he copied to make sense and scan, then it would not be surprising if he had suspected these lines to be corrupt. They are nothing but a sequence of nonsense words whose sole *raison d'être* is to read the same backwards as forwards, and only one of them could be mistaken for any sort of verse. This rather than ordinary corruption may be why A left them out in the first place (his exemplar perhaps contained only seven of them).

---

[32] Gallavotti thought that Planudes took his palindromes from some other source, a larger collection of palindromes: *Boll. Class. Lincei*, 3rd ser., x (1989), 49–69, at 53. But the fact that later apographs of *APl* add more palindromes (as Gallavotti interestingly illustrates) proves nothing about Planudes' own sources.

[33] With the marginal note τοῦ κυροῦ στυλ(ιανοῦ). Which Stylianos?

The main objection to this hypothesis is that between 158 and 159 might not seem a particularly obvious or suitable context for such a section. But a case can be made out. With 157 closes the first Meleagrian section of the book, and 158–78 comprise a brief miscellaneous section before the pattern of the first half of the book is repeated. Now Nicodemus' ἀναστρέφοντα occur inside the second miscellaneous section at the end of the second half, and a certain parallelism at least would be won if the palindromes were fitted into the first one.

We have strayed a little from E and Σ^π—and given freer rein to conjecture than might seem proper in a rigorous inquiry. But my purpose was less to fill in the gaps in *AP* than to demonstrate how very closely a particular book of *AP* reflects the contents of Cephalas. With just one major exception, *APl* and the minor *syllogae* have almost nothing to add to *AP*. The exception, of course, is the nearly 400 ecphrastic poems which we have already seen must have stood originally in a lacuna in *AP*'s exemplar. There can be no serious doubt that these ecphrastica go back to Cephalas. To this category we should probably add the new paederastica in S (Ch. X), which may represent another accidental loss from the source of *AP*.

Σ^π provides an excellent illustration. Its 57 poems were solely designed to supplement omissions which its scribe had detected in *AP*. Nine of these poems do in fact appear in *AP* already, but of the remaining 48 no fewer than 45 are ecphrastica that reappear in *APl* iv, and one other should almost certainly be traced to the same ultimate source, Cougny III. 179. It is a description by Julian the Egyptian of a statue of Adonis (shown, apparently, looking at his hunting dogs despite the presence of Aphrodite):

ἄγριος οὗτος ῎Αδωνις, ὃς εἰς κύνας ὄμματα βάλλει·
σχέτλι᾽ ῎Ερως, Παφίης ἄγχι παρισταμένης.

This presumably reached Σ^π via, in succession, Agathias' *Cycle*, Cephalas, and the original *sylloge Euphemiana*; it is one of the many probable Cephalana that should be included as an appendix to future texts of the Planudean Appendix. The two remaining non-Palatine poems in Σ^π are the likewise probably Cephalan Simonidea already dealt with. For the sake of completeness it should be added that the original E cannot have been either identical with or derived from either of the two redactions of Cephalas on which *APl* is based, since both E and Σᵐ contain material from both.

For *AP* vi, as we have seen, the rest of the Cephalan tradition does not provide enough even to fill the gaps in *AP*. As for *AP* vii, epitymbia, there is nothing new in either E or S as we have them. *APl* iii has just three to offer, and even here, whereas *APl* 26 and 29 are no doubt Cephalan in origin, 27, the well-known epitaph on Sardanopalus, must be held doubtful.[34] Gow has suggested the possibility that Planudes found it in some subsidiary source (it is widely quoted),[35] unaware of two factors that transform his guess into virtual certainty: (*a*) the poem appears already in L (Planudes' first attempt of 1280)—but as an addendum in a different ink;[36] (*b*) the only other passage which gives the same version as Planudes is the scholia on Strabo (xiv. 672A), a manuscript which, equipped with this scholion, Planudes is known to have owned and studied with some care.[37]

There is not much positive that can be said about the remaining 'new' poems in E. E 74 (Cougny III. 145) is the, presumably, Cephalan poem by Palladas (μῆνιν ἄειδε) discussed above. E 61 (C. III. 166) is an elegant and interesting description of a statue of Dionysus ascribed in another manuscript (unidentified) to Proclus:[38]

Ῥηγίνου μελάθροισι τὸν εὐαστὴν Διόνυσον
δέρκεο, δεξιτέρῃ χειρὶ κυπελλοφόρον,
ξανθὴν μὲν σφίγγοντα καρήατος αἴθοπι κισσῷ
χαίτην καὶ λαιῇ θυρσοφόρον παλάμῃ,
βαπτὰ δὲ πέπλα φέροντα κατὰ χροὸς αἵματι κόχλου
καὶ στικτὴν νεβρίδων ἀμφικρεμῆ χλαμύδα.
αὐτὸν Βάκχον ἄνακτα δόμων ἔντοσθε δέδορκας
εὐξείνων, εὐχαῖς ἵλαον ἑσταότα.

On grounds of both style and date it might be reckoned a possible candidate for Agathias' *Cycle* and appears in a solidly Cephalan context in E; but that is as far as we can go. E 76 (C. IV. 77) is a

---

[34] On the shorter, unquestionably Cephalan version *AP* vii. 325 see below, p. 296.
[35] For the many Byzantine testimonia see Preger, *Inscr. gr. metr.*, no. 232, pp. 183–7 and *SH* 335.
[36] Gallavotti, *Boll. Class. Lincei*, NS vii (1959), 46.
[37] A. Diller, *Traditio* x (1954), 40, publishing the scholion and referring to two other manuscripts where Planudes copied the poem in his own hand.
[38] Cougny III. 166.

24-line iambic poem on old age by the ninth-century writer Leo the philosopher; E 82 is the poem by Marcos Mamunas; and E 80 and 81 are fragments of Euripides. Even though there is one other Euripidean gnome in *AP* (x. 107, 107*b*) and other (though shorter) poems by Leo the philosopher (*AP* ix. 200–3, 214, 361, 578–9; and one each in *ABV* and *AP* xv),[39] this concentration of basically unCephalan material together at the very end of the collection (together with the obviously post-Cephalan dedications to Euphemius) would certainly seem to justify the suspicion that they are all post-Cephalan additions.

It is (of course) hardly surprising that E, like the other Cephalan derivatees, should contain a certain number of idiosyncratic additions from secondary sources (for some more examples see below). In general, however, there can be no doubt that E is based on the anthology of Cephalas. If so, then since E was compiled before the death of Leo the Wise in 912, then Cephalas' anthology must have been published before then.

More generally, we have reinforced a conclusion to which other lines of inquiry have long been pointing. Contrary to one of Aubreton's main theses, we have seen that (excluding a few additions here and there), L, S, E (and Σ^{π}), the two sources of *APl*, and *AP* are all based on Cephalas. Contrary to Aubreton's other main thesis, there is no reason to believe that the abundant material in *AP* absent from these other collections was derived from fresh research not available to their compilers. On the contrary, a variety of considerations, above all the distribution of Planudean omissions and C's corrections from Michael Chartophylax, make it clear that virtually all these poems also come from Cephalas. *AP* is simply a much fuller copy of Cephalas. Even Michael Chartophylax's copy, as we saw, was in some respects actually less complete than *AP*. Collation of the various Cephalan derivatees has revealed a very small number of probably Cephalan poems that were apparently omitted from *AP*. Some of these no doubt stood in *AP*'s source, which presumably also once contained the 400-odd ecphrastica lost before *AP* was copied from it. This manuscript must have been one of the fullest exemplars of Cephalas that ever existed (the small time interval suggests that it cannot have been made at more than one or two removes from the original).

[39] See below, p. 333.

Anthologies tended not to be regarded as protected texts. Most anthologies of epigrams are much reduced redactions of or even excerpts from Cephalas. *AP*, however, is not an example of this tendency. It is still equipped with all the original Cephalan prefaces to individual books, and it was scrupulously collated against Michael's copy of Cephalas by C poem by poem. *AP* v–xiv should be regarded not as an independent compilation, but as a slightly defective but otherwise conscientious early copy of Cephalas.

XII

The Suda

THE Suda is a lexicon compiled some time probably during the second half of the tenth century, a product of the antiquarianism and research that characterized the age of Constantine Porphyrogenitus.[1]

In the matter of epigrams the contrast with the mid-ninth-century lexicon of Photius[2] is striking. There are a mere five quotations from epigrams in Photius, three of which are absent from the Cephalan tradition.[3] The fourth appears in a different form as *AP* ix. 700[4] and the fifth as *AP* xiii. 29.[5] In the Suda, by contrast, there are 1,076 epigram quotations, from 430 different epigrams, *all* of which appear in *AP*.[6] In addition, the Suda

---

[1] Lemerle, 297–9; Hunger, ii. 40–2; the fullest study of the source question is Adler's entry in *PW* ivA (1931), 675–717; cf. too Emily Hanawalt, 'The Suda on the Pagan Gods', *East European Quarterly* xiii (1979), 385–94. I am using A. Adler's edition, 5 vols. (1928–38).

[2] Lemerle, 185–9; Hunger, ii. 39–40, both urging the early rather than the late date. No epigrams were quoted in the substantial new portions of the Lexicon published by Reitzenstein in 1907, and there are none in that part of C. Theodoridis's new edition (*Photii Patriarchae Lexicon*, i (*A–Δ*) [Berlin and New York 1982]) that is based on the complete manuscript discovered by L. Politis. Nor is there any indication that there are any in the still unpublished portions (see Politis, *Griechische Kodikologie und Textüberlieferung*, ed. D. Harlfinger [Darmstadt 1980], 653–5). This has nothing to do with the regrettable fact that the scribe of the Lavordensis tended to abbreviate his quotations (Theodoridis, pp. lxi–lxxi); there were simply no epigram quotations to be abbreviated, but (for example) many new quotations from the comic poets. And nothing to do with Gibbon's well-known remark that poetry 'was foreign to this universal scholar'. This may have been largely true of Photius' own reading (cf. Baldwin, *Byzantine and Modern Greek Studies* iv [1978], 9 f.), but the Lexicon was naturally full of quotations from the classical poets, almost all taken over from earlier lexica (on the sources of the Lexicon, see now Theodoridis, pp. lxxii–lxxvi).

[3] s.v. Κυψελιδῶν (i. 362–3 Naber) = Preger, *IGM* 53; s.v. σαυτὴν ἐπαινεῖς (ii. 148N) = Preger, *IGM* 158; s.v. ὑπὲρ τὰ ἐσκαμμένα (ii. 243N) = Preger *IGM* 142.

[4] s.v. θάσιος παῖς (i. 273N) = Simonides 160B = Page *EG* 48, with the painter's name correctly given.

[5] s.v. ὕδωρ δὲ πίνων (ii. 237N). See Gow and Page (*HE* ii. 421–3) on the bewildering variety of ascriptions.

[6] For the complete list see the index auctorum in Adler's edition, v (1938), 76–80.

quotations reflect exactly the same wide and idiosyncratic range of poets as all the other Cephalan derivatees discussed in the preceding chapters: both the *Garlands*, the *Cycle*, Rufinus, the Diogenes Laertius sequence (vii. 83 f.), the Anacreon and Simonides sequences (vi. 134 f., 212 f.), even vi. 322 by the Emperor Hadrian.

Now the compilers of the Suda did not usually excerpt ancient texts directly. Their quotations from the historians, for example, are taken from the historical excerpts made a generation earlier by Constantine Porphyrogenitus.[7] So we can hardly doubt that all these epigram quotations were taken from the compilation of Cephalas.

The text of the Suda quotations is often identical with that of *AP*, even in idiosyncratic error. Indeed Basson argued (pp. 26–31) that the Suda drew directly on *AP* itself.[8] He claims that the Suda readings agree with the text of *AP* as corrected by C: or (to be more precise) with the alterations C made directly in the original text of *AP* (at this point the work of A), but *not* with the corrections C wrote in the margins. Even if this were true, it would hardly prove Basson's thesis. Quite the reverse, in fact. If the Suda quotations really had been excerpted from *AP* as corrected by C, then we should expect it to reflect *all* of C's corrections. It is difficult to believe that anyone excerpting *AP* could have missed or would have rejected C's marginal corrections. In any case, Basson himself quoted two cases that refute his claim.

First, *AP* vi. 27. 2:

μήτ᾽ ἐρατῶν κώμων ἄνδιχα μήτε λύρης

nor without (ἄνδιχα) lovely revels or the lyre

ἐρατῶν is undoubtedly correct: so *APl* and in effect the original text of *AP*, though with a false word division that produced μητέρα τῶν. Perceiving that this was nonsense yet evidently not realizing how to correct it, C erased the letters ρατῶν and substituted the conjecture ἄτερ. Now the Suda offers μήτ᾽ ἄρα τῶν. How and why? If the excerptor had been faced with the present text of *AP*, how could he so have misread C's μήτε ἄτερ? The early date of C excludes the possibility that he saw an uncorrected text of *AP*, and even if (improbably enough) he took the trouble to decipher the

---

[7] C. de Boor, 'Suidas und die Konstantinische Exzerptsammlung', *BZ* xxi (1912), 381–424; xxiii (1914/19), 1–127.
[8] So too Adler, i (1928), xxii and in *PW* ivA.

original text beneath C's erasure, why should he then have written something different again? His μήτ᾽ ἄρα τῶν is in fact surely a miscopying of the true reading μήτ᾽ ἐρατῶν.

Note too l. 8 of the same poem, where the bibulous Anacreon is represented, with his robe drenched in wine,

ἄκρητον θλίβων νέκταρ ἀπὸ στολίδων

wringing unmixed nectar from its folds.

It is the Suda alone that offers the certainly correct στολίδων. στολίδες are the folds created by tying a girdle round a loose-fitting garment, according to Pollux (7. 54; cf. πέπλων στολίδες at Eur. *Bacch.* 935–6). *AP* has the absurd σταλίδων (with δω written by C over two letters no longer legible), 'stakes'; *APl* σταλίκων, another form of the same word.

Then there is vii. 19. 3, two pages earlier in *AP*. For the final word, the original text of *AP* gave the probably corrupt λοῖσθος. C erased the οι and substituted an upsilon (λύσθος). The Suda quotation (s.v. λοῖσθος) gives λοῖσθος, not λύσθος. Puzzling though λύσθος is,[9] it seems impossible to believe that the excerptor would have gone to the lengths of deciphering and copying the scarcely less puzzling λοῖσθος instead. Here then are two poems that the Suda excerptor cannot have read in *AP*.

The very fact that the Suda quotations sometimes agree with the original text of *AP* and sometimes with C's corrections is clear proof that they do not derive directly from either *AP* or the exemplar of C. Moreover, in addition to the coincidences between *AP* and Suda to which Basson drew attention, there are also a great many divergences. Many of these divergences have no probative value, of course. For example, take the following random selection from *AP* vi (the reading of *AP* given first in each case): vi. 224. 3, εὑρόμενος] εὕραμ-; 239. 5, εὖ] ἐκ; 246. 6, ῥοίζου] ῥοίζης; even (for example) 277. 2, λέλοιπε] ἀνέθηκε, or 69. 2, νηοῦ] κείνου. The compiler of the Suda was a careless fellow not much bothered about sense or metre, and he can and often must be held to be responsible for such corruptions himself. But it scarcely seems probable that he regularly 'normalized' dialect forms (for example, vi. 113. 2; 141. 1); note particularly 55. 3, βωκόλος] βουκόλος, where the latter is also the form given in *APl*.

---

[9] The problems of the last couplet seem insoluble: see Stadtmueller and Waltz ad loc. and Gow and Page, *HE* ii. 366.

There are in fact three clear examples of unquestionably true readings in the Suda where *AP* is corrupt: vi. 112. 2, ἔγκεινται] ἄγκεινται; 297. 1, φιλοδάπου] φιλοδούπου; and above all no fewer than three times in the very corrupt vi. 226: 1. 1, ὀλιγόλαυξ] ὀλιγαύλαξ; 1. 2, λεῖτος δ'] λιτός θ'; 1. 2 again, σχεδὼν] σχεδόν. Note too v. 150. 1, where for *AP*'s unmetrical nonsense-word ἠπιβότης C offers the certain correction ἡ 'πιβόητος, and the Suda has ἐπιβόητος. It is surely impossible to believe that all these readings are the product of conjecture.

There is in addition one passage to which Basson himself draws attention, his usual good sense deserting him. At vi. 153. 1–2 *AP* offers the proper name Ἐριασπίδα υἱός / Κλεύβοτος. In the Suda we find the jumble Ἐραππίδαυλος Κεύβοτος. Rightly conceding that *AP* is perfectly legible at this point, Basson gave away his whole position with the astounding conclusion 'Suidam non ex ipso codice Palatino . . . sed e lectoris cuiusdam apographo, ubi verba falso transcripta erant, descripsisse recte et iure statuas' (p. 29). If the Suda was copied here (as it surely was) from a manuscript where the words were less clearly written than in *AP*, why should this manuscript have been an apograph of *AP*? In view of the other factors listed above it must surely be presumed an independent copy of Cephalas. Certainly not (as Waltz suspected) Michael Chartophylax's exemplar (despite the numerous agreements with C), since there are two quotations from the one poem we know to have been omitted by Michael (vi. 269).

It is the anathematica that are best represented in the Suda. No fewer than 225 out of the 358 poems in *AP* vi are quoted, some of them many times (e.g. 165 twelve times). The poems quoted run from vi. 3 to 335, spread evenly through the greater part of the book but falling off sharply towards the end (for example, from 307 to 358 only three are quoted, 332, 334, and 335). As we saw earlier, the distribution of Planudean quotations and corrections by C lend no support to the idea that Cephalas' anathematic book was ever shorter than the 358 poems of *AP* vi, and this falling off is doubtless to be attributed to the waning industry of the lexicographer.

We must likewise be wary of drawing from the pattern of his takings from other books the sort of conclusions drawn by Waltz, Beckby, Basson, and others. Of the 310 erotica in *AP* v only 68 are quoted, but they run from v. 6 to v. 301. And if the anathematic book in the lexicographer's source was as full as *AP* vi why should his erotic book have been significantly smaller? From the epitaphia he quotes 135 epigrams (out of 748 in *AP* vii), but almost all from the first third of the book up to 259; from the rest only 10 (325, 413, 433, 531, 588, 620, 713, 727, 736). Waltz typically took it for granted that the lexicographer's exemplar 's'arrêtait évidemment aux environs de 250 ou de 260'—and then confessed himself at a loss to account for the quotations from the rest of the book![10] The lexicographer's treatment of vii was not really so 'remarquable' as Waltz found it. By vii. 259 he had excerpted nearly as many epitaphia as he had anathematica and erotica. He now had an adequate sample of the vocabulary, nomenclature, and *Realien* of classical epigrams, and decided not to plough through the rest of Cephalas' monstrously long epitaphic book. He just skipped through the remaining pages and took the merest handful of quotations that happened to catch his eye. He then did the same with the even longer epideictic/ecphrastic book (taking only ix. 61, 75, 397, 447, 448, 497, 503, 569) and called it a day.

Basson pointed out that there are no quotations from the Planudean ecphrastica absent from *AP*, in which he naturally saw confirmation of his own contention that the Suda's source was *AP* itself. But the short sequence taken from *AP* ix stops well before 583/4 where the lacuna falls. So we should not expect to find any Planudean ecphrastica in the Suda.

It is *possible* that the exemplar of Cephalas on which the Suda drew was both abbreviated and defective. But there is no real indication that it was either. On the other hand the quotations from *AP* i. 4, i. 99 and the three from i. 34 point to an exemplar that contained a counterpart to *AP* i. Whether or not the book is Cephalan, it was evidently not unique to *AP*. It is true that the quotations from i. 4 and i. 99 seem to be additions to the original text of the Suda,[11] but that does not eliminate their status as witnesses. Whatever their date, neither can derive from *AP*. The quotation from i. 4 comes with a different lemma;[12] that from i. 99 preserves a different and superior reading in l. 3 that cannot possibly be ascribed to conjecture.[13]

[10] Waltz, i (1928), pp. lx–lxi.
[11] s.vv. Στούδιος and ἀναίμονες with Adler's app. crit.
[12] Discussed by Mango, 'The Date of the Studius Basilica at Istanbul', *Byzantine and Modern Greek Studies* iv (1978), 117 f.
[13] See *Yale Classical Studies* xxvii (1982), 252 n. 122.

XIII

Arethas and Cephalas

MUCH the best documented library of the age belonged to Arethas of Patras, archbishop of Caesarea from 902 or 903 to the early 930s.[1] Did he have a copy of Cephalas? What did he know of the ancient epigram?

First a passage from the Scholia to Dio Chrysostom in Vat. Urb. 124 (s. XI) which A. Sonny published in 1896 and showed beyond all reasonable doubt to be the work of Arethas, no doubt copied directly from his own manuscript and probably written in 916 or 918.[2] Against Dio's quotation in *Or.* ii. 63 of the skolion εἴθε λύρα καλὴ γενοίμαν (*PMG* 900) Arethas quoted (as he put it) ἕτερα παροίνια σκολιά (p. 98 Sonny):

I. εἴθ' ἄνεμος γενόμην, καὶ σὺ στείχουσα παρ' αὐγὰς
    στήθεα γυμνώσαις καί με πνέοντα λάβοις.

    (= *AP* v. 83; Anon. P, Dionysius, Pl)

II. εἴθε ῥόδον γενόμην ὑποπόρφυρον, ὄφρα με χερσὶν
     ἀραμένη χιονοῖς στήθεσσιν χαρίσῃ.

     (= *AP* v. 84)

III. εἴθε κρίνον γενόμην ἀργέννααον, ὄφρα με ῥισὶν
      ἀρσαμένη μᾶλλον σῆς χροτιῆς κορέσῃς.

      (= *AP* xv. 35; Theophanes)

---

[1] P. Lemerle, *Le Premier Humanisme byzantin* (Paris 1971), 205–41; N. G. Wilson, *Scholars of Byzantium* (London 1983), 120–35. Unless otherwise indicated, references to Arethas' own writings are to L. G. Westerink's Teubner edition, *Arethae Scripta Minora*, i (1968) and ii (1972).

[2] *Ad Dionem Chrysostomum Analecta* (Kiev 1896), p. 98. For Arethas' authorship (inferred from numerous verbal parallels with Arethas' other scholia and the range of authors quoted, especially Plato, Aristotle, Lucian, and Marcus Aurelius) see pp. 85–94; the date is inferred from the note on Dio, *Or.* vi. 121, wondering whether the Bulgars have captured Thebes. As Sonny rightly saw, this must refer to Symeon's invasion of N. Greece as far as the gulf of Corinth known from *Vita S. Lucae Minoris*, *PG* cxi. 449–50, which Sonny dated to 917. But the true date is either 916 (S. Runciman, *The Emperor Romanus Lecapenus* (Cambridge 1929), 84 n. 2) or, more probably, 918 (G. Ostrogorsky, *History of the Byzantine State* (Oxford 1968), 264 n. 1). Cf. too now J. Koder, *JÖB* xxv (1976), 77–8.

Editors quote the passage, anonymously, among the testimonia for v. 83 and 84 though not, inconsistently enough, for xv. 35, but without observing that it is an earlier witness by twenty or thirty years than *AP*, and without realizing that it preserves a preferable reading for at least the second and third poems. Maas thought that Arethas was actually quoting from *AP*.[3] We need only compare their texts for the first line of III, ascribed in *AP* to Theophanes, to see that this cannot be so.

Theophanes' poem is not quite so feeble a reworking of (2) as has been supposed. The author of II wrote χερσὶν ἀραμένη (from ἀείρω), 'picking me up in her hands'. Theophanes wrote ῥισίν as in Urb. 124, not the flat χερσίν of *AP*, *APl*, and all editions; and then the participle ἀρσαμένη (from ἀραρίσκω, 'fit'): 'putting me [the white lily] to her nostrils'. It is hardly surprising that a scribe who had perhaps failed to recognize the letters ρισιν as a word at all 'corrected' them, perhaps unconsciously, on the basis of the ending to the otherwise virtually identical first line of the preceding poem. Though manifestly inferior by comparison, χερσίν makes perfectly tolerable sense in itself, a classic example of the corruption that, once made, was never likely to be detected. Arethas' reading must be transmitted truth, not conjecture.

The case of II. 2, where *AP* offers χαρίσῃ στήθεσι χιονέοις, is less clear cut. By classical standards it goes without saying that *AP*'s text is superior, but *utrum in alterum*? One of the two versions must be the result of deliberate and skilful rewriting. More than simple transposition would have been required to convert either version into the other. Which is more likely, that Arethas rewrote a metrically unexceptionable pentameter to obtain a spondee in the second half of the line, a feature quite alien to ancient elegiacs though somewhat affected in tenth-century verse (for example, *APl* 281, quoted below); or that some reader more sensitive than Arethas to classical practice (no doubt through study of the material made available by Cephalas) recognized the metrical anomaly and corrected it? II and III balance each other so perfectly that it is tempting to attribute both to the same poet, Theophanes, author of xv. 14; in which case both would be tenth-century work. If so, then it might well be Arethas who preserves

---

[3] *JRS* xxxv (1945), 146 (= *Kl. Schr.* [Munich 1973], 140). In fact *AP* must be at least twenty years later than the scholia.

the original reading, taken from a text which must be earlier than either *AP* or the source of *APl.*

On the other hand, Arethas' καὶ σύ in I. 1 looks like a conjecture to repair *AP*'s metrically defective σὺ δέ, better than Planudes' feeble σὺ δέ γε but less good than Jacobs's now generally accepted σὺ δὲ δή. If so, then Arethas was apparently faced with the same defective text as *AP*—the text of Cephalas.

Only I and II appear in *AP* v; III is absent from the Cephalan portion of the manuscript. If *AP* had been Arethas' source, we should have to suppose that it was Arethas himself who spotted the connection between II and III over nearly 600 pages of *AP*, which is improbable in itself and rendered less probable still by the occurrence of all three together in the same order in *APl* (vii. 153, fo. 74ᵛ). Not only this. Since he erroneously ran all three together into one poem, it was clearly not Planudes who put II and III together either. The presumption is that both Arethas and Planudes found them already so juxtaposed in their sources. Planudes' main source, we know, was Cephalas, and if Arethas was writing *c.*918, it would certainly be the obvious source for him too. There is no problem about the absence of III from *AP* v. II. 1 and III. 1 are virtually identical (especially after the corruption of III. 1), and omission by parablepsy scarcely strains belief. It might be added that the corruption of the original ῥισίν in III. 1 presupposes an original arrangement in which III followed II. The compiler of *AP* xv included just III in his collection because it happened to be the work of a poet known to him personally. The probability is that he, Arethas, *AP*, and Planudes all derive here from the erotic book of Cephalas.

The next passage to be considered is from the scholia to Clement of Alexandria, this time written in Arethas' own hand in his own text of the Apologists, the famous (and expensive) Par. gr. 451 copied for him by the scribe Baanes between September 913 and August 914.[4] Against Clement's account of the Locrian minstrel Eunomus and his grasshopper (*Protr.* 1. 1), Arethas made the following annotation:[5] (Εὔνομος) εἰς ὃν καὶ ταυτὶ τὰ στιχελεγεῖα· "Εὔνομον, ὤπολλον, σὺ μὲν οἶσθά με" καὶ ἑξῆς. This is the beginning of *AP* ix. 584, a sixteen-line anonymous epigram describing how

---

[4] *Clemens Alexandrinus* i³ (GCS), ed. O. Stähelin, rev. U. Treu (Berlin 1972), xvi–xxiii: cf. Lemerle, p. 234.

[5] p. 296. 28 f. Stähelin–Treu.

the grasshopper helped Eunomus win his contest at the Pythia. The only other passage where this poem is cited (apart from *API*) is in the scholia to Strabo, who also had occasion to mention the statue of Eunomus and his helpmeet (vi. 260D):[6] (εἰκόνα) ἐφ᾽ ἧς καὶ τὸ ἐπίγραμμα τοῦτο "Εὔνομον, ὤπολλον, σὺ μὲν οἶσθά με, πῶς πότε νικῶ / Σπάρταν ὁ Λοκρὸς ἐγώ" καὶ ἑξῆς.

In an important paper published in 1954 Aubrey Diller argued that a certain number of these Strabo scholia went back to Arethas: some show knowledge of the region around his native Patras, and Strabo is quoted in two other sets of indisputably Arethan scholia, one autograph.[7] At the time he did not connect the two citations (closely parallel in form) of *AP* ix. 584, but the connection once made it certainly looks as if this note too derives from Arethas, virtual proof that he had a hand in the Strabo scholia. It was Arethas' regular practice, as Sonny put it, 'ut easdem res apud varios scriptores obvias eisdem fere verbis illustraret'.[8]

The few extra words in the Strabo quotation are particularly valuable for our purpose. First, the same impossible πότε νικῶ as *AP*; a past tense is required, and editors rightly print Planudes' ποτ᾽ ἐνίκων. Second, an interesting and otherwise unattested variant for the name of Eunomus' rival in the contest: Σπάρταν for the Σπάρτην of *AP*, corrected *metri gratia* to Σπάρτιν by Planudes. The fullest version of the story,[9] that of Timaeus, gives the rival's name as Ariston. The only other alternative on offer is in a poem by Paul the Silentiary, ὁ δ᾽ ἀντίος ἵστατο Πάρθης (*AP* vi. 54. 3), where Planudes has Πάρθυς, once more surely a conjecture, and a poor one (what would 'a Parthian' be doing at Delphi?). The very similarity of the original readings in the two passages in *AP* (Σπάρτης/Πάρθης) is suspicious; surely both are corruptions of one and the same name (hence Brunck's unlikely Πάρθις in both places).

This is why the Σπάρταν of the Strabo scholia for ix. 584. 1 is so

---

[6] A. Diller, 'The Scholia on Strabo', *Traditio* x (1954), 36.

[7] Op. cit. p. 44, and now *The Textual Tradition of Strabo's Geography* (Amsterdam 1975), 81–2. (Diller argued that the majority of the Strabo scholia go back to Photius, a hypothesis not well received at the time—see Lemerle, p. 218—but persuasively reformulated by him in *Textual Tradition*, 30–1.) I am most grateful to Professor Diller for drawing my attention to the connection between the Clement and Strabo scholia before the appearance of his book.

[8] *Ad Dionem . . . Analecta*, p. 90, quoting many examples of such often verbatim repetitions between the various scholia of Arethas.

[9] For which see the Budé edition, vol. iii, pp. 171–2 and vol. viii, p. 101 n. 1.

interesting. For C quotes exactly the same form as a variant for vi. 54. 3: γρ(άφεται) Σπάρτας. C does not usually employ this formula; it implies that this was either the reading of Michael's exemplar or a variant there recorded—that is to say that it probably derives from Cephalas himself. Spartas is no more improbable a name than Spartis or Parthes, and does have the advantage of being transmitted independently in both passages by sources earlier than *AP* (Michael, Arethas). And it is easy enough to see how it came to be corrupted in both cases: in ix. 584. 2 Σπάρταν was 'corrected' to Σπάρτην on the assumption that the Laconian city was meant; and at vi. 54. 3 the conjecture Πάρθης was substituted to avoid the 'improper' shortening ἵστατο before σπ (tolerable in a proper name).

That Arethas derived his Clement scholion from Cephalas would have been a reasonable assumption on its own. But if he is the author of the Strabo scholion too, then reasonable assumption becomes reasoned probability. The corrupt πότε νικῶ it shares with *AP* we may presume to have stood in Cephalas, who may also have offered the Σπάρταν already corrupted in *AP* but supported by Michael's variant for vi. 54. 3. If the argument is accepted, then we can push back Cephalas' *terminus ante quem* from the *c*.918 of the Dio scholia to 913/14 at least.

And there is another passage that points to an even earlier date. In a letter to Stephen ἐπὶ τοῦ κανικλείου (i. 294 Westerink) who was dilatory in sending a promised gift, Arethas quotes anon. *AP* x. 30 in its entirety:

ὠκεῖαι χάριτες γλυκερώτεραι· ἢν δὲ βραδύνῃ
πᾶσα χάρις κενεή, μηδὲ λέγοιτο χάρις.

It is a gnomic piece which might easily have been quoted here or there in Classical or Byzantine literature. But nowhere we know of. All we do know is that it was certainly in Cephalas (in Σᵖ as well as *AP* and *APl*). In this it is like all the other four epigrams quoted by Arethas: anonymous, unremarkable, unknown outside anthologies based on Cephalas.

S. Kougeas identified Stephen with the Stephen *a secretis* (a higher official in the same bureau) of Arethas, *Op*. 51 (i. 324W), which Westerink dated to *c*.900. If both identification and date hold, then it would seem that Waltz was right after all to put Cephalas before 900. Both are conjectural, and the date, though a

reasonable inference, is perhaps not to be pressed. But the identification seems likely enough, and since Arethas' other letter to
Stephen *a secretis* belongs early in 907 (ii. 94W), we are still in the
first decade of the century.[10]

The last fairly certain passage comes in another autograph
scholion, on fo. 27ʳ of Mosqu. Mus. Hist. gr. 394 (231 Vladimir) of
932, at this point containing some anonymous questions and
answers on theological subjects:[11] πρὸ παντός, writes the now
eighty-year-old Arethas, ἐκεῖνο ἐρεῖν ἐν τοῖς τοιούτοις ἁρμόδιον, τὸ
"ἵνα σοί τι μέλῃ, δαίμονι τοῦτο μέλει", a verbatim quotation from
Palladas, *AP* x. 34. 4, found in *AP*, *APl*, and L. It is conceivable
that, like J, Arethas had a copy of Palladas, but he did not in
general collect poetical books, and in the light of the preceding
examples it seems more natural and economical to suppose that,
once again, he was quoting from his Cephalas.

Two other passages call for brief mention. First the two poems
that follow the subscription to Arethas' Euclid (Bodl. 301, fo.
397ᵛ), both in his own hand. The first, as Westerink rightly
remarks, betrays all the 'quaesita inelegantia' of Arethas himself.
Comparison with Arethas' undoubted elegiacs *AP* xv. 32 and 34
leaves no doubt that it is indeed his own work (Westerink, op. cit.
(n. 1) ii, p. xv). But the second poem is quite another matter:

Εὐκλείδης μέτρων ἀψευδέας εὗρε κελεύθους
γραμμῇ καὶ κέντρῳ κύκλον ἐρεισάμενος.

This is a concise and elegant piece quite unlike anything else
Arethas wrote and it seems inconceivable that he is the author. But
since it is not to be found in any of the extant Cephalan anthologies
there seems no reason to suppose that it was ever in Cephalas. In
any case, Bodl. 301 is dated by its scribe Stephen to September
888. Cephalas can scarcely be put as early as this. Whoever the
author was, as Westerink pointed out, he was familiar with the
following couplet from Paul the Silentiary, *AP* ix. 782. 3–4:

ὕδασι δ' ἠελίοιο ταλαντεύουσι κελεύθους
ἐς πόλον ἐκ γαίης μῆτιν ἐρεισάμενοι.

---

[10] For the letters to Stephen, see S. Kougeas, ὁ Καισαρείας Ἀρέθας (Athens 1913),
114–17; R. J. H. Jenkins and B. Laourdas, *Hellenika* xiv (1956), 366; Lemerle, pp.
221–3; and Westerink's notes ad loc. There is also a Stephen μυστικὸς καὶ ἐπὶ τοῦ
κανικλείου of *Ep.* 29 of Nicetas Magister, written in 946/7, according to Westerink
(*Nicétas Magistros: lettres d'un exilé* [Paris 1973], 138) probably the same man,
though the date is rather against this.

[11] L. G. Westerink, *Byz.* xlii (1972), 212.

Where and when did he read Paul? If in the 880s, not in Cephalas and hardly in a complete text of the *Cycle*. Not that the poem is a likely product of that age. Most probably Arethas found it in the manuscript from which his Euclid was copied, written perhaps as early as the sixth century, when copies of the *Cycle* were more freely available and widely read. *AP* ix is full of book-epigrams of about this date. So no connection with Cephalas at all.

The other passage is another scholion on Strabo (xiv. 672A), citing a six-line version of the epitaph on Sardanapalus.[12] Yet despite the fact that this same version appears as *APl* 27, there can be little doubt that it did not appear in Cephalas. It is one of the poems Planudes added from a subsidiary source that for once can be identified: this very scholion on Strabo (p. 215). Furthermore, there is nothing to connect this particular scholion with Arethas. So no connection here either between Arethas and Cephalas.

This is perhaps the place to mention another scholiast of the age who can be shown to have drawn on Cephalas: the anonymous commentator who added the latest items to the so-called *Scholia vetera* on Apollonius of Rhodes.

In lines 1241–2 of book iii, Apollonius lists among places sacred to Poseidon, Taenarum, and the 'water of Lerna' (Λέρνης ὕδωρ). The relevant note runs as follows:[13] Ταίναρον ἀκρωτήριον τῆς Λακωνικῆς. Λέρνη δὲ κρήνη τοῦ Ἄργους ἱερὰ Ποσειδῶνος, followed by line 4 of *AP* ix. 688, five hexameters originally inscribed on a gate built or rebuilt somewhere in Argos by a hierophant of the mysteries of Lerna:

τήνδε πύλην λάεσσιν ἐυξέστοις ἀραρυῖαν,
ἀμφότερον κόσμον τε πάτρῃ καὶ θάμβος ὁδίταις,
τεῦξε Κλέης Κλεάδας ἀγανῆς πόσις εὐπατερείης,
Λερναίων ἀδύτων περιώσιος ὀργιοφάντης,
τερπόμενος δώροισιν ἀγασθενέων βασιλήων.

Argive provenance could have been inferred from Lerna, but B's lemma (εἰς πύλην τοῦ Ἄργους) is shown to be more than a Byzantine guess by the epigram inscribed on a statue base from Athens by the same Cleadas:

Δηοῦς καὶ Κούρης θεοείκελον ἱεροφάντην
κυδαίνων πατέρα στῆσε δόμοις Κλεάδας,
[Κ]εκροπίης σοφὸν ἔρνος Ἐρώτιον· ᾧ ῥα καὶ αὐτός
Λερναίων ἀδύτων ἶσον ἔδεκτο γέρας.

---

[12] Diller, *Traditio* x (1954), 40.
[13] C. Wendel, *Scholia in Apollonium Rhodium vetera* (Berlin 1935), 254. 20–2.

Cleadas, himself hierophant of the Mysteries of Lerna, honours his father Erotius, hierophant of the Eleusinian Mysteries some time in the late third century.[14] The connection between Lerna and Poseidon which Apollonius had in mind is evidently the spring Amymone, named after a nymph he is supposed to have seduced. Poseidon had nothing to do with the Mysteries of Lerna under the Roman Empire, associated with Dionysus and (later) Demeter.[15] The inappropriate citation of the Kleadas epigram cannot have stood in any of the ancient commentaries. It was added by the Byzantine who copied it into the archetype of the scholia tradition, and he added it from Cephalas.

Like a number of other poems in the immediate context (ix. 670–6; 678–80; 686; from Smyrna, Alexandria, Assos, Antioch, and Thessalonica), ix. 688 was copied on the spot from the monument named. Compare ix. 686, where there is nothing in the text of the epigram itself to suggest that it was inscribed, as the lemma states, 'on the East Gate of Thessalonica'. The lemmata to the numerous epigrams from Constantinople that follow also give precise locations not identified in the epigrams (ix. 689–99). We know that Gregory Magister collected epigraphic poetry in Asia Minor as well as in mainland Greece,[16] and C's lemma to vii. 340, 'found in Thessalonica' ($\epsilon\dot{v}\rho\dot{\epsilon}\theta\eta$ $\dot{\epsilon}\nu$ $\Theta\epsilon\sigma\sigma\alpha\lambda o\nu\dot{\iota}\kappa\eta$), makes it clear that this was one of the places he searched. In any case, whether or not Gregory himself was the source of this particular batch of epigraphic material, it is a tiny fraction, a personal and arbitrary selection from the countless thousands of inscriptional epigrams available on buildings and statue bases all over the Byzantine world. Modern scholars have published thousands Gregory missed or ignored.

It is highly unlikely that any other Byzantine copied Cleadas' five hexameters from their gate somewhere in Argos. We may take it as axiomatic that Cephalas' was the only Byzantine Anthology in which they appeared. It follows that the latest stratum in the Apollonius scholia must be dated after Cephalas.[17] The earliest

---

[14] *IG* II² 3674; K. Clinton, *The Sacred Officials of the Eleusinian Mysteries* (Trans. Amer. Philos. Soc. 64. 3; Philadelphia 1974), 42–3. The second epigram confirms Jacobs's correction of P's $K\lambda\epsilon\dot{a}\delta os$ and Pl's $K\lambda\epsilon\dot{a}\delta\eta s$.

[15] K. Meuli, *PW* xii. 2 (1925), 2090–3; C. Wendel, *Hermes* lxxvii (1942), 217–18.

[16] Weisshäupl (1889), 29–32.

[17] The bulk of the *scholia vetera* derive, as a subscription in L directly states, from the commentaries of Theon, Lucillius, and Sophocleus, the first named Augustan, the last from late antiquity: C. Wendel, *Die Überlieferung der Scholien zu Apollonios von Rhodos* (Abh. Göttingen 1932), 105–6.

manuscript to carry these scholia is Laurentianus 32. 9 (L), which also happens to be the oldest and most important witness to the text of Sophocles and (under the alias Mediceus) of Aeschylus too. Until recently this manuscript was assigned to the late tenth or early eleventh century. Following a brief but important palaeographical discussion by A. Diller, it is now generally dated 'soon after the middle of the tenth century'.[18]

L is clearly not the archetype, as may be illustrated from this very quotation. In line 4 both P and Pl offer the meaningless ἀργιοφάντης, which must therefore have been Cephalas' text, as confirmed by its persistence in two of the scholia manuscripts, V and A. The scribes of two other scholia manuscripts tried to make sense of the transmitted text by emendation: the sixteenth century P conjectured[19] the Homeric Ἀργεϊφόντης, which makes no better sense of the poem as a whole; and L ingeniously restored the original text.[20]

If L dates from c.950, then its source must have been earlier still. So the archetype of the scholia tradition has to be dated between c.900 and 950. The man responsible must have been a contemporary of Arethas. It might even have been Arethas himself. It is usually assumed that he had little taste for the poets,[21] but our knowledge of his library is very incomplete. There is some evidence that he possessed an annotated Pindar,[22] and he might easily have owned, and occasionally annotated, a text of the tragedians and Apollonius. Maas drew attention to the odd Byzantine addition to the Sophocles scholia in L, for example on *Antigone* 264: τοῦτο μέχρι σήμερον οἱ Ῥωμαῖοι ποιοῦσιν, Ἑλληνικῶς πλανώμενοι καὶ ἐν ἄλλοις πλείστοις, 'the Romans still do this today, raving like pagans in countless other ways as well'. As Maas put it, this 'sounds just like Arethas'.[23] Of course, it also sounds like J and

[18] H. Lloyd-Jones and N. G. Wilson, *Sophoclis Fabulae* (Oxford 1990), vii; Diller 1974, 522.

[19] On this tendency in P, see Wendel's preface: 'maxime in eo operam posuit, ut sententias traditas in elegantiorem formam redigeret, difficultates aut rerum aut verborum removeret . . .' (p. xv).

[20] As Maas pointed out (*BZ* xxxvi [1936], 107), Wendel's app. crit. obscures this point, and does not cite the Cephalan witnesses. Both modern editions of *AP* ix likewise mistate the facts. J. Irigoin's Budé does not cite the Apollonius scholia at all; and while Beckby gives the reference, he does not quote L's text, giving Scaliger the credit for ὀργιοφάντης.

[21] For such evidence as there is for his knowledge of ancient poets, see Wilson (1983), 131.

[22] J. Irigoin, *Histoire du texte de Pindare* (Paris 1952), 128; Lemerle (1971), 232.

[23] 'klingt nach Arethas', *BZ* xxxvi (1936), 106.

no doubt many other scholars of the age, many of them pupils of Cephalas or readers of his Anthology.

But the six Cephalan poems studied above are surely enough to establish the case. Arethas must have had a copy of Cephalas, which he consulted off and on from at least 907 (and perhaps as early as *c.*900) till 932. It does not look as if Cephalas' anthology can have appeared much later than 900, perhaps a year or two before then, leaving plenty of time for the *sylloge Euphemiana* to be produced from its contents before the death of Leo the Wise in 912.

XIV

Constantine Porphyrogenitus

THE tenth century was an age of encyclopaedias and anthologies, the most ambitious and certainly the largest of which was the series of fifty-three volumes[1] of excerpts from the Greek and Byzantine historians, planned and produced at the direction of the Emperor Constantine Porphyrogenitus himself.[2]

That there were fifty-three volumes we know from the preamble to the *de legationibus*, the only one to have come down to us complete, though we also have substantial portions of three more, *de sententiis, de insidiis,* and *de virtutibus et vitiis*. In addition, we know the titles of nineteen more, thanks to frequent cross-references in the extant parts of the form ζήτει ἐν τῷ περὶ στρατηγη-μάτων, δημηγοριῶν or the like.[3] Now among these references there is one in an excerpt from Diodorus Siculus concerning Sardanapalus (*Exc. de virt. et vit.*, ed. Büttner-Wobst, i (1906), 207), ζήτει ἐν τοῖς ἐπιγράμμασιν.

It has generally been assumed that one of the fifty-three was a volume περὶ ἐπιγραμμάτων. As Büttner-Wobst put it,[4] 'just as historically important public speeches and letters were treated under special headings (he means the now lost περὶ δημηγοριῶν and περὶ ἐπιστολῶν), so we must suppose a heading περὶ ἐπιγραμμάτων for historically significant epigrams'. There are a number of objections to this assumption.

In the first place, the standard formula for cross-references from one volume of the excerpta to another is ζήτει ἐν τῷ περὶ, ἐν περὶ, or εἰς τὸ περὶ, followed by the relevant name in the genitive, 'concerning ——'.[5] This is *not* the form of this reference. Second, περὶ

---

[1] ὑπόθεσις when viewed from the point of view of subject matter, τεῦχος when viewed as a physical volume; the *de legationibus*, then as now, was in more than one τεῦχος.

[2] For a general account with bibliography, see Lemerle, pp. 280 f.

[3] For the list, see Büttner-Wobst, *Hermes* xv (1906), 108 f.; Lemerle, pp. 283–4.

[4] *Hermes* xv (1906), 112.

[5] See Büttner-Wobst, op. cit. 107.

ἐπιγραμμάτων would not be at all an appropriate title; such a volume would not be 'concerning epigrams', it would simply *be* epigrams. Third, this would be the only volume classified by literary genre instead of subject-matter. And last, all the other volumes consist of excerpts from historical writers. Now there are many hundreds of historically important epigrams, but scarcely any of them are quoted by Greek or Byzantine historians. All in all this supposed volume 'concerning epigrams' would have been very much an odd man out.

Let us for the moment content ourselves with the observation that ἐν (τοῖς) ἐπιγράμμασιν is the standard formula used by the compiler of the Suda to refer to Cephalas, and pass on to the other passages in the writings of Constantine Porphyrogenitus[6] where epigrams are quoted.

First *De admin. imp.* 21. 57 f., describing how an Arab general dismantled the Colossus of Rhodes (in ruins for almost nine hundred years) in 654 and sold it to a Jew from Edessa who carted it off on 980 camels. The Colossus, Constantine writes, was a brazen statue of the Sun 80 cubits high, 'as the inscription on the base of its feet bears witness':

τὸν ἐν Ῥόδῳ κολοσσὸν ὀκτάκις δέκα
Λάχης ἐποίει πήχεων ὁ Λίνδιος.

There are three things wrong with this epigram. In the first place, as was rightly perceived so long ago as Scipione Maffei, it is hardly likely that what the world at large quite properly knows as the Colossus of Rhodes was so described *in situ* at Rhodes. Our only other independent witness to the epigram, Strabo, unfortunately did not quote it all verbatim—ὁ τοῦ ἡλίου κολοσσὸς ὅν φησιν ὁ ποιήσας τὸ ἰαμβεῖον ὅτι ἑπτάκις δέκα Χάρης ἐποίει πήχεων ὁ Λίνδιος (xiv. 2. 5, p. 652)—but as Bergk saw, it looks as if the version he knew began something like τὸν ἡλίου κολοσσόν. Preger rightly objected that 'demonstrativum pronomen desideratur',[7] and accordingly I propose the modification τόνδ' ἡλίου κολοσσόν. Either a lemma (like the one to *APl* 82) εἰς τὸν ἐν Ῥόδῳ Κ. intruded itself into the text—or perhaps the beginning was simply invented to supplement the defective text offered by Strabo. Both the other faults in Constan-

---

[6] I am assuming that all these works are in their essentials products of Constantine's own pen; on the general question, Lemerle, pp. 270 f.

[7] T. Preger, *Inscr. graecae metricae* (1891), 229, no. 280.

tine's text are also revealed by comparison with Strabo: the builder's name was certainly Chares, not Laches; and earlier sources agree that the thing was 70, not 80 cubits tall. Significantly enough, however, all three corruptions appear in the version offered by *APl* 82. And the reason is simple; this is surely what stood in their common source, namely Cephalas.

Then there is *De Thematibus* i. 2 (p. 66. 70 f. Pertusi), where Constantine quotes two epigrams on the bad reputation of Cappadocians; first *AP* xi. 238. 1–4, introduced by the familiar ἐν ἐπιγράμμασιν, and then xi. 237, prefaced by ἄλλως, one of the standard formulas for introducing a variation on a theme. He is clearly quoting from a collection of epigrams. Now xi. 237 comes in *AP* at the end of a short series of attacks on different nationalities ascribed to the fifth- or fourth-century BC poet Demodocus. *AP* xi. 238 is a lampoon on an (unnamed) fifth- or sixth-century AD (?praetorian) prefect, quoted by John the Lydian (*de magg.* iii. 57), where Cephalas probably found it. Even if the two poems had chanced to be juxtaposed by someone before Cephalas, which is improbable, their juxtaposition in both Constantine and *AP* clearly points to Cephalas as the common source.

De Thematibus i. 5 (p. 70. 19 f.) quotes Agathias' poem on the Sangarius bridge (*AP* ix. 641). Despite the seemingly circumstantial detail that the epigram 'was written on one of the stone slabs', it is scarcely likely that the emperor, no traveller, copied the poem *in situ*. Agathias himself may well have proudly recorded in his lemma the honour paid to his poem. We can hardly doubt that Constantine found it in a literary source, and if so where but Cephalas?

There are two other cases, both epigrams that Constantine might equally have found elsewhere. *AP* vii. 169, which is also quoted in full in Hesychius of Miletus (*Patria Cpoleos.* pp. 12–13 Preger) and elsewhere. And an epigram commemorating the battle of Casulinum in 554 which is only otherwise known from Agathias' *History* (ii. 10. 8). It is clear from Agathias' account of how he was given the poem by a local that he had not already published it in his *Cycle*, and there is no reason to suppose that it appeared in Cephalas. Constantine is bound to have known both Hesychius and Agathias, though that does not mean that he did not get *AP* vii. 169 from Cephalas.

Let us return now to the cross-reference in the excerpt from

Diodorus. The subject is Sardanapalus, and the excerptor quotes the following line from his supposed epitaph:

ταῦτ᾽ ἔχω ὅσσ᾽ ἔφαγόν τε καὶ ἔπιον καὶ μετ᾽ ἐρώτων
καὶ τὰ ἑξῆς. ζήτει ἐν τοῖς ἐπιγράμμασι.

The epitaph is quoted in the original text of Diodorus, but (as Büttner-Wobst saw) it was not from Diodorus that the excerptor took his version (ταῦτ᾽ ἔχω ὅσσ᾽ ἔφαγον καὶ ἐφύβρισα καὶ μετ᾽ ἔρωτος). But for the first word (τόσσ᾽) it coincides exactly with the unique version of *AP* (vii. 325. 1), down to the unmetrical ἔπιον.

But there is a complication. Another version of the epitaph is quoted in another excerpt, from the chronicle of George the monk (*Exc. de virt. et vit.* i. 23, 13 f.):

τοσσ᾽ ἔχω, ὅσσ᾽ ἔφαγόν τε καὶ ἔπιον καὶ μετ᾽ ἐρώτων
τέρπν᾽ ἐδάην, τὰ δὲ πολλὰ καὶ ὄλβια πάντα λέλειπται.
καὶ γὰρ νῦν σποδός εἰμι, Νίνου μεγάλης βασιλεύσας.

Here too (as Büttner-Wobst again saw) this quotation cannot have been taken from George's own garbled quotation or rather (for the first two lines) paraphrase:

τόσσ᾽ ἔχω ὅσ᾽ ἐφύβρισα, ἔφαγόν τε καὶ ἔπιον καὶ μετ᾽ ἔρωτος
τερπνὸν ἐπολιτευσάμην, παθόντα δὲ πολλὰ καὶ ὄλβια πάντα λέλειπται·
καὶ γὰρ νῦν σποδός εἰμι, Νίνου μεγάλης βασιλεύσας

(i, pp. 13. 8 f. de Boor)

The excerptor evidently realized that something had gone badly amiss with George's first two lines and substituted a metrical version. His first line coincides exactly with *AP* vii. 325. 1, including the τόσσ᾽ this time: and his τερπν᾽ ἐδάην in l. 2 is likewise only otherwise found in the *AP* version (the other versions give τέρπν᾽ ἔπαθον *vel sim.*; ἐδάην seems guaranteed by the 'reply' *AP* vii. 326. 2). I suggest then that the excerptor took the actual text of his quotation from Cephalas. It is true that l. 3 of his second version is absent from the *AP* version, but this line he surely did take from George, reasonably enough (*a*) because (unlike ll. 1–2) it scans perfectly and (*b*) because it *was* absent from the *AP* version, to supplement it. καὶ γὰρ . . . βασιλεύσας is always elsewhere l. 3 of the long version of the epitaph; only George and the excerptor place it after instead of before the couplet τόσσ᾽ ἔχω . . . λέλειπται (ll. 4–5 in the long version).

I suggest then that when the excerptor wrote ζήτει ἐν τοῖς ἐπιγράμμασι he was referring to Cephalas. Whether or not the excerptor was Constantine himself (we need not doubt that he did some of the excerpting in person), it may well be that it was the same copy of Cephalas from which Constantine quoted in the *de them.* and the *de admin. imp.* If so, then it did not contain only 'historically significant' epigrams. It may be that some pieces of this sort that Cephalas had missed were added (the Casulinum epigram, for example), but there seems no good reason to believe that Constantine had a special collection of historical epigrams made, an anthology that was in any material respect different from Cephalas and uniform with the historical excerpts.

XV

AP xv, Constantine the Rhodian, and J

1. *AP* xv

THERE remains the collection of epigrams on pp. 664–706 of the Palatine MS misleadingly known as *AP* xv.[1] Misleadingly, because there can be no question of it actually forming a part of Cephalas' anthology. Contrary to what printed editions imply, it does not even follow *AP* xiv.

The central epigrammatic corpus of *AP* is preceded and followed by some notable specimens of early Byzantine ecphrastic poetry. On pp. 1–48 stand two ecphraseis by Paul the Silentiary and some poems of Gregory Nazianzen; on pp. 643–64. 20, following *AP* xiv, John of Gaza's ecphrasis of the world map in the winter baths at Gaza. It is not till p. 664. 24 f. that *AP* xv begins. Whatever we decide about *AP* i–iv, it seems clear that, for the Palatine scribes at least, xv had nothing to do with the main epigrammatic books v–xiv. Add to this the facts that it lacks a 'Cephalan' preface, consists disproportionately of ninth- and tenth-century rather than classical epigrams, and contains one poem (xv. 15) written if not (as commonly supposed) after the death of Leo the Wise, at any rate not before 908, and so after the appearance of Cephalas (before 907), and the conclusion is inescapable that xv is not Cephalan.

But before we can assess its character and relationship to the other anthologies of the age, we must first establish its contents and arrangement. According to *AP* as it is now bound up (the original sequence, as we shall see), the sequence of poems in the last forty-five pages runs as follows:[2]

---

[1] Beckby iv[2] 253–7 and Buffière, Budé *Anth. gr.* xii. 103–22, provide useful introductions, though Buffière is to be handled with caution.

[2] Preisendanz (1911), cols. xliii–xliv.

end of quaternion 42 (J), pp. 664. 24–674: *AP* xv. 1–27, plus (repeated)
AP i. 122; ix. 400, 180, 181; x. 87, 95; ix. 197, 196

quaternion 43 (J), pp. 675–90: *Anacreontea*

quaternion 44 (reversing the outside sheet):
  pp. 705–6: *AP* xv. 40 and 28. 1–9 (B3)
  pp. 693–5. 13: xv. 28. 10–14; 29–39*b* (B3)
  pp. 695. 14–704: Gregory Nazianzen, closing with *AP* viii. 85. 1–4 (J)
  pp. 691–2: more Gregory, beginning with *AP* viii. 85. 5–7 (J)
  pp. 707–9: *AP* xv. 41–51 (in fact Σ″).

The correction of the binding error in quaternion 44 is an improvement, though it is still surprising that so sizeable and self-contained a collection as the *Anacreontea* should intrude into an otherwise relatively homogeneous sequence of epigrams. Almost certainly this is another error of the binder, who inserted what is now quaternion 44 one quaternion too early. They should belong *after* the epigrams and the Gregory. If so, then the *intended* order was *AP* xv. 1–27, 40, 28–39*b* (plus the repetitions); then the Gregory; then the *Anacreontea*.

But this is not the order of J's index to the manuscript. After John of Gaza, J promises the *Syrinx* of Theocritus and other figure poems (referring to *AP* xv. 21, 22, 24, 25, 26, and 27); then the *Anacreontea*; and then excerpts from Gregory 'including epigrams by Arethas, Anastasius, Ignatius, Constantine, and Theophanes'. Though not an exhaustive list, this is a not misleading guide to the order of *AP as now bound*;[3] that is to say, epigram sequences each side of the *Anacreontea*. This alone is enough to disprove Preisendanz's ludicrous notion that J's index is not the index to *AP* at all but to its source (what would be the point of equipping one book with the index to another?). J certainly saw *AP* in its bound state, since on p. 693 (B3), where the binding error left xv. 28 lacking its first nine lines, J repeated them in the margin.

Before we leave the index, it should be made clear that there is no justification whatever for Boissonade's generally accepted emendation and repunctuation of J's description of *AP* xiv, ἀριθμητικὰ καὶ γρήφα [i.e. γρῖφα] σύμμικτα, τὸ ἀριθμητικὰ καὶ γρῖφοι· σύμμικτα, taking σύμμικτα, 'medley', to refer to xv. The heteroclite neuter is an acceptable (and attested: Hesych., s.v. γρῖφος, v.l.) Byzantine variant, and 'mixed puzzles' is an entirely appropriate

³ So too Aubreton (1968), 55–6.

description of the non-arithmetical part of *AP* xiv, embracing the oracles as well as the riddles. It would in any case be intolerably far-fetched to punctuate before σύμμικτα and then refer the word to another book not due till after John of Gaza—especially when the other book is then elaborately described after the entry for John of Gaza. We must accept that J did not supply a title for xv, either in his index or *suo loco* in the body of the manuscript. We cannot even be sure that he regarded the *Anacreontea* and the Gregory as integral parts of the collection of epigrams we know as *AP* xv.

It is in fact a pretty random assemblage. Even the epigrams are anything but homogeneous: a few more or less classicizing poems (mainly inscriptional) of the Roman age, some Palladas, the hellenistic technopaegnia (figure poems in the form of axes, altars, wings, and the like) and a preponderance of occasional pieces by poets of the ninth and tenth century, one fifty-seven lines long (no. 40). There is neither heading nor introduction nor epilogue; 1 refers back to John of Gaza (perhaps therefore to be excluded from the 'book' proper), 2 celebrates the emperor Marcian's enlargement of the walls of Myra in Lycia, and the last is a trifle addressed to an unnamed student of Plato (39*b*). About the *Anacreontea*,[4] since we cannot even be sure where in the manuscript they were originally intended to stand, we simply cannot say. Their inclusion certainly reflects a taste of the early tenth century (Ch. X). The Gregoriana, to which we shall be returning, may well have been intended to form part of the collection, just as the Gregoriana of *AP* viii were added in the source of *AP* as a supplement to *AP* vii (above, p. 108).

II. CONSTANTINE THE RHODIAN

The latest and most famous of the poets included is Constantine of Rhodes,[5] to whom are ascribed xv. 15, 16, and 17. Constantine is best known for his dreary but not unimportant ecphrasis of the Seven Wonders of Constantinople and the Church of the Holy

---

[4] Known only from *AP*, of course (see Ch. VIII).

[5] See G. Downey's useful sketch, 'Constantine the Rhodian: his life and writings', in *Late Classical and Medieval Studies in honour of A. M. Friend Jr.* (Princeton 1955), 212–21 (though the suggestion made at p. 214 n. 9 that the ἀπολογία of Matranga *Anecd. gr.* ii. 557–9 is by this Constantine is certainly mistaken: see above, p. 245).

Apostles, written some time between August 931 and December 944. The first datable reference to him comes in connection with the libel he wrote against a court favourite of Leo the Wise in 908 in the interests of his then patron, the Arab chamberlain Samonas. Like others of his age, Constantine evidently had a taste for polemic. He also wrote a scurrilous and rather silly poem against Leo Choirosphactes, perhaps in 907 (Matranga, *Anecd. gr.* ii. 624–5) and engaged in a protracted iambic controversy with an otherwise unknown Theodore the Paphlagonian (ibid. 625–32; eight items by Constantine, five by Theodore).

AP xv. 15, on a cross (or crucifix) he dedicated at Lindos in Rhodes (so the lemma), tells us most of what we know about the poet's background:

Κωνσταντῖνος Ἰωάννου ἠδ' Εὐδοκίης με
τέκνον ἔτευξεν ἀγακλυτόν, ὃν Λίνδος μεγάλαυχος
ἤνεγκε προτέρης γενεῆς προφερέστερον ἄνδρα
καὶ πιστὸν θεράποντα σκηπτούχοιο Λέοντος·
5 ᾧ Ἀλέξανδρος ἀδελφεὸς ἠδ' υἱὸς Κωνσταντῖνος
[σκῆπτρα Βυζαντιάδος συμμεθέπουσι Ῥώμης]
σκῆπτρα θεοστήρικτα συνεξαγέτην βασιλείης.

Constantine was born at Lindos, the son of John and Eudocia, and was a faithful servant of the Emperor Leo. It has always been assumed that these lines were written after the death of Leo (12 May 913) thus providing rather narrow limits for their composition, since Leo's brother Alexander died just over a year later (6 June 913). This assumption rests in part on a mistranslation of l. 3 and a false emendation in l. 5. Line 3 means, not 'whom proud Lindos bore, the foremost man of the former generation' (Paton, followed by Downey), but 'whom proud Lindos bore, more outstanding than his forbears'. The προτέρη γενεή is the preceding generation of his own family, namely the parents mentioned in l. 1. This is a normal claim in local inscriptional poetry of this sort (for example, *AP* vii. 698. 12, Christodorus on John, prefect of Illyricum in the 480s; *APl* 48. 6, Proclus, quaestor under Justin I). In l. 5 most editors print Boissonade's (hesitant) οὗ for P's ᾧ, thus giving a sharper break between Leo and the co-emperors of l. 6: 'Leo, whose brother and son . . . ruled together'. There is no call to tamper with ᾧ, which is governed by συνεξαγέτην. Translate as follows: 'Leo, with whom his brother and son . . . ruled together'. That is to say, Alexander and Constantine VII are being described as co-emperors with Leo rather than just with each other. Leo, then, was still alive when the poem was written.

The past tense συνεξαγέτην is not to be pressed; on no interpretation (least of all with οὗ) can it be made to imply that Leo was dead and the other two alive. It certainly does not mean that all three were dead, since Constantine VII lived till 959, by which time the poet himself must have been long dead. And by 927 at least (and probably earlier) we find the poet as the 'faithful servant' of Romanus Lecapenus, Constantine's co-emperor from 920 to 944. If the poem had been written after the death of the despised Alexander, either Constantine VII alone or (after 920) Constantine and Romanus would have been named. In his later ecphrasis (lines 22–6) Constantine alludes to the four co-emperors then reigning (between 931 and 944), namely Constantine VII, Romanus, and Romanus' sons Stephen and Constantine. It should be added that, if the lines had been written (as most commentators assume) between the deaths of Leo and Alexander, no poet who had been close to Leo would have been so tactless as to name the dead Leo first and then bracket Alexander and the six-year-old Constantine together as co-emperors. Alexander had been junior co-emperor throughout the long reign of the brother he hated and naturally proclaimed himself senior emperor on Leo's death.[6]

The poem must have been written during the period when Leo, Alexander, and Constantine were joint emperors; that is to say between the date of Constantine's coronation, 15 May 908,[7] and the death of Leo on 11 May 912. The past tense is used (as often in dedications) because the poet is looking back on the moment of his dedication from the point of view of future readers.

The next poem, xv. 16, runs as follows:

> ἅπαν μὲν ἔργον οὐ πρὸς ἀξίαν πέλει
> τὴν σήν, ὑπερθαύμαστε κόσμου δεσπότι·
> ἔργων γὰρ ἔξω καὶ φθορᾶς τὸ σὸν κλέος·
> τὸ δ' ἔργον, ὃ προσῆξέ σοι Κωνσταντῖνος,[8]

---

[6] G. Ostrogorsky, *History of the Byzantine State* (1968), 261 n. 1.

[7] So P. Grierson and R. J. H. Jenkins, *Byz.* xxxii (1962), 133 f., rather than 9 June 911, as previously supposed.

[8] There is no call to doubt that Constantine both wrote and intended the properispomenon accent on his own name (editors 'correct' *metri gratia* to paroxytone); see Cameron (1973), 192–3, where I would of course now revise my statement that *AP* 'is perhaps no more than half a century younger than Constantine'.

ἐπάξιον πέφυκεν, εἰ δή, Παρθένε,
τοῦ σοῦ τόκου τὸ σκῆπτρον εὖ διαγράφει,
καὶ σαρκὸς αὐτοῦ τὸ τρισόλβιον πάθος.

At first sight the poem itself, which is addressed to the Virgin, does not appear to bear out the claim of the lemma that it is 'about the same cross'. But it clearly concerns a dedication made by Constantine (l. 4), and the reference to it representing the 'sceptre' (i.e. kingly power) of her son (5) and the 'thrice blessed passion of his flesh' (6) suggest that the dedication consisted of a crucifix in a church of the Virgin at Lindos. It had long been a common practice to write two or more epigrams in different metres for a statue base or dedication.[9]

Constantine is not the only poet of his age to be able to handle the more congenial iambic (or rather dodecasyllable) so much more satisfactorily than the hexameter.[10] *AP* xv. 17, again iambics, on a picture of the Theotokos, is an altogether—indeed unexpectedly—superior example of his art:

εἰ ζωγραφεῖν τις ἤθελέν σε, Παρθένε,
ἄστρων ἐδεῖτο μᾶλλον ἀντὶ χρωμάτων,
ἵν' ἐγράφης φωστῆρσιν, ὡς φωτὸς πύλη·
ἀλλ' οὐχ ὑπείκει ταῦτα τοῖς βροτῶν λόγοις·
ἃ δ' οὖν φύσις παρέσχε καὶ γραφῆς νόμος,
τούτοις παρ' ἡμῶν ἱστορῇ τε καὶ γράφῃ.

It is less a description of a particular picture than a development of a conceit woven round a *topos* of the genre (the Virgin as the 'gate of light' who should be depicted with stars rather than colours), but none the less an elegant and pleasing poem. Though it is the sort of thing that could have been written at any time or place, not necessarily for inscription, it is perhaps worth suggesting the possibility that it was in fact inspired by a painting or mosaic of the Theotokos in the same church at Lindos.

These are the only poems ascribed to Constantine in *AP* xv, but there is one other that we may be justified in connecting with him: no. 11, a much earlier dedication describing how the priest Aglochartos planted olive trees round a temple of Athene, 'on the castron of Lindos', as the lemma says—quite correctly too, since

---

[9] Cf. *Athenaeum* xlv (1967), 145.
[10] Cf. *GRBS* xi (1970), 344; the fluent hexameter epitaph of the Synkellos Michael (below, p. 319) is quite exceptional.

the epigram (plus four others) is still to be read there today.[11] It
does not appear in any earlier anthology, and M. Rubensohn long
ago saw that, especially in the light of its immediate context in *AP*,
the most likely person to have transcribed such an out-of-the-way
inscription is the only Byzantine literary man from Lindos we
happen to know of, Constantine the Rhodian.[12]

Rubensohn, however, taking it for granted that *AP* xv was
Cephalan, supposed that Constantine gave it to Cephalas. But
what we shall see to be the crucial poem, xv. 15, was written *after*
the appearance of Cephalas. A simpler possibility suggests itself:
perhaps Constantine himself is the compiler of the collection.

It should be observed in this connection that xv. 15 is ascribed,
in the hand of J (who is writing text, ascriptions, and lemmata
here), τοῦ ταπεινοῦ Κωνσταντίνου τοῦ ʽΡοδίου. Now ταπεινός,
'humble' is a common enough epithet in Byzantine literary ascriptions—but invariably when an author is signing his *own* work.[13] We
may compare mock modest first person formulas such as ἡ ἐμὴ
ταπεινότης in letters.[14] This is the only self-ascription in the whole
of *AP*, and Constantine is the latest dateable poet to appear in *AP*.

But if Constantine is the redactor of at any rate this part of *AP*
xv, what is his relationship to J, undoubtedly the redactor of *AP* as
we have it? J's work on the manuscript has been assigned a date
perhaps a little before 950 (cf. p. 116). All we can say about the
latter stages of Constantine's career is that his ecphrasis may have
been as late as 944 (though could have been as early as 931); he
need not have been more than 70 by 950. If J was a pupil of
Cephalas (as argued above, p. 110), he can hardly have been much
younger by then. So J and Constantine must have been fairly close
contemporaries.

It might therefore seem perfectly reasonable in itself to assume
that J used an anthology compiled by Constantine. But there are

[11] *IG* xii. 1. 783, 'in arcis clivo qui occidentem versus spectat supra oppidum
hodiernum . . . rupi incisum'; cf. too ibid. 779–82, other poems by the same
Aglochartos or his poet inscribed on other rocks in the area.

[12] *Berl. Phil. Woch.* xiii (1893), 1661.

[13] K. Krumbacher, 'Die Akrostichis in der griech. Kirchenpoesie', *Sitz.-Ber. der
Bay. Akad. d. Wiss.*, Philos.-Philol. Kl. 1903, 642; the epithet often (though not
invariably) implies that the writer is a monk.

[14] L. Dinneen, *Titles of Address in Christian Greek Epistolography* (Diss. Washington 1929), 80; see also the lexica of Lampe and Sophocles s.vv. The index to the
Jenkins–Westerink edition (p. 318 n. 44 below) shows that Nicholas Mysticus used
ταπεινο- words more than seventy times in his letters, invariably referring to
himself. For many more examples see Darrouzès' *Épistoliers byzantins du Xᵉ siècle*
(1960), 422.

difficulties. In view of the attention J accorded Gregory's epigraphic finds, we might have expected Constantine to be awarded some credit for xv. 11 (the poem copied on the acropolis of Lindos), if not for more of the collection. Yet (as we have seen) *AP* xv has no overall title, ascription, or introduction. The only mention of Constantine is contained in the self-ascription to xv. 15. This is the more surprising in that Constantine was apparently still alive when J was writing. Elsewhere when referring to contemporaries J is always careful to add τοῦ μακαρίου or μακαρίτου after the names of those who had recently died, most relevantly in his ascriptions to the two poems that immediately precede xv. 15, xv. 13 to 'the late Constantine the Sicilian', and xv. 14 to 'the late Theophanes' (on whose dates see further below).

The key is provided by a closer study of xv. 15. It has every appearance of being a genuine inscriptional epigram; its modest purpose is to convey the requisite information about the person of the dedicator and the occasion of the dedication. This information (following a well-established classical tradition) is cast in the form of a speech by the dedicated object (Κωνσταντῖνος ... με ... ἔτευξεν), a crucifix. It was presumably written to be inscribed on the crucifix itself, or more probably its base. Yet it can scarcely have been copied from the crucifix in its present form. No editor has hesitated to delete l. 6. It is certainly superfluous (and metrically defective), but how did it come to get there? There are a variety of reasons why scribes and editors interpolate lines in poems of some antiquity or consequence, but why should anyone have taken it into his head to interpolate a manifestly superfluous and unmetrical line in a very inferior run-of-the-mill inscriptional epigram by a living poet?

The answer to this question at least is simple enough if we attend to the punctuation of *AP* itself, which no editor has recorded. The poem originally ended with l. 6; its last word is followed by the colophon with which J invariably indicates the conclusion of a poem, a cross with a dot in each corner followed by a dash (✳ —). It is with this conclusion (to his shame) that we must presume Constantine had the poem engraved on his crucifix. But modern editors were anticipated in their recognition of its shortcomings. It is unmistakably marked for deletion with J's usual sign in the left hand margin, and the metrically flawless l. 7, followed by a repetition of the colophon, was clearly intended to replace it (see the frontispiece).

But who was responsible for the deletion and the new last line? If Constantine, then we should have to suppose that J failed to perceive and execute the instructions in his exemplar and copied out both versions—together with the now inappropriate self-ascription. J is not usually so unalert. If J, it would be unusually high-handed treatment of another's work, nor is he elsewhere so anxious to palliate the inelegancies of others (see below for his treatment of the unhappy Cometas).

I suggest a very simple solution: J *is* Constantine the Rhodian. What happened here is that, when recopying in his old age this poem of his youth, he felt dissatisfied with its original conclusion, marked the line for deletion, and there and then wrote l. 7 to take its place.

Three other points might be made. First, of the six technopaegnia included in *AP* xv, the last and longest, the *Egg* (27), is ascribed by J to 'Besantinus the Rhodian', though in a subscription at the end, after repeating 'Besantinus the Rhodian' he adds 'or Dosiadas, or Simmias; both Rhodians'. On the evidence of our other witnesses to the technopaignia Simmias is the most likely name,[15] but what is relevant here is the interest shown in Rhodes. This is the only reference to the native land of the otherwise unknown Dosiadas (author of xv. 26).

Second, the aside about J's uncle quoted apropos *AP* vii. 348 (p. 113 above). Over and above the no doubt genuine parallelism of 'mentality and style' between Timocreon and J's uncle, was it not the fact that Timocreon was a Rhodian (as J himself had already noted in his lemma proper) that put the idea in his head?

Third, there is J's list of recent and contemporary poets in *AP* xv in his index: Arethas, Anastasius, Ignatius, Constantine, and Theophanes. There are three omissions (the despised Cometas perhaps deliberate), but it is surprising to find no specific mention of so prominent a living contemporary as Constantine the Rhodian. The Constantine named, to judge from his juxtaposition with Theophanes, is the Sicilian (cf. xv. 13–14).

The first two indications are trifling enough in themselves, of course, but the third is perhaps a real problem, neatly enough solved if J is Constantine. *AP* was not a finished work destined to bring its redactor credit through publication. It was his own personal copy of Cephalas with an appendix of related material

---

[15] A. S. F. Gow, *Theocritus* ii^2 (1952), 552.

assembled from here and there. This is why it is not put together in a more orderly form under a proper title. There was no call for J to place his own name at the head of personal jottings, though when actually quoting his own poems he naturally used a self-ascriptive formula, thereby quite incidentally revealing his identity. Byzantine literary men did not normally sign their books. Arethas is unusual in this respect. We would give much to know the name of the owner and annotator of the so-called Paris Plato corpus, perhaps a contemporary of J.[16]

III. THE OTHER CONTRIBUTORS TO *AP* XV

Immediately preceding Constantine's three poems stand one each by Constantine the Sicilian (xv. 13) and Theophanes (xv. 14), both described as 'the late' (τοῦ μακαρίου).[17] As elsewhere the presumption is that both were men known to the compiler (or to J, if they are not one and the same person) who had only recently died.

Unfortunately, we have no firm dates for either. All that can be said of Constantine the Sicilian, if we take away from him the attacks on Leo the philosopher published by Matranga, is that his erotic ode is probably post-Cephalan (above, Ch. X). There are two ninth-century poets called Theophanes, both hymnographers: the prolific Theophanes Graptos, who lived from c.775 to 845,[18] and may therefore be excluded from consideration; and Theophanes the Sicilian. The dates of the latter are quite uncertain.[19]

[16] On whom see now L. G. Westerink, *The Greek Commentaries on Plato's Phaedo* (1976), 30–1. Like J he too wrote punning dodecasyllables in the margins of his books. There is no chance, however, that he is actually to be identified with J; on the basis of photographs lent me by Professor Westerink I can report that the hand is quite different from J's. Leo Choirosphactes is one possibility, a Platonist and a poet, but certainty is hardly possible 'as long as the relationship between the owner, the scholiast and the revisor has not been firmly established' (Westerink, p. 30).

[17] Buffière, op. cit. n. 1, note complém. ad loc. (p. 107), incredibly takes μακάριος to mean 'canonisé', and on this ground alone identifies Constantine the Sicilian with St Constantine-Cyril, the apostle of the Slavs!

[18] Th. Xydes, *Νέα 'Εστία* lix (1956), 155–60; cf. H.-G. Beck, *Kirche und Theol. Literatur* (1959), 516–17. We may likewise exclude Beckby's suggestion of the chronographer Theophanes, who died in 818 and was a man of no education and small culture (see Cyril Mango, 'Who wrote the Chronicle of Theophanes?' *Zbornik radova Vizant. Instituta* xviii (1978), 11–12).

[19] For all that is known of him, see A. Papadopulos-Kerameus, *BZ* ix (1900), 370–8; S. Petrides, *Échos d'Orient* iv (1900/1), 284–7; M. Thearvic, ibid. vii (1904), 31–4, 164–71; Beck, 602; C. A. Trypanis, *Fourteen Early Byzantine Cantica* (Wien. Byz. Stud. v, 1968), 52.

One of his hymns alludes to a miracle that took place at Mineo in Sicily in 829,[20] which might be thought to point to a mid-ninth rather than early tenth-century *floruit*. And if the Theophanes of *AP* xv. 14 had been, like Constantine the author of 13, known as 'the Sicilian', one might have expected J to add καὶ αὐτοῦ Σικελοῦ or the like to his ascription.[21] More important, Theophanes' only other epigram, the classicizing eroticon xv. 35, though absent from *AP* v, almost certainly stood in Cephalas (Ch. XIII). If so, then we should have another example of a contemporary of Cephalas who was also known to J.

Leo the philosopher (author of xv. 12) died in the 870s. Ignatius (author of xv. 29, 30, 31, and probably 39) is Ignatius the deacon, biographer of the patriarchs Nicephorus and Tarasius, who flourished in the first half of the ninth century. Despite the lack of epithet or ethnic and the existence of other Ignatii, this identification is certain.[22] Matranga published from Barb. gr. 310 an ancreontic poem Ἰγνατίου διακόνου γραμματικοῦ εἰς Παῦλον τὸν ἴδιον μαθητήν (*Anecd. gr.* ii. 664–7). *AP* xv. 30 is an epitaph from the tomb of a monk Paul who, like the Paul of the anacreontic poem, had died young. Both Leo and Ignatius, then, had been dead three quarters of a century when J began work on *AP*.

Cometas too, author of xv. 36–8, was a figure of an earlier generation, if he was the Cometas who was appointed professor of grammar at the re-established 'University' of Constantinople around the middle of the ninth century. Though to judge from his spirited marginalia, it looks as if J had some personal bias against him; 36–8 describe how Cometas produced a corrected and punctuated edition of both *Iliad* and *Odyssey*, the most explicit being 38:

εὑρὼν Κομητᾶς τὰς Ὁμηρείους βίβλους
ἐφθαρμένας τε κοὐδαμῶς ἐστιγμένας,
στίξας διεσμίλευσα ταύτας ἐντέχνως
τὴν σαπρίαν ῥίψας μὲν ὡς ἀχρηστίαν,
γράψας δ' ἐκαινούργησα τὴν εὐχρηστίαν.
ἐντεῦθεν οἱ γράφοντες οὐκ ἐσφαλμένως
μαθητιῶσιν ὡς ἔοικε μανθάνειν.

I, Cometas, found the books of Homer in a state of ruin and lacking punctuation. I punctuated and polished them according to the rules,

---

[20] Thearvic, op. cit. 168.   [21] See further below on *AP* xv. 35.
[22] See below, p. 331.

throwing away the rubbish as useless waste, and giving them a new usefulness with my script. May those who write without error be eager to learn as they should learn.

Aubreton has argued that Cometas' text was not only the first transliteration of Homer but the first transliteration of a secular text. On this assumption he was a figure of capital importance, nothing less than the pioneer of the first Byzantine Renaissance.[23] Lemerle has rightly rejected so extreme a claim.[24] The emphasis laid on both punctuation and writing certainly suggest that Cometas did transliterate Homer into minuscule, but whether he was the first to do it and whether the result was satisfactory, that is another matter. Note, for example, the ominous boast in l. 4 that he had 'thrown away the rubbish', suggesting a somewhat cavalier attitude to a no doubt venerable uncial manuscript.[25] Was such confidence well founded? Our only other evidence for Cometas' powers is xv. 40, a fifty-seven-line poem on the Resurrection. It is perhaps the single most unmetrical poem in the Anthology; εὐήνορες might be judged a venial slip in the light of current pronunciation, but, not to mention such monstrosities as ἔμπνοῦς, no one who could write οὖσᾱι καί for a dactyl could have had much understanding of the principles of epic correption—poor qualification for a 'restorer' of the text of Homer. The other objection to taking Cometas too seriously is the attitude of J. Against 37 he wrote in the margin:

Κομητᾶ, ταῦτα δυσκόμιστα πάντ᾽ ἔπη.

Against 40 he gave much fuller vent to his feelings (with a different pun in the first line):[26]

---

[23] 'La translittération d'Homère', *Byz.* xxxix (1969), 13–34.

[24] pp. 166–7.

[25] According to Aubreton (op. cit. n. 23, p. 21), this 'rubbish' is not just a reference to the dilapidated state of Cometas' uncial exemplar: 'Ne trouve-t-il pas ces éditions antiques noyées sous un fatras de commentaires, scholies et gloses, qui empêchent la lecture du texte par des non-initiées?' Maybe; but if so, Cometas' edition could not be an ancestor of the earliest extant Byzantine manuscript of Homer, the early tenth-century Venetus A of the Iliad, which is very fully equipped with scholia. Moreover the tone of the passage would imply a contempt for scholiastic learning rather surprising in a Byzantine university professor. For all the obvious importance of Homer throughout Byzantine education we know too little about the history of the text in the ninth century to reach any proper verdict on Cometas' activity. In general see R. Browning, *Viator* viii (1975), 15–33.

[26] Compare the puns on proper names in the dodecasyllabic marginalia in some manuscripts of the 'Paris Plato' corpus (op. cit. n. 16) and in the dodecasyllabic

ἄκοσμα ταῦτα τοῦ Κομητᾶ πάντ᾽ ἔπη.
Κομητά, Θερσίτης μὲν ἦσθα. πῶς δέ γε
Ἀχιλλέως πρόσωπον εἰσέδυς, τάλαν;
ἄπαγε ταῦτα τῆς ἀμούσου καρδίας,
καὶ βάλλε γ᾽ ἐς κόρᾱκας ἢ κύφων᾽ ὕπερ
τὰ κοπρίας γέμοντα σαθρίαν ἔπη.

We may begin by anticipating the traditional assumption that J is merely reproducing the verses of some predecessor. We have already encountered other (if shorter) examples of his apostrophes to the poets of *AP*. In l. 6, though he wrote σαθρίαν, he presumably meant σαπρίαν. σαθρός and σαπρός mean much the same and σαπρός is one of J's favourite words of censure: for example, ἀναίσχυντον καὶ σαπρότατον at p. 93. 18, σαπρὸν καὶ μυσαρόν at p. 433. 2, and note particularly the similar iambic attack (with similar disregard of classical rules of prosody) on Antipater of Sidon's fictitious epitaph on Anacreon *AP* vii. 23:

τὸν σαπρὸν ἄνδρα σαπροῖς ἐπαίνοις στέφεις.

J is obviously picking up Cometas' claim (36. 4) to have stripped the σαπρία from the text of Homer. Cometas' own verses, he retorts, are κοπρίας γέμοντα σαθρίαν. Puzzled by the construction of these words, Buffière made the unmetrical conjecture σαθρᾶς. The answer is provided by J's scholia on p. 93. 8–10, ἀναίσχυντον καὶ σαπρὸν καὶ ὅλον γέμον ἀναιδείαν, and on p. 129, πᾶσαν γέμον ἔρωτος ἀκοσμίαν. J construed γέμω with an accusative, not a genitive; line 6, then, means 'verses full of the rottenness of dung'.

Why such indignation? *AP* xv. 40 is certainly a poor production, but 36–8 are if anything rather better than much of the other ninth- or tenth-century work included in *AP* xv. According to Aubreton, J's (as Aubreton interprets it) unfair and ill-informed attack on Cometas provides further proof of his eleventh-century date for *AP*. For, he argues, if J had been writing 'des environs de 930–980 . . . aurait-on oublié, à l'Université de Constantinople, les titres de gloire d'un de ses membres les plus illustres?' But after two centuries had passed 'le renom de Cométas ait pu s'estomper et disparaître'. On the contrary, the basis of J's criticism is

poems (i. 9, 33–4; ii. 15) prefaced to the medical corpus in the early tenth-century Laur. lxxiv. 7 (H. Schoene, *Apollonius von Kitium* (1896), xii–xiv). Both the poems and the medical corpus (oddly overlooked by both Lemerle and Hunger) deserve to be better known: it was compiled by one Nicetas, of the hospital attached to the Church of the Forty Martyrs.

precisely Cometas' performance as editor of Homer. Aubreton's argument must be stood on its head. It was not through the ignorance of distance that J wrote as he did, but rather out of the animosity of proximity.

The date of the foundation of the 'University' of Bardas in the Magnaura Palace is notoriously uncertain; the latest opinions favour the 840s rather than the 850s.[27] Even if Cometas had been a young man when appointed to his chair, he is not likely to have lived later than *c*.880, perhaps before J was born. But it is likely enough that either Gregory Magister or Cephalas would have known him. The Magnaura Palace was only a stone's throw from the New Church, and a certain rivalry between the two schools would be understandable. It would not be surprising if pupils at the New Church (such as J) had been brought up on the vices rather than the virtues of Cometas' Homer. It was apparently controversial from the first; as even Aubreton recognized, there is a distinctly defensive note in the claim (37. 6) that his labours were for the benefit of 'those who have intelligence'—οἷσιν ἔνεστι νόος. The criticism reflected in J's verses may have been unfair and even malicious; but it was surely *contemporary*. Why should he have felt so strongly about someone of whose work and personality alike (on Aubreton's hypothesis) he was completely ignorant?

AP xv. 28 is a set of fairly respectable hexameters on the crucifixion ascribed to 'Anastasius the Stammerer (τραυλός)'. All Beckby's index of poets has to say on Anastasius is that he 'lebte in byzantinischer Zeit'. We can do a little better than this. From a letter of Arethas we learn that an unnamed person had been criticizing Arethas for using the verb ταλαιπωρεῖν transitively. Arethas in turn made fun of something his critic had written. A helpful marginal scholion explains that the critic was 'Anastasius, then quaestor, known as the stammerer (ᾧ τὸ τραυλὸς γνώρισμα ὑπάρχον)', and that Arethas was mocking an epigram Anastasius had written on a painting of a quadriga above the kathedra of the prefect in the hippodrome (i. 322W). He seems to have been more generally known as Anastasius the quaestor. It is under this name that he is credited with a not contemptible corpus of hymns, mostly in the iambic metre.[28]

---

[27] Lemerle, 160; Speck, 9.
[28] A. Papadopulos-Kerameus, *Viz. vrem.* vii (1900), 55.

In this corpus, embodying an acrostic to a canon of hymns on the Annunciation, is an elegiac quatrain worth quoting as one of the better specimens of the revival of the form:

ἄγγελος οὐρανόθεν πολυήρατον ἄρτι καταπτὰς
παιδοφόρον Μαρίῃ φθέγξατο γηθοσύνην·
ἣ δ' ὑποκυσσαμένη θεὸν ἄμβροτον εἰς φύσιν ἀνδρὸς
παρθενικῷ τοκετῷ κοσμοχαρῶς ἐχάρη.

To Anastasius' quaestorship at least we can attach a date, thanks to a letter he wrote as quaestor from Constantinople to Leo Choirosphactes in Bagdad at the end of 906, expressing admiration of Leo's culture, apprehension at his recent illness, and his hopes for an early return to the capital.[29]

We also possess some iambic lines he wrote on the death of one of Photius' arch-enemies, Metrophanes metropolitan of Smyrna, himself a hymnographer of some distinction.[30] The date of Metrophanes' death is unfortunately not known, but the poem, together with another on the same theme by Leo Choirosphactes, was added after one of Metrophanes' hymns in a manuscript written by his disciple Arsenius in the year 912. Since Metrophanes was in possession of his see at least as early as 857,[31] it may be doubted whether his death was recent in 912, but since Anastasius is described in the title of the poem as protospatharius as well as quaestor, the presumption is that he acquired the title after 906.

There is also something to be won from *Op.* 25 of Arethas, in which the bishop defends himself against a false accusation laid against him by an unnamed person whose wickedness of soul and ugliness of body were symbolized, he claimed, by his stammering (γνώρισμα . . . τὴν τῆς γλώττης τραυλότητα, i. 228. 8 f.W). This hint is presumably meant to be enough to identify the man, and it is certainly tempting, with S. Kougeas, to suppose that he is the one man of the age we know to have been called by precisely this sobriquet.[32] The same surely applies to a poem on a stammerer published by L. Sternbach:[33]

---

[29] G. Kolias, *Leon Choirosphactes: magistre, proconsul et patrice* (Texte u. Forsch. zur byz. u. neugr. phil. 31, Athens 1939), 93.

[30] Published by S. G. Mercati, *BZ* xxx (1929/30), 54 f. = *Coll. Byz.* i (1970), 443 f.

[31] H.-G. Beck, *Kirche und theol. Literatur* (1959), 543–4.

[32] ῾Ο Καισαρείας Ἀρέθας καὶ τὸ ἔργον αὐτοῦ (Athens 1913).

[33] 'Analecta Byzantina', *České museum filologické* vi (1900), 297 f.

ὦ τραυλορῆμον, τραυλεπίτραυλε γνάθε,
τραυλόλαλον, πάντραυλον, ἔντραυλον στόμα,
τραυληγοροῦν ἄναρθρα τρυγόνος τρόπον,
σύριζε, κράζε, τρύζε σὸν τραυλὸν μέλος,
κροῦ κροῦ κεκραγὼς ἐν πρυμνοῖς δένδρων κλάδοις.

The reference to his μέλος in l. 4 clearly suggests that the stammerer is a poet (τραυλὸν presumably implies a criticism of the quality as much as the oral presentation of his poetry). One of Sternbach's three manuscripts preserves the title Λέοντος φιλοσόφου εἰς τραυλὸν μαθητὴν αὐτοῦ. Anastasius can scarcely have been known to Leo the philosopher, last attested alive in 869, but we know that he was acquainted with another poet of that name, Leo Choirosphactes. It is only to be expected that two such near-contemporary homonyms should be confused from time to time, and there can be little doubt that the poem on the stammering poet was written by Leo Choirosphactes about Anastasius the quaestor—presumably before Leo's disgrace and exile in 913. It would not be surprising to find a friend of the Leo Choirosphactes whom Arethas had so bitterly attacked in his *Op.* 21 of 907 attacking Arethas in turn (though if the poem is to be taken seriously, Leo and Anastasius were not always on the best of terms). Arethas' *Op.* 25 was written some time after 921, by when his stammering accuser had evidently died. So it would seem that Anastasius lived till *c*.920.

We come now to Arethas himself, author of xv. 32–4. Arethas lived till *c*.932. Now the original heading to 32, written by B3, reads 'Arethas the deacon'. To this J added 'who also became (γεγονότος δὲ καί) archbishop of Caesarea in Cappadocia'. Arethas was promoted to his archbishopric in 902 or 903,[34] and there is no reason to doubt that the poems were written this early in his career. 32 and 33 commemorate the death of his sister Anna at the age of 23, when their parents were still alive. Arethas was born probably not later than *c*.860; he may have been several years older than his sister, but even so a date before 902/3 seems indicated. Poems 32–3 were written for Anna's tomb, presumably at the family home in Patras. *AP* xv. 23, from the tomb of a nun called Febronia, presumably dates from the same period.

The poems were evidently copied into *AP* (by B3) from some contemporary source (whether the tombs themselves or an early manuscript copy). It was the knowledgeable J who brought the

---

[34] R. J. H. Jenkins, B. Laourdas, C. A. Mango, *BZ* xlvii (1954), 3.

ascription up to date, and the manner in which he did so is instructive. The addition of a title to a name with the formula γεγονώς in contemporary usage, as J. Darrouzès pointed out on the basis of a number of passages in tenth-century epistolographers, means: 'who became but is no longer'. The clearest illustration is the heading to the letters of Alexander of Nicaea: Ἀλεξάνδρου τοῦ γεγονότος μητροπολίτου Νικαίας. As Darrouzès explains: 'L'expression γεγονότος signifie qu'Alexandre *a été* métropolite de Nicée mais qu'il ne l'était plus',[35] the point here being that all these letters were written after Alexander's deposition. So when J made his addition, Arethas was no longer bishop of Caesarea, and since he is not known to have retired or been deposed, no longer alive. On the assumption that he was dead, might the absence of a τοῦ μακαρίου imply that he had not died recently? Practice regarding mention of the recently dead no doubt varied among the Byzantines as it does among us, often depending on how well the dead person was known to the writer. By the date here assumed for *AP* Arethas would have been dead for nearly twenty years, and it may be doubted whether he was personally known to J.

Beneath the *Axe* of Simmias (22) on p. 670 J wrote the following lines, in what may most simply be analysed as the hephthemimeres κατὰ στίχον ($- \overline{UU} - \overline{UU} - \overline{UU} \times$), 'on the book of Marcus':

εἰ λύπης κρατέειν ἐθέλεις,
τήνδε μάκαιραν ἀναπτώσσων
βίβλον ἐπέρχεο ἐνδυκέως,
ἧς ὕπο γνώμην ὀλβίστην
ῥεῖά κεν ὄψεαι ἐσσομένων,
ὄντων ἠδὲ παροιχομένων,
τερπωλήν τε ἀνίην τε
καπνοῦ μηδὲν ἀρειοτέρην.   (23)

It is also transmitted *in situ* in a manuscript of Marcus' *Meditations* (Vat. gr. 1950, fo. 392ᵛ). Now we know that, again while still a deacon, Arethas came across an old manuscript of the *Meditations*, which (as he wrote to Demetrius, metropolitan of Heraclea) he had transcribed (that is to say, presumably, transliterated into minuscule).[36] Maas argued that Byzantines used no metres κατὰ στίχον but hexameters, elegiacs, iambics, and anacreontics after the fifth century, and that the poem was therefore ancient, of the first or

---

[35] *Épistoliers byzantins* (1960), p. 67 n. 1; further examples on p. 402.
[36] See Lemerle, 230–1.

second century at any rate.[37] But we can hardly rule out the possibility of the odd Byzantine experiment, especially at a period when ancient occasional poetry was being rediscovered. Moreover, since an early imperial poet would certainly have elided the first τε in l. 7, Maas was obliged to consider the line defective, and proposed a final ⟨νόει⟩ or ⟨λέγων⟩ to fill it out. But tenth-century poets would not have been troubled by the hiatus; compare, for instance, l. 2 of Arethas' poem on Euclid (to which we shall be returning), πάντα τε ἀτρεκέως (and Cometas, xv. 40. 40). If we leave the first τε unelided, the line scans quite satisfactorily, if clumsily, with a spondee in the third foot (the iota of ἀνίη can be long or short). If Maas had been right, it would be an odd coincidence if, even in its defective state, the line could still be made to scan. There is a similar hiatus in l. 3, typical of ninth- or tenth-century hexameters, especially Arethas'. In view of the probability that Arethas' transliteration is the source of our extant manuscripts of the *Meditations* (including Vat. gr. 1950), I am inclined (with Westerink) to ascribe the poem to Arethas himself).[38] We may compare the poem he composed for and himself wrote in his famous manuscript of Euclid.

Maas thought that Arethas found the poem in his old manu-script of Marcus and passed it on to Cephalas, whom Maas supposed a member of the 'circle' of which Arethas was 'der geistige Führer'. The two men were certainly contemporaries, but if Arethas himself is the author of the poem, then a direct connection between him and either Cephalas (who in any case had nothing to do with *AP* xv) or J/Constantine the Rhodian seems unlikely. For in *AP*, as in Vat. gr. 1950, the poem is left anony-mous. The presumption is that J/Constantine found the poem unattributed (as such book-epigrams usually are) in a manuscript of Marcus—presumably *not* Arethas' own copy, or he might have been expected to make the connection. Note too the fact that 32-4 are all ascribed to Arethas as deacon still, although on the earliest date for xv. 15 (908), *AP* xv was put together when he had been an archbishop for nearly a decade. Constantine and Arethas had more than literature in common; both wrote scurrilous (extant) attacks

[37] *Hermes* xlviii (1913), 297-9 (= *Kl. Schriften* (1973), 137-8).
[38] i, p. xvi. Maas himself had second thoughts when reviewing Farquharson's *Marcus Aurelius* in *JRS* xxxv (1935), 146 (= *Kl. Schriften* (1973), 140).

on Leo Choirosphactes.[39] But there is no evidence for a personal relationship. Arethas had a finger in many literary pies, but there seems little to be said for Maas's conjecture that he was behind the revival of interest in the ancient epigram.

There are no firm conclusions to be drawn from these indications, but a consistent and plausible picture emerges if we assume a date in the 940s for J—and a date not much later for C. It would perhaps be rash to infer that all those styled μακάριος or μακαρίτης by J (or C) outlived Arethas (who died c.932), although the converse does seem to hold; that is to say, all those *not* so styled (including Anastasius the quaestor) certainly died before Arethas. There is no objection to supposing that Theophanes, Constantine the Sicilian, Gregory Magister, Michael Chartophylax, and even Cephalas himself (active in 917) lived into the 930s. So far, then, nothing inconsistent with the hypothesis that J is Constantine the Rhodian.

IV. PLA, PLB, AND *AP* XV

AP xv. 4–8 are two six- and three eight-line epigrams on the tomb of a second-century AD priest called Sacerdos and his wife Severa at Nicaea.[40] None of them appears elsewhere in the Byzantine anthology tradition, nor do they exhibit the sort of textual corruptions one might have expected from a long manuscript transmission. Add to this the fact that the lemma provides exact information about the location of the tomb[41] that could not have been deduced from the epigrams (ἐν Νικαίᾳ πλήσιον τῆς λίμνης ἐν τῷ ὀβελίσκῳ), and it becomes reasonable to guess that they were transcribed direct from the monument by some post-Cephalan collector.

There is of course no means of knowing who this collector might have been, but one possibility does suggest itself. Among the

---

[39] Arethas, *Op.* 21 (i. 200–12W) and Constantine in Matranga, *Anecd. gr.* ii. 624–5.

[40] See L. Robert, *Hellenica* viii (1950), 90; the earthquake mentioned is that of 120, not that of 368 (as supposed, e.g., by W. Peek, *GV* i. 1999; cf. Robert, *Gnomon* 1959, 24).

[41] There is no trace of the obelisk today, nor is it mentioned in any of the early travellers. There is, however, another funerary obelisk of roughly the same period extant at Nicaea, that of Cassius Philiscus: see A. M. Schneider, *Die römischen und byzantinischen Denkmäler von Iznik-Nicaea* (Istanbuler Forsch. 16, 1943), 7, 27, and pls. I, II.

addenda to his Book iv Planudes quotes the following poem (*APl* 281):

οὐ βαλανεῖον ἔην προπάροιθε τὸ νῦν βαλανεῖον,
ἀλλὰ τόπος σκυβάλων, χῶρος ἀποκρίσιος·
νῦν δὲ τὰ τερπνὰ τὰ πᾶσι βοώμενα καὶ χαρίεντα
ἀγλαΐῃ προφέρει· καὶ γὰρ Ἀλέξανδρος,
Νικαέων ἱερεύς, σοφίης ἐρικυδέος ἀστήρ,
τεῦξέ μιν οἰκείοις χρήμασι καὶ δαπάναις.

There can be no doubt that the builder of this bath was Alexander, metropolitan of Nicaea between ?919/25 and *c*.944 and at one stage of his career professor of rhetoric at Constantinople.[42] Once more it is obviously a genuine inscription copied from the monument, which (as we learn from the lemma) was situated at Prainetos, a stopping point on the road from Constantinople to Nicaea. If it was not written by Alexander himself, it was evidently written to his orders and taste. It has been much debated whether Alexander was bishop or professor first. I myself am inclined to agree with Maas that σοφίης ἐρικυδέος ἀστήρ alludes to (and therefore implies the priority of) the chair, but either way the poem is certainly post-Cephalan, perhaps as late as *c*.944. Maas argued that it was modelled on Agathias' poem on the Smyrna lavatory, *AP* ix. 662. This is probable (if not as certain as Maas supposed); if so, then it was presumably in Cephalas that the writer read the poem. Apart from the fashionable spondaic pentameter ending to l. 4,[43] *APl* 281 reveals more of a feel for the classical elegiac metre and a greater familiarity with the conventions of the genre than most ninth- or tenth-century attempts. The signs are that its author had profited from a study of Cephalas. Just the sort of man to collect classical epigrams from monuments in the neighbourhood of Nicaea—and pass them on to a friend who was making an anthology.

How did *APl* 281 reach *APl*? It has so far been assumed that all non-Cephalan material in *APl* was added by Planudes himself. Planudes was a man of exceptionally wide reading, and in general this is a reasonable assumption. But there is another possibility.

If Planudes' sources had followed the usual pattern of post-Cephalan anthologies, we might expect them to have contained the

[42] P. Maas, *Byz.-neugr. Jhb.* iii (1922), 333–6 (= *Kl. Schriften* (1973), 468–72); R. Browning, *Byz.* 24 (1954), 424–7; J. Darrouzès, *Épistoliers byzantins* (1960), 27–32.
[43] See p. 284.

odd post-Cephalan poem, comparing the batch at the end of E or Constantine the Sicilian's erotic ode in S—and of course *AP* xv.

In addition to the poem on Alexander's bath at Prainetos (from Pl*b*), there is another pair of inscriptional epigrams (again from Pl*b*), on a patriarch called Nicholas:

ὃς βασιλεῖς ἐδάμασσε καὶ ἠνορέην κατέπαυσεν
ἀντιπάλων, πατέρων εἵνεκεν εὐνομίης,
οὗτος ὑπὸ σμικρῷ κατάκειται σήματι τῷδε,
ἀρχιερεὺς Χριστοῦ Νικόλεως γεγαώς.
ἀλλ' ἀρετὴ πολύολβος ἐπέπτατο πείρατα κόσμου,
καὶ ψυχὴ μακάρων ἀμφιπολεῖ θαλάμους.
τοίην γὰρ βιοτὴν ποθέεσκεν ἐὼν ἐπὶ γαίης
σῶμα καλὸν πιέσας κυδαλίμοις καμάτοις.   (*APl* 21)

στήλην εὐνομίης καὶ σωφροσύνης ἀνάθημα
εἰκόνα Νικολέω στήσατο Γρηγόριος.   (*APl* 22)

According to Planudes' lemma this man was patriarch of Alexandria. Now apart from the fact that no patriarch of Alexandria called Nicholas happens to stand on record before 1210, it would be surprising if *any* Byzantine patriarch of Alexandria could claim to have 'tamed emperors' (21. 1). Surely it is Nicholas Mysticus, patriarch of Constantinople 901–7 and 912–25, the man who resisted Leo VI's fourth marriage and, indeed, barred the emperor from the doors of Hagia Sophia in 906/7. Nicholas was deposed by Leo but reinstated by (probably) Alexander,[44] and a council of 920 vindicated his stand against Leo's marriage, whereupon he proclaimed himself 'unifier' of the Church. It is surely to this ἕνωσις rather than simply to his orthodoxy in general (so the Loeb translator) that the εὐνομίη of 21. 2 and 22. 1 alludes. Planudes' lemma might be a mistaken expansion of an original lemma abbreviated, (say) εἰς Νικόλαον πατριάρχην, Ἀλεξανδρ(ου), 'on the patriarch Nicholas, *by* Alexander'—not impossibly Alexander of Nicaea, who was a friend of Nicholas. A common link with Alexander might explain why just these poems, 21–2 and 281, were added to Pl*b*. The Gregory who provided the icon (22) could be another friend, Nicholas' correspondent Gregory metropolitan of Ephesus.[45]

---

[44] R. J. H. Jenkins and L. G. Westerink, *Nicholas I Patriarch of Constantinople: Letters* (Washington 1973), xix; cf. I. Ševčenko, *DOP* xxiii/xxiv (1969/70), 200.

[45] Jenkins and Westerink, op. cit. n. 44, p. 594.

Nicholas was buried in his own monastery of Galacrenae. It is there (we may presume) that the two epigrams were inscribed, 22 perhaps beneath his image above the tomb and 21 on the tomb itself (cf. l. 3). It was probably in the ruins of this monastery that was discovered in 1943 a sarcophagus bearing the epitaph (in surprisingly competent Nonnian hexameters) of a certain Michael who had been syncellos of the patriarch Nicholas:[46]

τύμβος ἐγὼ προλέγω βιοτήν, τρόπον, οὔνομα τοῦδε·
σύγκελλο(ς) Μιχαὴλ μοναχό(ς), σοφός, ὄλβιος, ὧδε
ἄχθος ἀπορρίψας βεβαρηότα δεσμὸν ἀλύξας
πόσσιν ἐλαφροτάτοισι διέστιχεν, ἧχι χορεύει
5 πιστότατος θεράπων μεγαλήτορος ἀρχιερῆος
Νικολέω γεγαὼς πινυτόφρονος, ὅστις ἔτευξε
τόνδε νεὼν ὑψίστῳ ἐπουρανίῳ βασιλῆι.

The νεώς which Nicholas built and where Michael was buried must be the Galacrenae. It will be observed that the emphasized words in ll. 5–6 echo l. 4 in *APl* 21—hardly surprising if the two tombs lay side by side in the same monastery.

Then there is *APl* 379 (Pl*a*) on the charioteer Anastasius by 'Thomas the patrician, logothete of the drome'. The chances are high that this is the Thomas who was logothete in 907 and again in 913. This man was son of Constantine the Armenian, *drungarios* of

---

[46] A. M. Schneider, *Arch. Anz. 1944/5* (1949), col. 78; cf. F. Halkin, *Anal. Bolland.* lxxi (1953), 97–8. ἀλύξας, l. 2, is a Nonnian word (Peek, *Lex. zu Nonnos*, 84); with πόσσιν ἐλαφροτάτοισι, l. 3, cf. *Dion.* 28. 278; διέστιχεν in l. 3 is a favourite Nonnian word (Peek, 391); with πινυτόφρονος in l. 5, Peek, 1336. The earliest medieval manuscript of the *Dionysiaca* is Laur. 32. 16 (our L), and before then it is only quoted (anonymously, as in L) by Eustathius and auct. Et. Magn. (testim. in the prefaces of Ludwich and Keydell; cf. too Maas, *Kl. Schriften* (1973), 168). R. Browning has gone so far as to suggest that in L, Planudes had made 'the first and only transliteration into minuscule' (*BICS* vii (1960), 17). But the author of this epitaph surely knew the *Dionysiaca* (whether or not he knew its author's name), and his contemporary Joseph Genesius (mentioned below) quotes from it a number of times (A. Diller, 'Nonnus Dionysiaca in Genesius Regna', *CP* xvi (1951), 176–7). Reference might also be made to Erika Simon's ingenious and elaborate attempt to show that the carvings on the Veroli casket of *c*.1000 were influenced by an illustrated manuscript of the *Dion.* ('Nonnos und das Elfenbeinkästchen aus Veroli', *Jahrb. d. deutsch. arch. Inst.* lxxix (1964), 279–336). Nonnus' *Paraphrase of St John* originally stood in *AP*, which still contains the highly Nonnian Christodorus, John of Gaza, and Paul the Silentiary. I would suggest that the *Dionysiaca* was originally transliterated, together with the *Paraphrase*, in the age of Cephalas, and then largely forgotten in the eleventh and twelfth centuries. Planudes may have rediscovered it, as he did Cephalas' Anthology (though not John of Gaza and Paul, known only from *AP*). See addenda.

the Watch under Michael III, brother of Genesios the magister, and father of Joseph Genesios the historian.[47] He was a correspondent of Leo Choirosphactes (as also was his brother)[48] and of Arethas as well. The exchange between Leo and Genesios *frère* is dated by Kolias to 'fin 906', but it is interesting to note that while Leo's letter is addressed Γενεσίῳ ἀνθυπάτῳ πατρικίῳ (*Ep.* xv), Genesios in his reply (*Ep.* xvi) styles himself μάγιστρος, ἀνθύπατος καὶ πατρίκιος and takes care to congratulate Leo on the recent award of some mark of honour from the emperor. It is clear that Genesios himself had only just been promoted—soon to be followed by his brother. Thomas' letter to Leo (*Ep.* xviii), also dated 'fin 906', is headed just Θωμᾶς πατρίκιος, as is his exchange with Arethas (*Opp.* 15–16), dated by Westerink 'haud multo post m. Febr. a. 907' (i. 178). His first tenure of office as logothete must fall rather later in the year. It was natural that brothers should rise together in the emperor's service; Thomas' letter commends to Leo another kinsman, Procopios the *spatharios*.

Thomas' epitaph on Anastasius must then be later than 907. Early editions of *APl* ascribed the whole of the series *APl* 380–7, iambic epigrams on charioteers, to Thomas. This is an error. Planudes left them anonymous; but they are probably of about the same date.[49]

It is suggestive that the only demonstrably post-Cephalan poems to be found in *APl* date from the second or third decades of the tenth century. Why did Planudes find nothing to add from the eleventh or twelfth centuries, when the epigram was being both more widely and more proficiently cultivated in Byzantine literary circles? I would suggest that Planudes added only classical epigrams to his two main sources; the poems we have been discussing were already present in those sources, which were typical early post-Cephalan anthologies (like E and S), containing a selection of Cephalas' material together with the odd. recent poem that had come the redactor's way.

---

[47] D. A. Miller, *Byzantion* xxxvi (1966), 438 f.; J. B. Bury, *Eastern Roman Empire* (1912), 460; Cameron (1973), p. 189.

[48] Kolias, op. cit. n. 29, 95.

[49] See Cameron (1973), pp. 191–200.

V. J AND THE STRUCTURE OF *AP* XV

AP xv is another post-Cephalan anthology. The difference is that it is not an excerpt from or amplification of Cephalas, but rather a supplement. Such Cephalan poems as it contains (a handful of repetitions from *AP* ix and x and one from *AP* i) serve a rather special function in the structure of the book: they are space-fillers.

The most spectacular feature of *AP* xv, in *AP* itself as in most printed editions, is the technopaegnia. In order that their shape should be fully appreciated, it was obviously desirable that each one should be written on a fresh page, starting at the top. However, unlike the modern printer, the Byzantine scribe was seldom prepared (on aesthetic as much as economic grounds) to leave blank spaces at the bottom of his pages. With one exception, all the duplications in xv (and one other piece) conveniently occupy the blank spaces left by the artful disposition of the technopaegnia on pp. 668–74.

Theocritus' *Syrinx* (xv. 21) and its scholia took up the whole of p. 669, so the problem did not arise till p. 670, where Arethas' poem on Marcus' *Meditations* inappropriately enough fills the space beneath Simmias' *Axe*.[50] On p. 671, either momentarily at a loss for a stopgap or reckoning that he could do better at a second attempt, J filled the space beneath Simmias' *Wings* by writing the poem out again, this time in maiuscule. Besantinus' *Altar* and its scholia took up the whole of p. 672, as Simmias' *Egg* did 674, but the shorter *Altar* of Dosiadas left some 10 lines free at the bottom of p. 673. Here J repeated ix. 197 and 196, both on Marinus' *Life of Proclus*, followed by a line of (presumably) his own composition,

τεχνικοῖς κανόνεσσιν ἐφεσπόμενος τάδ᾽ ἔγραψα.

These 'technical canons' according to which J wrote the line were surely (as Maas saw) the canons of calligraphy. J is explaining why he has repeated these poems in such an inappropriate context.

At first sight this explanation seems not to apply to p. 668, with five repetitions and no figure poem. But the answer may very well be that J wanted to set out his first two figure poems to best advantage on the facing pages 669–70, and did not have quite enough new material to fill up the preceding page.

---

[50] It was Maas who first pointed this out (*Hermes* xlviii (1913), 295 = *Kl. Schr.* [1973], 135).

Where did he find the repeated poems? Presumably in his copy
of Cephalas. The couple of slight variants between the first and
second occurrences of ix. 196–7 are not more than might be
expected from two different scribes (A and J) copying from the
same exemplar. But the following sequence on p. 668 is rather
more of a puzzle:

ix. 400:	on Hypatia, ascribed to Palladas
ix. 180 and 181:	iambic poems by Palladas on Tyche
xv. 18:	anon., on Palamedes' invention of the game of draughts
xv. 19:	anon., iambics on a fatal wedding party
x. 87:	iambic poem by Palladas on Tyche
xv. 20:	anon., iambics on silence
x. 95:	iambic poem by Palladas on duplicity.

Of the five earlier ascribed to Palladas, ix. 400 and ix. 180–1 are
here anonymous. Of the rest, xv. 20 is by implication ascribed to
Palladas, xv. 18 seems to me entirely in his spirit and style, and xv.
19 is a variation on a fictitious epitaph by Palladas (*AP* vii. 610) on
the man who 'stole' his bride and was punished by his house
collapsing during the wedding and killing all the guests; if not by
Palladas it is certainly an imitation of his poem. Whether or not all
eight are actually by Palladas (ix. 400 at least is most probably not)
it looks as if the sequence might at least be characterized as
'Palladan'.

Where then did J find it? Gow supposed that the three 'new'
poems came from his source for *AP* xv and the five repetitions
from a text of Palladas.[51] This seems unnecessarily complicated,
nor is there any evidence for a complete collected edition of
Palladas extant this late. But his note on vii. 339 shows that J did
have a manuscript, separate from the exemplar of *AP*, that
contained some Palladas along with other poets (Ch. IV, end). The
simplest explanation is that J took all eight from this book. The
two occurrences of ix. 400 at least (both in the hand of J) must in
any case derive from different sources: for the first time he wrote
τῶν λόγων εὐμορφία, the second τ. λ. εὐφημία, with the marginal
variant εὐφορβία. If he had been copying from the same exemplar
the second time, or even referred back to the first occurrence in
AP, he could hardly have missed the obviously correct εὐμορφία.

[51] Gow (1958), 61–2.

Indeed, it is not difficult to trace the process of corruption: εὐμορφία corrupted by metathesis to the *vox nihili* εὐφορμία, which was corrected to the closest proper word εὐφορβία, which in turn was emended in the interests of sense (perhaps by J himself) to εὐφημία. Clearly this chain had not even begun in the source from which the first occurrence was copied. Since there is neither evidence nor probability that J had more than one copy of Cephalas, it seems natural to conclude that the second source was this other book we know him to have consulted for at any rate vii. 339.

J may have intended but simply forgotten to add a general ascription to Palladas at the top of the page. On the other hand, to judge from J's statement that vii. 339 stood 'among the epigrams of Palladas' and his guess that it was 'perhaps by Lucian', it looks as if this other book contained sequences of poems by Palladas interspersed with unascribed poems, quite possibly by other poets. In fact a state of affairs remarkably like that which we meet here. There is no way of knowing whether xv. 18–20 are by Palladas or not, but it may not be amiss to say a word or two about ix. 400:

ὅταν βλέπω σε, προσκυνῶ καὶ τοὺς λόγους
τῆς παρθένου τὸν οἶκον ἀστρῷον βλέπων·
εἰς οὐρανὸν γάρ ἐστί σου τὰ πράγματα,
Ὑπατία σεμνή, τῶν λόγων εὐμορφία,
ἄχραντον ἄστρον τῆς σοφῆς παιδεύσεως.

Though here (and in *APl*) anonymous, at their first appearance in *AP* these lines are ascribed to Palladas and said to be addressed to the pagan philosopher Hypatia, murdered by the monks of Alexandria in 415. There are strong grounds for doubting this ascription. In the first place the adulatory tone is quite out of keeping with the characteristically cynical and flippant manner of Palladas. Secondly, though Palladas' prosody is shaky by classical standards,[52] would he have reversed the proper quantities of the last two syllables of Hypatiā̆? More important, on the revised chronology proposed by Sir Maurice Bowra,[53] Palladas would have been 80 by the earliest date (c.400) at which Hypatia, born c.370, could have been thought worthy of such a eulogy. Lastly, and perhaps most important, anyone familiar with Byzantine ecphrastic poetry

[52] Palladas' prosody is treated in detail by A. Franke (1899), 99–100; briefly by Page (1978), 42.
[53] *Proc. Brit. Acad.* xlv (1959), 266–7; cf. *CQ*, NS xv (1965), 219 f.

will at once recognize that it is unquestionably a *Christian* poem.
What is the 'starry house of the Virgin' in l. 2? Hardly Hypatia's
own home in Alexandria; nor her zodiacal sign, as Jacobs quaintly
suggested. Compare the opening of *AP* i. 121:

ἔδει γενέσθαι δευτέραν Θεοῦ πύλην
τῆς Παρθένου τὸν οἶκον ὡς καὶ τὸν τόκον

Even closer is the opening of Theodore the Studite's epigram εἰς
τὸν ναὸν τῆς Θεοτόκου,

τῆς Παρθένου τὸν οἶκον ὁ βλέπων νόει

Line 2 of the Hypatia poem must surely refer to a *church* of the
Virgin Theotokos.[54] For a close parallel to l. 1 from a Byzantine
ecphrastic poem cf. John Mauropus 18. 1 on a picture of St
Nicholas: αὐτὸν, πατέρ, σε προσκυνῶ τε καὶ βλέπω. Literally
hundreds of such pieces end with βλέπω or βλέπων, self-consciously
evoking the relationship of the spectator to the picture.

The poem is undeniably somewhat incoherent, as are many
specimens of the genre, tissues of clichés, but the outline is fairly
clear. The poet is addressing a virgin called Hypatia who was well
known for her religious writings (λόγοι in ll. 1 and 4 and εἰς οὐρανόν
in l. 3) and somehow associated with a church of the Theotokos.
There was a μονὴ τῆς Ὑπατείας in Constantinople,[55] presumably
founded by a saintly lady called Hypatia. I suggest that, like the
more famous Kasia, Hypatia was a nun who wrote religious poetry,
and that this poem described a picture of her in a church of the
Theotokos attached to her monastery.

The first stage in the misattribution was presumably the identification with Hypatia the daughter of Theon.[56] Well before Cephalas' day the poem had apparently been added to the collected works
of Palladas. It appears in a different Palladan context in both *AP* ix
and *AP* xv, in both cases (if I am right) taken from Palladan
sequences, by Cephalas and J respectively. Both J and C (who was
in some doubt about 399) explicitly ascribe it to Palladas on the
first occurrence.

It would thus appear to be pure coincidence that on the second
occurrence it immediately follows Constantine the Rhodian's three

[54] As seen by G. Luck, *HSCP* lxiii (1958), 465.
[55] R. Janin, *Églises et monastères*[2] (1969), 491.
[56] On whom see Alan Cameron and Jacqueline Long, *Barbarians and Politics at
the Court of Arcadius* (Berkeley 1992), ch. ii.

poems on the Virgin and a repetition of *AP* i. 122 on the Virgin and child by Michael Chartophylax, the only repetition that cannot plausibly be connected with the technopaegnia—and the only one that appears in an appropriate context the second time. J probably just forgot that he had already written Michael's poem on p. 63 more than seven hundred pages before[57]—just as he evidently forgot the first time he wrote ix. 400. It is worth adding, however, that ll. 1–2 of Michael's poem are squashed into one line to fit it in at the bottom of p. 667, and the third line is centrally placed beneath them with a double asterisk on each side, as though to serve as a colophon. The implication is that this was intended to be the end of a section.

There seems little doubt that *AP* xv was designed as a supplement to the Cephalan books of *AP*. This is why it is such an ill-assorted collection; all the obvious sources had already been very thoroughly exploited by Cephalas. What it does contain is a few more or less classical (late Roman) epigrams that Cephalas might have included if he had known them (xv. 2–11, 18–20); some ninth- or tenth-century epigrams he would probably not; the technopaegnia, (probably from a manuscript of the Bucolici), not epigrams but by poets such as Theocritus, Simmias, and Besantinus who did write epigrams and feature in Cephalas; the *Anacreontea*, again not epigrams, but an appropriate enough supplement to *AP* v and xi. But it is the repeated Gregorian epitaphia that perhaps best illustrate the purpose of *AP* xv.

From the tenth century on we find a number of manuscripts that carry funerary epigrams by Gregory in varying numbers and combinations.[58] It is tempting to speculate that the revival of interest in Gregory's Christian epigrams is to be traced to the stimulus towards epigrammatic poetry in general provided by the publication of Cephalas. The fullest is the eleventh-century

---

[57] Though if he worked on the second half of the manuscript first (see Ch. VI) we cannot be sure which he actually wrote first.

[58] They have not yet been studied in full. For a useful list see P. Waltz's preface to the Budé edition of *AP* viii. It was also about this time that Gregory's prose works became serious objects of stylistic study and comment, added to the long-standing canons of pagan models (cf. G. L. Kustas, *Studies in Byzantine Rhetoric* (Thessalonica 1973), 21 f.). Another sign of the revived interest in Gregory is the long life of him by Arethas' friend Nicetas Paphlago, recently published by J. J. Rizzo (*The Encomium of Gregory Nazianzen by Nicetas the Paphlagonian* (Subsidia Hagiogr. 58, Brussels 1976)).

Medic. VII. 10, which contains all but one of the poems in *AP* viii and others besides. The next fullest is *AP* (viii) itself, with about 260 (many poems are differently divided in different manuscripts). Clark. 12, also of the tenth century, has 128. *AP* xv has 68, arranged in the same order as *AP* viii (= viii. 2, 5–11*b*, 76, 80, 83–5*b*, 105–27, 131–48, 150–8, 161–5). So the second batch in *AP* would seem to be a selection from the same selection as *AP* viii, though not from the same copy, since there are too many textual differences. Here at least then we do find J having a separate exemplar from A (though interestingly enough he seems not to have used it when revising *AP* viii).

Now it has already been pointed out that J would hardly have wasted so much time and paper copying these sixty-eight epigrams if he had realized that all of them and more already stood in *AP* viii. It follows that he did not expect to find any among the Cephalan epitaphia that he gave, unread, to his scribe A (see p. 108). On the contrary, he thought that Gregory's (more or less) classicizing epigrams would make a suitable supplement to the Cephalan epitaphia—not realizing at the time that the same thought had already occurred to the man responsible for his own exemplar of Cephalas.

VI. CONCLUSION

We have already seen that the lemma to xv. 15 and the provenance of xv. 11 point to the compiler of at any rate the epigrammatic portion of *AP* xv being Constantine the Rhodian (pp. 304–6). We have now seen that various aspects of the layout of the book in *AP*, the way J matches poems to pages, inserts space fillers and (in particular) his addition of the Gregoriana, all conspire to suggest that the compiler is J. Thus there are excellent reasons of logic and economy for identifying J and Constantine quite independently of the grounds advanced above.

Indeed nothing we know of either man is opposed to the identification. Several further points of contact between them can be added.

Both had a taste for writing invective in verse, and though Constantine's iambics in *AP* xv (pp. 302–3) are faultlessly 'classical' in their prosody, his ecphrasis of the Holy Apostles contains hundreds of 'false' quantities, just like J's lampoons on Cometas.

The principal contents of *AP*—apart from Cephalas—are the poems of Paul the Silentiary and John of Gaza, elaborate verse ecphraseis of works of Byzantine art and architecture. *AP* is in fact our only source for these poems, where they are copied in J's own hand.[59] The next example of the genre to have come down to us, almost certainly the first to be written on that scale since those swan-songs of the age of Justinian, is Constantine's poem on the Holy Apostles. There can be little doubt that Constantine knew Paul's poem. His description of the different marbles in the Holy Apostles (636–74) is clearly influenced by Paul's description of the marbles in Hagia Sophia (617–46).[60] It was only natural that he should want his own copy.

In the course of his poem Constantine makes it clear that, as a good Christian, he despised pagan works of art as the vain errors of the 'hellenes' (cf. τοίαις πλάναισιν Ἑλλάδος μωρὸν γένος / ἐξηπατεῖτο) just as J put Christian before pagan epigrams in *AP* i, to spite the 'hellenes' (p. 247). Such a limited and condescending appreciation of classical literature and art is by no means unknown to what P. Lemerle has recently called 'le premier humanisme byzantin': the bigoted invectives which fill the margins of Arethas' books (often paralleled by J's in *AP*) are another good illustration. But there is a more precise concordance in Constantine's contemptuous reference to the Artemision of Ephesus (128 f.), which evoked a similar remark from J, who had probably been there in person (see p. 155).[61]

---

[59] Except for the end of John's poem, finished off by A2.

[60] T. Reinach, *RÉG* ix (1896), 98.

[61] So the parallel with the 'renaissance' in Byzantine art that art historians postulate at this period is not nearly as close as (for example) Kurt Weitzmann assumed in his well-known essay 'The Character and Intellectual Origins of the Macedonian Renaissance', reprinted in *Studies in Classical and Byzantine Manuscript Illumination* (1971), 176–223: 'The artistic accomplishment of the Macedonian Renaissance consisted not only in the precise copying . . . of ancient art works' but was also characterized by the desire 'to unite the ancient physical world with Christian unworldliness and to bring the classical idea of beauty into harmony with Christian transcendentalism' (221–3). In the field of literature there is little evidence for this unqualified admiration for classical work that Weitzmann assumes in the field of art. The analogy between the art and literature of the age that he develops at such length breaks down because, perhaps misled by the very word renaissance, he saw as a revival of classical literature what was in fact a revival of classical *learning*. As A. Kazhdan remarked, 'Das Wort Renaissance passt für diese Epoche gar nicht, es war vielmehr die Zeit der Sammlung, des Ordnens, des Enzyklopädismus' ('Der Mensch in der byz. Literaturgeschichte', *JÖB* xxviii (1979), 19). Whether there really was a sudden and deliberate 'return to excellent, very early sources' (Weitzmann, p. 203) in book illumination under Leo VI and

If J is indeed Constantine the Rhodian, then we can add one or two details to Constantine's biography. We can say, for example, that he lived into (probably) the late 940s, after the deposition of Romanus Lecapenus in 944. We can also say that he had a bibulous, greedy, and slanderous uncle—the latter quality at least inherited by Constantine. More importantly, however, we can fill out our picture of his knowledge of classical and late antique poetry as for no other figure of the age.[62]

Constantine VII must remain uncertain at least until the relevant manuscripts can be assigned a secure date. Anthony Cutler's recent suggestion that ancient gems were imitated by Macedonian artists ("The mythological bowl in the Treasury of San Marco at Venice', *Near Eastern Numismatics, Iconography, Epigraphy and History: Studies in Honor of George C. Miles* (1974), 235–54) is more in keeping with the antiquarian, collector's ethos of the age. Compare too now the verdict of Cyril Mango: 'Pseudo-classical rather than classical, the illuminated manuscripts of the Macedonian Renaissance reflect the artificial and anaemic antiquarianism of court circles' (*Byzantium: the Empire of New Rome* (1980), 273); see too C. Walter, 'Expressionism and Hellenism', *RÉB* 42 (1984), 265–87.

[62] See further addenda.

XVI

Conclusion

No one has yet written the history of the Byzantine epigram[1] or of the classical epigram at Byzantium, nor is it my purpose or within my competence to do either here. But it may be a helpful start to indicate the role played by the anthology of Cephalas in both.

The *Cycle* of Agathias represents the swan-song of the classicizing elegiac epigram. A few competent elegiacs continued to be written down to the end of the sixth century, but by the beginning of the seventh the pattern of the Byzantium epigram for centuries to come had been firmly established by George of Pisidia: anything from two to a dozen or more iambic (dodecasyllabic) lines on a religious theme.[2]

The genre reached such heights as it was to attain at the turn of the eighth and ninth centuries in Theodore the Studite (759–826).[3] Its practitioners were often prominent ecclesiastics—for example, the patriarchs Methodius (843–7) and Ignatius (847–58)[4]—and show no familiarity with classical themes and models (of which they strongly disapproved). At a literary level, of course, this need not be at all a bad thing. Indeed, the strength of Theodore's poetry lies precisely in the fact (as Trypanis has put it) that 'there, at last,

---

[1] There is a brief sketch in F. Dölger, *Die byzantinische Dichtung in der Reinsprache* (Berlin 1948), 23–7 (inaccurate on the earlier period), and see too C. A. Trypanis, *Medieval and Modern Greek Poetry* (Oxford 1951), xx–xxiii; and especially now H. Hunger (1978), ii. 165–73, 180.

[2] George's epigrams were published by L. Sternbach, *Wien. Stud.* xiv (1892), 51–68; there is a useful survey of its themes, with bibliography, in A. D. Kominis, 'L'epigramma sacro ed i problemi dell'arte epigrammatica bizantina', *Actes du XIIe Congrès Intern. d'Études byzantines* ii (Belgrade 1964), 365–71 and Τὸ ἱερὸν Βυζ. ἐπίγραμμα (Athens 1966). There are countless anonymous epigrams of uncertain date, many usefully published in S. G. Mercati's *Collectanea Byzantina* ii (1970); for the corpus of epigrams to the miniatures in Vatic. Reg. gr. 1 see now T. F. Matthews, *Orient. Christ. Period.* xliii (1977), 94 f. See too V. Laurent, *Les bulles métriques dans la Sigillographie byzantine* (Paris 1932); Hunger II. 165–73; W. Hörandner, *Byz. Forsch.* 12 (1987), 235–47; B. Lavagnini, *DOP* 41 (1987), 339–50.

[3] P. Speck, *Theodoros Studites, Jamben* (Berlin 1968).

[4] Their epigrams were published by Sternbach, *Eos* iv (1898), 150–63.

we meet first-hand experiences and emotions, instead of those
which are conventional and determined by a long and in many
respects remote literary tradition.'[5]

The first sign of a change of direction comes with the romantic
figure of the nun Kasia, whose pertness cost her a throne. In
addition to her religious poetry she wrote a number of secular
epigrams on a variety of mostly moral themes: friendship, envy,
riches, poverty, pretence—and above all stupidity.[6] She was familiar with the Menandrean monostichs and had some knowledge of,
if not classical, at any rate late classicizing epigrams. There are two
clear examples. First A. 71–3 (p. 359 Krumbacher):

εἰ τὸ φέρον σε φέρει, φέρου καὶ φερε·
εἰ δὲ τὸ φέρον σε φέρει καὶ σὺ οὐ φέρεις,
σαυτὸν κακώσεις καὶ τὸ φέρον σε φέρει,

which is an almost verbatim adaptation of a distich attributed in
slightly differing versions to Palladas, the Emperor Julian, and
Basil the Great:

εἰ τὸ φέρον σε φέρει, φέρε καὶ φέρου· εἰ δ' ἀγανακτεῖς,
καὶ σαυτὸν λυπεῖς καὶ τὸ φέρον σε φέρει. (*AP* x. 73).[7]

It has indeed been suggested that she was strongly influenced by
Palladas,[8] but the similarities are probably best explained by their
common dependence on Menandrean sententiae.[9] The second
example is from her attack on the Armenians, C. 37–42, expressly
introduced as the saying of 'some wise man':

εἶπε τις σοφὸς περὶ τούτων εἰκότως·
Ἀρμένιοι φαῦλοι μὲν, κἂν ἀδοξῶσι,

---

[5] Op. cit. n. 1, xxi.
[6] See K. Krumbacher's preface to his edition in *Sitzungsberichte der philos.-
philol. und der histor. Classe der. k. bayer, Akad. d. Wiss.* (1897), iii. 333 f.
[7] Kasia's version is closer to this version than the one attributed to Julian (J.
Bidez and F. Cumont, *Iuliani Epistulae Poematia Leges* (Oxford and Paris 1922),
p. 220 (ὡς ἐθέλει τὸ φέρον σε φέρειν, φέρου).
[8] G. Luck, 'Palladas—Christian or Pagan?', *HSCP* lxiii (1958), 470 n. 71.
[9] This is particularly clear in the case of Kasia's 'Hassgedichte' all beginning
μισῶ (pp. 363 f.Kr) where the Menandrean models are quoted by Krumbacher,
pp. 342–5. For Palladas' Menandrean imitations cf. J. M. Raines, 'Comedy and the
Comic Poets in the Greek Epigram', *TAPA* lxxvii (1947), 83 f.; his conclusion that
of all the epigrammatists 'the most persistent imitator of Menander is Palladas'
(p. 95) is strikingly borne out by *AP* xi. 286, where ll. 1–2 are actually transmitted
among the *Monosticha* (197 and 609 Jäkel). For some further examples see 'Notes
on Palladas', *CQ* NS xv (1965), 228.

φαυλότεροι δὲ γίνονται δοξασθέντες,
πλουτήσαντες δὲ φαυλότατοι καθόλου,
ὑπερπλουτισθέντες ⟨δὲ⟩ καὶ τιμηθέντες
φαυλεπιφαυλότατοι δείκνυνται πᾶσι.

It has long been seen that this is adapted from *AP* xi. 238 on the Cappadocians:

Καππαδόκαι φαῦλοι μὲν ἀεί, ζώνης δὲ τυχόντες
    φαυλότεροι, κέρδους δ᾽ εἵνεκα φαυλότατοι.
ἢν δ᾽ ἄρα δὶς καὶ τρὶς μεγάλης δράξωνται ἀπήνης,
    δὴ τότε γίνονται φαυλεπιφαυλότατοι.
μή, λίτομαι, βασιλεῦ, μὴ τετράκις, ὄφρα μὴ αὐτὸς
    κόσμος ὀλισθήσῃ καππαδοκιζόμενος.

This poem is clearly an attack on a particular Cappadocian, whose identity would have been obvious to contemporaries from the reference to three (allegedly misused) tenures of high office.[10] The concluding prayer that he should not be given a fourth opportunity is an inversion of the sort of wish expressed in normal honorific epigrams, as for example, in *AP* ix. 696. 2 on Theodorus Teganistes, prefect of Constantinople for the third time in 520:

ἄξιός ἐστι πόλιν καὶ τέτρατον ἡνιοχεῦσαι.

Kasia removed all the particularizing details in her model, thus— typically—transforming a classicizing *pièce d'occasion* into a timeless moralizing ethnic commonplace.

Of the classical epigram proper she had no knowledge—still less of classical technique. She wrote only dodecasyllables (more or less), and was perhaps the first Greek poet to ignore the classical quantities completely.[11]

The first person we know of to have written elegiac poetry again is Ignatius the deacon early in the ninth century.[12] And there is perhaps enough evidence to justify the hypothesis that it was Ignatius who actually revived the metre.

Three specimens have come down to us, all in *AP* xv. First, xv. 29, 'on himself':

[10] I shall be discussing the identity of the subject of this poem elsewhere.

[11] See P. Maas, 'Metrisches zu den Sentenzen der Kassia', *BZ* x (1901), 54–9 (= *Kl. Schriften* [Munich 1973], 420–6), remarkable for a first publication at the age of twenty-one.

[12] For his biography see W. Wolska-Conus, 'De quibusdam Ignatiis', *Travaux et mémoires* iv (1970), 351 f. and P. Speck, *Die Kaiserliche Universität (Byz Archiv* 14, München 1974), 56 n. 3 and 74 f.

'Ιγνάτιος πολλῆσιν ἐν ἀμπλακίῃσι βιώσας
ἔλλιπον ἠδυφαοῦς ἠελίοιο σέλας·
καὶ νῦν ἐς δνοφερὸν κατακεύθομαι ἐνθάδε τύμβον,
οἴμοι, ψυχῇ μου μακρὰ κολαζόμενος·
ἀλλά, κριτά (βροτός εἰμι, σὺ δ' ἄφθιτος ἠδ' ἐλεήμων),
ἵλαθι, ἵλαθί μοι ὄμματι εὐμενέι.

Then xv. 30, lacking a lemma but evidently on the tomb of a certain Paul:

Σῶμα μέν, οὐκ ἀρετὴν ὅδε τύμβος νέρθε κέκευθε
κεδνοῦ Παύλοιο· ὥστε γὰρ ἠελίου
τοῦδέ γ' ἀπαστράπτουσιν ἀριπρεπέες λόγοι αἴγλῃ,
ἠδ' ἀρετῆς κάματοι εὖχος ἔχουσι μέγα.
εἴκοσιν ἐς λυκάβαντας ἰδὲ τρισὶν ἤρκεσε γαίῃ,
ζήσας δ' αὖ λογικῶς ἐσθλὸν ἔδεκτο τέλος.

Lastly, 31, 'on Samuel the deacon of the Great Church':

Ἱερὸς ἐν λαγόνεσσι Σαμουὴλ κεύθεται γαίης
πάντα λιπὼν βιότου, ὅσσα περ εἶχε, θεῷ·
καὶ νῦν εὐσεβέων εἰσέδραμε φαίδιμον αὐλὴν
δόξαν ὑπὲρ μεγάλων ληψόμενος καμάτων.

Now Ignatius' Suda-entry, one of the first for a post sixth-century literary figure, ascribes to him in addition to his biographies of the patriarchs Tarasius and Nicephorus and an iambic poem on the usurper Thomas the Slav, some 'sepulchral elegies' (ἐπιτύμβιοι ἔλεγοι)—among them presumably those quoted above. The implication of this separate listing of such seemingly mundane items is that they are unusual. Then there is Ignatius' own account of his education in the school of the future patriarch Tarasius, where he was 'initiated into the essentials of trimeters, trochaic tetrameters, and anapaests and "heroic" poems' (i.e. hexameters and elegiacs).[13] Study of the classical metres must surely have been exceptional at this period. It may be added that Ignatius also wrote an extant dirge on (presumably) the same Paul in anacreontics (Matranga, ii. 664–7), perhaps the first man since the early seventh century to write this metre too.

Of course, by classical standards some of Ignatius' lines do not scan at all (for example, 29. 6, 30. 2, and 31. 3, where we must certainly reject Jacob's αἴης; there are several similar misunder-

---

[13] *Vita Tarasii*, ed. I. A. Heikel (*Acta Soc. Sci. Fenn.* 17, Helsinki 1899), p. 423, 5 f., with, on the nature of this school, Speck, op. cit. n. 12, p. 52.

standings of the principles of epic correption in tenth-century hexameters). But the language and style is definitely classicizing: πολλῇσιν, ἠελίοιο, Παύλοιο, ἠδὲ, ἰδὲ, λαγόνεσσι.

More technically competent and distinctly less Christian in tone is the work of Leo the Philosopher, who died some time in the 870s. The epic centos already mentioned (Ch. X) are interesting because, though scarcely epigrams, they are erotic.[14] More interesting still is the curious autobiographical poem *AP* xv. 12, in thirteen hexameters, again not a piece with any obvious affinities to ancient epigram as such, but classicizing and fairly correct in style and metre. His main claim to be considered an epigrammatist in at any rate the late antique tradition is the several book epigrams ascribed to him: on Porphyrius (ix. 214); on a *Mechanica* by Cyrinus (ix. 200); on the *Astrologica* of Paul of Alexandria (201); on Theon and Proclus, apparently bound up together in one volume (202); and on the novel of Achilles Tatius (203). The poem on Achilles Tatius is oddly ascribed to 'either Photius the Patriarch or Leo the Philosopher', presumably in fact Leo, given Photius' known disapproval of the book (*Bibl.* cod. 87) and Leo's known (and in that age unusual) interest in erotica. Many other book epigrams certainly or probably derive from this period, such as two or three by Arethas (pp. 288 and 315), those on the *Tactica* of Urbicius (p. 149), and probably the poem on Apollodorus' *Bibliotheca* quoted by Photius (*Bibl.* p. 142*b*); doubtless also many of the anonymous epigrams in the Anthology and in extant manuscripts, though it is often impossible to decide on stylistic and metrical grounds alone whether such a poem is late antique or Byzantine, so fossilized is the genre. Most of the specimens attributed to Leo are in Byzantine dodecasyllables, none in elegiacs, and only two in hexameters (ix. 200–1). None the less, he is the only writer of the age to whom such pieces are ascribed by name, and it seems likely that he played a major role in reviving this particular subspecies of the ancient epigram.

It will be remembered that a pupil of Leo's called Constantine who later fell under the influence of Photius bitterly reproaches Leo, in elegiacs full of classical motifs, for introducing him to the snares of pagan poetry (pp. 246–8). The role of Leo in the revival

---

[14] It was perhaps Leo who wrote the two parallel erotic centos *AP* ix. 381 and *ABV* 7 (p. 172 above), both now anonymous. On Leo and his epigrams, see now L. G. Westerink, *Illinois Classical Studies* xi (1986), 193 f.

of classicizing poetry is thus clearly established—as too is the suspicion of pagan ways that it aroused (pp. 246–7). It is surely significant that Leo is the only post seventh-century poet included by Cephalas; the compilers of E and *AP* xv also included pieces by him. Cephalas may well have felt that Ignatius' elegiacs (if he knew them) were too Christian in tone for an anthology of classical and classicizing epigrams.

The first sign of a serious scholarly interest in classical epigrams proper comes with Gregory of Campsa, whose epigraphic forays presumably date from about the 88os. It was probably Gregory who kindled the interest in his younger colleague at the New Church, Constantine Cephalas, who carried out a systematic search among all the available literary sources. Whether or not Gregory in any sense published his epigraphic findings himself, they were incorporated in the massive anthology that Cephalas published perhaps a little before 900. Cephalas did not himself rediscover the classical epigram. He was responding to an interest that had been growing for half a century. The pre-Cephalan 'vasta epigrammatum collectio' postulated in the nineteenth century and now conjured up afresh by Aubreton would have to be placed implausibly early in the century. 900 seems just about the right moment for such a venture.

'La façon dont opéra Képhalas est caractéristique et de Byzance et de son temps: partant des anciens recueils, il constitua le sien, qui tient à la fois d'une encyclopédie épigrammatique et du genre des Excerpta, en disloquant les collections antérieures pour intro-duire un classement rigide par sujet, au mépris de ce que nous appelons l'"histoire littéraire".'[15] Cephalas' thematic categories were certainly crude in design and often careless in execution. But we have seen in Ch. VI that this was not his only method of classification. He frequently incorporated relatively long se-quences from his major sources more or less intact, thereby allowing us—and of course his Byzantine readers—to form a fairly accurate idea of the sophisticated organization of the two *Garlands* and the *Cycle*. And many of his own thematic sequences (notably *AP* x. 1 f.) are so arranged as to permit a good 'diachronic' view of the differing ways a particular motif is treated from hellenistic down to Byzantine times. The result is hardly a satisfying artistic

---

[15] Lemerle, p. 268.

unity, but it is simply not true to suggest that Cephalas was altogether blind to literary considerations.

The nature of his undertaking places him firmly in the encyclo-paedic movement of the age—and his date in its van—but he stands apart from it in his concern with the literary and historical as much as the moral and didactic aspect of his material. I give just one illustration. For the Suda, the many hundreds of quotations from epigrams are assigned no more helpful a label than ἐν ἐπιγράμμασιν, and several later anthologies provide few or no ascriptions for individual epigrams. An epigram was an epigram; it did not matter who wrote it or when. Cephalas, on the other hand, as we can see from the ascriptions in *APl*, E, *ABV*, and above all *AP*, enriched by the successive ministrations of J and C, took great pains not only to equip every poem he could with its author's name but where possible to distinguish between homonyms. Indeed, as Gow pointed out, it was presumably Cephalas who added many of the ethnic adjectives attached to authors' names:[16] it was not till the two *Garlands* were combined that there was any danger of (for instance) Antipater of Sidon being confused with Antipater of Thessalonica. The fact that (inevitably) he sometimes does confuse them is less important than his evident conviction that it mattered to distinguish them. If Cephalas had shared the incurious and unhistorical attitude of the compiler of the Suda, what would literary historians have been able to make of the thousands of unidentifiable and undatable epigrams he had preserved for their tantalization?

Cephalas' success was immediate and overwhelming. In an age when books were few and expensive[17] it is remarkable how many different early copies can still be identified besides the one that has come down to us, *AP* (1). First there is *AP*'s source (2), which cannot have been Cephalas' autograph because of the numerous additions and corrections C was able to import from the copy of Michael Chartophylax (3), which *was* taken from Cephalas' auto-graph. The source of the Suda (4), though closely similar to *AP* (at least up to vii) was not either *AP* itself or Michael Chartophylax (see Ch. XII). Then there are X (5) and Z (6), the ultimate (if not immediate) sources of L and *ABV*, two more versions evidently

---

[16] *The Greek Anthology* (1958), 18 f.
[17] N. G. Wilson, 'Books and Readers in Byzantium', in *Byzantine Books and Bookmen* (Dumbarton Oaks 1975), 3–4; cf. C. Mango, ibid. 38–9.

similar to though not identical with *AP*. (Obviously it is possible that *X* is identical with *Z*; and that one or the other (if they are not identical) was Michael's copy or the source of *AP* or the Suda; but this would hardly be a safe assumption.) Pl*a* and Pl*b* (7 and 8), the two sources of *APl*, cannot have been *AP* or the source of the Suda or L, and though it was suggested above that one of them might have been *Z* (the source of *ABV*), this is no more than a guess. Another very early redaction we have identified is the one used by Arethas (9); where we are able to compare, it was clearly not identical with at any rate *AP*, Michael, Pl*a*, or Pl*b*. Nor is it likely that the copies used by the emperor Constantine VII and his excerptors (10) or the exile Nicetas Magister (11) were identical either with each other or with any of the foregoing. Lastly, there are the early epitomes E (12), from the lifetime of Leo VI, and S (13), perhaps not much later, both containing poems we have seen reason to suppose Cephalan not known from any other version; neither derives from *AP*, Pl*a*, or Pl*b*, and though we cannot rule out the others listed above, the chances are that at least one further early copy of Cephalas (14) lies behind them.

We have in addition compiled an impressive list of early tenth-century literary men who actually wrote hexameter or elegiac epigrams, in some cases demonstrably under the influence of poems included by Cephalas: Alexander of Nicaea, Anastasius the quaestor, Arethas, Constantine the Rhodian, Constantine the Sicilian, the patriarch Nicholas' friend Gregory (? of Corinth), Theophanes, Thomas the patrician, Euphemius' friend the compiler of E, an anonymous military writer in the reign of Leo VI, and other anonymous writers of book epigrams. Thomas and Anastasius take us into the circle of Leo Choirosphactes, all of whose extant poems are in iambics or anacreontics[18] (not necessarily implying any coolness to the classicizing vogue, since the one poem each we have from Michael Chartophylax (*AP* i. 122) and Cephalas (v. 1) is likewise in iambics). Cyriacus, Metropolitan of Chonai early in the tenth century, seems to quote *AP* ix. 401. 3 by Palladas in a letter.[19] The quotations in Nicetas have been discussed earlier.

---

[18] To the list compiled by G. Kolias, *Léon Choirosphactès* (Athens 1939), 71–3, 131–3, add the epitaph on Metrophanes quoted above, p. 312.

[19] Text in G. Karlsson, *Idéologie et cérémonial dans l'épistolographie byzantine* (Uppsala 1962), 89; cf. 93.

But by the middle of the tenth century this enthusiasm for the classical epigram seems to be on the wane. The epigrammatists of the later tenth and eleventh centuries, John Geometres, John Mauropus, and Christopher of Mytilene, continue to write a fair number of poems in hexameters and elegiacs, but they are less classical in subject-matter, treatment, and style than has sometimes been supposed. At a technical level their versification marks little advance on the early tenth century and it is seldom possible to trace the direct influence of any particular classical model.

Take poem 16 of John Geometres (*PG* cvi. 917), evidently written for a copy of Simplicius' commentary on Aristotle's *Categories*:

Σιμπλίκιος μέγ᾽ ἄεισμα κατηγορίαισι φαάνθη,
ἐκ δ᾽ ὁ κατηγορίας λῦσεν Ἀριστοτέλους.

Compare too l. 3 of his third hymn on the Theotokos (*PG* cvi. 860),

Χαῖρε, Κόρη, μέγ᾽ ἄεισμα.

ἄεισμα is an exceptionally rare word, and at this position in the line the student of hellenistic poetry will at once think of Callimachus' famous epigram on another writer, Aratus,

Ἡσιόδου τό τ᾽ ἄεισμα καὶ ὁ τρόπος
(*AP* ix. 507).

But what John had in mind was an earlier echo (if echo it be) of Callimachus. Compare (noting the decisive μέγα), Gregory Nazianzen, *AP* viii. 9. 1,

Καισαρέων μέγ᾽ ἄεισμα, φαάντατε, ὦ Βασίλειε

and viii. 113. 1,

Καππαδοκῶν μέγ᾽ ἄεισμα, φαάντατε Μαρτινιανέ.

It was from Gregory that John got the idea of using ἄεισμα in the sense 'glory' rather than just 'song' (not realizing this T. W. Lumb made the neat but disastrous conjecture μέγα σῆμα).[20] F. Scheidweiler has already pointed out a number of echoes of Gregory's poetry in John,[21] to which these may now be added. Note too poem 15, transcribed by successive editors without a word of comment:

[20] *Notes on the Greek Anthology* (London 1920), 130.
[21] *BZ* xlv (1952), 277 f.

ἔνθεος ἦν ὁ Σύρος, πολυγράμματος ἦν δὲ ὁ Φοῖνιξ,
Καππαδόκης δ᾽ ἄμφω καὶ πλέον ἀμφοτέροις.

This is a versification of a pseudo-pythian 'oracle' quoted by late
neoplatonists, ἔνθους ὁ Σύρος, πολυμαθὴς ὁ Φοῖνιξ.[22] The allusion is to
the great divide in later neoplatonism, typified by the polymath
Porphyry from Tyre (the 'Phoenician') and the mystic Iamblichus
from Coele Syria.[23] The 'Cappadocian' is Gregory Nazianzen, who
(so John asserts) excels both in both areas. We have already seen
how the revival of interest in classical epigrams carried the
epigrams of Gregory back into circulation, and it is hardly surprising that ultimately they proved more to the Byzantine taste.[24]

It is interesting to notice that it is in his prose *Progymnasmata*
rather than in his epigrams that we find John actually quoting from
hellenistic epigrams: Antipater of Sidon (vii. 2), Asclepiades or
Archelaus (*APl* 120), and (possibly) Zonas (ix. 312).[25] In his
poems, where we can point to a specific earlier model, where it is
not Gregory it is usually some other late antique poem. For
example, the δῆμος φιλοκέρτομος of the hippodrome in *Ep.* 46
probably derives from the sixth-century charioteer epigram *APl*
366. 5. And especially revealing is *Ep.* 142 (*PG* cvi. 964), 'On life':

τὴν ἀρετὴν χθὲς εἶδον ἐν μέσῃ πόλει,
μελαμφοροῦσαν καὶ κατηφείας ὅλην·
Τί δ᾽, ἠρόμην, πέπονθας; ἡ δέ· Νῦν ἔγνως
τόλμα, φρόνησις, γνῶσις ἐν ταῖς γωνίαις,
ἄγνοια δ᾽ ἄρχει καὶ μέθη καὶ δειλία.

It has not been noticed that this is a free adaptation of Palladas *AP*
xi. 386:

στυγνὴν τὴν Νίκην τις ἰδὼν κατὰ τὴν πόλιν ἐχθὲς
εἶπε, Θεὰ Νίκη, τίπτε πέπονθας ἄρα;

---

[22] David, *In Isag. prooem.*, p. 92. 4 Busse; Aeneas of Gaza, *Theophrastos*, p. 12. 12
Colonna.

[23] See H. D. Saffrey and L. G. Westerink, *Proclus: Théologie platonicienne* i
(Paris 1968), lix, with n. 3.

[24] I had already reached this conclusion before reading W. Hörandner's general
formulation about the practice of eleventh-century poets: 'On n'aime pas insérer
des citations dans les poésies, et nombre d'auteurs dont les lettres et discours sont
des véritables trésors de citations tendent à s'abstenir dans leurs poésies' (*Travaux
et mémoires* vi (1976), 259). However, my own argument is based less on the absence
of direct citations in Geometres than on its generally quite unclassical character.

[25] A. R. Littlewood, *Progymnasmata of Ioannes Geometres* (Amsterdam 1972), 22.
24, 25. 11; and see also Littlewood in *JÖB* xxix (1980), 133–44.

ἡ δ' ἀποδυρομένη καὶ μεμφομένη κρίσιν εἶπεν·
Οὐκ ἔγνως σὺ μόνος; Πατρικίῳ δέδομαι.
ἦν ἄρα καὶ Νίκη πολυώδυνος, ἣν παρὰ θεσμὸν
Πατρίκιος ναύτης ἥρπασεν ὡς ἄνεμον.

Editors have been unnecessarily puzzled by this poem. There can be little doubt that Patricius is a charioteer;[26] Victory is distressed because he won her by cheating (παρὰ θεσμόν). ἥρπασε νίκην is the Greek equivalent of the stock Latin formula 'eripuit et vicit' of a last-minute victory, and cf. too ἥρπασε νίκην of a narrowly victorious charioteer in Nonnus, *Dion.* x. 424. Like Kasia, John took a whimsical *pièce d'occasion* and turned it into a timeless piece of dodecasyllabic moralizing.

The most technically competent corpus of Byzantine epigrammatic poetry is the *Paradisus*, a sequence of ninety-nine elegiac quatrains on the desert fathers, adapted from the *Apophthegmata patrum*. Half the manuscripts attribute it to the early fifth-century monastic writer Nilus of Ancyra; the other half to Geometres. The joke about cooking on Mount Athos in no. 48 is enough to eliminate Nilus.[27] The poet cannot be earlier than the tenth century. On the other hand he cannot be Geometres either. It is not just that his versification (by which I mean observance of pauses and caesuras as much as prosody) is far above the level of John's. He has a feel for the structure of the classical epigram that is not only missing in Geometres but without parallel in the entire Byzantine age. Consider (taken almost at random) no. 80:

ἄνδρε δύο κατὰ Χριστὸν ἐνήθλεον· εἷς μὲν, ἀγῶνας
θερμοτέρους· ὁ δὲ δὴ δεύτερος ἀργοτέρους.
πρῶτα δὲ οἱ σκήνωσε Θεός. τίνος εἵνεκα; λέξον·
ἦτορ ἁπλοῦν ποθέει Κύριος ἢ καμάτους.

God prefers a simple heart to extravagant feats of asceticism. A Christian theme, but the technique and structure are thoroughly classical. There is nothing remotely like this in John's epigrams.

This poet was certainly familiar with hellenistic and early imperial epigram. For example, no. 30. 4, γνῶθι καιρὸν, ἔφη

---

[26] As I pointed out in *JHS* lxxxiv (1964), 58.
[27] P. Speck, 'Zur Datierung des sogenannten Paradeisos', *BZ* lviii (1965), 333–6. It is curious the way the name Nilus served as a sort of catch-all for ownerless and cast-off Byzantine texts: see *GRBS* xvii (1976), 194–5. But it is not likely that he wrote poetry.

Πιττακὸς Ὑρραδίου, is a patent reminiscence of Callimachus *Ep.* 1 (*AP* vii. 89), read in a version that already contained the corrupt Ὑρραδίου in l. 2 for the misunderstood patronymic Ὑρράδιον.[28] His technique may be nicely illustrated by no. 9:

Ἀρσενίῳ τις ἔφη· σὺ τὸ "μῆνιν ἄειδε" διδάξας
τούτους εἰρωτᾶς τοὺς ἀμαθεῖς τί μαθεῖν;
ἀλλ᾽ ἐγώ, εἰφ᾽ ὁ γέρων, ἔτι δὲ [surely δὴ] νῦν οὐ δεδάηκα
τῶν ἀμαθῶν τούτων οὐδὲ τὸ ἄλφα μόνον.

Arsenius was a professor of grammar, tutor to the sons of Theodosius I, who at the age of forty had given up everything to retire into the desert. There are many anecdotes about him in the *Apophtheg-mata patrum* (*PG* lxv. 78–108), no. 6 of which is clearly the model for this poem: ἀββᾶ Ἀρσένιε, πῶς τοσαύτην παίδευσιν Ῥωμαϊκὴν καὶ Ἑλληνικὴν ἐπιστάμενος, τοῦτον τὸν ἀγροῖκον περὶ τῶν σῶν λογισμῶν ἐρωτᾶς; ὁ δὲ εἶπε πρὸς αὐτόν· τὴν μὲν Ῥωμ. καὶ Ἑλλ. ἐπίσταμαι παίδευσιν, τὸν δὲ ἀλφάβητον τοῦ ἀγροίκου τούτου οὔπω μεμάθηκα. But for the colourless reference to 'Roman and Greek culture' in his source the poet substituted a striking phrase he had borrowed from an earlier schoolmaster, Palladas (Cougny III. 145):

"μῆνιν ἄειδε" μαθὼν καὶ "μῆνιν ἄειδε" διδάξας.

'The later Byzantine writers paid much attention to the epigrams', wrote James Hutton in 1935.[29] I do not myself possess the first-hand knowledge of eleventh- to fourteenth-century literature either to confirm or disprove such a claim; and the detailed research into classical sources on which a balanced verdict could be based has scarcely begun. But the examples which Hutton quotes hardly suffice to prove that copies of Cephalas were in general circulation.[30] The two prime exhibits, John Tzetzes and Nicetas Eugenianos, are not perhaps to be taken as typical representatives of the educated public. The eleven epigrams quoted by Tzetzes are mostly quoted in one or more other sets of scholia and are often devoted to the poet who is the subject of the scholia.[31] It would be going too far to suggest that he did not know Cephalas at all, but

---

[28] And so is to be added to the testimonia collected by Gow and Page, *HE* ii. 205.

[29] Hutton (1935), 7.

[30] Nor is anything relevant quoted by W. Hörandner, 'La poésie profane au XIᵉ siècle et la connaissance des auteurs anciens', *Travaux et mémoires* vi (1976), 245–63.

[31] *AP* vi. 213; vii. 3, 54, 77, 433; ix. 448; xi. 442; xiv. 64; *APl* 92, 115, 120. 3–4.

we may probably assume that it was from the scholiastic tradition that he derived most of his quotations. And though the nineteen epigrams adapted by Nicetas Eugenianos unquestionably derive from a text of Cephalas, none the less they cannot be considered the casual fruits of a wide reading. As pointed out above (p. 129), it is clear that Nicetas rewrote them into his own dodecasyllables one after another from just two or three pages of his Cephalas, in the course of a calculated but very limited search for erotic motifs for his own erotic poem. It might be added that most Byzantine writers who quote epigrams do so for historical rather than literary reasons: for example, ix. 641 and 657 on the Sangarios bridge and the Sophianae palace in Zonaras xiv. 7 and 10 respectively. The most prolific epigrammatist of the age, Theodoros Prodromos, betrays only the slightest acquaintance with the anthology.[33]

Only one even nearly complete copy of Cephalas has come down to us—*AP*. And it is perhaps significant that that copy dates from the 940s, the heyday of Cephalas' popularity. Most if not all the other copies we have identified likewise seem to date from about this period. There is nothing to show that fresh copies continued to be made in later centuries.[32] When Maximus Planudes, the most celebrated scholar of the fourteenth century, decided to make a new anthology of his own, he could not lay his hands on a single copy even as complete as *AP* (Pl*a* and Pl*b* between them contained only 2,400 epigrams as against the 3,700 of *AP*). It has already been suggested that the two abridgements he did find were likewise of the tenth century. It is tantalizing that we do not know more of the man who in the eleventh or twelfth century collated *AP* against E/Σ" and added to it the poems we know as Σ".

Such a decline in popularity might seem surprising in a society that was not conspicuous for rapid changes of literary fashion. But perhaps it is less the success of a book we have been tracing than the personal influence of its author. For Cephalas was not just a

---

[32] We might compare the almost complete loss of the Constantinian historical excerpts, another tenth-century compilation that found few later readers.

[33] He quotes xi. 186 in a prose work (*PG* cxxxiii. 1295), but none of the imitations alleged by W. Hörandner, *Theodoros Prodromos: historische Gedichte* (Wien. Byz. Stud. xi, Vienna 1974), 575, survives critical scrutiny. Some undeniable quotations may have been taken from well-known intermediaries; e.g. Constantine Manasses' quotation of *AP* xi. 237 and Cedrenus' of *APl* 82 may derive from Constantine Porphyrogenitus. Aubreton's claim (*L'Ant. class.* xxxviii (1969), 459 f.) that *AP* xiv. 5, 35, and 58 were actually written by Psellus is quite untenable; see *GRBS* xi (1970), 340 f.

scholar and man of letters; he was a *school-teacher*. And we know from C's note on vii. 429 that he taught his speciality, classical epigrams. J's note on vii. 327 implies that Gregory of Campsa did so too. This surely puts our problem on quite a different footing. No longer do we need to explain the sudden popularity of a book. For a period of perhaps two or three decades while Gregory and Cephalas taught at the New Church, classical epigrams were part of the school curriculum. No longer do we need to suppose that it was pure enthusiasm for classical elegiacs that impelled so many Byzantines of the early tenth century not merely to read and copy them but actually to write in a metre that came so unnaturally to their pens. No doubt it was Gregory and Cephalas who dinned hexameters and pentameters into their heads in the classroom. It should also be borne in mind that, unlike the Planudean Anthology, Cephalas' collection seems not to have been treated as a regular book credited to its compiler's name. Not even in *AP* does Cephalas' name appear in the original book-headings written by A and B—which presumably means that it did not appear in their exemplar either. But for the marginalia of J and C and the colophon of Michael Chartophylax reproduced by C, we should have had no idea that the ur-anthology we should still have been obliged to postulate was the work of Cephalas. Its anonymous state may have encouraged and accelerated the perhaps inevitable process of excerpting and abbreviation that (as represented in E) was already under way before the death of Leo VI.

By contrast, the Planudean Anthology managed permanently to maintain both its name and its integrity, partly no doubt because of the fame of Planudes, partly too because it appeared at a more propitious moment. Not to mention countless sets of excerpts, numerous complete copies were made and continued to be made well down into the sixteenth century,[34] both in the original Planudean and in a slightly later Triclinian redaction.[35] Indeed, until the final publication of *AP* by Jacobs in 1813–17, the Planudean Anthology *was* the Greek Anthology, surely the most celebrated and influential product of Byzantine scholarship. Yet

---

[34] For the excerpts, see Hutton (1935), pp. 33–5, Aubreton, pp. 77 f., Turyn, pp. 426–8, and Appendix IV. For the complete copies, see Hutton, pp. 30–1; Turyn, pp. 429 f.; Mioni (1975), p. 264. For one early reader see V. Tiftixoglu, 'Die griechische Anthologie in zwei Gedichten des Johannes Chortasmenos', *BZ* lxx (1977), 2–21.

[35] See Appendix II.

seldom has such success been won so easily. For what did Planudes do but rearrange and bowdlerize an already abridged copy of the anthology of Cephalas? In all probability Planudes did not even know the name of the original discoverer of his treasures. It was only pupils and contemporaries such as J and C and Michael Chartophylax who were able and eager to preserve the few priceless facts that enable us to set the activity and achievement of Cephalas in their true perspective.

APPENDIX I

Marc. gr. 481 and BM Add. 16409

UNTIL the first proper publication of *AP* in the form of Jacobs's second edition of 1813–17, the anthology of Maximus Planudes (*APl*) was *the* Greek Anthology. And yet during all the period since the *editio princeps* of 1494, not one editor made use of Planudes' own certified autograph copy, fos. 2^r–100^r of Marcianus gr. 481. Philippe d'Orville, whose projected edition of the Anthology was never completed, recognized it as Planudes' autograph in a letter dated 6 April 1728, published by Chardon de la Rochette in 1812 (Hutton, 1946, 281). But his discovery was evidently unknown to F. Dübner, whose first volume appeared in 1864. All readings ascribed to 'Plan' in editions before Stadtmueller (*AP* i–ix. 563, 1894–1906) are merely the readings of late manuscript apographs of *APl* or early printed editions, and this long-established but ill-founded vulgate still occasionally imposes even on editors who have consulted the Marcianus. In particular, it must regrettably be stated that the collation K. Preisendanz supplied for H. Beckby's edition of 1958 (second edition 1967/8), the only complete collation of the Marcianus, perpetuates a large number of these old errors. This serious defect seems not to have been noticed so far. It is in fact because of these errors that Beckby was led to formulate the mistaken view that we shall be discussing in this appendix.

In 1955 Douglas Young drew attention to a manuscript of *APl* in the British Museum (Add. 16409) which was made (he claimed) directly from the Marcianus before Planudes had made his own final revisions (*Parola del Passato* x, 197–214). This manuscript (hereafter Q) has now been read by Beckby for his revised second edition of 1967/8. Beckby, however, while acknowledging that it is indeed a witness to an earlier state of *APl* than the Marcianus (hereafter Pl) as we now possess it, denies that it is a direct apograph. He claims that there are 'several hundred' divergent readings, and prefers to posit at least one intermediary. It would not be without value for future editors to explain why he is wrong.

1. Let us begin with what would appear to be Beckby's strongest piece of evidence, the double appearance in Q of *AP* vii. 502 by Nicaenetus. Here is the poem as given in *AP* and at fo. 37ᵛ of Pl:

'Ηρίον εἰμὶ Βίτωνος, ὁδοιπόρε· εἰ δὲ Τορώνην
λείπων εἰς αὐτὴν ἔρχεαι Ἀμφίπολιν,
εἰπεῖν Νικαγόρᾳ, παίδων ὅτι τὸν μόνον αὐτῷ
Στρυμονίης Ἐρίφων ὤλεσε πανδυσίη.

As would be expected, it appears in the same form in the corresponding place in Q. But then it appears again among the addenda on fo. 101ʳ, between vii. 654 and 506, with a number of variants: l. 1, *Βίωνος* for *Βίτωνος* and ὁδοιπόροι for ὁδοιπόρε; l. 3, ἠνδαγόρῃ (*sic*) for *Νικαγόρα*; l. 4, *Στρυμονίη* for *Στρυμονίης*, δυομένων for πανδυσίη. In themselves, the variants are worthless: ὁδοιπόροι would remove a hiatus, but that is no problem (see Gow and Page on Mnasalces, *HE* 2625 (*AP* vi. 264. 5)). However, where do they come from?

AP vii. 502 has been collated four times in the Marcianus: by Stadtmueller, by Waltz, by Preisendanz, and finally by Gow and Page. Yet no one, apparently, has yet noticed that it appears again there too, on fo. 94ᵛ, between vii. 654 and 502, with exactly the variants offered by Q, right down to the nonsensical ἠνδαγόρῃ.

2. vii. 187 is ascribed in *AP* to Philip—twice, in fact, for it appears again after vii. 344. In Q it is ascribed to Leonidas. In the Marcianus, according to Beckby, it is ascribed to Simonides: indeed, he adds an exclamation mark in brackets, his usual way of indicating that whatever earlier editors (in this case Stadtmueller and Waltz) might say, this is what Planudes wrote. It is of no intrinsic importance, since the Palatine ascription to Philip is almost certainly correct, but nevertheless Planudes, like Q, does definitely ascribe the poem to Leonidas.

3. At *AP* ix. 81. 2 (Crinagoras), Q gives ἑτέρων where *AP* and (according to Stadtmueller and Waltz as well as Beckby) Pl gives ἕτεραι. In fact Pl plainly gives ἑτέρων too (as correctly noted by Gow and Page).

4. Lines 3–4 of a rather feeble epigram (ix. 187) on Menander as given in the Palatinus:

αὐταὶ καὶ Χάριτές σοι ἐδωρήσαντο, Μένανδρε,
στωμύλον εὐτυχίην δράμασιν ἐνθέμεναι.

I cannot say that I am happy with εὐτυχίην, though it is accepted by Stadtmueller and Waltz. Q has εὐστιχίην; Pl εὐστοχίην, according to Waltz and Beckby (who prints it), and Stadtmueller too, though he admits that 'litt. o parum clare nec tamen vox εὐστιχίην exarata est'. I am not so sure, but whether or not Planudes did actually intend εὐστιχίην, it is understandable that the scribe of Q should have thought that he did.

εὐστοχίην is attractive (cf. G. Luck, *Gnomon* xxxiii (1961), 778): it would be used in a meaning not given by *LSJ* (or the new *Supplement*) but borne by εὔστοχος in Ps-Longinus and Dionysius of Halicarnassus (cf. D. A. Russell on Περὶ Ὕψους 34. 2): 'aptness'. Damocharis, writing in the age of Justinian, claims that the face of a painting of Sappho δηλοῖ φαντασίην ἔμπλεον εὐστοχίης, but he perhaps had no very precise notion in mind.

All the same, εὐστιχίη, though not attested at all in such a context, could be right.

5. At vii. 368. 1 (Erycius), where Planudes wrote ἐμή, Q, according to Beckby, has ἐμοί. In fact Q too has ἐμή. It is an outsize and ungainly eta to be sure, but there are many similar on neighbouring pages.

6. *APl* 94. 7 (Archias): θωρήσσεο *AP* and Q, θωρήσσε (*sic*) Pl. The merest of slips, but copied faithfully by the original scribe of Q: for the omicron was added in a different ink by a later hand (quite possibly by Planudes himself: see below)—a fact no doubt invisible in Beckby's photograph.

7. *APl* 251. 1 (anon): πτανῷ Q, πτανῶ Pl, according to Beckby. It is a tiny detail, but the iota subscript is in fact clearly visible in Pl.

8. *APl* 276. 4: κτεινόμεθ' Q, κτείνομεθ' allegedly Pl. An even tinier point, but the accent in Pl is in fact exactly as in Q.

9. *AP* ix. 246. 1: οἰνοπόταισι *AP* and allegedly Pl; οἰνοπότῃσι Q. Once more this is the reading of Pl too.

10. *APl* 47. 2: Πράσινοι Q, Πράσιοι allegedly Pl. In fact Πράσινοι too Pl.

11. *APl* 367. 4: Pl, like Q, has ἀμφέθετο.

12. *APl* 380. 5: Pl, like Q, has ἄνεισιν.

13. Palladas, addressing Τύχη:

> μάνθανε καὶ σὺ φέρειν τὰ σὰ ῥεύματα, καὶ σὺ δίδαξον
> τὰς ἀτυχεῖς πτώσεις, ἃς παρέχεις ἑτέροις   (ix. 182. 3–4)

δίδαξον is obviously unsatisfactory ('learn', not 'teach' is the meaning required), and all editors give the passive form διδάσκου, which is alleged by Waltz, Stadtmueller, and Beckby to be what Planudes wrote. In fact Planudes wrote (what Q copied from him) the same as *AP*: δίδαξον. διδάσκου may be what Palladas wrote (though I am not wholly convinced): but it is only an early conjecture, which Turyn has recently tracked down to its source: the copy in Vat. Barb. gr. 123, a manuscript owned by J. Lascaris, whence it was entered as a correction in Paris. gr. 2891, a manuscript written by Lascaris, and (not surprisingly) printed in his edition of 1494.

14. *APl* 104. 5: πάντας Ἔρως Pl, πάντα σ᾽ Ἔρως Q, subsequently conjectured by Scaliger, and (rightly) the modern vulgate (to the extent that Gow and Page do not indicate that it is not the reading of Pl). Obviously a conjecture in Q—but not of the scribe himself, who dutifully copied the πάντας of his exemplar. The apostrophe is added in the same different ink and later hand (?Planudes') we have already met.

15.

> δορκάδος ἀρτιτόκοιο τιθηνητήριον οὖθαρ
> ἔμπλεον οἰδοῦσα πικρὸς ἔτυψεν ἔχις.   (ix. 1. 1–2)

The calf then suckles the poisoned breast with the result that (l. 6) ἦν ἔπορεν γαστήρ, μαστὸς ἀφεῖλε χάριν. For the both grammatically and metrically unsatisfactory οἰδοῦσα of Pl, *AP* offers the even less promising εἰ δοῦσα. From this Burguière constructed and Waltz printed εἰλύσας, 'enfolding', while Beckby prints Scaliger's οἰδούσης. Both are surely impossible. But whatever the true reading, Q seems to anticipate Scaliger's οἰδούσης. Yet again, however, this is the work of the later hand: the original reading is exactly as in Pl.

16. *APl* 93. 5: Αὐγείαν ἐδάη Pl; Αὐγείας μ᾽ ἐδάη Q, according to Beckby, who prints it. In fact Q has the same as Pl, nor is there any call to doubt the reading (cf. Gow and Page on Philip, *GP* 3088).

17. *AP* ii. 58: Pyrrhus is eager to shake the weapons τὰ μή νύ οἱ ὦπασε τέχνη (i.e., the maker of the statue did not provide him with any). νύ is Stadtmueller's conjecture, based on his (hesitant) decipherment of Pl as μήν. The Palatinus gives μιν, but a negative is required (the poem continues γυμνὸν γάρ μιν ἔτευξεν—whence, incidentally, P's μιν).

Q has μή ῥ. Pl is not easy to make out here, but I should

definitely read μή, with a rho added as an afterthought, no doubt *metri causa*. This would point to τὰ μή οἱ being the original reading in Pl, an unlikely hiatus in so strict a Nonnian poet. F. Baumgarten, *De Christodoro poeta Thebano* (Diss. Bonn 1881), p. 32, could find no parallel, and accepted Jacobs's unlikely τὰ μὴ ἑοῖ. Stadtmueller's νύ finds strong support (as he saw) in Nonnus, *Dion.* xxvi. 155, ἐπεί νύ οἱ, in the same position in the line.

The list of alleged divergences between Q and Pl that can be eliminated by a closer inspection of the two manuscripts could no doubt be extended. Some genuine divergences do remain, it is true, but it would be strange indeed if during the whole course of his work the scribe of Q had made no slip himself nor essayed any correction of what he took to be a slip in his exemplar.

I would suggest that all the outstanding differences are of this nature. First a few minor corrections:

ὦ τῆς ταχίστης ἁρπαγῆς τῆς τοῦ βίου (*AP* xi. 289. 1, Palladas). ὦ Pl, ὦ Q. According to Thomas Magister, ὤ was the form with an exclamatory genitive, ὦ with a vocative (cf. *LSJ* s.v. ὦ). It was no doubt with some such school rule in mind that Q corrected Pl's accent here—if he did not do it unconsciously.

APl 105. 2 (anon.) 1, on Theseus and the Marathonian Bull:

Θαῦμα τέχνης ταύρου τε καὶ ἀνέρος, ὧν ὁ μὲν ἀλκᾷ
θῆρα βίῃ βρίθει, γυῖα τιταινόμενος

Planudes wrote just βίῃ, Q adds the iota. βίῃ is certainly clumsy after ἀλκᾷ, but Planudes cannot seriously have intended his βίῃ as a nominative. Thus Q's greater punctiliousness ought scarcely be counted as a genuine variant—barely even a deliberate correction.

APl 118. 3 (Paul Sil.) on Aeschylus' brother Kynaigeiros:

ἁνίκα που Κυναίγειρε, φυγάς ποτε φορτὶς ἐκεῖνα.

So Pl. Q emends *metri causa* to Κυνέγειρε. An obvious enough correction, especially since the name occurs twice in the immediately preceding poem, where Planudes had originally written Κυναίγειρ' (-ον), but then made the same correction himself by writing ε above the line. The name occurs twice elsewhere in epigrams copied by Planudes, in vii. 741. 1 and xi. 335. 1, where he wrote Κυνέγειρε both times. Both poems come from the ἕτερον βιβλίον he used for his addenda. Perhaps it was only after discovering the 'poetical' by-form of the name here that he went back and corrected his own earlier spelling, missing however *APl* 118. 3, where the scribe of Q did the job for him.

Lastly, a simple error in Q: at *AP* ii. 120 (Christodorus), where Pericles is described as μόθον ἐντύνων Πελοπήϊον, Q has μόνον. It is not so much a question of whether our scribe could have misread Pl's perfectly clear theta as a nu. It is just that he unconsciously substituted the commoner of two very similar looking words.

It is hardly necessary to prolong the inquiry further. I would submit that there is nothing in Q to warrant the hypothesis that it is anything but a direct apograph of the Marcianus. It is indeed the earliest apograph, the more privileged still since Alexander Turyn identified the hand in which various additions and corrections to Q were made as that of Planudes himself (see Appendix II). Evidently the copy was made during Planudes' lifetime and revised by him. It must be re-examined with care and fully exploited by future editors of the Anthology.

APPENDIX II

BM Add. 16409 and Par. gr. 2744

PLANUDES' autograph of his anthology (Pl) falls (as we have seen) into two parts. After (as he thought) completing his task, Planudes came across another and fuller (though still abridged) redaction of Cephalas. So he appended a substantial section of addenda (Pl*b*), carefully arranged in the same or similar categories, with an introductory note asking the next copyist to unite them with the main body of the Anthology (Pl*a*).

Unfortunately, however, he neglected to give the scribe deputed to make the copy Q advance verbal instructions, and as a consequence the man did not discover what he was supposed to have done till he reached the written instructions on fo. 81^v, when of course it was too late. So the two sections remain separate in Q. Until recently, the earliest unified edition known was contained in Paris. gr. 2739, written by Michael Apostoles *c*.1450. But in 1968 (*Scriptorium* xxiii, 69–87) Aubreton discovered a much earlier unified edition, Paris. gr. 2744, hereafter (in this appendix) C.

But how early? According to Aubreton himself (and later Mioni, 1975), it is the work of another pupil of Planudes, written, like the botched Q (which it was commissioned to replace), before Planudes' death. But a meticulous piece of research (*EEBS* xxxix–xl (1972–3), 403–50) by the doyen of such studies, Alexander Turyn, has identified the copyist of C with a man who worked under Demetrius Triclinius at Thessalonica, and places the writing of the manuscript between *c*.1315 and 1320. He has also identified a number of metrical and textual notes in the hand of Triclinius himself. That C is a Triclinian manuscript may now be regarded as certain. Nor should the idea seem surprising: Nigel Wilson uncovered several more indications that Triclinius was familiar with the work of Planudes (*GRBS* xix (1978), 389–94; xxii (1981), 395–7). Less self-evident, however, is Turyn's assumption that it is the first definitive unified Planudean Anthology, prepared under Triclinius' direct supervision.

J. Irigoin (*Annuaire de l'École Pratique des Hautes Études* 1975/6 (1977), 289–94) drew attention to the fact that the paper on which C was written is oriental, the sort that was still in use at Constantinople—by Planudes and his school, for example—whereas all the other Triclinian manuscripts we know of are written on filigraned Italian paper (including at least two with contributions from the scribe of C), which apparently became available at Thessalonica rather earlier than in other eastern centres. Prima facie, then, C was copied at Constantinople, and as a consequence Irigoin rejects Turyn's view: 'Loin d'être due à l'initiative de Démétrius Triclinius, l'édition unifiée de l'Anthologie Planudéenne paraît avoir été faite à Constantinople par quelque disciple de Planude soucieux de respecter la volonté de son maître.' C he takes to be no more than a copy of this original unified edition, made by a scribe Triclinius sent to Constantinople for the purpose.

This is not in fact the only alternative to Turyn's view. Turyn himself has already argued on other grounds (which can be strengthened) that C was written at Constantinople. I venture to suggest a compromise solution.

Whether or not the school of Planudes produced its own unified edition (see below), it can I think be shown that C is not just a copy of such an edition but was itself based directly on both Pl and Q.

Turyn insisted that C was copied from Pl alone. He further argued—mistakenly, as I hope to show—that the scribe of C occasionally looked at one of the sources from which Planudes had compiled Pl, and for this reason suggested that 'Triclinius travelled with his scribe C from Thessalonica to Constantinople' for the purpose. But if they really did this, and the oriental paper lends strong support to the suggestion, they are more likely to have found Q than these sources (one at least of which we know Planudes had to borrow from a friend). If Planudes took the trouble to revise Q himself, this is surely because it was a copy he intended to keep and use.

Whether or not Planudes' school survived his death, there is no reason to suppose that his library was immediately dispersed. It is a reasonable assumption that for a few years at least Pl and Q stood side by side on the same shelf in the Akataleptos monastery where Planudes signed Pl and spent the last years of his life.[1] Nothing is

[1] Most of Planudes' working life was spent in the Chora monastery, but by *c.*1300 it had become rather dilapidated and Planudes moved to the Akataleptos.

known of the vicissitudes of Pl before it passed into the possession of Cardinal Bessarion and was presented by him to San Marco in 1468 (Turyn, *Dated Greek MSS* (1972), 90–6). Even less is known of the history of Q, which was purchased by the British Museum as late as 1846 from the Italian collector L. M. Rezzi.

So if C was copied in Constantinople as early as 1315–20, then it is likely (*a*) that it was copied at the Akataleptos, and (*b*) that its scribe would have had access to Q as well as Pl. Four items suggest that he did.

1. The first is the case of Nicarchus' mildly amusing quatrain on the contradictory qualities of the fart (xi. 395). Planudes originally wrote it in a section with a lemma εἰς πορδήν all to itself. At a later stage, however, it was completely erased in the Marcianus—while still appearing not only in Q but also in C.

It is easy to see how it got into Q, which was evidently copied from Pl before the poem was erased. But what of C? According to Aubreton and Turyn the poem was not erased from Pl till *after* C had been copied from it; that is to say, it was not erased by Planudes. Turyn refers to Aubreton, who bases his argument on the facts (*a*) that the poem is in C, and (*b*) that 'Planude a reservé un lemme particulier à cette epigramme', whence he concludes 'ce n'est donc pas lui qui l'a effacée'. The first point is obviously not compelling (C could have got it from Q), and the second I do not understand. Certainly Planudes gave the poem a lemma to itself, both in the table of contents to his second Book on fo. 21^r, and in the margin ad loc. on fo. 27^r. The hand that erased the poem erased the first of these lemmata but left the second. I cannot see any reason to ascribe such inconsistency to anyone other than Planudes. On the contrary, considerations of probability unmistakably point to Planudes, the 'Dr Bowdler of Byzantium', as Douglas Young once called him. The point will bear illustration.

But many of his books appear to have remained in the Chora, which was renovated *c.*1316 by Theodore Metochites (I. Ševčenko, "Theodore Metochites, the Chora and the Intellectual Trends of his Time', in *The Kariye Djami* iv, ed. P. A. Underwood (Princeton 1975), 29). Metochites owed much to Planudes' writings and editions (Ševčenko, pp. 41–2), and it is possible that he subsequently reunited the whole of Planudes' library at the Chora. Did Metochites work on the Anthology? Now that his hand has been identified, marginalia and corrections in both Pl and Q could be re-examined. If traces of his hand were found in both books, there would be a strong presumption that they did indeed remain together for a while.

In the introduction to his Book vii (erotica) Planudes frankly admits that he has deliberately omitted a large number of poems in his exemplar that πρὸς τὸ ἀσεμνότερον καὶ αἰσχρότερον ἀποκλίνεται (fo. 68). Just how many he did omit can easily be estimated by a comparison with the two erotic books of *AP*, most of whose contents we may suppose to have stood in Planudes' two sources. Of the 311 heterosexual poems of *AP* v, *APl* vii has only 194; of the 258 homosexual erotica in *AP* xii Planudes took only 17. Furthermore, there are at least six passages in poems he did take where the text of the Marcianus has been deliberately bowdlerized.

With *AP* v. 35 (Rufinus) Planudes began, drastically enough, by omitting the first four couplets. Then at l. 5, εἰ ταύτας ὁ κριτὴς ὁ θεῶν ἐθεήσατο πυγάς, he substituted κούρας for πυγάς, girls for bottoms. Cf. *AP* v. 84 (anon.): 'would that I were a purple rose, so that you could pick me up in your hands and χαρίσῃ στήθεσι χιονέοις.' κομίσαις for χαρίσῃ Planudes, evidently to tone down the sensuality. The last couplet of v. 245 (Macedonius) is omitted in Pl, presumably because of its promise of promiscuity. Homosexual poems particularly troubled him. *AP* v. 6. 5 (Callimachus), ἀρσενικῷ θέρεται πυρί, becomes ἄλλης δὴ θέρεται πυρί. At xii. 19 (anon.) οὐ δύναμαί σε θέλων θέσθαι φίλον, he substituted φίλην, *contra metrum*. At xii. 136 (anon.) too, moral overrode metrical considerations; for τὸν τρυφερῇ παιδὸς σαρκὶ χλιαινόμενον he desperately substituted τρυφερῆς παρθένου. Here the unashamed carnality of the line seems to have induced a moment of panic in the good monk; a moment's cool reflection would at least have supplied κούρης. Much more calculating is his treatment of Agathias v. 269. 1:

δισσῶν θηλυτέρων μοῦνός ποτε μέσσος ἐκείμην.

Here Planudes skilfully removed the clear implication that the poet and his two girl-friends were in bed together by substituting μέσσα καθήμην, 'sat between them'.

We may compare the Byzantine version of Ovid's *Amatoria* recently published by E. J. Kenney and P. E. Easterling, which Kenney has plausibly argued to be an early work of Planudes. What has come down to us is clearly an excerpted version of the postulated Planudean original. Curiously enough the extensive and often comical bowdlerizing (e.g. φίλος for *puella*, προσειπεῖν for *oscula ferre*, τόδε τι ποιεῖν for *servire puellae*, τὸ ἔργον for *Venus*, etc.) that is so notable a feature of the version is ascribed by Kenney to the excerptor, on the grounds that 'Planudes himself was not in the habit of bowdlerizing'. The original was not bowdlerized, he argues, because a certain number of risqué passages (e.g. *AA* ii. 361 f. on adultery) are fully and accurately translated—or, as Kenney puts it, 'allowed to pass without revision' by his editor. The existence of the editor is not in doubt, but the argument is clearly invalid. Inconsistency is the hallmark of bowdlerization, and Planudes is no exception. He included in his Anthology, for example, many an epigram at least as obscene as any he omitted or bowdlerized, whether because he read them too carelessly, with too pure a mind, or too readily discerning a moral purpose not intended by the poet. To quote but one example, he included *AP* v. 302 (in L as well as Pl), Agathias' *tour de force* assessment of all forms of sexual gratification, concluding that masturbation was simplest and best. Perhaps he felt that this was a healthy principle.

Reference might also be made to Young's conjecture that, in some leaves of the Marcianus that have been physically removed, Planudes first copied and then suppressed the homosexual Book ii of Theognis; and to the evidence that Planudes lightly bowdlerized one branch of the manuscript tradition of Plutarch's *Moralia* (Wilson, *Antike und Abendland* xvi (1970), 72–3).

Nicharchus' epigram was included in every known manuscript copy of Planudes' anthology and every printed edition (Aubreton, Budé x, 213 n. 3, oddly claims that it was deleted in D). It became a favourite with Renaissance translators (Hutton (1935), 613–14). It is merely a little indelicate—not a poem so grossly obscene that any pure-minded person might have felt in duty bound to save posterity the embarrassment of reading it. If the Marcianus had chanced to fall into the hands of so excessively pure-minded a reader, why no other and more justified traces of his blue pencil? The simplest and most likely explanation is surely that it was Planudes himself who, regretting his earlier broadmindedness, struck it out *pudoris causa* when making his final revisions.

2. The next item comprises the two lines *AP* ix. 538–9, which Planudes treated as a single poem:

ἁβροχίτων δ' ὁ φύλαξ θηροζυγοκαμψιμέτωπος.
ἁβρὸς δ' ἐν προχοαῖς Κύκλωψ φθογγάζετο μύρμηξ.

These are nonsense-lines, whose sole *raison d'être* is that they contain all the letters of the alphabet (εἰς τὰ κδ' γράμματα, as the lemma remarks). Like Nicarchus' poem on the fart, they were subsequently erased in Pl but are still to be read in Q and (presumably) C. We no longer have the relevant leaf of C itself, but both lines are to be found in two apographs (Ambros. A. 161 sup. and Laur. 31. 28) and the *editio princeps*.

Once more, for Turyn they were 'obviously' copied into C from Pl *before* being erased there.

There are only two reasons I can think of why anyone should have wanted to erase such harmless trifles. First, their very silliness. Second, their location. The rest of the poems in this section are all concerned with grammarians, as its title (εἰς γραμμα-τικούς) promises. *AP* ix. 538–9 might well be thought typical enough products of Byzantine grammarians, to be sure; strictly speaking, however, they do not belong. But these are not the sort of objections that would prompt a *reader* to such drastic measures. It is only the *editor* who might feel his taste or judgement sufficiently impugned by the misclassification of such trivia to justify their excision.

There is no need to assume that the copyist of C (or Triclinius himself, for that matter) collated Q throughout. Granted that he had access to Q his attention was directly drawn to it in both these cases by the mere fact that Planudes had conspicuously obliterated the poems. The blue pencil always suggests that what was struck out is worth the trouble of a little research to track down.

3. The third case, ix. 128, is rather different. This poem Planudes himself omitted from the Marcianus—a simple case of haplo-graphy, since ix. 129, the next poem in P as also, no doubt, in Planudes' source, began with the same word εἶρπε. That Planudes had intended to include it is proved by the fact that he added it in his own hand (evidently direct from his source) in the upper margin on the appropriate page of Q. It was also added in the upper margin of fo. 9ʳ of the Marcianus—in the hand of the scribe C. Proof positive that the scribe C had Pl in his hands, of course. But where.did *he* find the poem?

According to Turyn there were two quite separate operations. First Planudes added it to Q. Then, *independently* (since, on Turyn's hypothesis, he had no knowledge of Q), the scribe added it to Pl *from the same source that Planudes had used*. There are three serious objections to such a hypothesis.

First, the sheer improbability of both Planudes and the scribe C independently spotting the absence of the same poem in different manuscripts with the aid of the same source.

Second, the uncertain availability of Planudes' original source.

Third, if C used the source of Pl as well as Pl, we should certainly have expected him to add thence more than just one poem—and that a poem he could equally have read in the margin of Q. In the matter of erotica at least he could considerably have amplified Planudes' meagre selection. Turyn argues that he did supply one more poem from this source: *AP* v. 18 (Rufinus), which is added in a different hand (that of Demetrius Triclinius' younger brother Nicolaus) at the end of Book vii in C (fo. 28^v). It seems to me that this one poem is far from sufficient evidence to support so potentially far-reaching an assumption. In P *AP* v. 18 stands next to another poem by Rufinus, v. 19, which Planudes included in his Book vii. Presumably they stood together in the source of Pl as well. If so, then by analogy with the case of *AP* ix. 128 and 129, we might have expected v. 18 to be inserted in both the margin of Pl and the text of C *next* to v. 19. In fact it is added out of context at the end of the book in C alone by someone other than the copyist of the rest of the Anthology. It is, I would suggest, both simpler and more probable to conclude that Nicolaus Triclines chanced to find the poem in some quite separate source, and added it himself to the already completed work of his colleague C. I have in fact suggested above (Ch. VIII) that he found it in *ABV*.

The truth about ix. 128 is then probably as follows. Planudes himself, revising Q with his source(s) rather than Pl to hand, noticed his omission and inserted the poem in the margin, intending to add it in Pl later but forgetting to do so. The scribe C, working with both Pl and Q open on his desk, noticed the addition in the margin of Q, and thought it proper to repair the omission in Pl before transcribing it into his own copy.

It is now time to reconsider the implications of the later manuscripts of the Planudean Anthology. As Turyn (*passim*) and Mioni (1975, 286) have made clear, alongside what we may call the 'C-tradition', manuscripts copied directly or indirectly from C (of which at least three are known from the fifteenth century), we also find another tradition, of which the earliest datable representative is Paris. gr. 2739 (hereafter D), written by Michael Apostoles *c.*1450 (there are at least four others from the fifteenth century). This latter tradition Turyn christened the 'Apostoles tradition', 'just as a matter of convenience . . . without prejudging whether Michael Apostoles was its very first originator' (p. 430). Mioni was sure that Apostoles 'instaura una nuova tradizione'. In fact, as Irigoin has suggested and I hope to be able to confirm, though with a significant refinement of Irigoin's own argument, it may be presumed to go back to the school if not the person of Planudes himself.

The features that distinguish the C- from the 'Apostoles-tradition' are (*a*) certain differences in the order of the epigrams, and (*b*) the presence or absence of *AP* v. 18 (Nicolaus Triclinius' addition in C at the end of the erotica). Now according to Turyn, Michael Apostoles' version on the one hand followed 'the basic arrangement of the unified Triclinian edition of C' while on the other restoring so far as possible the original order of Planudes' autograph where C had altered it, on the basis of a careful study of Q. In addition Michael 'naturally' omitted *AP* v. 18 because, not finding it in Q, he recognized it to be an 'alien addition'.

The facts here are certain, the interpretation less so. Why should Michael have been so preoccupied with the order of the epigrams as to undertake this painstaking collation between his C manuscript and Q? He was no Planudes or Triclinius but (after his exile) a professional calligrapher, for whom time was money. If he had a unified manuscript why should he bother with a divided text as well? And whereas Apostoles might have been sufficiently impressed by Planudes' signature to read Pl itself if he had chanced on it (by then presumably in Italy), Turyn insists that it was from Q, not Pl, that D derives. Above all it would be editorial scrupulosity of an unparalleled order to have excluded *AP* v. 18 from what was after all an anthology, not an original work by Planudes. Most readers would have welcomed this addition to Planudes' notoriously bowdlerized erotic section.

Irigoin suggests that both D and C derive from a now lost earlier unified edition. D is presumed to be a more or less faithful copy of this edition (let us call it *d*), whereas C contains 'un petit nombre de retouches' introduced by Triclinius.

This hypothesis has certain advantages over Turyn's. For example, v. 18 may be presumed absent from the D tradition because it was absent from *d*; it is present in the C tradition because it was a Triclinian addition to C. But why and on what principles did Triclinius make these in themselves quite unimportant changes in the order of poems?

It seems to me that there is a more satisfactory explanation. There was no one definitive unified edition. There were *two* independent unified editions, one Planudean and one Triclinian.

These occasional and in themselves insignificant variations in the order of the epigrams between the C and D traditions are surely not the result of deliberate tampering by Triclinius with the definitive Planudean version, but the natural and inevitable consequence of two *independent* attempts to unite the two halves (Pl*a* and Pl*b*) of two already slightly different versions, Pl and Q. There were at least four confusing factors. First Planudes' occasional failure to give clear instruction for the location of marginal addenda. Consider the case of *APl* 4, which Planudes wrote in the upper margin of fo. 3ʳ of Pl, though neglecting to indicate whereabouts on the page it was to be inserted. The scribe of Q took the trouble to study both the poem and the context, shrewdly perceived that its natural fellow there was *AP* ix. 476 (both on the theme τί ἄν εἴποι Ἕκτωρ) and placed it after that poem. As a consequence, this is where it appears throughout the D tradition (Mioni (1975), p. 282). In the C tradition *APl* 4 does *not* appear after *AP* ix. 476, but at the end of the chapter εἰς ἀνδρείαν. It was evidently Pl, not Q, from which the scribe of C was copying at this point; in the absence of specific instructions he used his discretion in a different way, and just added the poem at the end of the relevant chapter, his regular policy with addenda.

The second confusing factor was the failure of one or the other of the two scribes to understand or follow such instructions as Planudes gave. Third, the different possibilities for combining the addenda from Pl*b* with the material in the appropriate chapters in Pl*a* (i.e. next to matching poems or at the end). And fourth, the uncertainty when confronted with a chapter in Pl*b* which had no counterpart in Pl*a*. It would be astonishing if any two scribes had produced the same results when confronted with such a task, and what we find in the C and D traditions is exactly what we should expect under the circumstances.

The C tradition originated in the school of Triclinius *c.*1315–20, whether in Constantinople or Thessalonica. Did Apostoles originate the D tradition as late as the mid-fifteenth century? With Irigoin, I hypothesize a source *d* for D, and I would assign it to the school of Planudes.

According to Douglas Young, the Theognis portion of D derives directly from Q. But two more cautious editors, F. R. Adrados and

M. L. West (who kindly lent me his collations), were sufficiently impressed by textual differences between D and Q to hypothesize derivation from Pl instead (hypothesize, since by an unexplained mishap Pl's Theognis text is missing). Adrados drew attention to three passages (discounting one where his collation was in error) where D has what is either the true reading or at any rate (and more significantly from the transmissional point of view) the vulgate, while Q, according to Young its source, does not. Where then did D obtain these readings?

Young replied that in every case they may be presumed conjectures by Michael Apostoles. This seems doubly improbable. First there is the intrinsic implausibility of this explanation in all five of the cases I shall discuss:

79: αἱρήσεις Q, εὑρήσεις D and all other MSS. A correction made 'currente calamo', according to Young. But αἱρήσεις makes perfectly adequate sense, and it is hard to see why Michael should ever have suspected it.

347: Q has πήχεων for the vulgate τειχέων and αὐλήσαντες for συλήσαντες. No one could have thought that these readings made sense, but it is doubtful whether the correction is in either case easy or inevitable.

312: Q omitted the word ὀργήν (presumably just through carelessness, since he did not, as he does elsewhere when in doubt, leave a gap), and later added the guess γνώμην above the line. D has ὀργήν none the less. According to Young ὀργήν would 'come easily to mind from 214 written a few minutes earlier'. But once again, without another exemplar to check against, why should Michael have suspected the perfectly tolerable γνώμην?

463: εὔμαρε [blank] χρῆμα Q, where D has the vulgate εὐμαρέως τοι χρῆμα. τοι is by no means the only or most obvious way to fill the gap.

Second, these vulgate readings are also to be found in two other copies of the Planudean recension, Ur (as far as it goes) and I, according to Young independent copies of Pl itself. It follows that they were the readings of Pl. Now it would be a remarkable coincidence if D had in every case restored by conjecture the original text of the source of his own supposed source. So D cannot have been copied direct from Q. On the other hand it cannot have been copied direct from Pl either.

D, like Q and Pl, contains one other relevant text, the Menandrean *Monosticha* (it is another of the distinguishing marks of the D tradition that its representatives contain the whole original contents of Pl and Q; Triclinius seems only to have been interested in the Anthology). Now l. 151 in Jäkel's edition of the *Monosticha* runs as follows:

γυναῖκα θάπτειν κρεῖσσόν ἐστιν ἢ γαμεῖν.

This is what Planudes must originally have written in Pl and it is what appears in Q and the D tradition. But at some later stage, apparently distressed by the denigration of marriage, he erased the last three words and substituted the feeble conclusion ἢ ζῆν ἀθλίως. This is on quite a different footing from the simple erasures discussed above, where the blank spaces in Pl would have prompted any curious scribe to check with Q. In this case the scribe's suspicions were not likely to be alerted by what he would naturally take to be a straightforward correction.

Since Apostoles preserves the original text, he cannot have got it from Pl. Nor is it even much help to suppose that he had both Pl and Q to hand; even if he had thought to check with Q, he would still probably have followed Planudes' correction, rightly perceiving that it represented the editor's final thoughts. *Mon.* 151 he might have got direct from Q—but not his text of Theognis.

The simplest solution is that Apostoles' direct source was neither Pl nor Q but our postulated *d*, which conflated the text of both. Now it is not likely that Pl and Q were available together indefinitely, and the presumption is that *d* was an early copy. And why not the copy Planudes himself must have commissioned? It was natural that he should have given the scribe both Pl and Q, since Q, though imperfect, was neater and had at least incorporated the marginal additions and straightened out the mess in the alphabetical arrangement on fo. 46ʳ. On the other hand, when Triclinius' man arrived to make his copy, it was equally natural that he should have considered the editor's autograph to be more authoritative and used Pl as his base text.

If *d* was copied before Planudes' death, then it is theoretically possible that the original text of *Mon.* 151 that it passed on to D was taken from Pl *before* Planudes erased and rewrote the line. Yet it seems improbable that Planudes should have bothered to make such alterations in what was after all only his rough copy after a satisfactory fair copy had been made. More probably he made his few final modifications to Pl before, and with a view to, giving it once more to his copyist. There are in any case other proofs—the placing of *APl* 4, for example—that the scribe of *d* had Q as well as Pl before him.

It is to be hoped that before long someone will undertake a full collation of at any rate Pl, Q, C, and D. But it will have to be a more accurate collation than any Planudean manuscript has so far received.

APPENDIX III

The two exemplars of Marc. gr. 481

THE problem of the elimination or restoration of Doric forms is one of the most 'tiresome and insoluble' to confront the editor of the Anthology (Gow and Page, *HE* xlv). While hardly a reliable guide, P is certainly more consistent than Pl, where countless Doric forms offered by P have been eliminated. Since Planudes is notoriously as much an editor as a copyist, the common assumption or implication is that such tinkerings are to be laid at his own door. W. Seelbach, for example, editing the Doric poets Mnasalces of Sicyon and Theodoridas of Syracuse, on principle took P as his only guide in such matters, ignoring and on occasions actually suppressing Doric variants in Pl.

In this case at least the inference is perhaps premature. It is instructive to collate the few relevant cases where Planudes by oversight duplicates among his addenda (Pl*b*) poems he had already included in his Anthology proper (Pl*a*), for they come (as he explicitly remarks on fo. 81ᵛ) from a second exemplar. I set out below the readings for Doric forms in three epigrams found in P, Pl*a*, and Pl*b*:

		P	Pl*a*	Pl*b*
ix. 375.	6:	αὐξαμέναν	-ην	-αν
		εὐφροσύναν	-ην	-αν
	8:	κάδεος	κήδεος	κήδεος
vii. 388.	2:	ἄκρην	-ην	-ην
	3:	Δίκα	-η	-α
	5:	αἰδομένα	-η	-α
	6:	γᾶ	-η(?)	-ᾶ
		ἑᾶς	-ῆς	-ᾶς
		ἐλευθερίης [*sic*]	-ης	-ης

In company with some early editors and Gow and Page we should probably read ἐλευθερίας, but this still leaves some Ionic forms presented by all three manuscripts.

	P	Pl*a*	Pl*b*
ix. 154. 2:	ἁ τλάμων	ἡ τλήμων	ἁ τλάμων
5:	θνάσκειν	-η-	-η-
6:	τᾶς πάτρας	τῆς -ης	τᾶς -ας

Pl*a* reveals a clear tendency to normalize, while Pl*b* retains Doricisms almost as consistently as *AP*.

At ix. 333 indeed, a relatively authentic Doric poem by Mnasalces of Sicyon, Pl*b* alone preserves the surely correct ᾶς in l. 3 where Pl*a*, *AP*, and S all have ῆς. Not aware of the general superiority of Pl*b* in this matter, Seelbach anomalously printed P's ῆς. At vii. 464. 2 Pl*b* has a Doric form normalized by the first hand in *AP* (but reinstated by the Corrector).

Compare too vii. 212 (Mnasalces) where we have only P and Pl*b*:

	P	Pl*b*
1:	Αἰθυίας	-ης
2:	τᾶς	τᾶς
3:	ἤνυσε μᾶκος	ἄνυσε μᾶκος
4:	δολιχάν	δολιχάν

At vii. 529 (Theodoridas) Pl*b* is likewise more consistently Doric than *AP*; note particularly πυρᾶς in l. 2, where Seelbach (*Die Epp. des Mnasalkes und Theodoridas* (1964), 7) prints P's πυρῆς, not even mentioning πυρᾶς in his apparatus.

Compare vii. 170, a Doric poem by Callimachus or Posidippus that appears twice in *AP* (again after vii. 481); the first occurrence has Doric α throughout, the second η. We can also compare the original text of *AP* with C's corrections in this respect: e.g. at v. 148. 1, v. 307. 2, and vii. 221. 3 C corrects η in *AP* to α (with Pl); at vii. 257. 2 and 489. 3 he corrects η in P and Pl to α, while at vii. 129. 3, with Pl, he corrects α in P to η. Such examples could be multiplied; they do little to suggest that there is any straightforward sense in which *AP* as a whole can be said to be more reliable. Many different sources lie behind *AP* as they do behind *APl*, and at all periods the practice of scribes varied in this matter (note the vacillation from line to line in the Doric epigrams in P. Oxy. 662).

For *APl* 8 we do not have P, but we do have two versions in Pl (Beckby's apparatus unfortunately confuses Pl*a* and Pl*b* here):

	Pl*a*	Pl*b*
3:	Ἀθήνης	Ἀθάνας
6:	θνητὸς . . . θείην	θνατὸς . . . θέιαν
8:	Ἀΐδην	Ἀΐδαν

The sample is small, of course, but such evidence as it provides all points the same way. It is hard to resist the inference that the difference between Pl*a* and Pl*b* in this respect does reflect a genuine difference between the two manuscripts Planudes used, not his own vagaries as copyist or editor.

Consider too the following case, *APl* 291. 3 (Anyte):

Pl*a*: αἱ μιν ὑπὸ ζαθέοιο θέρευς
Pl*b*: οὕνεχ' ὑπ' ἀζαλέου θέρεος

Both versions have had their champions (Gow and Page, *HE* ii. 93; D. Geoghegan, *Liv. Class. Monthly* i (1976), 56–7), but whichever we choose it is by no means as obvious as some have supposed that the rejected version has to be written off as Planudean conjecture. Why should Planudes have chosen to rewrite when copying a second time a poem that had not bothered him the first time? Editors may or may not be right to be suspicious of the appropriateness of ζάθεος to θέρος, of the epic genitive ζαθέοιο, and of the contracted genitive θέρευς. But it is hardly likely that such fine details would have prompted Planudes to rewrite the line. It is surely more likely that Planudes found both versions in his two exemplars. We might even conjecture that they went back to the two redactions of Meleager used by Cephalas (Ch. VI).

The source of Pl*b* was apparently fuller than the source of Pl*a*, if we may judge from the number of addenda it supplied (though of course we cannot be sure that it contained all the poems in the source of Pl*a*), but not necessarily more accurate or reliable in other respects. For example, there are fewer ascriptions in Pl*b* (see Aubreton [1968], 35–6): for all its superiority in dialect, Mnasalces' poem ix. 333 is left anonymous in Pl*b*.

Lenzinger has compiled some very useful tables comparing the readings of Pl*a* with Pl*b*,[1] Pl*a* with *AP*, and Pl*b* with *AP* (pp. 32–55). These tables need careful control, but no one who has studied them at all carefully will feel able to prefer the Palatine text as a matter of principle where there is a conflict. There is no question that Planudes indulged freely in conjecture, especially where he thought he could repair metre or morals. But in matters of dialect, ascription, and text alike, we must always be ready to allow the possibility that he is merely reproducing his sources.

---

[1] It is curious to reflect that Lenzinger would probably not have compiled the interesting and valuable comparison between the text of poems duplicated in Pl*a* and Pl*b* (pp. 32–5) had he not been under the misapprehension that Basson had argued 'dass Planudes gar nicht zwei verschiedene Vorlagen sondern zweimal die selbe benutzt haben konnte' (p. 31). Basson made no such foolish claim: cf. p. 18 'non duo diversi fontes sed duo eiusdem anthologiae Cephalanae exemplaria'.

APPENDIX IV

Laur. 91. 8 and 32. 50

Two small post-Planudean anthologies merit more accurate description than they have so far received. First the fifty-two (not fifty) epigrams written on fos. 32ᵛ–37ᵛ of the (according to Aubreton) sixteenth-century Laur. 91. 8, fitfully and incompletely quoted by Beckby but first given a letter of their own by Aubreton (pp. 75–6), namely F. Its contents are as follows:

1	vii. 145	19	x. 37	37	x. 31
2	vii. 670	20	30	38	74
3	ix. 39	21	ix. 530	39	106
4	C III. 33	22	*APl* 152	40	ix. 230
5	*APl* 174	23	vii. 471	41	451
6	ix. 576	24	*APl* 200	42	452
7	387	25	ix. 47	43	498
8	388	26	v. 94	44	367
9	389	27	*APl* 14	45	461
10	vii. 44	28	151	46	462
11	70	29	vii. 8	47	473
12	xi. 375	30	ix. 253	48	463
13	vii. 674	31	93	49	476
14	149	32	359	50	*APl* 4
15	46	33	360	51	ix. 477
16	13	34	257	52	vii. 151
17	*APl* 141	35	*APl* 3		
18	vii. 152	36	ix. 111		

According to Aubreton, despite the late date of the manuscript (consisting in fact of fifty-four leaves added to an *editio princeps* of Theocritus) 'on ne peut penser que cette *sylloge* . . . soit en dépendance de l'œuvre de Planude; la succession des épigrammes ne correspond nullement à l'ordre planudéen; mais un bon nombre se lit dans la *sylloge Σ*, dans un ordre toutefois tout à fait différent'. On these grounds alone he makes F equal (with E) earliest extant Byzantine anthology of epigrams, derived not even from Cephalas but from a pre-Cephalan anthology.

But as we have often seen (especially in the case of *Σ*: Ch. VII) sequence of poems alone cannot disprove (though it may prove) dependance of one anthology on another. It is convenient for the *Quellenforscher* if an anthologist follows the arrangement of his source, but it is obviously open to him to rearrange his material how he pleases.

In this case the decisive points are the following. All but three of these fifty-two epigrams appear in *APl*. Of those three, two (ix. 388–9) appear in *Σ* (for their source, above, Ch. VII), ix. 389 lacking the last line as in *Σ*. The text of the poems is heavily influenced by Planudean conjecture; indeed it is clearly influenced (for the worse) by *Σ* as well as *APl*. It is hardly necessary to give more than a handful of examples: e.g. at vii. 44. 4 F has τραγικήν for P's Μουσέων, with *APl* and *Σ*; at vii. 471. 1, Callimachus' εἶπας, ἤλιε χαῖρε, where Planudes first copied εἶπας and then wrote εἰπών above the line (perhaps dubious of the 1st aor. part.), the scribe of F ridiculously conflated the two readings into the nonsense-word εἴπασων; at v. 94. 4 F shares *APl*'s miscopying of συνῶν as συρῶν; at ix. 476. 1 F has οὐ σθενῶν with *APl* and *Σ* (a patent conjecture) for *AP*'s ἀσθενῶν; at ix. 367. 1 F has παρ' ἐλπίδας (with *APl*) for *AP*'s περὶ φρένας (Planudes originally wrote περὶ φρένας and only later added what is plainly his own conjecture); lastly *APl* 152, where F has *Σ*'s unmetrical miscopying -ευσον for *APl*'s -εσον. It should be added that there are also clear traces of the Planudean sequence of epigrams: e.g. nos. 45–51 are only in very broken Palatine order, with an intruder; yet they are in perfect unbroken Planudean sequence, *APl* ia. 5. 9–15.

So F is not after all a pre-Cephalan anthology of the ninth century. Not only is it post-Planudean; it is later than *Σ* too and so at earliest of the early seventeenth century.

Then there is the smaller collection at Laur. 32. 50, fos. 13ʳ–17ʳ, which Aubreton by an oversight took to be another copy of F. It does open with the same poem as F and nos. 3 and 6 also appear in F; but the other twenty-seven are all different:

1	vii. 145	11	v. 147	21	*APl* 331
2	ix. 129	12	148	22	v. 139
3	576	13	142	23	141
4	346	14	ix. 47	24	143
5	66	15	48	25	v. 155. 1/148. 2
6	357	16	39	26	v. 82

7	xii. 51. 3–4	17	*APl* 387c5	27	xii. 60
8	ix. 163	18	223	28	ix. 365
9	*APl* 172	19	224	29	vii. 20
10	ix. 122	20	xi. 323		

Once more there are clear traces of Planudean order: i.e. the broken erotic sequence nos. 11–13 and 22–5, while a random selection from the middle of the erotic book of *AP*, are in fact taken directly from the beginning of Planudes' erotic book (*APl* vii. 6, 7, 3, 1, 2, 4, and 11). Note too that the pederastic poems nos. 7 and 27 (*AP* xii. 51 and 60) are *APl* vii. 190–1. Once more, however, the decisive point is the influence of *APl* and *Σ* on the text. For example, at vii. 45. 4, κρεῖσσον ἐμοῦ with *APl* and *Σ*; at ix. 576. 2, with *APl* and *Σ* a transposition which may even be correct; at ix. 323. 3, *Σ*'s wild οὐκοῦν for the λοιπόν of *AP* and *APl*; and at ix. 346. 2, *Σ*'s nonsense πηκτίδι νεοσσοτροφεῖς.

Once more, then, an anthology of the early seventeenth century. It is doubtless not a coincidence that, like the two manuscripts of *Σ* that so much influenced them, both manuscripts are (still) to be found in Florence, where they were all perhaps written, an interesting testimony to the contemporary vogue for Greek epigrams.

I am grateful to M. Aubreton for the loan of his photographs of both manuscripts.

APPENDIX V

The *Soros*

As Reitzenstein noticed long ago (*Epigramm und Skolion*, 96–102), there are a number of connections between the early third-century epigrammatists Asclepiades (also apparently known as Sicelides), Posidippus, and Hedylus. Since Reitzenstein's day these connections have increased both in extent and variety:

1. There are numerous Meleagrian sequences in *AP* (especially v and xii) where epigrams by Asclepiades and Posidippus either directly follow each other or are separated only by contributions from Meleager, the editor of the *Garland*. No other pair of Meleagrian poets is linked so frequently, and it was not without reason that Reitzenstein conjectured that Meleager found their poems already juxtaposed in whatever source he took them from. According to a more elaborate analysis by W. and M. Wallace, with only six exceptions (I count seven) the sequence *AP* v. 134–215 'is to all intents and purposes an edition of Meleager's own verse interspersed with similar poems by Asclepiades, Posidippos, and Hedylos' ('Meleager and the Soros', *TAPA* lxx (1939), 193).

2. An early first-century papyrus unknown to Reitzenstein, P. Tebt. 3, probably a Meleagrian excerpt (see Ch. I above), contains traces of four epigrams, one identifiable as *AP* ix. 588 by the Meleagrian Alcaeus of Messene. The third, apparently on a literary work by a friend of the author, is ascribed to a damaged name ending -*ppos* (-ππου), and the fourth to a name ending -*iades* (-ιᾴδου). The only other epigrammatists who might be considered theoretical possibilities (Philiades, Dosiades, Hegesippus) are quite obscure, and as Gow has already observed (*HE* ii. 151), the regular juxtaposition of poems by Asclepiades and Posidippus in *AP* 'lends considerable support to the view that they were the authors of these two epigrams'.

3. Six epigrams attributed to Asclepiades bear an alternative ascription to Posidippus (for the fullest and most accurate

presentation of the evidence see Gow and Page, *HE* ii. 117). Shared ascriptions are otherwise rare in Meleager's *Garland*, and as many as six cases where the ascription is shared between the same two poets seems to go beyond the permissible limits of coincidence. It might also be thought more than coincidental that the two names are regularly separated by the rare formula ἤ rather than the stock scholiastic οἱ δέ. In his study of shared ascriptions in 1958 Gow concluded (rightly, I think) that 'the origin of at least the great majority of them is a disagreement between exemplars employed' (p. 33). In these cases, however, he was prepared to concede that the uncertainty went back to Meleager rather than Cephalas.

4. Of the three poems (in *AP*) plausibly ascribed to the less prolific Hedylus, one is ascribed jointly to Hedylus or Asclepiades (v. 161: cf. Gow and Page, *HE* ii. 143–4).

5. These connections are not just external. Posidippus was clearly much influenced by Asclepiades, and Hedylus by both Posidippus and Asclepiades. In addition to the Gow and Page commentary see especially P. M. Fraser, *Ptolemaic Alexandria*, i (Oxford 1972), 556–75. They wrote on the same subjects in the same manner and even use the same names.

6. Asclepiades and Posidippus are numbered (accepting the standard and natural restoration, Ἀσκλη[πιάδη τῷ Σικε]λίδη καὶ Ποσειδίππῳ) among Callimachus' literary enemies in the celebrated diegesis to the *Aetia* preface (I p. 3 Pfeiffer).

7. That both poets were justly so numbered is suggested by the epigrams both wrote praising that *bête noire* of Callimachus, the *Lyde* of Antimachus (ix. 63; xii. 168). The obscene poem that so neatly perverts a solemn line from Callimachus' *Bath of Pallas* is, perhaps significantly, one of those ascribed to both (v. 202). A corrupt poem of Hedylus may also allude to the *Lyde*: I would suggest τῆς Λύδης for the intolerably flat δὴ πολύ at Gow–Page VI. 5 (bizarrely misinterpreted by Giangrande, *L'Épigramme grecque*, 158–63).

8. According to *Etym. Gen.* B, s.v. ἀλυτάρχης, Hedylus wrote a commentary on Callimachus' epigrams. Gow and Page were disposed to believe that this was another, later Hedylus, grammarian rather than epigrammatist (*HE* ii. 153, cf. 289), but at this period poets were frequently grammarians (or vice versa), and it is surely significant that it was Callimachus' epigrams he chose to comment on. The publication of the oyster papyrus (Parsons, *ZPE*

xxiv (1977), 1–12) has proved the existence of near-contemporary commentaries on third-century epigrammatists. If this is the same Hedylus, then all three of our trio appear as critics of Callimachus.

9. The names Asclepiades and Posidippus appear together on a proxeny list from Delphi datable to either 276/5 or 273/2: *Fouilles de Delphes* iii. 3. 192 (not mentioned by Gow and Page); cf. Trypanis, *CR* lxvi (1952), 68–9; Fraser, *Ptolemaic Alexandria* (1972), ii. 796 n. 45. It is true that neither is styled poet nor identified by ethnic, but Posidippus is similarly honoured on a proxeny list from nearby Thermos in Aetolia, datable to 262/3 (*IG* ix. 1². 17. 245; cf. Fraser, ii. 796 n. 44), where he is explicitly styled 'the epigrammatist from Pella'. Date and place would both suit, and in the light of the evidence here assembled it would not be surprising if the two poets had been travelling together.

10. All three poets were active in Alexandria. Fraser, op. cit. i. 556 f., has collected most of the evidence, though the case for Asclepiades can be strengthened. It seems not to have been noticed that the dark-skinned girl called Didyme praised by Asclepiades in v. 210 is surely Didyme the mistress of Ptolemy Philadelphus, 'one of the native women' (Athenaeus xiii. 576e–f) and so—to a Greek—dark-skinned. (See *GRBS* xxxi [1990], 287–91.)

11. Asclepiades and Hedylus were both born on Samos.

12. Hedylus wrote on the temple of Arsinoe-Aphrodite (Gow–Page IV), as did Posidippus (XII, XIII)—and Callimachus (XIV). Both Asclepiades and Posidippus wrote (as I have shown elsewhere) on mistresses of Ptolemy Philadelphus (*GRBS* xxxi [1990], 287–304).

13. Whatever may be the exact point of Hedylus VI, it appeals to Asclepiades as a master of the genre ('sweeter than Sicelides').

14. Last (but not least), even if Reitzenstein was not justified in his claim that Meleager in his preface (*AP* iv. i. 45–6) gave all three poets the same flower, he certainly seems to have thought of them as a trio:

ἐν δὲ Ποσείδιππόν τε καὶ Ἡδύλον, ἄγρι' ἀρούρης,
Σικελίδεώ τ' ἀνέμοις ἄνθεα φυόμενα.

There is an obvious and unmistakable convergence of evidence, both internal and external. One conclusion at least seems beyond doubt. Whether or not 'the three friends lived and loved and drank and wrote verse together' (W. and M. Wallace, *Asclepiades of*

Samos (Oxford 1941), p. xi), we may safely assume both a literary and a personal relationship of some sort between them, though surely at Alexandria rather than (as the Wallaces believed) at the 'friendly court' of Duris of Samos.

But the juxtaposed poems and especially the alternative ascriptions require a more specific explanation, and the only comprehensive solution so far proposed is that of Reitzenstein, recently followed and elaborated by I. G. Galli Calderini, *Att: dell'Accademia Pontiana* xxxi (1983), 239–80. His point of departure was the A scholion on *Iliad* xi. 101 (Erbse iii. 144. 13 f.):

αὐτὰρ ὁ βῆ ῥ᾽ Ἶσόν τε καὶ Ἄντιφον ἐξεναρίξων]

Ζηνόδοτος ἔξω τοῦ ῥ᾽ βῆ Ἶσον, μὴ ἐμφερεσθαι δέ φησιν ὁ Ἀρίσταρχος νῦν ἐν τοῖς Ποσειδίππου ἐπιγράμμασι τὸν Βήρισον, ἀλλ᾽ ἐν τῷ λεγομένῳ Σωρῷ εὑρεῖν. εὔλογον δέ φησιν ἐλεγχόμενον αὐτὸν ἀπαλεῖψαι.

Zenodotus ⟨reads⟩ βῆ Ἶσον without the rho, and Aristarchus says that the Berisus ⟨poem⟩ is not now to be found in the Epigrams of Posidippus, but he did find it in the so-called Soros ['Heap']. It is likely that he deleted it on being criticized.

Apparently Posidippus had construed (or affected to construe) the variant reading βῆ ῥ᾽ Ἶσον as a proper name Βήρισον, and used it in a poem of his own, published in a work known as the *Soros*. Aristarchus had also looked for it among Posidippus' Epigrams, but without success.

Reitzenstein suggested that the *Soros* was a *joint* collection published by Asclepiades, Posidippus, and Hedylus, in which individual epigrams were not distinguished by the author's name. This collection was used by Meleager, who assigned individual poems to their authors 'from their placing or style, and perhaps also from separate editions of their author's works'. The shared ascriptions are cases where he could not decide between two possible claimants. Reitzenstein saw a further trace of this uncertainty about authorship in a curious passage in which Strabo cites some elegiac lines with the ascription 'Hedylus or whoever it was' (εἴθ᾽ Ἡδύλος ἐστίν εἴθ᾽ ὁστισοῦν, xiv. 6, p. 683).

If the Homer scholion correctly reports Aristarchus searching for the Berisus poem among Posidippus' Epigrams as well as in the *Soros*, publication of one at least of his epigrams in two different books is certainly implied—though of course it might just be that Aristarchus could not remember which of the two books it appeared in and looked in the wrong one first. It should also be noted that the wording of the scholion does not suggest that the *Soros* contained poems by anyone other than Posidippus—though it does not exclude the possibility either.

As formulated, this ingenious hypothesis is certainly neither plausible in itself nor does it adequately account for the facts. In the first place, such a joint collection would be without parallel, and though the lack of a parallel is not decisive by itself, it does seem incredible that the collaborators should have been prepared to leave their respective contributions unsigned. In the second place, as Gow objected, 'a separate edition of any one of the three should have secured that he did not appear in any double attribution; and if there were no separate editions all ascriptions in *AP* are guesswork' (*HE* ii. 116). All three names do appear in double ascriptions, and no one will believe that all the ascriptions in *AP* are guesswork. The logic is impeccable—but perhaps too rigorously applied. As the Wallaces pointed out (*TAPA* lxx, 195), there may have been epigrams that appeared only in the *Soros*, and so anonymously. Yet if this had been the case, we should have expected at least a few *triple* ascriptions. How was it that Meleager apparently knew when *Soros* epigrams were at any rate not by Hedylus? The Wallaces somewhat implausibly replied that Meleager must have decided that (e.g.) v. 194 and 209 must be by either Asclepiades or Posidippus because they were 'too flowery, too delicate, too straightforward for the more brutal and ironic approach of Hedylus'. Yet even so they conceded that there 'must have been some poems which Meleager was unable to assign even to one or two out of the three'. These, they suggest, are the six poems in their alleged *Soros* sequence that are marked ἄδηλον, which they take to be Meleager's own acknowledgement of defeat.

But this amounts to saying that all double ascriptions are Meleagrian guesswork. And even if the ἄδηλον headings do go back to Meleager, a simpler explanation is that the poems were straightforwardly anonymous in his source, as so often on extant papyri. There is also a more basic flaw in the entire Reitzenstein-Wallace hypothesis here. They assumed that the Meleagrian sequence in *AP* v could be treated as a more or less direct excerpt from the *Garland*. Yet as we have already seen in Chs. II and X, the original Meleagrian erotic section comprised not just the (mainly) heterosexual sequence from *AP* v but also the pederastic Meleagrian sequence from *AP* xii, not consecutively but mixed up together in one sexually undifferentiated sequence. Thus the apparent integrity of the Reitzenstein-Wallace '*Soros* sequence' is illusory: in the original *Garland* its groupings would have been constantly interrupted by scores of other poems by other poets—including another 30-odd ἄδηλα, which Gow (1958, p. 25) referred to Meleager's source, which he took to have contained a number of anonymous paederastica.

I venture to propose a modified and more modest version of Reitzenstein's hypothesis, one that would eliminate most of this postulated guesswork. While a joint collection by three contemporary poets would be unparalleled, there would be nothing at all strange in the latest of a series of epigrammatists producing a collection of his own and his predecessors' work. What else did Meleager, Philip, and Agathias do? His obvious familiarity with the work of Asclepiades and Posidippus makes it clear that Hedylus was the latest of our trio. And if he is the Hedylus who commented on Callimachus' Epigrams, it would not be surprising if he had also published a collection of the work of Asclepiades and Posidippus, the two other most distinguished epigrammatists of the age, adding for good measure a selection of his own work in the same vein.

Then there is Strabo's puzzling citation of 'Hedylus or whoever it was'. In view of the fullness of the citation (two couplets quoted and a summary of the rest of the poem), Reitzenstein was right to observe that the uncertainty is not to be put down to defective recollection. The presumption is that either Strabo or his source was copying directly from some source which somehow suggested this uncertainty. On the other hand 'Hedylus or whoever' hardly suggests a quotation from the supposedly undifferentiated poems of three authors. Above all, why guess the most obscure and least prolific of the three? But what if Strabo (or his source) had been using a collection of which Hedylus had been co-author and editor? The uncertainty may then have arisen from one of the standard hazards of such collections, the omission of headings to individual poems or the ambiguity of τοῦ αὐτοῦ or ἄλλο headings. Given Hedylus' role as editor, when doubt arose 'Hedylus or whoever' would have been a perfectly reasonable form of citation. We have already noted an exactly parallel tendency for poems cited from Agathias' *Cycle* to be ascribed to Agathias himself (Ch. XIV).

It might be added that, to judge from Strabo, this poem of Hedylus (cited as an 'elegy') must have been longer than the average epigram, which would not have been anomalous in a third-century epigram collection (see Ch. I).

The difference between my hypothesis and Reitzenstein's is that in the collection I postulate all epigrams would have been ascribed to their respective authors. Naturally, however, as copy succeeded copy some poems are bound to have acquired false ascriptions in one or another of the ways so fully illustrated in the pages of this book. Meleager's double ascriptions will have arisen when he collated this collection with separate editions of the three epigrammatists—or perhaps with another copy of the collection (compare the often discrepant ascriptions of the poems repeated in the two sources of Planudes, or between Planudes and *AP*).

This seems to me the simplest explanation of the constant juxtaposition of poems by the trio (still striking even if we allow for the missing paederastica), the double ascriptions, and the Strabo citation. Whether or not this edition was the *Soros* is perhaps another matter. A collection of short poems might without absurdity have been likened to a 'heap of winnowed grain' (Gow on Theocritus vii. 155). According to Matthew Santirocco, 'that the collection is winnowed (i.e. that the chaff has been removed) suggests Alexandrian polish and labor' (*Arethusa* xiii (1980), 47). One might add that the ear of grain well suggests the smallest literary creation, the epigram; and a heap of them a collection of epigrams. But since Aristotle uses σωρός for a random as opposed to a definite number or quantity (*LSJ*, s.v. 2), there would presumably be no implication of artistic arrangement (as, e.g., with στέφανος). Fraser suggests rather the meaning 'treasure' (op. cit. ii. 801 n. 72), comparing σωρευτής 'one who heaps up wealth' (*LSJ*), but this meaning is not attested for σωρός itself.

If this collection was the *Soros*, there is one last observation to make. According to Reitzenstein, Posidippus' own edition of his epigrams must have appeared *after* the *Soros*, because it did not contain the Berisus epigram. Even Gow assigned both books to Posidippus' lifetime. But neither conclusion really follows. It was clearly no more than a *guess* of Aristarchus' (εὔλογον) that Posidippus himself eliminated or revised the Berisus epigram in the light of Zenodotus' criticism. Is it credible that Posidippus would have retracted so tamely? Did he really believe in the reading *Βήρισον*?

What bad luck if it was by mere chance that he hit on such a ghost name when looking for a Homeric warrior for his epigram! Surely he was *deliberately* alluding to a controversial passage, knowing full well that such as Zenodotus would bristle at the implied Homeric interpretation. R. Merkelbach has vividly sketched a hypothetical scenario, a symposiastic contest ('Wettdichten beim Wein') among our three poets:

Man dichtete reihum Epigramme auf Helden des trojanischen Krieges, wie wir sie aus dem aristotelischen Peplos kennen: der erste auf einen Griechen, dessen Name mit dem Buchstaben A anfing; der zweite auf einer Trojaner mit A; der dritte auf einen Griechen mit B; und nun kam Poseidipp an die Reihe und sollte ein Epigramm auf einen Trojaner mit B machen. Es fiel ihm keiner ein: kurz entschlossen dichtete er ein Epigramm auf 'Berisos'. Als die Zechbrüder einwandten, einen Berisos gäbe es doch gar nicht in der Ilias, sagte Poseidipp: 'Doch, in dem Vers αὐτὰρ ὁ BH P ΙΣΟN τε καὶ Ἄντιφον ἐξεναρίξων' (Λ 101). Man kann sich den Jubel der Runde vorstellen (*Rhein. Museum* xcix [1956], 123–4).

As already remarked, there are many reasons why the poem might not have appeared in both books.

APPENDIX VI

Planudea IV: Urbinas gr. 125

THIS miscellaneous book (hereafter U), consisting mainly of prose texts (especially Libanius, Aristides, and Philo), was written by as many as nine different scribes of the late thirteenth and early fourteenth century and completed by five more in the fifteenth. But most of the work, according to the Russian scholar B. L. Fonkič (*Viz. vrem.*, NS xi (1979), 251; cf. ibid. xli (1980), 215–16) was done by Planudes himself. While noticing a ligature 'not prominent in the usual script of Planudes', Nigel Wilson accepts the identification as 'probably secure enough' (*GRBS* xxii (1981), 396–7).

There are four brief sections containing epigrams, on fos. 197ᵛ (2 poems); 203ᵛ–204ᵛ (24 poems); 303ᵛ (11 poems); and 307ᵛ (3 poems). On Fonkič's identifications all but the last of these sections are in Planudes' hand.

All 40 of these items are to be found in the epigrammatic portions of L: 39 in Part I (see p. 203 above), and the other in Part II(*b*) (see p. 204).

(*a*) On fo. 197ᵛ stand *AP* xi. 401 and the riddle poem xiv. 9, the latter with the same lemma and text as L (see the addendum to Beckby iv². 771).

(*b*) The 24 poems on fos. 203ᵛ–204ᵛ are an excerpt from the sequence of 57 poems on fos. 3–4ᵛ of L, in the same sequence throughout except for the first two pairs (dots indicate where U omits poems present in L): *AP* vii. 56; vii. 89; v. 297; v. 302 [L has the sequence v. 297; v. 302; vii. 56; vii. 89] . . . vii. 336; ix. 394 . . . x. 98 . . . xi. 50 . . . xi. 238; xi. 251; xi. 252; xi. 292. 3–4; xi. 293; xi. 294; xi. 303 . . . xi. 391 . . . x. 28 . . . x. 32; *Paroem. gr.* 2. 167. 11 . . . ix. 165; ix. 166 . . . ix. 359; ix. 360. The section is closed by ix. 440, Moschus' *Runaway Love*, from elsewhere in L (see Maas, *Kl. Schriften* (1973), 168 and above, Ch. X).

(*c*) On 303ᵛ, x. 79, 80, and 84, in the same sequence as on fo. 6–6ᵛ of L.

(*d*) On 307^v are eleven poems apparently not in Planudes' hand. The other difference is that although all eleven appear in L, the original order has been more disturbed, at both the beginning and end of the sequence: xi. 432; ix. 120; x. 27; x. 29; x. 30; x. 28; xi. 172*b*; ix. 23. 7–8; xi. 156; xi. 193; x. 58.

There is no epigram in U that is not in L. It can hardly be doubted that the epigrammatic portions of U were excerpted from the epigrammatic portions of L, in part by Planudes himself, in part by one of his team of fellow workers.

Gallavotti (1959, 48–50) long ago drew attention to a short epigrammatic sequence on fos. 169–70 of Barberinus gr. 4, which he dated to *c*.1300. Here too the sequence is exactly as in L, with only five omissions: v. 297; v. 302 . . . vii. 89 . . . vii. 126; ix. 61; vii. 309; vii. 327. 1–2; vii. 336; ix. 394; ix. 499; ix. 527 . . . ix. 642; ix. 768; x. 98 . . . xi. 50; xi. 61; xi. 156; xi. 193 . . . xi. 251; xi. 292. 3–4.

Evidently both manuscripts must have been written after the compilation of L, that is to say after 1280–3. It also seems logical to infer that both were written before Marc. 481 (that is to say, before 1301). It would be strange if Planudes had been content to refer back to the tiny and textually worthless selection in L after he had found even one let alone both of the much fuller and more authoritative redactions of Cephalas that he utilized for the compilation of his definitive anthology in Marc. 481. Not surprisingly, it was this collection, not L, that dominated the subsequent Byzantine epigram tradition, as Turyn (1973) and Mioni (1975) have so abundantly illustrated.

APPENDIX VII

P. Oxy. 3724

P. Oxy. 3724 consists of fragments from a first-century-AD papyrus roll listing the first two or three words of about 175 epigrams, arranged in eight columns.[1] Columns i–vi are written on what may be the end of a roll, on the recto of the papyrus, cols. vi–vii on the verso (a fact which may be of significance for the interpretation of the list). Of these 175 incipits only thirty-one can be identified, and of these thirty-one at least twenty-five and probably twenty-seven are epigrams of Philodemus. Two are by Asclepiades, and two more anonymous (though one of these, ii. 29 = *AP* xii. 103, was closely imitated by Philodemus, vii. 13 = *AP* v. 107). Here is the list:

i	15–20	*AP* v. 145	Asclepiades (again vi. 18)
ii	2	Cougny VI. 77	anonymous oracle
	5	xi. 34	Philodemus
	14	xi. 41	Philodemus
	18	v. 126	Philodemus
	19	v. 121	Philodemus
	21	? x. 103	Philodemus (again iv. 16)
	28	xii. 103	ἄδηλον
iii	7	xi. 30	Philodemus (deleted, again v. 31 ?)
iv	4	xi. 44	Philodemus
	7	ix. 570	Philodemus
	10	v. 4	Philodemus
	16	x. 103	Philodemus
	17	v. 24	Philodemus
	18	vii. 222	Philodemus
	19	vi. 349	Philodemus
	28	v. 150	Asclepiades
	31	v. 80	'Plato' or Philodemus

[1] Published with his characteristic learning, economy, and judgement by Peter Parsons (P. Oxy. vol. LIV [1987], 65–84), to whom I am most grateful for the opportunity to study this intriguing document before publication. This appendix is a revised and updated version of a letter to Parsons dated 9 Dec. 1985. The papyrus is cited as P.

v	3	? v. 123	Philodemus
	11	v. 112	Philodemus
	13	v. 306	Philodemus
	14	v. 131	Philodemus
	20	v. 132	Philodemus
	31	? xi. 30	Philodemus
vi	4	v. 308	Antiphilus or Philodemus
	18	v. 145	Asclepiades
vii	7	v. 115	Philodemus
	13	v. 107	Philodemus
	15	v. 46	Philodemus
	17	xi. 35	Philodemus
	21	ix. 412	Philodemus
	25	? v. 13	Philodemus
viii	2	x. 21	Philodemus
	9	v. 120	Philodemus

Thirty-five epigrams are attributed to Philodemus in *AP*, two or three of which are doubtful (Gow and Page, *GP* ii. 371, from whom I differ in two cases discussed below). Now the Philodeman poems preserved in *AP* and the other Cephalan derivatives come from Philip's *Garland*, itself preserved in much reduced compass by *AP* (Ch. II). And Philip himself presumably included no more than a representative selection from the work of this prolific writer. On the other hand we have in the two *Garlands* a similar representative selection from the work of all the other leading hellenistic and early imperial epigrammatists. And yet almost all we know of Philodemus appears among the Oxyrynchus incipits, and virtually nothing by all the rest. We may surely infer that many, perhaps most of the unidentified incipits are to unknown poems of Philodemus.

Of these new poems, 'one probably mentions Philodemus, and may be by him (ii 12); so possibly ii 15. iii 15 makes a pair with ii 19 (Philodemus); ii 8, iv 1, and iv 21 do or may have names (Antigenes, Xanthion, Demo) which recur in Philodemean poems. Other incipits mention Roman names, places or institutions' [iv 24, v 7, v 25, vi 2, vii 23, viii 4] (Parsons, p. 67). Note particularly the two poems on Naples (iv. 14–15), where Philodemus is known to have lived. If we turn to the themes of the new poems, 'there are perhaps forty whose subject could, with all proper reserve, be inferred; almost all look to wine and love' (ibid.), the principal themes of Philodemus' epigrams. Two recent articles, by D. Sider (*ZPE* lxxvi [1989], 229–36) and M. Gigante (*SFIC* lxxxii [1989],

129–51) have adduced a number of arguments of various sorts why a great many other incipits should, could, or might be assigned to Philodemus.

Some of these arguments are fragile: clearly a substantial number of the unknown incipits *might* come from other poets. A certain scepticism is in order. But it is equally important to recognize that scepticism is not in itself a virtue. A list of incipits that are mostly but not entirely from Philodemus is harder to explain than a list that is all Philodemus. Gigante writes of the source of P as an 'anthology' that 'closed with Philodemus' (p. 134). But it would be odd to describe as an 'anthology' a collection that consisted of just two poets, with twenty or thirty times as many poems by Philodemus as Asclepiades.[2]

It is worth exploring the possibility that *all* the incipits are Philodeman. On this hypothesis there would be two perfectly reasonable explanations for the (apparent) presence of Asclepiadean and other incipits in the list. The first is that the poems of Asclepiades in question served as models for variations by Philodemus, and were included for that reason. The second is that these incipits may *not* in fact be Asclepiades, but parodies or variations beginning with the same or similar words.

Lest this seem too far-fetched, there are in fact three examples in the Oxyrynchus and one in the Vienna list. (A): the first two words of col. v 28 (ἡδὺ θέρευς) suggest Asclepiades' famous poem ἡδὺ θέρους διψῶντι χιὼν ποτόν; but P adds a third word, ἕλκει. Evidently a different poem that took Asclepiades' opening words as its point of departure. (B): col. iv 8 (οὐ μισέω τὸ πόημα) is a variation on Callimachus' well-known ἐχθαίρω τὸ ποίημα τὸ κυκλικόν, though in this case the quotation comes in the middle of the line rather than the opening words. (C): if all we had was the initial traces Εὔφρων καὶ θ[. . . of Vienna list no. 113, who would have hesitated to correct and supplement Εὔφρω καὶ Θαΐς καὶ Βοΐδιον, αἱ Διομήδους = Hedylus or Asclepiades, *AP* v. 161? In fact the papyrus resumes after the gap . . .]ξ δύο ἀδελφεοί, once again evidently a different poem.[3] Lastly, a less clearcut case (D): col. vi 12 (ἰξὸν ἔχεις τὸν)

---

[2] A *private* anthology might reasonably contain a disproportionate preponderance of personal favourites, but that would not be an anthology of epigrams in the same sense as the *Garlands* of Meleager and Philip.

[3] The only metrically possible supplements suggested by F. Dornseiff and B. Hansen, *Rückläufiges Wörterbuch der griechischen Eigennamen* (repr. Chicago 1978), 120–1 are Thornax, Tharrax, and (most promising) Thraix (the three ladies in *AP* v. 161 are described as daughters of the Thracian king Diomedes).

looks like (and was taken by Parsons to be) the beginning of *AP* v. 96 by Meleager, ἰξὸν ἔχεις τὸ φίλημα. The τὸν of the papyrus *might* just be an error for Meleager's τὸ. But we cannot exclude the possibility that, once more, this is a different poem. If so, either a variation by Meleager, or by a later poet. If by a later poet, then the only two post-Meleagrian erotic epigrammatists of any note are Philodemus and Argentarius, and we cannot be certain that Argentarius wrote in time for the collection behind the incipits. In favour of Philodemus one could compare, for the metaphor (ἰξόν, bird-lime), col. ii 12, ἰξεύειν φιλόδη[μος]. For two further examples in Mnasalces, see above, p. 4.

The most puzzling item in the list on any hypothesis is the first (col. ii 2), εἴκοσι τὰς πρὸ κυ(νός). On the face of it, this must be the opening of the fake Delphic oracle quoted (from Chamaeleon) by Athenaeus (22 E: H. W. Parke and D. E. W. Wormell, *The Delphic Oracle*, ii [Oxford 1956], 167, no. 414; J. Fontenrose, *The Delphic Oracle* [Berkeley 1978], 392, L103):

> εἴκοσι τὰς πρὸ κυνὸς καὶ εἴκοσι τὰς μετέπειτα
> οἴκῳ ἐνὶ σκιερῷ Διονύσῳ χρῆσθαι ἰητρῷ.

For twenty days before the dog [namely the rising of Sirius], and twenty days after, use Dionysus the Physician [namely wine] in a shady house.

It is easy to see how this advice could have been exploited in a sympotic poem. Sider points out that in his prose works Philodemus twice quotes Chamaeleon, and suggests that the incipit might be the opening of 'an epigram by Philodemus that begins with a quotation from this oracle' (p. 231). Gigante was wrong simply to dismiss this as 'troppo fantasiosa' (p. 137). It may be mistaken (as Sider was well aware), but it could also be right. If it is, the incipits might indeed all be Philodemus.

But if this approach should turn out to be mistaken, what sort of collection might we then identify behind the incipits? Taking the four non-Philodeman incipits at face value, apparently not an edition of Philodemus alone. On the other hand, if it were any sort of anthology, in the light of our knowledge of the *Garlands* of Meleager and Philip we should expect to be able to identify far more poems by other epigrammatists. Philip himself may not have published by the date of the papyrus (the Philodeman incipits show no trace of Philippan order),[4] but many of his contributors would have been available to earlier anthologists.

---

[4] According to Gigante, Philip's *Garland* was 'certamente nota al nostro Autore'

Furthermore, we might have expected either Philodemus or an anthologist to have arranged his material in some sort of artistic sequence. Yet there is little sign of such artistry in the incipits. With the eye of faith a few pairs might be conjured up out of the incipits alone. For example, col. iv 3–4 might both concern dinners, 10–11 witnesses to love, and col. v 16–17 perhaps symposia (like many others); more securely, col. iv 4–15 both begin with a reference to Naples and vi 8–9 both allude to harping (but then so do the poems referred to at col. ii 5 and v 14). Col. ii 15–16 both have πρότερον second word, but then so do ii 21 and vii 4. And when we have the actual text of the poems referred to, the evidence mostly points the other way. For example, the ἄδηλον *AP* xii. 103 (col. ii 29) is nowhere near Philodemus' adaptation *AP* v. 107 at col. vii 13. At col. vi 16–19 we have four consecutive poems by Philodemus (*AP* xi. 103; v. 24; vii. 222; vi. 349), a long enough sequence (it might have seemed) to reveal at least something of the verbal and thematic links between neighbouring poems that we regularly find in the Meleagrian and Philippan sequences in *AP*. Yet there are no significant links between these four poems, whether by community or even contrast of theme. Nor between *AP* v. 306 and 131 at col. v 13–14. And though *AP* v. 132 follows 131 in Palatine (here = Philippan) sequence in col. iv (14 and 20), there is a gap of five poems, and, again, no verbal or thematic connection at all.

Three Philodeman poems with close and important thematic links are *AP* xi. 34, 41 and v. 112. v. 112 makes the same point as xi. 41 about grey hairs being συνετῆς ἄγγελοι ἡλικίης while xi. 34 shares with xi. 41 the renunciation of women, wine, and song, collectively designated as μανίη. A. H. Griffiths wanted xi. 34 to be the first and 41 the last poems in a book (*BICS* xvii [1970], 37–80). We do not have to accept that (see Giangrande, *Grazer Beiträge* i [1973], 143–7), yet it is difficult to doubt that Philodemus consciously wrote each of these poems with reference to the other two, and that he put them in some sort of significant sequence in the book in which he originally published them. This original sequence was thoroughly broken up before the poems reached *AP*,

(p. 133), without further comment. But if Philip published under Nero rather than Gaius (Ch. IV), that is already the 'later first century' to which Parsons assigns the papyrus (p. 65).

first when Philip rearranged them in his alphabetical categories,[5] and then again when Cephalas arbitrarily divided them between his erotic and sympotic categories. It is difficult to believe that their positions in the incipit list (ii 5, ii 14, v 11) reflect the arrangement of either Philodemus or any competent anthologist.

One curious feature of the incipits is not infrequent repetition: 'some items are deleted and reappear later (ii 4 and 24; iii 7 f. and v 31 f.; others stand twice (ii 15 and vii 4, ii 21 and iv 16 (?), vi 7 and vii 14)' (Parsons). If the incipit list is the index to a sequence of poems written out in full, it is not easy to believe that so relatively short a sequence contained so many duplications. Note (for example) that ii 4 is repeated in the same column as ii 24. Even if it did, why delete the duplications in the incipit list? Nor is it easy to believe that the duplications and deletions were attempts to correct the order of the original sequence; for then it would cease to be an accurate index. But then perhaps it was not intended to be an index.

In favour of the hypothesis that it is an index is the fact that one of the epigrams featured in the incipit list (*AP* v. 145 by Ascle-piades, at vi 18) is also written out in full by another hand near the bottom of col. i, above the traces of another, unidentifiable epigram, also written in full. It is tempting (with Mark Caponigro) to identify these traces with the next and last incipit in col. vi. Caponigro goes on to suggest that the incipits are nothing more than the index to a collection written in the missing remainder of P. Oxy. 3724. On this hypothesis col. vi, the last column on the recto of the papyrus, is the last column of the index, which would then begin with col. vii on the verso. An index of incipits would certainly be a useful conclusion to any collection of epigrams.

---

[5] It is worth emphasizing how completely Philip's alphabetical rearrangement must have broken up whatever principle of arrangement Philodemus himself used—or any other Philippan poet, for that matter. *AP* xi. 34 and 35 (for example) are about very different themes, though superficially linked by their common reference to symposia—and by the fact that they begin with consecutive letters of the alphabet (lambda and kappa). That was enough for Philip to place them together, but there is no reason to believe that Philodemus himself exploited these unimportant links in whatever context he first published the poems. So there is no particular significance in the fact that they are widely separated in the incipits (ii 2 and vii 17). No significance either in the fact that *AP* v. 132 follows (though not immediately) v. 131 at col. v 14 and 20, since the poems have no significant verbal or thematic links, and owe their juxtaposition by Philip solely to the fact that they begin with consecutive letters of the alphabet (psi and omega). Given the obvious independence of the incipits from Philip, there is no point in looking among them for traces of the Philippan sequences of *AP*.

Caponigro's hypothesis does not explain the duplications, but then nothing seems to explain them very well. However, it does have the advantage of giving the list a simple, mundane function—one that would take it out of the scope of this book.

The alternative is Parsons' suggestion that the incipits were intended as a list of contents for a projected personal anthology of erotic and sympotic epigrams (even the Delphic 'oracle' concerns the medicinal use of wine). I should prefer to substitute the word 'selection' for anthology, given the very limited range of authors included. Such a list might have been compiled from more than one source. At first glance it might seem that the duplications support the hypothesis of careless consultation of two or more sources, and at some stage a plurality of sources must presumably be invoked, if some of the poems are indeed non-Philodeman. But several of the duplicated incipits are poems of Philodemus, and it seems natural, if not inevitable, to infer that the Philodeman poems at least all came from the same source. Other factors to take into account are the occasional check-marks (in groups of five) and the occasional sequences of numbers (in groups of ten) in the margins. The check-marks might be taken as an indication that the epigrams corresponding to those incipits had been located and copied. Here we might compare the abbreviation ϵv found against a number of the Vienna incipits. *If* (as Harrauer suggests) this stands for $\epsilon \hat{v} \rho o v$, ('found' or 'located'), that might suggest that the Vienna incipits are likewise a list of contents for a projected anthology, some (but not all) of which the writer has already located. But when so little is known of the contents and purpose of the Vienna incipits, they cannot safely be used to interpret the Oxyrhynchus incipits. We are not entitled to assume that both were intended for the same purpose. The heading to the Vienna incipits suggests that they are only a selection from a unified pre-existing collection (p. 10 above); there seems no reason to make the same assumption about the Oxyrynchus incipits.

All in all, the new papyrus seems to offer little to the historian of anthologies in the wider, more literary sense employed in this book.

I append some notes on three cases of controversial ascriptions, in each of which the new papyrus supports Philodeman authorship.

AP v. 80 (col. iv 31) must surely now be assigned to Philodemus rather than Plato (or even Pseudo-Plato, since surely no one any longer believes that Plato himself wrote hellenistic epigrams). The facts as I see them are as follows (for some different arguments in favour of the attribution to Plato, see now David Sider, *AJP* cvii [1986], 321). At some point before Diogenes Laertius wrote, both *AP* v. 80 and its pair v. 79 got attributed to Plato, presumably because of the name Xanthippe. W. Ludwig (*GRBS* iv [1963], 75–7) inferred from Diogenes iii. 29–32 that Diogenes took them from the περὶ παλαιᾶς τρυφῆς of Pseudo-Aristippus, and that they were part of Aristippus' campaign to blacken Plato's name by means of discreditable sexual liaisons—in this case with his master's wife. But Diogenes only directly names Aristippus as his source for the poems on Aster, Dio, and Phaedrus. We are not entitled (with Ludwig) to attribute all the remaining epigrams quoted by Diogenes (including an innocuous epitaph on the Eretrians) to this source (so Page, in his valuable discussion in *FGE* 126–7). Nor is it plausible to argue that the Xanthippe epigrams were deliberate forgeries maliciously foisted on Plato, since they purport to concern the seduction of a virgin; and not even the most incompetent forger can have supposed a disciple of Socrates born early enough to seduce Xanthippe before she married Socrates. Nor would Plato really have deserved the accusation of treachery that is supposed to have been the point of the operation if Xanthippe had still been single at the time. It follows that *AP* v. 79–80 were originally written by another poet for another Xanthippe. Philodemus wrote at least four poems about a lady called Xanthippe; Planudes directly attributes v. 80 to Philodemus; and here we find v. 79 in an overwhelmingly Philodeman context on the new papyrus. Diogenes wrote long after Philodemus, as too probably did the Pseudo-Aristippus from whom he derives his Pseudo-Platonic epigrams (so Page *FGE* 127, against the earlier date assumed by Ludwig). It is perfectly possible that the misattribution took place (accidentally) as late as the first century AD, especially since (as the papyri confirm) epigrams were so often quoted without any attribution. There can be no doubt that *some* of the allegedly Platonic epigrams Diogenes quotes from Pseudo-Aristippus are malicious forgeries. But *AP* v. 79–80 hardly fit in this category. I suggest that they were later additions to the pseudo-canon, once Pseudo-Aristippus' efforts had established Plato as an erotic epigrammatist.

The incipit runs μῆλον ἐγὼ πέμ(πει), where *AP* and *APl* offer βάλλει. We need entertain no doubts that the incipit is indeed the

first three words of *AP* v. 80. Nor do we need to explain πέμ(πει) as
an error for βάλλει. For Philodemus did not write βάλλει. No recent
editor or critic seems to have noticed that the Latin translation
preserved as *Epigr. Bob.* 32 offers *mittit*:

> malum ego: mittit me quidam tibi munus amator.

So our earliest witness apart from the papyrus actually supports
πέμπει. If we consider the pair v. 79–80 together, 'The first
contains words which a lover might say while throwing the apple.
The other pretends to be an inscription scratched into the apple
itself' (Ludwig 75). The inscription does not need to specify the
means whereby the apple reaches Xanthippe. But it is easy to see
how the βάλλει of v. 79 could have come to oust the less vivid
πέμπει.

Next there is *AP* v. 308 = col. vi 4, with conflicting ascriptions
to Philodemus and Antiphilus. Plainly the poem was written as a
pendant to *AP* v. 46 by Philodemus. In v. 46 the streetwalker is
unusually co-operative, in v. 308 unusually unco-operative; and
there are also clear verbal parallels (see Gow and Page, *GP* ii
125–6). Gow and Page believed that Antiphilus wrote in imitation
of Philodemus; but why not the simpler alternative, that Philodemus wrote both poems? It should be observed that, while a
banale mechanical error (misapplication of a τοῦ αὐτοῦ) will explain
how a poem of Philodemus got ascribed to Antiphilus or vice-versa
in Philip's *Garland*, Cephalas or *AP*, where the two poets regularly
appear in sequence, that error cannot be assumed here. It seems
quite clear that the incipits show no knowledge of Philip's
Garland. Indeed, the papyrus may well be earlier than the *Garland*; earlier too than Antiphilus, the latest datable poet in the
Garland except for Philip himself.

At col. iv 18 stands *AP* v. 24, attributed by both *AP* and *APl* to
Philodemus, but transferred to Meleager by Jacobs, followed by
both Beckby and Gow and Page. Even before the appearance of the
poem in the Philodeman context of the incipits, there was no
serious argument in favour of Meleagrian authorship. Why should
not Philodemus, like Lucillius (*AP* xi. 256), have used the Meleagrian name Heliodora? As for style, even Gow and Page concede
that 'Philodemus can write very like M.' (*HE* ii 631). And while
confusion of Meleager and Philodemus would be a routine error in
anthologies deriving from Cephalas, who combined the two
Garlands, once more we cannot make the same assumption here.

APPENDIX VIII

The *Peplos*

LOOSELY related to the question of early epigram collections is a
curious lost work ascribed to Aristotle under the name Πέπλος (V.
Rose, *Aristotelis fragmenta* [1886], 394–407; C. A. Forbes, *PW* xix.
1 [1937], 561–2). It was clearly a work of antiquarian research. The
long fr. 637 (schol. Aristides, *Panath.* p. 323 Dind.) shows that
among other things it discussed a number of Greek festivals, a
known interest of Aristotle. The ecclesiastical historian Socrates
cites it as a source for erotic myths (*HE* iii. 23). For my purposes
the most relevant testimonium is preserved from Porphyry (*c*.300)
by Eustathius (*Eustathii Commentarii*, ed. M. van der Valk, I
[1971], 439. 23 f.). According to Porphyry, the *Peplos* 'set out the
genealogies of the [Greek and Trojan] leaders and the number of
ships of each and epigrams on them'. So while basically a prose
work of scholarship, it also included epigrams.

The title implies a miscellany, presumably taken from the varied
mythological scenes woven into the robe of Athena for the Pan-
athenaia every fourth year (L. Deubner, *Attische Feste* [1932],
30–2); in earlier times scenes from the Gigantomachy, later mortals, such as Antigonus and Demetrius (G. Leroux, Daremberg–
Saglio, iv. 385–6). Schol. Arist. *Vesp.* 827 describes the πέπλος as
παμποίκιλος. Cicero described the *Imagines* of Varro, an illustrated
biographical work that again included epigrams (surely modelled
on the *Peplos*), as a πεπλογραφία (*ad Att.* 16. 11. 3: Schanz–Hosius,
Gesch. d. röm. Lit. I⁴ [1927], 561–3). Aulus Gellius, when justifying
the title *Noctes Atticae* that he gave his own miscellany, lists a
number of fancy titles others had used for miscellaneous works
(*nam quia variam et miscellam et quasi confusaneam doctrinam
conquisiverunt, eo titulos quoque ad eam sententiam exquisitissimos
indiderunt*), instancing *Musae, Silvae*, Λειμῶνες, and Πέπλος (*pr.* 6).
In the appendix to the list of the *Vita Menagiana* stands an entry
πέπλον· περιέχει δὲ ἱστορίαν σύμμικτον (p. 257 Moraux).

Such a work had fifth-century predecessors. Damastes of

Sigeum is said to have written a Περὶ γονέων καὶ προγόνων τῶν εἰς Ἴλιον στρατευσαμένων in two books (Suda Δ 41; Jacoby, *FGrH* 5 T 1); and Polus of Acragas (best known from Plato's *Gorgias*) is credited with a Γενεαλογία τῶν ἐπὶ Ἴλιον στρατευσάντων Ἑλλήνων καὶ βαρβάρων καὶ πῶς ἕκαστος ἀπήλλαξε and a Νεῶν κατάλογος (Suda Π 2170; *FGrH* 7 T 1). W. Nestle could not believe that the sophist Polus wrote such a work (*PW* xxi. 2 [1952], 1985), but Jacoby was rightly critical of such scepticism (Nachträge to his Komm., Ia [1957], 542–3). The growth of local historiography must have added to the available sources for such an enterprise. Frivolous though the reference in Socrates makes it seem, the *Peplos* may in fact have embodied a serious study of the Catalogue of Ships. This is clearly why Porphyry turned to it for his own Homeric researches.

Porphyry included the epigrams in his book 'because they were simple and contained nothing extravagant or inflated; they are all distichs except for the one on Ajax'. Eustathius quotes 'the one on Ajax' in full, and gives details from several others, though none entire. At some stage (whether or not in antiquity is unclear) someone excerpted the epigrams alone. A thirteenth-century Laurentian manuscript (56. 1) preserves a sequence of 48 epigrams, mostly epitaphs on Greek and Trojan heroes. Just as Eustathius reports from Porphyry, they are all distichs except for the quatrain on Ajax. In addition there are the Homeric commentaries of John Tzetzes, which quote 14 of the epigrams in the Florentine manuscript together with 15 more (text in Rose; Bergk, *PLG* ii.⁴ 338 f.; Diehl, *Anth. Lyr.* ii. 171 f.). And lastly we have Ausonius, who himself produced a series of free Latin versions of funerary epigrams on heroes of the Trojan war (*titulos sepulchrales heroum qui bello Troiano interfuerunt*, p. 72 Peiper = p. 56 Prete). Ausonius says only that his Greek originals were 'old poems he came across in a certain scholar' (*apud philologum quendam*), presumably meaning Porphyry (Wendling, p. 47 n. 1), but afraid to name the anti-Christian polemicist.

The epitaphs (as Porphyry rightly remarked) are concise and simple to the point of baldness, but not on that account fourth century rather than hellenistic. They scarcely look like genuine inscriptional poetry, and in the unlikely event that one or two were ever inscribed on monuments, they were surely monuments of the hellenistic age. Their stylistic and thematic homogeneity suggests that they were composed specially for the *Peplos*. That in turn suggests a single author (though according to Symmachus, *Epp.* 1. 2. 2, the epigrams in Varro's *Imagines* were by *diversis auctoribus*). On the other hand, there are sometimes two epitaphs on the same hero. In the case of Agamemnon and Nestor, they give the same version. But no. 4 has Achilles 'honoured on the White Isle', no. 5 buried at Troy. To be sure epigrammatists liked to ring variations on their themes, but the ostensible purpose of these poems is to convey information. Since doublets are the exception rather than the rule, we might compromise in the conclusion that the compiler wrote one epigram on each hero, occasionally adding others when he found them in his sources—or perhaps writing a second himself when his sources gave two versions (as in the case of Achilles).

Some elements of the work look Aristotelian enough. The two most detailed studies, by F. G. Schneidewin ('De peplo Aristotelis Stagiritae: Accedunt pepli reliquiae', *Philologus* i [1846], 1–45) and Ae. Wendling (*De peplo Aristotelico quaestiones selectae*, Diss. Strasburg 1891), decided in favour of the authenticity of the *Peplos* itself, but argued that the epitaphs were a later addition. This is obviously a possibility, though systematic interpolation of several score poems in a treatise of Aristotle might be thought improbable. It is perhaps worth noting that, after naming Aristotle when describing the contents of the *Peplos*, in his discussion of the Ajax epigram Eustathius goes on to refer to 'the epigrammatist', as though this might have been a different person. But that need only imply that he saw Aristotle as the collector of epigrams by others. At all events, if the *Peplos* is (whether in its entirety or as interpolated with the epigrams) a later product of the Peripatetic school, how much later? Although not named in Diogenes Laertius' list of the Aristotelian works, it is included in the list of the *Vita Menagiana*, which contains very little that is demonstrably inauthentic. P. Moraux inferred accordingly that it was at any rate relatively early (*Les Listes anciennes des ouvrages d'Aristote* [Louvain 1951], 238). It is also perhaps significant that Theophrastus too is credited with a work called Πέπλος (Dirk Obbink, in R. W. Sharples *et al*. [edd.], *Theophrastus of Eresus* [Leiden 1991], fr. 727. 10). The best clue to date may in fact lie in the relationship of the *Peplos* to Meleager's *Garland*.

The only one of these distichs to be cited by an ancient writer is no. 15 in the Florentine sequence, on Idomeneus and Meriones, by

Diodorus Siculus (v. 79). There can be little doubt that Diodorus got it from the *Peplos*; he gives the genealogy of the heroes first, then the number of their ships and finally the epigram itself—the topics Porphyry lists and in the order he gives. More interesting still, this is the only distich from the *Peplos* to appear in the Anthology tradition, as *AP* vii. 322. Significantly enough, *AP* offers ὁρᾷς and τοῦ in line 1 with Diodorus as against the ὅρα and τοι of Laur. and Tzetzes. The natural inference is that Cephalas got it from Diodorus rather than a text of the *Peplos*. Indeed, Cephalas seems not to have known the *Peplos*. Bergk (p. 517) quotes three distichs in *AP* (vii. 615–17) which in style and content are certainly very similar to *Peplos* distichs, but all three are also quoted in Diogenes Laertius, whom we know Cephalas to have excerpted with great care. Even if their ultimate source was the *Peplos*, Cephalas' source was surely Diogenes.

But we can go further. The complete absence of *Peplos* distichs from all *Garland* sequences in *AP* suggests that it was not known to Meleager either. Cephalas' failure to use it is easy to explain; the book had long since perished by then, superseded by the no doubt more comprehensive work of Porphyry. We have already seen that Eustathius only knew it through Porphyry. But Meleager would surely have used such a source if he had known of it. The distichs are far from distinguished work, but some are neat enough. One example will suffice, no. 26 on Podarces the brother of Protesilaus, buried in Sicyon:

Γῆ μὲν Ἀχαιὶς ἔθρεψε Ποδάρκην, Ἄκτορος υἱόν·
ὀστέα δ' αὖ Σικυὼν γῆ κατέχει φθίμενον.

It would be surprising if Meleager had rejected every epigram in a collection attributed to Aristotle.

The one quatrain in the *Peplos* (no. 7) is also transmitted in *AP* (and *APl*) under the name of Asclepiades. It stands apart from the distichs not only in length but in its totally different character. Not a simple epitaph specifying the whereabouts of the tomb, but a much more ambitious conception, with Virtue in mourning because Deceit has bested her (alluding to Odysseus' foul play). It is difficult to resist the conclusion that the Ajax epigram was not written by the author of the rest of the distichs. If so, it seems natural to accept the other ascription, to Asclepiades, not least because it was clearly known to Mnasalces of Sikyon (who flourished perhaps a generation later than Asclepiades). Here is the poem (*AP* vii. 145 = *HE* 946–9):

ἅδ᾽ ἐγὼ ἁ τλάμων Ἀρετὰ παρὰ τῷδε κάθημαι
Αἴαντος τύμβῳ κειραμένα πλοκάμους,
θυμὸν ἄχει μεγάλῳ βεβολημένα εἰ παρ᾽ Ἀχαιοῖς
ἁ δολόφρων Ἀπάτα κρέσσον ἐμεῦ δύναται.

And here is Mnasalces' imitation (*HE* 2671–4 = Athen. 163 A):

ἅδ᾽ ἐγὼ ἁ τλάμων Ἀρετὰ παρὰ τῇδε κάθημαι
Ἀδονῇ αἰσχίστως κειραμένη πλοκάμους,
θυμὸν ἄχει μεγάλῳ βεβολημένη εἴπερ ἅπασιν
ἁ κακόφρων τέρψις κρεῖσσον ἐμοῦ κέκριται.

In Asclepiades, Virtue sits by Ajax's tomb, cutting her hair in mourning and wailing because cunning Deceit has got the better of her. In Mnasalces, Virtue is sitting beside Pleasure (Ἀδονή), mourning and wailing because all men have judged τέρψις (presumably a synonym or function of Ἀδονή) superior. According to Porphyry/Eustathius, Mnasalces 'parodied' the poem, but this does not seem at all the right word. Mnasalces is not making fun of either Asclepiades' poem or its sentiments. He has taken its form and much of its language to extend the basic idea from one limited situation (Ajax's defeat) to a cynical comment on human society at large. All we are concerned with here is one detail of his adaptation, the final word in both poems. Where Asclepiades (according to *AP*) complains about the *power* of Deceit, Mnasalces complains that all men *prefer* Pleasure (judge her superior) to Virtue. Compare now the version in the *Peplos*:

ἅδ᾽ ἐγὼ ἁ τλάμων Ἀρετὰ παρὰ τῷδε κάθημαι
Αἴαντος τύμβῳ κειραμένα πλοκάμους,
θυμὸν ἄχει μεγάλῳ βεβολημένα ὡς παρ᾽ Ἀχαιοῖς
ἁ δολόφρων Ἀπάτα κρέσσον ἐμεῦ κέκριται.

The Asclepiadean version, but with Mnasalces' final κέκριται. If the argument may be pressed, the Asclepiadean poem was taken, not from a copy of Asclepiades, but from a text in which it was closely followed by Mnasalces' imitation. And that was surely Meleager's *Garland* (unfortunately, the Mnasalces poem has not survived in the Anthology tradition to test this assumption). So the *Peplos* may actually be later than Meleager.

Of course, the Asclepiadean poem might be a later interpolation into a pre-existing sequence of distichs. But since it clearly stood in the copies of both Porphyry and Ausonius, it must at any rate have been an ancient rather than a Byzantine interpolation. And assuming that the compiler of the *Peplos* was not Aristotle, there is a good reason why he might have chosen to add this particular poem: for Aristotle himself wrote a famous poem praising Ajax' death in pursuit of Ἀρετή (*PMG* 842; cf. *FGE* 31–2, 93–5). There are indeed points of contact between Aristotle and Asclepiades (not noticed in Gow and Page), but the more natural explanation (of course) is that Asclepiades wrote with Aristotle's poem in mind. A further argument is the absence of a distich on Ajax. Gow and Page suggested that the Asclepiades poem 'replaced' the original distich, but we have seen that the compiler did not in the least mind duplications. If Eustathius' comment that the poet's aim in writing a longer poem was to praise Ajax more highly than the other heroes reflects, by way of Porphyry, something in the *Peplos* itself, the link between this poem and Aristotle might have been made clear.

So either the *Peplos* as a whole or at any rate the epigrams of the *Peplos* may be no earlier than the end of the second century BC. They must have been in circulation well before Varro wrote his *Imagines* (in production by late in 44, the date of Cicero's letter), and the researches of Diodorus take us back to *c*.60 BC. Given the homogeneity of theme and treatment and perhaps even single authorship of the epigrams, it would be misleading to call them an anthology. To quote an extant Greek parallel rather than the lost *Imagines* of Varro, Diogenes Laertius included in his *Lives of the Philosophers* 52 epigrams of his own composition on selected philosophers, which he also published in a separate volume. These epigrams, though usually longer than distichs and in a variety of metres, are similarly functional and unadorned, with few literary pretensions (J. Mejer, *Diogenes Laertius and his Hellenistic Background* [Hermes Einzelschr. 40; 1978], 46–50).[1]

---

[1] This Appendix has benefited from suggestions by Stephen A. White.

BIBLIOGRAPHY

THIS is neither a complete bibliography of the Greek Anthology, nor a complete index of works cited, but a list of the most important or representative works consulted during the writing of this volume. For a useful bibliography of works on individual epigrammatists, see Beckby, i². 110–13. Information about editions of the text of the Greek Anthology, and other standard texts and reference works, is included in the Abbreviations section at the front of the book.

AUBRETON, R., 'La tradition manuscrite des épigrammes de l'Anthologie grecque', *RÉA* lxx (1968), 32–81.

—— 'L'archétype de la tradition planudéenne de l' "anthologie grecque"', *Scriptorum* xxiii (1969), 69–87.

—— 'Michel Psellos et l'Anthologie palatine', *L'Antiquité classique* xxxviii (1969), 459–62.

—— 'La translittération d'Homère', *Byzantion* xxxix (1969), 13–34.

—— 'Le livre XII de l'Anthologie palatine: la muse de Straton', *Byzantion* xxxix (1969), 35–52.

—— 'La sylloge Barberino-Vaticana', *RÉA* lxxx (1978), 228–38.

—— 'La tradition de l'anthologie palatine du xviᵉ au xviiiᵉ siècle', *Revue d'histoire des textes* x (1980), 1–52; xi (1981), 1–46.

BALDWIN, B., 'The Date of the *Cycle* of Agathias', *BZ* lxxiii (1980), 334–40.

BARIGAZZI, ADELMO, 'Sopra alcuni nuovi epigrammi ellenistici', *Hermes* lxxx (1952), 494–6.

BASSON, J., *De Cephala et Planude syllogisque minoribus* (Diss. Berlin 1917).

BIRT, T., *Das antike Buchwesen* (Berlin 1882).

BOAS, M., *De Epigrammatis Simonideis pars prior: commentatio de epigrammatum traditione* (Groningen 1905).

—— 'De sylloge Rufiniana', *Philologus* lxxiii (1914), 1 f.

BROWNING, R., 'The Correspondence of a Tenth-Century Byzantine Scholar', *Byzantion* xxiv (1954), 397–452.

CAMERON, AVERIL and ALAN, 'The Cycle of Agathias', *JHS* lxxxvi (1966), 6–25.

CAMERON, ALAN, 'The Garlands of Meleager and Philip', *GRBS* ix (1968), 323–49 [a completely revised version of this paper has been incorporated in Ch. II].

—— 'Michael Psellus and the Palatine Anthology', *GRBS* xi (1970), 339–50 [partially incorporated in Ch. IX].

CAMERON, ALAN, 'Crinagoras and the Elder Julia', *Liverpool Classical Monthly* v (1980), 129–30.

—— 'The Garland of Philip', *GRBS* xvi (1980), 43–62.

—— 'Strato and Rufinus', *CQ*, NS xxxii (1982), 162–73.

—— *Porphyrius the Charioteer* (Oxford 1973).

—— 'Sir Thomas More and the Greek Anthology', *Florilegium Columbianum: Essays in Honor of Paul Oskar Kristeller*, Italica Press, New York, 1987, 187–98.

CLARKE, W. M., 'The Manuscript of Straton's *Musa Puerilis*', *GRBS* xvii (1976), 371–84.

DARROUZÈS, J., *Epistoliers byzantins du Xe siècle* (Paris 1960).

DAY, A. A., *The Origins of Latin Love Elegy* (Oxford 1938).

DEVREESSE, ROBERT, *Introduction à l'étude des manuscrits grecs* (Paris 1954).

DILLER, AUBREY, 'The Scholia on Strabo', *Traditio* x (1954), 25–50.

—— 'The Age of Some Early Greek Classical Manuscripts', *Serta Turyniana* (Univ. of Illinois Press 1974), 514–24.

DILTHEY, K., *De epigrammatum Graecorum syllogis quibusdam minoribus* (Göttingen 1887).

DOWNEY, G., 'Constantine the Rhodian: His Life and Writings', *Late Classical and Medieval Studies in Honor of A. M. Friend Jr.* (Princeton 1955), 212–21.

Épigramme grecque, L', see Raubitschek.

FRANKE, ALFREDUS, *De Pallada Epigrammatographo* (dissertatio inauguralis, Leipzig 1899).

FRIEDLÄNDER, P., and HOFFLEIT, H. B., *Epigrammata: Greek Inscriptions in Verse from the Beginnings to the Persian Wars* (Berkeley and Los Angeles 1948).

GALLAVOTTI, CARLO, 'Planudea', *Bollettino del Comitato per la preparazione dell'Edizione Nazionale dei Classici Greci e Latini* (1959), 25–50.

—— 'Planudea II', *Boll. Class. Lincei*, NS viii (1960), 11–24.

—— 'Planudea III', *Boll. Class. Lincei*, 3rd ser., ii (1981), 2–27.

—— 'Planudea IV', *Boll. Class. Lincei*, 3rd ser., iii (1982), 63–86.

—— 'Planudea V', *Boll. Class. Lincei*, 3rd ser., iv (1983), 36–56.

—— 'Planudea VI', *Boll. Class. Lincei*, 3rd ser., iv (1983), 101–28.

—— 'Planudea VII', *Boll. Class. Lincei*, 3rd ser., viii (1987), 96–128.

GARDTHAUSEN, V., *Griechische Palaeographie* i–ii (Leipzig 1911).

GEANOKOPLOS, D. J., *Greek Scholars in Venice: Studies in the Dissemination of Greek Learning from Byzantium to Western Europe* (Cambridge, Mass., 1962).

GOW, A. S. F., *The Greek Anthology: Sources and Ascriptions* (Hellenic Society supplementary paper 9, London 1958).

——, and PAGE, D. L., *The Greek Anthology: Hellenistic Epigrams* i–ii (Cambridge 1965) [*HE*].

——, —— *The Greek Anthology: The Garland of Philip* (Cambridge 1968) [*GP*].

GRONEWALD, MICHAEL, 'Ein Epigramm-Papyrus', *ZPE* xii (1973), 92–8.

HARRAUER, H., 'Epigrammincipit auf einem Papyrus aus dem 3 Jh. v. Chr.: P. Vindob. G 40611. Ein Vorbericht', *Proceedings of the XVI Int. Congress of Papyrology* (Chico, Calif., 1981), 49–53.

HIRSCH, ERHARD, 'Zum Kranz des Philippos', *Wiss. Zeitschrift d. Univ. Halle* xv (1966), 401–17.

HUNGER, H., *Die hochsprachliche profane Literatur der Byzantiner*, i–ii (Munich 1978).

HUTTON, J., *The Greek Anthology in Italy to the Year 1800* (Cornell Studies in English 23, Cornell 1935).

—— *The Greek Anthology in France and in the Latin Writers of the Netherlands to the Year 1800* (Cornell Studies in Classical Philology 28, 1946).

IRIGOIN, J., 'Philologie grecque', *Annuaire de l'école pratique des hautes études* 1975–6, 1977, 281–95.

LAURENS, P., 'Martial et l'épigramme grecque du Iᵉʳ siècle après J.-C.', *RÉL* xliii (1965), 315–41.

LEMERLE, P., *Le Premier Humanisme byzantin: notes et remarques sur enseignement et culture à Byzance des origines au Xᵉ siècle* (Bibliothèque byzantine: Études 6, Paris 1971).

LENZINGER, FRANZ, *Zur griechischen Anthologie* (Diss. Bern, Zürich 1965): cf. B. Turlington, *AJP* lxxxviii (1967), 377–9.

LUCK, GEORG, 'Palladas, Christian or Pagan?', *Harvard Studies in Classical Philology* lxiii (1958), 455–71.

—— review of *The Greek Anthology: Hellenistic Epigrams*, edited by A. S. F. Gow and D. L. Page, in *GGA* ccxix (1967), 23–61.

LUDWIG, W., 'Plato's Love Epigrams', *GRBS* iv (1963), 59–82.

MAAS, PAUL, 'Das Epigramm auf Marcus εἰς ἑαυτόν', *Hermes* xlviii (1913), 295–9 (= *Kleine Schriften* (Munich 1973), 135–8), with *JRS* xxxv (1945), 146 (140).

MANGO, CYRIL, 'The Availability of Books in the Byzantine Empire, AD 750–850', *Byzantine Books and Bookmen* (Dumbarton Oaks 1975), 29–45.

—— *Byzantium: the Empire of New Rome* (London 1980).

MATRANGA, P., *Anecdota Graeca e MSS. Bibliothecis Vaticana, Angelica Barberiniana, Vallicelliana, Medicea, Vindobonensi deprompta* (Rome 1850).

MATTSSON, A., *Untersuchungen zur Epigrammsammlung des Agathias* (Lund 1942).

MERCATI, G., 'Sopra Giovanni Clement e i suoi manuscritti', *La bibliofilia* xxviii (1926), 81–99 (= *Opere minori* iv (Studi e Testi 79, 1937), 292–315).

MIONI, ELPIDIO, 'L'Antigrafo dell'"Appendix Barberino-Vaticana" all'Antologia Planudea', *Miscellanea*, i (Padua 1978), 69–79.

—— '*L'Antologia Greca* da Massimo Planude a Marco Musuro', in *Scritti in onore di Carlo Diano* (Bologna 1975), 263–307.

NISSEN, THEODOR, 'Die byzantinischen Anakreonteen', *Sitzungberichte der Bayerischen Akademie der Wissenschaft* (Philosophisch-historische Abteilung, 1940, Heft 3), 3–81.

NOLHAC, P. DE, *La Bibliothèque de Fulvio Orsini* (Paris 1887).

PACK, R. A., *Greek and Roman Literary Texts from Greco-Roman Egypt*, 2nd edn. (Ann Arbor, Mich., 1965).

PAGE, D. L., *Greek Literary Papyri* (London and Cambridge, Mass.: Loeb 1961).

—— 'Five Hellenistic Epitaphs in Mixed Metres', *Wiener Studien* lxxxix (1976), 165–76.

—— *The Epigrams of Rufinus, Edited with an Introduction and Commentary* (Cambridge 1978).

—— *Epigrammata Graeca* (Oxford 1975).

—— *Further Greek Epigrams*, revised and prepared for publication by R. D. Dawe and J. Diggle (Cambridge 1981).

PASSOW, F., *Quaestio de vestigiis coronarum Meleagri et Philippi in Anthologia Constantini Cephalae* (Breslau 1827).

PFEIFFER, R., *Callimachus*, i–ii (Oxford 1949, 1953).

PREGER, T., *Inscriptiones graecae metricae ex scriptoribus praeter anthologiam collectae* (Leipzig 1891).

PREISENDANZ, C., *Anthologia Palatina: codex Palatinus et codex Parisinus phototypice editi*, i–ii (Leiden 1911).

—— review of Gow, *The Greek Anthology*, in *Gnomon* xxxiv (1962), 653–9.

RADINGER, K., *Melagros von Gadara* (Innsbruck 1895).

RAUBITSCHEK, A. E., GENTILI, B., GIANGRANDE, G., ROBERT, L., LUDWIG, W., LABARBE, J., DIHLE, A., and PFOHL, G., *L'Épigramme grecque* (Entretiens sur l'antiquité classique 14, Fondation Hardt, Vandœuvres-Geneva 1968).

REITZENSTEIN, R., *Epigramm und Skolion: ein Beitrag zur Geschichte der alexandrinischen Dichtung* (Giessen 1893).

—— 'Epigramm', in *PW* vi. 1. 71–111.

REYNOLDS, L. D., and WILSON, N. G., *Scribes and Scholars: A Guide to the Transmission of Greek and Latin Literature* (Oxford 1974).

ROSS, DAVID O., *Style and Tradition in Catullus* (Cambridge, Mass. 1969).

SCHNEIDEWIN, F. G., *Progymnasmata in Anthologiam Graecam* (Göttingen 1855).

SPECK, P., *Die Kaiserliche Universität von Konstantinopel* (Byzantisches Archiv 14, Munich 1974).

STELLA, L. A., *Cinque poeti dell'antologia palatina* (Bologna 1949): cf. W. C. Hembold, *CP* xlvi (1951), 102–3.

STERNBACH, L., *Anthologiae Planudeae Appendix Barberino-Vaticana* (Leipzig 1890).

TURNER, ERIC G., 'Two Greek Epigrams', *Journal of Juristic Papyrology* iv (1959), 235–8.

TURYN, ALEXANDER, 'Demetrius Triclinius and the Planudean Anthology', in *ΛΕΙΜΩΝ, Προσφορὰ εἰς . . . N. B. Τομαδάκην* ('Επετ. 'Εταιρ. Βυζ. Σπουδ. 39–40, 1972–3, Athens 1973), 403–50.

VAN SICKLE, J. B., 'The Bookroll and some conventions of the Poetic Book', *Some Augustan Poetry Books* (= *Arethusa* xiii, 1980), 5–42.

WEISSHÄUPL, RUDOLF, *Die Grabgedichte der griechischen Anthologie* (Arch. Semin. d. Univ. Wien 7, 1889).

—— 'Zu dem Quellen der Anthologia Palatina', in *Serta Harteliana* (1896), 184–8.

WENDEL, CARL, 'Planudea', *BZ* lx (1940), 406–45.

WEST, MARTIN L., *Studies in Greek Elegy and Iambus* (Berlin/New York 1974).

WIFSTRAND, ALBERT, *Studien zur griechischen Anthologie* (Lunds Univ. Årsskr. xxiii. 3, 1926).

WILAMOWITZ-MOELLENDORFF, U. VON, *Sappho und Simonides* (Berlin 1913).

—— *Hellenistische Dichtung in der Zeit des Kallimachos* (Berlin 1924).

WILSON, NIGEL G., 'Books and Readers in Byzantium', *Byzantine Books and Bookmen* (Dumbarton Oaks 1975), 1–15.

—— 'Planudes and Triclinius', *GRBS* xix (1978), 389–94; ibid. xxii (1981), 395–7.

—— *Scholars of Byzantium* (Baltimore 1983).

WOLTERS, PAUL, 'De Constantini Cephalae anthologia', *RhM* xxxviii (1883), 97–119.

YOUNG, D. C. C., 'On Planudes' Edition of Theognis and a Neglected Apograph of the Anthologia Planudea', *Parola del passato* x (1955), 197 ff.

ADDENDA

p. 10: Thanks to the courtesy of its future editors (Guido Bastianini and Claudio Gallazzi), I am able at the very last moment to mention an almost complete roll of epigrams dating from the late third century BC recently purchased by the Università Statale of Milan (P. Mil. Vogl. inv. 1295). The editors warn that at the time of writing (July 1992) they have not fully deciphered the text, but communicate the following provisional results. It contains *c*.100 epigrams, many complete, totalling *c*.600 lines, all apparently new. Individual epigrams vary in length from four to fourteen lines, thus bearing out my claim (p. 13) that Ptolemaic epigrams were often very long. All are in elegiacs. There are no ascriptions to individual epigrams, and (in the provisional judgement of the editors) language and style suggest that all are by a single poet, unfortunately not named in the surviving part of the roll. They do not therefore represent an anthology as defined in this book.

p. 12. On P. Oxy. 662 see now my article 'Philip V and his Poets' forthcoming in *GRBS*.

p. 29. The epigrams in P. Mil. Vogl. inv. 1295 are divided into thematic groups by centrally placed titles, some generic (ἀναθεματικά), some more specific (shipwrecks, women). This is obviously relevant to my suggestion that Meleager's *Garland* was subdivided into much larger thematic categories. It will be interesting to see how individual epigrams are arranged within these categories.

pp. 80–2, 90–2, and 389. On Ausonius' translations from Greek epigrams, see now the commentary on individual epigrams in R. P. H. Green, *The Works of Ausonius* (Oxford 1991), 363–420. On a priori grounds Green suggests that they may be 'relatively early works', while allowing that they could be 'much later' (p. 376).

p. 101. Given his interest in ecphraseis (see p. 327), it is perhaps not surprising that J copied the title of Nonnus' *Paraphrase* in error as ἔκφρασις instead of παράφρασις. For views on the date and circumstances of its loss from *AP*, see now E. Livrea, *Nonno di Panopoli: parafrasi del Vangelo di S. Giovanni, XVIII* (Naples 1989), 69–71.

p. 150: Theodosius Diaconus too seems to imitate Agathias' preface (*AP* iv. 46) in the preface to his *de Creta capta* (l. 30) written soon after 961 (ed. H. Criscuolo 1979), as well as *AP* ix. 677. 7, also by Agathias (l. 114). Since he also imitates the *Anacreontea* (15. 29–30, cf. l. 226, with Criscuolo p. 65), it looks as if he too used a copy of Cephalas that resembled *AP*.

p. 184: See now Anna Meschini's detailed study in *Boll. class. Linc.* 1982, 23–62, with a fuller list of readings from *AP* on pp. 58–60. She disputes Mioni's claim that both MSS are in the same hand, showing that 1169 was written by the wealthy Siennese manuscript collector Lattanzio Tolomei (1487–1543). Meschini also claims that the Palatine readings derive from Tolomei rather than Musurus: 'il fatto che soltanto in questo codice si trovino epigrammi e lezioni che possono derivare unicamente da P dimostra che questo fu noto solo al suo redattore, e non anche alle fonti di cui si servì' (p. 57 n. 65). But Tolomei may have had sole use of a source that was lost or destroyed; after all, no such manuscript of Musurus has survived. Meschini's hypothesis also ignores the evidence presented above that *AP* was in London and Louvain at the time.

p. 243: The improbable-looking Περπούρου is more likely to have spawned the flat but straightforward τερπνὸν ὅλως than vice versa. Περπούρου itself may well be corrupt, though Greek names ending in -ουρος and -ουριος are found (L. Zgusta, *Kleinasiatische Personennamen* [Prague 1964], 672, 674). Possibly Purpureus (-ius). Strato does not elsewhere use Roman names, but that very fact might explain the corruption.

p. 254: There is no indication that Constantine Cephalas is connected to the Cephalas family prominent from the late eleventh century on: *Prosopographisches Lexikon der Palaiologenzeit* I (Vienna 1976), nos. 11667–80.

p. 304, n. 11: The Aglochartos inscriptions (3rd or 4th century AD) were republished, with a new one discovered in 1941 by Ch. Blinkenberg, by J. Bousquet, 'Les oliviers de Lindos', *Recueil Plassart* (Paris 1976), 9–13; for earlier generations of the family, Ch. Habicht, *ZPE* 84 (1990), 113–20. Even allowing for the fact that, being carved high in the living rock, they are rather inaccessible, Constantine's transcription is remarkably inaccurate, with 14 errors in ten lines.

p. 319: Michael's epitaph has been republished with photo and commentary by I. Ševčenko, *DOP* 41 (1987), 461–8 (reading ἐγώγ ... προλέγωγ in l. 1). He points out that ἄχθος ἀπορρίψας in l. 3 comes from Leonidas *AP* vii. 19. 4 and πινυτόφρονος in l. 6 perhaps from Simmias *AP* vii. 22. 5; furthermore, Metrodorus *AP* xiv. 125 and Gregory viii. 224, 230, and 239 all open τυμβὸς ἐγώ. That is to say, the writer (? Alexander of Nicaea, cf. p. 317) was another reader of Cephalas. To be described as Nicholas' syncellus, Michael cannot have died before 901.

p. 328: J's marginalia to John's ecphrasis of the painting in the winter baths reveal knowledge of other products of the school of Gaza that cannot plausibly be ascribed to a hypothetical earlier source: 'this city was devoted to the Muses, and attained the highest distinction in literature; among its celebrities were John and Procopius and Timothy, who wrote on the animals of India, and various anacreontic poets.' Timothy of Gaza did indeed write such a work, and excerpts were included in a zoological compilation dedicated to Constantine Porphyrogenitus (Lemerle 1971, 297; Hunger 1978, ii. 265–6), and so of the 940s/950s, exactly contemporary with J's work on *AP* and a generation later than Cephalas. A couple of later MSS preserve six anacreontics by John grammaticus of Gaza and a further eight by George grammaticus (Bergk, *PLG* iii⁴ 342–8, 364–75). George's poems are so similar in both themes and style to John's, as well as to the prose sophists of Gaza, that George too has generally been assigned to the school of Gaza (R. Anastasi, *Siculorum Gymnasium*, xx [1967], 209–53). J himself in another scholion claims that John's painting was also mentioned by Procopius, presumably in his lost lament on the destruction of Antioch in the earthquake of 526. For at the end of the poem he queries his earlier assumption that John's winter baths were in Gaza by adding 'or in Antioch', no doubt on the basis of his recollection of Procopius (Cameron, *CQ* forthcoming). All in all, remarkably well-informed notes, evidently based on first-hand knowledge—just the sort of texts we should expect to be familiar to Constantine the Rhodian.

Some further illustrations of J's culture. First, his knowledge of late antique poetry. On *AP* i. 19 by Claudian, J wrote: οὗτος ὁ Κλαυδιανός ἐστιν ὁ γράψας τὰ πάτρια Ταρσοῦ, Ἀναζάρβου, Βηρύτου, Νικαίας. This information is preserved nowhere else, and yet it is entirely plausible that a 'wandering poet' such as Claudian wrote in the fashionable genre of city origins (*Historia* xiv [1965], 489–90, 492); the examples cited find strong support in Nonnus' familiarity with the mythical origins of three out of these four cities (see my *Claudian* [1970], 7–11). On *AP* ix. 136 by Cyrus of Panopolis he wrote: τοῦ μεγάλου ποιητοῦ, ἡνίκα ἔμελλεν ἐξορίζεσθαι ἐκ τῆς πόλεως, θρῆνος ὃν εἶπε πρὸς αὐτῇ τῇ πύλῃ τῆς ἀκροπόλεως. Since Cyrus was indeed exiled from Constantinople (*Yale Class. Stud.* xxvii [1982], 254–70), once again there seems no reason to doubt the information. When we add the inclusion in *AP* of long hexameter poems by Nonnus, Christodorus, Paul, and John of Gaza, it seems clear that J was familiar with a substantial corpus of late antique poetry.

Second, on *AP* vii. 304 (Pisander) J claims that the poem was 'quoted for its excellence' by Nicolaus of Damascus. Preisendanz characteristically ascribed this note to J's 'source' (*neque enim lemmatistam legisse Nicolaum credere in mentem veniet cuiquam*, col. xcix). Yet most of what survives of Nicolaus is preserved in the Constantinian excerpts (*Exc. de virt.* i. 329–53 B-W, *de insid.* 3–33 de B, collected in *FGrH* 90; cf. Jacoby, *Komm.* p. 230), with cross-references to more in volumes now lost (F 70 fin.), and so again dating from the 940s/950s, contemporary with J's work on *AP* and substantially later than Cephalas. It is therefore more likely that J found his quotation (F 40) here than in his exemplar.

GENERAL INDEX

Since the sources and methods of Cephalas and Planudes are mentioned or discussed on almost every page of Chapters V–XV, and Planudean manuscripts throughout Appendices I–IV and VI, it has not seemed useful to attempt a full index of these topics. The same applies to the discussions in Chapters VII–XV *passim* of the debt of the various later anthologies to Cephalas. See too the other indexes and the table of contents.

INDEX OF PASSAGES

This index lists only texts singled out for comment, not those mentioned in passing or included in lists; see too entries for individual authors in the General Index.

SELECT INDEX OF GREEK WORDS

9 780198 140238